WORLD WAR II
AT SEA

WORLD WAR II AT SEA

A GLOBAL HISTORY

CRAIG L. SYMONDS

OXFORD
UNIVERSITY PRESS

OXFORD
UNIVERSITY PRESS

Oxford University Press is a department of the University of Oxford.
It furthers the University's objective of excellence in research, scholarship,
and education by publishing worldwide. Oxford is a registered trade mark of
Oxford University Press in the UK and certain other countries.

Published in the United States of America by Oxford University Press
198 Madison Avenue, New York, NY 10016, United States of America.

Library of Congress Cataloging-in-Publication Data

Names: Symonds, Craig L., author.
Title: World War II at sea : a global history / Craig L. Symonds.
Description: New York : Oxford University Press, [2018] |
Includes bibliographical references.
Identifiers: LCCN 2017032532 | ISBN 9780190243678 (hardback : alk. paper)
Subjects: LCSH: World War, 1939–1945—Naval operations
Classification: LCC D770 .S87 2018 | DDC 940.54/5—dc23 LC record available at
https://lccn.loc.gov/2017032532

10

Printed by Sheridan Books, Inc., United States of America

For Marylou, again

CONTENTS

List of Charts and Graphs   ix
Author's Note   xi
Prologue: London, 1930   xiii

PART I: THE EUROPEAN WAR   1
  1. *Unterseebooten*   3
  2. *Panzerschiffe*   18
  3. Norway   39
  4. France Falls   61
  5. The Regia Marina   78
  6. The War on Trade, I   103
  7. The *Bismarck*   130

PART II: THE WAR WIDENS   153
  8. The Rising Sun   155
  9. A Two-Ocean Navy   173
  10. Operation AI: The Attack on Pearl Harbor   195
  11. Rampage   216
  12. The War on Trade, II   240

PART III: WATERSHED   267
  13. Stemming the Tide   269
  14. Two Beleaguered Islands   294

15. A Two-Ocean War   322
16. The Tipping Point   348
17. The War on Trade, III   373

PART IV: ALLIED COUNTERATTACK   401
18. Airplanes and Convoys   403
19. Husky   421
20. Twilight of Two Navies   443
21. Breaking the Shield   469
22. Large Slow Target   497

PART V: RECKONING   517
23. D-Day   519
24. Seeking the Decisive Battle   538
25. Leyte Gulf   562
26. The Noose Tightens   589
27. Denouement   613
Epilogue: Tokyo Bay, 1945   637

Afterword   641
Acknowledgments   649
Abbreviations used in Notes   651
Notes   653
Bibliography   717
Index   743

CHARTS AND GRAPHS

Relative Sizes of Royal Navy Warships in the 1930s   xvii

The Cruises of the *Graf Spee* and *Deutschland*,
August–December 1939   28

The Campaign in Norway, April 1940   44

The Mediterranean, 1940–41   80

The Pursuit of the *Bismarck*, May 18–27, 1941   136

Japanese Attack on Pearl Harbor,
November 26–December 7, 1941   201

Japan Moves South, December 1941–March 1942   219

The *Kidō Butai* in the Indian Ocean, April 3–10, 1942   237

The Battle of the Coral Sea, May 7–8, 1942   277

Fleet Movements Prior to the Battle of Midway,
June 3–5, 1942   284

The Battle of Savo Island, August 8–9, 1942   305

Operation Pedestal, August 10–16, 1942   315

Operation Torch, November 8–11, 1942   350

Naval Battles off Morocco, November 8–10, 1942   357

Allied Shipping Losses vs. Construction of
New Ships, 1942–44   390

The Battle of the Bismarck Sea, March 1–4, 1943   406

Planning the Invasion of Sicily   423

The Dual Advance in the South Pacific,
June–November 1943   476

The Battle for Italy   501

The Normandy Beachhead, June 6, 1944   528

Battle of the Philippine Sea, June 19–21, 1944   545

The Battle of Leyte Gulf, October 23–26, 1944   570

The Noose Tightens   596

AUTHOR'S NOTE

THE SECOND WORLD WAR was the single greatest cataclysm of violence in human history. Some sixty million people lost their lives—about 3 percent of the world's population. Thanks to scholars and memoirists of virtually every nation, it has been chronicled in thousands, even hundreds of thousands, of books in a score of languages.

Many of those books document the naval aspects of the war. Unsurprisingly, the winners have been more fulsome than the vanquished—Stephen Roskill and Samuel Eliot Morison emphasized the particular contributions of the Royal Navy and the United States Navy in multivolume sets. Others have examined the role of navies in a particular theater or a particular battle, especially in the Mediterranean and the Pacific. Yet no single volume evaluates the impact of the sea services from all nations on the overall trajectory and even the outcome of the war. Doing so illuminates how profoundly the course of the war was charted and steered by maritime events.

Such is the ambition of this work, and it is one with challenges. The story of the global war at sea between 1939 and 1945 is a sprawling, episodic, and constantly shifting tale of conflicting national interests, emerging technologies, and oversized personalities. Telling it in a single narrative is daunting, yet telling it any other way would be misleading. There was not one war in the Atlantic and another in the Pacific, a third in the Mediterranean, and still another in the Indian Ocean or the North Sea. While it might simplify things to chronicle the conflict in such geographical packets, that was not the way the war unfolded or the way decision-makers had to manage it. The loss of shipping during the Battle of the Atlantic affected the availability of transports for Guadalcanal; convoys to the besieged island of Malta in the Mediterranean meant fewer escorts for the Atlantic; the pursuit of the battleship *Bismarck* drew forces from Iceland and Gibraltar as well as from Britain. The narrative here, therefore, is chronological. Of course, leaping about from ocean to ocean day to day is both impractical and potentially bewildering, so there is necessarily some chronological overlap between chapters.

Whenever possible, I allow the historical actors to speak for themselves, for my goal in this book is to tell the story of World War II at sea the way contemporaries experienced it: as a single, gigantic, complex story, involving national leaders and strategic decision-makers, fleet commanders and ship drivers, motor macs, gunners, pilots, merchant seamen, and Marines; as a worldwide human drama that had a disproportionate and lasting impact on the history of the world.

PROLOGUE

London, 1930

THE MURMUR OF CONVERSATION ceased abruptly and there was a rustle of movement as the assembled delegates stood when King George entered the Royal Gallery, followed by the lord chamberlain and the prime minister. The king walked slowly but purposefully toward the ornate throne that dominated one end of the House of Lords, and he waited there while the delegates resettled themselves. That he was here at all was noteworthy, for George V had been ill for some time (very likely with the septicemia that would later kill him) and had retired to Craigweil House, in Bognor, on the Sussex coast, to recuperate. Unhappy and frustrated by his confinement there, he had made a special effort to be present for this ceremony.

The House of Lords, with its gilded coffered ceiling and stained glass windows, offered a suitable stage for the king's public reappearance, though the windows admitted little light on this occasion because on January 20, 1930, London was blanketed by a thick fog; local authorities had been compelled to turn on the streetlights in the middle of the day. The hall was crowded, not with peers of the realm, but with more than a hundred delegates from eleven nations. Six of those nations were dominions within Britain's far-flung empire, including Canada, Australia, and New Zealand, though the audience also boasted representatives from the military powers of three continents. From Europe there were delegates from both France and Italy (though, significantly, not from either Weimar Germany or communist Russia). In addition to Canada, a delegation from the United States represented the Western Hemisphere, and from Asia there was a substantial contingent from the Empire of Japan, though not from China. Each delegation was headed by a high-ranking civilian, and the audience included two prime ministers, two foreign secretaries, and one secretary of state. The men—and they were all men—were mostly in their fifties and sixties, and they constituted a somber audience in their dark suits with stiff white collars.[1]

Scattered among them, however, and lined up across the back of the hall, were the uniformed officers of a dozen navies, the fat and narrow gold stripes ascending their sleeves from cuff to elbow revealing their exalted rank. There was less variation in their attire than might have been expected from such a polyglot assemblage because all of them, including the Japanese, wore uniforms modeled on the Royal Navy prototype: a double-breasted dark blue (officially navy blue) coat with two vertical rows of gold buttons. Here was unmistakable evidence of the extent to which the Royal Navy was the archetype of all modern navies.

Many of the officers also wore gaudy decorations—stars and sashes— earned over a lifetime of service at sea and ashore, and the bright splashes of color among the dark suits suggested songbirds among ravens. Even the junior officers, tasked with note-taking, translating, and providing technical support, stood out by sporting thick aiguillettes of gold braid draped over their shoulders and across their chests, ornamentation that identified them as belonging to the staff of one or another of the gold-striped admirals.

George V, too, might have worn a naval officer's uniform, since in addition to being the Sovereign of Great Britain, Ireland, and British Dominions Beyond the Seas, he was also a five-star admiral in the Royal Navy. He had decided instead to wear a plain black frock coat. Solemnly he took his position in front of the distinguished audience to offer a brief welcoming address. Speaking in what the London *Times* called "a firm and resonant voice," he noted that every nation there was proud of its navy—and rightly so. But, he said, competition among navies had been a major factor in provoking what he called the "grim and immense tragedy" that had erupted in 1914. He hardly had to remind these men that the battleship construction race between Britain and imperial Germany from 1905 to 1914 had been a central feature of the mounting distrust that culminated in the outbreak of war.[2]

Indeed, in recognition of that, the victorious powers had met in Washington in 1921, a few years after the end of the war, to place limits on future battleship construction. Germany had not been invited to that conference (or to this one, either) since the Versailles Treaty already forbade her both battleships and submarines. The Washington conference had been a success nonetheless, producing a treaty in 1922 that established limits on the size and number of battleships that could be possessed by the major powers, limits that were enshrined in the subsequently famous formula 5:5:3, denoting the ratio of battleship tonnage allowed to Britain, the United States, and Japan, respectively, with France and Italy each accorded smaller totals. Now, the British monarch told the assembled delegates, it was time to go further and complete the job so nobly begun—to extend the limits to all classes of warships: cruisers, destroyers, and especially submarines.

The impetus behind this renewed effort had two sources: one of them philosophical and idealistic, the other pragmatic and economic. The philosophical touchstone was the Kellogg-Briand Peace Pact, signed two years earlier by sixty-two nations, including all of those represented here. That agreement had outlawed war as an instrument of national policy. Years later, after regimes in Germany, Japan, and Italy had made a mockery of such high-principled declarations, it became popular to dismiss the Kellogg-Briand Pact as a fatuous exercise in wishful thinking. But in 1930 it was still being taken seriously, at least publicly.

A more pragmatic spur to action was the fact that the previous October, a stock market crash in New York had triggered a worldwide economic recession, the depths of which had not yet been plumbed. With employment and revenue falling, governments the world over were seeking ways to trim their expenses, and warships were one of the most expensive items in any nation's budget. Additional naval arms limitation, therefore, seemed both philosophically admirable and fiscally responsible. In view of these circumstances, George V urged the delegates to lift "the heavy burden of armaments now weighing upon the peoples of the world" by finding a way to reduce warship construction.[3]

BATTLESHIPS REMAINED the universally accepted measuring stick of naval power, which was precisely why they had been the focus of the 1922 agreement. More than six hundred feet long and displacing more than 30,000 tons of seawater, battleships were operated by crews of twelve to fifteen hundred men, making them virtual floating cities. Heavily armed as well as heavily armored, their principal weapon consisted of large-caliber guns housed in rotating turrets fore and aft. The largest of these guns had grown from a diameter of 12 inches to 14, and recently to 16 inches, and they fired shells that weighed nearly two thousand pounds at targets ten to fifteen miles away. Indeed, the range of these massive guns was so great that most battleships carried airplanes that were used not only to scout for the enemy but also to spot and report the fall of shot. These planes were propelled into the air by an explosive charge, and because they were equipped with pontoons they could subsequently land alongside their host vessel and be hoisted back aboard.

Battlecruisers were in some cases even longer than battleships, though they had slightly smaller guns and considerably less armor, which meant they displaced less tonnage. The largest warship in the Royal Navy in 1930 was the battlecruiser HMS *Hood*, which at 860 feet was the pride of the fleet. Her eight 15-inch guns gave her exceptional offensive power, but her Achilles' heel was her relatively thin armor, which made her more vulnerable than any battleship. British battlecruisers had fared badly in the 1916 Battle of Jutland, when three of them had blown up spectacularly with the loss of almost all hands. That had provoked Royal Navy Admiral David Beatty to comment, with characteristic British sangfroid, "There seems to be something wrong with our bloody ships today." After that, most naval planners began to think of battlecruisers not so much as light battleships as oversize cruisers.

Relative sizes of
Royal Naval warships in the 1930s

Battleship HMS *Nelson* (1927)

Battlecruiser HMS *Renown* (1916)

Aircraft Carrier HMS *Ark Royal* (1938)

Heavy cruiser HMS *York* (1930)

Light cruiser HMS *Leander* (1931)

Destroyer HMS *Gallant* (1936)

Submarine HMS *Starfish* (1933)

Cruisers looked much like battleships, with their characteristic super-structure amidships and rotating gun turrets fore and aft, and differed primarily in their smaller size. Heavy cruisers generally displaced about 10,000 tons (a third that of battleships) with guns that were 8 inches in diameter. Indeed, the Washington Treaty had specified that any ship displacing more than 10,000 tons or carrying a gun larger than 8 inches would count as a battleship, which led most nations to build heavy cruisers that conformed to those precise specifications.

Light cruisers were smaller yet, usually displacing about 6,000 tons and carrying guns that fired 6-inch shells. The British preferred these smaller cruisers because they were cheaper, which meant they could build more of them to patrol the extensive sea-lanes of their far-flung imperial possessions, from Gibraltar to Suez and from India to Singapore.

Destroyers were the workhorses of twentieth-century navies. Initially built to combat small torpedo boats, they were christened "torpedo-boat destroyers." If cruisers were about a third the size of battleships, destroyers were about a third the size of cruisers, displacing between 1,200 and 2,000 tons. Too small to slug it out with the bigger ships, they were generally used as escorts, scouting out ahead of the battleships to patrol for submarines, or performing that same function for merchant convoys. They had guns that varied in size from 4 to 5 inches, but their most effective anti-ship weapon was the torpedo. Though the reliability of the torpedoes was sometimes problematic, a destroyer armed with them could be fatal even to the largest of warships.

THE OSTENSIBLE GOAL of the delegates in London was to extend the limits that had been applied to battleships in the 1922 treaty to cruisers and smaller ships as well, especially the heavy cruisers. The U.S. Navy's General Board had instructed its delegates that the United States needed no fewer than twenty-seven of the big cruisers to ensure the security of its Pacific outposts at Hawaii, Wake, Guam, and the Philippines, though the board acknowledged confidentially that it could get by with twenty-three. The British preferred to have fewer of the big cruisers and more of the smaller, 6-inch-gun cruisers. One difficulty, then, was to devise a formula by which some number of smaller cruisers could be equated to one heavy cruiser.

Japan's case was unique. Back in 1922, Japan had reluctantly accepted the formula embedded in the Washington Treaty that allowed her only three-fifths of the battleship tonnage allotted to the Americans and the British. On one level this was logical: the British and Americans had interests in both the Atlantic and the Pacific as well as the Caribbean and the Mediterranean, and in Britain's case, the Indian Ocean, too. Japan's interests were almost exclusively in the western Pacific, so her apparent subordination to the British and Americans actually gave her a strong relative position in her home waters. To the Japanese, however, it was a matter of national pride. Japanese newspapers remarked that the 5:5:3 Washington formula equated to "Rolls-Royce, Rolls-Royce, Ford." The Japanese delegation had come to London with strict instructions to accept no less than 70 percent of the number of heavy cruisers allotted to Britain and the United States. As Katō Kanji, head of the Supreme Military Council, put it: "The real issue at stake is no longer our naval power per se, but our national prestige and credibility."[4]

In hindsight, it seems curious that so much effort and energy were focused on cruisers, and so little on aircraft carriers. Such ships were less than a decade old in 1930, and the major naval powers continued to think of them as experimental ships that functioned as auxiliaries to battleships. The British suggested that perhaps they and the United States could each accept a limit of 100,000 tons of carriers, but American delegates nixed that proposal in part because two of the existing American carriers—*Lexington* and *Saratoga*—displaced more than 36,000 tons each and would use up more than two-thirds of the total allotment, leaving little room for experimentation.

Nor was there any substantive agreement about submarines, the unrestricted use of which had nearly brought England to her knees in the last war, and which had played a major role in triggering American belligerency in 1917. Given that, it was not surprising that during the ensuing conversations both the Americans and the British urged the abolition of submarines altogether. Like germ warfare and gas warfare, submarine warfare would be banned entirely. Henry Stimson, the secretary of state, who headed the U.S. delegation, declared that "the use of the submarine revolted the conscience of the world," and noted presciently that regardless of any international rules that might be adopted for their use, "those who employ the submarine will be under strong temptation, perhaps irresistible temptation, to use it in the way which is most effective for immediate purposes," which was the destruction of unarmed merchant ships.[5]

Italy and France, however, rejected that argument. They insisted that submarines were defensive craft, invaluable to weaker naval powers, and that abolishing them would only increase the naval dominance of the English-speaking superpowers. The French minister of marine, Georges Leygues, argued that it was not the submarine itself that was evil, but the way it was used. Noting that airplanes could be used to bomb cities, he asked if they should be banned because they were capable of such acts. In the end, the only limit that all of the delegates could agree to was that individual submarines would be limited to no more than 2,000 tons displacement. Since most submarines displaced less than half that, this was, in effect, no limit at all. The delegates did adopt new rules for the humane use of submarines: captains were to provide their victims with sufficient time to abandon ship and get well away before attacking. Of course, since such rules were unenforceable, they were also largely meaningless.[6]

IN ALL THESE DISCUSSIONS, the unseen and unacknowledged specter was Germany. This was especially true for the French, who had been invaded twice by Germany within the lifetime of the French delegates in the room. There was no German delegation in London because the Versailles Treaty already detailed the size and type of navy that Germany was allowed to have, so what was there to discuss? The Kaiserliche Marine, the old imperial navy, no longer existed. In October 1918, with the war virtually lost, the commander of Germany's battleship fleet, Admiral Reinhard Scheer, had ordered it to sea, presumably to engage in one last sacrificial battle for the sake of honor. The sailors refused to do it, some of them raising the red flag of the Bolsheviks in open rebellion. Consequently, when the armistice was signed on November 11, 1918, the German fleet was still at anchor at Wilhelmshaven, the principal German naval base on the southern rim of the North Sea, between Holland and Denmark. During the negotiations at Versailles, that fleet steamed under skeleton crews to intern itself at the Royal

Navy's roadstead at Scapa Flow, north of Scotland. When it became evident that the British intended to demand those ships as spoils of war, the German crews scuttled them, opening the sea cocks below decks and sending them to the bottom of the chilly waters of Scapa Flow. Eleven years later, as the delegates met in London, they were there still.

That did not stop the French from worrying about a German revival. If France was expected to weaken her defenses in any way—by giving up her submarines, for example—the French government wanted a commitment from the British and the Americans that they would come to her aid, or at least consult with her, if she was attacked again. Given their tradition of insularity, the British were unwilling to make such a guarantee, and the Americans, firmly entrenched in a policy of isolationism, adamantly refused.

The biggest stumbling block at the conference concerned the Japanese. The Japanese were determined to secure no less than 70 percent of the number of heavy cruisers allocated to the British and Americans, who in turn were just as determined to hold the percentage at 60. In the end, a somewhat complicated compromise allocated the Americans eighteen heavy cruisers and the Japanese twelve—66 percent. While this seemed a middle-ground position, it was complicated by other factors. One was that the Japanese already had twelve such cruisers, and the Americans had only four. The practical effect of the agreement, then, was that the Americans could build fourteen new heavy cruisers, while the Japanese total was frozen at twelve. On the other hand, the Japanese would be allowed to replace their existing cruisers with new ones over the ensuing five years, while the Americans could not build the last of their new cruisers until 1935. The overall effect was that the Japanese would actually possess a de facto cruiser ratio of near 70 percent for the life of the treaty. In consideration of these factors, and unwilling to let the conference collapse, the head of the Japanese delegation, former prime minister Reijirō Wakatsuki, accepted the compromise. That infuriated most of the Japanese naval officers who had accompanied the delegation, especially the younger officers, who denounced Wakatsuki to his face. Back in Tokyo, however, the sitting prime minister and, crucially, the emperor, supported the arrangement, and the treaty was ratified.[7]

On the final day of the conference, Wakatsuki rose to thank the British for their hospitality and to offer some concluding remarks. He knew full well that despite the incremental gains he had secured, the treaty would be unpopular with the Imperial Japanese Navy, as the reaction of the officer delegates had already demonstrated, and that it was possible, perhaps even likely, that he would lose his position, or even his life, in consequence. He nevertheless praised the agreement as "a historic and lasting monument on the path of peace and human progress."[8]

The Germans, of course, had no opportunity to say anything at all. The new agreement offered no easing of the strangling restrictions that the victors of the Great War had imposed on the German navy, and German resentment at the Versailles humiliation continued to rankle. In national elections held five months later, the National Socialist German Workers Party, Nazi for short, won 18.3 percent of the popular vote and 107 seats in the Reichstag, making it the second-largest political party in Germany.

PART I

THE EUROPEAN WAR

Adolf Hitler assumed power in Germany less than three years after the signing of the London agreement. He did not seize power violently, as he had tried to do back in 1924; he was invited to become chancellor by virtue of the Nazi Party's success at the polls. Hitler then consolidated his power in a series of emergency decrees, and the Weimar government effectively disappeared. Two years later, in March 1935, Hitler publicly renounced the Versailles Treaty, including the restrictions it imposed on the size of the German navy. There were no repercussions to his unilateral announcement, and Hitler was confirmed in his view of the fecklessness of the Western democracies.

The renunciation of the Versailles Treaty was important, but the decisive moment in the rebirth of the German navy came three months later with the signing of the Anglo-German Naval Agreement. By then, many in Britain actively sought an accommodation with Germany. British diplomats saw Hitler's regime as a useful buffer to Stalinist Russia and welcomed the idea of an Anglo-German rapprochement. On June 18, 1935, without consulting either France or Italy,

Britain agreed to lift most of the naval restrictions that had been imposed on Germany at Versailles.

The new agreement permitted Germany to build a navy whose total tonnage was 35 percent that of the Royal Navy. While that would keep it subordinate to the British, it also opened the door for substantial new growth. The treaty even allowed for the construction of the first German submarines since 1918. By its terms, Germany could build its submarine force up to 45 percent of the British total, and there was an escape clause that allowed Germany to build up to 100 percent of Britain's total in the event of a national crisis, though what kind of crisis might justify such an expansion was not stipulated. The German navy also got a new name. Under the old empire it had been the Kaiserliche Marine (Imperial Navy); during the Weimar Republic, it was the Reichsmarine (National Navy). Now, under Hitler, it became the Kriegsmarine (War Navy).

On September 1, 1939, Hitler's revitalized German army, the Wehrmacht, invaded Poland. The naval war began the same day when a German warship opened fire on the Polish garrison of Gdansk (Danzig). Two days later, British prime minister Neville Chamberlain went on the radio to announce that since he had received no response to the Anglo-French ultimatum calling on Hitler to withdraw German forces from Poland, a state of war now existed between Britain and Germany. The lugubrious tone of his announcement underscored the reality that almost everyone in the British government—and in the British public, for that matter—dreaded the resumption of hostilities. Chamberlain had labored mightily to prevent war, and he had failed largely because he had underestimated both the breadth of Hitler's ambition and the perversity of his ideology. So now, barely twenty years after the last war had ended, war had come again.

CHAPTER 1

UNTERSEEBOOTEN

THE NORTH SEA WAS ROUGH in October 1939, as it often was in the fall months, especially this far north. Strong winds whipped froth from the crest of the dark waves and turned it into a stinging spray that drenched the three men who stood precariously on the small conning tower of the actively rolling submarine U-47, wetting them thoroughly despite their oilskins. One of those men was the sub's captain, thirty-one-year-old Günther Prien (pronounced Preen), who had joined the merchant service as a cabin boy at the age of fifteen and almost literally grown up at sea. On an early cruise he had faced down and physically pummeled a much larger and older deckhand who had sought to intimidate him. As long as he lived, Prien considered that triumph over a bully to have been a defining moment in his life. At twenty-four, he had obtained his master seaman's license, but that was in 1932, during the depths of the Depression, and he had been unable to find work, a circumstance he blamed on the harsh terms of the Versailles Treaty and the hapless Weimar government. His bitterness led him to join the Nazi Party, and by 1933—the year Adolf Hitler became chancellor—Prien was an officer candidate in the slowly reviving German navy. Now, six years later, he was a *Kapitänleutnant* (lieutenant) in that navy, commanding his own submarine, and embarked on a very special mission.[1]

As Prien later recalled the moment, he had to steady himself against the railing of the U-47 as he peered through his Leitz binoculars, searching for a recognizable landmark at the edge of the gray sea and the equally gray sky. And he found it: there on the horizon were the Orkney Islands, a forlorn archipelago off the northern tip of Scotland that embraced the commodious Royal Navy fleet anchorage known as Scapa Flow.

Despite its isolation, Scapa Flow was the very heart of the Royal Navy. It was from there that the British Grand Fleet had sortied in 1916 to meet the German High Seas Fleet in the Battle of Jutland; after the war, it was in Scapa Flow that fifty-two ships of the interned German fleet had been scuttled by their crews. Along with Spithead, below Portsmouth on the Channel coast, Scapa Flow was one of the Royal Navy's most important bases.

What made it so valuable was its location. Any vessel seeking the open Atlantic from the North Sea or the Baltic had to pass either through the English Channel past Portsmouth and Plymouth or around the northern tip of Scotland past Scapa Flow. Moreover, the anchorage at Scapa Flow was enormous, more than a hundred square miles—able to accommodate all the navies of the world with room to spare. It was well protected by the group of rocky islands that surrounded it, as well as by coastal batteries, booms, submarine nets, and minefields. Only three well-defended passages allowed access: Hoy Sound to the west, Hoxa Sound to the south, and the narrow channel of Kirk Sound to the east. The British Admiralty believed that the only vulnerable point in the defenses of Scapa Flow was from the air, for it was just within the extreme range of German bombers.[2]

Barely a week before, only a month after the declaration of war, the British commander at Scapa Flow, Admiral Sir Charles Forbes, had learned that two German cruisers, the *Gneisenau* and *Köln*, accompanied by nine destroyers, had ventured into the North Sea, and he at once ordered the Home Fleet out in pursuit. An impressive armada of battleships, battlecruisers, and cruisers set out from Scapa Flow to find and destroy the interlopers, while the battleship *Royal Oak*, with two escorting destroyers, had steamed northward to block the escape route through the somewhat incongruously named Fair Isle Channel, between the Orkneys and the Shetlands. As it happened, the German cruisers had swiftly retreated, and so the British, too, returned to port, with the main body dropping anchor in Loch Ewe, on the western coast of Scotland beyond the range of German aircraft, while the *Royal Oak* and her escorts returned to the sanctuary at Scapa Flow.[3]

Now, four days later, on October 13, Prien studied the entrance to Scapa Flow through his binoculars. He had kept the object of the sub's mission a secret from everyone on board during the long journey northward, but now his first officer, Engelbert Endrass, risked a rebuke by venturing to ask him: "Are we going to visit the Orkneys, sir?"

It was time to let the cat out of the bag. "Take hold of yourself," Prien told Endrass. "We are going into Scapa Flow."[4]

THE U-47'S AUDACIOUS MISSION was not the spontaneous idea of an enthusiastic young lieutenant. It had been carefully planned in Berlin by Rear Admiral Karl Dönitz, the thin, pinch-faced, and reedy-voiced commander of the German navy's submarine force. Forty-seven years old in 1939, Dönitz had joined the German navy in 1910 at the age of eighteen. Commissioned three years later, he spent two years in surface ships before requesting a transfer to submarines (in German, *Unterseebooten*, or U-boats). While he had been commanding a U-boat in the Mediterranean near Malta in October 1918, a mishap in the engine room compelled him to surface in the middle of a convoy and he was taken prisoner, spending the last few weeks of the war in England. In spite of that experience, or perhaps because of it, he dedicated the rest of his life to the U-boat service.[5]

When Dönitz returned to Germany after the peace in 1919, he wanted to remain on active service in the navy even though the Versailles Treaty restricted the size of Germany's postwar navy to six older battleships, six light cruisers, and twenty-four smaller craft (destroyers and torpedo boats), banning submarines entirely. Convinced that these circumstances would not be permanent, Dönitz opted to remain in uniform, serving in a variety of billets in the small surface navy of the Weimar government while he waited for the time when U-boats would again become part of the service.[6]

Karl Dönitz was an ardent champion of U-boats throughout the interwar period and he commanded Germany's U-boat force after war began in September 1939. He regularly pressed Hitler to make U-boats the highest priority in the German military economy.

U.S. Naval Institute

It was a long wait. For fifteen years Dönitz served in a number of surface craft, rising to the rank of *Kapitän zur See* (captain) and commanding the light cruiser *Emden,* and still Germany possessed no U-boats, though all that time Dönitz never doubted that the day would come. During this interregnum, several clandestine efforts within Germany succeeded in sustaining and even expanding the kind of technical expertise that would be needed to revive the U-boat arm if the ban was ever lifted. A Dutch company acted as a cover for German naval architects and engineers who experimented with new submarine designs, and German firms built submarines for both Spain and Finland.[7]

Even before Hitler renounced the Versailles Treaty in 1935, Germany actively tested the boundaries of the restrictions. The first such test was the construction of the small battleship *Deutschland,* begun in 1929 and still under construction when the delegates met at the London Conference in 1930. While the Versailles Treaty allowed Germany to replace its six battleships as they aged, it specified that the replacement ships were not to exceed

10,000 tons displacement, even though the battleships of other Western nations were up to three times that size. In spite of that, the *Deutschland* exceeded the 10,000-ton limit by at least 20 percent, and her 11-inch guns and ten-thousand-mile cruising range suggested that she had been designed for missions other than coastal defense. Launched in 1931, she was bigger than any cruiser, yet smaller than a battleship, and she was colloquially known as a "pocket battleship," or in German, a *Panzerschiff* (literally "armored ship"). Her construction was a relatively minor transgression of the Versailles limits—the international equivalent of putting a cautious toe over a dare-mark line on the playground. Neither Britain nor France formally objected, and Germany soon constructed two more *Panzerschiffe*. Along with two new cruisers, the *Köln* and the *Karlsruhe*, they became "symbols of hope and spiritual rebirth" to champions of a German naval revival, including Dönitz.[8]

With the signing of the Anglo-German Naval Agreement in June 1935, Germany's naval revival accelerated. In particular, Germany began to build its first U-boats. The British were willing to tolerate the rebirth of the German U-boat arm that had nearly starved them into submission in the last war in large part because British scientists had developed a counterweapon. It was called Asdic, an acronym for the Anti-Submarine Detection Investigating Committee, which had helped to develop it in the 1920s. By sending out repeated electronic impulses, or pings, then timing and measuring the echo, Asdic equipment could locate and track submerged submarines. The Americans later developed a similar technology that they called sonar (sound navigation and ranging), but the British, for whom the technology was crucial, were a full decade ahead of them. Before Asdic, the first notice a surface ship was likely to have that a submarine was nearby was the explosion of a merchant ship struck by a torpedo. Now, Asdic could find and track a submerged submarine while it was still several thousand yards away. In some quarters, it was believed that Asdic made submarines all but obsolete as anti-ship weapons. A 1936 Admiralty memo claimed that thanks to Asdic, "the submarine should never again be able to present us with the problem we were faced in 1917." As subsequent events would demonstrate, such conclusions were wildly optimistic.[9]

The first German U-boats were small (250-ton) coastal craft, colloquially called *Nordsee Enten* or "North Sea ducks," which were clearly intended
for harbor defense. Several were assembled in secret even as the 1935 agreement was being negotiated, and the first of them was launched the day after
the treaty was signed. Soon enough, 500-ton and 750-ton boats began to
join the fleet. (Submarines, then as now, are generally called boats rather
than ships.) By 1939, the most common version was the Type VII, which
was 220 feet long, displaced 769 tons, and carried fourteen torpedoes that
could be fired from four forward tubes and one tube astern. Powered by
twin 1,400-horsepower diesel engines, Type VII-B boats had supplementary external tanks that nearly doubled their fuel capacity and extended
their range to 7,400 miles. They had a speed of seventeen knots on the surface, faster than any merchant ship or convoy, and possessed a 124-cell battery that enabled them to cruise for eighty miles while submerged, where
they could make 7.6 knots, though four knots was the best speed for conserving battery power. The Germans were able to produce these new boats
quickly once the new naval treaty was signed, because they had stockpiled
the components in advance, anticipating the lifting of the ban. Within
weeks of the signing of the Anglo-German Naval Agreement, Dönitz surrendered his command of the cruiser *Emden* to assume control of the
swiftly growing U-boat arm of the new Kriegsmarine.[10]

The British did seek to impose a different kind of restraint on the German
U-boats. In November 1936, Britain, France, Germany, and Italy all signed an
agreement in London that specified the protocols to be used by submarines
in time of war. All four signatories agreed that submarines were to act under
the same rules of engagement as surface ships. That is, they were to stop the
vessel in question and send a boarding party to examine its papers; if satisfied
of its belligerent status, they were to allow the crew and any passengers time
to escape into lifeboats. Only then could a submarine sink the ship with a
torpedo or with gunfire. Though all parties solemnly affixed their signatures
to this document, it is unclear whether any of them genuinely believed that,
should it come to war, those protocols would be strictly observed.

In 1938, citing the threat of Russian forces in the Baltic, Hitler invoked
the emergency clause in the Anglo-German treaty that authorized Germany

The U-36, seen here, was a Type VII-A U-boat built in 1935–36 after the Anglo-German Naval Agreement once again allowed Germany to build submarines. It was dangerous work—the U-36 went down with all hands in December 1939, sunk by the Royal Navy submarine *Salmon* off Norway.

Naval History and Heritage Command

to build U-boats up to the total possessed by Britain. Thus on September 3, 1939, when Chamberlain announced that war had begun, Dönitz had a total of fifty-seven U-boats—the same number as Britain—though only forty-six of them were ready for immediate operations, and half of those were the smaller coastal *Enten*. That gave Dönitz only about two dozen of the larger Type VII boats to begin the war.

Worse, from his perspective, was the fact that at any given moment, two-thirds of them would necessarily have to be en route to or from enemy shipping lanes, undergoing repairs, or taking on stores, so only a paltry eight or nine could be on station at a time. Dönitz had made it clear to Hitler that an effective trade war against Britain would require at least three hundred such boats. As late as August 28, only three days before the invasion of Poland, and six days before war with Britain began, he submitted a memorandum to the Führer stating bluntly that the German navy, and the U-boat arm in particular, were not "in a position to fulfill the tasks which will be allotted to them in the event of war." Hitler, however, was impatient, openly skeptical of British and French resolve, and he ordered German forces across the Polish frontier on September 1.[11]

Hitler had been astonishingly successful in calling the bluff of the Western powers concerning Austria, the Sudetenland, and Czechoslovakia, and he more than half expected that Britain and France would back down once again. For that reason, even after Britain and France declared war, he ordered Dönitz to abide strictly by the Hague convention and the 1936 London treaty concerning submarine warfare—at least for now. He did not want some untoward event to galvanize British attitudes and make a return to the negotiating table more difficult. Despite that, on the very first day of the war, Oberleutnant (lieutenant junior grade) Fritz-Julius Lemp, commander of the U-30, espied a ship a few hundred miles off the Irish coast that was proceeding blacked out and zigzagging, circumstances that suggested to Lemp that it must be either an armed merchant cruiser or a military transport ship and therefore a legitimate target.

The ship was, in fact, the commercial liner *Athenia*, with more than fourteen hundred passengers on board. Hit by two torpedoes, it went down quickly with over a hundred killed, including twenty-eight Americans. Only after he surfaced to witness the ship's death throes did Lemp discover the true character of the ship he had targeted. Hitler was furious, worried that the incident would derail a possible rapprochement with Britain. Officially, Germany denied responsibility and the German propaganda minister, Joseph Goebbels, suggested that the *Athenia* had very likely been sunk by the British themselves in order to elicit American sympathy, though few outside Germany took such claims seriously.[12]

For his part, Dönitz was only moderately disappointed that the Führer placed limits on his submarines, since with the small number of boats he had available, all he could do was deliver what he called "a few odd pin-pricks." Soon enough it became evident that the British were not going to reconsider their declaration of war after all, and Hitler lifted the restrictions, informing Dönitz that his U-boats could now attack without warning any vessel identified as hostile. Of course, warships had always been approved targets, and two weeks before Hitler lifted the ban on attacking merchant ships, Dönitz sent word to Lieutenant Prien that he had a special mission in mind for him.[13]

PRIEN WAITED UNTIL DARK before attempting to enter Scapa Flow. Quitting the tiny conning tower of the U-47 for the relative quiet of the control room, he called the crew forward and explained the mission. Then he ordered them to their diving stations. In his subsequent memoir, he recalled the moment vividly: the hatch cover dropping into place with a muffled clang, and the change in his ears as the boat pressurized. Crewmen closed the exhaust valves as the diesel engines were shut down, and a low-grade hum indicated that the electric motors had kicked in. Until the submarine surfaced again, the engines, lights, fans, and all other onboard machinery would run off the boat's batteries.[14]

Prien ordered the tanks flooded, and four kneeling men pressed down on levers that drove air from the ballast tanks. The hissing sound of escaping air was followed by the noise of seawater burbling into the tanks, and the U-47 inclined forward and downward. Instead of tossing on the surface, the U-boat was now suspended in the sea, producing what Prien described as "a sensation of floating as in a balloon." The noisome violence of the outside weather was replaced by an unnatural quiet as the submarine descended through the frigid North Sea waters and settled gently on the bottom, where Prien intended to wait until the following evening. The engines were cut and lights extinguished to save battery power. Though there was no logical reason for it, men instinctively spoke in whispers.[15]

At four o'clock the next afternoon, which was October 14, the crew of the U-47 was awakened and fed a rather extravagant meal (for a submarine) of veal cutlets and green cabbage. After that, the men checked the engines and the torpedoes to ensure that everything was in good order. At 7:00 p.m. Prien calculated that it would be full dark this far north in mid-October, and he ordered the U-47 to periscope depth—about forty-five feet. Once there, he ordered the scope raised and put his face to the eyepiece, swiveling the scope around 360 degrees. Seeing nothing, he ordered the boat to surface.

As the U-47 broke the surface, it rocked back and forth in the choppy sea, almost, Prien recalled, "as if half drunk from the immersion." Prien and Endrass climbed out onto the conning tower, so small it could barely accommodate them. They stood stock still and listened for the sound of screws in the water. Nothing. As their eyes adjusted, the shoreline became visible. Indeed, it seemed much *too* visible. Dönitz had timed Prien's sortie to coincide with the new moon, when it would be darkest, but the skies were unnaturally light. Orange and green flashes lit up the sky, and after a moment of confusion, Prien understood: it was the aurora borealis, the northern lights, of which he had heard but which he had never seen. He briefly considered calling off the operation and submerging again, then decided to go ahead. He ordered half speed, and as the U-47 approached the entrance to Holm Sound, Prien noted that one of the topside lookouts was staring upward at the flickering lights, his eyes wide in wonderment.[16]

The British, too, may have been staring skyward, for as the U-47 passed through Holm Sound and into the narrow channel of Kirk Sound, there was no challenge from the shore. The British had sunk several unmanned hulks in Kirk Sound to block the channel. More hulks were scheduled to be placed there soon, but on this night there was just enough room for the U-47, still on the surface, to squeeze between the northernmost of the hulks and the coastline. Visibility was limited despite the northern lights, and that made the slow passage difficult as the submarine threaded its way between the blockships and the rocky coast. At one point the U-47 became entangled with an anchor chain from one of the blockships, and not long after that the boat briefly touched bottom. A car driving along the coastal road passed by so close that its headlights washed across the sub's conning tower. Then, suddenly, the U-47 emerged from the narrow passage and into the wide expanse of Scapa Flow. Half surprised, Prien said in a loud whisper, "We are inside!"[17]

A number of tankers were at anchor in the lower bay, and while they would constitute a worthy target under any other circumstance, Prien was after bigger game. He turned the U-47 northward toward the upper reaches of the anchorage, and just past midnight, he saw it. Silhouetted against the shore—"hard and clear, as if painted into the sky with black ink"—was the unmistakable profile of a Royal Navy battleship.[18]

HMS *Royal Oak* was an older ship, launched in 1914 on the eve of the First World War. She was a battleship nonetheless, displacing some 30,000 tons, with a crew of over a thousand men, and armed with a main battery of eight 15-inch guns plus a secondary battery of fourteen 6-inch guns. Even one of her two 3-inch guns could blow the fragile U-47 out of the water. The *Royal Oak*'s major weakness was that her speed topped out at twenty-three knots, which was why she had been sent on her solitary mission to patrol Fair Isle Channel the week before instead of accompanying the task force sent to pursue the *Gneisenau* and *Köln*. Given the presumed security

HMS *Royal Oak* was one of five *Revenge*-class battleships in the Royal Navy, all of which bore names that started with the letter *R*, and all of which were old enough to have fought in the First World War. Though slow, the *Royal Oak* had heavy armor, including a thirteen-inch armor belt along her waterline.

Naval History and Heritage Command

of the anchorage in Scapa Flow, none of the Royal Navy ships had its Asdic system in active mode, though even if they had it would have done little good, for Asdic had been designed to track U-boats under water, and the U-47 was on the surface.

Excited by the spectacle of an enemy capital ship only four thousand yards away, Prien felt the blood hammering in his temples and found that he could hardly breathe. He quietly called down the hatch to prepare a spread of four torpedoes. There was a muffled gurgling sound as water ran into the opened tubes, a hiss of compressed air, and a metallic click as the levers snapped into position. Prien gave the order, and the U-47 lurched backward as the first torpedo left the tube, then two seconds later another, then a third. The fourth torpedo misfired. The torpedo officer counted off the seconds aloud as Prien and everyone else on board waited silently. After an interminable three and a half minutes, there was a muffled explosion near the bow of the *Royal Oak*, but no reaction from the battleship—no searchlights, no gunfire, and no secondary explosion.[19]

As it happened, two of the U-47's torpedoes had missed entirely, and the third struck only the *Royal Oak's* forward anchor cable, cutting the cable and sending up a geyser of seawater that splashed up onto the foredeck, but doing no evident structural damage. The men of the battleship's duty section instinctively looked skyward, the only conceivable direction from which danger was likely to come. They had heard no aircraft sounds, however, and were uncertain about what had happened. One suggested that perhaps a CO_2 tank had exploded; others wondered if the anchor chain had run out and splashed noisily into the sea. The commanding officer of the *Royal Oak*, Captain William G. Benn, who had been asleep in his cabin, came topside to see what the commotion was. He at once suspected an internal explosion, and sent a team below to discover the cause and report. He did not order the ship to general quarters. Indeed, many on the crew did not even hear the explosion, and most of those who did simply turned over in their bunks, assuming that if it was important, there would be an announcement. There was no announcement. Based on the reports he received, Benn concluded, as he later testified, "that some explosion must have occurred in the Inflammable Store from internal causes."[20]

Prien, meanwhile, turned the sub around and fired again with his stern tube. That torpedo, too, either missed the target or failed to explode. Undaunted, Prien then headed southward, away from the *Royal Oak*, to reload his bow tubes. An hour later, just past 1:00 a.m., with the crew of the battleship still no wiser about his presence, he returned to fire three more torpedoes.

This time the results were spectacular. A massive plume of water, as high as the ship's superstructure, erupted amidships, followed in quick succession by two more. Pieces of the ship flew skyward, and flames in a variety of colors—blue, red, and yellow—shot up into the night. Black smoke roiled up from the spaces below, and the big ship began listing heavily to starboard. Within minutes she was sinking. Several of the watertight doors had been dogged shut for safety, and now they blocked the way as hundreds of men tried to scramble out from the lower decks. As the big battleship slowly rolled over, the giant 15-inch gun turrets broke off and toppled into the sea. As they did, more flames shot up from inside the ship. Those of the crew who had managed to make their way topside jumped into the frigid water.

The great battleship rolled majestically over onto its starboard side, with the escaping air producing a noise that, to at least one witness, sounded exactly like a forlorn sigh. Three hundred and seventy men survived; more than eight hundred did not.[21]

Elated by this vista of destruction, Prien called down through the hatch into the control room, "He's finished!" and the announcement provoked wild cheering until Prien ordered them to be silent. By now the British knew this was no internal accident, and Prien assumed that they would be eager to seek out the deadly menace that had found its way into their midst. Searchlights probed from a nearby seaplane carrier (which Prien mis-identified as another battleship), and several ships that Prien assumed to be destroyers got under way. It was time to leave.

He kept the U-47 on the surface, where it could make seventeen knots, as opposed to only seven knots when submerged, and raced for the exit. A surface ship behind him was perceptibly gaining, and Prien ordered "extreme speed," only to be told that the engines were already at extreme speed. It would be only moments before the destroyer—if that's what it was—was on them. Despite the northern lights, however, the skipper of the pursuing ship did not see the low silhouette of the sub running on the surface, and turned away. As Prien gripped the safety rail and silently urged the boat to go faster, the U-47 pressed on for the narrow exit.

The tide was falling now and, recalling the shallow water along the north-ern coastline, Prien decided to hug the southern edge of the sound on the way out. He squeezed past another blockship and maneuvered around a jutting promontory. Gradually the sounds of the *Royal Oak* breaking apart grew more distant. By two-fifteen in the morning of October 15, the U-47 was back in the open sea. Prien set a course southward for Wilhelmshaven, and told his men they could now cheer all they wanted.[22]

The trip back was not without incident. British patrol boats caught up with the U-47 in the Moray Firth, on the east coast of Scotland, and forced it to dive. Prien tried to escape by changing course while submerged, but the British ships were equipped with Asdic and tracked him underwater. The men in the U-47 could hear the eerie and insistent *ping...ping...ping* of the searching Asdic, and soon enough, depth charges began to detonate nearby, sounding like a hammer smashing against the hull: a sharp metallic clang followed by a deafening wham. The fragile sub shuddered like a rat shaken by a terrier; lightbulbs shattered, and one of the boat's two drive shafts, sheared in half by the concussion, broke free from its bearings. Prien again took the U-47 to the bottom and stayed there hoping to outlast his pursuers. Those crewmen not working to repair the broken shaft bearings tiptoed around in slippers to avoid making any sound. The British continued their search, and the men in the U-47 could hear both the pinging of the active Asdic and the whir of propellers passing overhead. Eventually, however, the pinging ceased and the sound of the propellers moved away. With both air and battery power running low, Prien took the U-47 to periscope depth to discover that his tormentors had left. With the shaft repaired, he again set a course for Wilhelmshaven.[23]

PRIEN'S TRIUMPH in Scapa Flow was not the first U-boat success of the war. Despite the long voyages necessary for them to reach their cruising grounds west of Ireland, Dönitz's handful of U-boats sank more than sixty Allied ships in the first six weeks of the war—ten ships a week. Most of them were merchant ships, though that number also included the British aircraft carrier *Courageous*, sunk by the U-29 off Ireland in mid-September four weeks before Prien's exploit in Scapa Flow. Hit by three torpedoes, the *Courageous* went down in a mere fifteen minutes with the loss of 519 men. That was especially worrisome because the Royal Navy had only five carriers in commission at the time. The sinking of the *Courageous*, therefore, represented the loss of 20 percent of her carrier force. Yet Prien's accomplishment in Scapa Flow was unique. It was chilling to the British Admiralty that a solitary U-boat had managed to penetrate the inner sanctum of the Royal Navy, sink one of its battleships at anchor, and get clean away—bearding the British lion in its den. For Germany it was wonderful propaganda, and Goebbels made the most of it. Both Dönitz and his boss, Grossadmiral Erich Raeder, the head of the Kriegsmarine, came on board the U-47 when it arrived in Wilhelmshaven to congratulate Prien and his crew, and Hitler sent his personal airplane to fly Prien to Berlin for a parade from Templehof Airport to the Kaiserhof Hotel.[24]

Dönitz was under no illusions that sinking one carrier and one battleship would significantly affect the trajectory of the war. He was convinced that the real target of his U-boats was not the Royal Navy but Britain's merchant trade, and he was aware that it would be many months, if not years, before he possessed a sufficient number of operational U-boats to mount the kind of campaign he believed necessary to have a strategic impact on the war. Then, too, the first several weeks of war had revealed flaws in the torpedoes that were the U-boats' principal weapon. The triggers in the warheads were magnetic, and when operating in northern latitudes, they often failed to work. Dönitz estimated that during the first six weeks of war, "at least 25 percent of all shots fired have been torpedo failures." He worried that if U-boat crews lost confidence in their torpedoes, it would erode their morale and their willingness to take risks. He resolved to do all he could "to keep up the fighting spirits" of the U-boat crews. He did not sugarcoat it. He warned his officers that the war would be neither swift nor easy. It could last for seven years, he told them, and even then it might end with a negotiated settlement rather than outright victory. Still, he was determined to do what he perceived as his duty, and that meant building up the U-boat arm as swiftly as possible so that it could destroy not ten ships a week, but twenty, thirty, or more, cutting off British trade altogether.[25]

PANZERSCHIFFE

O N THE DAY THAT KAPITÄNLEUTNANT PRIEN AND THE U-47 entered Scapa Flow, the German pocket battleship *Graf Spee* was more than five thousand miles almost due south in the middle of the Atlantic Ocean, halfway between Africa and Brazil. In contrast to the bitter cold of the North Sea, the water temperature here was in the high seventies. The *Graf Spee* was one of the three *Panzerschiffen* that Germany had built in the early 1930s. In August, Hitler had authorized Grossadmiral Erich Raeder, the administrative and operational head of the Kriegsmarine, to pre-position two of them—*Deutschland* and *Graf Spee*—in the Atlantic, where they would inaugurate a campaign against British shipping in the event that Britain followed through with its threat to declare war if Germany invaded Poland.

Since then, the invasion had taken place as planned, and the British had indeed declared war, yet for three weeks the *Graf Spee* had stayed out of the shipping lanes and scrupulously avoided contact with other vessels. The reason was Hitler's conviction that the British could be enticed back to the negotiating table once Poland had been dispatched by a swift German victory. Just as he had ordered Dönitz's U-boats to pull their punches, Hitler ordered Raeder to restrain his surface raiders. Finally on September 26, with the war in Poland all but settled (Warsaw would fall the next day), Hitler decided that the British were not going to be reasonable after all, and he authorized the *Deutschland* in the North Atlantic and the *Graf Spee* in the South Atlantic to begin offensive operations.[1]

The *Graf Spee* was under the command of Kapitän zur See Hans Langsdorff, a career officer with a high-domed forehead who was something of a throwback in the Kriegsmarine: a gentleman warrior of the old school, correct, punctilious, and unwilling to let war interfere with good manners. He adopted a benign demeanor with his subordinates, and even with his foes. Langsdorff had been inspired to join the navy in 1912 at the age of eighteen because of his admiration for a Düsseldorf neighbor, Admiral Maximilian von Spee, a Prussian nobleman who bore the title of count (in German, *Graf*). Von Spee had been killed in the 1914 Battle of the Falklands, and in a curious coincidence Langsdorff now commanded the ship that subsequently had been named for him. Almost certainly Langsdorff would have preferred combat operations to stalking and sinking unarmed merchantmen, but that was his assignment and he was willing, if not altogether eager, to do what was necessary for victory.[2]

Once Langsdorff received orders to commence active operations against British shipping, he began to search for prey. On September 30, lookouts reported a thin trace of smoke on the horizon. Langsdorff ordered the ship's scout plane catapulted off its rail amidships, and turned the *Graf Spee* toward the contact. The smoke was from the stack of a British merchant ship, the *Clement*, an undistinguished steamer of some 5,000 tons displacement characterized by one contemporary as "a typical tubby, ocean-going, tramp."[3]

The captain of the *Clement*, F. P. C. Harris, had only a bows-on view of the swiftly approaching warship, and at first he thought it might be the British cruiser *Ajax*, which he believed to be operating in the area. He appreciated his error when the *Spee*'s scout plane flew past, spraying his bridge with machine gun fire. At once Harris stopped his ship's engines, ordered the lifeboats hoisted out, and began to destroy the *Clement*'s confidential documents, which included Britain's naval codes. He also sent out a distress signal over the wireless radio, repeatedly flashing the letters "RRR" to indicate that he was under attack by a surface raider, and providing the coordinates.* Langsdorff was disappointed that the British ship had managed to get off a radio signal, but he was all courtesy when Harris was brought on board the *Graf Spee*. Langsdorff saluted him and remarked in perfect English, "I am sorry, Captain, but I will have to sink your ship. It is war."[4]

Langsdorff saw to it that Harris and the *Clement*'s chief engineer were comfortably settled on the *Graf Spee*, and ensured the safety of the rest of the *Clement*'s crew in their lifeboats, even reporting their location to the nearest ports on the Brazilian coast. Then he ordered the *Clement* sunk by torpedoes. The first torpedo missed, as did the second, and rather than expend more of these expensive (and apparently unreliable) weapons on a tramp steamer, Langsdorff decided to use the *Graf Spee*'s secondary 5.9-inch guns. After twenty-five rounds, the *Clement* remained stubbornly afloat, and Langsdorff ordered the *Graf Spee*'s big 11-inch guns to finish her off. After five rounds, the *Clement* finally slipped beneath the waves.[5]

LIKE PRIEN'S MISSION TO SCAPA FLOW, Langsdorff's presence in the South Atlantic was part of a larger operational scheme. The orders that had sent him there were a product of Admiral Raeder's vision of a war on British trade carried out by dozens of swift surface raiders. If Dönitz was a lifelong advocate of U-boats, Raeder was a dedicated champion of the surface navy. He had spent the First World War in battleships and cruisers, and had participated in both of the great surface battles of that war at Dogger Bank and Jutland. In the latter battle, he had been the chief of staff to Vice Admiral Franz von Hipper.

---

* Rather than the conventional SOS, established in 1905 as a universal distress signal, the British Admiralty adopted a new protocol with the outbreak of war. As noted above, RRR (or RRRR), repeated several times, indicated an attack by a surface raider; SSS indicated a submarine attack, and AAA an air attack. After that, the vessel in distress provided its identity in a series of code letters, and then its position in latitude and longitude.

Grossadmiral Erich Raeder, head of the German navy since 1928, hoped to create a traditional surface navy centered on battleships and battlecruisers. He crafted a long-range plan to achieve that goal based on Hitler's assurances that war would not begin until 1946 or 1947.

U.S. Naval Institute

Raeder was fifteen years older than Dönitz, and very different in both appearance and temperament. Unlike the cadaverous Dönitz, Raeder was robust and handsome. Indeed, to many he was the idealized personification of Prussian manhood. He admired strict discipline and formal protocols, and possessed a strong work ethic that he imposed on others as well as himself. He later listed his core values as "fear of God, love of truth, and cleanliness." Raeder was skeptical of the relaxed, comradely environment that Dönitz encouraged among his U-boat crews where, in Dönitz's words, "every man's well-being was in the hands of all and where every single man was an indispensable part of the whole." Such communal claptrap did not appeal to Raeder, who was a product of the Kaiserliche—the old imperial navy—and preferred to maintain what he considered a dignified professionalism.

As one example of that, he sought to reestablish the requirement, abolished during the Weimar years, that all navy personnel attend formal religious services every Sunday. On this, as on other issues, Raeder occasionally clashed with Hitler, who had little interest in religious services—or in a large surface navy, for that matter—and at least twice Raeder submitted his resignation in response to one of Hitler's tirades. In both cases Hitler prevailed upon him to withdraw it and stay on.[6]

Despite their differences, Raeder shared Dönitz's commitment to a revived German navy, as well as a hope that any future war could be postponed until at least 1944 or 1945 so that they would have time to develop the kind of fleet they believed necessary for victory. Raeder had become chief of the Admiralty in 1928, and from the start he had focused his efforts on building a balanced fleet centered on battleships and battlecruisers— the kind of navy that defined sea power in the first half of the twentieth century. In another divergence from Dönitz, be believed that submarines were useful auxiliaries, but hardly a foundation for naval greatness. Once the 1935 Anglo-German Naval Agreement opened the door for expansion, Raeder got to work to produce the kind of navy he envisioned.

In addition to the three pocket battleships built in the early 1930s, Raeder championed a far more ambitious construction program that included battleships, heavy cruisers, and even aircraft carriers. The first step in the fulfillment of this vision was the construction of two sleek new battlecruisers, subsequently christened the *Scharnhorst* and the *Gneisenau*. At 771 feet, they were longer than the newest British battleships; they were designated as battlecruisers rather than battleships because they had 11-inch guns instead of 15-inch guns, and less protective deck armor. That also made them both lighter (though still quite large at 32,000 tons) and faster (thirty-one knots) than most battleships. Laid down in 1935 within days of the naval treaty with Britain, they were commissioned in 1938 and 1939, just in time for the war. Raeder also presided over the construction of two even larger warships: the battleships *Bismarck* and *Tirpitz*. Displacing more than 40,000 tons empty and over 50,000 tons when fully equipped, they were each armed with eight 15-inch guns, making them the largest and most powerful battleships in the world when they were laid down in 1936. Both remained under construction when the war began, though they were only months from completion.[7]

In constructing this new navy, Raeder envisioned a possible future conflict with Poland over Danzig—a war that might easily involve France—or perhaps a war with Russia for control of the Baltic Sea. He did not, however, envision a war against Britain. Like many other Kriegsmarine officers, Raeder believed that fighting Britain in the First World War had been "a tragic mistake which should never be repeated," and that a future war with Britain was out of the question. Hitler assured him that he shared in this view, repeatedly telling Raeder that Britain was not a potential foe in any future war. Not until November 1937, in a secret meeting with his service chiefs, did Hitler announce that the admirals and generals should begin to plan for a war with Britain as well as with France, and that such a war could begin well before 1944.[8]

Raeder was annoyed by this volte-face, which he attributed to Hitler's "self deception" about British determination. There would be no opportunity now to build the kind of balanced fleet that Raeder believed the country needed and deserved. In his private diary, he wrote bitterly that the new circumstances doomed his beloved Kriegsmarine to proving that it could "die gallantly." Raeder nevertheless embraced a program crafted by a young staff officer, Commander Helmuth Heye, which called for a fleet composed of ten large battleships to tie down the British main fleet, and fifteen of the swift *Panzerschiffe* to savage British commerce. Even this less ambitious plan was doomed to failure, since Hitler's timetable for a confrontation over Poland ensured that it could not be completed before the outbreak of war.[9]

Denied the opportunity to challenge British supremacy with a daunting surface fleet, Raeder embraced a plan to starve her into capitulation. Trade was Britain's lifeline, and during the First World War, U-boats had been the principal tool by which Germany had sought to strangle that trade. While Raeder did not discount the importance of U-boats in this new war, he also wanted to sow mines in the sea-lanes around the British Isles, and employ a fleet of swift surface raiders. The mines, mostly dropped by airplane, proved especially effective in the first few months of war, in part because the

Germans had developed a sophisticated magnetic mine that detonated when a ship passing overhead disturbed the magnetic field. By the end of 1939, of the 422,000 tons of shipping lost by the British, more than half of it was to magnetic mines. The British countered this new technology by demagnetizing their ships, wrapping electrical cables around them in a protocol known as degaussing. This dramatically reduced the effectiveness of the mines, though they remained a serious threat throughout the war.[10]

In addition to U-boats and mines, Raeder also counted heavily on surface raiders, though his resources were limited. He had only the three pocket battleships, two battlecruisers, a handful of cruisers, and (as soon as they were complete) the two big battleships. Still, he hoped that these modest assets, if deployed creatively, would compel the British to disperse their own warships in order to protect their convoys and thereby weaken themselves elsewhere. "By scattering our forces all over the globe," he wrote in his postwar memoir, "we might hope to hit damaging surprise blows before the enemy would bring up superior forces to meet us."[11]

Forewarned by Hitler of the imminent invasion of Poland, Raeder obtained permission to dispatch two of the pocket battleships into the Atlantic, the *Deutschland* in the North Atlantic south of Greenland, and the *Graf Spee* in the South Atlantic. Should Britain determine to challenge German ambitions, these two ships would begin a campaign of destruction against British trade. For all his disappointment at the turn of events, Raeder was determined "to use all possible means to damage and disrupt the enemy."[12]

IN CONDUCTING A CAMPAIGN OF COMMERCE RAIDING, Langsdorff and the *Graf Spee* acted in conformance with a long-standing maritime tradition. More than seventy-five years earlier, in May and June 1863, the Confederate raider CSS *Alabama*, which had been built and fitted out in England, had conducted a commerce-raiding cruise against American shipping in these same waters, destroying a dozen merchant ships off the eastern tip of Brazil. The captain of the *Alabama*, Raphael Semmes, had been unable to bring his prizes into port for adjudication, and so, after removing the crew and any passengers, he had set the ships afire. Periodically

Semmes had spared a prize, filled it with his accumulated prisoners, and sent it off as a cartel. That 1863 campaign was very nearly a template for Langsdorff and the *Graf Spee*. One great difference between 1863 and 1939, however, was the advent of wireless radio, which enabled the victims to report the location of a raiding warship even as it approached, as Harris had done on the *Clement*. Langsdorff knew that his campaign against British shipping would be effective only if he remained elusive, and that would not be possible if every ship he stopped immediately reported his position.

Langsdorff's sinking of the *Clement* provoked a reaction in England. The distress signal sent out by Captain Harris had been picked up by a Brazilian ship and relayed onward, reaching London the next day. On October 4, Admiral Sir Dudley Pound, the British First Sea Lord, presided over a meeting at Admiralty House in London to determine how to respond to this new danger. Pound had spent nearly half a century in the Royal Navy. Like Raeder, he had fought at Jutland, where he had commanded the battleship *Colossus* with considerable distinction. Though the sixty-four-year-old

Admiral of the Fleet Sir Dudley Pound became First Sea Lord in June 1939, just three months before the outbreak of war. He had served in the Royal Navy for forty-six years, and his indifferent health was a concern even at the time of his appointment.

U.S. Naval Institute

Pound was Raeder's chronological contemporary, he looked at least a decade older, in part due to his indifferent health. Arthritis in his hip caused him to walk with a slight limp, and he had a tendency to doze off during lengthy staff meetings. At least one Royal Navy officer thought he was "a worn out old man." Even less charitably, others described him as "pig-headed" and temperamentally unsuited for the job of First Sea Lord. Then, too, he was relatively new to the job. Whereas Raeder had been in charge of the German navy since 1928, Pound had become First Sea Lord in the summer of 1939, only four months before the war began.[13]

In response to the news from the Atlantic, Pound and his advisors in the Admiralty considered their options. Though a convoy system had already been implemented for the vital transatlantic shipping from Canada and the United States, the small escort vessels assigned to North Atlantic convoy duty had no chance against a pocket battleship, so the first decision made by Pound and the Admiralty was to send several older battleships to Halifax to serve as additional escorts. As for the South Atlantic, there were simply not enough escorts to establish a network of convoys there. The Admiralty did, however, send a battlecruiser, HMS *Renown*, plus the aircraft carrier *Ark Royal*, escorted by a small cruiser, into the South Atlantic to look for what they believed was a different pocket battleship, the *Admiral Scheer*.[14]

More broadly, Pound and the Admiralty developed a whole new protocol for defending British commerce from surface raiders. Instead of using warships to patrol the sea-lanes as if they were police cruisers on oceanic highways, the British created half a dozen hunter-killer groups, most of them composed of two cruisers each. One (dubbed Force F) headed for North America, another (Force H) headed for South Africa, a third (Force G) went to the east coast of South America, and a fourth (Force M) steamed for Dakar, in French West Africa, to join French forces there, including the new battlecruiser *Dunkerque*. This, of course, was exactly what Raeder had hoped to achieve: the dispersion of Royal Navy assets in pursuit of a few surface raiders.[15]

The written orders for these hunter-killer groups stated bluntly that "the strength of each hunting group is sufficient to destroy any armored ship of the DEUTSCHLAND class or armored cruiser of the HIPPER class." That assertion—that two Royal Navy cruisers would be "sufficient" to defeat a pocket battleship—reflected the lingering faith in Whitehall, and indeed throughout the service, that Royal Navy ships could prevail over forces that were nominally more powerful because of superior British skill and élan. This legacy of the Napoleonic era continued to influence British thinking despite the disappointment—even the embarrassment—of the Battle of Jutland during the First World War, when the German High Seas Fleet had more than held its own against the British Grand Fleet. Most of the cruisers now being sent to confront the *Admiral Scheer* (actually the *Graf Spee*, of course) were heavy cruisers with six 8-inch guns plus a substantial secondary battery. The *Graf Spee*, however, had six 11-inch guns that could outrange the British cruisers by thirty-five hundred yards—nearly two miles. The Germans could probably get off a dozen or more salvos during the three or four minutes it took for the cruisers to get close enough to open fire. Of course, if the British cruisers operated in pairs, the Germans would have multiple targets to deal with, while the British could focus all their fire on the pocket battleship. In any case, it was evident that the Admiralty fully expected that by attacking together, the British cruisers could overmaster the German raider.[16]

ON OCTOBER 14, 1939, the same day that Prien and the U-47 slipped into Scapa Flow, Langsdorff kept a scheduled rendezvous with his supply ship, the modified tanker *Altmark*, which had been sent into the Atlantic in August precisely to act as Langsdorff's floating base. By then, the *Graf Spee* had sunk four ships including the *Clement*, and the pattern of her rampage was well established. The *Graf Spee* was one of only four ships in the Kriegsmarine that had radar, a technology that was still in its infancy. Even so, more often than not, Langsdorff had to rely on visual sightings to discover his quarry. Spotting a wisp of smoke on the horizon or receiving a sighting report from his floatplane pilot, Langsdorff steamed at full speed toward the contact, ordering it by blinker light—in English Morse code—to stop, and not to transmit any wireless signals. Despite that, in most cases the captain of the steamer at once began to send a radio message. That inaugurated a test of wills in a potentially deadly cat-and-mouse game.

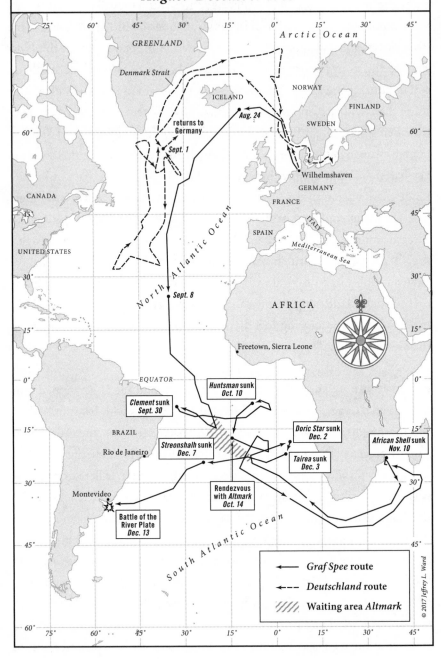

THE CRUISES OF THE *GRAF SPEE* AND *DEUTSCHLAND*
August–December 1939

Arctic Ocean

GREENLAND

Denmark Strait

ICELAND

NORWAY

Aug. 24

SWEDEN

FINLAND

returns to
Germany

Sept. 1

Wilhelmshaven

GERMANY

CANADA

North Atlantic Ocean

FRANCE

SPAIN

ITALY

Mediterranean Sea

UNITED STATES

AFRICA

Sept. 8

Freetown, Sierra Leone

EQUATOR

**Huntsman sunk
Oct. 10**

**Clement sunk
Sept. 30**

**Doric Star sunk
Dec. 2**

**African Shell sunk
Nov. 10**

BRAZIL

**Streonshalh sunk
Dec. 7**

**Tairea sunk
Dec. 3**

Rio de Janeiro

Montevideo

**Rendezvous
with Altmark
Oct. 14**

**Battle of the
River Plate
Dec. 13**

South Atlantic Ocean

— *Graf Spee* route

---- *Deutschland* route

//// Waiting area *Altmark*

© 2017 Jeffrey L. Ward

As one example of that, on October 22 when the *Graf Spee* stopped the steamer *Trevanian* in mid-ocean, Langsdorff sent his usual warning ("If you transmit on your wireless I will fire"). Almost immediately, however, the radio operator on the *Graf Spee* detected an outgoing message from the *Trevanian*, and Langsdorff ordered his machine gunners to spray her bridge. That seemed to do the trick, as the transmission suddenly ceased. On board the *Trevanian*, however, the ship's captain, J. M. Edwards, went into the radio room and asked the wireless operator if he had managed to send out the complete message. The nervous operator said no, that he had stopped sending when the gunfire started. Edwards ordered him to send it again, and stood by him while he did so. When the renewed transmission was detected on the *Graf Spee*, Langsdorff ordered the machine guns to open fire again. This time, despite bullets flying into and past the radio room, the wireless operator completed the message.[17]

Rather than resent this British defiance, Langsdorff admired it. As one of his officers wrote later, "When there are brave men on the other side, the machine-gun fire is of little use." For Langsdorff, the good news was that his own radio operators did not detect an acknowledgment of the *Trevanian's* distress signal, so he could hope that perhaps it had not been received by anyone. In any case, when Edwards was brought on board the *Graf Spee*, Langsdorff offered his usual apology, telling him, "I am sorry I have to sink your ship. War is war." When Edwards remained stubbornly silent, Langsdorff reached out, seized his hand, and firmly shook it.[18]

Having sunk five ships in less than four weeks, Langsdorff decided to change his hunting grounds by passing around the Cape of Good Hope into the Indian Ocean, and after another prearranged rendezvous with the *Altmark* near the tiny and remote island of Tristan de Cunha, he headed eastward, giving the cape a wide berth in order to stay beyond the range of British reconnaissance aircraft. Once in the Indian Ocean, however, he found slim pickings. For a week he searched fruitlessly for a likely victim, finally stopping the small tanker *Africa Shell* in the Mozambique Channel. Her captain protested that his ship was within three miles of Portuguese Mozambique, and since Portugal was neutral, the capture was illegal. Langsdorff took a careful survey and insisted that the *Africa Shell* was seven miles from shore and therefore a legitimate prize. Having revealed his presence in the Indian Ocean, however, Langsdorff turned south again to reenter the Atlantic.[19]

By then it was November. The *Graf Spee* had been continuously at sea for nearly four months and had cruised more than thirty thousand miles, equivalent to a circumnavigation of the globe. The *Deutschland*, after a disappointing cruise that resulted in the destruction of only two ships, had already been recalled from her cruising grounds in the North Atlantic, and Langsdorff suspected that he, too, would soon have to return to Germany. On the other hand, he still had sufficient fuel and supplies to last through January, and he began to think that a fine way to cap off his cruise would be to defeat an enemy warship. On November 24, he told his officers that with the cruise so near its end, it was no longer necessary to avoid enemy warships so scrupulously. Indeed, Langsdorff's actions after November suggest that he was actively seeking a battle. For one thing, he disguised the *Graf Spee* with a false smokestack amidships and a dummy gun turret made out of wood and canvas, modifications that so changed his ship's profile that from a distance she could well be mistaken for the British battlecruiser *Renown*. That might allow him to get within gun range of an unsuspecting British cruiser.[20]

Another clue that Langsdorff might be seeking a fight was his apparent unconcern about revealing his location. On the afternoon of December 2, several hundred miles off the coast of Namibia in the South Atlantic, the *Graf Spee* encountered the *Doric Star*, a large (10,000-ton) steamer of the Blue Star line, carrying a cargo of mutton and wool from New Zealand to Britain. Abandoning his usual protocol of steaming up to the quarry while flashing a signal not to employ the wireless, Langsdorff instead fired a number of warning shots from long range. That gave the captain of the *Doric Star*, William Stubbs, time to send off several detailed and repeated distress calls while the *Graf Spee* closed the range. When he got closer, Langsdorff did send his usual signal: "Stop your wireless or I will open fire." By then, however, Stubbs had already sent off repeated signals and had received acknowledgments from several vessels.[21]

After sinking the *Doric Star*, Langsdorff barely had time to contemplate his next move before lookouts espied yet another potential victim—the steamer *Tairoa*. Once again, Langsdorff's warning not to transmit had little impact, and even after the *Graf Spee*'s guns opened fire, the *Tairoa*'s wireless operator, lying prone on the deck, got off several messages, even identifying the attacker as the *Admiral Scheer*. The capture of two ships so quickly, each of which managed to send out detailed reports, provided the British with more information than they had previously had. For more than two months, the enormous size of Langsdorff's cruising ground had allowed him to hide in plain sight. That was about to change.[22]

THE REPORTS from the *Doric Star* and the *Tairoa* reached the bridge of the Royal Navy light cruiser *Ajax* on December 3. The *Ajax* was the temporary flagship of Commodore Henry Harwood, commander of the hunter-killer group Force G. Comfortably plump and somewhat jowly, with impressive bushy eyebrows, Harwood was a thirty-six-year veteran of the service. His command included a total of four cruisers, though on December 3 they were spread out all over the South Atlantic. Two of them were heavy (8-inch gun) cruisers, and two others, including the *Ajax*, were light (6-inch gun) cruisers. Collectively they could well prove more than a match for the *Graf Spee*, as the British Admiralty had assumed, but only if Harwood could concentrate them in the right place at the right time. He was aboard *Ajax* on that December 3 because his regular flagship, the heavy cruiser *Exeter*, was undergoing a much-needed refit at Port Stanley in the Falklands, more than four thousand miles from the scene of the *Graf Spee*'s latest predation. His other heavy cruiser, the *Cumberland*, was a thousand miles to the north and en route back to the Falklands for her own refit. Besides the *Ajax*, Harwood's other light cruiser was the *Achilles*, manned predominantly by New Zealanders. It had come from the South Pacific through the Straits of Magellan in late October and was now in Rio de Janeiro.*

In receipt of the twin sighting reports, Harwood tried to put himself in the mind of his adversary. He was sure that the German captain, whoever he

---

* The New Zealand navy was not formally constituted as a separate service until September 1941, so in 1939 the *Achilles* technically belonged to the New Zealand Division of the Royal Navy.

was, would vacate the area of his recent captures as soon as possible. Most likely he would head west again, recrossing the Atlantic toward South America. If the German captain wanted to have the maximum impact on South Atlantic commerce, he would very likely go where the shipping lanes converged. There were two such places on the South American coast: Rio de Janeiro and the wide estuary at the mouth of the river Plate that led up to Montevideo, the capital of Uruguay. Doodling possible routes on a piece of message paper, Harwood calculated that, at a cruising speed of fifteen knots, the German pocket battleship might be expected to arrive on the South American coast somewhere between those two cities early on the morning of December 12. Making the plunge, he ordered the ships of his command, less the *Cumberland*, which still had to complete its refit, to rendezvous at seven o'clock on the morning of December 12 at a designated position halfway between Montevideo and Rio. If he had guessed right, he intended to attack the German pocket battleship immediately with all three of his cruisers. His orders to his ship captains read: "Attack at once by day or night."[23]

Harwood's assumptions about the movements of the *Graf Spee* were incorrect, for the German raider headed west not at fifteen knots but at twenty-two knots. On the other hand, Langsdorff stopped en route to effect another meeting with the *Altmark*, and he also made another capture—of the steamer *Streonshalh*—and these activities slowed his westward journey, so even though Harwood's calculations were wrong, his conclusion turned out to be very nearly spot on. As it happened, a Buenos Aires newspaper retrieved from the *Streonshalh* informed Langsdorff that the British were using Buenos Aires as a gathering spot for convoys, and a radio update from Berlin informed him that a convoy from the river Plate, escorted by one cruiser and two destroyers, was soon to depart from there. To intercept it, Langsdorff set a course for the coast of South America.

Meanwhile, Harwood successfully concentrated three of his four cruisers (*Cumberland* was still en route) at the designated rendezvous, and at 6:10 on the morning of December 13, lookouts spotted a trace of smoke on the horizon. Harwood sent the *Exeter* to investigate, and the resulting report was electrifying: "I think it is a pocket battleship." Harwood at once ordered all three of his ships to increase speed and spread out in order to attack the *Graf Spee* from different quarters.[24]

Langsdorff, too, decided to attack. Based on the report he had received from Berlin, he believed he faced the convoy escort of one cruiser and two destroyers. Even after the two smaller ships were correctly identified as light cruisers, Langsdorff held his course, remarking to his senior gunnery officer, Commander F. W. Raseneck, "We'll smash them." What a fine culmination to his cruise this victory would make.[25]

Langsdorff conducted the battle from the foretop, a small (three-by-five-foot) platform above the bridge. From there he could track the course of all three British ships, though it also cut him off from the plotting table and the advice of other officers—only his young flag lieutenant stood with him. The greater range and firepower of the *Graf Spee*'s 11-inch guns gave him an early advantage. Shells from the *Graf Spee*'s second salvo straddled the *Exeter*, and on the fifth salvo, an 11-inch shell struck squarely on *Exeter*'s second forward turret (the B turret), just below the bridge. The turret was utterly wrecked, its twin 8-inch guns thrown drunkenly askew, and the explosion smashed up the bridge as well, killing everyone there except the ship's captain, Frederick S. Bell, and two others. It also cut off all internal communication. Bell had to quit the bridge and carry on the fight from the after control room, using messengers for communication. Hit seven times in twenty minutes, the *Exeter* was soon left with only one working gun, taking on water and listing badly to starboard. Bell nevertheless continued the fight until Harwood ordered him to retire and make his way to Port Stanley under best speed. That left Harwood with only the two light cruisers to face a pocket battleship, and they, too, had received serious damage. *Ajax* took an 11-inch shell in her stern that put both of her rear turrets out of action, and another shell took down her mast. On *Achilles*, an 11-inch shell blew shrapnel across the bridge, creating a horrible execution. It was some minutes before anyone on the bridge realized that the range-finding operator, hunched over his equipment, was in fact dead.[26]

Of course, *Graf Spee* had been hurt, too. The most serious damage had resulted from the *Exeter*'s 8-inch shells, three of which hit home, and one of which penetrated the *Graf Spee*'s 3.1-inch-thick armor belt. The 6-inch shells from the light cruisers hit more frequently but did less damage. Nevertheless, thirty-seven of the *Graf Spee*'s crew had been killed, and fifty-seven more were wounded, including Langsdorff, who was knocked unconscious and probably suffered a concussion, though after coming to he remained at his post in the foretop.[27]

When Harwood ordered his two cruisers to launch torpedoes, Langsdorff turned away to avoid them. That created a respite in the battle during which the opposing commanders assessed their circumstances. Harwood concluded that it would be folly to continue the attack with only his two smaller ships, and he remained out of range. As for Langsdorff, rather than finish off the *Exeter* or attack the two small cruisers, he instead allowed the British ships to withdraw. He conducted a quick inspection of the *Graf Spee* and concluded that she could not get back to Germany in her condition. The galley had been destroyed, so feeding the thousand-man crew was problematic; the main battery range finder had been smashed as well, which meant that the 11-inch guns were unreliable, and the ammunition hoists for the ship's secondary battery had been wrecked. The ship also had a six-by-six-foot hole in her port bow that might not withstand a voyage across the North Atlantic. Without consulting his officers, he decided to head into the river Plate to effect repairs.[28]

Harwood followed at a distance, shadowing his foe and sending out radio messages to the *Cumberland* to hurry, and other messages to the battlecruiser *Renown* and the carrier *Ark Royal* to come join the fight as soon as possible. The *Cumberland* would arrive the next day, but it might be five days before the *Renown* or the *Ark Royal* could get there. How long would the *Graf Spee* stay in the river before coming out again? And if she did come out, could Harwood's two small battered cruisers deal with her? Even if the *Cumberland* arrived in time, it would be another desperate fight. Whatever the answers to those questions, Harwood was determined to stay where he was and find out.[29]

LANGSDORFF HAD TRAPPED HIMSELF. International law held that a belligerent warship could remain in a neutral port for no more than twenty-four hours unless it was unseaworthy. Langsdorff tried hard to convince Uruguayan authorities that the *Graf Spee* was not seaworthy—that he would need two weeks to effect repairs. The *Graf Spee*'s real problem, however, was less its seaworthiness than its battle-worthiness. From the start, Harwood had speculated that even if he failed to destroy his foe, he could effectively pull its teeth by crippling it or even forcing it to use up its ammunition. The *Graf Spee* was not quite toothless, but its offensive capability had been dramatically compromised, and because of that, Langsdorff petitioned local officials to allow him to stay longer in Montevideo.

Ironically, Harwood wanted the same thing. If the pocket battleship came out now, even compromised as she was, she might still be able to fight her way past two small cruisers, each of which had also expended most of its available ammunition. Even after the *Cumberland* arrived the next day (December 14), it was by no means certain that the British could prevail, and it would be five more days before the *Renown* and *Ark Royal* arrived. In the end, the Uruguayan government gave Langsdorff until 8:00 p.m. on the seventeenth to leave port or face internment, a decision that disappointed everyone. Harwood and the British consul in Montevideo, Eugen Millington-Drake, engaged in an elaborate program of disinformation to convince Langsdorff that the *Renown* and the *Ark Royal* had already arrived and were hovering just over the horizon.[30]

Above all else, Langsdorff wanted to avoid internment. Not only would that mean the loss of his ship and the imprisonment of his crew, but it was possible that Uruguay would eventually turn his ship over to the British. He did not think he could fight his way out, and he clearly could not stay where he was. Since radio silence was useless now, Langsdorff reported his dilemma to Raeder in Berlin, and Raeder, unwilling to second-guess a commander five thousand miles away, told him to use his best judgment: to fight his way out if he could, or to scuttle his ship if he must, but under no circumstances to let it fall into the hands of the British. Almost at once, Langsdorff concluded, "Under the circumstances I have no alternative but to sink my ship." Just minutes before the deadline given him by local authorities, Langsdorff raised the large German battle flag and took his ship out beyond the four-mile mark. As they had done on so many merchant ships, demolition specialists set charges around the ship while the crew evacuated. At six minutes to eight on December 17, six separate explosions turned the *Graf Spee* into a pyrotechnic display. British sailors on the cruisers ten miles out to sea lined the rails and cheered.[31]

The German officers and men, watching from tugboats and launches as well as from the German merchant steamer *Tacoma*, were silently grim. Langsdorff, too, had evacuated the *Graf Spee*, and he watched as well while the big ship settled to the bottom, with much of her superstructure still showing. His goal had been to ensure the safety of his men and to get them to Argentina, whose government he expected to be more accommodating. He was disappointed in that, too, however, for most of the *Graf Spee*'s crew was interned by Uruguay for the duration of the war. That might have been Langsdorff's fate as well, but on December 19, he put a pistol to his head and pulled the trigger. The bullet missed, only grazing his skull. He then raised the pistol a second time, and this time he was successful.

Only hours before, in a conversation with an Argentinian naval officer, Langsdorff had mused aloud that the whole concept of using surface raiders to attack British commerce was misplaced. "Germany should abandon

The wreck of the *Graf Spee* lies on the bottom of the Rio de la Plata following her destruction at the hands of her own crew. Langsdorff's decision to scuttle his own ship was controversial at the time and remains so today.

Naval History and Heritage Command

that method of warfare on commerce," he told Commander Edwardo Anamann, "and instead dedicate all effort to submarine war."[32]

Dönitz could not have agreed more.

———

THERE WAS A POSTSCRIPT. Though the *Graf Spee* never escaped the South Atlantic, her consort, the *Altmark*, did. With 299 British prisoners on board, collected from many of the *Graf Spee's* captures, she steamed northward through the center of the Atlantic Ocean, passed east of Iceland, and turned toward Norway. Once her captain, Heinrich Dau, got the *Altmark* into Norwegian territorial waters, he dismounted the ship's guns and sent the prisoners below so that he could claim sanctuary as a merchant ship in neutral waters. Of course, Dau and the *Altmark* still had to steam the roughly six hundred miles south along Norway's treacherous coast to make it to a German port.

Meanwhile, the British conducted a search for her, and on February 19, their persistence was rewarded when a scout plane found her anchored near Jøssing Fjord, south of Bergen. Not long afterward, three Royal Navy warships appeared off the Norwegian coast. Undeterred by Norway's neutral status, one of them fired two warning shots across the bow of the *Altmark*. That led Dau to move his ship well into the fjord, convinced that the British would not openly violate Norwegian neutrality by attacking him there.[33]

He was wrong. Like Langsdorff, Dau had trapped himself. Back in London, Winston Churchill, who had been recalled to his old job as First Lord of the Admiralty, personally composed the orders authorizing British destroyers to search the *Altmark* to see if she did indeed hold British prisoners. If the *Altmark's* captain did not allow a thorough search, Churchill wrote, Royal Navy forces were authorized to "board *Altmark*, liberate the prisoners and take possession of the ship," regardless of her presence in neutral waters.[34]

Just before midnight on February 19, the British destroyer HMS *Cossack*, under the command of Captain Philip Vian, steamed boldly into Jøssing Fjord, brushing past two Norwegian torpedo boats. As the *Cossack* approached, Dau ordered the *Altmark* full astern, hoping to back into the British destroyer and force her aground. Instead it was the *Altmark* that ran aground, hard up against the ice. Vian maneuvered the *Cossack* alongside, and, in an act reminiscent of the age of fighting sail, sent a boarding party charging onto the deck of the *Altmark*. In the bright glare of the *Cossack*'s searchlight, there was a spattering of small arms fire. Eight members of the German crew were killed, and the rest fled inland across the ice. The boarding party then began a search of the ship. Opening a hatchway down into the hold, Lieutenant Bradwell Turner called out, "Any British down there?" which elicited a rousing cry of "Yes! We're all British!" "Come on up then," Turner called back, "the Navy's here." Years later, Vian remembered the scene vividly: "The long shadows on the ice and snow cast by *Altmark*'s upper works; in the foreground her brightly lit decks, on which there began to emerge the prisoners, laughing, cheering, and waving in satisfaction at the turn of events."[35]

Hitler was infuriated ("indignant" was the word Raeder used) that Langsdorff had decided to blow up his ship instead of going out to fight. Had he done so, Hitler insisted, he at least might have taken some British ships down with him. Unconsciously echoing Langsdorff's last words, the Führer told Raeder that using battleships, even pocket battleships, for commerce raiding was a waste of resources; U-boats could do it cheaper and more effectively. Somewhat defensively, Raeder suggested that Langsdorff's cruise had yielded significant secondary benefits by keeping a large number of Royal Navy warships busy looking for him, which was true enough. Hitler was not to be mollified, however, and Raeder was compelled to issue a new general order to the fleet: "The German warship," the new orders read, "fights with the full deployment of its crew until the last shell, until it is victorious or goes down with flag flying." It was, as Raeder had predicted two years earlier, to "die gallantly."[36]

Hitler was also infuriated that the Norwegians had stood by and done nothing to stop HMS *Cossack* when she had so flagrantly violated their neutrality by boarding the *Altmark*. On this, at least, Raeder was in complete agreement. The Norwegians had failed to live up to their obligations as neutrals. There would be consequences.[37]

CHAPTER 3

NORWAY

ADMIRAL RAEDER HAD BEEN URGING HITLER to authorize the occupation of Norway for months, almost since the war began. One reason was that basing Dönitz's U-boats out of Norwegian ports would put them several hundred miles closer to the passage around the north of Scotland to gain the Atlantic sea-lanes, which would greatly extend their time on station. Raeder was also eager to demonstrate the importance of his beloved Kriegsmarine to the burgeoning war effort.

The main reason, however, was iron, the principal ingredient of steel, used to make everything from tanks to warships. Germany's economy consumed thirty million tons of iron ore annually—a number that was sure to rise with the onset of hostilities, and despite dramatic increases during the 1930s less than half of that iron came from domestic sources. Prior to September 1939, Germany imported ore from France, Spain, Luxembourg, and even Newfoundland, and all these sources were cut off once the war began. Most of the rest came from northern Sweden—over nine million tons of it in 1939. With the onset of war, it was vital for Germany to increase its own domestic ore production and to guarantee the security of its imports from neutral Sweden.[1]

During the summer months, ships carried Swedish ore from Luleå down the length of the Gulf of Bothnia to German ports on the Baltic Sea (see map page 44). In winter, however, the northern half of the gulf was frozen, and the ore was transported westward by rail to the Norwegian port of Narvik, which thanks to the Gulf Stream was ice-free all winter. From there, German ships carried the ore southward along the coast. Norway's neutrality protected them from hostile interference as long as they stayed within territorial waters. That protection was a thin reed, however. The *Altmark* incident underscored the fact that, in Raeder's words, Norway "did not have the requisite firmness to resist British violations of her neutrality." If the British decided to interfere with those ore shipments, Norwegian neutrality would not deter them. Raeder convinced Hitler that

Winston Churchill twice served as First Lord of the Admiralty prior to becoming prime minister. During his first tour (1911–1915) he sponsored the ill-fated invasion of Turkey at Gallipoli; in his second, in 1940, he directed the campaign in Norway.

Naval History and Heritage Command

the occupation of Norway was essential as a defensive move, and in March, the Führer approved what was named Operation Weserübung. Raeder ordered the invasion to begin during the dark of the new moon in the first week of April 1940.[2]

Raeder's concerns about British intentions in Norway were justified. Even as the German admiral secured Hitler's approval to seize Norway by force, the new British First Lord of the Admiralty, Winston Churchill, was urging the British government to conduct its own intervention. Almost the first decision that Prime Minister Neville Chamberlain made once the war began was to recall Churchill to his old post as First Lord, a position he had held during the first fifteen months of the First World War.* Churchill had lost that job in November 1915 because of his role in promoting the Gallipoli campaign, which had been an unmitigated disaster for French, Australian, and British forces. That misadventure notwithstanding, his eloquent pleas for British rearmament throughout the 1930s, along with his instinctive love of the Royal Navy, made him popular with officers and enlisted men alike, and when the news of his reappointment was sent out to the fleet, the message read simply: "Winston is back."

The presence of the sixty-four-year-old Churchill in Admiralty House infused new energy and purpose into the Royal Navy and reenergized the cabinet as well, though his assertive personality and aggressive instinct often alarmed its members. Moreover, Churchill had a penchant for getting personally involved in operational planning down to and including the tactical level, a tendency his critics labeled as meddling. Churchill's orders to board the *Altmark* were but one example of that. Such behavior naturally caused occasional friction with the First Sea Lord, Dudley Pound. Interestingly, both Churchill and Pound had American mothers and both had been raised in privileged circumstances. Pound also shared with Churchill a capacity for long hours and hard work, but unlike Churchill he was tolerant of and even receptive to divergent opinions.

---

* The First Lord of the Admiralty is the civilian head of the service and a member of the cabinet, a position akin to that of secretary of the navy in the United States. The First *Sea* Lord, by contrast, is an active-duty naval officer who commands the operational navy, much like the American chief of naval operations.

As a result, Churchill generally overbore the accommodating Pound, who was relegated to acting as a kind of naval chief of staff to the uncompromising force of nature that was Winston Churchill.[3]

To interdict the ore shipments, Churchill's first instinct was to send a powerful Royal Navy surface fleet through the narrow passage between Denmark and Sweden (the Kattegat) and into the Baltic Sea to shut down the trade altogether. The whole idea was completely unrealistic both tactically and logistically, and Pound was horrified. For once, Pound stood up to Churchill, arguing that a sortie into the Baltic would almost certainly result in the loss of most or all of the warships involved, losses that could jeopardize Britain's naval superiority in the North Sea and elsewhere. Churchill next urged a landing at Narvik and a ground campaign along the railroad line to seize the Swedish ore fields themselves. The pretext for this would be the need to deliver supplies to the embattled Finns, who were resisting a Russian invasion in the so-called Winter War. The cabinet toyed with that notion until Finland's capitulation in March, which rendered the idea moot. Churchill then asserted that at the very least they should mine the inlets and fjords of coastal Norway. "British control of the Norwegian coast-line," he insisted, was "a strategic objective of first-class importance." Mining the fjords would violate Norway's neutrality, but it would also force the German ore ships to venture out into the North Sea, where they could be seized or sunk. With some trepidation, the cabinet agreed, and Churchill issued orders for a mine-laying expedition to set out on April 5.[4]

Thus it was that in the first week of April 1940, both Germany and Britain prepared to launch nearly simultaneous naval expeditions to neutral Norway. The German plan was by far the more ambitious—even audacious, for it was nothing less than a full-scale invasion and occupation of the entire country, and of Denmark as well, which was included mainly on the urging of Hermann Göring, the head of the German air force or Luftwaffe, who wanted the airfields in Jutland. German occupation of Denmark would also have an effect on the war at sea, especially if Germany somehow managed to gain control of Iceland, which, though officially independent, was linked historically and culturally to Denmark. Raeder knew, however, that seizing Norway would be challenge enough for the Kriegsmarine and that

Iceland was, for now, beyond its reach.* Germany shared a land border with Denmark, so the occupation of that country was primarily a matter of marching. Norway, however, was necessarily the responsibility of Raeder's Kriegsmarine.

Unlike Pound, who was loath to risk Britain's naval supremacy by sending a substantial part of the fleet into the cul-de-sac of the Baltic, Raeder was willing to commit virtually all of the Kriegsmarine to a campaign in the North Sea, which was very nearly a British lake. It was an audacious, even foolhardy risk. Raeder acknowledged that it was "a bitter decision," but he insisted that "Germany had no other choice." The success of the operation would depend almost entirely on secrecy, surprise, and precise timing, plus more than a little luck.[5]

The invasion plan was both detailed and complex. During the first week of April, scores of German ships would sail both independently and in groups in an intricate maritime quadrille. Some were supply ships disguised as merchant vessels that would be pre-positioned inside various Norwegian ports to support the invasion forces after they arrived. The soldiers themselves would be crowded aboard warships, mostly destroyers, that would sail in six groups and rendezvous at five widely separated Norwegian ports simultaneously. The idea was to present the British (and the Norwegians) with a swift fait accompli before the British Home Fleet could sortie from Scapa Flow to interfere. Of course, even if the plan worked to perfection, the British were certain to react swiftly afterward, and because of that Raeder wanted all the warships to return to Germany immediately after delivering the invasion forces. Otherwise, he feared, many of them might not get back at all.[6]

A central element of the plan was the dual role Raeder scripted for Germany's two new battlecruisers, *Scharnhorst* and *Gneisenau*. Raeder had

---

* A month after the German strike at Norway, a contingent of British Royal Marines occupied Iceland. Since they had not been invited, it was technically an invasion and the local government protested. Because the British offered financial compensation and promised to evacuate the troops as soon as the war ended, the Icelanders resigned themselves to occupation. A year later, after Pearl Harbor, American forces replaced the British, and Iceland remained in Allied hands throughout the war, playing an important role in the Battle of the Atlantic.

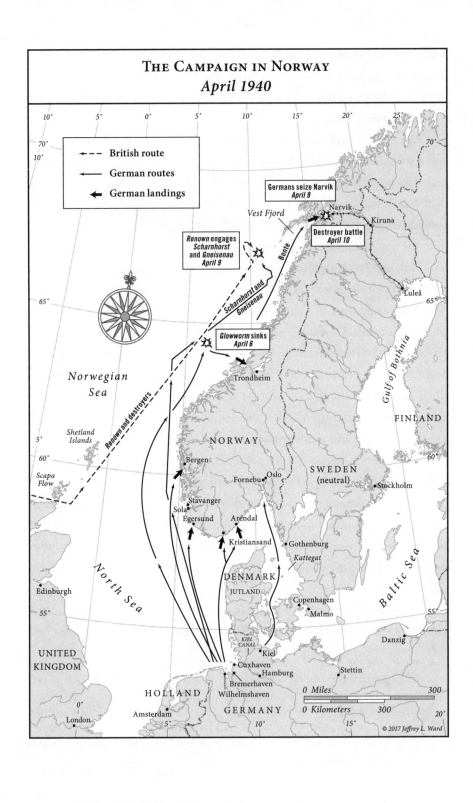

THE CAMPAIGN IN NORWAY
April 1940

- - - → British route
——→ German routes
◄—— German landings

Germans seize Narvik
April 9

Vest Fjord

Narvik

Kiruna

Renown engages
Scharnhorst
and *Gneisenau*
April 9

Destroyer battle
April 10

Bonte

*Scharnhorst and
Gneisenau*

Luleå

65°

Glowworm sinks
April 6

Trondheim

Renown and destroyers

*Norwegian
Sea*

Shetland
Islands

5°

NORWAY

FINLAND

Gulf of Bothnia

60°

Bergen

SWEDEN
(neutral)

Scapa
Flow

Fornebu• Oslo

Stockholm

Stavanger

Sola
Egersund

Arendal

Kristiansand

Gothenburg

Kattegat

Baltic Sea

Edinburgh

North Sea

DENMARK

JUTLAND

Copenhagen

55°

Malmo

Danzig

UNITED
KINGDOM

*KIEL
CANAL*

Kiel

Cuxhaven

Stettin

Hamburg

0 Miles   300

Bremerhaven

Wilhelmshaven

HOLLAND

GERMANY

0 Kilometers   300

Amsterdam

London

© 2017 Jeffrey L. Ward

noted that whenever German surface units sortied, the British responded quickly by sending forces in pursuit. In November, for example, when Raeder dispatched the *Scharnhorst* and *Gneisenau* into the North Sea to draw British attention away from the *Graf Spee*, it had provoked a swift response by the Royal Navy. On that occasion, the German battlecruisers had sunk the British armed merchant cruiser *Rawalpindi* north of the Faroe Islands, triggering a massive, though ultimately unsuccessful, search for them by the Home Fleet. Raeder counted on a similar reaction this time. After covering the invasion force for Narvik, therefore, the battlecruisers were to maneuver menacingly in the Norwegian Sea as a kind of decoy.[7]

Other capital ships would spearhead invasions elsewhere in Norway. The heavy cruiser *Hipper* and four destroyers, loaded with 1,700 German soldiers, would execute a landing at Trondheim, and the pocket battleship *Deutschland* would lead the expedition against Oslo. On Hitler's order, the *Deutschland* had been recently rechristened the *Lützow* because the Führer did not want to run the risk that she might be captured or sunk, which, given her name, would provide the British and her allies a major propaganda victory. In addition to the *Deutschland/Lützow*, the Germans also committed the brand-new heavy cruiser *Blücher*, a light cruiser, and various smaller craft to the Oslo expedition. Other cruisers, and quite a few destroyers, were committed to landings at Bergen and Kristianstad. Dönitz also employed his entire U-boat force, even the six smaller coastal boats that were normally used for training, though privately Dönitz considered this a misallocation of resources. Altogether, Raeder devoted almost the entire Kriegsmarine to the operation.[8]

Even as the various elements of the German invasion force departed Wilhelmshaven and Kiel, the British mine-laying force also put to sea. The minelayers themselves were four modified destroyers (without torpedoes to make room for the mines) accompanied by four fully armed destroyers as an escort. These eight destroyers were covered by the battlecruiser *Renown*, now back from the South Atlantic, herself escorted by four more destroyers, all under the command of Vice Admiral Sir William Whitworth, an urbane fifty-six-year-old career officer who was called "Jock" by his friends. Whitworth's orders were straightforward: he was to offer protection to the mine-laying destroyers off the coast of northern Norway in case the Norwegians felt obliged to intervene.

Almost immediately, however, the simultaneous sortie of the various German invasion groups utterly transformed Whitworth's assignment. Indeed, the new circumstances triggered a frenzied reassessment by the Admiralty, including its energetic First Lord, and over the next several weeks orders and counterorders from Whitehall added a layer of confusion and uncertainty that did much to undermine Britain's response to the German invasion.

SINCE MOST OF THE SHIPS INVOLVED on both sides still lacked radar, and because of the poor visibility in the North Sea in April, it is not surprising that the first encounter between the opposing units occurred by accident. On April 6, the Royal Navy destroyer *Glowworm*, part of *Renown*'s escort, lost a man overboard, and turned out of the formation to recover him. Given the sea state, the recovery took some time, and the *Glowworm* soon found herself alone. After completing the rescue, the *Glowworm* had just turned north again when lookouts spotted two destroyers amidst the morning haze and intermittent snow flurries. They were two of the four German destroyers assigned to the invasion group for Trondheim along with the cruiser *Hipper*. Lookouts on the German ships espied the *Glowworm* at about the same time, and the opposing forces exchanged several long-range salvos, though the severe weather conditions resulted in poor marksmanship. Reports of the contact from the German destroyers, however, led Captain Hellmuth Heye on the heavy cruiser *Hipper* to turn back in support.

At 9:00 a.m., with visibility improving, *Hipper* unleashed a full salvo from her 8-inch guns at the *Glowworm*, whose largest guns were 4.7 inches. It was a dramatically unequal contest, and after only a few salvos the *Glowworm*'s captain, Commander Gerard B. Roope, fired a spread of torpedoes, laid a smokescreen, and turned away. Believing that the British destroyer was in full flight, Heye pursued. Then, suddenly, the *Glowworm* dashed out from the bank of smoke at point-blank range and smashed into the side of the *Hipper*, ripping off 130 feet of her armor plate. The collision severely damaged the cruiser, but it was fatal to the *Glowworm*, whose bow was crushed. Powerless and ravaged by fires, she blew up a few minutes later. The Germans rescued thirty-eight of the *Glowworm*'s crew of 147, though not Roope, who slipped back into the sea while attempting to climb aboard. Heye and the *Hipper* continued to Trondheim and successfully landed the embarked invasion force, though afterward the *Hipper* had to return to Germany for extensive repairs. Years later, after the war was over, Roope was posthumously awarded the Victoria Cross for gallantry.[9]*

That proved only the opening round. Roope's radio report alerted both Whitworth on the *Renown* and the Admiralty in London that major German surface forces were abroad in the North Sea. Conforming to new orders from Whitehall, Whitworth united his *Renown* task force with the eight destroyers of the mine-laying group and led all of them northward toward Narvik, the strategic objective of the entire campaign. Whitworth's new orders from Churchill, which were labeled "Most Immediate," directed him "to concentrate on preventing any German force proceeding to Narvik."[10]

Arriving there in the midst of a blinding snowstorm late on April 8, Whitworth assumed that the Germans would not attempt to enter the narrow fjords under such conditions in the dark, and he maneuvered off the coast to await the dawn. It was a consequential miscalculation, for that very evening, Admiral Günther Lütjens, the grim-faced and humorless German commander of Group One, which included the ten German destroyers headed for Narvik as well as the *Scharnhorst* and *Gneisenau*, arrived off Vest Fjord, which Lütjens ordered the destroyers, crammed with the invasion troops, to enter at once despite the weather. Then, like Whitworth, he took his two big ships off to the northwest to gain sea room.

Though he was unaware of it, Lütjens and his two battlecruisers were following in the track taken only hours earlier by Whitworth and the *Renown*. At 3:00 a.m., Whitworth had just completed a 180-degree turn to head back toward the Norwegian coast when a lookout spotted the two German battlecruisers emerging out of the heavy snow ten miles away. Whitworth identified them, incorrectly, as a battlecruiser and a cruiser,

---

* Roope's VC citation was based on the assumption that he deliberately rammed the *Hipper*, which is entirely possible and perhaps even likely. Given the circumstances, however, it is also possible that the two ships merely collided.

The German battlecruisers *Scharnhorst* (seen here) and her twin the *Gneisenau* were brand-new when the war began. With their nine 11-inch guns and a speed of thirty-one knots, they were more powerful than a heavy cruiser and faster than most battleships. Note the two seaplanes—one atop the stern turret, and one just forward of the mast.

Naval History and Heritage Command

mainly because he had seen intelligence reports indicating that two such ships were abroad. That may have encouraged him to accept battle, though he might have done so even if he had known that he was facing two battlecruisers. In either case, it was a bold decision. The *Renown* had 15-inch guns, but only six of them, and the two German battlecruisers had three times that number of 11-inch guns. Whitworth also had nine destroyers in company, while Lütjens had none, though that was unlikely to affect the battle because the British destroyers had only 4.7-inch guns, and in any event, they could not keep up with the battlecruisers in seas with waves so high they occasionally broke over the top of the destroyers' superstructures.

Accepting—even forcing—a battle, Whitworth increased speed from twelve to twenty knots and opened fire. Breasting the heavy seas, which sent icy spray flying as high as the bridge, the *Renown* plunged forward to close the range, and her fifth salvo straddled Lütjens's flagship, the *Gneisenau*. One shell disabled the *Gneisenau*'s range finder and fire-control director, rendering her guns all but useless. Lütjens ordered the *Scharnhorst* to make smoke to cover their withdrawal, and the Germans fled to the northwest, drawing Whitworth further from Narvik. That may have been Lütjens's intention from the start, or he may have been influenced by the long row of gun flashes from Whitworth's destroyers in the distance, which suggested that there were more heavy ships behind the *Renown*. Whitworth pursued, leaving his laboring destroyers behind, thus creating the odd circumstance of one battlecruiser chasing two others. Nevertheless, by six-fifteen in the morning the German ships were out of sight. Eventually both of them made it safely back to port, arriving in Wilhelmshaven on April 12 along with the damaged *Hipper*.[11]

There were several British and Norwegian tactical successes in these first few days of the invasion. On that same April 9, during the German attack on Oslo, Norwegian coastal batteries sank the brand-new heavy cruiser *Blücher*, which was only three days into her operational life; the next day, the British submarine *Spearfish* torpedoed the *Lützow*, which barely made it back to Kiel, where she would undergo repairs for nearly a year. Another British sub, the *Truant*, mortally wounded the light cruiser *Karlsruhe*. Finally, British Skua dive-bombers based in the Orkneys sank the cruiser *Königsberg*, the first destruction of a warship by dive-bombers in the history of warfare. These successes against major elements of the *Kriegsmarine* were gratifying. Yet even as Whitworth and the *Renown* chased the *Scharnhorst* and *Gneisenau* over the horizon, the ten destroyers that Lütjens had sent into Vest Fjord were securing the principal strategic prize, Narvik.

THE COMMANDER OF THOSE TEN DESTROYERS was Friedrich Bonte, a forty-four-year-old veteran of the First World War, who had been promoted to *Kommodore* just two months before. Bonte was a bold and capable mariner, but he was conflicted, even tormented, by his skepticism about the Nazi regime. Like every other Kriegsmarine officer, he had taken the oath of loyalty to the Führer, and he felt honor bound to obedience. There was, however, a hint of fatalism in his orders and actions. That may have made it easier for him to accept with equanimity Lütjens's daunting order to lead his ten destroyers up the narrow Vest Fjord, and then the even narrower Ofot Fjord toward Narvik in a blinding snowstorm in the dark. Surviving that harrowing passage, Bonte took five of his ships directly into the harbor at Narvik. Two of them stopped to land their troops, while Bonte took the other three into the crowded anchorage, which was filled with twenty-three merchant ships from five countries. The harbor also hosted a pair of forty-year-old Norwegian coastal defense ships, *Eidsvold* and *Norge*, each armed with two 8.2-inch guns and a secondary battery of 5.9-inch guns, though their fire-control systems were badly out of date.[12]

As Bonte's three destroyers approached the anchorage, Norwegian navy Captain Odd Isaksen Willoch in the *Eidsvold* fired a warning shot. That caused Bonte to stop, though another of his destroyers continued toward the jetty to land its embarked soldiers. Meanwhile, Bonte sent an envoy to the *Eidsvold* in a small boat. The only message he carried, however, was an assertion that the Germans had come to protect the Norwegians from the British and that "all resistance was useless." When Willoch peremptorily refused the demand to turn his ships over to the Germans, the envoy departed, and as soon as he was clear of the target, he fired a red flare, the signal for Bonte to fire a spread of torpedoes. Two of them struck the *Eitsveld*, breaking her in half, and she went down in a matter of seconds, taking 177 men down with her. Only eight survived. The other Norwegian defense vessel, the *Norge*, traded salvos with the German destroyers amidst the crowded anchorage until she, too, was hit by torpedoes, going down almost as quickly as the *Eitsveld* with the loss of more than a hundred men. That effectively ended the battle, and the Germans took control of both the harbor and the city.[13]

The German seizure of Narvik changed Whitworth's assignment yet again. Instead of keeping the Germans from getting in, he was now tasked with preventing them from getting out. Indeed, the news that the Germans were in Narvik provoked alarm and not a little confusion up and down the British chain of command. The Admiralty sent out a flurry of orders (most of them dictated by Churchill) that bypassed Whitworth and went directly to two of his subordinates: Captain George D. Yates, who commanded the light cruiser *Penelope*, and Captain Bernard Warburton-Lee, commander of the Second Destroyer Flotilla. Boyish-looking at forty-four, Warburton-Lee was known as "Wash-Lee" or simply "Wash," and his orders were especially fateful. Noting that "press reports" indicated that a German ship had

Two German destroyers are moored next to the pier in Narvik harbor in April 1940 prior to the attack by Warburton-Lee's destroyers. Two German minesweepers are moored at right. By the time British forces arrived at Narvik, the Germans were already in possession of both the town and the harbor.

Naval History and Heritage Command

reached Narvik Harbor, Churchill ordered Wash-Lee to "proceed Narvik and sink or harass enemy ship. It is at your discretion to land force and capture Narvik from enemy present."[14]

For both Whitworth, who received an information copy of those orders, and Warburton-Lee, it should have been evident that, press reports notwithstanding, the orders had been composed with incomplete knowledge. For one thing, there was clearly more than one German ship at Narvik, and Warburton-Lee's small command of five H-class destroyers was only a small portion of the Royal Navy forces that were available. Better coordination within the chain of command might have assembled a more suitable attack force. As it was, dispatching Warburton-Lee's flotilla of small destroyers into the narrow fjords to ferret out the German invaders was like sending a beagle into a wolf's lair. Whitworth did not intervene, for he assumed the Admiralty knew what it was doing.

In receipt of the orders to "capture Narvik" at his discretion, Warburton-Lee conducted a swift reconnaissance of Vest Fjord, learning from a Norwegian pilot station ashore that at least six large German destroyers and one submarine had passed into the fjord, and that a strong German land force held the town. Warburton-Lee's five ships were all smaller destroyers, displacing less than 1,500 tons each and armed with four 4.7-inch guns, whereas the six German destroyers displaced over 2,200 tons each and had five 5-inch guns. Despite that, Warburton-Lee knew it would have been unseemly for him to protest his orders, so he contented himself with sending the Admiralty the information he had secured along with a statement of intent: "Norwegians report Germans holding Narvik in force, also six destroyers and one U-boat are there and channel is possibly mined. Intend attacking at dawn." Such a message at least allowed the Admiralty (in this case, Churchill) to reconsider the orders. Warburton-Lee may even have expected a change in orders, but what he got instead was a confirmation: "Attack at dawn, all good luck."[15]

Later that night—actually early the next morning, just past 1:00 a.m.—more orders arrived for Warburton-Lee that emphasized finding out how the Germans had managed to land, and whether they had captured the shore batteries. That suggested that he was to conduct a reconnaissance rather than an attack. Another follow-up message noted that the Germans might also have seized the two Norwegian defense ships in Narvik, in which case, the Admiralty message read, "you alone can judge whether, in these circumstances, attack should be made." Of course the only way Warburton-Lee could discover whether the Germans had taken possession of either the shore batteries or the Norwegian warships was to go into the harbor and see if they fired at him. The last Admiralty message closed with the assurance that "we shall support whatever decision you make." Theoretically, that left it up to Wash-Lee. Given the burden of four centuries of Royal Navy tradition, however, it was certain what decision he would make.[16]

Well before dawn on April 10, with the snow still falling heavily, Warburton-Lee led his five small destroyers through Vest Fjord and into Ofot Fjord. His ships crept into the harbor at six knots at 4:30 a.m. virtually unseen. Five of the German destroyers were in the harbor, two of them refueling at the oiler *Jan Wellem*, one of the supply ships the Germans had pre-positioned there. The other five German destroyers were anchored up adjacent inlets. Still undiscovered, Warburton-Lee in HMS *Hardy* fired a spread of torpedoes at one German destroyer to starboard, and HMS *Hunter* fired a spread at another to port. Within minutes, both targeted ships exploded and went down. One of them was Bonte's flagship, the *Wilhelm Heidkamp*, and Bonte himself was killed, his reservations about his duty now irrelevant. After that, it became a wild melee in the dark, with 5-inch and 4.7-inch shells flying across the anchorage while torpedoes furrowed the water. There was significant collateral damage to the merchant ships, and the British destroyers sank six of the German supply ships, though not the *Jan Wellem*. The three other German destroyers that were in the harbor were hit as well, some seriously. After forty minutes, it appeared that against all odds Warburton-Lee's audacious predawn sortie had badly crippled the German invasion force, opening the way for a swift British recapture of the town.[17]

Alas for Warburton-Lee, there were not five, or even six, German destroyers in Narvik—there were ten. As the British destroyers began their return trip back up Ofot Fjord, the other five German warships darted out from inlets to both port and starboard. One 5-inch shell smashed into the bridge of the *Hardy*, and Warburton-Lee received a mortal head wound. Reportedly, his last words were "Keep on engaging enemy." Soon afterward the burning *Hardy* ran aground and was lost, with members of its crew escaping ashore. HMS *Hunter* was hit so many times no accurate count was possible. Unable to steam or steer amidst the blinding snow, she was rammed by HMS *Hotspur* coming up behind her. The *Hotspur* herself was hit seven times by German shells, though, incredibly, she managed to stay afloat. Bad as it was for the British, it might have been worse. The three U-boats assigned to Vest Fjord conducted multiple attacks on the British destroyers, both on their way in and on their way out, but none of their torpedoes exploded. Dietrich Knorr, captain of the U-51, fired four torpedoes at one of the destroyers from point-blank range. Two exploded prematurely, and two did not explode at all. Clearly, there was something very wrong with the German torpedoes.[18]

HMS *Havock*, commanded by the appropriately named Lieutenant Commander Rafe E. Courage, covered the retreat of the two surviving British destroyers, and on the way out *Havock* also destroyed the German ammunition ship *Rauenfels*, which exploded in a spectacular fireball. Afterward, both opposing commanders, Bonte and Warburton-Lee, were posthumously honored with the highest medals their countries offered: Bonte with the Knight's Cross, and Warburton-Lee (like Roope) with the Victoria Cross.[19]

ELSEWHERE ALONG THE NORWEGIAN COAST, Admiral Sir Charles Forbes, with the bulk of Britain's Home Fleet, sought to interfere with German landings at Trondheim and Bergen, south of Narvik. Despite his superiority in battleships, he found himself in daily peril of German aircraft flying from captured Norwegian airfields. Göring committed more than seven hundred planes to the campaign, and they harassed British ships daily, sinking the destroyer *Gurkha* and damaging the battleship *Rodney*, which Forbes was using as his flagship. Britain had only one carrier in the area (*Furious*) when the campaign began, and she carried only torpedo planes, no fighters. *Ark Royal* and *Glorious* were quickly ordered from the Mediterranean, but they did not arrive until April 24. In addition, the sea made carrier operations difficult, and in any case the British planes were mostly relatively slow Gloster Gladiator and Swordfish biplanes and Skua fighter-bombers, which were both outnumbered and outperformed by the Germans.[20]

Initially, Forbes's orders were to prevent the Germans from landing at Trondheim and Bergen, but, as at Narvik, the Germans were well ashore before the Royal Navy arrived, and Forbes's new orders were "to maintain a patrol off the entrance to Bergen to prevent enemy forces from escaping." With so many German threats along the coast, however, Whitehall (that is, Churchill) used Forbes's main body as a pool of reinforcements for operations elsewhere, periodically detaching one ship or another to threatened areas until Forbes's "fleet" consisted of only two battleships, the *Furious*, and six destroyers.[21]

On April 11, in the wake of Warburton-Lee's sortie into Narvik harbor, Forbes received an order to diminish his fleet further by sending the

Admiral Sir Charles Forbes in a formal portrait by Sir Oswald Birley painted in 1947. According to historian Correlli Barnett, Forbes was "the human equivalent of the eighteenth-century 74-gun ship-of-the-line": stolid, reliable, and very much the product of an earlier era.

Britannia Royal Naval College Museum

battleship *Warspite* and the *Furious* to Whitworth for another try at Narvik. There would be no surprise in this second attack, though that mattered less now because instead of a beagle the Royal Navy was sending an Irish wolfhound into the harbor. Flying his flag on the *Warspite* with her eight 15-inch guns, Whitworth led his force into the fjords toward Narvik on April 13. As the *Warspite* steamed majestically up the fjord, her spotter aircraft sighted and sank the U-64, which was lying in wait in Ofot Fjord, and then the pilot provided target information for the *Warspite*'s big guns. The surviving German destroyers gamely came out to engage, but they were quickly overwhelmed. After expending most of their torpedoes and virtually all of their 5-inch ammunition, they were driven into Rombaks Fjord, a smaller arm of Ofot Fjord, where they beached themselves, their crews taking to the forest. Damage on the British side was much less severe. The destroyer *Cossack*, commanded now by Robert St. Vincent Sherbrooke, was hit seven times in two minutes and drifted ashore, though she was subsequently salvaged, and a torpedo blew off most of the bow of the destroyer *Eskimo*, which had to back out of the fjord to avoid further damage.[22]

With German naval assets at Narvik destroyed, Churchill laid plans to recapture the town itself. Initially he hoped that Whitworth might be able to land a party of sailors from the warships. Given the presence of two thousand elite Tyrolean mountain troops, augmented now by another two thousand crewmen from the abandoned and scuttled German destroyers, he decided to dispatch a regular landing force. Major General Piers Mackesy commanded the embarked troops, escorted by seven cruisers and five destroyers under Admiral William Boyle (who bore the Irish title of Lord Cork and Orrery and who was known simply as "Lord Cork"). In contrast to the carefully planned German invasion, this expedition was what the British called a "lash-up"—that is, quickly thrown together using whatever resources were close to hand. The troops consisted of a Scots Guards Brigade, units of Irish Borderers and Welshmen, French Foreign Legion troops, and two battalions of expatriate Poles. Moreover, their equipment and supplies were thrown aboard the transport ships as it arrived on the docks rather than being "combat loaded" so that the material needed first was loaded last. Few even knew which ships held what equipment. Even more remarkably, there was no joint commander. Mackesy and Cork were supposed to cooperate even though they never met face-to-face before sailing.[23]

Almost at once, the cabinet began to have second thoughts about the expedition. The foreign minister, Lord Halifax, argued that a successful defense of Trondheim would have greater political impact, and insisted that it should be the focus of British efforts. In a swift turnabout, Churchill supported him, and elements of the Narvik invasion force were diverted en route to sites above Trondheim (at Namsos) and below it (at Åndalsnes) with an eye to launching a pincer movement against the city. The troops were successfully landed, but they encountered deep snow and difficult terrain, and they were bombed almost daily by the Luftwaffe, so they made little progress. To support them, Churchill urged Forbes to launch a naval assault on Trondheim itself with his remaining battleship, an effort he code-named, rather optimistically, Operation Hammer. Forbes resisted, largely because of the absence of air cover. Indeed, Forbes dared to lecture the First Lord on the subject, suggesting that "to carry out an opposed landing…under continued air attack, was hardly feasible." Grudgingly, Churchill backed down, though he would remember Forbes's defiance.[24]

Meanwhile, Mackesy, with the rest of the Narvik invasion force, landed at Harstad, near Narvik, on April 15. There was more than a little confusion getting ashore, and the landings took longer than anticipated. In one case, it took five days to unload two ships, and meanwhile German aircraft continued their harassing attacks. The *Furious*, along with the newly arrived *Glorious*, flew two squadrons of British aircraft ashore, but they had little luck against the Luftwaffe, which claimed six British ships. Pressured by Churchill, Cork urged Mackesy to undertake a land assault, but Mackesy, whose troops were floundering in snow up to their waists, was not to be hurried, and instead began a slow encirclement of the city. As he had with Forbes, Churchill then pressed Cork to undertake a bombardment of the town with his big ships. Cork did so on April 24, though with little effect. By the end of the month the British, French, and Poles had thirty thousand men in the Narvik area, yet the Germans continued to hold the town.[25]

EVEN AS THE ALLIED BUILDUP CONTINUED, unambiguous intelligence began to arrive in London that a far more serious buildup was taking place on the Continent, where German armored divisions were gathering along the border with France and Belgium. Though the land war in Europe had remained quiescent since the fall of Poland in September, it now appeared that the Germans were about to initiate a major offensive. That led Chamberlain and the rest of the cabinet, including Churchill, to wonder if the Royal Navy was not overextended in Norway. As early as April 24, the day that Cork's naval forces bombarded Narvik, the cabinet secretly voted to terminate the Norway campaign. The government shared this decision with the French, though they did not tell the Norwegians.

In the first week of May, Chamberlain called for a vote of confidence from the House of Commons. Somewhat defensively, he asked members "not to form any hasty opinions on the result of the Norwegian campaign," which by now had become an apparent quagmire. Chamberlain narrowly won the vote but, recognizing that a change in government might revitalize

British morale, he resigned anyway. Most of the errors of the Norwegian campaign could be traced to Churchill's unfortunate meddling, but his reputation as an ardent and unyielding foe of Nazism (which he often pronounced as if it derived from the word "nausea"), made him the only suitable candidate as Chamberlain's successor, and on May 10, the king asked him to form a government. As prime minister, Churchill also kept the portfolio of defense minister in his own hands, and of course he continued to exercise significant influence over naval affairs, so throughout the war he had near complete dominance of military and naval strategy as well as government policy.[26]

On that same May 10, German armored columns, backed up by tactical aircraft, charged across the frontiers of France and Belgium. The swiftly unfolding campaign in France necessarily became Churchill's most immediate priority, though he still hoped to complete the capture of Narvik before withdrawing from Norway. In part, he wanted to destroy the ore piers and railroad facilities there, but he also hoped that the seizure of Narvik would somehow validate the decision to go into Norway in the first place, which would demonstrate that the campaign had not been a complete failure—another Gallipoli. He replaced the cautious Mackesy with the more energetic Claude Auchinleck, and pressed Lord Cork to "get Narvik cleaned up as soon as possible."[27]

The Allied ground attack on Narvik took place on May 27. Hitler ordered the German defenders to fight to the last man, though they withdrew inland instead, destroying the railroad tunnels as they did so, thus actually aiding the British objective of making Narvik all but useless as an ore terminal. By the next day, Narvik was at last in British hands, though by then its importance had been overwhelmed by events elsewhere, and almost immediately the British prepared to evacuate not only Narvik but all of Norway. Norway's King Haakon VII accepted a British offer to carry on a government in exile and was spirited out of Tromsø (along with fifty tons of Norway's gold reserves) on June 1. At least as important, a handful of Norwegian warships and more than a thousand merchant vessels joined him. Given the worldwide dearth of shipping—on both sides—that was a significant boost to the British war effort.[28]

Admiral Raeder had achieved his goal. Norway—or at least the principal port cities of Norway—had been occupied. To accomplish it, however, he had risked most of his surface navy and it had been severely crippled. Three cruisers, including the brand-new *Blücher*, and all ten of the destroyers sent to Narvik plus a dozen other ships had been sunk, and nearly every major combatant that survived the campaign had been damaged. By June 1940, the Kriegsmarine had fewer than a dozen surface combatants that were fit for service, and it no longer posed a meaningful threat to the Royal Navy in the North Sea or anywhere else. Raeder was also disappointed by the political outcome in Norway. From the start he had hoped that once the shooting stopped, it would be possible to adopt "a warm and friendly attitude" toward the Norwegians. Instead, Hitler's appointed deputy treated Norway as a conquered province, a circumstance that gnawed at Raeder, who repeatedly tried to convince Hitler to adopt a more conciliatory policy, though with no success.[29]

Finally, and ironically, the circumstances that had made Norway important enough to justify risking the entire German navy changed dramatically almost immediately. Once the Wehrmacht overran France, Dönitz's U-boats obtained access to French ports on the Atlantic, which made those in Norway of little value, and the seizure of the enormous iron mines in French Lorraine made the mines in northern Sweden far less important. In the end, despite what looked to many like a German victory, Raeder had risked everything, lost much, and gained little.[30]

THE BRITISH, TOO, LOST MUCH in the Norway campaign, and for them there was one more tragedy to endure. On June 8, the aircraft carrier HMS *Glorious*, accompanied by two destroyers, *Ardent* and *Acasta*, was returning to Britain from the evacuation of Trondheim. The *Glorious* had just recovered a squadron of Hurricane fighters from Norway that had managed to get aboard despite the fact that RAF planes lacked trailing hooks to catch the arrester wires. With her deck crowded with the Hurricanes, she had no fighters aloft when the *Scharnhorst* and *Gneisenau* suddenly appeared on the horizon. Raeder had sent the battlecruiser twins to sea four days earlier under Wilhelm Marschall with orders to attack British shipping off Narvik.

Though it was too late for that, Marschall stumbled into an unforeseen opportunity.

With the Hurricanes crowding her flight deck, the crew of the *Glorious* could not get any fighters or bombers aloft. There was no explanation at all, however, for the fact that there were no topside lookouts on duty that day; the captain of the *Glorious*, Guy D'Oyly-Hughes, did not even order general quarters until twenty minutes after the German warships were in sight. The result was that the *Glorious* achieved the inglorious distinction of being the first aircraft carrier in history to be sunk by surface gunfire. Only thirty-four minutes after the *Scharnhorst* opened fire, the *Glorious* rolled over onto her starboard side and went down.[31]

The two British destroyers did all they could, speeding toward the battlecruisers to launch torpedoes and fire their small deck guns. It was a forlorn hope. One of them, the *Ardent*, was sunk almost immediately, and the other, the *Acasta*, commanded by Charles E. Glasfurd, fought on alone, making smoke and banging away with her 4.7-inch guns to the very end. As Glasfurd told a fellow officer, "The least we can do is make a show." The *Acasta* even hit the *Scharnhorst* with a torpedo, doing significant damage, though almost immediately afterward *Acasta* herself was struck by a salvo of 11-inch shells and went down. Every member of her crew, save one, was killed. Glasfurd himself was last seen on the bridge calmly lighting a cigarette. Of nearly fifteen hundred men on the three British ships, only forty-five survived.

News of this disaster was late in reaching London. Because an early hit put her wireless out of action, the *Glorious* had not even managed to get off an intelligible radio report, and as a result, Churchill did not learn of her loss until it was announced by German radio several days later. It was a disgrace at every level, and might well have become a national scandal except that far more serious events were occurring that week in the English Channel.[32]

CHAPTER 4

FRANCE FALLS

A T SEVEN-THIRTY IN THE MORNING ON MAY 15, 1940, French president Paul Reynaud placed a phone call to Winston Churchill at 10 Downing Street. Never an early riser, Churchill was still asleep, and it was several moments before he came to the phone. Reynaud's first words jolted him fully awake: "We have been defeated."`

Churchill's immediate instinct was to reassure him. Surely things were not that bad; the German offensive had begun only five days before; the news would get better. Reynaud was not to be consoled. "We have been defeated," he said again, "we have lost the battle." The next day, Churchill flew to Paris, where he found everyone there in the same frame of mind as Reynaud.[1]

Their despondency was justified. The long-delayed German ground attack, spearheaded by eighteen hundred tanks, had knifed through the supposedly impenetrable Ardennes Forest north of the Maginot Line, mauled the French Ninth Army in the Battle for Sedan, and advanced swiftly across the open fields northeast of the Somme River, the tanks and aircraft working in partnership. Two decades earlier, during the First World War, the opposing armies had fought over this ground for years, measuring their progress in yards. This time, the German armored columns reached the Channel in ten days. Because the British Expeditionary Force and the French First Army had rushed into Belgium at the start of the offensive in order to confront the Germans as they advanced, those forces were now cut off. By May 20, half a million British, French, and Belgian troops were pinned inside a coastal pocket that extended from Calais to Ostend. Halfway between those cities was the port of Dunkirk.[2]

The men inside that enclave got an unexpected respite on May 24 when the columns of German panzers paused to allow the infantry to catch up. That bought the Allies a few precious days, and the British commander, General John Vereker, known by his title as Lord Gort, sent Group Captain Victor Goddard to London with orders to talk personally to Admiral Pound and brief him on the seriousness of the crisis. Pound agreed at once that it was essential to rescue the trapped British soldiers, and he authorized a program subsequently code-named Operation Dynamo. To run it, he turned to the commander of Royal Navy forces at Dover, Vice Admiral Bertram Home Ramsay.[3]

Ramsay—"Bertie" to his friends—was an unprepossessing man of average height with a plain round face and thinning hair. The son and brother of army officers, he had asserted his independence at the age of fifteen by choosing the Royal Navy over the British Army. He was an effective administrator who spent much of his subsequent career on the staff of one or another senior admiral. His career hit a bump in the 1930s when, as a rear admiral, he had resigned as chief of staff to Admiral Sir Roger Backhouse because he felt that Backhouse was doing most of the staff work himself. Soon afterward, Ramsay was placed on the retired list and he enjoyed a brief hiatus as a gentleman farmer. He was recalled to active service in 1938 during the Munich crisis, and when the war began he was flag officer in charge at Dover and therefore the nearest naval commander to the developing crisis at Dunkirk. That proved fortuitous for the Allies, because Ramsay's administrative skill and relentless work ethic proved essential. Pound and the other admirals at Whitehall initially hoped that it might be possible to rescue as many as 40,000 of the nearly 400,000 men trapped on the French coastline. In the end, Operation Dynamo saved more than 338,000 of them.[4]

RAMSAY COORDINATED THE EFFORT from a headquarters that had been carved out of the chalk cliffs at Dover. Dug by French prisoners during the Napoleonic Wars, it featured a balcony that offered a splendid view of the Channel.* From there Ramsay could see the smoke and hear the rumble of heavy artillery on the Continent, less than twenty miles away. Over the next two weeks he rarely left that cliffside office. He and his staff worked, quite literally, around the clock. "No bed for any of us last night," the fifty-seven-year-old Ramsay wrote to his wife on May 23. "I'm so sleepy I can hardly keep my eyes open." Surviving on sandwiches and coffee, Ramsay and his subordinates simply kept at it—gathering the resources and manpower, scheduling

Admiral Sir Bertram Ramsay examines the beaches in Flanders from Admiral's Walk in Dover Castle. Ramsay orchestrated both the Dunkirk evacuation in 1940 and the Allied return to the continent four years later on D-Day.

Imperial War Museum

* During the First World War, one of the rooms in what became Ramsay's headquarters had hosted a dynamo that produced electricity for Dover Castle. That was the origin and inspiration for designating the evacuation effort as Operation Dynamo.

the shipping, and coordinating the near chaos of an unprecedented evacuation effort. It was like running the D-Day invasion—backward.[5]

Ramsay's first task was to assemble the shipping. Despite the traditional assumption that the British Expeditionary Force was evacuated from Dunkirk by a motley armada of yachts and fishing boats, the lion's share of the work was done by a score of transports and two score Royal Navy destroyers. One of Ramsay's first acts was to recall the destroyers from Norway as well as from every other command within reach; he even ordered the destroyers that were escorting the vital Atlantic convoys to abandon their flocks and steam at flank speed for the Channel. By such means, he quickly assembled a flotilla of 39 destroyers, 36 minesweepers, and 34 tugs, plus 113 freighters and trawlers. He appointed Rear Admiral Frederic Wake-Walker to command the ships, and Navy Captain William George "Bill" Tennant to coordinate the loading ashore.[6]

The evacuations began on May 26. For the most part, the Allies were denied use of the harbor facilities at Dunkirk. During the pause in the German advance after May 24, Göring convinced Hitler that his Luftwaffe bombers could wipe out the Dunkirk pocket without having to risk the panzers, and while that boast proved vain, the Luftwaffe did wreck the piers and jetties in the harbor so thoroughly they could hardly be used at all. Tennant reported that the streets of Dunkirk were "littered with wreckage of all kinds," every window was smashed, and the docks had been rendered useless. When two transports attempted to enter the harbor, one was sunk and the other so badly damaged it had to withdraw. Ramsay concluded that the men would have to be evacuated over the beach.[7]

That was problematic because the beach gradient at Dunkirk was so gradual that the destroyers, which drew twelve feet or more, could get no closer than six or eight hundred yards from the coast. As a result, troops had to be ferried from the beach out to the destroyers in small boats, a tedious and time-consuming process. Often when a small boat approached the beach, desperate soldiers immediately clambered into it and the additional weight caused it to be grounded firmly in the sand. When that happened, the last few men to board had to climb back out again, and of course they were reluctant to do so. Once the boat reached the destroyer or transport offshore, the men then had to climb up nets or ladders, often while Luftwaffe planes were strafing them. Finally, as the day wore on, the rowers became exhausted and the trips slower. It was, as one destroyer officer put it, "dreadfully inefficient."[8]

A partial solution to this bottleneck was the use of forty Dutch canal barges, called *schuitjes*, but which the British Tommies, who could not get their tongues around the Dutch word, called "skoots." Manned by Royal Navy personnel, they could get close enough to the beach for the soldiers to wade out to them. Once loaded, the skoots then ferried the soldiers out to the waiting destroyers and trawlers, or in some cases all the way to England. More small craft were needed, however, and on May 27, Tennant urged Ramsay to "send every available craft to beaches east of Dunkirk immediately." Ramsay's team gathered more than three hundred small craft, including yachts from the Royal Ocean Racing Club and cockleshell boats from the Thames River. Motorized lifeboats from the lifeguard service were towed across the Channel in long strings at night and used to ferry troops from the beach to the destroyers. To man these small craft, Ramsay's deputies recruited retired navy officers, fishermen, even yachtsmen. Though there were many enthusiastic volunteers, there were also some who required convincing. After their first trip through the barrage of bombs and shells off the beach, some of the volunteers adamantly refused to make another and had to be persuaded at bayonet point to repeat the experience.[9]

Even more important than the skoots and the flotilla of small craft were the two long breakwaters, or moles, built of large boulders that reached out into the English Channel from either side of Dunkirk harbor like spindly arms seeking to embrace arriving ships. Built to shelter the harbor from periodic Channel storms, they had not been designed for use as piers. Nevertheless, a narrow wooden walkway along the top of the eastern breakwater allowed soldiers to line up in a long queue that stretched more than two miles from the beach to the tip of the breakwater. It required remarkable patience and a certain stoicism for the soldiers to wait passively in those long lines, for once they stepped out onto the breakwater, there was no going back, and they were completely exposed to strafing German aircraft. A survivor recalled the wait: "One hour, two hours, three, four, five, six hours, waiting there on the beach. At last we were moving? Yes! Yes! Towards the Mole." It was precarious for the destroyer skippers, too, who had to come alongside the exposed breakwater while battling twenty-foot tides and a three-knot current. Nevertheless, the breakwater proved essential. On May 28, the first day it was used, Royal Navy destroyers boarded soldiers at a rate of two thousand men an hour, and by the end of the day, they had rescued nearly eighteen thousand men.[10]

While Ramsay and his team scrambled to embark as many men as possible, the Wehrmacht renewed its offensive against the Allied perimeter. For the Belgians the pressure became irresistible, and on May 28 Belgium capitulated. Since the Belgian army had been holding the eastern flank of the salient, Lord Gort had to contract his defenses. More than ever, it was now a race to see if the shrinking perimeter could hold back the Germans long enough for the trapped soldiers to escape. To win that race, Ramsay petitioned the Admiralty for even more destroyers, and on May 29 Pound gave him command authority over every destroyer in the Royal Navy.[11]

The French destroyer *Bourrasque*, crowded with soldiers just rescued from the beach, sinks off Nieuport on May 30, 1940. Note the soldier jumping off the bow.

U.S. Naval Institute

Once the weary Allied soldiers were taken aboard ship, many thought their trial was over. Instead, the crossing often proved as dangerous as the beach. Due to the severe losses the Kriegsmarine had suffered in the campaign for Norway, the Germans lacked the surface capability to interfere with the withdrawal directly. There were other perils at sea, however, including the Luftwaffe, mines, Dönitz's U-boats, and something called *Schnellbooten* (literally, "fast boats"), which the Allies called S-boats or E-boats. A hundred feet long and powered by twin 7,500-horsepower Daimler-Benz engines, the German E-boats were a slightly larger version of what the Americans called PT boats. Though they carried 20 mm machine guns, their principal weapon was the torpedo, and each E-boat carried four torpedoes with a range of nearly four miles. Because the boats themselves were small and fragile, they relied heavily on stealth and operated almost exclusively at night.[12]

Just past midnight on May 28–29, the destroyer HMS *Wakeful*, which had already made one cross-Channel run that day, was setting out on a second trip with a full load of soldiers when a torpedo from an E-boat (the S-30) struck her amidships. The explosion broke her back and she went down in less than a minute. Only 25 of her crew of 110 could be rescued. The real tragedy, however, was below decks, where 640 soldiers were packed in like sardines. The men had been plucked from the breakwater at Dunkirk only hours before, and all but one of them perished as the *Wakeful* plunged quickly to the bottom. The destroyer HMS *Grafton*, herself encumbered with a load of seven hundred soldiers, stopped to pick up survivors, and while thus engaged, she, too, was struck by a torpedo. Unlike the *Wakeful*, the *Grafton* stayed afloat long enough for a third destroyer, HMS *Ivanhoe*, to take off most of her crew and passengers before she sank. *Ivanhoe* delivered her human cargo to Dover, though three days later, on June 1, she was herself bombed off Dunkirk Harbor and compelled to limp back to England under her own power. The next day, a French destroyer, the *Bourrasque*, also packed with Allied soldiers, struck a German mine and went down with the loss of 150 men.[13]

Altogether, six British and three French destroyers were lost and nineteen more Royal Navy destroyers were damaged. That put twenty-five of the original thirty-nine Royal Navy destroyers involved in Operation Dynamo out of action. Such losses were horrifying and provoked Pound to recall some of the newer destroyers from the operation with the idea of conserving them to resist the expected German invasion. Ramsay appealed the decision and got Pound to reverse it.[14]

By now, Operation Dynamo was rescuing fifty to sixty thousand men a day, almost all of them British. The few French ships in the area, such as the *Bourrasque*, evacuated French infantrymen, but most of the French fleet was in the Mediterranean, and it seemed to many Frenchmen that the British were simply abandoning them. An ugly incident took place on May 29 when a group of French soldiers rushed to board a landing craft and were driven back at gunpoint by British soldiers. Recognizing that such incidents could irreparably damage what remained of the Anglo-French alliance, Churchill directed that French troops were to have equal priority with British troops in the evacuation schedule. Lord Gort protested; his priority was to save his command, and he insisted that British ships should carry British soldiers and French ships carry French soldiers. Churchill overruled him, and Gort grudgingly complied.[15]

On June 1, the number of Frenchmen evacuated from Dunkirk exceeded the number of British soldiers for the first time, though by then most of the British troops had already been evacuated. The British rear guard of 4,000 men escaped during the night on June 2–3, and when the operation officially ended on June 4, only 265 British soldiers, most of them too badly wounded to move, remained. In nine days, Operation Dynamo had rescued a total of 338,226 men from the Dunkirk pocket. That included 123,095 Frenchmen, though more than 40,000 French soldiers were left behind. For the most part, they stoically accepted their fate and, still holding the lines outside Dunkirk, awaited the arrival of the Germans.[16]

Operation Dynamo was not a victory. Despite the relief felt in Britain at the improbable rescue of so many men, almost immediately enshrined as the "Miracle of Dunkirk," there was no disguising the fact that it marked the culmination of a disastrous campaign. Though many men had been saved, the British had abandoned all their heavy equipment, including more than 120,000 vehicles, 2,472 artillery pieces, 445 tanks, and 90,000 rifles, plus hundreds of tons of ammunition.* As Churchill himself acknowledged in a moving speech to the House of Commons, "wars are not won by evacuations."[17]

Indeed, only in hindsight did the escape of the British Expeditionary Force from Dunkirk come to be perceived as a kind of triumph. At the time, the expulsion of the BEF from Europe, along with the loss of the *Glorious* on June 8, marked a low point in British fortunes and a high point for the triumphant Germans. Two days later, Italy declared war on both Britain and France, and twelve days after that, on June 22, France formally capitulated. In only a few weeks, the Germans had conquered Norway, Denmark, Holland, Belgium, and now France. The damage to so many Royal Navy destroyers, both at Narvik and during Operation Dynamo, threatened the security of the Atlantic convoys on which Britain depended for its very survival. Then, too, because Britain had relinquished control of the western Mediterranean to the French navy before the outbreak of hostilities in order to concentrate Royal Navy forces in the North Sea, the collapse of France and the entry of Italy into the war jeopardized the security of the Mediterranean, a locus of British naval power since the War of the Spanish Succession. If Britain lost the Mediterranean, it would sever the vital sea route from Gibraltar to Suez and force British ships bound for India, Singapore, or the Middle East to steam twenty thousand miles around the Cape of Good Hope, extending the journey by weeks. From Churchill's perspective, there was no time to rest and recover. Urgent measures were needed: first to ensure that the French navy did not fall into the hands of the Germans, and second to confront the threat of the Italian navy.

THE FRENCH CAME FIRST. In June 1940 the French navy was a substantial one, boasting eight capital ships, including two new and powerful *Richelieu*-class battleships, with 15-inch guns, and two *Dunkerque*-class battlecruisers,

---

* Following the Dunkirk evacuation, President Franklin Roosevelt obtained a ruling from his acting attorney general that "surplus" weapons could be sent to Britain without violating the Neutrality Laws. That allowed him to send six hundred thousand rifles, nearly nine hundred 75 mm field pieces, and eighty thousand machine guns to Britain, which helped replace some of what was lost on the beaches.

each armed with eight 13-inch guns mounted in two enormous quad turrets forward. France also had thirty-two supersized destroyers, nearly as large as light cruisers, that they called *contre-torpilleurs*. They displaced over 3,000 tons, and some carried 5.5-inch guns. Among the world's naval powers, France ranked fourth behind only Britain, the United States, and Japan. Hitler's decision to allow the French to retain nominal autonomy with the creation of what came to be known as Vichy France was motivated in large part by his concern that if he occupied all of France, the French fleet would go over to the British and thus augment British naval superiority. A neutral French fleet was more desirable than one arrayed against him.[18]

Not so for Churchill. To him, the existence of a powerful unaligned naval force in the Mediterranean was intolerable. A century and a half earlier, at the height of Britain's war with Napoleon, a British fleet under Admiral Horatio Nelson had attacked the battle fleet of neutral Denmark at Copenhagen because the Admiralty worried that Napoleon would somehow get control of those ships and use them to challenge British naval mastery. Nelson virtually annihilated the Danish fleet, doing so even after his nervous superior, Admiral Hyde Parker, watching from a distance, ordered him to discontinue the fight. On that occasion Nelson allegedly put his telescope to his blind eye and declared that he could not see the recall signal. Inspired by that example, Churchill contemplated doing much the same thing to the French fleet.

According to the surrender document signed at Compiègne on June 22, the ships of the French navy were to be "demobilized and disarmed under German and Italian control." It was not entirely clear what that meant. The French word *contrôle* used in the agreement implied supervision and verification, but the British tended to read it as the English word "control," and feared that the Germans would somehow come to possess and operate the ships. Though the Germans solemnly declared that they did not "intend to use [the French navy] for its own ends," Churchill had no faith in the solemn declarations of Nazis. When he had left Paris on June 12 after talking with Reynaud, Churchill had pulled aside a French admiral, Jean-François Darlan, and told him that even if France was forced to capitulate, "you must never let them get the French fleet." Darlan had agreed. No matter what happened, he told Churchill, "we will never hand it over to Germany or Italy. Orders to scuttle will be given in the event of danger." Churchill worried nonetheless. "It is a matter so vital to the safety of the whole British Empire," he wrote later, "we could not afford to rely on the word of Admiral Darlan."[19]

Several French warships did make their way to England after June 22 to avoid being turned over to the Germans. These included two older battleships (*Courbet* and *Paris*) and several of the oversized destroyers, as well as seven submarines. Most of the rest left their European bases and steamed to ports in Africa, with the biggest concentration of them at Mers-el-Kébir, on the coast of French Algeria just west of Oran. By the end of the month the French naval force there consisted of two older battleships (*Bretagne* and *Provence*), both of the new battlecruisers *Dunkerque* and *Strasbourg*, plus a seaplane carrier and half a dozen destroyers. The *Richelieu* went to Dakar, on the west coast of Africa, and the *Jean Bart* to Casablanca. Other, smaller groups of French warships were at Oran and Algiers, and a squadron called Force X was actually part of a combined Anglo-French naval force at Alexandria, Egypt, that was under the overall command of a British admiral, Sir Andrew Browne Cunningham. Allies and partners on June 21, the French ships became technically neutral on June 22, and there was at least a possibility that they could become foes. Churchill would not risk it; to him, the loss of the Mediterranean would be nearly as disastrous as the loss of the English Channel.[20]

The first imperative was to fill the void in the western Mediterranean created by the French capitulation. Pound suggested pulling Cunningham's squadron at Alexandria back to Gibraltar, essentially abandoning the eastern Mediterranean. Churchill would have none of it. He convinced the cabinet to leave Cunningham where he was and send a new squadron to Gibraltar. Dubbed Force H, it included two battleships (*Valiant* and *Resolution*) the huge (48,000-ton) battlecruiser *Hood*, and the carrier *Ark Royal*, plus two light cruisers and eleven destroyers. The dispatch of such a force, drawn mainly from the Home Fleet, was possible at all because of the attrition suffered by the Kriegsmarine during the Norway campaign. The commander of this new force was Vice Admiral Sir James Somerville, a popular and experienced officer with a knack for attracting the loyalty of his colleagues and subordinates. Somerville had retired in 1939 due to suspected tuberculosis, from which he soon recovered, and he was restored to active duty when the war broke out later that year.[21]

Even with Somerville's squadron at Gibraltar, the unsettled status of the French fleet continued to worry Churchill, who invoked Nelson's 1801 attack at Copenhagen during a decisive cabinet meeting on June 27. The French warships, he insisted, must be neutralized or destroyed. The ideal solution was for the French naval commanders to repudiate the surrender of their government and join the British in the war against the Nazis. Failing that, they could intern their ships in British ports, sail them to the West Indies, or scuttle them as the Germans had done in Scapa Flow in 1919. If they rejected all these options, Churchill insisted, they had to be eliminated. Despite serious concerns expressed by several cabinet members, Churchill succeeded in obtaining their unanimous consent for what was dubbed Operation Catapult, and that same day he sent new orders to both Somerville at Gibraltar and Cunningham at Alexandria.[22]

Cunningham's situation was especially fraught. The French squadron there (Force X) consisted of one older battleship (the *Lorraine*), three heavy cruisers, a light cruiser, and three destroyers. All these ships were under the direct command of Admiral René-Emile Godfroy, but they were

Admiral Andrew Browne Cunningham, who was later the First Sea Lord, commanded the Royal Navy Squadron at Alexandria, near Suez, when the French capitulation presented him with a delicate set of circumstances.

Britannia Royal Naval College Museum

also a part of the Anglo-French squadron under Cunningham. Even before Churchill's new orders arrived, Godfroy and Cunningham confronted an extraordinarily awkward situation. On June 23, Godfroy received orders from Darlan to leave Alexandria and take his squadron to a French port in conformance with the armistice agreement. That same day, Cunningham got orders from Pound not to let Godfroy leave port at all.[23]

Cunningham's reputation was not that of a diplomat. He was a man with exacting standards, a confident manner, and an assertive physiognomy (the naval historian Correlli Barnett described him as having "a jawline like a battleship's bow"). Nevertheless, he found the Admiralty's orders unnecessarily confrontational and believed that attacking Godfroy's ships would be "an act of sheer treachery which was as injudicious as it was unnecessary." He therefore approached Godfroy sympathetically to discuss the various options. Despite periodic orders from Churchill to get on with it ("Do not, repeat NOT, fail"), Cunningham quietly continued to discuss various options with his French colleague. He even asked his ship captains to visit their French counterparts to consider possible solutions. It worked. After several days, Godfroy agreed to disarm and intern his ships, and afterward both sides praised the principals for their diplomatic forbearance. Even Churchill came to appreciate Cunningham's management of the crisis, eventually sending his congratulations, though he did so through a third party.[24]

THE FRENCH FLEET at Mers-el- Kébir was the more serious problem. It was both larger than Godfroy's squadron and independent of any association with an Allied command. Like Cunningham, Somerville hoped and expected to resolve the issue short of violence. He even dispatched a memorandum to London suggesting a less confrontational approach. Churchill rejected it, informing Somerville that it was "the firm intention" of the government that unless the French accepted the alternatives presented to them, "their ships must be destroyed."[25]

One factor in Churchill's hard line was his eagerness to demonstrate British resolve. It was to quash growing disquiet at home and uncertainty abroad that he offered the fighting speech he delivered in the House of Commons on June 4. In his fierce growl he told the members: "We shall defend our Island whatever the cost may be. We shall fight on the beaches, we shall fight on the landing grounds, we shall fight in the fields and in the streets, we shall fight in the hills. We shall never surrender." Aggressive action against the French fleet would underscore that determination.[26]

It was an emotional issue for the French, too. Like Godfroy, Vice Admiral Marcel-Bruno Gensoul at Mers-el-Kébir felt the defeat of his country as a deep personal humiliation. When the British commander at Gibraltar, Admiral Sir Dudley North, visited Gensoul on June 24, he found the Frenchman "in a state of stupefied misery." Several times North thought Gensoul was close to tears. At the end of their conversation, the French admiral pledged that he would never surrender his ships to the Germans or the Italians. The problem was that for Churchill, promises, however sincere, were not enough.[27]

Churchill ordered Somerville to resolve the crisis by July 3. A swift solution was essential because it seemed likely that the Germans might soon attempt a cross-Channel invasion, and if they did, Somerville's ships would be needed in the Channel. Somerville sent Captain Cedric Holland ahead of the main fleet in the destroyer *Foxhound* to meet with Gensoul and present the alternatives that had been crafted in London. In one sense, Holland (called "Hooky" by his friends in tribute to his large hooked nose) was a good choice, for he had spent two years as the Royal Navy attaché in Paris and spoke French fluently. On the other hand, the proud Gensoul saw it as a snub that Somerville sent a subordinate rather than come himself, and initially he declined to meet with Holland. Determined to deliver the message he carried, Holland entrusted it to Gensoul's flag lieutenant. Only after Gensoul read the documents did he begin to appreciate the seriousness of the crisis and agree to meet with Holland. Even then, however, an emotional Gensoul was in no mood to bow to an ultimatum. He told Holland he would never let any of his ships fall into the hands of the Germans, but neither would he turn them over to the British; he would meet "force with force."[28]

That afternoon, Gensoul received a message from French navy headquarters in Toulon supporting his defiant response and implying that French naval forces throughout the Mediterranean would rally around him. That message was intercepted in London, and an alarmed Churchill fired

The French built both of their new fast battlecruisers, *Dunkerque* (seen here) and *Strasbourg*, with all their big guns pointing forward in two massive four-gun turrets. That proved disastrous when the British assailed them at Mers-el-Kébir.

U.S. Naval Institute

off a wireless message to Somerville directing him to settle things swiftly: "French ships must comply with our terms or sink themselves or be sunk by you before dark." Somerville ordered Holland to break off the talks. As the disappointed Holland left the *Dunkerque* at 5:25 in the afternoon, he heard bugles sounding general quarters.[29]

Somerville opened fire as soon as Holland's destroyer cleared the harbor. Despite the lengthy talks, Gensoul had never quite believed the British would actually attack him. All four of his capital ships, including the two new battlecruisers, were tied up facing landward. Since they had been designed with all eight of their 13-inch guns facing forward, none of those guns could be brought to bear against an attack from the sea until the ships unmoored, got under way, and turned around. Meanwhile, Somerville's battleships pounded them with thirty-six unanswered salvoes from their 15-inch guns.[30]

The two older French battleships fared the worst. The *Bretagne*, which had been laid down in 1912 before the First World War, was hit four times in rapid succession. The fourth shell exploded in her magazine and the *Bretagne* blew up spectacularly, rolling over and sinking quickly with the loss of nearly a thousand men. Her sister ship, *Provence*, was sunk as well, though with less loss of life. Gensoul's flagship, *Dunkerque*, was badly damaged, too, and might have gone down had her crew not maneuvered her into shallow water, where she went aground. The battlecruiser *Strasbourg* and five destroyers managed to get under way. In the growing dark they steamed out of the harbor and headed eastward along the coast before turning north toward Toulon. Somerville pursued them in the battlecruiser *Hood* and ordered an air strike by planes from the *Ark Royal*. Despite that, the *Strasbourg*, though damaged, made it to Toulon, where she arrived on the evening of July 4.

Somerville felt wretched afterward, writing his wife, "We all felt thoroughly dirty and ashamed." Still, he followed up the initial attack three days later, ordering planes from the *Ark Royal* to carry out a torpedo assault on the now grounded and abandoned *Dunkerque*. A thousand miles away at Dakar, in West Africa, planes from the small carrier *Hermes* launched torpedoes at the French battleship *Richelieu* on July 7. In that more measured attack, torpedoes damaged the *Richelieu*'s rudder and propellers, thus making her inoperative without inflicting a heavy loss of life. The *Jean Bart*, at Casablanca, was still incomplete, lacking most of her armament, and was therefore left alone.*

At Mers-el-Kébir, the French lost 1,297 men killed, most of them when the *Bretagne* blew up, plus another 351 wounded. Gensoul himself survived the attack and was even promoted to full admiral in a tribute to his defiance, though he never again served at sea and refused to talk about the events of July 3 for the rest of his life.[31]

On that same July 3, by prearrangement, British forces in Portsmouth and Plymouth boarded and seized the French warships that had come there voluntarily. It was mostly bloodless, though a few men on each side were killed when some Frenchmen resisted. The rest were presented with the alternative of joining the British cause or being interned; those who chose the latter were treated largely as prisoners of war.[32]

---

* Other French warships were stranded overseas when France fell. The aircraft carrier *Béarn* (launched in 1920) was in port at Martinique in the West Indies, where her existence concerned both the British and the Americans. U.S. Navy planners even developed a plan (Operation India) to invade and occupy Martinique if necessary. It never came to that, as the French admiral, Georges Robert, agreed to accept the presence of American onboard observers. The *Béarn* remained in Martinique until June 1943, when she and her crew formally joined the Free French, though she never engaged in combat.

While tactically successful, the British attack at Mers-el-Kébir under-standably provoked French anger. An infuriated Darlan issued orders for French warships to "attack all British warships met," though he rescinded that hot-tempered directive the next day. Over the next several weeks, the two nations—and the two navies—managed to restore a kind of chilly cor-diality. Officially and legally, the French remained neutrals, though the uncertainty and precariousness of the new relationship became especially evident during what was called Operation Menace. One of Churchill's many enthusiasms, this was an attempt by a British task force of two battleships (*Resolution* and *Barham*) and the carrier *Ark Royal* to seize Dakar from Vichy control and establish a Free French stronghold there. What might have been a fairly easy occupation was compromised by the arrival of three French light cruisers and three destroyers from the Toulon fleet. Admiral North at Gibraltar had allowed them to pass through the strait on September 10 in the belief that amicable relations with France had been restored. After the British and Free French invasion attempt at Dakar collapsed, Churchill made North the scapegoat and had him dismissed from the service.[33]

CHURCHILL NEVER APOLOGIZED FOR MERS-EL-KÉBIR. He believed that the circumstances had given him no other viable option. Command of the sea was essential to Britain's survival, especially now that she stood vir-tually alone against the Axis juggernaut. Though the French were entirely sincere in pledging that they would never let their warships fall under con-trol of the Germans, Churchill would not stake the future of the empire on their promise. As he told the House of Commons, he was willing to let his-tory judge him. "I leave it to the nation," he said. "I leave it to the United States. I leave it to the world and to history."[34]

Two years later, the French had an opportunity to demonstrate their fidelity to the Allied cause. When German forces swept over Vichy France in the wake of the Allied invasion of North Africa in November 1942 (see Chapter 16), the French fulfilled the pledge they had made two years before by scuttling seventy-seven of their own warships, including both the *Dunkerque* and the *Strasbourg*. As Darlan had promised, no major French warships ever served the Nazi regime.[35]

CHAPTER 5

THE REGIA MARINA

NEUTRALIZING THE FRENCH FLEET did not ensure control of the Mediterranean for the Royal Navy. Benito Mussolini, the Italian dictator, had declared war on both Britain and France on June 10, waiting until after the fall of Paris to do so in order to share in the spoils of the German victory. Mussolini's decision was purely opportunistic, but Italian belligerence dramatically shifted the balance of naval power in the Mediterranean because the Italian navy was nearly as large as the French. The Regia Marina, as the Italian navy was called, included 6 modern battleships, 19 cruisers, and 59 destroyers plus 116 submarines, though many of the subs were smaller coastal boats. It was the fifth-largest navy in the world—significantly larger than Germany's. Many of the Italian ships were beautiful and built for speed, though they tended to be underarmored, and because of limited steaming time due to chronic fuel shortages, their crews were less experienced and therefore less efficient than those of the Royal Navy. Still, with the French removed from the strategic chessboard, Italy's was the most powerful naval force in the Mediterranean.

Moreover, control of Libya, consolidated in the 1930s, gave Italy a dominant position athwart the Sicilian narrows, and Mussolini was determined to expand that dominance and turn the Mediterranean into an Italian lake. As in the days of the Roman Empire, it would become Mare Nostrum, "our sea."[1]

A key geographical reality that profoundly affected Anglo-Italian naval warfare was the simple fact that virtually all of the Mediterranean was within range of land-based aircraft (see map pages 80–81). The Italian naval high command, the Supermarina, counted heavily on airplanes from bases in the Italian boot as well as in Sardinia, Sicily, and Libya to provide cover for its surface fleet, which was why Italy had not invested in building any aircraft carriers. The British, too, had important air bases in the Mediterranean: at Gibraltar, at the western end; at Alexandria, Egypt, at its eastern end; and on the island of Malta, a tiny outpost of the empire just fifty miles south of Sicily, very nearly in the center of the Mediterranean. In addition, however, the British had several aircraft carriers, which proved crucial. Another crucial factor was that in 1939, on the eve of war, a reorganization of the British Ministry of Defence had returned control of naval aviation from the Royal Air Force to the Admiralty. That ensured effective cooperation between British air and surface forces, whereas in Italy they remained entirely separate.

In order to support their important outposts—Libya for the Italians, and Malta for the British—both sides had to run regular convoys through contested seas. This would appear to be a much easier prospect for the Italians, since it was only 170 miles from Marsala, Sicily, to Tunis, Tunisia, whereas it was more than 1,000 miles to Malta from Alexandria, Egypt, and nearly 1,200 miles from Gibraltar. There were other factors, however, that affected the effectiveness of Italian convoys to North Africa. One was that Mussolini had failed to notify the nation's merchant marine of his intention to declare war, and a full third of Italy's merchant shipping was seized in foreign ports on the day the war began. Another was the limited capacity of port facilities in Tunisia and Libya, which restricted Italian convoys to no more than three or four vessels at a time. Often, Italian "convoys" consisted of only two ships. Finally and decisively, there was Italy's persistent fuel

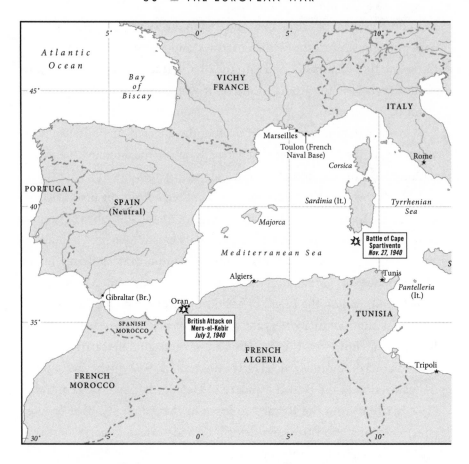

shortage. Her handsome warships often languished in port because there was simply not enough fuel oil for them to operate. A problem from the beginning, the fuel crisis worsened as the war lengthened.[2]

The British had plenty of fuel, but their convoys to Malta from either Gibraltar or Alexandria had to make that perilous thousand-mile trek under a nearly constant barrage of Italian, and later German, air attack. Some in the Admiralty suggested that these daunting logistical circumstances dictated that Malta should be given up as indefensible. Churchill would not hear of it, and Malta remained a nexus of naval combat in the Mediterranean throughout the war. The initial phase of the fighting consisted of a series of large and small naval engagements through the summer and fall of 1940, sporadic combat that one authority has likened to a guerilla war.[3]

THE MEDITERRANEAN, *1940–41*

ROMANIA

YUGOSLAVIA

Black Sea

Adriatic Sea

BULGARIA

British air attack on Taranto *Nov. 11, 1940*

ALBANIA

GREECE

Aegean Sea

TURKEY

Ionian Sea

Athens

Sicily

Battle of Calabria (Punta Stilo) *July 9, 1940*

Malta(Br.)

Battle of Cape Matapan *March 27-29,1941*

Crete

CYPRUS

SYRIA

Suda Bay

British evacuation of Crete *May 28- June 1, 1941*

LEBANON
Beirut

Mediterranean Sea

0 Miles   300

0 Kilometers   300

Haifa

Tobruk

PALESTINE

Benghazi

Alexandria (Br.)

Port Said

LIBYA

EGYPT

© 2017 Jeffrey L. Ward

In that war, Mussolini believed that Italy's superiority in land-based air gave him a critical advantage. That proved a vain hope for two reasons. One was that, as noted above, the Regia Marina and the Italian air force, the Regia Aeronautica, were bureaucratically independent. They had no overlapping command structure, no common signal code, not even a tactical communications link. This was an astonishing shortcoming. It meant that when an Italian naval commander required air support, he had to pass his request up the naval chain of command to the Supermarina in Rome. Officials there then contacted the headquarters of the air force, the Superaereo, which sent orders down its own chain of command to the operational air commanders. This cumbersome protocol, which one authority has labeled "organizational dysfunction," made tactical cooperation all but impossible. Mussolini's foreign minister and son-in-law, Galeazzo Ciano, noted in his diary, "The real controversy in naval conflicts is not between us and the British, but between our air force and our navy."[4]

The second problem was that Italian pilots were trained primarily for land combat. Their planes had proved devastating against ground targets during the conquest of Ethiopia, but attacking moving warships was far more difficult. The Italian protocol for attacking ships at sea was for the bombers to fly at high altitude in a tight formation over the target and drop their bombs all together in the expectation that one or more of them surely would hit something. This had the advantage of keeping the planes beyond the reach of shipboard anti-aircraft fire, and Cunningham was impressed by the discipline of the Italian pilots who executed such maneuvers. Yet in the Mediterranean, as elsewhere throughout the Second World War, attempts to bomb maneuvering ships from high altitude proved ineffectual to the point of futility.[5]

THE FIRST NAVAL ENGAGEMENT between the opposing forces occurred in the second week of July, just five days after Somerville crippled the French fleet at Mers-el-Kébir. On July 6, an Italian troop convoy left Naples for Benghazi with an escort of two light cruisers and eight destroyers. To cover it, an Italian battle fleet under Vice Admiral Inigo Campioni put to sea with two battleships, six heavy cruisers, eight light cruisers, and sixteen destroyers. At about the same time, a British convoy left Malta for Egypt, and to cover it Cunningham sailed from Alexandria with three battleships, the aircraft carrier *Eagle*, five cruisers, and fifteen destroyers. The covering fleets collided on July 8 thirty miles off the toe of Italy (see map) in what the British called the Battle of Calabria and the Italians called the Battle of Punta Stilo.[6]

The British had the advantage in battleships, three to two, while Campioni had a clear advantage in heavy cruisers if he could get them close enough to engage. Cunningham ordered an attack by torpedo planes from the carrier *Eagle*, though it did little more than disrupt Campioni's formation. The opposing battleships flung heavy shells at one another from long range, generating great clouds of smoke and huge shell splashes but inflicting little damage. Then at 4:00 p.m. a 15-inch shell from Cunningham's flagship—

the Narvik veteran *Warspite*—struck Campioni's flagship, the *Giulio Cesare*. The explosion knocked out four of the *Giulio Cesare's* eight boilers, and the big ship slowed to eighteen knots. Campioni turned away and ordered his destroyers to conduct a torpedo attack and make smoke to cover his withdrawal. He still hoped that planes from the Italian mainland would arrive to even the odds, though when they did appear forty minutes later they dropped their bombs indiscriminately among the ships of both fleets. From ten thousand feet, the flash of the bomb explosions and the great geysers of water they generated looked quite impressive, and the pilots claimed multiple hits. In fact, they achieved only a few near misses, though one of them damaged the hull plates of the *Eagle* below the waterline. Frustrated by the lack of air support, Campioni returned to port, and Cunningham returned to Malta. Though the British claimed a victory, the convoys of both sides made it safely to port and the engagement had little impact on the strategic balance in the Mediterranean.[7]

Over the next few months the British gained a significant technological advantage when several of their ships were equipped with a new device that the British called a radio direction finder (RDF) and the Americans called radar. The technology was so new that it initially provoked skepticism about its practical utility. On the last day of August, the radar-equipped British cruiser *Sheffield* radioed the carrier *Ark Royal* to warn her of an inbound enemy air strike. The duty officer on the *Ark Royal* ignored the message. When the carrier came under attack shortly afterward, it encouraged a reevaluation. The *Sheffield* radioed another warning later that afternoon, and this time the *Ark Royal* launched fighters that met the attackers en route and fought them off. Soon after that, officers from the *Ark Royal* visited the *Sheffield* to learn more about this amazing new apparatus, and by October British carriers, too, were equipped with radar sets. Initially they were rudimentary and not always reliable, though over time operational commanders grew to trust them.[8]

Meanwhile, Mussolini repeatedly pressed the commander of the Italian Tenth Army in Libya, Marshal Rodolfo Graziani, to cross the border into Egypt and begin a drive on Alexandria and Suez. Graziani insisted that his forces were too weak for such a campaign and that his supply line across the

Sicilian Narrows was too precarious. Mussolini ordered him forward none-theless, and Graziani dutifully invaded Egypt on September 9. Ciano opined in his diary, "Never has a military operation been launched with such opposition from the commanders."[9]

As Graziani had feared, Cunningham responded to the move by attacking his supply lines, not only the ship convoys across the Sicilian Narrows to Libya, but also the truck convoys on the long coastal road from Benghazi to the fighting front. Cunningham's cruisers and destroyers shelled the coastal road, and planes from the aircraft carrier *Illustrious* conducted air strikes on truck convoys and supply depots.

The planes that carried out those strikes were Swordfish biplanes, designed and built by the Fairey Aviation Company in the 1930s. With their twin cloth-covered wings, open cockpit, and fixed landing gear, they looked very much like something left over from the last war. Because their wings were con-nected by struts and wires, many assumed that their nickname, "Stringbags," derived from that design feature. Instead, it was a tribute to their versatility: a reference to the habit of British shoppers to carry their purchases in

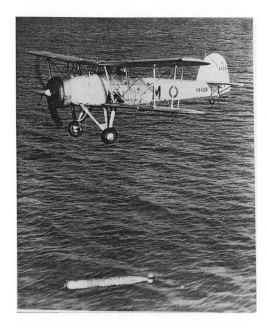

A Fairey Swordfish biplane drops a torpedo during fleet exercises in 1939. Despite their outdated look, these all-purpose aircraft operated as long-range scouts, dive-bombers, and torpedo planes and were the backbone of the British naval air fleet.

Naval History and Heritage Command

expandable string bags. Though the Swordfish had been designed as a scout plane, it proved capable of operating effectively as a dive-bomber and as a torpedo bomber. Despite the planes' archaic appearance, they were the standard attack aircraft of the Fleet Air Arm.[10]

In August, only weeks before Graziani began his invasion, three Swordfish took off from Sidi Barrani, in the Egyptian desert, to attack Italian shipping in the harbor at Bomba, between Tobruk and Benghazi. With only three torpedoes, they sank four ships when the explosion of a sub tender wrecked both the tender and the submarine alongside it.[11]

Impressive as that was, the decisive—even revolutionary—moment in the emergence of carrier-based aviation as a principal striking arm of modern navies occurred three months later when a score of Swordfish attacked the main Italian battle fleet at Taranto, on the inner heel of the Italian boot. The idea of conducting a raid by carrier-based planes on a battleship fleet at anchor had been part of Royal Navy planning since the 1930s. Drawing on that planning, Rear Admiral Lumley Lyster, who commanded Royal Navy carriers in the Mediterranean, petitioned Cunningham for permission to attack Campioni's six battleships moored in the harbor at Taranto. Campioni kept his fleet there rather than at Naples because it was closer to the British convoy routes, though of course it also put him closer to any air threat. Initially, Lyster wanted to use two carriers to conduct the strike, but the damage suffered by the *Eagle* at Calabria (Punta Stilo) meant that he had to go ahead with just the *Illustrious*, though five planes from the *Eagle* were transferred temporarily to the *Illustrious* for the raid.

After escorting yet another convoy to Malta, Cunningham detached the *Illustrious* with a substantial escort of four cruisers and four destroyers to make a high-speed run northward on November 11, Armistice Day. Lyster had hoped to conduct the raid on October 21, Trafalgar Day, but a fire on board *Illustrious* damaged a number of aircraft and forced a postponement. Meanwhile, the Swordfish were fitted with sixty-gallon auxiliary fuel tanks for the long flight, and the pilots rehearsed night attacks.[12]

Just past eight o'clock, already full dark in mid-November, the *Illustrious* turned into the wind to launch planes. It was not a large raid by later standards. Only twenty-one of the Stringbags took off, half of them armed with bombs and half with torpedoes. Lieutenant Commander Kenneth Williamson led the first wave of twelve planes, and Lieutenant Commander J. W. "Ginger" Hale led nine more in the second wave. For two hours the planes lumbered along at five thousand feet at ninety miles per hour, their most fuel-efficient speed when carrying a heavy ordnance load, and they arrived over the target just before 11:00 p.m. The Italians had no radar, but one of the Stringbags that had become separated from the group arrived early and alerted the defenders, who put up a cloud of anti-aircraft fire, reminding one pilot of an eruption from Mount Etna.[13]

The first planes dropped parachute flares to illuminate the harbor, then bombed the fuel tanks ashore. Given the oil-starved status of the Regia Marina, the destruction of those tanks was a heavy blow. The dive-bombers had little luck against the ships: only one bomb hit a ship—the destroyer *Libeccio*—and it failed to explode. Then the torpedo planes arrived. Eleven of the twenty-one planes carried the Mark XII torpedo, which was just over sixteen feet long and weighed 1,548 pounds. To launch such a weapon, the pilot had to approach the target low and slow, for if the torpedo was dropped from an altitude above 150 feet or at a speed greater than seventy knots, the impact with the water could render it inoperable. The Stringbags flew so low that at least one pilot claimed his wheels actually touched the water. That created a dilemma for the gunners on the Italian ships, for if they depressed their guns to shoot at the low-flying planes, they risked shooting one another. The boldness of the British pilots might have been in vain if the Italians had had torpedo nets in place, but to prepare for a sortie the next morning, the nets had been removed.

Sub-Lieutenant P. J. D. Sparke lined up his plane on the *Conte di Cavour*, an older battleship displacing 23,000 tons. He felt the lurch as he released the torpedo, which ran straight and true and exploded at 11:14, creating a twenty-seven-foot hole below the waterline, sinking the *Conte di Cavour* at her moorings. Only minutes later, another torpedo hit the newer and larger *Littorio*, which displaced 40,000 tons and had 15-inch guns. As the *Littorio*'s crew fought the ensuing fires, another torpedo struck. When the second wave of Swordfish arrived just before midnight, the *Littorio* was hit a third time. Though she stayed afloat, the extensive damage kept her out of the war for

The Italian battleship *Conte di Cavour* rests on the bottom of the harbor at Taranto following the British raid on November 11–12, 1940. Though the Italians raised her, repairs took longer than anticipated and she was still in the repair yard at Trieste in September 1943 when she was seized by the Germans.

U.S. Naval Institute

five months. Still another torpedo hit the older battleship *Caio Duilio*, which had to flood both of her magazines to prevent the fires from igniting them and ran herself aground to avoid sinking. Two Swordfish were lost in the attack; two men were killed and two, Williamson and Lieutenant Norman Scarlett-Streatfield, were made prisoner. Yet in a matter of minutes a handful of Stringbags had rendered three battleships, exactly half of Italy's capital ship navy, unusable. As Cunningham put it, twenty airplanes "inflicted more damage upon the Italian fleet [at Taranto] than was inflicted upon the German High Seas Fleet" at Jutland. In his diary, Ciano wrote simply: "A black day."[14]

Among those professing special interest in the effectiveness of this dramatic raid was a delegation of Japanese visitors who arrived on a formal visit to Taranto the following May. They took particular note of the fact that torpedoes had proved effective in the relatively shallow waters of Taranto Harbor.[15]

There were political repercussions as well. Admiral Domenico Cavagnari, who had led the Regia Marina as chief of staff since 1934 and had promoted battleship construction at the expense of aircraft carriers, lost his job to Arturo Riccardi, who would remain in that post until the Italian surrender. In London, Churchill was thrilled. The raid on Taranto, he told the House of Commons, "affects decisively the balance of naval power in the Mediterranean, and… the naval situation in every quarter of the globe."[16]

THE EVENTS OF NOVEMBER 11 led the Supermarina to order Campioni to relocate the surviving elements of his fleet from Taranto to Naples, two hundred miles to the west. They did not, however, discourage Campioni from making further attempts to intercept British convoys. Barely a week afterward, he learned from pro-fascist spies in Spain that elements of Somerville's Force H had left Gibraltar to cover an eastbound convoy headed for Malta. Somerville's force was greatly reduced from what it had been in July. He now had only the battlecruiser *Renown* (which he used as his flagship), the carrier *Ark Royal*, and some light cruisers. Campioni decided to sortie from his new base at Naples and attack this force with two battleships and six heavy cruisers. He knew there was a second British surface force in the vicinity, for Cunningham, too, was at sea, approaching from the east with the old R-class battleship *Ramillies*, three cruisers, and three destroyers. Rather than discourage him, however, Campioni saw this as more opportunity. He would destroy Somerville's force, and if that went well, and depending on his own battle damage, he would then turn and attack Cunningham. Italian prospects seemed excellent.[17]

Somerville learned of the approach of Campioni's force on the morning of November 27. He continued eastward nonetheless, accepting the possibility of a battle at long odds in order to cover the valuable convoy, which included seven hundred Royal Air Force personnel being sent to Alexandria. Only later that morning did he learn, to his great relief, that Cunningham's force was just thirty-four miles away and closing. Campioni also learned of Cunningham's proximity, and that led him to reassess his situation. Instead of two isolated elements of the British fleet, he now faced the possibility of confronting the combined power of both Somerville and Cunningham.

He might have pressed on anyway—his two battleships were newer and faster than those of the British, and he would still have an edge in heavy cruisers—but his opportunity to split the British forces and defeat them separately had passed. He decided to call off the attack and return to base.[18]

That should have been easy enough, since Campioni's battleships could steam in excess of thirty knots and the twenty-five-year-old *Ramillies* could make barely twenty-one. Somerville pursued him nonetheless and tried to slow Campioni down by ordering an airstrike by eleven Swordfish from the *Ark Royal*. Hitting ships maneuvering at high speed, however, was far more difficult than attacking ships at anchor, and they scored no hits. If they had managed to damage one of the Italian battleships and slow it down, Somerville no doubt would have continued the chase, but as Campioni's much faster ships pulled away, Somerville decided to let them go. His primary mission, after all, was to cover the convoy, and it was always possible that Campioni might be leading him into an ambush by Italian submarines.[19]

This second inconclusive skirmish, known as the Battle of Cape Spartivento, pleased no one in either Rome or London. The admirals at Supermarina were disappointed and frustrated that a sortie that had begun with such high hopes had ended so meekly, and on December 10, Campioni was transferred to a new job as assistant chief of staff, so that command of the fleet could be turned over to Vice Admiral Angelo Iachino, the commander of Campioni's cruiser force.

Churchill was even more disappointed. Instinctively impatient with men he considered insufficiently aggressive, he thought Somerville should have pursued Campioni to the death. Recalling the admiral's qualms about attacking the French at Mers-el-Kébir, the prime minister concluded that Somerville lacked the killer instinct. He convened a board of inquiry and suggested that Somerville should be replaced by Henry Harwood, the victor over the *Graf Spee* in the Battle of the Plate. This time, however, the service rose up to defend the popular Somerville, and for once Churchill did not get his way. Though Somerville kept his job, the incident underscored Churchill's unforgiving standard of performance.[20]

Churchill's disgruntlement notwithstanding, the crippling blows that the Royal Navy dealt to the French in July and the Italians in November

successfully reclaimed British naval superiority—if not quite dominance—
in the Mediterranean. Convoys to and from Malta, or from Gibraltar to
Alexandria, still had to run a gauntlet of air attacks, but there was no more
talk of abandoning the Mediterranean. Moreover, on December 8, British
armies in Egypt began a counterattack against Graziani that would last two
months, drive the Italians six hundred miles back to El Agheila, and end
with Graziani's dismissal. As Cunningham put it, "the year 1940 ended
in high hope" for British prospects in the Mediterranean. Indeed, the
strategic situation there had been so completely reversed that Mussolini
found himself overextended and had to appeal to Hitler for support. The
Führer responded by sending the 15th Armored Division under General
Erwin Rommel to Africa, where he would build his reputation as the
"Desert Fox."[21]

ALL THIS TIME, Churchill and the British people steeled themselves for
the expected cross-Channel invasion, which the German high command
had dubbed Operation Seelöwe (Sea Lion). To conduct it, the Germans
needed to transport half a million men plus their ammunition and equipment across the Channel, and in pursuit of that they assembled two hundred large transport ships and more than seventeen hundred motorized
barges in the Channel ports. It could not happen, however, unless and until
Göring's Luftwaffe gained control of the skies over the Channel. Göring
repeatedly assured Hitler that his aircraft were making splendid progress,
but in fact the pilots of the Royal Air Force were more than holding their
own, inflicting heavier losses on the Luftwaffe than they suffered themselves. Moreover, at the end of August, British bombers began making regular night runs against the collected shipping of the invasion fleet on the
coast of France and Holland, destroying twenty-one of the transports and
nearly two hundred motorized invasion barges.

The air war over Britain entered a new phase after the British conducted
an air raid on Berlin on August 25. Infuriated, Hitler ordered Göring to
change his target from British airfields to cities, including London. Despite
the devastation that wrought on London and Londoners, it gave the hard-
pressed Spitfire and Hurricane pilots a respite, and by mid-September it

had become evident that the Luftwaffe had failed to win the air battle over Britain. Though Churchill did not learn of it until later, Hitler shelved his invasion plans on September 17. He decided instead to turn his attention eastward.[22]

The Führer had always believed that the ultimate struggle for mastery in Europe would be with the Soviet Union, whose vast territory would provide the German *Volk* with the *Lebensraum* he had promised in *Mein Kampf*. Almost as soon as it became evident that Operation Sea Lion was impractical, he ordered his generals to reposition their forces from the Channel coast to the eastern frontier and prepare to execute Operation Barbarossa—the invasion, conquest, and occupation of Soviet Russia. He hoped to begin that invasion in mid-May 1941, though events in the Mediterranean and the Balkans forced a delay.

The delays were a direct consequence of his troublesome Italian ally. Despite the disappointments of the Egyptian campaign in September 1940, barely a month later Mussolini ordered his army and navy to invade Greece, doing so without informing Berlin. Il Duce was annoyed that the Germans had invaded Romania without telling him in advance, and he resolved to turn the tables on his senior partner by invading Greece without telling Hitler. As he said to his son-in-law, "He will find out from the papers that I have occupied Greece." It was characteristic of the Axis coalition that these putative partners acted unilaterally. They were on the same side, but they were never true allies.[23]

Mussolini's invasion of Greece started off well enough. The Regia Marina successfully transported half a million men and half a million tons of equipment and supplies across the Adriatic to Albania. The ground campaign, however, did not go well. The Greek army not only resisted but threw the Italian invaders back into Albania. The British, eager for allies in their solitary war against the Axis, immediately offered Greece their support, and soon convoys of men, equipment, and supplies were making regular runs northward across the eastern Mediterranean from Alexandria to Piraeus as part of what was called Operation Lustre. Raeder was disgusted. In a memo to the Führer in November, he labeled Italy's invasion of Greece as "a serious strategic blunder" and stated bluntly, "Italian leadership is wretched."[24]

Italian fortunes did not improve over the winter, and it became evident that Mussolini's legions had once again charged into a quagmire. To salvage the situation, Raeder urged Hitler to take over the campaign altogether, even pushing for a German army-navy operation to seize the Suez Canal. Though Hitler's eye remained fixed on the Russian steppes, the bungled Italian campaign in Greece, plus a threatened anti-Axis coup in Yugoslavia, compelled him to order German ground forces into the Balkans. The Führer was annoyed, not only because he once again had to pull Italian chestnuts out of the fire but also because doing so forced him to postpone Barbarossa.[25]

AS THE GERMANS prepared their Balkan intervention, they pressed the Italians to do something about those British convoys carrying supplies to the Greeks. The Regia Marina had been mostly idle over the winter. Officially, at least, that was because of the scarcity of fuel oil, though the Germans suspected, not without justification, that the Italians sometimes used that as an excuse for inaction. Mussolini, already looking ahead to postwar peace negotiations, wanted to preserve as much of his navy as possible so that when the negotiations began he would have increased leverage. The Germans, of course, had no sympathy for such equivocation, and at a strategic conference at Merano in the Italian Alps on February 13–14, 1941, Raeder pressed his Italian counterpart, Arturo Riccardi, to authorize a surface raid into the eastern Mediterranean. Riccardi implied that such a raid might be possible if the Germans supplied the Regia Marina with more fuel oil from the Romanian oil fields. Raeder said he would look into it, though he had to know that with Barbarossa pending, increasing oil shipments to Italy was unlikely.[26]

German pressure for a raid into the eastern Mediterranean increased after a corps of Luftwaffe bombers, transferred from Norway to Sicily in January, had marked success against British surface convoys near Malta. The primary assignment of the German bombers, which belonged to the Tenth Fliegerkorps, was to cut the British supply line to Malta. Though British escorts for the convoys had become increasingly robust, the Germans—especially the Stuka dive-bombers—proved remarkably effective.

On January 11 they sank the British light cruiser *Southampton* and severely damaged the carrier *Illustrious*, hitting her with no fewer than six bombs, thus partially avenging her attack on Taranto. The wounded carrier limped into the harbor at Malta still burning, and eventually had to be sent to the United States for extensive repairs. By the end of the month the Germans had more than two hundred planes in Sicily and Italy, and their numbers continued to grow into the spring.[27]

By March, German naval representatives could claim—accurately—that German bombers were doing more to interdict British convoys in the Mediterranean than the Italian navy was. The Luftwaffe damaged two of Cunningham's battleships—*Barham* and *Warspite*—which they believed left the British with only one undamaged battleship in the eastern Mediterranean. Yet despite that, the Germans pointedly noted that Greek forces continued to receive "constant reinforcements in men and equipment" from Alexandria. The German naval liaison officer in Rome hinted broadly that these convoys offered "a particularly worthwhile target for the Italian naval forces." It was very nearly a taunt.[28]

As it happened, Admiral Iachino had already petitioned the Italian naval staff for permission to conduct a sweep of the eastern Mediterranean and had been turned down, officially because of the fuel shortage. Now, however, he was called to Rome and informed that his proposal was to be implemented after all. As he planned the mission, Iachino's principal concern, besides fuel, was the lack of reliable air cover. The Italian air force remained a doubtful partner, and venturing into the eastern Mediterranean within easy range of British aircraft from both Egypt and Greece would be especially perilous without air support. The admirals on the Italian naval staff assured Iachino that long-range planes from bases in Sicily, including planes of the Tenth Fliegerkorps, would be available to support him. Iachino was skeptical, but could not say so without risking a rebuke, and he got under way from Naples after dark on March 26.[29]

Iachino's force was a substantial one. His flagship was the 40,000-ton *Vittorio Veneto*, armed with nine 15-inch guns and capable of thirty knots, plus six heavy cruisers, two light cruisers, and thirteen destroyers. Relying on German reports, he believed that Cunningham had only one operational

Iachino's flagship during his sortie into the eastern Mediterranean was the new battleship *Vittorio Veneto*, photographed here soon after her commissioning in 1940. Note the torpedo blister along her port side.

Naval History and Heritage Command

battleship—the *Valiant*—and some smaller ships at Alexandria, a force far too weak to challenge him.[30]

In fact, the damage that German aircraft had inflicted on Cunningham's battleships was not as devastating as the enthusiastic German pilots had reported, and all three British battleships were fully operational. They were elderly ships, veterans of the 1916 Battle of Jutland, and slow as well, but they each carried 15-inch guns—assuming they could get close enough to use them given their indifferent speed. Cunningham also had operational control of four light cruisers and four destroyers out of Piraeus near Athens. Cunningham's weakness was that he had no heavy cruisers at all, and that was because of one of the most daring exploits of the campaign, or indeed of the entire war.

The same night that Iachino got under way from Naples, eight Italian commandos piloting tiny motorboats called *motoscafo turismos* (MTs) crammed with explosives ventured into the long, narrow inlet at Suda Bay, on the north coast of Crete, where the heavy cruiser HMS *York* lay at anchor. In an operation suggestive of Günther Prien's penetration of Scapa Flow in the first months of the war, the commandos crept into the protected harbor at low throttle, lined up their tiny craft toward the anchored ships, then pushed the throttles forward, jumping off just before impact. The commandos swam to shore and were taken prisoner, but only after their MTs reached their targets. Two of them hit the *York*, and the ensuing explosions flooded her boilers and engine room, so the cruiser had to be beached to prevent her from sinking. As a consequence of that daring raid, when Cunningham's three battleships put to sea the next night they did so accompanied only by nine destroyers.[31]

Significantly, however, Cunningham also had the new aircraft carrier *Formidable*, sent from home waters to replace the damaged *Illustrious*. To get there, the *Formidable* conducted a lengthy voyage around the southern cape of Africa and then north through the Indian Ocean to the Red Sea. There was some delay there since German planes had dropped mines in the Suez Canal, but eventually the mines were neutralized, and the *Formidable* arrived at Alexandria on March 10, just two weeks before Iachino set out from Naples.[32]

Iachino passed through the Straits of Messina between Italy and Sicily late on March 26 and headed eastward into the Ionian Sea. The next morning, a British long-range Sunderland flying boat, used before the war to carry passengers and mail across the Atlantic, spotted one element of Iachino's command and reported to Cunningham that three enemy cruisers and a destroyer were steaming eastward eighty miles east of Calabria. In fact, Cunningham had already placed his fleet on high alert as a consequence of one of the earliest examples of operationally useful code breaking during World War II. British cryptanalysts at Bletchley Park, a top-secret facility fifty miles northwest of London, had intercepted and decoded messages about Iachino's sortie and passed them on to the Admiralty.*

* Iachino sent his orders by landline, which was secure from electronic interception, but the Regia Aeronautica used wireless transmissions to several airfields about conducting reconnaissance flights over the area between Crete and Alexandria. These were the messages that the code breakers at Bletchley Park intercepted and decrypted. The subsequent role of code breaking, and especially what was known as Ultra intelligence in the naval war, is developed in Chapter 12.

Cunningham's first reaction to that news was to cancel all scheduled convoys to Greece. Since those convoys were Iachino's principal target, that decision by itself deprived him of any likely success. After that, Cunningham issued orders for his own fleet to prepare to get under way. To disguise his plans from prying eyes, he made a point of taking a suitcase with him that afternoon when he left the *Warspite*, ostensibly for a night ashore, then doubled back to reboard his flagship surreptitiously after dark. Later that night, his fleet put to sea.[33]

By then, Iachino was already having second thoughts. Between ten-thirty and eleven-thirty that night he received an updated intelligence report that Cunningham had not one but three battleships at Alexandria, and that the British were aware of his approach. In spite of that, Iachino decided to continue eastward until morning, then to reverse course. His force proceeded in three groups: the flagship with her destroyer escorts constituted the main battle force, and the six heavy cruisers proceeded in two groups of three each. It was one of those cruiser groups that had been sighted by the Sunderland that morning and reported to Cunningham.[34]

Cunningham also divided his forces, sending the four light cruisers and four destroyers from Piraeus a hundred miles out ahead of the battleships as a scouting force under Rear Admiral Henry Daniel Pridham-Whippell. Throughout the dark hours of the night, the opposing forces steamed toward each other on converging tracks, though neither knew the location or the strength of the other.

THE ENSUING BATTLE is known to history as the Battle of Cape Matapan, which is the middle promontory of the three peninsulas that extend southward from mainland Greece (see map pages 80–81). The action began shortly after dawn on March 28, with each side conducting air reconnaissance in an effort to find and identify its foe. Unsurprisingly, perhaps, the promised Italian air support from Sicily never arrived, and Iachino had to rely on the floatplane from his own flagship to conduct the search. A serious limitation for the Italians was that whereas British battleships could recover their floatplanes by hoisting them back aboard afterward, the *Vittorio Veneto* lacked that equipment, so after making his scouting run, the

Italian pilot had to depart the area and land at a shore base. In effect, Iachino and the Italians had only one chance to locate the enemy.[35]

Even so, it was Iachino's scout plane that made the first sighting at 6:35 that morning, when its pilot radioed a report of Pridham-Whippell's group of light cruisers. Twenty minutes later, one of the eight British planes from the *Formidable* sighted the foremost of the two Italian cruiser groups. Curiously, neither sighting clarified the strategic situation for the opposing commanders. The Italian pilot initially mistook Pridham-Whippell's ships for one of the Italian cruiser groups, and back on the *Warspite*, Cunningham wondered if the cruisers reported by the plane from the *Formidable* might be the ships of Pridham-Whippell's squadron. Nor did the situation become much clearer when a second British aircraft reported seeing *another* cruiser group twenty miles away from the first. Was this a second group of enemy cruisers, or the same group that had already been reported? Or was *this* Pridham-Whippell?[36]

All doubt was erased at 8:00 a.m. when lookouts on the three heavy cruisers under Vice Admiral Luigi Sansonetti visually sighted Pridham-Whippell's light cruisers. At almost the same moment British lookouts on the light cruisers spotted the Italians. The British had four ships to Sansonetti's three, but the 8-inch guns on the Italian heavy cruisers easily outranged the 6-inch guns on the British light cruisers, so that even as he reported the contact to Cunningham ("3 unknown vessels distant 18 miles"), Pridham-Whippell turned away and increased speed, doing so partly to open the range, but also to draw the Italians toward Cunningham's battleships. Cheered by the sight of fleeing British warships, Sansonetti ordered a pursuit, opening fire at 8:12. Pridham-Whippell's ships zigzagged to avoid the shells splashing all around them until 8:30, when Sansonetti received orders from Iachino to break off the pursuit and close on the flagship. Iachino recalled Sansonetti because he was suspicious that the British were leading him into a trap, which of course they were, though Iachino suspected the trap consisted of lurking British submarines, for he did not know that Cunningham's battleships were so close.[37]

When Sansonetti turned away, Pridham-Whippell reversed course to follow him, taking care to stay beyond range of the Italian guns. Both groups steamed northward until about eleven o'clock, when Pridham-Whippell received his second surprise of the morning as the topmasts of the *Vittorio Veneto* appeared above the horizon. An officer eating a sandwich on the bridge of Pridham-Whippell's flagship *Orion* gestured off to the northwest and said, "What's that battleship over there? I thought ours were miles away." Once again Pridham-Whippell ordered an abrupt turn and fled to the southeast, reporting (incorrectly), "Two battleships in sight."[38]

Cunningham ordered the Fleet Air Arm to attack the Italian battleships. The *Formidable* turned into the wind and launched a half dozen attack planes. The planes were Albacores (or, as the pilots called them, "Applecores"), which were a modest improvement over the utilitarian Stringbags. Though still biplanes, they were slightly faster, had a longer range, and could carry a heavier bomb load than the Swordfish. They also had an enclosed cockpit. The six Albacores found the *Vittorio Veneto* at about eleven-thirty and attacked with torpedoes. Though they scored no hits, they confirmed Iachino's suspicion that whatever opportunity there had been to catch a British convoy by surprise was now gone. In addition, the continued absence of any Italian air support, especially in the face of a British air attack, suggested that continuing the sortie now would entail more risk than benefit. He ordered his surface groups to turn around and head west.[39]

The hunter now became the hunted. British aircraft attacked again that afternoon. Indeed, Iachino's flagship was attacked eight times that day by both carrier-based torpedo bombers from the *Formidable* and high-level bombers from Greece. Late that afternoon, three of the torpedo bombers attacked from out of the sun on the battleship's starboard side. Seeing them too late to avoid them, Iachino could only watch. "An interminable interval of time seemed to pass," he recalled, "during which we all had our hearts in our mouths and our eyes fixed on the aircraft." Two of the torpedoes missed, but one hit the *Vittorio Veneto* just above her port-side screw, jamming her rudder. The big Italian battleship began taking on water and listed slightly to port. Stopped temporarily, she managed to get under way again six minutes later using only her starboard engines, and by five o'clock she was making nineteen knots. Only after that did ten German Messerschmitt fighters appear overhead to provide the promised air cover, though they stayed for only fifty minutes before they had to fly off to refuel.[40]

Fifty-five miles behind the *Vittorio Veneto*, Cunningham feared that this tempting target would get away, and he ordered another air strike that would arrive over the Italian battleship at dusk. Six more Albacores plus three Swordfish found that the Italian surface ships had closed up on the battleship in a single formation. The handful of British aircraft attacked in the last few moments of twilight. One of the pilots recalled that "the Italians [were] silhouetted against the last glow of light in the west." In the fading light it was difficult to tell what impact the attack had, and several of the pilots reported that they thought they had scored a hit. In fact, the only hit was on the heavy cruiser *Pola*, but it proved to be the decisive blow of the battle, for it disabled five of the *Pola*'s boilers, broke her main steam pipeline, and cut off all electricity. She was dead in the water. Iachino continued westward with the main body and did not even learn that the *Pola* had been hit for more than half an hour. When he did, he ordered Rear Admiral Carlo Cattaneo's cruiser force to go back and remain by the *Pola*, to salvage her if possible or rescue her crew if necessary.[41]

All that day, and especially after receiving Pridham-Whippell's electrifying report of "two battleships," Cunningham had been trying unsuccessfully to coax his three battleships to a speed greater than a plodding twenty-two knots. When the *Vittorio Veneto* suffered the torpedo hit, he thought he might catch her, but once she was back up to nineteen knots, it seemed unlikely. He sent his swift destroyers ahead to execute a torpedo attack but did not expect to be able to use his 15-inch guns. Iachino's decision to send Cattaneo's cruisers back to succor the crippled *Pola* created a new and unlooked-for opportunity.[42]

As early as 8:15 p.m., first the *Pola* and then the other vessels of Cattaneo's command began to appear on the radar screens of those British warships that had radar. Because the Italians did not have radar, Cattaneo had no idea that enemy surface ships were so close. Unseen and unsuspected, the British battleships closed on the Italian cruisers in the dark. Cunningham remembered the moment vividly. There was a profound silence on the flag bridge of the *Warspite*, he recalled, a silence "that could almost be felt," broken only by "the voices of the gun control personnel putting the guns on the new target." Looking toward the bow, he saw "the turrets swing and steady when the 15-inch guns were pointed at the enemy cruisers." For a battleship man, it was the zenith of a career. "Never in the whole of my life," he later wrote, "have I experienced a more thrilling moment."[43]

Cattaneo and his fellow officers were focused on the crippled and drifting *Pola* when at 10:28 a bright white finger of light from a British searchlight suddenly pierced through the darkness and illuminated Cattaneo's flagship, *Zara*. Seconds afterward, orange stabs of flame issued from a dozen 15-inch guns. At only 3,800 yards, virtually point-blank, the British could hardly miss. Of the *Warspite*'s initial salvo of six shells, five hit the heavy cruiser *Fiume*. Because the initial salvo was often used merely to determine the range and bearing of the target, the *Warspite*'s senior gunnery officer, Captain Douglas Fisher, was startled by it: "Good Lord!" he declared. "We've hit her!" Before the officers and crew of the *Fiume* could even process the fact that they were in a fight, her superstructure was smashed to pieces and her rear turret blown over the side. The *Zara* took twenty hits in less than five minutes. From the bridge of the *Warspite*, Cunningham could see "whole turrets and masses of other heavy debris whirling through the air and splashing into the sea."[44]

Utterly overwhelmed, the *Zara* was sinking by the bow, and Cattaneo made his way to the stern to address those crew members who were gathered there. He told them he had ordered teams to place charges around the ship to ensure that she did not fall into the hands of the enemy. He then called for three cheers for Italy and ordered abandon ship. As the men went over the side, he made his own way back toward the bridge to go down with his ship. His flag captain, Luigi Corsi, followed him, stopping to ask an engineer officer for a cigarette. He was handed the whole pack. Aware that he would not have time to smoke more than one, he smiled wanly and said, "These are too many." The *Zara* went under at 2:40 a.m. with the loss of 783 men, including both Cattaneo and Corsi.[45]

The Allied destroyers, commanded by an Australian navy man, Captain Hector Waller, got into the action, too, sending torpedoes into the burning wreckage and attacking the Italian destroyers, sinking two of them. As

Cunningham put it in his report, the destroyers "had an exciting time and did considerable execution." At eleven o'clock Cunningham recalled his dispersed warships; of Cattaneo's entire force, only two destroyers survived. Two British destroyers, *Nubian* and *Jervis*, went alongside the stricken *Pola* and took off survivors just minutes before she rolled over and sank at 4:10 a.m. Other destroyers picked up more men from the water. All told, British ships rescued some nine hundred Italian officers and men. Rescue operations were terminated when several German bombers belatedly appeared and began strafing the ships. Cunningham then retired eastward, though he radioed the coordinates of the site to the Italian navy, and the Italian hospital ship *Gradisca* eventually picked up 160 more survivors.[46]

That morning—March 29—as Cunningham returned triumphant to Alexandria, Iachino finally obtained the robust air cover he had been promised. Now that it was much too late, more than a hundred Italian and German aircraft arrived overhead to escort his ships home. Though Iachino escaped with the damaged *Vittorio Veneto*, he had lost three heavy cruisers, two destroyers, and more than 2,400 men in the Battle of Cape Matapan. The British lost one airplane. It was a shattering blow, not only to Italian hopes of commanding the Middle Sea but also to Italian morale and prestige. After the Battle of Cape Matapan, Mussolini decreed that the Regia Marina should operate only in coastal waters within range of land-based aircraft.[47]

Six days later, Hitler's legions invaded the Balkans.

GERMAN INTERVENTION IN THE GREEK WAR WAS DECISIVE. Within days, British and Greek ground forces were in full retreat. If the Germans had failed to provide adequate air cover for Iachino's fleet, their aircraft proved devastatingly effective in the land war, and Stuka dive-bombers and Junkers level bombers dominated the skies. In a kind of mini Dunkirk, British transports and destroyers sought to rescue the hard-pressed Allied forces. More than fifty thousand men were successfully evacuated from mainland Greece and carried 250 miles southward to the island of Crete, though four thousand British soldiers and two thousand colonial troops from British Palestine had to be left behind to become prisoners of war.

Cunningham issued orders that "no enemy forces must reach Crete by sea." Nor did they. Absent a surface navy, the Germans could not pursue their foes across the Aegean. But on May 20, thirteen thousand German paratroopers jumped onto the island from the air. The paratroopers suffered horrific casualties, and initially the British and Greek commanders believed they could contain them. But poor Allied coordination allowed the Germans to secure the airfields, and that enabled them to fly in transport planes filled with reinforcements and supplies. Within days, the Allies had to evacuate Crete as well.[48]

As at Dunkirk the year before, every available destroyer was assigned to the task, and as at Dunkirk, the evacuation had to take place at night due to German control of the skies. For four consecutive nights, from May 28 to June 1, the destroyers crept in at midnight and loaded troops from the jetties, putting to sea well before dawn filled with exhausted and hungry soldiers. Some 16,500 men were evacuated, though once again more than 5,000 had to be left behind. The Luftwaffe pursued and attacked the Allied ships all the way across the Mediterranean, and the toll on Cunningham's fleet was shocking—greater than Italian losses in the Battle of Cape Matapan. Altogether the British lost three light cruisers and six destroyers sunk and sixteen more ships severely damaged, including the battleships *Warspite* and *Barham*, as well as the new carrier *Formidable*. More than 2,400 British sailors lost their lives.[49]

Despite efforts by the Regia Marina, the British still commanded the sea, but the Germans controlled the air, so—much like the Italians—the Royal Navy could not operate effectively beyond the umbrella of land-based air cover. Arthur Tedder, head of the Royal Air Force, observed that "any excursion [by warships] outside a radius of about 150 miles to the east and north of Alex[andria] is an expensive adventure." The Royal Navy retained its presence in the eastern Mediterranean, but its reach had been severely limited.[50]

CHAPTER 6

THE WAR ON TRADE, I

W HILE THE ROYAL NAVY contended with the Axis for supremacy in the Mediterranean, the struggle for control of the North Atlantic took a new and dangerous turn. On June 23, 1940, the day after France capitulated, Karl Dönitz headed west by train, crossing a defeated and dejected France to visit seaports along the Atlantic coast and assess their suitability as possible U-boat bases. U-boats operating from ports on the Bay of Biscay would be nearly five hundred miles closer to the Atlantic sea-lanes, which would dramatically shorten the transit time to their hunting grounds and lengthen the time they could remain on station. Two weeks later, on July 7, the U-30 entered Lorient Harbor, on the southwest coast of Brittany, and in August the Germans began building a bombproof U-boat headquarters at Kernevel near the harbor's entrance.* By the fall,

---

* Royal Air Force bombers regularly targeted the U-boats in their new bases, which led the Germans to construct massive concrete U-boat "pens" with roofs that were more than sixteen feet thick. Because of that, the U-boats remained secure in their Biscay ports despite repeated air attacks.

German U-boats were operating from five ports on the Bay of Biscay: Brest, Lorient, St. Nazaire, La Rochelle, and Bordeaux. It marked a dramatic change in the character and the intensity of Germany's war on British trade.[1]

The home islands of Great Britain produced only about half the food necessary to feed its population. From the start, Dönitz had argued that Britain could be starved into surrender if his U-boats could sink Allied ships faster than they could be replaced by new construction. It did not matter if the ships were inbound and filled with vital war materials from the United States, or outbound and carrying mostly ballast. The key was to sink the ships. To measure progress, Dönitz established monthly goals for his U-boats. In 1940 he initially set a goal of 100,000 to 200,000 tons per month. Later, after the United States joined the war, he doubled that objective, and by 1943 he was suggesting that the U-boats needed to sink 700,000 tons a month. Whatever the standard, it was clear that to implement this so-called tonnage strategy (*Tonnageschlacht*), he needed many more U-boats than he had, and he insisted that all of them should operate in the North Atlantic and target only merchant ships. On both of these issues, Dönitz clashed with Erich Raeder.

Dönitz also implemented a new tactical protocol for his U-boats, one that he had been thinking about since 1918. Rather than send the boats out one by one to conduct solitary patrols, he planned to coordinate them in operational groups, eventually called wolf packs. The idea was to deploy the U-boats in a long reconnaissance line along a north-south axis, making it more likely that one of them would encounter a transatlantic convoy and report its location. Initially, Dönitz imagined that the U-boat commanders would communicate directly with one another by radio, and he experimented with that in the fall of 1939. He soon concluded, however, that it was more efficient and effective if he coordinated them himself from his new headquarters at Kernevel. It was a game changer. Whereas previously a solitary U-boat might sink one or two merchant ships in a convoy, a wolf pack could potentially sink ten or fifteen ships—even destroy the convoy altogether.[2]

The German occupation of northern France also meant that the U-boats could benefit from sighting reports sent in by long-range Focke-Wulf 200

Condor aircraft operating from coastal bases. These sleek four-engine planes, built originally to carry well-heeled passengers nonstop from Berlin to New York, could fly well out to sea to locate, track, and occasionally attack British convoys. This partnership of airplane and U-boat never fully developed, however, in part because of a shortage of Condor aircraft, and in part because Göring was jealously proprietary of his Luftwaffe. While the relationship between the Kriegsmarine and the Luftwaffe was never as dysfunctional as the one between the Regia Marina and the Regia Aeronautica, it fell well short of full cooperation. Then, too, by July, Göring was focused almost entirely on the air war against British cities—the Blitz. On the British side of the Channel, the Royal Navy and the airplanes of what was called Coastal Command established a joint headquarters at Liverpool in February 1941, but like the Germans, the British had a limited number of long-range aircraft, and the Royal Air Force preferred to use most of them to bomb Germany, a priority shared by the prime minister. In the end, the bulk of the responsibility for trade defense fell on the hard-pressed escorts at sea.[3]

Before he could launch his onslaught on British trade that summer, Dönitz first had to solve two problems, one of them technological, the other institutional. The technological problem was the continued unreliability of the torpedo warheads. Dönitz had attributed the multiple failures of the magnetic triggers in the torpedoes during the Norway campaign to the proximity of the magnetic north pole. Yet throughout April and into May, U-boats operating further south reported that their torpedoes didn't work, either. The U-boat skippers were frustrated to the point of anger when, after carefully lining up a shot and firing a spread of four torpedoes at point-blank range, the torpedoes either exploded prematurely or ran too deep to have any effect. Angrily Dönitz wrote in his war diary: "I do not believe that ever in the history of war men have been sent against the enemy with such a useless weapon."[4]

Ironically, it was the British who provided at least a partial solution. In early May, German engineers examined the torpedoes taken from the captured British submarine *Seal* and found that the British trigger design was both simpler and more reliable than their own. Soon afterward, Dönitz ordered that German torpedoes be retrofitted with the British-style contact trigger. The tendency of the torpedoes to run deep was not fully resolved until early in 1942, when the engineers discovered that there was a slow leak in the torpedoes' balance chamber.

The institutional problem was not so easily solved. This was an almost crippling shortage in the number of available U-boats. Indeed, Dönitz had no more U-boats in June 1940 than he had had the previous September, when the war began. Though twenty-eight new U-boats had been built, twenty-eight others had been lost to enemy action. From the start, Dönitz had insisted that "the building of a powerful U-boat fleet was the German Navy's most urgent task." Yet despite obtaining official agreement from Raeder—and, more important, from Hitler—to build twenty-five new U-boats a month, that goal was not met. At first the invasion of England got top priority, though even after Hitler shelved those plans in September, a shortage of skilled workers and machine tools hampered U-boat construction. As a result, Dönitz was able to deploy only twenty-one U-boats from his new Atlantic coast bases.[5]

Even with that limited number, the U-boats sank thirty-one ships off Ireland and Britain in June alone—Prien's U-47 sank seven of them by itself. In July, Otto Kretschmer in the U-99 returned to Lorient having sunk a record 65,137 tons in a single patrol. U-boat skippers labeled this the *glückliche Zeit* or "happy time," and upon their return to Lorient or Brest, Dönitz distributed medals to the commanders and congratulations to the crews. Their success helped to restore the morale of the U-boat crews dispirited by the series of torpedo failures. Morale was important in the U-boat service, where forty-five or so officers and men lived and worked in a claustrophobic iron tube so small that men sometimes had to crawl on their hands and knees from one compartment to another. For weeks at a time, they went without showers and breathed one another's stale air, sleeping in shifts on shared bunks. In such an environment, crews either became brothers or turned on one another.[6]

The surge of U-boat success in June did not last through the summer mostly because Dönitz simply did not have enough boats to keep a significant number of them at sea. Then, too, three more U-boats were lost that month, and several others had to be laid up for repairs. As a result, by July Dönitz had only four boats operating in the decisive area off Britain. After

Italy joined the war, it seemed possible that the Regia Marina's 116 submarines could supplement the U-boats, and one squadron of Italian submarines did operate out of Bordeaux that summer. They were large and impressive-looking, but they performed indifferently, sinking only four ships in August, and Dönitz mentally dismissed them as all but useless. Nevertheless, the early success by German U-boats operating from French ports demonstrated the potential of an all-out U-boat war on trade.[7]

THE BRITISH RESPONSE to the U-boat threat was to establish a convoy system. Though convoys had been used by maritime powers to protect trade since the Age of Sail, the Admiralty had been initially reluctant to embrace the concept during the First World War. After all, a convoy conveniently clustered all the merchant ships together, thus creating a target-rich environment for a stalking U-boat. Then, too, convoys necessarily had to proceed at the speed of the slowest vessel. Despite these apparent defects, however, the events of 1917–18 had proved that convoys were by far the most effective countermeasure to a U-boat threat, and in 1939 the British established a convoy system even before the war began.

From the start, each convoy was identified by a code that indicated its origin, destination, and numerical sequence. The first outbound convoy from Liverpool, for example, was OB-1. Eventually, regular convoys were established for routes from Gibraltar (HG), Jamaica (KJ), Freetown, Sierra Leone (SL), and scores of other places, though the busiest and most important route was the transatlantic one between Halifax, Nova Scotia, and either Liverpool or the Firth of Clyde (Glasgow) in Scotland. Eastbound convoys from Canada to Britain were designated as HX convoys (homebound from Halifax), and westbound convoys were ON convoys (outbound to North America). Typically they consisted of twenty to forty merchant ships organized into seven to ten columns of four or five ships each. To avoid collision in rough seas or heavy fog, the ships in each column steamed at intervals of four hundred to six hundred yards, and the columns themselves were a thousand yards apart. As a result, a forty-ship convoy filled a rectangle of ocean five miles wide and two or three miles long, an area as large as fifteen square miles.[8]

The merchant ships were under the supervision of a convoy commander, a civilian who was usually a retired Royal Navy officer and who rode one of the merchant ships as commodore. His job was to maintain order within the convoy and issue the periodic course changes by flag hoist or blinker light that kept it zigzagging across the sea, a protocol designed to throw potential attackers off their stroke. Maintaining order in a convoy was often difficult since civilian merchant captains were unused to making the precise tactical maneuvers required to reorient forty ships simultaneously on a new course. The commodores necessarily had to adjust their expectations of instantaneous execution when ordering a course change.

In the van and on the flanks of this large rectangle of ships, and often maneuvering independently as well, were the armed escorts. If Dönitz was frustratingly short of operational U-boats, the British were equally deficient in the number of available escorts. Destroyers were the most effective convoy escorts, but destroyers were needed everywhere, and the heavy losses during the Norway campaign and especially off Dunkirk meant that the

HMS *Gentian*, seen here, was one of the first Flower-class corvettes built in 1940 for convoy escort. These small and uncomfortable vessels were especially valuable during the first two years of the war. The *Gentian* herself participated in more than seventy convoys in the North Atlantic.

Imperial War Museum

Royal Navy had a severe shortage of these critical workhorse warships. To make up the shortfall, all sorts of vessels were called into service for escort duty.

Among them was a new type of small warship called a corvette. Because the first generation of corvettes were all named for flowers, they were known as Flower-class ships and they bore such unwarlike names as *Azalea*, *Begonia*, *Bluebell*, and *Buttercup*. At only 940 tons each, they were tiny and carried only a single 4-inch gun on their foredeck plus twin .50-caliber machine guns; against virtually any conventional warship they were all but helpless. They were not only small, they were also slow. With a maximum speed of sixteen knots, corvettes were no faster than a surfaced U-boat. They were nearly as uncomfortable as well, especially in the volatile North Atlantic, where even in a moderate sea they bounced around like so much flotsam. A crewman on the *Rhododendron* recalled that being on a corvette "was like a terrier shaking a bit of rag. The old ship [would] corkscrew up on top of a wave and you'd be up and you'd look down into this trough and you'd think *crikey*, and the next thing you'd be down in there and a bloomin' great wave'd come over the top." That, plus the fact that a crew of fifty men was crammed into a 190-foot hull made service in a Flower-class corvette a challenge to one's constitution and endurance. The novelist Nicholas Monsarrat, who served three years in corvettes, vividly recalled the challenge of simply eating a meal: "When you drink, the liquid rises toward you and slops over: at meals the food spills off your plate, the cutlery will not stay in place. Things roll about and bang, and slide away crazily." Standing topside watch was an ordeal. "Every night for seventeen nights on end," Monsarrat wrote, "you're woken up at ten to four by the bosun's mate, and you stare at the deck-head and think: *My God, I can't go up there again in the dark and filthy rain, and stand another four hours of it*. But you can of course."[9]

On the plus side, the corvettes were inexpensive, could be built quickly, and had both Asdic and depth charges. Churchill extolled them as the "Cheap and Nasties," meaning that they were cheap to build and nasty to the enemy. Fifty-six of them were laid down prior to September 3, 1939, and forty-one more soon after the war began. Eventually, Britain and Canada built 269 of them, including 130 for the Canadian Navy. Despite their floral names, minimal armament, and cramped quarters, they played a crucial role in sustaining Britain's maritime lifeline to the outside world.[10]

Other vessels served in the escort role as well. Two of them bore names that harked back to the Age of Sail. One was a "sloop-of-war," which in 1940 designated a small (1,000-ton) destroyer with two 4-inch guns, one forward and one aft. The other was a slightly larger ship (1,350 tons) that was initially dubbed a twin-screw corvette but was subsequently labeled a "frigate." Though the British eventually built hundreds of these small ships, in 1940 they were so strapped for escorts they also employed something called an armed merchant cruiser (AMC).

This was a much larger vessel (often 14,000 to 16,000 tons) that was essentially a cargo ship or a passenger vessel retrofitted with a few 6-inch guns and then rechristened a warship. The very existence of such ships was a measure of Britain's desperation, because the day when a freighter could be turned into an effective warship merely by installing some guns had long passed. These merchant cruisers had no armor, and the guns they carried were

The former Anchor Line passenger ship *Cilicia* was one of many ships converted into armed merchant cruisers (AMCs) in 1940–41. In that capacity, the *Cilicia* was rechristened the HMS *Atlantic Isle*. Later in the war, when more conventional escorts became available, she became a troop transport.

Naval History and Heritage Command

old, unprotected, and often manned by indifferently trained volunteers. Sailors on these ersatz warships claimed that the initials AMC stood for "Admiralty-made coffins." The crews of the AMCs often consisted of the same men who had served aboard them as merchant sailors. Because the document they signed to enter the naval service was numbered T-124, they were occasionally referred to as T-124 sailors. Merchant Marine officers who accepted duty in this service received a commission in the Royal Navy Voluntary Reserves (RNVR) and wore traditional navy blue uniforms except that the gold stripes on their sleeves undulated like the waves of the ocean, which led to their nickname as members of the "Wavy Navy."[11]

Even with these additions, Britain remained desperately short of escorts. One source of support was Canada. In 1940, however, what was grandly called the Royal Canadian Navy was tiny—as recently as 1933, the Canadian government had seriously proposed abolishing it altogether as a cost-saving measure. Now the Canadian navy began to expand, slowly at first, then dramatically. In September 1939, when the war began, it boasted only six destroyers and ten corvettes, though within days Canada authorized the construction of fifty-four new corvettes and twenty-five minesweepers. It would be many months before any of those vessels were operational, and the need was immediate.[12]

Because of that, Churchill looked longingly to the United States, which had 120 mothballed World War I–era destroyers moored in long rows in ports all along the East Coast. The dominant characteristic of these ships was that they had four funnels, and so they were called four-pipers or four-stackers. They were old, inefficient, and greatly in need of a refit, but they were better than nothing, and Churchill all but begged Roosevelt for them, calling it a "matter of life and death." Even King George put in a word, writing the American president, "I am certain you will do your best to procure them for us before it is too late." Roosevelt was convinced that America's own security was bound up in the fate of Britain, and he very likely would have been willing to give the ships away, but a suspicious Congress compelled him to strike a hard bargain.[13]

What emerged was the so-called bases-for-destroyers agreement in September 1940, by which the United States turned over fifty of the four-stackers to Britain in exchange for ninety-nine-year basing rights in Bermuda, Antigua, the Bahamas, and elsewhere in the Western Hemisphere. British critics thought it was a stiff price to pay, but Churchill was grateful, writing Roosevelt, "Every destroyer that you can spare to us is measured in rubies." Brought into the Royal Navy, these vessels were designated as Town-class destroyers because all of them were renamed for towns that existed in both the United States and the British Commonwealth, including one that was christened HMS *Churchill*, which was the former USS *Herndon* (DD-198). In 1944 she was transferred to the Soviet Navy, became the *Deyatelny*, and was sunk by the U-286 in January 1945. Even more well-traveled was the USS *Yarnall*, which went into British service as HMS *Lincoln*, then into the Norwegian navy, and finally into the Soviet navy as the *Druzhny*. The Soviets returned her to Britain in 1952, and she

HMS *Lincoln* (formerly the USS *Yarnall*) was one of 50 four-stack destroyers the United States turned over to the Royal Navy in exchange for long-term leases on naval bases in the Western Hemisphere. Although they were old and in great need of updating, they nevertheless helped the British sustain their transatlantic convoys.

U.S. Naval Institute

was sold for scrap after a service life of forty-four years. These former American destroyers were nearly as uncomfortable to serve in as the Flower-class corvettes, for they rolled excessively and were awkward to handle. They did, however, give the British fifty more seagoing platforms for convoy defense.[14]

Just as each convoy had a commodore on one of the merchant ships, each also had an escort commander, an active-duty officer, usually a Royal Navy captain or commander. The relationship between the civilian commodore and the escort commander was a nuanced one. The commodore of the merchant ships was often a retired flag officer who was generally much older than the active-duty escort commander and vastly senior in rank as well. On the other hand, he was also retired and therefore could not give orders to the escort commander regardless of their respective ranks. Still, some escort commanders were reluctant to issue peremptory orders to a former flag officer. Despite the potential for confusion or conflict, for the most part this divided command system worked well enough.[15]

During the first six months of the war, the long journey from Wilhelm-shaven around the northern tip of Scotland kept most of the U-boats from venturing too far into mid-ocean; aware of that, the escorts accompanied the outbound convoys only as far as 12 degrees west longitude—just beyond Ireland. After that, the merchant ships were sent on their way and the escorts waited to meet an inbound HX convoy from Halifax for the dangerous run into port. These nearly constant handovers were choreographed by an office in the Admiralty called Trade Plot. There, routing officers coordinated the complicated matrix of British global trade, working in shifts around the clock to track every convoy and escort vessel worldwide.[16]

After the fall of France and the establishment of the new U-boat bases in the Bay of Biscay, the Admiralty pushed the meeting point for inbound convoys four hundred miles further west, out to 20 degrees west longitude. For the rest of the war, the area between this invisible line and the British Isles was known as the Western Approaches, and it became a killing ground as the convoys and their overworked escorts engaged the U-boats in a constant and deadly cat-and-mouse game.

The coordination of the convoys and their escorts through the Western Approaches was an imperfect science. The convoys operated under strict radio silence, so calculating the time and place of their arrival was difficult for the schedulers in Trade Plot. Then, too, there were simply never quite enough escorts, which meant that they were sometimes shuttled from convoy to convoy as the routers borrowed from Peter to pay Paul. On one occasion in September 1940, when convoy HX-72 was approaching the 20 degree longitude exchange point, the Admiralty ordered its lone escort, the armed merchant cruiser *Jervis Bay*, to abandon it and speed back to Halifax to pick up another convoy. Since the relief escorts from Britain were not due for another twenty-four hours, the ships in HX-72 plodded along unescorted for most of a day and a night. As fate would have it, that night Günther Prien, still in U-47, spotted them and radioed their location to several other U-boats. Over the next twenty-four hours, Prien and the other U-boat skippers sank eleven ships with a gross tonnage of more than 72,000 tons. It was a foretaste of what was to come.[17]

THE BATTLE OF THE ATLANTIC is something of a misnomer, for it implies that the confrontation between convoys and wolf packs was a single event. It was instead a recurring and relentless struggle that lasted more than four years and passed through a number of different phases marked by shifting geographical boundaries and technological innovations, including efforts on both sides to read the naval codes of the other. In the fall of 1940, as Luftwaffe bombs fell nightly on London and other British cities, the dynamics of the initial phase of this protracted conflict were just emerging. A useful example of those dynamics is the confrontation that took place in the Western Approaches during the third week of October 1940.

Convoy SC-7 departed Nova Scotia for Liverpool on October 5. The SC designation indicated that the convoy originated in Sydney (S) on Cape Breton (C), at the northwestern tip of Nova Scotia, some two hundred miles northeast of Halifax. For all that, it might as well have stood for "slow convoy," since all of the thirty-five merchant ships in it had failed to qualify for the regular HX convoy from Halifax, which required ships to be able to maintain an average speed of nine knots.* Officially, that meant that HX convoys were "fast convoys," though at nine knots it was a rather generous characterization. SC-7's designation as a slow convoy, however, was entirely appropriate. In theory, slow convoys were supposed to proceed at an average speed of seven knots, though they did not always achieve that goal. In one such convoy (ON-126), a "howling gale" forced the ships to reduce speed first to 4 knots, then to 1.25 knots, until it seemed, as one sailor put it, "the convoy is just about standing still." For SC-7, the average speed was 6.6 knots.[18]

Most of the thirty-five ships in SC-7 were British, though like most convoys it included several ships of foreign registry, including in this case a total of sixteen: six Norwegian, four Greek, three Swedish, two Dutch, and one Danish. The ships ranged in size from 1,500 to 10,000 tons, and they carried a variety of cargos from trucks to grain. Many carried what were called "pit props": timbers cut from the Canadian forests that were used to hold up the roofs of coal tunnels so that British miners could maintain the supply of coal needed to heat British homes in the winter.[19]

The commodore of SC-7 was a former Royal Navy vice admiral named Lachlan MacKinnon who had retired from active service only two years before and who at one point back in the 1920s had commanded the battlecruiser *Hood*. MacKinnon flew his commodore's pennant on board the freighter *Assyrian*, which ironically enough had been built in Germany. Despite the large number of ships gathered in Sydney Harbor, the initial escort of SC-7 consisted of only a single ship, the sloop HMS *Scarborough*, whose captain was a forty-year-old Royal Navy commander named Norman Dickinson. The *Scarborough* had been refitted as a survey ship in the 1930s and then quickly recommissioned as a warship after war broke out. As a result, she carried only one 4-inch gun rather than the two usually found on sloops-of-war. Nor was she equipped with an Asdic system, though as it turned out that hardly mattered.[20]

---

* Ships that could steam at fifteen knots or better sailed independently because although U-boats could make sixteen or seventeen knots on the surface in good weather, it was difficult, if not quite impossible, for them to get in position for a shot against a surface vessel that was proceeding at fifteen knots.

Early in the crossing, four of the merchant ships left the convoy due to either bad weather or engine problems. Though neither MacKinnon nor Dickinson knew it, two of those four were subsequently discovered by U-boats and sent to the bottom. The convoy encountered the usual gut-wrenching sea conditions characteristic of the North Atlantic. As one described it, "The stern is submerged occasionally as we slip over the crest [of a wave], balance precariously for a moment high in the air & then slither down in a mixture of white spume and green lather." After eleven days of that, on the night of October 16, Dickinson was greatly relieved to see two new escorts coming out to join him for the perilous run through the Western Approaches. The new arrivals were the sloop *Fowey* and the corvette *Bluebell*. Their arrival not only allowed Dickinson to cover both sides of the convoy as well as the van, but the newcomers were equipped with Asdic. Dickinson may have thought that with their arrival the worst was past, but if so, he was soon disabused of that notion.[21]

The very next night, just before midnight, a lookout on board the U-48 spotted several dark objects off the port bow. The skipper of the U-48, Kapitänleutnant Heinrich Bleichrodt, climbed up to the conning tower to see for himself, and he shadowed the ships for some time to satisfy himself that this was, in fact, a British convoy before employing the new protocol and sending a radio message to Dönitz at Kernevel. Then he maneuvered for an attack.

No one in any the merchant ships or any of the three escorts was aware that the U-48 was stalking them. Though the Asdic systems on the newly arrived escorts were in active mode, they revealed nothing because the U-48 was running on the surface. None of the ships in the convoy was equipped with radar, and the low profile of a U-boat at night was all but invisible to the human eye. The first indication that danger was near came at 4:00 a.m., when the 10,000-ton *Languedoc*, loaded with fuel oil, suddenly exploded. Only minutes later, the smaller *Scoresby*, whose deck was piled high with a cargo of pit props, was also hit. MacKinnon ordered an emergency turn to starboard, and Dickinson directed the three escort ships to the scene of the torpedoing. Asdic revealed nothing, and all the escort skippers could do was peer into the darkness searching vainly for the profile of a U-boat and rescue the survivors from the two sinking ships.[22]

There were no more explosions that night, and a few hours later, with the sun coming up, Dickinson received a report from a long-range British Sunderland flying boat that a surfaced U-boat was only a few miles away. It was the U-48, and Dickinson went after it. He forced Bleichrodt to dive, and he blanketed the area with depth charges. Though he scored no hits, he kept the U-48 submerged for an extended period, draining her batteries and keeping her away from the convoy, which continued eastward.[23]

At Kernevel, Dönitz was disappointed that Bleichrodt had attacked without waiting for the rest of the wolf pack because in doing so he lost contact with the convoy. Even so, Dönitz calculated the convoy's probable course and ordered five more U-boats to converge on the coordinates. The five boats Dönitz sent included three commanded by men who were already famous in Germany (and infamous in Britain) for their prowess as U-boat skippers. They were Otto Kretschmer in the U-99, Joachim Schepke in the U-100, and Prien's former first officer, Engelbert Endrass, now in command of his own boat, the U-46.

As they closed in on SC-7, two more escorts arrived from Britain, raising the total number of escorts to five. One of them was the sloop HMS *Leith*, whose captain, Commander Roland C. Allen, was senior to Dickinson and who therefore succeeded to the role of escort commander. Such abrupt changes in supervisory authority necessarily weakened the effective partnership of the escort vessels. Of course the U-boats, too, lacked a cooperative tactical plan. Dönitz's wolf pack strategy brought them together, but once in contact with the enemy, each U-boat skipper attacked independently.[24]

The attacks began near midnight when Endrass fired a spread of four torpedoes into the convoy. One hit the Swedish steamer *Convallaria*, a small (2,000-ton) cargo ship carrying pulpwood that went down in less than five minutes. Another hit the British steamer *Beatus*, loaded with timber, steel, and crated airplanes. Then, one after another, other ships were hit. It was impossible to tell where the danger lurked. As the survivor of a later convoy noted, "A ship of the convoy could be torpedoed and sunk whilst other ships of the convoy were unaware of it....Explosions would occur, to be heard or felt, but would only indicate that action was taking place somewhere." Once again, Asdic proved useless since all of the U-boats attacked on the surface. It was obvious that there was more than one of them; men on the merchant ships caught glimpses of them, low shadows flitting past in the darkness. Most of the merchantmen had a single 4-inch gun aft, and many of them opened fire, though with no effect. The escorts fired star shells into the night that floated down by parachute to illuminate the darkness, and the escorts, too, opened with their 4-inch guns, but like the gunners on the merchantmen, they scored no hits. The white phosphorus glare from the star shells and the occasional orange muzzle flash lit up the night and reflected off the black water. Then, periodically, there was a much brighter flash when another ship exploded. In his war diary, Kretschmer described the effect of one of his torpedoes when it struck the 6,000-ton *Empire Miniver*: "The explosion of the torpedo was immediately followed by a high sheet of flame and an explosion which ripped the ship open as far as the bridge, and left a cloud of smoke 600 feet high." Several minutes later, he added: "Ship still burning fiercely with green flames."[25]

In the two hours between midnight and 2:00 a.m., nine ships of the convoy went to the bottom. Kretschmer sank six of them himself. The escort commanders were reduced to the role of lifeguards, plucking men from the water until the number of rescued seamen outnumbered the crew. The corvette *Bluebell* eventually hosted 203 survivors, more than four times the number of men in her crew. And still the torpedoing continued. By dawn, the U-boats had sunk sixteen ships. Counting the four lost previously, the final toll was twenty ships sunk out of the thirty-five that had left Nova Scotia. And the slaughter wasn't over yet.[26]

None of the U-boats had been damaged, though three of them had expended all their torpedoes and headed back toward the Biscay ports to reload. Schepke's U-100 and Endrass's U-46 still had some fish on board, as did Bleichrodt in the U-48. Within hours they received a message from Lorient that a second convoy was coming their way. Dönitz vectored two more U-boats toward its reported location, one of which was Prien's U-47.

The target of this reconstituted wolf pack was a "fast" convoy, HX-79. It was also an especially large one, consisting of forty-nine merchant ships. It had left Halifax on October 8 with an escort of two armed merchant cruisers and, like SC-7, it had been reinforced just prior to the wolf pack assault by a particularly large contingent of escorts including two destroyers, four corvettes, an armed minesweeper, and three armed trawlers. Once again the attacks began just past midnight in pitch darkness with the U-boats attacking on the surface. Thirteen more ships were sunk, including the *Caprella*, loaded with 13,500 tons of fuel oil. Despite the oversize escort, not a single U-boat was damaged.[27]

Coming up behind HX-79 was HX-79A, with the overflow ships that could not be accommodated in the first convoy, and the U-boats found it, too. Seven more ships were sunk, and it would have been worse had the U-boats not run out of torpedoes. In less than three days, eight U-boats had sunk thirty-seven ships without suffering a single loss. If eight U-boats could wreak such havoc, what might eighty or a hundred do? It was a powerful argument for Dönitz's vision, and he renewed his pleas that U-boats be given the highest priority in Germany's war production program.

In the three months between September 2 and December 2, 1940, Dönitz's wolf packs sank a total of 140 British and Allied ships, most of them in the Western Approaches, and in that same period the small coastal ducks claimed another seventeen. The U-boats had destroyed nearly 850,000 tons of shipping. It was a rate of loss that Britain could not sustain.

Of course, the human loss was significant as well. The veneer of humanity that had characterized Langsdorff's treatment of his victims during the cruise of the *Graf Spee* had by now disappeared. In order to avoid any risk to his boats and their crews, Dönitz ordered his skippers not to attempt to rescue any survivors. "Concern yourself only with the safety of your own boat," he told them. "We must be hard in this war." That meant not only a heavy loss of life when the ships initially sank, but also unrecorded days and weeks of suffering as survivors slowly starved to death or died of thirst.[28]

Other ships in the convoys dared not stop to pick up survivors in the water. If they did, it not only upset the convoy formation but also often ensured that they became the next victim. As a result, the transports generally left the rescue mission to the escorts and held their positions in the convoy. It was hard to pass by men struggling in the water and calling for help, and many of the mariners who were forced to do so wondered if it would be their turn next to watch as other ships passed them by. A veteran of several crossings recalled the various reactions of the men in the water. "Some of them [were] swearing, some praying, and some mockingly sticking out their thumbs and calling 'Going my way, mister?' as we slid by not 100 feet from them."[29]

The only reprieve for the convoys came from the weather. The winter storms in the North Atlantic made life uncomfortable, but it was even more disruptive for the 750-ton U-boats, and in particularly harsh weather the number of sinkings dropped dramatically. There were, however, other dangers at sea that fall and winter.

WHILE DÖNITZ PLEADED FOR MORE U-BOATS, Raeder reprised his strategy of sending out heavy surface ships as commerce raiders. Though Hitler remained skeptical of using large and expensive warships to sink merchant vessels, Raeder hoped that surface raiders would compel the British to, in his words, "split up their heavy naval forces and scatter some of these out over all the high seas, thus weakening and wearing down their main fleet." In addition, Raeder envisioned the deployment of surface raiders as a kind of stopgap: they would keep the British back on their heels until Dönitz could acquire the U-boats he needed.[30]

In pursuit of these twin goals, four days after the slaughter of SC-7 and HX-79, Raeder dispatched the pocket battleship *Admiral Scheer*, commanded by Captain Theodor Krancke, into the North Atlantic on a commerce-raiding cruise. Aided by heavy weather that kept British reconnaissance flights

The pocket battleship (*Panzerschiff*) *Admiral Scheer*, a sister ship of the *Deutschland* (later *Lützow*) as she appeared during her commerce raiding cruise in 1941.

Naval History and Heritage Command

grounded, Krancke took the *Admiral Scheer* through the North Sea, around Scotland and Iceland, and then south through what was called the Denmark Strait, between Iceland and Greenland, without being discovered. By the first of November, he was in position south of Greenland, well west of the 20th degree of longitude, where the convoys believed they were relatively safe. Wireless intercepts relayed to Krancke from Berlin told him that two eastbound HX convoys were at sea, and he steered to intercept them. His lookouts sighted individual ships on both November 3 and 4, but Krancke let them go without getting close enough to be recognized. He was after bigger fish. On November 5 (Guy Fawkes Day back in Britain), the *Scheer* encountered the steamer *Mohan*, which was quite literally a banana boat, as it was loaded with 70,000 stems of bananas. After sinking it with gunfire, he launched his scout plane to search the most likely quadrant for convoys, and the plane soon returned, the pilot waggling his wings to indicate that he had important news. After the plane landed alongside and was hoisted aboard, the pilot literally ran to the bridge to report that there was a large convoy eighty-eight miles dead ahead.[31]

Composed of thirty-eight ships in nine columns, convoy HX-84 had left Halifax eight days earlier with an escort of two Canadian destroyers, though they had turned back once the convoy was well out to sea, leaving it with only the armed merchant cruiser *Jervis Bay* as a mid-ocean escort. This was the same vessel that Trade Plot had detached a day early from HX-72 in order to hasten back to Halifax to assume this new duty. The routers in Trade Plot had hoped to include three of the four-pipers recently obtained from the Americans as an additional escort, but those ships were still undergoing refits, including the installation of an Asdic system, and they were not yet ready for sea when the convoy sailed on October 28. Though the *Jervis Bay* had seven 6-inch guns, they were of uncertain utility since they were old, not connected to a central fire-control system, and instead of being housed in turrets they were simply bolted to the deck. The ship had neither radar nor Asdic, no torpedo tubes, and no depth charges. The skipper of the *Jervis Bay* was forty-nine-year-old Captain Edward S. F. Fegan, an Irishman from County Tipperary and a career Royal Navy officer who was the son and the grandson of naval officers.[32]

On November 5, Fegan received a message by blinker light from the SS *Briarwood*, the northernmost vessel in the convoy, reporting that the mast of what appeared to be a warship was visible on the northern horizon. As the vessel got closer, Fegan challenged her, blinking out that day's recognition signal: M-A-G. The stranger replied with the same three letters, which was not the correct response, and Fegan then did three things nearly simultaneously: he fired a red rocket as a signal for the ships of the convoy to scatter; he radioed a sighting report to the Admiralty that the convoy was under attack by a surface raider (RRRR); and he ordered the *Jervis Bay* to full speed, pulling ahead of the convoy and turning sharply toward the approaching warship. Fegan knew his ship stood no chance in a stand-up fight with a pocket battleship; in effect, he was willing to sacrifice himself and his ship in order to buy time for the merchantmen to escape.[33]

Fegan opened fire before he was within range in order to attract the attention of the raider to himself. And it worked. On the *Admiral Scheer*, Krancke saw that the *Jervis Bay* was the only vessel in the convoy with guns big enough to damage his ship, and in the mid-Atlantic, two thousand miles from a friendly base, even moderate damage would be troublesome. He therefore focused all his attention on the large armed freighter. Shell after shell from the *Admiral Scheer* smashed into the unarmored *Jervis Bay*—eventually Krancke expended more than three hundred rounds on her. Soon fires were burning out of control as the *Jervis Bay* drifted powerless, trailing a long plume of black smoke. Her guns continued to fire, though the closest any of her 6-inch shells came to the *Scheer* merely splashed some seawater up onto her deck. Krancke was impressed by his foe's determination. "Whoever he was," Krancke wrote later of Fegan, "he had the authentic Nelson touch."[34]

Soon enough, flames enveloped the *Jervis Bay* from stem to stern and all of her guns were knocked out of action. By then Fegan had been mortally wounded, and the senior surviving officer, himself mortally wounded, ordered abandon ship. The *Scheer* pounded the *Jervis Bay* with several more salvos before shifting fire to the nearest merchant ship. The battle, such as it was, had lasted twenty-two minutes, which at least gave the fleeing merchantmen a head start. For that, Fegan became the latest to receive a posthumous Victoria Cross.[35]

Krancke turned his attention to the merchant ships, now fleeing in all directions. Nearly all of them made smoke to cover their escape, and combined with the smoke from the burning *Jervis Bay*, visibility was poor. One ship, however, attracted Krancke's attention. It was one of the larger freighters and it was shooting at him with both a 4-inch gun on its stern and a 3-inch gun on its bow. The shells did no serious damage, though a near miss dislodged a few hatch coverings. Krancke decided to finish her off first, though that proved more difficult than he initially assumed. The ship was the SS *Beaverford*, commanded by a Scottish-born Canadian named Hugh Pettigrew. Dodging in and out of the thick smoke, Pettigrew and the *Beaverford* proved frustratingly stubborn. Eventually the *Scheer* pumped nineteen 11-inch and 5.9-inch shells into her, and even then Krancke had to finish her off with a torpedo. When the torpedo hit, it lifted the *Beaverford* right up out of the water. As Krancke later described it, "There was a great sound of bursting and cracking. . . . The stern rose high out of the water and then the whole vessel slid under the surface." The last radio message from the *Beaverford*'s wireless operator was: "It's our turn now. So long." There were no survivors.[36]

Like the *Jervis Bay*, the *Beaverford*'s prolonged fight bought time for the other ships of the convoy to flee. After chasing down four more ships, Krancke

Korvettenkapitän Theodor Krancke commanded the pocket battleship *Admiral Scheer* during its Atlantic cruise in 1940. Raeder believed that Krancke's success in that raid validated the strategy of using Germany's big surface warships to attack British commerce.

Courtesy of Alamy

decided to call it a night. In six hours he had sunk 52,000 tons of British shipping, more than Langsdorff had sunk in six weeks, and the toll might have been greater but for the sacrifices of the *Jervis Bay* and the *Beaverford*.[37]

At Whitehall, the flash RRRR signal from Fegan provoked the Admiralty once again to send out several hunter-killer groups to track down and destroy the rampaging pocket battleship. Because Churchill did not yet know that Hitler had canceled Sea Lion, he had some fears that this might be a diversion to draw attention away from the Channel. Even so, he approved Forbes's decision to send the battlecruisers *Hood* and *Repulse* plus three cruisers and six destroyers to hunt down the *Admiral Scheer*. At the same time, the battleships *Rodney* and *Nelson* were dispatched to patrol the waters northwest of Ireland to prevent the *Scheer* from getting back to Germany. As Raeder had hoped, a single German surface raider was attracting disproportionate attention from the Royal Navy.[38]

AMONG THE SHIPS attacked by the big guns of the *Admiral Scheer* on that Guy Fawkes night was the 8,000-ton Eagle Oil tanker *San Demetrio*, whose long journey to this mid-ocean catastrophe had begun on the Dutch island of Curaçao, in the West Indies. There it had filled up with 11,200 tons of high-octane aviation fuel for the Hurricanes and Spitfires that were fending off the Luftwaffe in the Battle of Britain. Given her cargo, she was almost literally a floating bomb. Her captain was Captain George Waite, described by one crewmember as "a big, robust man in his early fifties, a little wider round the girth than the shoulder." Waite knew that if an enemy shell ignited the cargo he carried, it would blow the ship and everyone in it to kingdom come. He decided, therefore, that if she was hit, he would order abandon ship at once. At about five-thirty, a shell from the *Admiral Scheer* struck the *San Demetrio* just above the waterline. "The ship shuddered, squeaked, and groaned," eighteen-year-old Calum MacNeil recalled. "Crockery and cooking utensils in the galley and messrooms crashed and clattered everywhere. Lights failed throughout the ship." Within seconds, a second shell hit amidships, starting several fires. It was time to go. The crew scrambled to launch the lifeboats and soon were pulling away from the crippled ship, which was dead in the water and burning furiously. Waite initially decided to stay on board and die with his ship, though after the lifeboats were well away, he yielded to entreaties from some men in a different lifeboat, and he, too, abandoned the *San Demetrio*. Eventually he made it safely back to Newfoundland.[39]

From their lifeboats, the crew of the *San Demetrio* watched while the *Scheer* attacked other ships in the convoy and twilight gradually turned to full dark. Meanwhile, they had to deal with the sea. "Spray and clots of foam came over us ceaselessly," a crewman recalled, "until we were all drenched and feeling the cold seeping through to us." The weather worsened through the night, and the men rigged sea anchors to ease the bucking and rolling of their small lifeboats.[40]

With the coming of dawn, the men saw nothing but empty sea. That afternoon, however, they spotted a smudge of smoke on the horizon. As they drifted closer, rowing occasionally, they saw that it was a ship. It was riding low in the water and black smoke poured out of it. Then one of the crew muttered aloud, "Well, I'll be goddamned," as he recognized the *San Demetrio*. The sea all around her was filled with high-octane fuel, and a single spark could still ignite it, so they waited through another cold night before deciding to go on board and try to put the fires out.[41]

The ship was a mess. The deck plating "was buckled and crumpled like cardboard and riddled with shell holes." The engine room and other critical spaces were waist deep in seawater. Nevertheless, under the direction of Second Officer Arthur Hawkins and the chief engineer, Charles Pollard, the crew got to work restoring electrical power to get the pumps working, and eventually they pumped out enough water to get the engines restarted. Steering by starlight because the compasses were broken, too, they limped along eastward. Five days later, at dawn on Wednesday, November 13, the man on lookout shouted that there was land ahead. The routers in Trade Plot were astonished to learn that a ship that had been reported sunk eight days before had arrived off the Irish coast. Eventually the *San Demetrio*, with most of her cargo intact, made port in Rothesay Bay, in the Firth of Clyde, as called for in her initial manifest.[42]

Krancke, meanwhile, had turned south and steamed into the South Atlantic, the scene of the *Graf Spee*'s rampage the year before. As Langsdorff had done, he rounded the Cape of Good Hope into the Indian Ocean and attacked shipping there. More important, he did something Langsdorff had not managed to do: return successfully to his base in Germany. After five months at sea, cruising forty-six thousand miles and sinking seventeen ships, the *Admiral Scheer* entered Kiel on April 1, 1941. Raeder himself came on board full of congratulations, and Krancke served him steak and eggs taken from the British refrigerator ship *Duquesa*.[43]

Raeder believed that the cruise of the *Admiral Scheer* validated his commerce-raiding strategy. Krancke's success, he wrote, created "advantageous preconditions for a new raid by other fleet units." To seize that opportunity, he dispatched the heavy cruiser *Hipper* on two raids, one in December 1940 and another in February 1941, though neither was particularly fruitful. He also sent out the battlecruiser twins *Scharnhorst* and *Gneisenau*, still under the command of Admiral Lütjens, for another raid on the Atlantic convoys. Over the ensuing three months (January–March 1941), those two battlecruisers sank twenty-one ships, sixteen of them in just two days on March 15–16, before safely making port in Brest on March 22. Again, Raeder was pleased, declaring that the entire cruise had been "singularly successful," especially in causing the Royal Navy to disperse its assets. Almost certainly that perception contributed to the pressure the Germans put on Riccardi to send Iachino's surface force on the sortie that culminated in the Battle of Cape Matapan in the Mediterranean.[44]

IN ADDITION TO U-BOATS AND SURFACE RAIDERS, there was a third danger to British trade that fall from what were called auxiliary cruisers (*Hilfskreuzer* in German). These were former merchant ships that were modified for use as raiders by adding a suite of naval guns and increasing the size of their fuel tanks for extended cruising. In some ways, they were the German version of British armed merchant cruisers such as the *Jervis Bay*, except that the *Hilfskreuzers* paraded as something else entirely. Their naval guns were hidden behind false bulkheads or what appeared to be crates of deck cargo, and they went to sea disguised as innocent neutrals, dropping their disguise at the last minute to open fire on British and Allied shipping. Germany sent out a dozen such ships in the summer and fall of

1940, and between May and November they sank or captured more than eighty British and Allied ships displacing more than half a million tons. Ship for ship, they proved more destructive to Allied trade than the U-boats.[45]

The first of them went to sea in the early spring when Leutnant Bernhard Rogge, commanding the *Atlantis*, formerly the cargo ship *Goldenfels*, followed the route used by the *Admiral Scheer* and other surface raiders through the Denmark Strait, then headed south for the Cape of Good Hope. Steaming at ten knots to save fuel, the *Atlantis* underwent several chameleon-like transformations during the journey. Her masts and even her stacks could be raised or lowered, and the crew used wood framing, canvas sheeting, and paint to reconfigure her silhouette and appearance. During her passage through the North Sea, she was the Norwegian freighter *Knute Nelson*; as she traversed the route above Scotland toward Greenland, she became the Russian naval auxiliary *Kim*; and by late April, now in the South Atlantic, she was the Japanese *Kasii Maru*. A few weeks after that, in the Indian Ocean, she adopted the configuration and color scheme of the Dutch freighter *Abbekerk*.[46]

Atlantis made her first capture on May 3, only days before the German ground offensive in France began. Steaming innocently up to the 6,200-ton freighter *Scientist*, Rogge dropped the false bulkheads, showed his guns, and ordered the freighter not to use its wireless. Despite that, the captain of the *Scientist*, G. R. Windsor, immediately broadcast the alarm using the code QQQ , to indicate that he was under attack by an armed merchant raider.* The *Atlantis* opened fire, and the crew of the *Scientist* abandoned ship. After securing the prisoners, Rogge sank the freighter with a torpedo.[47]

Atlantis laid ninety-two mines in the waters off Cape Town, then over the next six months she sank ten ships displacing 72,640 tons and capturing three others displacing another 21,300 tons. One of her victims was the Egyptian passenger steamer *Zam Zam*, which had 140 Americans on board.

---

* The QQQ signal code derived from the use during World War I of what were called Q-ships, merchant vessels armed with hidden deck guns. In 1914–15, the British had employed such vessels to decoy U-boats to the surface, where the Q-ships would then sink them.

Though no Americans lost their lives, the incident provoked anger and protest in the United States. The most consequential success of the *Atlantis*, however, was the capture of the British steamer *Automedon* in the Indian Ocean on November 11, 1940. The captain of the *Automedon* sent out an RRRR radio warning, and the *Atlantis* opened fire. The first salvo killed everyone on the bridge, ripping it apart, as a member of the German boarding party recalled, "like a tin can pried open with a bayonet." Consequently, when the boarding party arrived, no one on the *Automedon* had destroyed her large cache of secret documents, which included detailed information about British defenses in the Pacific. A month later, when the *Atlantis* put in at Kobe, Japan, Rogge handed the information over to the Japanese, still officially neutral but already looking hungrily at British and Dutch colonies in the South Pacific.[48]

The *Atlantis* was not the only German auxiliary raider to operate in the Pacific. Two of them (*Orion* and *Komet*), aided by an icebreaker, successfully completed an improbable journey from the North Cape of Norway through the Arctic Ocean along the north coast of the Soviet Union and then southward through the Bering Strait into the Pacific. There they attacked British, Dutch, and Australian shipping before returning to Germany by rounding Cape Horn, thus completing a circumnavigation of the globe. Another merchant cruiser, the *Kormoran*, fought a desperate battle off the west coast of Australia with the Australian light cruiser HMAS *Sydney*. After a furious gun battle, the *Sydney* sank the *Kormoran*, though the Australian cruiser was also badly wounded. With both of her forward gun turrets knocked out and the two aft turrets jammed, she limped away from the scene of her costly victory on fire and listing, and was never seen or heard from again. Her sunken wreckage was discovered off Shark Bay on the west coast of Australia in 2008.[49]

This combination of U-boats, surface raiders, and auxiliary cruisers severely strained, but did not quite break, Britain's maritime lifeline in the summer and fall of 1940. Moreover, the cruel North Atlantic weather, so often cursed by the men on the merchant ships and escorts alike, proved an invaluable ally that winter, since it weakened the efficiency of the commerce raiders. January 1941 was the least productive month of the entire war for the U-boats until mid-1944.

Far worse, from Dönitz's viewpoint, three of his best U-boat command-ers, Günther Prien, Otto Kretschmer, and Joachim Schepke, were all killed or captured in early March. Prien was lost on March 7 while attacking out-bound convoy OB-293 west of Ireland. Two British destroyers, *Wolverine* and *Verity*, working as a team, used Asdic and depth charges to pursue Prien's U-47 relentlessly as it twisted and turned underwater. After repeated attacks, the commander of the *Wolverine*, James Rowland, saw a "faint orange light" just under the surface, which might have been the U-47 break-ing apart, though he could not verify it. Almost certainly he was right, how-ever, for Prien was never heard from again.[50]

Ten days later, Kretschmer's U-99 and Schepke's U-100, along with the U-70, attacked eastbound convoy HX-112, which had a particularly strong escort of five destroyers and two corvettes (*Bluebell* and *Hydrangea*). Kretschmer sank five ships before his engines were damaged by depth charges and he was forced to surface. Unable to maneuver, he was a sitting duck, and he reluctantly ordered abandon ship. He and most of his crew were taken prisoner. Schepke's fate was more dramatic. Once again, British destroyers worked in tandem to force his U-100 to the surface, where it was spotted by HMS *Vanoc*, one of the first Royal Navy destroyers to be equipped with surface-search radar. That enabled the *Vanoc* to find and ram the U-100. Schepke had only enough time to call out "Abandon ship!" before the bow of the *Vanoc* sliced through his conning tower, killing him instantly. Afterward, the convoy escorts pursued and sank the U-70 as well. Dönitz was shocked by the loss of three of his most experienced and suc-cessful U-boat commanders, all recipients of the Knight's Cross, and four U-boats. Prien's loss was especially dispiriting, and news of his death was kept secret from the German public for more than two months out of con-cern for its impact on national morale.[51]

These losses were sobering. Raeder, however, had an ace up his sleeve—actually two aces. He had a plan to send out both of Germany's brand-new battleships, *Bismarck* and *Tirpitz*, with orders to rendezvous with the *Scharnhorst* and *Gneisenau* at Brest. That would create a battle force power-ful enough to make the Atlantic all but untenable for British shipping.

CHAPTER 7

THE *BISMARCK*

Back in the summer of 1936, when the keels of the battleships *Bismarck* and *Tirpitz* were laid down, Raeder had envisioned a time when they would be merely the first of an entire fleet of super-battleships. Plan Z, which Hitler had approved in 1939 just before the outbreak of war, called for a total of ten such ships. Instead, the unforgiving timetable of war dictated that for at least the near term they would remain the only two such vessels in the Kriegsmarine. Still, Raeder hoped that if they proved their value by making a significant contribution to victory, he might yet fulfill his dream of building a world-class surface navy. The immediate goal, however, was to get these two ships finished, fitted out, and commissioned.[1]

They were built a hundred miles apart: *Bismarck* at the Blohm and Voss naval shipyard across the Elbe River from Hamburg, and *Tirpitz* at the old imperial shipyard near Wilhelmshaven where the *Scharnhorst* and all three of the *Panzerschiffe* had been built. From the start, the British Admiralty kept careful track of their progress, aware of the impact two such ships could have on the naval balance of power. Both were launched early in

1939—*Bismarck* in February, *Tirpitz* in April—though it took another two years to complete them, and they were not ready for service until 1941.[2]

They were enormous. Displacing more than 50,000 tons each when fully armed and fueled, they were the largest warships afloat. The British battle-cruiser *Hood*, commissioned twenty years earlier in 1920 and the pride of the Royal Navy, was seventy-one feet longer, but the *Hood* had significantly less armor and therefore displaced less tonnage. Like the *Hood*, each of the German battleships was armed with eight 15-inch rifles in a quartet of two-gun turrets, two forward and two aft. Each of the gun barrels was fifty-seven feet long and weighed 122 tons, and they fired shells weighing 1,764 pounds up to twenty miles. Moreover, improved fire-control technology made the guns on the German battleships more accurate and more reliable than those on the *Hood*. Both German ships also carried a wide array of second-ary guns: twelve 6-inch, sixteen 4-inch, and sixteen more 1.5-inch guns. They had been designed with a warren of internal watertight compartments and a belt of armor that was nearly 13 inches thick, characteristics that Raeder believed made them (his word) "unsinkable."[3]

The war was more than a year old when the *Bismarck* left the building yard near Hamburg and passed through the Kiel Canal to conduct her sea trials in the Baltic under the watchful eye of her captain, Ernst Lindemann, who reported her ready for active service in mid-January 1941. Completion of the *Tirpitz* took longer, and she was not commissioned until March. Even then, problems encountered during her sea trials made it evident that the *Tirpitz* would not be ready for active service for several more months. Raeder was loath to wait for her. He had hoped to send both battleships into the North Atlantic in a supersized version of the raid recently con-ducted by the *Scharnhorst* and *Gneisenau*, and he appointed the man who had led that raid, Admiral Günther Lütjens, to command the two-battle-ship task group. In Raeder's conception, Lütjens would first conduct a raid against the Atlantic convoys, then head for Brest to rendezvous with the *Scharnhorst* and *Gneisenau*. Once united, the four ships would constitute a surface force so powerful it could command the Atlantic sea-lanes.[4]

That enticing vision began to evaporate almost immediately. In addition to the problems with the *Tirpitz*, British air strikes in April badly damaged the *Gneisenau* as she lay in Brest Harbor, and her skipper reported that she would not be ready for service until October. The *Scharnhorst* had problems of a different kind: her boiler tubes were so corroded that her power plant had to be disassembled, and so she, too, would be unavailable for several months. Thus of the four capital ships Raeder planned to use to demonstrate the capability of his new surface navy, only the *Bismarck* would be ready that spring. It was, he confided to his diary, "a crippling blow."[5]

Raeder might have postponed the sortie until one or more of the other ships was made seaworthy, and Lütjens himself argued that Raeder should at least wait until the *Tirpitz* was fully operational. Instead, in what he later described as "one of the most difficult decisions I personally had to make during the war," Raeder decided to send out the *Bismarck* without the *Tirpitz*. Several considerations led him to this fateful decision. The first was his eagerness to demonstrate the utility of large surface combatants in the war on trade. Hitler remained skeptical of the whole idea of using surface warships to attack convoys, and he said as much when Raeder briefed him on the plan in April, though he left the final decision in Raeder's hands. By then, Hitler was preoccupied with the pending invasion of the Soviet Union—Operation Barbarossa—and that, too, fed Raeder's sense of urgency. New triumphs by the Wehrmacht might further eclipse the accomplishments of the Kriegsmarine. If Raeder's big ships did not demonstrate their utility soon, Hitler's already tepid support for the navy might evaporate altogether. "If they [the battleships] are not sent into action," Raeder told Admiral Wilhelm Marschall, "we will not get any more."[6]

In addition, Raeder was haunted by the memory of the final disposition of the ships of the Imperial High Seas Fleet in 1919. They had sat uselessly at anchor throughout the last two years of the First World War while the morale of their crews eroded; when the fleet was eventually ordered to sea, the sailors refused to go. He feared that might be the fate of the *Bismarck* as well if she remained idle throughout the summer, a summer during which the strategic circumstances in the Atlantic would almost certainly change. Raeder considered it at least possible, even likely, that the United States would soon become an active belligerent, and if that happened, the combined Anglo-American fleet might keep Germany's big battleships locked

The 50,000-ton *Bismarck* was the pride of Raeder's revived German navy. She is seen here in a photograph taken from her consort, the heavy cruiser *Prinz Eugen*, on May 19, 1941, while en route to Norway to begin her commerce-raiding cruise.

Naval History and Heritage Command

up in the Baltic indefinitely. Better to sortie now with only one of them than risk having both of them rendered impotent by changing circumstances.[7]

In place of the unavailable *Tirpitz*, Raeder added the new heavy cruiser *Prinz Eugen* to Lütjens's command. If the *Prinz Eugen* was no battleship, she was, at 18,000 tons, half again as large as the *Panzerschiffe*, and would constitute a suitable consort for the *Bismarck*. And it was always possible, Raeder thought, that by the time Lütjens completed his cruise against British shipping, the battlecruisers at Brest might be ready to join him. A battle group composed of the *Bismarck*, *Scharnhorst*, *Gneisenau*, and *Prinz Eugen* would constitute a force powerful enough to contend with anything in the Royal Navy except the Home Fleet itself. As a first step toward the realization of this ambition, the *Bismarck*, *Prinz Eugen*, and three destroyers got under way from Danzig on May 19, 1941, and steamed west through the Kattegat, the narrow passage between Denmark and Sweden, toward the North Sea.[8]

BY THEN, THE BRITISH HOME FLEET had a new commander. As part of his ceaseless effort to endow the Royal Navy with aggressive and uncompromising leadership, Churchill replaced the solid but colorless Charles

Forbes with Admiral Sir John Tovey. At fifty-five, the lean and rugged-looking Tovey was five years younger than Forbes and had clearly established himself as a fighting sailor. Indeed, Tovey was something of a wunderkind in the Royal Navy. He had conducted a daring torpedo attack against the German fleet during the Battle of Jutland in the First World War, which had won him a Distinguished Service Cross (DSC) and promotion to the rank of commander at the age of only thirty-one. Tovey was a Churchill man in other ways, too. He was an unapologetic champion of Britain's imperial interests, and had a gourmand's love of good food and good wine. In May 1941, it became Tovey's job to find, track, and ultimately destroy the *Bismarck*.[9]

The first intelligence Tovey got about the *Bismarck*'s sortie came in a roundabout way. Swedish observers who witnessed the *Bismarck*'s passage through the Kattegat on May 20 passed the news on to the Norwegians, who shared it with the British. The next day, an RAF pilot in a specially equipped long-range Spitfire reported the presence of "two cruisers" in Grimstadfjord, near

Admiral Sir John "Jack" Tovey, here being piped ashore from his flagship, *King George V*, replaced Charles Forbes as commander of the Home Fleet in November 1940. In May 1941 he orchestrated the pursuit of the *Bismarck*.

Imperial War Museum

Bergen. When the pilot returned to base and the photos were developed, it was clear that the "cruisers" were, in fact, the *Bismarck* and *Prinz Eugen*. The RAF immediately prepared a bombing mission, though before it could be launched, a weather front clouded the skies over Norway and reduced visibility to near zero. In consequence, the bombers failed to find the German warships.[10]

Tovey thought it likely that Lütjens would take advantage of the foul weather to make a dash for the Atlantic, though he was less certain which route he might take to get there. The shortest and quickest was due west past the Shetland Islands, then south along the west coast of Ireland. That would take Lütjens directly into the Western Approaches, but it was perilously close to Tovey's main base at Scapa Flow, and a more likely alternative was that Lütjens would pass north of the Faroe Islands and turn south through what was called the Faroe-Iceland Gap. Or he might take the long route through the Denmark Strait that he had used before. That was the most indirect route, but it was also the farthest from the British Isles and the most difficult to watch. With the RAF now grounded by weather, Tovey sent a small surface force to each of these routes to act as lookouts. They were not to engage the big battleship or its consort, Tovey told their commanders, only to find them, report their location, and then shadow them until Tovey's big ships could get there. To watch the most likely passage through the Denmark Strait, Tovey relied upon the heavy cruisers *Norfolk* and *Suffolk* under the command of Rear Admiral Frederic Wake-Walker, who had played such a critical role in the evacuation of Dunkirk exactly one year before.*

A principal consideration in Tovey's thinking was that all of Britain's big ships had been designed primarily for service in the North Sea and were therefore "short legged," that is, they had a fuel capacity that restricted them to a maximum range of about four thousand miles, exactly half that of the

---

* To help find the *Bismarck*, Churchill also turned to the Americans. On May 23, he wrote Roosevelt to ask if U.S. Navy warships would keep an eye out for the *Bismarck* or for any German supply vessels that might have been sent out to replenish her. "Give us the news," he wrote FDR, "and we will finish the job." Privately, Churchill hoped the Americans would find the *Bismarck* first, exchange gunfire, and thus be drawn into the war. Roosevelt authorized reconnaissance by several long-range PBY aircraft and directed his naval commanders to pass on any intelligence they discovered, but he stopped short of ordering them to conduct an active search.

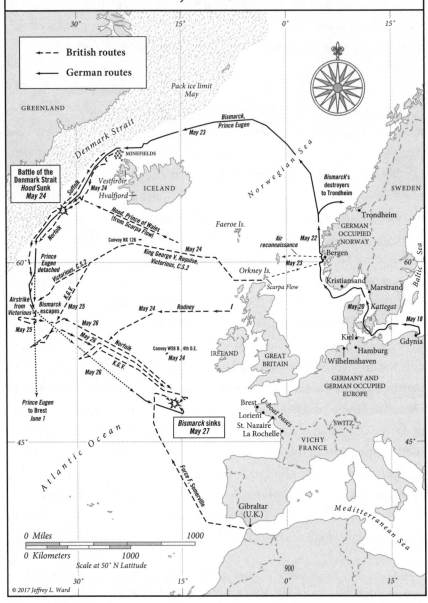

THE PURSUIT OF THE *BISMARCK*
May 18–27, 1941

- - - ▶ British routes

——▶ German routes

Pack ice limit May

GREENLAND

Denmark Strait

MINEFIELDS

Battle of the Denmark Strait *Hood* **Sunk May 24**

Suffolk

Vestfirðir May 24 *Hvalfjord* ICELAND

Bismarck, Prince Eugen May 23

Norwegian Sea

Bismarck's destroyers to Trondheim

SWEDEN

Trondheim

GERMAN OCCUPIED NORWAY

Hood, Prince of Wales (from Scarpa Flow)

Faeroe Is.

Air reconnaissance May 22

Convoy NX 126

May 24

King George V, Repulse, Victorious, C.S.2

Norfolk

Prince Eugen detached

Victorious, C.S.2

K.G.V.

May 23

Orkney Is.

Bergen

Kristiansand

Marstrand

Scarpa Flow

May 20 *Kattegat*

May 18

Baltic Sea

Airstrike from *Victorious* **Bismarck escapes** May 25

May 25

May 24 Rodney

Kiel

Gdynia

May 26

May 26 Norfolk

Convoy W58 B , 4th D.E. May 24

Hamburg

Wilhelmshaven

K.G.V. May 26

IRELAND

GREAT BRITAIN

GERMANY AND GERMAN OCCUPIED EUROPE

Prince Eugen to Brest June 1

Brest

Lorient

St. Nazaire

La Rochelle

U-boat bases

SWITZ.

Bismarck sinks May 27

VICHY FRANCE

Atlantic Ocean

Force F, Somerville

Gibraltar (U.K.)

Mediterranean Sea

0 Miles 1000

0 Kilometers 1000

Scale at 50° N Latitude

900

© 2017 Jeffrey L. Ward

Bismarck. Consequently, putting to sea at once with his big ships to conduct a lengthy search for the *Bismarck* could well mean running out of fuel before he found her—or, worse, in the middle of a fight. On the other hand, the Denmark Strait was more than seven hundred miles from Scapa Flow, and even at twenty-eight knots it would take him more than twenty-four hours to get there. Tovey decided to hedge his bets. Well before the Spitfire pilot reported the two "cruisers" in Grimstadfjord, he ordered two of his big ships to leave Scapa Flow and head west. The ships he sent were the battlecruiser *Hood* and the battleship *Prince of Wales*, which was so new that workmen sailed with her, their welding torches alight, as she steamed off to war. Tovey himself would sortie with the rest of the fleet as soon as it was certain that Lütjens had sailed.[11]

On the morning of May 22, another RAF reconnaissance flight over Grimstadfjord confirmed that Lütjens had indeed flown the coop, and Tovey left Scapa Flow at ten o'clock the next morning, heading west with his flagship, the battleship *King George V*, the battlecruiser *Repulse*, and the aircraft carrier *Victorious* plus seven destroyers. By then, the *Hood* and *Prince of Wales* were more than five hundred miles ahead of him and closing on the Denmark Strait.[12]

Tovey had put those two ships under the command of Vice Admiral Lancelot Holland, who was especially eager to bring the *Bismarck* to battle. Holland did not have the kind of warrior's resumé that Tovey did, and he had achieved promotion largely on the basis of excellent performances in staff and diplomatic positions. Here was an opportunity to augment that resumé. His eagerness was also fueled by the fact that just the year before, he had drawn critical scrutiny from Churchill while commanding a cruiser group under Somerville during the Battle of Cape Spartivento in the Mediterranean. On that occasion, Churchill had been disappointed by Somerville's decision not to pursue Campioni's fleeing battleships, and some of his displeasure had spilled over onto Somerville's subordinates as well, including Holland. Like Somerville, Holland had survived the subsequent inquiry, but the experience left him in no doubt that aggressive, even audacious action was the key to fulfilling Churchill's expectations.[13]

THE DENMARK STRAIT between Greenland and Iceland is more than two hundred miles wide, but in May the western two-thirds of it was clogged with an impassable ice shelf, and a British minefield stretched across its eastern side, so the navigable passage was less than fifty miles wide. If Lütjens elected this route, as he had before, he would have to pass through this relatively narrow funnel, which was why Tovey had positioned the *Norfolk* and *Suffolk* there under Wake-Walker to act as lookouts. Each of those British cruisers had been recently equipped with a radar set. The one on the *Suffolk* was more reliable, but it only scanned forward, and the *Suffolk* had just turned southward on her patrol when at 7:22 on the evening of May 23 a topside lookout spotted a large gray shape emerging out of the mist and fog astern. Wake-Walker immediately forwarded the sighting report, and by 8:00 p.m. the two British cruisers were shadowing the German warships, one on each flank, staying close enough to track them through the fog banks and intermittent snow showers while remaining just beyond range of the *Bismarck*'s 15-inch guns.[14]

Three hundred miles away on the battlecruiser *Hood*, which Holland was using as his flagship, officers leaned eagerly over the chart table and plotted the *Bismarck*'s position, which was almost due north of them. Holland might have continued westward to cut her off from the North Atlantic, but, aware of Churchill's penchant for aggressiveness, he chose instead to increase speed to twenty-eight knots and turn northwest to close on her as swiftly as possible, directing Captain John Leach in the *Prince of Wales* to follow his movements. Throughout the short Arctic night, the opposing battle groups steamed toward each other at a combined speed of nearly fifty knots.[15]

Sunrise came early in the Denmark Strait in late May, and the sun was already well up at 5:35 a.m. on May 24 when the opposing forces sighted each other almost simultaneously at about thirty-two thousand yards (just over eighteen miles). On board the *Prince of Wales*, the ship's chaplain, W. G. Parker, read a prayer over the ship's loudspeaker. It was the prayer that had been offered by Parliamentary forces at the Battle of Edgehill in 1642: "Oh Lord, Thou knowest how busy we must be today. If we forget Thee, do not Thou forget us."[16]

Unlike Henry Harwood, who had separated his ships to attack the *Graf Spee* from different angles back in 1939, Holland kept his two ships together, perhaps to create a concentration of fire. The *Hood* fired first, aiming her initial salvos at the lead enemy ship, which Holland thought must be the *Bismarck* but which was actually the *Prinz Eugen*. The *Prinz Eugen* fired back, and improbably landed an 8-inch shell on the *Hood's* signal rocket storage locker. It triggered a spectacular pyrotechnic display but caused no serious damage. On the *Bismarck*, Lütjens ordered Captain Lindemann to hold his fire until all eight of the ship's 15-inch guns could be brought to bear, and despite the impatient pleading of the senior gunnery officer, it was several minutes before the *Bismarck* responded. When it did, the weakness of the *Hood's* relatively thin armor was demonstrated in a spectacular way. At 5:55, a shell from the *Bismarck's* sixth salvo struck the *Hood*, penetrated to her magazine, and exploded.[17]

As if a giant hammer had smashed down on her amidships, the *Hood* broke in half, her bow jackknifing upward to a forty-five-degree angle while flames and smoke soared into the sky. Watching from the *Bismarck*, Lindemann's adjutant, Burkard Müllenheim-Rechberg, recalled seeing "a mountain of flame and a yellowish-white fireball bursting up between her masts and soaring into the sky. White stars, probably molten pieces of metal, shot out from the black smoke and followed the flame, and huge fragments, one of which looked like the main turret, whirled through the air like toys." Within seconds, she was gone. The biggest ship in the Royal Navy and the pride of the fleet for more than two decades simply disappeared. Of the more than fifteen hundred men in her crew, only three survived.[18]

With hardly a pause to contemplate this astonishing spectacle, Lindemann turned the *Bismarck's* guns on the *Prince of Wales*, and almost at once, a 15-inch shell struck the new British battleship on her bridge, killing everyone there except the captain, the chief yeoman, and the leading signalman. There was so much carnage on the bridge that blood ran down through the voice tube and dripped onto the plotting table. In quick succession, three more shells hit the *Prince of Wales*, knocking out her fire-control system, smashing her scout plane, and penetrating her hull below the waterline, which allowed four hundred tons of seawater to flow into her hull. At the same time, smaller shells—8-inch shells from the *Prinz Eugen* and 6-inch shells from the *Bismarck's* secondary battery—struck her repeatedly. Almost as bad, the giant four-gun turret on the stern became inoperable. With his main battery compromised and absorbing terrible punishment, Leach ordered the engine room to make smoke, and turned away.[19]

Lindemann was eager to pursue and finish her off, but Lütjens stopped him. Lütjens was a brooding and lugubrious figure for whom orders were sacred; Raeder had instructed him to avoid action with enemy surface units and focus on the war against shipping, and that was exactly what he intended to do. Lindemann could hardly believe it. Here was a chance to sink a second British capital ship, the newest and, next to the *Hood*, the largest in her fleet. Her destruction would put the stamp of immortality on an already glorious day. Lütjens, iron-faced as always, said no. Inevitably, Lütjens won the argument, and the *Bismarck* and *Prinz Eugen* continued southward while Lindemann quietly simmered.[20]

CHURCHILL WAS AT CHEQUERS, his country house north of London, and still asleep at 7:00 a.m. on May 24 when he was awakened with the startling news of the *Hood's* destruction. It was another bitter blow, and not the last of many that befell him during the war. Only later did he learn that after the *Hood* blew up, Leach had broken off the action and steered the *Prince of Wales* away. That, Churchill wrote later, was "a sharp disappointment." Once again, it seemed to him that his naval commanders had betrayed a disturbing reluctance to carry the fight through to the end. Pound, too, was disappointed, not only with Leach but also with Wake-Walker, who assumed the role of senior officer present after Holland was killed. Rather than renew the action with his two cruisers and the crippled *Prince of Wales*, Wake-Walker merely continued to shadow the German ships. He knew that Tovey was approaching from the east with the *King George V* plus a battle-cruiser and a carrier, and to him it seemed prudent to wait for them.[21]

Lütjens, too, had some decisions to make. A 14-inch shell from the *Prince of Wales* had opened a five-foot hole in the *Bismarck's* forward hull, and despite her watertight compartments, hundreds of tons of seawater had flowed in. As a result, she was markedly down by the bow and listing nine

Admiral Günther Lütjens at the time of his command of the *Bismarck* battle group. A reserved, even cold demeanor earned him the nickname "Iron-Face." Despite that, or perhaps because of it, both Raeder and Dönitz held him in high esteem.

Bundesarchiv

degrees to port. Equally perilous was that another shell had ruptured two of her fuel tanks. Not only did that leave a telltale streak of oil streaming out behind her, but the loss of fuel severely limited her cruising range, a potentially disastrous blow for a raider.

As always, Lütjens kept his own counsel; whatever thoughts went through his mind as he considered his circumstances, he did not share them with Lindemann or anyone else. If he continued south for a planned rendezvous with a pre-positioned German supply ship in the mid-Atlantic, it might help solve his fuel problem, but it would draw the shadowing British cruisers after him, and that made a successful rendezvous unlikely. The battle damage the *Bismarck* had suffered reduced her potential as a commerce raider, and as long as the *Prinz Eugen* sailed in company it would restrict her as well. Lütjens decided to divide his forces. He sent the undamaged *Prinz Eugen* south to the rendezvous and turned the *Bismarck* southeast toward the French coast to draw off British pursuit. After effecting repairs in Brest or St. Nazaire, the *Bismarck* might be ready to rejoin the *Prinz Eugen* on her cruise. Lütjens sent a lengthy signal to Raeder reporting the destruction of the *Hood* and his plan to make for a port in the Bay of Biscay. When Raeder shared that report with Hitler, the Führer wondered, as Churchill had done, why his naval commander had not continued the fight in the Denmark Strait and finished off the enemy battleship. Raeder explained—again—that the purpose of the mission was to raid British commerce, a reply that left Hitler unimpressed.[22]

The two German warships parted company in the middle of a rain squall at about 6:15 p.m., and from that point on the *Bismarck* sailed alone, occasionally exchanging long-range fire with the two British cruisers and the *Prince of Wales*, all three of which followed the German battleship rather than the *Prinz Eugen*. Meanwhile, Tovey was closing in from the east. *Bismarck* was now making only about twenty-one knots, principally to conserve fuel. To slow her down further, Tovey detached the aircraft carrier *Victorious* with an escort of four light cruisers to make a high-speed run toward the *Bismarck* and launch an aerial torpedo attack while his capital ships continued to the southwest to intercept her.

The *Victorious* was even newer than the *Prince of Wales*, having been commissioned only days before, on May 14. She had just nine operational aircraft, all of them Swordfish biplanes. Moreover, the pilots on the *Victorious* were untested rookies, most of them having made only one or two practice carrier landings prior to deployment, none of them at night. The sortie against the *Bismarck* would be their first combat mission, their first night mission, the first undertaken in severe weather, and the first while carrying the heavy Mark XII torpedo. Nevertheless, at 10:15 p.m. Captain Henry C. Bovell turned his ship into the wind and, perhaps holding his breath, launched all nine Swordfish into the air.[23]

Led by Lieutenant Commander Eugene Esmonde, the Stringbags and their rookie pilots flew westward into a stiff headwind amidst the gathering dusk, and in full darkness they found the *Bismarck* at about eleven-thirty. Esmonde broke his squadron into groups of three to conduct a formal attack. The *Bismarck* fired every gun it had, and green tracers lit up the night sky. Even the big 15-inch guns fired into the sea ahead of the Swordfish to create giant shell splashes in front of them as they made their slow and deliberate torpedo runs. A gunnery officer on the *Bismarck* recalled that the aircraft "were moving so slowly that they seemed to be standing still." The novice pilots nevertheless persevered and successfully launched their torpedoes. In the dark, and with the *Bismarck* maneuvering radically, only one of them found its mark, and it struck the battleship on her thick armor belt. The

Bismarck "gave a slight shudder" and one sailor was killed by the concussion, but there was no structural damage. Lütjens later boasted that all it did was scratch some paint. To Berlin he reported, "Torpedo hit immaterial."[24]

The attack concerned him nonetheless. It meant that in addition to the three ships following him, there was another Royal Navy task force within a hundred miles of him, and he was still more than twelve hundred miles from Brest or St. Nazaire. At twenty-one knots, it would take him forty-eight hours to get close enough to gain the protection of land-based Luftwaffe planes. In addition, the *Bismarck*'s wild maneuvering during the air attack had jarred loose the patches that the damage control parties had placed over the shell holes in her hull. Lindemann had to reduce speed temporarily to sixteen knots while the patches were repaired. Lütjens also received a message from B-Dienst, the German naval code-breaking service, informing him that the Royal Navy had deployed a veritable fleet to look for him, including not only the ships under Wake-Walker and Tovey but also Somerville's Force H from Gibraltar, which had been escorting a troop convoy but which the Admiralty now ordered to rush north to join in the hunt for the *Bismarck*. Altogether, the British committed four battleships, two battlecruisers, two carriers, thirteen cruisers, and twenty-one destroyers to the hunt.[25]

May 25 was Lütjens's fifty-second birthday, and just three hours into it he got something of a birthday present. Ever since the *Bismarck* had separated from the *Prinz Eugen*, the British cruisers following him had maintained a zigzag course to prevent being targeted by U-boats. This was a sensible precaution since Dönitz had sent out seven U-boats to assist the *Bismarck*, and part of Lütjens's plan was to lead his pursuers into a U-boat trap.* The cruisers therefore zigged away from the *Bismarck* out to the limit of the *Suffolk*'s Type 284 radar system, and then zagged back again. At 3:00 a.m., Lütjens waited until the *Suffolk* was at the outermost point of her zig, then abruptly turned away and increased to full speed. The blip representing

---

* Several of the U-boats Dönitz diverted to the area were returning from operational patrols and had expended all of their torpedoes. The captain of the U-556 spotted both the *Ark Royal* and the *King George V* on May 26, and wrote in his war diary: "I was just perfectly placed for an attack.... If only I had just a few torpedoes!"

the *Bismarck* disappeared from the *Suffolk's* radar screen, and the *Suffolk's* captain, Robert Ellis, guessing that she had turned west toward the shipping lanes, turned southwest to find her. In fact, the *Bismarck* executed a complete circle, heading first west, then north, and then around to the east again before settling back on a southeasterly course. She had slipped the leash. Large as she was, the *Bismarck* had simply disappeared.[26]

To boost morale aboard ship, Lütjens made a formal announcement at noon. He congratulated the men on the destruction of the *Hood* and assured them that they were now headed for France and would soon be under the cover of the Luftwaffe. He should have stopped there. Instead, in what he no doubt intended as a pep talk, he told them that the British would undoubtedly concentrate all their forces against them, and proclaimed his determination to "fight until our gun barrels glow red-hot and the last shell has left the barrels." He ended with a call for "victory or death!" Far from raising morale, his address convinced many in the crew that they were doomed.[27]

WHEN TOVEY GOT THE ALARMING REPORT that the *Bismarck* had disappeared, he had to guess where she might go. In making that calculation, he was guided not only by what was possible but also by what was most dangerous to British interests. An escape by the *Bismarck* into the Atlantic sealanes was by far the most perilous scenario, and because of that Tovey, like Wake-Walker, decided to search westward. At some point early on the morning of May 25, Tovey, heading southwest, actually crossed the wake of the *Bismarck* as she steamed to the southeast; they were, quite literally, ships passing in the night. Further south, Somerville's Force H was struggling northward through heavy seas and a fierce headwind. In this complex maritime matrix, the Royal Navy ship that was closest to the *Bismarck*, though no one knew it at the time, was the twenty-year-old battleship *Rodney*, commanded by Sir Frederick Dalrymple-Hamilton. The *Rodney's* big 16-inch guns could prove decisive if she could get close enough to use them; the problem was that the elderly *Rodney* had a top speed of only twenty-one knots, so even in her wounded state the *Bismarck* could easily run away from her. A final piece of the puzzle was the destroyer division of

Philip Vian, the officer who had seized the *Altmark* in Jøssing Fjord more than a year before. Because all of the British destroyers assigned to the hunt for the *Bismarck* had been forced to leave for lack of fuel, the Admiralty sent Vian's six destroyers to replace them, and on May 25 Vian was steaming toward the search area as fast as his destroyers could go in the heavy seas.[28]

Meanwhile, the object of all this activity continued alone and unseen on a direct course for St. Nazaire. Lütjens was all but in the clear, his location and course a complete mystery to his many pursuers. Ironically, however, Lütjens did not know that. The *Bismarck's* radar detector continued to indicate that impulses from the *Suffolk's* radar were still reaching the big German battleship. What neither Lütjens nor anyone else in the *Bismarck* knew was that those impulses did not have sufficient strength to get back to the *Suffolk*. Lütjens therefore assumed that he was still being shadowed, and consequently he did not bother to maintain radio silence. That was his undoing, for when his coded transmissions to Berlin were broadcast into the ether, British radio receivers afloat and ashore used high-frequency direction finders to track a bearing to the source of the broadcast.[29] With inputs from several different receivers, it was possible to triangulate his approximate location, and that allowed the Admiralty to notify Tovey that he was going in the wrong direction.*

Tovey ordered his staff to work out the data for themselves, and after some discussion, they concluded that the *Bismarck* was indeed making for the French coast. Tovey turned around just before 6:00 p.m., though by then the *Bismarck* had what might prove to be an insurmountable head start. Meanwhile, most of Tovey's accompanying ships, including the *Repulse* and the *Victorious*, had to break off the pursuit and head for Iceland to refuel. Tovey's destroyers had left earlier, so for a while Tovey and the *King George V* sailed on alone. The *Rodney* was on a parallel course, and

---

* In one of the earliest uses of decrypted Ultra intelligence, the code breakers at Bletchley Park informed the Admiralty at 6:12 p.m. that radio intercepts strongly suggested the *Bismarck* was headed for the French coast. By the time this news had been relayed to Tovey, however, he had already turned around.

eventually Tovey overtook her, effectively doubling his striking power. This was something of a mixed blessing, however. While Tovey was certainly happy to have the *Rodney*'s nine 16-inch guns, he had to reduce his own speed to keep company. The slower speed allowed Tovey to conserve his dwindling fuel supply, but with both the hunters and the hunted steaming at twenty-one knots, any chance of overtaking the *Bismarck* was now extremely unlikely. Absent a near-miraculous intervention, the *Bismarck* was almost certain to make good her escape.[30]

The intervention came from Somerville's Force H. Somerville, too, was operating without a destroyer escort. With only the battlecruiser *Renown*, the light cruiser *Sheffield*, and the carrier *Ark Royal*, he could not take on the *Bismarck* in a surface fight. He was determined, however, to slow her down and give Tovey a chance to catch her. He therefore ordered Captain Loben E. H. Maund, commanding the carrier *Ark Royal*, to carry out an aerial torpedo attack.

Conditions for an air strike, indeed for air operations of any kind, were all but prohibitive. Winds gusted to thirty-five miles per hour, and the *Ark Royal* plunged through ten-foot seas, her hull rising and falling up to fifty-six feet

HMS *Ark Royal* with a squadron of Stringbags overhead. The sea conditions in May 1941 were significantly more daunting than in this staged photograph, which was taken in 1939 before the war.

Naval History and Heritage Command

with each successive wave as wind-driven sea spray flew over her flight deck. The weather was so bad that Lütjens received a report that the Luftwaffe planes he had counted on for air cover had been grounded in France. Nevertheless, pilots from the *Ark Royal* not only took off that morning, they found and reported the location of the *Bismarck*. Two of the Swordfish remained above her, circling slowly and periodically reporting her location, while the others returned to the *Ark Royal* to be armed with torpedoes. Determined that the *Bismarck* would not slip away a second time, Somerville also sent the light cruiser *Sheffield* ahead to shadow her. By midafternoon, Maund had fifteen Swordfish refueled and armed with torpedoes, and at 3:00 p.m. he turned into the wind to launch them. The wind was so strong that as one Swordfish surged toward the bow, the wind lifted her almost straight up so that she seemed to levitate into the air. One by one, the other planes climbed skyward, formed up, and headed northward toward the target.[31]

The lead Swordfish was equipped with radar—a rarity at the time—and, given the poor visibility that day, it promised to be a godsend. Instead it very nearly led to a catastrophe. When his radar screen indicated a contact ahead, the radar operator, Sub-Lieutenant N. C. Cooper, assumed it must be the *Bismarck*. The radios on the Swordfish did not allow them to communicate directly with one another, so Cooper stood up in the open cockpit and waved his arms, pointing off to the right. When the planes descended through the cloud cover, several of the pilots saw at once that the ship was clearly not the *Bismarck*, and a few recognized her as the *Sheffield*.* Nevertheless, eleven of the pilots executed their torpedo run anyway. The *Sheffield* was saved by the volatile sea conditions, which caused most of the torpedoes to explode prematurely, and by quick action on the part of the *Sheffield*'s astonished captain, Charles Larcom, who managed to avoid the rest. Belatedly recognizing their error, the Swordfish pilots, much chastened, returned to the *Ark Royal* at around 5:20. There the planes were

---

* Coincidentally, the U.S. Coast Guard cutter *Modoc* was in the area searching for survivors of a sunken freighter, and at one point crewmen on board caught a brief glimpse of the big battleship. The *Modoc* did not, however, play a role in either finding or attacking the *Bismarck*.

refueled and rearmed—this time with contact triggers on the torpedoes—
and the pilots climbed back into their cockpits for another try.[32]

It was near seven o'clock when the Swordfish swooped down on the
Bismarck. Once again the German gunners opened up with everything they
had. Lindemann was on the bridge, and he maneuvered wildly, throwing
the rudders alternately hard to port and then hard to starboard and changing speeds as fast as the engine room could respond to his commands. The
pilots attacked in groups of three, coming in from different directions to
make it harder for the *Bismarck* to avoid all of their torpedoes. The attack
lasted half an hour, and afterward the flight commander radioed a gloomy
message back to the *Ark Royal*: "Estimate no hits." That report, however,
referred only to the lead aircraft, for in fact, the doughty Swordfish pilots
had made some hits—two of them. One torpedo struck the *Bismarck* amidships, where it was again defeated by the battleship's heavy armor belt. The
other hit near the stern, where the armor was thinner. And it was decisive.[33]

The torpedo that hit the *Bismarck* on her starboard quarter opened a
hole in her side and flooded an engine room. More critically, it jammed
both of the ship's huge rudders, which had just been positioned hard over
to starboard in response to Lindemann's most recent order. With the rudders stuck in that position, the *Bismarck* began to steam counterclockwise
in a giant circle. Lindemann tried to compensate by using the engines, but
they could not overcome the pressure of the big rudders. Unable to resist
using the radio again, Lütjens notified Berlin: "Ship no longer maneuverable." Though he was only four hundred miles from safety, he would get no
closer. Half an hour later, after desperate efforts to repair the rudders proved
unsuccessful, Lütjens sent another message—his last: "Ship unable to
maneuver. We will fight to the last shell. Long live the Führer."[34]

ON BOARD THE BRITISH WARSHIPS, the extent of the injury to the *Bismarck* was not completely understood for some time. Only after receiving
several reports of her erratic course did Tovey appreciate that she had been
struck a crippling blow. As that reality grew on him, his mood shifted from
deep dejection to near exultation. Rather than increase speed at once, however, and use up more precious fuel, he decided that as long as the *Bismarck*

was pinned in place, he could wait until dawn to attack. That would allow him to approach the Bismarck out of the west, hidden by the predawn darkness, while the German battleship was silhouetted against the rising sun. Meanwhile, other forces closed in as well. Vian's six destroyers arrived during the night and for several hours one or another of them periodically darted in to launch torpedoes at the crippled and slowly circling Bismarck—a wounded lion surrounded by gathering jackals.[35]

Dawn arrived at 7:22 on May 27, and an hour and twenty-one minutes later, a lookout on the King George V called out that most electrifying of reports: "Enemy in sight!" And there she was: wounded, perhaps, but still bristling with guns and flying her oversized battle flag. Four minutes later the Rodney opened the battle, and the King George V followed suit soon afterward. To the north, Wake-Walker on the Norfolk, who had been pursuing the Bismarck for most of four days, also opened fire. Bright orange stabs of flame issued from the muzzles of the guns on four ships. The thunderous concussions mixed with the higher-pitched smack of enemy shells landing nearby and flinging tons of seawater two or three hundred feet into the air. The gunners on the Bismarck had more difficulty adjusting their fire because Lindemann could not control the ship's movements, and the turrets turned constantly in an effort to track the targets.[36]

The Rodney drew first blood at 9:02, when a 16-inch shell struck the Bismarck's forward superstructure. Both forward turrets were knocked out, the guns of one sagging sadly toward the sea while those of the other aimed uselessly skyward. No orders came from the bridge after that, almost certainly because both Lütjens and Lindemann had been killed. The battle went on nonetheless. The Bismarck could use only her four rear guns now, and soon enough they were silenced, too. Some of her smaller guns continued to fire, and her battle flag still flew, and so the British battleships continued to hammer her. By 10:00 a.m., the Bismarck had been hit more than four hundred times. By then, men could be seen jumping over the side as the big ship listed heavily to port with fires burning out of control all along her lengthy hull.[37]

The British ceased firing at 10:21. The Bismarck still floated, but Tovey was anxious about his fuel supply and was eager to begin the trip back to England lest he be forced to accept the ignominy of being towed into port. As he

This depiction of the *Bismarck*'s final moments was painted by Montague Dawson in 1943. Though hopelessly battered and on fire, the *Bismarck* remains afloat. The Royal Navy cruiser *Dorsetshire* (in foreground) has just launched one of several torpedoes—the track of which can just be discerned—that finally sent her to the bottom.

U.S. Naval Institute

shaped a course northward, he ordered the heavy cruiser *Dorsetshire* to finish off the *Bismarck* with torpedoes, and after three of them exploded against her side, the unsinkable German battleship finally rolled languidly over to her port side and went down at 10:40. The *Dorsetshire* and one of Vian's destroyers picked up 110 members of her crew, but after that, the British ceased their rescue efforts, fearing the imminent arrival of U-boats. Five more survivors were subsequently rescued by the U-74. The rest, more than two thousand men, including both Lütjens and Lindemann, were lost.[38]

The House of Commons was in session on that historic May 27, though the members met in Church House, next to Westminster Abbey, rather than in the Houses of Parliament because German bombers had destroyed the Commons Chamber seventeen days before. Churchill had the floor and he had just finished explaining that a major battle with the *Bismarck* was taking place in the eastern Atlantic. After he took his seat, a messenger strode in and handed him a piece of paper. Churchill read it quickly, then reclaimed the floor. "I have just received news," he announced, "that the *Bismarck* is sunk." Members stood and cheered as a relieved Churchill stood quietly enjoying the moment.[39]

Hitler got the news at the Berghof, his home in the Bavarian Alps near Berchtesgaden. It was not a great surprise, for he had essentially written off the *Bismarck* the moment he received Lütjens's last report. Though at the time he had dictated an encouraging reply ("All of Germany is with you"), he was infuriated that Raeder's strategic planning had led to this disaster. He fell into one of his famous rages, vowing "he would never let another battleship or cruiser out into the Atlantic." Nor did he. With the arrival of the *Prinz Eugen* at Brest on June 1, the Kriegsmarine never sent another capital ship into the Atlantic sea-lanes. Raeder knew this was a turning point for him, too, and that his dream of a mighty German surface navy had died when the *Bismarck* slipped beneath the waves.[40]

EVEN AS THE *BISMARCK* WAS IN ITS DEATH THROES, Hitler continued to look eastward, where his generals were massing their forces along the Soviet border. For more than twenty years, Hitler had considered Bolshevik Russia as Germany's true enemy, both militarily and ideologically. It was there that the German people would find both raw materials and *Lebensraum*. Though Britain remained unbeaten and defiant in her island, Hitler considered her effectively neutralized, and so the long-awaited showdown with Germany's mortal enemy could now begin. To ensure victory, he assembled the greatest military force ever deployed. As the historian Andrew Roberts has noted, "The size of Operation Barbarossa dwarfs everything else in the history of warfare." By mid-June there were more than four million men and four thousand tanks in 183 divisions poised along the German-Soviet border. At 3:15 a.m. on June 22, they began to move forward.[41]

PART II

THE WAR WIDENS

Hitler was not the only one looking east. From their island empire halfway around the world, the Japanese fixed an uneasy and calculating eye across the broad Pacific to the United States. Economics and culture each played a role in defining Japanese policy toward the West generally and toward the United States in particular. The economic issue was a product of the cruel fate that had deprived Japan of most of the raw materials essential to sustain a modern industrial economy, including iron, copper, tin, zinc, rubber, and especially oil. These could be purchased from overseas, of course, including from the United States. The problem was that it created a dependency that was uncomfortable, and to many Japanese intolerable, especially after the Americans began to impose conditions on the continued sale of such items as a way of influencing Japanese foreign and military policy. By the 1930s, many Japanese had come to believe that they must choose between accepting whatever demands the Americans made as a condition for the privilege of purchasing the raw materials they needed and establishing their economic independence by finding those commodities elsewhere.

The cultural component of Japanese policy was more nuanced. Japan's historically swift transformation from a semi-feudal system into a modern industrial state at the end of the nineteenth century was a heady, even disorienting experience. As part of that transformation, the emperor Meiji (1867–1912) invited the British to mentor the development of a modern Japanese navy, and though Japan successfully retained its distinctive culture, her warships, weapons, uniforms, rank structure, watch-standing protocols, and most other aspects of the Imperial Japanese Navy mirrored those of the Royal Navy—even the bricks used to build the naval academy at Etajima were imported from England. Successive victories against China (1894–95) and tsarist Russia (1904–5), including the improbable and decisive victory over the Russian fleet in the Battle of Tsushima, established Japan as a world power, and her partnership with the Allies in the First World War confirmed it—so much so, in fact, that by 1930 Japan had become one of the three great naval powers in the world.

And yet the naval treaties signed at Washington in 1922 and in London in 1930 had consigned Japan to a decidedly subordinate position. This was especially difficult for the young and fiercely nationalistic junior officers, many of whom found the terms of the Washington agreement almost physically painful. These self-styled patriots were offended to the point of violent rebellion when the 1930 London Treaty confirmed Japan's inferior status. Almost at once, naval officers divided into two antithetical groups. Those who accepted the London agreement as a reasonable compromise and sought to cooperate with the English-speaking superpowers belonged to the "Treaty Faction"; those who found the treaty terms humiliating and dishonorable belonged to what was called the "Fleet Faction." Over the ensuing decade, the hostility between these blocs grew so heated as to constitute a fundamental crisis of identity.

CHAPTER 8

THE RISING SUN

EVEN BEFORE THE JAPANESE DELEGATION returned from the London conference in the summer of 1930, the opposing factions in the Imperial Japanese Navy had staked out their territory. Treaty Faction admirals dominated the Navy Ministry, the policy-making organ of the navy, while Fleet Faction admirals dominated the Naval General Staff, which oversaw operations. Though they wore the same uniform and pledged fealty to the same emperor, the distance between them was vast and all but unbridgeable.[1]

The head of the Naval General Staff and the principal spokesman for the Fleet Faction was Admiral Kanji Katō.* Sixty years old in 1930, Katō was a meticulous man whose close-cropped hair and trim mustache hinted at his serious demeanor. He had graduated at the top of his class from Etajima in

---

* In Japanese the family name precedes the given name. Thus Admiral Katō's name in Japanese would be rendered as Katō Kanji. Since this is likely to distract or confuse Western readers, all Japanese names herein are rendered in Western style, with the family name coming last.

1891 and served as commander of the Combined Fleet (1926–28) before becoming chief of the Naval General Staff as well as supreme military councilor. Though he had served a tour as naval attaché in London, he resented the way Britain had cast off its alliance with Japan after the First World War, and he was impressed by the resilience of Germany's naval leaders. In the 1920s, he secretly colluded with German naval architects to exchange information about submarine technology, though the Navy Ministry in Tokyo refused to validate the arrangement. Before the Japanese delegation left for London late in 1929, Katō had insisted that its goal should be to secure absolute parity with the British and Americans. Failing that, he said, the delegates must insist on a non-negotiable 70 percent ratio. The negotiators came close. The compromise formula embedded in the London Treaty actually granted Japan 69.75 percent of the U.S. total (367,050 tons to 526,200 tons). In protest, Katō made a grand gesture of submitting his resignation to the emperor. Such a maneuver—resigning, or threatening to resign—was a gambit frequently employed by senior officers of both the army and navy in Japan to bend government policy to their will.[2]

Not this time. Though Hirohito refused to accept Katō's resignation, the emperor agreed with the Navy Ministry and with Prime Minister Osachi Hamaguchi that Japan's fragile economy would benefit from reduced expenditures on the navy, and the treaty became law. The emperor's role in that decision remained secret, and because the emperor was divine and therefore infallible, it was unthinkable to attribute policy errors to him. Instead, Katō and the other Fleet Faction admirals directed their anger at Hamaguchi, and in the volatile climate of Japanese politics, that created a tangible and imminent danger. On November 4, 1930, a would-be assassin shot Hamaguchi as he stood on the platform of the Tokyo train station. The prime minister survived, but the attack underscored the reality that opposition to the military was dangerous, even potentially fatal.[3]

Like the navy, the Imperial Japanese Army was also divided into opposing camps. The more moderate group was the Tōseiha or "Control Faction," whose members were committed to a powerful military but sought to achieve that goal within the existing constitutional structure. The more radical faction was the Kōdōha or "Imperial Way Faction," whose adherents were impatient with what they perceived as the obstructionism of civilian bureaucrats. These so-called Spirit Warriors sought to lead the nation to ever greater heights by championing an idealized, mythological past. They embraced and promoted a narrative in which the emperor was a prisoner of his weak-willed advisors, and freeing him of their insidious influence would restore the glory of the empire. They were perfectly willing, even eager, to take unilateral action if necessary, and as an example of that, on September 19, 1931, Japanese soldiers detonated an explosion at Mukden near the Japanese-controlled railroad in Manchuria to create a pretext for the occupation of Manchuria itself.[4]

Young navy officers, too, were willing to take matters into their own hands. One year after the Mukden Incident, on the night of May 15, 1932, eleven young officer cadets of both the Japanese army and navy gathered at the Yasukuni Shrine near the Imperial Palace in Tokyo. This was a near-sacred place in Japan, dedicated to those who had given their lives in the service of the empire. After paying homage to their predecessors, the young officers made their way to the home of the new prime minister, seventy-seven-year-old Tsuyoshi Inukai. Upon gaining entrance, they told Inukai that the nation was asleep, and "the condition of the country could not be improved unless blood was shed." It was his blood they had in mind. Inukai begged for an opportunity to explain himself. His last words were "If I could speak, you would understand." To which the officer cadets replied, "Dialogue is useless," and they shot him to death. Then they took taxis to police headquarters in Tokyo and turned themselves in.[5]

The young men who committed this outrage justified their action in the name of what was called *gekokujō*, a kind of principled disobedience in which honorable men acted boldly to redeem the errors of their superiors. Though peculiarly Japanese, it was a concept not unknown in Western culture as well. As the naval historian Stephen Howarth has pointed out, Horatio Nelson embodied this principle when he put a telescope to his blind eye at Copenhagen to avoid acknowledging his superior's recall order. Within the Royal Navy, Nelson's behavior was universally applauded as heroic rather than mutinous or insubordinate, and it is held up today as an example of bold initiative. Of course, it helped a great deal that Nelson subsequently won the battle. In Japan, even the most outrageous acts of disobedience, including violence and murder, could be considered acceptable and even admirable if they were motivated by high-principled goals and conducted in the spirit of *yamato-damashii*, which roughly translates as the "spiritual soul of the Japanese people."[6]

At their trial, Inukai's murderers conducted themselves in compliance with the five basic virtues of Japanese soldiers and sailors: decorum, courage, obedience to the emperor, loyalty, and bravery. Their love for the emperor was so great, they insisted, they could no longer tolerate the craven policies of his civilian advisors. They professed their profound loyalty—not to the government, of course, since governments were transient—but to the emperor and to the spirit of *yamato-damashii*. Their professional deportment and naive youth evoked sympathy within the officer corps and the public at large. Even the moderate Admiral Kichisaburo Nomura, later Japan's ambassador to the United States, was sympathetic, commenting, "I was once a hothead myself." The perpetrators all received light sentences, and in some quarters were honored as heroes and martyrs.[7]

The May 15 Incident, as it came to be called, was a milestone in Japan's transition from a constitutional monarchy to a military dictatorship. Fleet Faction admirals warned darkly that unless the government acceded to the ambitions of the military services, it would become impossible for them to control their fiercely patriotic junior officers. Another factor in the political transition was that because the cabinet ministers representing the armed services were active-duty officers, the army or navy could topple a government simply by withdrawing its minister. The practical consequence was that the armed services exercised a kind of veto power over government policy. After the May 15 Incident, the Fleet Faction gained ascendency within the navy, and over the ensuing decade most of the Treaty Faction officers were purged from the service or marginalized.[8]

ONE OF THE FEW Treaty Faction admirals to survive the purge was Rear Admiral Isoroku Yamamoto, the diminutive (five-foot-three), brilliant, and supremely confident commander of the First Carrier Division. Yamamoto had been a delegate to the conference at London, and though he had initially opposed the compromise so despised by the Fleet Faction, he subsequently decided that the modified 10:10:7 ratio was the best Japan could expect, and for that matter all it could afford. Yamamoto was an outlier in other ways. He had spent two tours in the United States and had been profoundly impressed by its industrial strength, reflected by Henry Ford's automobile assembly plant in Detroit, and the fecundity of the Texas oil fields. War against such an opponent, he concluded, was foolish. Fleet Faction admirals such as Katō did not entirely discount America's material and economic superiority, but they insisted that the spirit of *yamato-damashii* could overcome mere wealth and numbers. Like Confederates after Fort Sumter who boasted that one Reb could lick five Yanks, they valued a martial culture over material superiority. When asked if he had any concerns that the Americans were likely to have more fighter planes than the Japanese, the commanding officer of a fighter squadron on the carrier *Akagi* replied: "We can handle three of their planes with one [of ours]." As Katō put it in a July 1934 speech, "the morale and self-confidence" of the navy would yield "certain victory

Admiral Isoroku Yamamoto, commander in chief of the Combined Fleet, was an iconoclast in the Imperial Japanese Navy who questioned both the ambitions of Fleet Faction admirals such as Katō and the supremacy of the battleship in naval combat.

Naval History and Heritage Command

over our hypothetical enemy, no matter how overwhelming the physical odds against us." Yamamoto found such notions naive and dangerous.[9]

Another area in which Yamamoto defied the reigning philosophy of the Fleet Faction was his skepticism about the preeminence of battleships. It was a near-universal assumption in the early twentieth century that large battleships with heavy guns constituted the principal index of naval power, an assumption epitomized by the construction of the *Bismarck* and *Tirpitz* in Germany and by the *King George V* class of battleships in Britain. It was an American naval officer, Captain (later Rear Admiral) Alfred Thayer Mahan, who had codified these assumptions in an influential book that had been published in 1890. Entitled *The Influence of Sea Power upon History, 1660–1783*, Mahan's book showed how England's possession of a fleet of ships-of-the-line (the battleships of the Age of Sail) had allowed her to defeat first the Dutch, then the French, and rise to world dominance. Her command of the sea had led to wealth, influence, and power. It was not lost on the Japanese that their homeland shared many of Britain's geographical circumstances, and Mahan himself implied that other nations could replicate Britain's success by committing themselves to the construction and maintenance of a battleship fleet. Mahan's book was quickly translated into Japanese, and its central argument became dogma within the Imperial Japanese Navy.[10]

Like every other Japanese naval officer of his generation, Yamamoto had read Mahan's book at Etajima, and he had initially embraced its tenets. By 1930, however, his natural skepticism led him to reconsider. Prior to his participation in the conference at London, he had been captain of the large aircraft carrier *Akagi*, and afterward he commanded the First Carrier Division, composed of the smaller carriers *Ryūjō* and *Hōshō*. Based in part on that experience, he became convinced that aircraft were poised to make battleships secondary, if not quite irrelevant. In 1934, he told a class of air cadets that battleships were like the expensive artwork that wealthy Japanese families put on display in their living rooms to impress visitors: beautiful, perhaps, but of no practical utility. On another occasion, he described the advocates of big battleships, the so-called Gun Club or *teppō-ya*, as "thick headed," and predicted that "big ships and big guns, will become obsolete." Nor did the Japanese Army escape his criticism. He questioned the ambitions and pretensions of the Kōdōha and openly opposed the war in Manchuria, once publicly referring to "those damn fools in the Army."[11]

Yamamoto seemed to take a particular joy in tempting fate by speaking his mind. He was a risk taker by instinct, and one manifestation of that was his willingness to bet on almost anything. He enjoyed games of skill, such as bridge and chess, and he especially liked American poker, which he could play for hours, often forgoing sleep in order to play all night. He knew that his outspokenness would provoke the anger of "hotheads" in both services, though it did not deter him from continuing to act the gadfly. It was a high-wire act. Luck was with him on one occasion when he left town on the very day that a group of conspirators planned to assassinate him.[12]

Yamamoto was not alone in his assertion that the airplane would supersede the battleship. Admiral Shigeyoshi Inoue, for one, lamented the "ratio neurosis" of Fleet Faction admirals such as Katō, and argued that land-based airplanes operating from scores of tiny islands in Micronesia could effectively turn back an enemy battle fleet. Inoue and Yamamoto supported the development of long-range, land-based bombers that could be used to attack an American fleet attempting to steam into the western Pacific. The first such plane was the twin-engine Mitsubishi G3M (officially the Type 96) that became operational in 1936 and which the Americans dubbed the "Nell," and it was followed four years later by the faster and better-armed G4M1 "Betty," which was also made by Mitsubishi. In addition, however, Yamamoto believed that the most effective way to deploy naval air power was on aircraft carriers.[13]

The British had advised and aided Japan in the construction of its first aircraft carrier, the Hōshō, back in 1922. Consistent with early British carriers, the Hōshō was relatively small, displacing fewer than 10,000 tons, and capable of carrying only fifteen aircraft. By the 1930s, however, both the United States and Japan possessed aircraft carriers so large that they dwarfed those of the Royal Navy. This had come about because both nations took advantage of a special exception in the 1922 Washington Treaty. That treaty required both Japan and the United States to scrap a number of brand-new or partially finished warships, though as compensation it allowed them to salvage several already completed hulls by converting them into aircraft carriers. The Japanese used the hull of the unfinished battleship *Kaga* for one carrier and that of the battlecruiser *Akagi* for another. The Americans, too, availed themselves of this opportunity, creating the oversized *Lexington* and *Saratoga*. Each of these four displaced more than 40,000 tons and could carry as many as ninety aircraft. They were so large, in fact, that they transformed the very function of aircraft carriers. Rather than act as auxiliaries to the battleships, they became powerful striking weapons in their own right. This was demonstrated in January 1929 when, in the midst of the U.S. Navy's annual fleet exercise, Admiral Mason Reeves took the *Saratoga* away from the main body to execute an independent "air strike" against the Panama Canal. His raid was a straw in the wind for those who were paying attention, though it fell short of a genuine revolution since in both Japan and in the United States most admirals remained committed to the principles of Mahan and concluded that Reeves's exploit was little more than a stunt.[14]

The Japanese aircraft carrier *Kaga*, seen here in a 1936 photograph, was built on the hull of an unfinished battleship. The Japanese and the Americans each built two such oversized carriers in the 1920s. Note the elevated flight deck, the relatively small island, and the stack exhausting smoke downward on her starboard side.

Naval History and Heritage Command

FRUSTRATED BY THE RESTRICTIONS OF the London Treaty, the Fleet Faction admirals who dominated the Japanese Naval General Staff sought to strengthen the navy as much as possible while staying technically within the treaty limits. This was done primarily through qualitative improvements. The Japanese modernized their existing battleships, including the *Fusō* (1932), *Kongō* (1935), *Ise* (1935), and *Mutsu* (1936), replacing their coal-fired boilers with new oil-fired boilers to improve their speed, even though it exacerbated the problem of oil resources. They also added protective torpedo blisters to each ship, and increased the thickness of their armor. A particular goal was to ensure that Japanese battleships could outrange their American counterparts, and to achieve that the turrets on all these battleships were modified so that the guns could be elevated to a forty-degree angle.[15]

Cruisers, too, were strengthened and enlarged. Since Japan was already at its allowable limit for 8-inch-gun cruisers, the Supplemental Building Program for the years 1931 to 1936 focused on the construction of a new class of heavily armed light cruisers. Though these *Mogami*-class cruisers carried no gun larger than 6 inches, they featured fifteen of them arrayed in five turrets, three forward and two aft. Moreover, those turrets were designed in such a way that the 6-inch guns could be quickly replaced by 8-inch guns in case of war.[16]

Another technological advance that did not fall within the strictures of the Washington or London treaties was the development of larger and more efficient torpedoes. By the mid-1930s, the Japanese had figured out how to use compressed oxygen as a propellant in torpedoes. That gave them a longer range and more punch than Western torpedoes, which relied on compressed air. The largest was the Type 93, which the British and Americans subsequently called the "Long Lance." Thirty feet long and weighing nearly three tons, Long Lance torpedoes had a maximum range of more than twenty miles, which meant they could be launched from beyond the range of all but the largest naval guns, and they had a thousand-pound warhead, nearly twice as powerful as American torpedoes. The Long Lance was intended for use by cruisers and destroyers, and smaller versions were developed for submarines (the Type 95) and airplanes (the Type 91). All of them performed better than their Western counterparts.[17]

The Japanese determination to keep its fleet fully up to the mark, combined with American disinterest in naval developments during the Depression, meant that by 1934 the Imperial Japanese Navy was approaching not 70 percent of the American total but nearer 80 percent. And because the United States had to divide its fleet between two coasts, the Japanese achieved de facto naval superiority in the Pacific. Even so, Japan's naval leaders, alarmed by American protests over the occupation of Manchuria, remained convinced that a showdown with the Americans was inevitable and pressed the government to abandon the treaty protocols altogether. That year, when the major powers began preliminary planning for another conference in London to renew the 1930 treaty, Japan's government instructed its delegates to obtain absolute parity with the West or walk out of the conference.[18]

Yamamoto, now a vice admiral, headed the Japanese delegation, but his instructions gave him no room to negotiate. He knew there was no chance whatsoever that the British or Americans would accept Japanese parity, and that the conference was doomed from the start. Afterward Japan gave the required two-year notice of its intention to withdraw from the Washington Treaty. It had already withdrawn from the League of Nations in protest of the league's condemnation of the occupation of Manchuria, so in effect Japan abandoned the policy of collective security altogether. Though the alternative was a naval arms race with the United States, the Fleet Faction admirals did not quail at such a prospect, and their domination of the government became even more complete that winter in the aftermath of another failed coup.[19]

On February 26, 1936, hundreds of Japanese army "Spirit Warriors," most of them junior officers in their twenties, conducted a series of full-scale assaults on government officials. In the belief that a recent election victory by the Liberal Party would mean a reduction in military appropriations, they determined to decapitate the government. They murdered the finance minister, the inspector general of military education, and the Lord Keeper of the Privy Seal, and they targeted the prime minister as well, though they mistook their man and inadvertently killed his brother-in-law instead.[20]

Unlike the perpetrators of the May 15 Incident, the killers this time were not seeking to make a statement about the soul of Japan; their objective was to seize power, and instead of public sympathy their rampage earned them general condemnation. Seventeen of the conspirators were sentenced to death, and the influence of the Kōdōha was greatly diminished. Ironically, however, the conspirators succeeded in their broader goal, for the regular army leadership now argued successfully that in order to maintain the strict discipline necessary to prevent further such uprisings, the army's power and authority must be increased. The prime minister, who had escaped assassination by pure chance, acknowledged that within the government the fear of another coup attempt was greater than the reluctance to surrender control to the army. By the end of 1936, Japan had become a de facto military dictatorship. Unlike Hitler's regime in Germany, where ultimate authority and control resided in the person of the Führer, Japan's dictatorship was a military oligarchy where national policy decisions emerged from a complex and often contentious negotiation between the army and navy General Staffs. Both the civilian office holders and even the emperor were largely reduced to approving decisions already made by those in uniform. The American ambassador to Japan, Joseph Grew, called it "a dictatorship of terrorism."[21]

In the meantime, "those damn fools in the army" started another war.

IN 1937, JAPAN EMBARKED ON THE SECOND SINO-JAPANESE WAR, so called because Japan and China had fought previously in 1894–95. This new war began when Japanese soldiers stationed at Peiping (now Beijing) exchanged gunfire with Chinese soldiers at the Marco Polo Bridge near the walled town of Wanping. Unlike the incident at Mukden six years earlier, it was not a deliberate provocation contrived to justify a war, though war came nonetheless mainly because neither side tried very hard to prevent it. Amidst heightened tensions a Japanese naval officer was shot and killed in Shanghai, and this acted as the trigger for open hostilities. The Japanese endowed this conflict with the rather benign name of the China Incident, though it marked the beginning of eight years of full-scale warfare. In due course it would merge into the broader conflict that the Japanese called the Great East Asia War and the West called the Second World War.[22]

The war in China was almost exclusively a land conflict, though the Japanese Navy did execute a number of mostly unopposed amphibious landings at Tsingtao, Amoy, Foochow, and Canton. In addition, Japan's blockade of the Chinese coast not only reduced the importation of needed military equipment, it also cut off customs duties, thus starving the Chinese government of revenue, which contributed to rampant inflation. On the other hand, the unexpected efficiency of Chinese fighter planes during the bombing raids encouraged Japanese designers to come up with a new long-range and highly maneuverable fighter escort for the bombers, and the result was the A6M2 Type 00 fighter, known then and throughout the subsequent Pacific War as the Zero. It was a remarkable airplane. When it was introduced in 1940, not only did the Zero have a longer range than any other fighter in the world, it could also climb faster and turn tighter. It carried an impressive suite of weapons, including two 20 mm cannon in the wings. It achieved all this, however, by having limited armor and was therefore highly vulnerable, so much so that when a Zero was hit the pilot was often lost as well.[23]

Even before the war in China began, the Japanese had promulgated a document entitled "Fundamental Principles of National Policy" that established a national goal of becoming "in name and in fact a stabilizing power for assuring peace in East Asia, thereby ultimately contributing to the peace and welfare of humanity." The Japanese framed this program as a kind of Japanese Monroe Doctrine, though most Americans perceived it as a declaration of Japanese determination to dominate East Asia and the western Pacific.[24]

The Imperial Japanese Navy played a secondary role in the China war, and most Japanese naval officers continued to keep their eyes fixed on the potential foe to the east. Most of them considered it likely that the Americans would use the war in China as a pretext to interfere, in which case the result would be a full-scale naval war with the United States, an outcome that many, especially in the Fleet Faction, considered inevitable—even desirable. To win such a war, the Japanese planned to use airplanes and submarines operating from their island bases in Micronesia to weaken the American fleet as it advanced toward a final showdown somewhere in the western Pacific. To ensure victory in that showdown, the Japanese conceived of a new weapon, and in 1937, the same year the war in China began, they began to build it.

THE INLAND SEA (Seto Naikai in Japanese) is the large navigable body of water formed by the close proximity of three of Japan's four main islands: Honshū, Shikoku, and Kyūshū. It is an enormous protected anchorage, 280 miles long and 30 miles wide, and, like Scapa Flow, it is accessible by only a few well-guarded passages, in particular what was known as the Bungo Channel (Bungo-suidō), between Shikoku and Kyūshū. Unlike Scapa Flow, however, the Inland Sea is also picturesque, dotted with nearly three thousand forested islands, one of which—Nomi Island—is home to Etajima, the Japanese naval academy. Around the rim of the Inland Sea are a dozen important seaports, including Kure, six miles southeast of Hiroshima.

Officially designated as the Kure Naval Arsenal, Kure hosted extensive ship repair facilities, its own steel works, an arms factory, and the largest shipbuilding dry dock in the country. Even so, in the late summer of 1937 hundreds of workers spent months expanding and deepening that dry dock, and on November 4, workers began laying the keel of a new battleship. Ordinarily, such an event would be the occasion for celebration and ceremony in a culture where formal rituals served as the milestones of national progress. Instead, a giant curtain made of sisal was erected around the landward side of the shipyard to conceal the work that was taking place. So much sisal was employed to erect this barrier that Japanese fishermen were unable to make or mend their fishing nets and for a while local seafood became both scarce and expensive. Workers assigned to the construction of the new ship had to take an oath of secrecy and were issued numbered armbands; armed guards at each gate verified that every individual who entered the work area was authorized to do so.[25]

Soon enough, the dimensions of the new ship became evident and the workers began to understand the reason for such precautions. It was enormous. Initially labeled only as Battleship No. 1, the vessel taking shape at Kure was forty feet longer, ten feet wider, and much heavier than the *Bismarck*, then under construction halfway around the world at Hamburg. Eventually the ship being built at Kure would displace more than 70,000 tons, making it nearly twice the size of British or American battleships. Its most striking aspect, however, was its armament. In place of the *Bismarck*'s 15-inch guns or the *Rodney*'s 16-inch guns, this new vessel was to have nine 18.1-inch guns arrayed in three triple turrets. Each of those guns was capable of firing a 3,200-pound shell more than twenty-five miles. They would outrange any American battleship, damaging or sinking it before it could even fire a shot. Just under six months later, on March 29, 1938, the keel of a second such ship, Battleship No. 2, was laid down at Nagasaki, at the western end of Kyūshū.* There, too, the work was shrouded in secrecy, so much so that hikers on the surrounding hills were detained and held for interrogation.[26]

The Japanese super-battleship *Yamato*, photographed here during her trials in October 1941 two months before the Pearl Harbor attack; it is one of the most beautiful warships ever built. The Japanese expected that the *Yamato*'s nine 18.1-inch guns would provide the edge in a decisive battle with the Americans in the looming war.

U.S. National Archives photo no. 80-G-704702

---

* It is one of history's many ironies that Japan's two super-battleships were constructed at Hiroshima and Nagasaki, cities destined to become historic for a quite different reason.

The ships at Kure and Nagasaki were eventually christened *Yamato* and *Musashi*, and they represented Japan's effort to neutralize American numerical superiority with size and quality. The Japanese were confident that the Americans would not be willing to match these giants because no such ship could fit through the Panama Canal. The *Yamato* and *Musashi*, therefore, would trump anything the Americans could produce, and they would secure the decisive victory in the inevitable confrontation. Alas for this vision, by the time the ships were commissioned in 1941 and 1942, battleships no longer defined the index of naval power. In acknowledgment of that, the third ship of the class, laid down in May 1941 (the same month Germany struck in the West), was converted in mid-construction into an aircraft carrier. In 1937, however, naval experts the world over continued to enshrine the battleship as the queen of naval warfare, and with the *Yamato* and *Musashi* the Japanese believed they had found the key to defeating their transpacific rival.[27]

THE WAR IN CHINA GROUND ON. Japanese armies won virtually all the battles, but in most cases the defeated Chinese, commanded by Generalissimo Chiang Kai-shek, merely gave ground and regrouped to fight another day. Frustrated by these tactics and convinced by their own propaganda that the ungrateful Chinese were refusing to accept benign liberation, the Japanese responded with unprecedented fury, unleashing their aircraft and artillery on Chinese cities, and conducting war against civilians as well as Chiang's elusive army. Notoriously, that included what the West called "the rape of Nanking" (now Nanjing) in December 1937, during which as many as two hundred thousand Chinese died, including many women and children. News photographs of this atrocity appeared in American newspapers and newsreels and further strained Japanese-American relations. That same month, Japanese warplanes attacked and sank an American gunboat, the USS *Panay*, that was operating on the Yangtze River near Nanking. The Japanese suspected, not without reason, that the American gunboat was there to gather information, and though they insisted the attack was a mistake, apologized, and offered an indemnity, the incident further soured American attitudes. In the meantime, Japanese armies pushed ever deeper into

China, and by 1939 they were having trouble administering the vast territory they occupied. Soon enough, Japanese army leaders began looking for a way out of what began to feel like a quagmire.[28]

By then the war in Europe had begun. Though Japan remained neutral in that war, Japanese army leaders were impressed by the way German forces rolled over Poland in September 1939, seized Norway in April 1940, drove the British from the beaches at Dunkirk, and overran France. Japan had previously signed an anti-Comintern pact* with Germany aimed at the Soviet Union, and now Japan's leaders went further. In September 1940, one year into the European war, representatives from Germany, Italy, and Japan signed what was called the Tripartite Pact in Berlin. The signatory nations agreed to "stand by and co-operate with one another." Japan acknowledged the preeminence of Germany and Italy "in the establishment of a new order in Europe," and Germany and Italy recognized "the leadership of Japan in the establishment of a new order in Greater East Asia." The agreement obliged the participants to "assist one another" if any of the three were attacked by "a power at present not involved in the European War." Only two major powers fit that description: the Soviet Union and the United States. Since Germany had signed a non-aggression treaty with the Soviet Union, the obvious target of the Tripartite Pact was the United States.[29]

The dramatic successes of German forces in Europe created opportunities for the Japanese in Asia. The defeat of France and Holland and the beleaguered circumstances of Britain meant that the South Asian colonies of these European states became virtual orphans. Borneo, Java, and Sumatra in the Dutch East Indies, as well as the British colony of Malaya, were all rich in oil reserves. French Indochina was a principal source of both rubber and tin. The temptation to seize these valuable and vulnerable colonies proved irresistible. To Imperial Japanese Army officers in particular, not only was a move into South Asia economically appealing, but they imagined that it could somehow provide a way out of the China mess. It was a curious and in many ways contradictory vision. To defeat China, they

---

* With the Anti-Comintern Pact of November 25, 1936, Japan and Germany labeled the Soviet state as "a menace to the peace of the world," and committed both nations to cooperate "against Communist subversive activities."

needed unhindered access to the resources of the European colonies in South Asia. If obtaining those resources meant war with Britain and Holland, and quite possibly the United States as well, army leaders saw that as acceptable if it enabled them to resolve the situation in China.[30]

It was by no means certain that a move southward to seize the European colonies meant war with the United States, since the Americans might prove unwilling to go to war in defense of Britain's colonial empire. The problem was that Japanese oil tankers carrying petroleum to Japan from Borneo, Sumatra, or Malaya would necessarily have to pass through or around the American-held Philippines. Because of that, the Americans would still have their hand on the valve that controlled the flow of essential resources to the homeland. It therefore seemed both necessary and logical to seize the Philippines as well, and that *did* mean war with the United States. Advocates of this logic argued that since such a war was inevitable in any case, a preemptive move southward would at least allow Japan to choose the timing and circumstances.[31]

If the Japanese army was eager for war, the navy was more cautious, though it was a muted caution. Despite the progress the navy had made since 1936, Japanese naval leaders knew their fleet was not strong enough to prevail over the United States Navy, especially in a protracted war. On the other hand, they also knew that if they admitted to that, the army generals

Admiral Osami Nagano, shown here as a vice admiral, replaced Katō as navy chief of staff in 1939. Though not as ardent for war as Katō, he was fatalistic about it, insisting that "the force of circumstances ... gradually compelled us to a war determination."
U.S. Naval Institute

who dominated the government might well cut off the funding needed to continue the naval buildup. As one naval officer put it after the war, "Inwardly we felt we could not fight with the Anglo-American powers, but we could not unequivocally say so. . . . We were afraid that the army would say, 'If the navy can't fight, give us your materiel and budget.'"[32]

Kanji Katō died in 1939, and the navy chief of staff in 1941 was Admiral Osami Nagano, a physical giant of a man whose nickname was "The Elephant." Despite his intimidating size, one of Nagano's primary goals was to avoid antagonizing his army counterparts. At a meeting in July 1941, ten days after Germany invaded the Soviet Union, the army generals insisted that a war with the United States and Britain was unavoidable. "Well," Nagano replied, "seeing that the government's made up its mind, I suppose we'll have to go along with it." Yamamoto was disgusted, telling a fellow officer, "Nagano's a dead loss." Still, he sounded his own fatalist note by saying, "There's nothing we can do now." If "those damn fools in the army" were going to take the nation into war against the Americans, Yamamoto was convinced that the best, and maybe only, chance Japan had to survive such a war was to strike a crushing preemptive blow at the outset. As early as January 1941, he began to work on what became a nine-page plan of operations that called for a raid by all six of Japan's large aircraft carriers against the American battleship fleet anchored at the Pearl Harbor naval base in Hawaii on the first day of the war.[33]

The wisdom of such a strike was still under consideration when Japanese-American relations reached a crisis in late summer. On August 1, after the Japanese sent troops into French Indochina, the United States announced an economic embargo of a long list of essential goods that Japan routinely imported from the United States. The moment had arrived when Japan had to choose whether to knuckle under to American demands or to seize their own resources from the British and Dutch colonies of South Asia. In October, army General Hideki Tojo assumed the position of prime minister. After that, there was hardly any doubt about the direction of Japan's future policy. The Naval General Staff ordered its operational commanders to prepare for hostilities, and carrier pilots began making practice runs against anchored ships in Kagoshima Harbor, whose topography resembled that of Pearl Harbor.

CHAPTER 9

A TWO-OCEAN NAVY

F RANKLIN D. ROOSEVELT had been a navy man all his life. Like his fifth cousin (and uncle by marriage) Theodore "Teddy" Roosevelt, who dispatched the Great White Fleet on its round-the-world cruise in 1907, FDR had been fascinated by naval history since boyhood. Growing up on the banks of the Hudson River at Hyde Park, he had learned to sail a small boat almost as soon as he could walk. He read his cousin Ted's history *The Naval War of 1812* as a boy, and at age fifteen he plowed his way through Alfred Thayer Mahan's tome about how possession of a battleship fleet determined national greatness. He was a devoted collector of both ship models and naval prints, especially from the Age of Sail. During the First World War, he served as Woodrow Wilson's assistant secretary of the navy, jovially hobnobbing with admirals and making himself entirely at home on the deck of a warship, even personally navigating a destroyer through the tortuous passages of the Maine coast. Later in life he routinely referred to his tenure as assistant secretary as "when I was in the Navy." On March 4, 1933, he took the oath of office as the thirty-second president of the United States.[1]

The country had elected him by an overwhelming margin in response to the ravages of the Great Depression, and Americans waited anxiously to hear how he planned to bring the country out of it. In fact, Roosevelt did not have a detailed or cohesive program to present in his inaugural address, so he sought to restore public confidence: "The only thing we have to fear is," he declared, pausing dramatically, "fear itself." His specific proposals, however, were a grab bag of mostly conventional ideas, including a bank holiday to stanch the bleeding of the nation's financial institutions, cuts in the salaries of government workers to help balance the budget, and even a reduction in military spending. Soon, however, the new president tacked sharply left and sponsored a series of innovative programs designed both to provide immediate relief to those in need and to stimulate the economy. He called for unemployment insurance, farm support, a public works program, and a National Industrial Recovery Act, all of which were quickly enacted by a compliant Congress during the subsequently famous first one hundred days of his administration.[2]

Though domestic economic woes dominated the new president's agenda, he did not ignore the emerging threats from abroad. The day after his inauguration, an election in Germany made the Nazi Party the only legal political organization in the country, confirming Hitler's absolute control of the government, while in Japan, the Kōdōha consolidated its dominance. Roosevelt continued the policy set by his predecessor's secretary of state, Henry L. Stimson, of refusing to recognize Japan's puppet state of Manchukuo in Manchuria, which if nothing else signaled America's disapproval of wars of conquest. On a more tangible level, Roosevelt acted to enlarge the U.S. Navy. In doing so, he was able to combine his commitment to public works with a desire to expand his beloved branch of service. Encouraged by the chairman of the House Naval Affairs Committee, Carl Vinson (D-Georgia), Roosevelt funneled $238 million of public works money to naval construction in the first year of his presidency, and the next year backed legislation to bring the U.S. Navy up to the limits allowed by the Washington and London Treaties. That legislation, the Vinson-Trammell

Act, authorized the construction of one new aircraft carrier, sixty-five destroyers, thirty submarines, and nearly twelve hundred aircraft. When two years later Japan announced its withdrawal from the treaty system, Roosevelt convinced Congress to fund two more aircraft carriers as well as six heavy cruisers that had been initially authorized back in 1929 but which had never been built due to the Depression. Naturally, these decisions added to the Japanese conviction that the United States was arming for an eventual showdown.[3]

THEY WERE NOT ENTIRELY WRONG. For more than twenty years, the U.S. Navy had focused much of its planning, training, and war-gaming on a possible war with Japan. For the most part this was simply the exercise of due diligence as naval officers prepared contingency plans for future eventualities. In the 1920s, the navy developed a whole series of so-called color plans, each color representing a possible foe: red for Britain, black for Germany, green for Mexico, orange for Japan, and several others. Still, just as most Japanese naval officers considered the United States their most likely future enemy, U.S. Navy officers concurred and focused most of their attention on Plan Orange.[4]

The first version of the plan was sketched out in 1911, and although it underwent regular revision and adjustment, its basic outline remained largely unchanged. It assumed a Japanese assault on the Philippines, in response to which American and Filipino ground forces would withdraw into a defensive position on the Bataan Peninsula near Manila and hold out there for six months. That would buy time for the U.S. battle fleet to gather in Pearl Harbor, Hawaii, and steam westward across the Pacific for a showdown with the Japanese battle fleet that would decide the war. Plan Orange was a contingency plan and not government policy, but for twenty years it informed the requests the U.S. Navy put forward for budget and planning purposes.

The problem was logistics. It was obvious that sending a battleship fleet five thousand miles from Hawaii to the Philippine Sea created a precarious supply line, and it was clear that it would be useful, and perhaps essential, to occupy and develop one or more island bases in the Pacific to support that advance. As early as 1921 Major Earl "Pete" Ellis of the U.S. Marine Corps drafted a paper entitled "Advance Base Operations in Micronesia," which marked the emergence of amphibious operations as the particular specialty of the U.S. Marine Corps. By the time Roosevelt became president, the latest version of Plan Orange included the seizure of at least two interim bases en route to Manila: Eniwetok in the Marshall Islands, and Truk in the Carolines. It would not be easy. Both islands were under Japanese supervision as part of a League of Nations mandate that had been granted after the First World War, and though the 1922 Washington Treaty forbade the construction of fortifications on those islands, the Japanese had clandestinely fortified them anyway. Once they renounced the Washington Treaty in 1936, they began to do so openly.[5]

In addition to developing war plans, the U.S. Navy also conducted large-scale exercises each year to test the readiness of the fleet. Planning, executing, and evaluating these fleet exercises was its central focus during the interwar years. To conduct them, the high command divided the fleet into two relatively equal task forces, one of them designated as friendly and usually dubbed the "White" Fleet or the "Blue" Fleet, and the other assigned the role of aggressor and commonly christened the "Black" Fleet or the "Orange" Fleet.* Officers acting as umpires kept track of presumed hits and hypothetical damage throughout the exercise. Often the exercise involved defending the Panama Canal, as it had in 1929 when Admiral Mason Reeves demonstrated the tactical flexibility of aircraft carriers by attacking the canal with planes from the carrier *Saratoga*. For 1937, the navy planned a particularly large exercise involving 152 ships and 496 aircraft in the northern Pacific between Hawaii and Alaska. The Japanese protested, arguing that conducting a full-scale war game so close to Japan was a deliberate provocation. The exercise went ahead nonetheless, and one noteworthy aspect of it was a carrier-borne air attack by the aggressor fleet on the Hawaiian Islands.[6]

---

* There were exceptions. In Fleet Problem XX, held in the spring of 1939, the friendly force was "Black," and the aggressor force (presumably German) was "White." Interestingly, in Japanese war games, the friendly (Japanese) forces were often labeled "Blue" while the enemy (American) force was "Red."

Already precarious, Japanese-American relations took a marked turn for the worse later that year with news of the "rape of Nanking" and the Japanese attack on the USS *Panay*. Within Roosevelt's cabinet, Claude Swanson, the usually serene secretary of the navy, insisted that the attack on the *Panay* was an act of war and that the United States should respond accordingly. Roosevelt, however, was unwilling to get ahead of public opinion, and decided instead to announce economic sanctions, though he chose to call them something else. "We don't call them economic sanctions," he told reporters, "we call them quarantines. We want to develop a technique which will not lead to war." He did, however, seek additional increases for military spending, and four months later, in May 1938, Congress agreed to another 20 percent across-the-board increase in the size of the U.S. Navy.[7]

THE OUTBREAK OF WAR IN EUROPE complicated American military and naval planning. If the Japanese saw opportunity in early German successes and rushed to cement their relationship with Hitler's regime, the American response was a near-universal determination to stay out of the war, and Roosevelt at once declared America's neutrality. It was neutrality, however, not indifference. From the start, Roosevelt saw Britain's survival as essential to American security. Churchill cultivated that view, sending the American president regular reports about the progress of the war, especially naval actions. After the destruction of the *Graf Spee* in the river Plate, for example, Churchill sent Roosevelt a lengthy and vivid description of the battle, and FDR wrote back to thank the "Former Naval Person" (as Churchill often subscribed his letters) "for that tremendously interesting account." A full year before Pearl Harbor, Churchill was asserting to his American counterpart "that the safety of the United States as well as the future of our two democracies and the kind of civilization for which they stand are bound up with the survival and independence of the British Commonwealth of Nations." Roosevelt agreed, and for more than two years of official neutrality, he did all he could to ensure the survival of Britain, testing and stretching the limits of the law, and even the Constitution, to achieve that goal.[8]

The Neutrality Acts of 1935 and 1937 forbade the United States from selling arms to Britain, or to any belligerent, on credit, or transporting them in American ships, and the best Roosevelt could do was get permission from Congress to sell arms to Britain on a "cash-and-carry" basis. What he could do—and did do—was use his executive authority to declare a security zone extending two hundred miles out from America's coastline that would be patrolled by the U.S. Navy. Publicly, he presented this as a defensive measure designed to keep the war away from American shores, though it also, and not incidentally, aided the British in their effort to track German warships. U.S. Navy ships monitored and reported—in uncoded English-language messages—the location and character of belligerent vessels within the American security zone. The captain of the American destroyer *Jouett*, Frank K. B. Wheeler, had no doubt that "the purpose of our position reports was to allow British naval ships to track" the reported contacts.[9]

One example of how U.S. Navy warships violated the spirit, if not the letter, of strict neutrality was the case of the German passenger liner *Columbus*. Stranded in the Caribbean when the war began, the *Columbus* took refuge in the neutral Mexican port of Vera Cruz. The passengers went ashore, but for nearly a year the ship itself remained there while U.S. Navy destroyers kept a vigil offshore. In December 1940, her captain received orders to bring the *Columbus* back to Germany despite the possibility that it might be intercepted by the British. When she left Vera Cruz, American warships shadowed her across the Gulf of Mexico and into the Atlantic, broadcasting her location every four hours. She was 425 miles off Cape May, New Jersey, when the British destroyer *Hyperion* showed up. With an American cruiser standing by, the *Hyperion* fired several shots across the bow of the *Columbus* to compel her to stop. Unwilling to be captured, the crew of the German liner scuttled the ship, setting fires and opening the sea cocks before taking to the lifeboats. The Americans picked up the German crewmen and took them back to the United States, where they were released. Though the U.S. Navy had not fired a shot during this episode, neither had it behaved with scrupulous neutrality.[10]

Over the ensuing months, Roosevelt gradually expanded the size of the American security zone as well as the freedom of action of American warships within it. When at a press conference reporters asked him how far the American neutrality zone might be extended, he airily replied that it would be as far as necessary. The assignment put some strain on the American peacetime navy, and the chief of naval operations, Admiral Harold Stark, reactivated several of the old First World War four-stack destroyers. Virtually all of them required extensive refitting, and once they got to sea they were manned mostly by novice crews. As a result, the so-called Neutrality Patrols got off to a sluggish start.[11]

The fall of France in June 1940 had a dramatic, even revolutionary impact on congressional attitudes. Though it did not affect the popular determination to stay out of the war, the startling defeat of the French army and the British evacuation from Dunkirk convinced many Americans that a German victory in Europe was likely and perhaps imminent. It seemed prudent, therefore, for the United States to make more strenuous military preparations—not to enter the war, but to defend the Western Hemisphere in the event of German victory. On July 19, less than a month after the French capitulation, Congress voted the single largest naval appropriation in American history, adding no fewer than 257 warships to the fleet, very nearly doubling its size. The Two-Ocean Navy Act, as it was called, authorized an astonishing 18 new aircraft carriers, 7 battleships, 33 cruisers, and 115 destroyers. It was a force that by itself was nearly as large as the entire Imperial Japanese Navy and utterly dwarfed the Kriegsmarine. Despite an enormous price tag of over $8.5 billion, the bill passed the House 316–0. Thus was the Japanese decision to abandon the treaty protocols and engage the United States in a naval building race revealed as monumentally ill-considered. Of course, none of the ships authorized that summer would be available for several years, which meant that the Japanese still had a narrow window of opportunity, during which their fleet would remain competitive with the Americans, especially since the United States had to divide its forces between the Atlantic and the Pacific. The Japanese calculated that their own navy would reach its apogee relative to the United States in mid-1942. After that, the Americans would surge to the forefront and their margin of superiority would rapidly widen. For those who believed that war with the United States was inevitable, the clock was already ticking.[12]

AS AMERICAN SHIPYARDS on both coasts resounded with new activity, the ships of the existing United States Navy continued the Neutrality

Patrols in the Atlantic. In September, Roosevelt announced the bases-for-destroyers deal with Britain (see Chapter 6). Unwilling to submit the plan to Congress for fear of being rebuffed, Roosevelt used his executive authority to conclude it. That put Stark in an awkward position. The American CNO, whose curious nickname was "Betty,"* was a conscientious naval officer, and he was reluctant to certify, as required by law, that the destroyers in question were "obsolete and useless." Old they might be, but several of them were even then participating in the Neutrality Patrols, which suggested that they weren't entirely "useless." Moreover, like almost everyone else that summer of 1940, Stark wondered if the British could hold out against the Nazi war machine. If they did not, the United States might need every old and out-dated destroyer it had. Roosevelt had known Stark since the First World War, and had appointed him to the top navy job over a number of his con-temporaries in part because of his presumed loyalty. Faithful to that expecta-tion, Stark in the end decided that the naval bases obtained from Britain added greater security to the nation than fifty old destroyers, and if the com-mander in chief wanted him to certify their uselessness, he would do so.[13]

Stark also played a central role in reorienting American war planning that fall. In November, he took it upon himself to prepare a lengthy memo-randum for Roosevelt's new navy secretary, the former Rough Rider and Chicago newspaper baron Frank Knox, in which Stark surveyed the drasti-cally changed world situation. It seemed to Stark that the United States had essentially four strategic alternatives:

    A. To rely on a strict defense of the Western Hemisphere
    B. To maintain the traditional focus on a possible war with Japan
    C. To try to maintain competitive naval forces in both oceans
    D. To focus on the threat from Germany

---

*   Stark came by the nickname as a plebe at the Naval Academy when an upperclassman asked him if he was related to General John Stark from the American Revolution. Midshipman Stark confessed ignorance about General Stark, and the upperclassman informed him that prior to the Battle of Bennington, the general had declared, "We will win today or Betty Stark will be a widow," and ordered the young plebe to make that an-nouncement on demand throughout his plebe year. Thenceforward, Harold Stark was universally known as "Betty." Ironically, General Stark's wife was actually named Molly.

President Franklin Roosevelt awards Admiral Harold "Betty" Stark a gold star to represent a second Distinguished Service Medal in the Oval Office in April 1942. Despite Stark's critical role in reorienting American strategic plans, once war began, he was eased out of his job as chief of naval operations in order to make room for Admiral Ernest J. King.

Naval History and Heritage Command

Despite the U.S. Navy's twenty-year obsession with the Japanese, Stark concluded that it was Hitler's Germany that posed the greater and more immediate danger, and he argued that the fourth of these alternatives—Plan D, or "Plan Dog" in navy lingo—was the country's best option. "Should we be forced into a war with Japan," he wrote, "we should...avoid operations in the Far East or the mid-Pacific that will prevent the Navy from promptly moving to the Atlantic forces fully adequate to safeguard our interests and policies in the event of British collapse." It was a near-reversal of twenty years of U.S. Navy planning.[14]

Moreover, because the defeat of Germany would necessarily have to be achieved in conjunction with the British, Stark also urged the initiation of

Anglo-American informal staff talks for joint planning. If this was sound strategy, it was also political dynamite. Even a hint that the United States was collaborating with a belligerent power would inflame the powerful isolationist lobby both in the public at large and in the Congress. Roosevelt therefore insisted that if the talks took place at all, they must be unofficial, low-profile, and nonbinding. Even so, it was another large step toward active American involvement.[15]

The staff conversations took place in Washington between January and March 1941. The British were delighted to hear the Americans agree that Germany was the principal foe, and equally pleased when the Americans agreed to "collaborate continually in the formation and execution of strategical policies and plans." To do that, each country agreed to maintain a senior naval liaison officer in the capital of the other. Roosevelt did not formally accept the recommendations—he remained leery of making any official commitment—but neither did he repudiate them. It was characteristic of his managerial style that he preferred to wait and see how things worked themselves out while keeping all of his options open. He did, however, send Rear Admiral Robert L. Ghormley to London to act as an informal liaison.[16]

That same fall, Roosevelt also reorganized the fleet. For a generation and more, the U.S. Navy had structured its fleet in accordance with Mahan's prescription that a great nation should never divide its battleship force. Consequently, the United States possessed one unified battle fleet, and a smaller "scouting force." Ostensibly, the battle fleet could be shuttled from one ocean to the other through the Panama Canal depending on where the threat was greatest, which was precisely why the canal was a linchpin of American security interests. Yet with the Japanese actively threatening to expand in the Pacific, and German U-boats savaging convoys in the Atlantic, the perils were simultaneous. Early in the new year, therefore, Roosevelt ordered that the U.S. Navy be divided into two commands: an Atlantic Fleet and a Pacific Fleet. (A third, much smaller Asiatic Fleet operated out of the Philippines.) It was an acknowledgment that shuttling the fleet from one ocean to another was no longer practicable.

Roosevelt named Admiral Ernest J. King, shown here in his formal navy portrait, to command the newly created Atlantic Fleet. King was a stern, no-nonsense commander who quickly put the fleet on a war footing. His daughter famously said of him that he was "the most even-tempered person in the United States Navy. He is always in a rage."

U.S. National Archives photo no. 80-G-K-13715

To command the Atlantic Fleet, Roosevelt named Rear Admiral Ernest J. King. The career officer was efficient and hardworking, but his behavior was notorious in the service. Cold and brusque, he had no patience with inefficiency and no tolerance for sloppiness, and he would publicly curse his own subordinates if they failed to meet his exacting standards. The army's chief of staff, George C. Marshall, called him "perpetually mean," and Marshall's planning officer, Dwight Eisenhower, who rarely had a bad word to say about anyone, called him "deliberately rude." These characteristics had derailed King's ambition to become chief of naval operations in 1937, a job that had gone instead to the more diplomatic and restrained Harold Stark. King assumed his naval career was over, and he spent several months in what he thought was a twilight tour on the navy's prestigious but only marginally influential General Board. Then in December 1940, Stark and Knox resurrected his career by convincing Roosevelt that King was just the man needed for the new Atlantic Fleet. King, Stark predicted, would "lick things into shape."[17]

He did exactly that, instituting wartime protocols, such as requiring warships to run blacked out at night and to zigzag while under way to throw off lurking U-boats. Crews were called to general quarters regularly, and gunnery drills and torpedo exercises became more frequent. Going much further than

Roosevelt had yet dared to, King issued a general order to his ship captains in which he declared, "We are preparing for—and are now close to—those active operations (commonly called war) which require the exercise and the utilization of the full powers and capabilities of every officer in command status." To make sure no one missed the point, a few days later he issued another message proclaiming, "We are no longer in a peacetime status."[18]

The Pacific Fleet was much larger than King's Atlantic Fleet, and its commander retained the title of commander in chief, U.S. Fleet, or CINCUS. In 1941, the CINCUS was Admiral James O. Richardson, a direct and assertive Texan who, like King, had fixed notions of how things should be managed. Richardson's tenure in command, however, was cut short. The Pacific battleship fleet had arrived in Pearl Harbor, Hawaii, the previous spring, and though the initial plan was for it to return to its permanent base on the West Coast after only a few weeks, Roosevelt decided it should remain there in order to exert a restraining influence on the Japanese. Richardson was unhappy about that, mainly because it complicated both his logistics and his training regimen. He was also annoyed that in order to disguise the reason for the extended stay, the administration had announced that the fleet was remaining in Hawaii because Richardson himself had requested it. Of course he had done no such thing, and he flew to Washington to protest both the decision and the way it had been presented to the public. At one point in his conversation with the president, he offered his unsolicited view that "the senior officers of the Navy do not have the trust and confidence in the civilian leadership of the country that is essential for a successful prosecution of a war in the Pacific." That was a shocking thing to say to the president of the United States, especially one who considered himself a navy man. Roosevelt did not react at the time, for he disliked and avoided personal confrontations, but from that moment on Richardson's days in command were numbered. On February 1, 1941, the same day King was elevated to the rank of full admiral, Roosevelt named Admiral Husband Kimmel to replace Richardson in command of the Pacific Fleet. Angered by his dismissal, Richardson demanded to know the reason. Knox told him: "The last time you were here you hurt the President's feelings."[19]

IN THE SPRING OF 1941, as Hitler's Wehrmacht overran Greece, stamped out opposition in Yugoslavia, and drove the British from Crete, the United States moved ever closer to full belligerency in the North Atlantic. In March, Roosevelt won an important political victory when a sharply divided Congress approved the crucial Lend-Lease Act, which opened the tap for a flood of American aid to Britain. That aid would hardly matter, however, if the Lend-Lease goods could not get to Britain across the North Atlantic. In April 1941, shipping losses to the U-boats nearly doubled from 365,000 tons a month to 687,000 tons, and Stimson urged the president to allow the U.S. Navy to escort convoys carrying Lend-Lease materials.

Two things held Roosevelt back. One was that on April 1, a Republican senator introduced a bill making it illegal for American warships to escort convoys, and the other was Japan's decision to sign a non-aggression pact with the Soviet Union, clearing the way for a Japanese move into the South Pacific. Amidst these pressures at home and abroad, Roosevelt backed away from authorizing active escorts in the Atlantic and instead simply expanded the area of America's Neutrality Patrols. He remained characteristically coy about exactly what it was those patrolling warships were doing. When at a press conference on April 25 he was asked about public criticism that he was using U.S. Navy warships to escort convoys, he insisted that "patrols" were not escorts. "If by calling a cow a horse... you think that makes the cow a horse?" he quipped to the reporters. "I don't think so." But of course it was FDR who was calling a cow a horse. When a reporter called him on it by asking, "Mr. President can you tell us the difference between a patrol and a convoy?" FDR shot back: "You know the difference between a cow and a horse?"[20]

Whatever they were called, King had to coordinate the expanded patrols, and to do that he openly declared a "war mobilization" for the Atlantic Fleet. Roosevelt bulked up King's command by transferring the aircraft carrier *Yorktown* and four destroyers from the Pacific to the Atlantic. An even larger force, including three battleships and four cruisers, followed in June. He made the transfers quietly, with the ships sailing a few at a time under sealed orders. He remained reluctant to do anything that might appear deliberately provocative. At a cabinet meeting on May 23 (the day before the *Bismarck* sank the *Hood*) he told his cabinet, "I am not willing to fire the first shot." Perhaps not, but he was walking a fine line. Interior secretary Harold Ickes assumed that Roosevelt was "waiting for the Germans to create an incident."[21]

Hitler wouldn't do it. Having decided to invade the Soviet Union as soon as the Balkans were pacified, he was determined to do nothing that might draw the United States into the war, at least not until Stalin was defeated. When the United States sent a brigade of Marines to occupy Iceland in June, only days before the scheduled invasion of Russia, Erich Raeder argued vehemently with Hitler that it was a virtual act of war and that the Kriegsmarine, and particularly its U-boats, should be unleashed against the meddlesome Americans. Hitler turned him down. The Russians came first, he told Raeder, and he instructed him to order the U-boat skippers that "weapons are not to be used" against the Americans regardless of the provocation.[22]

That same June, news arrived in Washington that a German U-boat (the U-69) had sunk a United States merchant steamer, the *Robin Moor*. There had been no casualties, for the German U-boat commander, in conformance with rules agreed to back in 1936, though seldom honored, had stopped the *Robin Moor*, demanded to see its papers, and then, deciding that it was carrying contraband goods (some target rifles and ammunition), ordered the passengers and crew into lifeboats before sinking the ship. The incident had occurred weeks earlier, but news of it had been delayed until the lifeboats were found and the passengers rescued. It lacked the drama and the carnage of the *Lusitania* sinking back in 1915, but it was an undeniable casus belli if Roosevelt wanted to make an issue of it. Instead, Roosevelt merely delivered a defiant message to Congress. Not only did he doubt the will of the country to back him in a more confrontational posture, he continued to hope that the British could prevail in the Battle of the Atlantic without the United States having to become an active belligerent.[23]

Once German divisions crossed the Soviet border on June 22 and it became clear that Hitler's full attention was directed eastward, Stark thought the moment had come for the U.S. Navy to begin the undisguised escort of Atlantic convoys. Roosevelt initially agreed, then backed away again when the Japanese occupied French Indochina. Facing a two-ocean crisis, he was reluctant to commit fully to the Atlantic while the situation in the Pacific remained so volatile. In a letter to Ickes, he bemoaned the fact that "I simply have not got enough Navy to go around."[24]

He did, however, finally decide to share escort duties with the British. A few weeks later, in mid-July, as he sat in the White House with Harry Hopkins, he tore a map of the Atlantic Ocean out of the pages of *National Geographic*. Spreading it out on a table, he took a pencil and drew a north-south line on it from a point two hundred miles west of Iceland down to the Azores, roughly approximating the 26th meridian. He told Hopkins to inform Churchill that the U.S. Navy would assume responsibility for convoy security west of that line, which would allow the thinly stretched Royal Navy to focus its efforts on the war zones closer to Europe. It was another tie linking the British and American navies.[25]

ON SEPTEMBER 4, 1941, the USS *Greer*, one of the recommissioned four-stack destroyers, was en route to Iceland carrying mail and supplies for the six thousand U.S. Marines who had been sent there in June. As it breasted the choppy seas, an RAF long-range patrol plane flew overhead and signaled by blinker light that a surfaced U-boat was ten miles away. The *Greer*'s commanding officer, Lieutenant Commander Laurence H. Frost, ordered a change in course to close on it. Frost had no intention of attacking the U-boat; his plan was to track and report its position in conformance with standing orders.[26]

The U-boat had submerged by the time Frost found it, and he began tracking it with his sonar. The skipper of U-652, with the *Greer*'s sonar pinging relentlessly in his ears and his batteries running low, had no way of knowing the nationality of the vessel that was pursuing him so relentlessly. The British patrol plane dropped several depth charges, all of which missed, but since he was submerged, the U-boat captain could not see the source of the explosives and concluded that they had come from the destroyer above him. After three and a half hours, he worked himself into position to fire two torpedoes at his tormentor. Both missed. Having been attacked, however, Frost responded by dropping a flurry of depth charges of his own. Neither vessel was damaged, but it was the first exchange of live ammunition between German and American naval forces.[27]

Roosevelt expressed outrage at the German affront in a fireside chat a week later. Whether his outrage was genuine or feigned, he told his radio audience that the *Greer* was "proceeding on a legitimate mission," and the German U-boat had fired the torpedo "with deliberate design to sink her." As a result, he announced, American vessels in the North Atlantic would no longer wait for a proximate threat before opening fire. "When you see a rattlesnake," he declared, "you do not wait until he has struck before you crush him." From now on, Roosevelt declared, American warships in the Atlantic would shoot first.[28]

Raeder understood this announcement to be a virtual declaration of war, at least at sea, and in a meeting with Hitler at Wolf's Lair, the Führer's military headquarters in East Prussia, he argued that Roosevelt's announcement meant there was "no longer any difference between British and American ships." He urged that the U-boats should be allowed to attack any warship escorting a convoy "in any operational area at any time." Again Hitler turned him down. He told Raeder that he expected a decisive result in Russia soon, and until then the U-boats must continue to exercise restraint.[29]

For his part, Roosevelt decided that the time had come for him to meet Churchill face-to-face. In the kind of cloak-and-dagger staging he enjoyed, he sneaked away from Washington on a supposed fishing trip and secretly boarded Admiral King's Atlantic Fleet flagship, the heavy cruiser *Augusta*, off Martha's Vineyard. The *Augusta* carried him to Placentia Bay, on the south coast of Newfoundland, where on August 5 he and Churchill met for a four-day conference. Churchill himself arrived on board the battleship *Prince of Wales*, the vessel that had tangled with the *Bismarck* in the Denmark Strait ten weeks before. Once the meeting had concluded and became public knowledge, it dominated the news on both sides of the Atlantic. It was not an alliance, and the only formal document that emerged was the so-called Atlantic Charter, a list of principles that both sides agreed on to guide them in any postwar settlement, including "the right of all peoples to choose the form of government under which they will live." The real significance, as Churchill certainly appreciated, was that the meeting had taken place at all.[30]

The next month, in accordance with the president's directive, the U.S. Navy began escorting convoys in the western half of the North Atlantic. The first of them was HX-150, a fast convoy out of Halifax originally composed of some fifty ships, though several dropped out early due to engine trouble. Canadian destroyers brought the convoy to a point south of Newfoundland, where on September 16, five U.S. Navy destroyers took over the escort duty. For ten days the convoy plowed eastward, zigzagging at nine knots through typically rough North Atlantic weather. Despite a number of imagined sightings and even the dropping of a few depth charges, there were no actual U-boat attacks, and on September 25, the Americans turned the convoy over to the British at a pre-designated mid-ocean meeting point (MOMP). There they received thanks and a brisk "cheerio" from their Royal Navy counterparts before the Americans turned north to Iceland to refuel.[31]

Convoy SC-48, which left Sydney two weeks later, was less fortunate. Again Canadians turned the convoy over to the Americans only a few days out. The trouble began late on the night of October 15. The presence of at least one U-boat became evident when a merchant ship in the convoy suddenly exploded. Over the next several hours, in what by now was an all-too-familiar pattern, U-boats attacked on the surface under the cover of darkness. The American escort commanders fired star shells into the night sky and steamed about purposefully, though to no avail, and periodic explosions continued throughout the night. Dawn brought a respite, and the convoy plowed doggedly eastward through the daylight hours of October 16.

That night, however, the U-boats were back. By now additional escorts from a westbound convoy (ON-24) had converged on the area, giving SC-48 an unusually strong escort of seven destroyers and seven Flower-class corvettes. One of the new arrivals was the USS *Kearny*, a relatively new *Gleaves*-class destroyer, thirty-four feet longer and 600 tons heavier than the old four-stackers. Amidst the confusion of a night battle imperfectly illuminated by drifting star shells and the occasional exploding ship, the skipper of the *Kearny*, Lieutenant Commander Anthony L. Danis, suddenly saw a British corvette cutting across his bow dead ahead of him, and he ordered emergency left rudder. Turning in a tight circle, and silhouetted against a burning freighter, the *Kearny* made an irresistible target for Kapitänleutnant Joachim Preuss in the U-568. Preuss fired a three-torpedo spread, and the middle torpedo hit the *Kearny* flush on her starboard side.[32]

The explosion destroyed the Number One Fire Room and sent jets of scalding steam as high as the bridge; it knocked out all electrical power and both internal and external communications. For a moment it seemed the ship might be lost. Instead, damage control teams shored up the collapsing bulkheads, and the engineering team (colloquially called the "black gang") managed to get the port-side engine working. Within an hour the ship was under way again at three knots, and by dawn it was making ten. Escorted by the *Greer*, the *Kearny* managed to limp into harbor in Iceland with eleven killed and twenty-two wounded.[33]

The incident marked the first official shedding of American blood in combat in World War II. Ignoring the fact that the *Kearny* had been actively engaged in combat operations, Roosevelt announced that "history has

The USS *Kearny* (in foreground) alongside the destroyer USS *Monssen* in Reykjavik, Iceland, after being torpedoed by the U-568 on October 17, 1941. Note the torpedo hole amidships on her starboard side.

U.S. National Archives photo no. 80-G-28788

recorded who fired the first shot." He insisted that "America has been attacked" and declared, "We do not propose to take this lying down," adding for dramatic emphasis: "Damn the torpedoes!" Roosevelt may have counted on his listeners to silently add the next line of Admiral Farragut's famous pronouncement at Mobile Bay in 1864: "Full speed ahead!"[34]

In the wake of this event, the leaders of both the German and American navies urged their governments to declare war. Raeder again pleaded with Hitler to remove the restrictions he had placed on U-boat operations. What was happening in the North Atlantic, he insisted, was open warfare, and the restraints on the U-boats only put them at an impossible disadvantage, assailed by a foe they were not allowed to fight. For his part, Stark urged Roosevelt to seize the moment to ask Congress for a declaration of war. Stark was convinced the British could not win the war unaided, and he was perfectly willing to jump into the conflict with both feet. Neither head of state would be moved. Hitler was determined to finish off the Russians first, and Roosevelt would not act without the assurance of public support.[35]

The convoys continued. Six days after the *Kearny* was torpedoed, HX-156 departed Halifax and rendezvoused with its American escort group the next day amid heavy seas and poor visibility. For a week the convoy steamed eastward, the tedious duty made more uncomfortable than usual by fierce weather. On the port wing of the convoy, the American destroyer *Reuben James* rolled precariously, and crewmen held fast to the lifelines as they made their way along the treacherous decks.

Around 3:00 a.m. on October 30, Kapitänleutnant Erich Topp of the U-552 caught a glimpse of the convoy through his Leitz binoculars. He radioed the coordinates to Dönitz at Kernevel and then began stalking it. Near five-thirty, just before dawn, he decided to make one quick attack before the sun came up, and the closest vessel to him was a four-stack destroyer guarding the port flank of the convoy. Topp fired a two-torpedo spread, then sent off another quick contact report before diving. The *Reuben James* had just begun a turn to port in response to the intercepted radio emission when one of the torpedoes struck her just ahead of the forward funnel. The torpedo explosion was followed immediately by a huge secondary explosion—almost certainly the torpedo had ignited the ship's magazine, directly below the bridge. Whatever the cause, the whole forward section of the *Reuben James* was blown to pieces. Surviving crewmen struggled to launch the life rafts or slipped into the frigid water, now coated with thick, heavy oil. As the stern of the *Reuben James* sank, the depth charges, which were preset to detonate at specified depths, began to explode, killing many of those struggling in the water. Altogether, 115 men lost their lives, including all of the officers, out of a crew of 160.[36]

In only a few months, the role of American warships in the Atlantic had escalated from conducting "patrols" to active escorting and then to full-scale warfare. Even now, however, neither side would officially acknowledge what was happening. Hitler was frustrated that his expected triumph in the east had been slowed by the Red Army's scorched-earth tactics. When, after a costly siege of Odessa, German divisions finally marched into the city on October 16 they found only smoldering ruins. Clearly the war in Russia would take longer, and cost more, than Hitler had planned. As for Roosevelt, there was still no popular consensus for the United States to enter the war. In his diary, Harold Ickes noted, "Apparently the President is going to wait—God knows for how long."[37]

AND THERE WERE STILL THE JAPANESE. On the same day the *Kearny* was torpedoed and German troops entered Odessa, General Hideki Tojo became Japan's prime minister, an event that signaled the final surrender of the Japanese government to army control. This greatly complicated Roosevelt's determination to keep Japan at arm's length while supporting Britain in the Battle of the Atlantic. So far the policies he had adopted to secure that goal—moving the U.S. Pacific Fleet to Hawaii, and imposing economic sanctions—had failed to impress the Japanese. On the other hand, Roosevelt held a trump card: American oil. In 1941 the United States was the world's leading producer and exporter of crude oil, and Japan's desperate need for that oil gave Roosevelt enormous leverage.* Roosevelt was loath to play that card, however, aware that doing so could provoke a final and irreversible crisis.

---

* In 1940, the United States produced nearly 1.5 billion barrels of oil. That was more than six times the output of the world's second-largest producer, which was Venezuela. Middle East oil production in 1940–41 was tiny by comparison.

Roosevelt warned the Japanese that there was a limit to his restraint. In July 1941, three months before Tojo assumed his position as Japan's prime minister, the Japanese used a skirmish between French and Siamese (Thai) soldiers as a justification for sending troops into Indochina. On the twenty-fourth of that month, Roosevelt met with the Japanese ambassador, Kichisaburo Nomura, to tell him bluntly that although he had thus far permitted the continued sale of oil to Japan in the hope of preserving peace, Japan's move into Indochina had created "a situation which necessarily must give the United States serious disquiet." The threat was implicit but unmistakable. Nomura responded with the Japanese government's official line that Free French elements and Chinese influence in Indochina had made it necessary for Japan to occupy the area for its own security. Roosevelt dismissed that rationalization out of hand, but he did offer a possible solution. He suggested that if Japan withdrew its forces from Indochina, the United States, Britain, and Japan could join together to guarantee Indochina's neutrality, turning the province into a kind of Asian Switzerland (Roosevelt's simile). Nomura confessed that "such a step would be very difficult at this time on account of the face-saving element involved on the part of Japan," but he dutifully forwarded the suggestion to Tokyo. There, however, the momentum toward war had become irreversible, and the idea was rejected.[38]

Roosevelt squeezed harder, ordering a freeze on Japanese assets a week later, on August 1, 1941. Even now, however, he refrained from playing the oil card. Hawks in the cabinet, such as treasury secretary Henry Morgenthau, pressed him to cut off all exports, though others warned that such a step would back Japan into a corner and trigger a war. Roosevelt literally threw up his hands and told them to work it out. What emerged was a plan to embargo high-octane aviation fuel, but to allow Japan to buy crude oil at the same level as in past years, though only for cash. As the historian Jonathan Utley has put it, Roosevelt wanted "to bring Japan to its senses, not its knees." Alas, while Roosevelt was meeting with Churchill in Newfoundland, another hawk, assistant secretary of state Dean Acheson, who headed the Foreign Funds Control Committee, suspended Japan's access to cash. The practical effect was that for more than a month Japan also lost access to American oil, which constituted 80 percent of her oil imports. After Roosevelt returned from his meeting with Churchill off Newfoundland and learned what had happened, it was too late to reverse the policy without looking irresolute, and so the de facto embargo stood.[39]

It was decisive. The Japanese had only about eighteen months of oil in reserve, and the embargo forced them to choose between backing down to the Americans or forging ahead with the conquest of South Asia. Tojo and the other generals insisted that there was no choice now but to obtain the essential oil from the orphaned European colonies of British Malaya and the Dutch East Indies. If that meant war with England, Holland, and even with the United States, so be it.[40]

Nomura, who was ignorant of both the government's decision and Yamamoto's Pearl Harbor attack plan, remained in Washington in a last-ditch effort to save the peace. The Tojo government sent him a new set of proposals on November 20, but the terms were so one-sided that Cordell Hull called them "preposterous." The Japanese considered the American counterproposals equally unacceptable. Hull himself concluded that further talks had become useless and that the Japanese were not serious about reaching an agreement.[41]

Hull also knew that Nomura was working under a deadline. For some time the American State Department had been privy to the diplomatic message traffic used by Japan's Foreign Ministry.* He knew that Tokyo had informed Nomura that he had to reach a diplomatic solution before November 29, because after that "things are automatically going to happen." That knowledge was enough to convince Stark to send an alert out to all Pacific commanders. The message, sent on November 27, minced no words: "This dispatch is to be considered a war warning. Negotiations with Japan toward stabilization of conditions in the Pacific have ceased and an aggressive move by Japan is expected within the next few days." The target of such aggressive moves, Stark suggested, might be the Philippines, Thailand, Malaya, or Borneo. In a follow-up message, he cautioned Pacific commanders not to jump the gun: "Undertake no offensive action until Japan has committed an overt act."[42]

By then, the Japanese carrier strike force was already at sea.

---

* These MAGIC, or Purple, intercepts, which concerned Japanese diplomacy, were different from Japanese operational codes, which are discussed in Chapter 13.

CHAPTER 10

OPERATION AI

The Attack on Pearl Harbor

COLD, DENSE, PENETRATING FOG and intermittent snow showers made Hitokappu Bay on Etorofu Island a particularly uncongenial anchorage in November. The largest of the Kuril Islands that stretch in a long chain from Japan's home islands north to the Siberian peninsula of Kamchatka, Etorofu is a lonely and remote outpost. Yet as the sun rose on November 26, 1941, Hitokappu Bay was crowded with warships: six aircraft carriers, two towering battleships, and two heavy cruisers, plus a dozen smaller warships and eight supply vessels, seven of them oil tankers. Assembled in secret, element by element, over a period of weeks, this Japanese battle force with more than four hundred combat aircraft was the largest concentration of naval air power in the world.

Even as Ambassador Nomura struggled hopelessly to salvage the negotiations in Washington, and the generals who ran the Japanese government worked out the details of the strike southward, Admiral Yamamoto had continued to insist that if war with the United States was unavoidable, a preemptive strike on the American battle fleet at Pearl Harbor was essential.

Such a strike would not ensure victory, he acknowledged, but it would incapacitate the Americans long enough to allow the Japanese to complete their conquest of the southern resource area without interference. Critics of Yamamoto's plan noted that sending all six of Japan's big carriers to Hawaii meant that the seizure and occupation of the islands of the South Pacific would have to proceed without them, and that in any case targeting Pearl Harbor, nearly four thousand miles away, was highly risky. Even if the carriers managed to get all the way to Hawaii undetected, which was uncertain at best, there was no assurance that the American battle fleet would be in Pearl Harbor when they arrived. Still Yamamoto had insisted, and in the end the power of his personality was decisive. The force gathered in Hitokappu Bay would be the instrument of that strike.

The concentration of six big carriers into a single unit was a significant departure from conventional views about the employment of aircraft carriers. Both the Americans and the British tended to deploy their aircraft carriers singly, as the Americans did in their fleet exercises, and as the British had done for the strike against the Italian battleships at Taranto. It was a mere commander in the Imperial Japanese Navy, the brilliant and precocious Minoru Genda, who conceived the idea of putting all of Japan's big carriers together into a single task force. He claimed later that he got the idea from watching an American newsreel film of four U.S. carriers maneuvering together. The film was merely a publicity shot, but Genda saw at once that deploying carriers that way for battle would allow Japan to apply Mahan's principle of mass to air warfare. When the two newest Japanese carriers joined the fleet in September, making a total of six, Yamamoto administratively grouped all of them into a single unit, the First Air Fleet. When deployed for combat, they were the Kidō Butai—a term that roughly translates as "Mobile Striking Force."[1]

The commander of this awesome concentration of naval air power was Vice Admiral Chūichi Nagumo. Unlike the confident and ebullient Yamamoto, Nagumo was a worrier by nature who fretted constantly over even the smallest detail. Occasionally he would call junior officers into his presence and solicit their reassurance that things were progressing as they should. Genda was dismissive of Nagumo as "very cautious," and Yamamoto's chief of staff, Matome Ugaki, confided to his diary that Nagumo was "not fully prepared yet to advance in the face of death and gain results two or three times as great as his cost by jumping into the jaws of death." In spite of that, Nagumo was now charged with executing Operation AI: taking a thirty-ship task force across the breadth of the Pacific Ocean to Pearl Harbor.[2]

Organizationally, the six carriers of the Kidō Butai were divided into three carrier divisions (CARDIVs) of two carriers each. CARDIV One was composed of the large but now rather old *Kaga* and *Akagi*, the latter of which Nagumo used as his flagship. Each of these oversized carriers had been built in the 1920s atop the hull of an unfinished battleship or battlecruiser, which gave them a displacement of more than 40,000 tons each. That proved to be something of a mixed blessing, however. On the one hand, they carried an

Japanese Vice Admiral Chūichi Nagumo commanded the carrier strike force (the Kidō Butai) for both the Pearl Harbor raid and the subsequent Battle of Midway. This 1942 photograph hints at his lugubrious outlook.

Naval History and Heritage Command

impressive number of airplanes—as many as ninety in the case of the *Kaga*—but at the same time they could make only about twenty-eight knots, even after they were modernized and updated in the 1930s. That compared unfavorably to newer carriers, which could steam at thirty-four knots.[3]

CARDIV Two was composed of the smaller carriers *Hiryū* and *Sōryū*, each of them displacing only about half the tonnage of the two big carriers. Still, having been built from the keel up as carriers in 1936–37, they could embark sixty to seventy aircraft each and could steam at thirty-four knots. CARDIVs Three and Four were made up of Japan's smaller carriers and were not part of the Kidō Butai. CARDIV Five consisted of Japan's two newest carriers, the *Shōkaku* and *Zuikaku*. Commissioned just two months before, in September, and displacing 30,000 tons, they carried seventy-two airplanes each. When all six carriers operated together, they could theoretically put as many as 430 planes in the air.

Each carrier hosted three types of aircraft—fighters, dive-bombers, and torpedo planes—and in 1941 they were among the most sophisticated carrier-borne airplanes in the world, a full technological generation ahead of British Fulmar and Skua fighters, or the Stringbags the Royal Navy used as attack planes. Japan's principal fighter was the already famous Zero, which had proven so effective in China. At sea, the job of the Zeros was to protect the task force from enemy bombers by flying combat air patrol (CAP) over the task force and escorting the attack planes to their target. On strike missions, they generally flew above the bombers and torpedo planes at fifteen thousand feet so they could dive down on any enemy aircraft that came out to challenge the attackers.

The dive-bomber on the Japanese carriers was the Aichi D3A1, Type 99, which the Americans code-named the "Val." It was a two-seat monoplane with a pilot in front and a radioman/gunner in the rear seat. It could carry one 250-kilogram (551-pound) bomb, plus two 60-kilogram (132-pound) bombs, one under each wing. It borrowed several design elements from Japan's German ally, having a low elliptical wing like the Heinkel and fixed landing gear like the Stuka dive-bombers that had proved so effective against Cunningham in the eastern Mediterranean. Like the Stuka, the Val was designed to approach the target from high altitude, say fifteen thousand

The Nakajima B5N2, Type 97 carrier plane, which the Americans nicknamed the "Kate," was the premier aircraft of the Japanese naval air arm. Capable of dropping either a heavy bomb or a Type 91 torpedo (shown here), it was the best torpedo plane in the world in 1941.

U.S. Naval Institute

feet, and then dive nearly straight down, using the momentum of the dive to aim the bomb it carried, which the pilot released at about fifteen hundred feet. The Val had proved a reliable weapon in China against ground targets and weak opposition, but its indifferent top speed of 242 miles per hour made it vulnerable to modern fighters.[4]

More impressive was the Type 97 carrier attack plane, which the Americans labeled the "Kate." Though the Kate was not significantly larger or faster than the Val, it could carry a much heavier ordnance package of up to two thousand pounds, which meant that it could function either as a level bomber, dropping a heavy 800 kilogram (1,760-pound) bomb from altitude, or as a torpedo plane coming in low with the even heavier Type 91 aerial torpedo. For the attack on Pearl Harbor, the Kates were slotted to act in both capacities. As high-altitude bombers, they were armed with specially modified 16-inch battleship shells weighing as much as 2,000 pounds. The thought was that when dropped from ten thousand feet, the momentum generated would enable them to smash through the armored decks of American battleships.[5]

As demonstrated at Taranto and elsewhere, air-launched torpedoes were ship-killers, and they were central to Japanese battle doctrine. Using them in the shallow waters of Pearl Harbor, however, posed a serious problem. When dropped from airplanes, torpedoes first plunged to a depth of eighty to a hundred feet before rising up to twenty or thirty feet for the run into the target, and Pearl Harbor was only about forty feet deep. For months the Japanese had sought a solution to this problem, carefully studying the success of the British Stringbags at Taranto, and they solved it quite literally in the nick of time. Breakaway wooden fins attached to the torpedoes arrested their descent so that they plunged to only about thirty or forty feet. The new torpedoes were distributed in Hitokappu Bay only days before the carriers began to haul up their anchors, and the attack on the ships in Pearl Harbor would be their operational debut.[6]

THE KIDŌ BUTAI GOT UNDER WAY at 6:00 a.m. on November 26. (That same day in Washington, President Roosevelt signed a law establishing the fourth Thursday in November as the official date of the Thanksgiving holiday.) Once the ships of the Japanese fleet cleared the harbor, the carriers sorted themselves into two columns of three ships each. The destroyers scouted ahead while the battleships and heavy cruisers took up positions to port and starboard. The essential oil tankers trailed astern.

A worrier by instinct, Nagumo was haunted by several concerns. The first was that his task force would be sighted somewhere along its nearly four-thousand-mile journey before it ever got close enough to Hawaii to launch planes. The need for stealth was the main reason the Kidō Butai had assembled so far north, above the 40th parallel, where shipping was scarce and frequent rain squalls provided a curtain of concealment. Of course, all of Nagumo's ships operated under strict radio silence, and to ensure it, the transmission keys on the ships were sealed shut. They could still receive messages, of course, which was critical, since in theory Nagumo's force could still be recalled if Nomura somehow convinced the Americans to retract their embargo, though no one expected that to happen.[7]

Nagumo also worried about fuel. His big carriers had been packed with extra fuel before departing, but even at a modest fourteen knots they could not make the seven-thousand-mile round trip to Hawaii without refueling several times at sea, a task that was difficult at the best of times, and especially

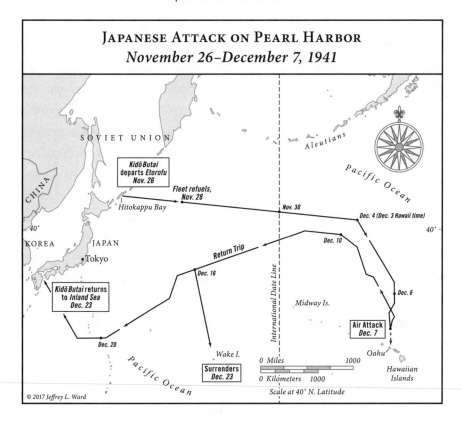

JAPANESE ATTACK ON PEARL HARBOR
November 26–December 7, 1941

fraught in the rough seas along the 40th parallel. The first refueling took place only two days out, on November 28. As the warships came gingerly alongside the tankers and fuel hoses suspended from support wires were passed between them, one of the wires snapped, whipping across the deck and sweeping several men overboard. It did little to improve Nagumo's lugubrious frame of mind.[8]

Another concern was that even if his force managed to get within striking distance of Pearl Harbor without being detected, the American battle fleet might not be there when his planes arrived. They could be at sea, or anchored in Lahaina Roads off Maui. Japanese intelligence estimated that the Americans had a total of four aircraft carriers and eight battleships in the Pacific, and Yamamoto had suggested to Nagumo that the destruction of half that force—two carriers and four battleships—would constitute a strategic success by rendering the Americans incapable of interfering with the move into the South Pacific that was already under way. The Japanese estimate of the number of battleships in Pearl Harbor was accurate enough, though there were only two American carriers, not four, at Pearl. As noted earlier, Roosevelt had quietly sent the *Yorktown* to the Atlantic, and the *Saratoga* was on the West Coast for a refit. Even more disastrous to Japanese plans, the two remaining American carriers departed Pearl Harbor even as Nagumo was en route. In response to Harold Stark's "war warning" of November 27, Husband Kimmel sought to beef up the defenses of two remote outposts—Wake and Midway—by sending a squadron of fighter planes to each. On November 28, he dispatched the *Enterprise* to Wake Island, two thousand miles to the west, and a week later, on December 5, he sent the *Lexington* to Midway, thirteen hundred miles to the north. From the outset, Yamamoto had insisted that "our prime target should be U.S. carriers," yet as Nagumo's force approached the launch coordinates north of Oahu on December 6, there were no American carriers at all in Pearl Harbor.[9]

THE AMERICANS WERE VERY MUCH AWARE that war with Japan could break out at any moment, though virtually no one in Washington or any-where else thought the flash point would be Hawaii. If American territories were in jeopardy, the Philippines seemed the most likely target. The war warning sent out on November 27 prompted the U.S. Army commander in Hawaii, Lieutenant General Walter C. Short, to guard against sabotage by Hawaii's 160 thousand residents of Japanese ancestry by ordering that the army's pursuit planes be clustered together in rows on the runways, where they could be closely guarded. For his part, Kimmel was thinking offensively. Officially, the defense of Pearl Harbor was the army's job, and Kimmel believed his primary responsibility was to ensure that the fleet was in a condition to attack Japanese possessions in the Marshall Islands. Consequently, he focused on an intensive training pro-gram, which was made difficult by virtue of regular transfers of sailors from the Pacific to the Atlantic. Neither American commander took seri-ously the idea that the Japanese might open the war with an attack on Hawaii. Rear Admiral Patrick Bellinger, commander of Patrol Wing Two, had several dozen long-range Catalina PBY aircraft at his disposal, but only seven of them were aloft, and four of those were engaged in exercises rather than searching.[10]

Meanwhile, American intelligence lost track of the whereabouts of Japan's big carriers. By using deceptive radio transmissions and committing Nagumo's force to the seldom-traveled northern route, the Japanese had effectively pulled a curtain across the activities of the Kidō Butai. When Kimmel asked his intelligence officer, Commander Edwin Layton, where Japan's carriers were, Layton had to confess that he did not know. Kimmel reacted with mock astonishment: "What!" he cried. "You don't know?" That was followed by a sentence that has been much quoted since: "Do you mean to say they could be rounding Diamond Head and you wouldn't know it?" Kimmel's comment was more banter than rebuke. He knew that Layton did the best he could with the tiny fragments of data available to him. The Americans had not yet cracked the Japanese operational code, and even if they had, the radio discipline of the Japanese would have disguised the location and activities of the Kidō Butai. Moreover, neither Kimmel nor Layton was a recipient of the diplomatic message traffic that was available in Washington.[11]

The first proof that the Japanese were on the verge of a major offensive came not from radio message traffic or the discovery of the Kidō Butai but from British observers in the South China Sea who spotted two large invasion fleets, one of them an armada of more than a hundred ships, heading south from Japanese home waters toward the Taiwan Strait. It was the largest naval deployment of the war to date, and Roosevelt was furious at this unmistakable evidence of Japanese double-dealing. Even as their diplomats in Washington talked peace, invasion forces were already at sea steaming southward. Stark wondered aloud if that was enough to justify an American military response. Even Harry Hopkins suggested that since war was apparently both unavoidable and imminent, "it was too bad we could not strike the first blow." Roosevelt nodded thoughtfully, then said, "No, we can't do that. We are a democracy and a peaceful people." As in his war with the German U-boats in the Atlantic, Roosevelt was determined that the United States would not fire the first shot.[12]

The Japanese were perfectly willing to fire the first shot, and at 6:00 a.m. on the morning of December 7, some 220 miles north of Oahu, the six carriers of the Kidō Butai turned into the wind and increased speed to twenty-five knots to launch planes. The Zeros lifted off first, climbing swiftly to circle above the task force while the heavily burdened Vals and Kates roared off six carrier decks in a carefully choreographed sequence. In only fifteen minutes, the Japanese launched 183 aircraft—a remarkable display of efficiency—and by 6:45, the entire formation was heading southward toward Oahu.[13]

At that very moment, a lookout on the American destroyer USS *Ward*, patrolling the entrance to Pearl Harbor, spotted what was clearly the feather of a submarine periscope. The *Ward's* skipper, Lieutenant Commander William W. Outerbridge, on only his second day in command, promptly opened fire, and the second shot punched through the sub's fragile hull. As the sub slipped into the *Ward's* wake, Outerbridge dropped several depth charges on it. Satisfied that he had sunk it, he sent a report at 6:53.

What the *Ward* had sunk was a midget submarine, one of five the Japanese committed to the Pearl Harbor attack. Carried piggyback all the way from Japan on top of five fleet submarines, the seventy-eight-foot-long, two-man subs had been uncoupled from their host vessels off the entrance to Pearl Harbor late on the night of December 6. Though Yamamoto thought the whole midget sub program a waste of resources, others on his staff were enamored of the idea of sneaking into the enemy lair and picking off survivors of the air attack. Yamamoto's chief of staff, Matome Ugaki, admired the young volunteers on the subs who were eager to sacrifice themselves for their country, and he expected great things of them. In the end, their only contribution was to provide what ought to have been an early warning of the coming air attack. Alas, Outerbridge's report did not cause alarm bells to ring. As his report worked its way up through the chain of command that Sunday morning, it met with skepticism, uncertainty, and caution at each step, until it was too late to make a difference.[14]

Another lost opportunity to sound the alarm occurred only minutes later, at 7:02, when a radar station on Kahuku Point, on Oahu's north shore, detected a large number of inbound planes coming from the north. The radar installation was new and the enlisted operators were inexperienced trainees, which may have sown doubt about the accuracy of their report.

Moreover, since a flight of B-17s was expected that morning from California along that same trajectory, the duty officer told the radar technicians to "forget about it."[15]

Other than the few destroyers patrolling off the entrance and three PBY Catalina seaplanes on routine patrol, the great American naval base at Pearl Harbor slumbered. Though Japanese intelligence informed Nagumo that there were nine American battleships in Pearl Harbor, one of the nine was the *Utah*, a former battleship now used as a target ship, and another, the *Pennsylvania*, was in dry dock for repairs. The other seven were moored on the southern rim of Ford Island in the middle of the anchorage. The *Nevada* was anchored at the eastern end of the line, with the *Arizona* just ahead of her inboard of the repair ship USS *Vestal*. Four more were tied up in pairs, with the *Tennessee* and *Maryland* inboard of the *West Virginia* and *Oklahoma*. *California*, like the *Nevada*, was moored by herself at the western head of the line. To the Japanese pilots swooping in from the north, it was a thrilling and glorious sight. To announce that the attack had achieved complete surprise, the flight leader, Commander Mitsuo Fuchida, broke radio silence for the first time since the Kidō Butai had left Hitokappu Bay to broadcast a predetermined code signal: "Tora, tora, tora" ("Tiger, tiger, tiger").[16]

The Japanese attack plan was for the bombers and the torpedo planes to make separate runs, but last-second confusion led them to attack simultaneously. It hardly mattered. The Kate level bombers flew in at ten thousand feet while the torpedo planes swept around the anchorage to approach from the south at five hundred feet. Almost every American who saw them assumed they were friendly aircraft engaged in maneuvers; a few officers were annoyed that some hotshot pilots were apparently showing off by flying so low on a Sunday morning, and they sought to read the plane numbers so they could report them to their squadron commanders. Then the first bombs exploded. In the midst of the excitement, formal protocols were omitted. On board the *Nevada*, a voice over the public address system announced: "This is a real Jap air attack and no shit!"[17]

Within minutes, the battleships *Maryland* and *Tennessee* were each hit by a pair of bombs; three more exploded close alongside the *Arizona*. A fourth was a direct hit. At 8:10, an armor-piercing 16-inch shell dropped from ten

The battleship USS *Arizona* was hit by a modified 16-inch shell dropped from altitude that ignited her forward magazine. She sank quickly with 1,177 men still trapped inside. She remains the final resting place for 1,102 American sailors and Marines.

Naval History and Heritage Command

thousand feet punched through the *Arizona*'s five-inch-thick armored deck, penetrated to the magazine, and exploded. The resulting fireball ripped the heart out of the ship. The *Arizona* sank almost immediately, taking most of her crew down with her.[18]

Meanwhile, the Kate torpedo planes that had circled around to the south came in low over the anchorage, untroubled by American fighters, to drop their specially modified torpedoes. Until that moment, the Kate pilots did not know if the torpedoes would work in the shallow waters of Pearl Harbor. They did. Seven of them struck the *West Virginia*, and five others hit the *Oklahoma*; a few hundred yards to the west, two torpedoes hit the *California*. The Japanese even expended several torpedoes on the target ship *Utah*.

The explosion of the *Arizona* left the water around the *Nevada* filled with debris and burning oil. The *Nevada*'s captain was ashore on that Sunday morning and the senior officer on board was Lieutenant Commander J. F. Thomas. He decided that the safest thing to do was get under way. Thanks to the duty officer, Ensign Joseph Taussig, the *Nevada* had two boilers on line, and that allowed her to head slowly out into the channel. Seeing this, the Japanese pilots sought to sink her in the harbor entrance in order to plug up the harbor. After she was hit by five bombs and one torpedo, Thomas realized he could not make it safely to open water, and he steered the *Nevada* toward Hospital Point, where the big ship grounded.[19]

The initial raid lasted about half an hour. Then, after a brief hiatus, a second wave of 167 more planes arrived. They focused on finishing off those capital ships that were still afloat or only partially damaged. The Americans were alert this time and succeeded in shooting down twenty-four of the planes, yet by ten o'clock four American battleships had been sunk and three more severely damaged. Altogether, the Japanese sank or damaged 18 ships and destroyed 188 American planes (96 army and 92 navy) while damaging 159 others. The attack caused the death of 2,403 U.S. servicemen, nearly half of them on the ill-fated *Arizona*.[20]

For the Japanese, it was a more complete triumph, and with fewer losses, than even the most optimistic planners had imagined. Pre-battle estimates had assumed the loss of two of their own carriers—a third of the Kidō Butai. Instead, only twenty-nine planes were lost in addition to the five midget submarines. The sole disappointment was that the American carriers had not been in port. Once the Japanese planes returned to their carriers, there was talk among the giddy pilots about staying around to finish the job. Having all but eliminated American airpower on Oahu, they had command of the skies and could take their time wrecking the Navy Yard and other targets of opportunity. Nagumo would have none of it. From the start he had conceived of the raid as a desperate long shot, and he was hugely relieved, and more than a little surprised, that it had gone so well. His assignment had been to cripple the American fleet to the point where it could not interfere with the movement into South Asia; having done that, he decided it was time to go. Once he recovered the surviving planes from the second strike, he set a course to take the Kidō Butai back to Japan.

None of the celebrating pilots aboard the six Japanese carriers could possibly have known that just the day before, on the other side of the world, Marshal Georgy Zhukov had directed a counterattack of half a million Russian soldiers against German forces outside Moscow. Before the winter was over, the Russians would push the Germans some two hundred miles to the west. Japan had joined the war at almost the precise moment that the German juggernaut was exposed as vulnerable after all.

ROOSEVELT LEARNED OF THE JAPANESE ATTACK while it was still in progress. Navy secretary Frank Knox called the White House at 1:17 in the afternoon, Washington time, with the news. The president was initially incredulous. "No!" he shouted, slamming his hand down on the top of the desk. Soon enough, however, his surprise and skepticism turned to grim determination. For his part, Churchill found out about the attack several hours later from a radio report while he was at Chequers. Coincidentally, he was hosting the American ambassador, John G. "Gil" Winant, at dinner. Churchill immediately placed a telephone call to Roosevelt. "Mr. President," he said when Roosevelt was on the line, "what's this about Japan?" "It's quite true," Roosevelt replied, calm by now. "They have attacked us at Pearl Harbor. We are all in the same boat now."[21]

However tactically successful, the Japanese raid on Pearl Harbor stands alongside Hitler's invasion of the Soviet Union as one of the most reckless and irresponsible decisions in the history of warfare, and along with the Russian counterattack outside Moscow marked a decisive turning point in the Second World War. It brought the United States and its vast industrial resources fully into the conflict and galvanized American public opinion in such a way as to ensure not only an eventual Allied triumph, but what Roosevelt in his December 8 speech to Congress called "absolute victory."[22]

In view of that, it is easy to overlook the fact that the raid on Pearl Harbor was only one element of Japan's grand strategy. In fact, the Japanese began to seize the southern resource area—the actual target of all their planning—at virtually the same moment their aircraft were crippling the American battle fleet. On December 4 and 5, as Nagumo turned his carriers to the southeast (and Zhukov assembled his divisions outside Moscow), Japanese invasion flotillas left Hainan Island, in the South China Sea, and Cam Ranh Bay, in Indochina, to steam southward into the Gulf of Siam. Even as the first plane lifted off from Nagumo's carriers, a Japanese invasion force of twenty-one transports, escorted by a light cruiser and four destroyers, began landing soldiers on the north coast of British Malaya at Kota Bharu, just below the border with Thailand (formerly Siam). Ninety minutes later (as Fuchida's planes were lining up for their attack run on Battleship Row), a second invasion force of twenty-two transports, escorted by a battleship and five cruisers plus seven destroyers, began landing soldiers at Singora Beach inside Siam, 130 miles up the Kra Peninsula.[23]

THE KRA PENINSULA is an oversized appendix that extends southward from the Asian mainland toward the principal islands of the Dutch East Indies. The upper (northern) half of the peninsula was part of Siam; the southern half was the British colony of Malaya, and at its southernmost tip was the bastion of Singapore, which the British often referred to as the Gibraltar of the Pacific since, like Gibraltar, it guarded a critical maritime choke point: the Strait of Malacca, the most direct route from the Pacific to the Indian Ocean. Because of that, and because it outflanked planned Japanese operations in the Dutch East Indies, Singapore was a particular target of Japan's move southward. The British had ruled Singapore politically and socially for a hundred years, often treating the native population with casual condescension. Those circumstances had bred self-assurance if not smugness among the decision-makers and contributed to what one author labeled a "sluggish and uncoordinated" response to the Japanese threat. When he learned that the Japanese had landed at Kota Bharu in British Malaya, the British commander in Singapore, Lieutenant General Arthur Ernest Percival, urged British imperial troops to drive the "little fellows" into the sea.[24]

At Singora, the Thai defenders fought half-heartedly for several hours before the Thai government decided that the wisest course was to accept Japanese occupation. Eventually Siam signed an agreement granting the Japanese the run of the country and full use of its transportation system.

The fighting was more sustained at Kota Bharu, where the British 8th Indian Brigade sank one Japanese transport and damaged two others before being forced to give way. Bad weather interfered with British attempts to counterattack from the air, and in any case the Japanese Zeros were vastly superior to the American-made Brewster B-339 Buffalo fighters flown by the British. By December 9, the Japanese were in full control of the beachhead at Kota Bharu and moving inland.[25]

British planners in London, including Dudley Pound and Churchill, had long been aware of the Japanese threat to Malaya, but given the press of war in Europe, they were loath to add another front or another enemy, and, like the Americans, they had focused their efforts on deterring Japan from launching an attack in the first place. To do that, Pound had suggested sending several of the Royal Navy's older battleships, which he felt could be spared, to Trincomalee, on the east coast of Ceylon. There they could not only act as a deterrent to Japan but also carry out convoy escort duties in the Indian Ocean.[26]

Churchill rejected the idea. He did not think that a handful of older battleships would have the same psychological effect on the Japanese as a few of the new and more powerful *King George V*–class battleships. In particular, he wanted to send the *Prince of Wales*, the ship that had fought the *Bismarck* in the Denmark Strait and then had carried him to Newfoundland to meet Roosevelt. The foreign secretary, Anthony Eden, agreed, writing in his diary that nothing could be more salutary to Anglo-Japanese relations "than [the] arrival of [a] modern battleship or two at Singapore." Pound wanted to keep the *Prince of Wales* in home waters to counter the *Tirpitz* in the Baltic or the battlecruiser twins *Scharnhorst* and *Gneisenau* at Brest. As usual, however, he gave way before the confident assertions and powerful personality of the prime minister. Consequently, the *Prince of Wales* headed south, first to Cape Town, South Africa, then into the Indian Ocean to pick up the battlecruiser *Repulse* as a consort, before steaming on to Singapore.[27]

Like all battlecruisers, the *Repulse* was heavily armed but weakly armored. She had a powerful battery of six 15-inch guns, but only one to two inches of deck armor, which made her vulnerable to plunging fire or to air attack. Initially Churchill had wanted to add the new aircraft carrier *Indomitable* to this task force, but the *Indomitable* had run aground in the West Indies while undergoing sea trials, and had to go into the yards for repair. In the end, therefore, only the *Prince of Wales* and *Repulse*, plus four destroyers, made it to Singapore, where they arrived on December 2. The absence of a carrier was deemed acceptable on the grounds that planes from shore bases in Malaya could provide the necessary air cover. Besides, the purpose of sending these ships—dubbed Force Z—was to impress the Japanese, not to fight them.[28]

Captain John Leach still commanded the *Prince of Wales*, but the overall commander of Force Z was Admiral Tom Phillips, who due to his small stature (five feet four inches) was known in the fleet as "Tom Thumb." His first action upon arrival in Singapore on December 2 was to fly to Manila to coordinate plans with his American naval counterpart, Admiral Thomas C. Hart. He returned to Singapore on December 7. Within hours, he learned that the Japanese had wrecked the American battle fleet at Pearl Harbor and that the new common enemy was landing in force at Kota Bharu. That completely exploded the notion that his ships could serve as a deterrent, and in light of these new circumstances, it was unclear what his duty was. One option was to withdraw from Singapore and combine his force with the Dutch and the Americans to constitute what Mahan would have called a "fleet in being," a force strong enough that it might at least complicate further Japanese moves. That struck Phillips as timid. He was a no-nonsense disciplinarian and traditionalist of the old school who had spent occasional weekends with Churchill. He understood and appreciated Churchill's preference for bold and courageous action. It was perhaps inevitable, then, that he should decide instead to sally forth into the Gulf of Siam and challenge the Japanese invaders. With luck, he might catch the enemy invasion fleet in a vulnerable state off the beaches.[29]

PHILLIPS PUT TO SEA on the evening of December 8 with his two capital ships and four destroyers, and headed northeast into the South China Sea. He intended to steam north until he was opposite the Japanese beachhead, then turn west and descend on the invasion fleet from seaward. As the two ships left port, the captain of the *Repulse*, William Tennant, offered a short address to the crew: "We are off to look for trouble," he began. "I expect we shall find it."[30]

Barely seven hours into his deployment, at a few minutes before eleven o'clock, he received a startling radio report from Singapore: "Fighter protection on Wednesday, 10th, will not, repeat not, be possible." The Japanese had overrun the airfield at Kota Bharu, and the surviving British aircraft had fallen back southward. Despite that, Phillips thought he still might be able to spring a surprise on the invaders if he could avoid early detection. His best hope—indeed, his only chance now—was to find the enemy fleet before he was himself spotted by Japanese aircraft. What he did not know was that he had already been identified by a Japanese submarine, the I-56, which had reported his position, course, and speed.[31]

Alerted by that report, Rear Admiral Sadaichi Matsunaga, commanding the 22nd Air Flotilla in southern Indochina, readied an air strike by land-based Nell and Betty bombers. There were some delays in getting the big two-engine bombers rearmed with armor-piercing ordnance for use against warships, and by the time they took off, it had become a cloudy and moonless night. As a result, they were unable to find the British ships. In part this was because Phillips, concluding that he had somehow missed the retiring Japanese fleet, decided not to press his luck further, especially without air cover, and had turned south to return to base.

Then, just past midnight, he got another radio message from Percival in Singapore that the Japanese were landing at Kuantan, halfway down the peninsula from Kota Bharu, and only 150 miles west of his current position. Phillips assumed that Percival's message was suggestive as well as informative, and he assumed, too, that Percival would send planes from Singapore to attack the invaders. He did not confirm this, however, in order to maintain radio silence. He turned west toward the Malay coast, intending to fall upon the landing flotilla at dawn. Still maintaining radio silence, he did not notify Percival of his movements. If Günther Lütjens on the *Bismarck* had been entirely too free in his use of the wireless in the North Atlantic, Phillips erred in the other direction by refusing to use it at all, and because Percival did not know that Phillips was closing on Kuantan, he did not order a supporting air strike.[32]

Dawn arrived at 6:00 a.m. on December 10 with the *Prince of Wales* and *Repulse* closing quickly on the Malay coast. Within the hour, Phillips could see for himself that there were no Japanese forces at Kuantan, nor had there ever been. Percival had passed along an unconfirmed report that proved incorrect. It also proved fatal. Even as Phillips gazed on the unmolested shoreline at Kuantun, Matsunaga was sending out his air fleet of Nell and Betty bombers for a second attempt to locate the British battleships. This time, shortly after ten in the morning on December 10, they found them.[33]

Just over twenty years before, in 1919, the American Brigadier General William "Billy" Mitchell, pressing the case for an independent U.S. air force, had claimed that land-based aircraft could sink battleships at sea. If true, it would make the navy largely redundant as a defender of the American coastline, and the champions of naval power were instinctively skeptical, even scornful. One of those who found such claims "pernicious" was the assistant secretary of the navy at the time, Franklin Roosevelt. To test Mitchell's theory, the army and navy agreed in 1921 to allow planes under Mitchell's direction to bomb an anchored battleship offshore, the former German dreadnaught *Ostfriesland*. After being pummeled from the air for two days, the *Ostfriesland* did indeed sink, though naval observers discounted the test as meaningless since she had been almost literally a sitting duck: at anchor, unmanned, and not shooting back. Twenty years later, the success of torpedo bombers at Taranto and again at Pearl Harbor were a better measure of the capabilities of aircraft against battleships, but in those cases, too, the ships had been at anchor and caught by surprise. On December 10, however, the *Prince of Wales* and *Repulse* were under way, fully alert, and manned by crack crews. Though Billy Mitchell had died in 1936, here, at last, was a true test of what land-based airplanes could do against battleships.[34]

The Japanese sent eighty-eight planes, sixty-one of them armed with torpedoes, to attack the two British ships. In the first attack, nine Nells dropped their bombs from ten thousand feet in a tight pattern. The sea around both ships fairly boiled with the explosion of near misses, and one bomb actually struck the *Repulse* amidships, though it did only minor damage. Fifteen minutes later, sixteen Bettys conducted a torpedo attack on the *Prince of*

This photograph, taken from a Japanese bomber during the morning high-level attack on December 10, 1941, shows the *Prince of Wales* (at top) bracketed by near misses, while the *Repulse* (at bottom) maneuvers to throw off the bombers.

Naval History and Heritage Command

Wales through a cloud of anti-aircraft fire. With so many planes attacking from different vectors, it was impossible for Leach to maneuver to avoid them all. A lieutenant on the *Prince of Wales* watched as "a narrow, pale green streak of rising bubbles " headed directly for the bow of the ship. "Never have I felt so helpless," he recalled. It struck with "a resounding thud." Then came another. And another. One of the torpedoes struck near the stern and, as on the *Bismarck* seven months earlier, the result was catastrophic. Both propellers on the port side were destroyed; the outer propeller shaft was sheared in half, though it continued to turn, and so it sliced through the skin of the ship's hull. The rudder was jammed in place and the ship could not maneuver. As tons of seawater poured in, the *Prince of Wales* took on a thirteen-degree list and slowed to fifteen knots. Leach raised the signal flag for "ship not under control." Like the *Bismarck*, the *Prince of Wales* was pinned to the sea, providing her enemies the opportunity to complete her destruction at their leisure.[35]

An hour later, the Japanese were back again. The *Repulse* at last broke radio silence to report: "Enemy aircraft bombing." That led authorities in Singapore to launch fighters, though they would arrive far too late. Three more torpedoes hit the *Prince of Wales*—one forward, one amidships, and one aft—and soon afterward, three more struck the *Repulse*. The captain of the *Repulse*, William Tennant, ordered the ship's crew up from below, which certainly saved several hundred lives, for at 12:33 the big battlecruiser rolled over and went down. The *Prince of Wales* stayed afloat for only another forty-five minutes, sinking at 1:18 p.m. The accompanying British destroyers, unmolested by the Japanese, picked up more than 2,000 survivors, though 840 men were lost, including both John Leach and Tom Phillips. The Japanese, having lost only three aircraft, retired just as the squadron of Buffalo fighters from Singapore arrived.[36]

Back in London, the news struck Churchill like a body blow. "In all the war," he wrote later, "I never received a more direct shock." It was more than the loss of two important capital ships, more even than the loss of those 840 men. It was the realization that this defeat completely uncovered the British Empire in South Asia. Combined with the destruction of the American fleet in Pearl Harbor, there were now no Allied capital ships between Ceylon and Hawaii, a distance of eight thousand miles, more than a third of the earth's circumference. "Over all this vast expanse of water," Churchill later wrote, "Japan was supreme, and everywhere we were weak and naked."[37]

The next day, Hitler declared war on the United States.

CHAPTER 11

RAMPAGE

ALL THROUGH THAT HISTORIC DECEMBER OF 1941 the Western Allies staggered under successive blows by the Japanese war machine. The almost effortless string of their conquests stunned even the Japanese. On December 10, the same day that the *Prince of Wales* and *Repulse* went down in the Gulf of Siam, Japanese bombers destroyed many of the American planes on the ground at the U.S. Army's Clark Field in the Philippines. That day, too, Japanese forces landed on the north coast of Luzon, the largest of the Philippine Islands, and two days later another force landed on its southern coast. A week after that a third, much larger Japanese army—more than fifty thousand men in eighty-four troopships and transports—landed at Lingayen Gulf, on the west side of Luzon. The American commander in the Philippines, General Douglas MacArthur, rather than fall back to prepared defenses in Bataan in accordance with Plan Orange, instead tried to meet the invaders on the beaches. It was a mistake. In the end, he had to fall back anyway, losing much of his equipment in the process.

The hammer blows continued. On December 14, the Japanese invaded British-held North Borneo, and on the twentieth they landed at Davao on Mindanao, the southernmost of the Philippine Islands, which they turned into a major base. Hong Kong surrendered on Christmas Day, and the next day MacArthur abandoned Manila, declaring it an open city. The small American naval force in the Philippines, commanded by Admiral Thomas C. Hart, had to evacuate south to Surabaya, on the north coast of Java. For the Western Allies it was a dizzying string of defeats and setbacks. As one British historian put it, it was a period of "defeat and retreat, confusion and loss, death and misery."[1]

There were a few fleeting rays of hope for the Allies during these eventful weeks. One was the initial American defense of Wake Island, more than three thousand miles east of the Philippines in the mid-Pacific. Roughly 450 U.S. Marines occupied the tiny island along with twelve hundred construction workers. The Marines nevertheless managed to turn back the initial Japanese landing on December 11 by holding their fire until the Japanese ships were within point-blank range, then opening up with camouflaged 5-inch guns, sinking one Japanese destroyer and severely damaging another. The four American planes that had survived the Japanese air strike managed to sink another destroyer. They were the first warships lost by the Imperial Japanese Navy in the war.

Encouraged by that, Admiral Kimmel organized a relief force (Task Force 14) built around the aircraft carrier *Saratoga* and sent it toward Wake Island on December 16. Even as it was en route, however, the Japanese renewed their assault on Wake, this time committing two of their big carriers—the Pearl Harbor veterans *Hiryū* and *Sōryū*—as well as a cruiser division. That so escalated the degree of risk that on December 22, with the *Saratoga* still 725 miles from Wake, Kimmel's temporary replacement, Admiral William S. Pye, ordered her to turn around. When he got the message, the American task force commander, Rear Admiral Frank Jack Fletcher, flung his service cap to the deck in frustration, but he obeyed. Wake surrendered the next day.[2]

Another moment that offered encouragement, at least briefly, occurred a month later at Balikpapan, an important oil port on the east coast of Borneo.

Japanese forces had seized it with little difficulty on January 24, though they were infuriated to find that the Dutch had sabotaged both the oil fields and the refinery, setting them on fire before the invaders could take possession. That night, the Japanese transports and support ships in the harbor were silhouetted by fires ashore when four U.S. destroyers led by Commander Paul H. Talbot arrived. "It was a destroyer sailor's dream," a crewman on one of them recalled, to be "in the middle of the enemy invasion fleet, apparently no enemy combat ships to oppose [us] and to the complete surprise of the foe." The American destroyers launched all of their torpedoes—forty-eight of them—to both port and starboard, then got away unscathed except for a single 4-inch shell that struck the destroyer *John D. Ford*. The American torpedoes sank four freighters, one of them an ammunition ship that blew up spectacularly, though given the circumstances the Americans had hoped for more.[3]

A third minor success for the Western Allies occurred in the mid-Pacific when Admiral Chester Nimitz, who replaced Pye as the permanent commander of the Pacific Fleet on December 31, ordered all three of his aircraft carriers—operating in separate task groups—to raid Japanese bases in Micronesia. One of the carriers had to be recalled when it encountered fuel issues, but on February 1, 1942, American bombers from the *Yorktown* inflicted minor damage on Japanese outposts in the Gilbert Islands, and planes from the *Enterprise* attacked Japanese shipping in Kwajalein lagoon, in the Marshalls, sinking a transport and a sub chaser and damaging several other vessels. During that raid, the Americans exacted the first mortal casualty of the war on a Japanese flag officer when one of the bombs at Kwajalein killed Rear Admiral Sukeyoshi Yatsushiro.[4]

─────────

THE JAPANESE SHRUGGED OFF THESE PINPRICKS. They had been planning the southern campaign for months, and their forces executed it with clocklike efficiency, advancing in carefully measured steps, seizing and expanding airstrips at each invasion site so that every subsequent move took place under an umbrella of air superiority. Throughout January and into February, Japanese forces captured one lightly defended outpost after another: Sarawak and Jolo, Brunei and Jesselton, Tarakan and Ambon. On January 23, they

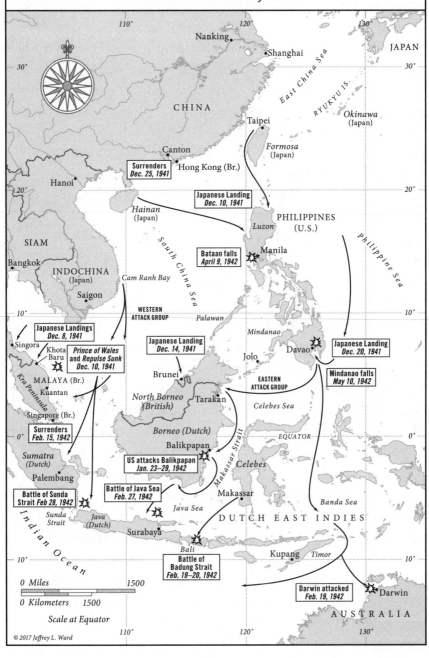

JAPAN MOVES SOUTH
December 1941–May 1942

CHINA

Nanking

Shanghai

JAPAN

East China Sea

RYUKYU IS.

Okinawa
(Japan)

Taipei

Formosa
(Japan)

Canton

**Surrenders
Dec. 25, 1941**

Hong Kong (Br.)

**Japanese Landing
Dec. 10, 1941**

PHILIPPINES
(U.S.)

Luzon

Philippine Sea

Hanoi

Hainan
(Japan)

**Bataan falls
April 9, 1942**

Manila

SIAM

South China Sea

Bangkok

INDOCHINA
(Japan)

Cam Ranh Bay

Saigon

WESTERN
ATTACK GROUP

Palawan

Mindanao

**Japanese Landings
Dec. 8, 1941**

Singora

Khota
Baru

**Prince of Wales
and Repulse Sunk
Dec. 10, 1941**

**Japanese Landing
Dec. 14, 1941**

Jolo

Davao

**Japanese Landing
Dec. 20, 1941**

MALAYA (Br.)

Kuantan

Brunei

EASTERN
ATTACK GROUP

**Mindanao falls
May 10, 1942**

Kra Peninsula

Singapore (Br.)

North Borneo
(British)

Tarakan

Celebes Sea

**Surrenders
Feb. 15, 1942**

Borneo (Dutch)

EQUATOR

Sumatra
(Dutch)

Balikpapan

Palembang

**US attacks Balikpapan
Jan. 23–29, 1942**

Celebes

Makassar Strait

**Battle of Sunda
Strait Feb 28, 1942**

**Battle of Java Sea
Feb. 27, 1942**

Makassar

Banda Sea

Indian Ocean

*Sunda
Strait*

Java
(Dutch)

Surabaya

Java Sea

DUTCH EAST INDIES

Bali

**Battle of
Badung Strait
Feb. 19–20, 1942**

Kupang

Timor

0 Miles   1500

0 Kilometers   1500

Scale at Equator

**Darwin attacked
Feb. 19, 1942**

Darwin

AUSTRALIA

© 2017 Jeffrey L. Ward

occupied the key port of Rabaul, at the northern tip of New Britain Island in the Bismarck Archipelago, more than three thousand miles east of Singapore. The Allies barely had time to catalog these advances, let alone respond effectively.[5]

The ultimate objective of the Japanese campaign—indeed of the whole war—was the Dutch East Indies, composed of four large islands (Borneo, Celebes, Java, and Sumatra) plus innumerable smaller ones. In addition to their value as exporters of sugar, pepper, rice, and tea, those islands produced 35 percent of the world's known supply of rubber and boasted some of the most productive oil fields outside the United States. Then, too, Sumatra and Java, along with the Kra Peninsula, constituted what was called the Malay Barrier, a convex shield behind which the Japanese planned to establish what they hoped would be an unassailable maritime empire: the Greater East Asia Co-Prosperity Sphere.

The Dutch were not helpless in defending their Asian possessions. Though their homeland had been overrun by the Nazis eighteen months before, Queen Wilhelmina and the Dutch government had escaped to London to carry on the war from there, and a handful of Dutch warships joined the vessels of other occupied countries, such as Norway and Poland, to cooperate with the Royal Navy in the war against the U-boats. As noted in Chapter 4, Dutch *schuitjes* played a crucial role in the evacuation of British troops from Dunkirk. In the Far East, the Royal Netherlands Navy had a squadron of three light cruisers and seven destroyers plus a number of submarines, all under the command of Vice Admiral Conrad Helfrich.[6]

Since it was self-evident that Helfrich's little squadron could not stand toe-to-toe with the Imperial Japanese Navy, British and Dutch military officials had initiated staff talks in November about how best to cooperate. After Pearl Harbor, more discussions took place in Washington, and what emerged was an organization known as ABDA, an acronym that stood for the combined forces of the Americans, British, Dutch, and Australians. It was a measure of their desperate circumstances that these allies all agreed to accept a unified commander. As a rule, naval officers were reluctant to place their ships under the supervision of an army general, especially a *foreign* army general. Yet in January 1942, all four countries agreed to accept General Sir Archibald Wavell, the British commander in India, as the overall ABDA commander.* Wavell dutifully took up the assignment and set up his headquarters on Java, though he did so with little hope and few expectations. As the British historian Stephen Roskill noted, "Rarely can a Commander-in-Chief have assumed great responsibilities in less auspicious circumstances."[7]

Though the formation of ABDA theoretically created a unified command, it was impossible to stifle national jealousies altogether. At least one American sailor thought Wavell was "another pompous general right out of Gilbert & Sullivan" and characterized his chief of staff, Sir Henry Pownall, as "a snotty bastard." The Americans questioned Wavell's decision to use ABDA warships to escort convoys to and from Singapore rather than to attack the advancing Japanese. Nor were the Australians entirely pleased, noting ruefully that "the arrangement did not provide for any direct consultation with Australia." The Dutch resented the fact that the command of ABDA naval assets had gone to an American (Admiral Hart) and that another American (Rear Admiral William Glassford) was named commander of what was called the ABDA Striking Force of cruisers and destroyers, including all the Dutch warships. In late January, however, Glassford got a promotion to vice admiral and a new job. That made room for a Dutch officer, Rear Admiral Karel Doorman, to assume command of the Striking Force. Helfrich was unmollified and continued to grumble about Hart's overall exercise of command.[8]

Helfrich's unhappiness derived in part from the intensity of his commitment. Among all the Allied naval leaders in ABDA, he was the only one who was native to Java, having been born there in 1886. Though he had studied and taught at the Dutch naval academy at Den Helder, near Amsterdam, Helfrich considered the East Indies his homeland. To him, the defense of the Malay Barrier was not merely a strategic gambit; it was a crusade to defend his native soil. Then, too, it is possible that the short,

---

* Curiously, it was the Americans, and particularly U.S. Army chief of staff George C. Marshall, who were the strongest advocates for unified command, and the British, especially Prime Minister Winston Churchill, who were initially resistant. "What does an army officer know about handling a ship?" Churchill asked Marshall challengingly. In the end, however, Churchill gave way: "It was evident," he wrote, "that we must meet the American view."

Dutch Rear Admiral Conrad Helfrich (left) was a fierce defender of his homeland who was annoyed that an American commanded the ABDA naval force. In part to pacify him, American Admiral Thomas C. Hart (right) was recalled to the United States. Hart resented it. A year later, during a visit to the United States by Queen Wilhelmina, he initially refused to receive a decoration the queen was scheduled to present to him until Roosevelt asked him to accept it as a personal favor.

Naval History and Heritage Command

jowly, and double-chinned Helfrich looked upon the tall, handsome, and aristocratic-looking Hart as more of a show pony than a workhorse. In part due to pressure from the Dutch, Hart was recalled to Washington, ostensibly because of failing health, and Helfrich assumed the job as ABDA naval commander. With more determination than calculation, he resolved to fight it out to the last Allied soldier and sailor.

Doorman, the ABDA Strike Force commander, was not native to Java; he had come out to the East Indies in 1940 just as the Nazi legions were sweeping across Holland. A quietly intense man, not unlike Günther Lütjens, the German admiral who had gone down with the *Bismarck* the previous May, Doorman was determined to fulfill Helfrich's expectations, however unrealistic.

Doorman had no battleships or carriers in his small surface fleet, though his English-speaking allies did provide him with two heavy cruisers. One was HMS *Exeter*, the ship that had battled the *Graf Spee* off Montevideo in the first months of the war, and the other was the USS *Houston*. Both were older ships that had been laid down in 1928 as so-called treaty cruisers, which meant they displaced 10,000 tons and carried 8-inch guns—nine of them in the case of the *Houston*, though only six were operable after her rear turret had been struck by a Japanese bomb during an air attack in the Makassar Strait on February 4. In addition to the two heavy cruisers, Doorman also had ten light cruisers—four British, two American, two Australian, and two Dutch, one of which, the *De Ruyter*, he used as his flag-ship. All these ships were based out of Surabaya, in eastern Java.[9]

The real weakness of the ABDA Striking Force, however, was the absence of any standing protocols for cooperation, or even a reliable communications system. Having been thrown together so quickly, the ships of Doorman's command did not even share a common signal code. Doorman himself spoke fluent English as well as Dutch, but few others in his command did. Liaison officers had to translate and decode messages from other ships before they could be acted upon, which made timely tactical maneuvering all but impossible. As the official historian of Australian forces in the campaign put it, "Tactically the ships of the Combined Striking Force were capable of little more than following each other in line ahead."[10]

Nor was there any effective cooperation between naval and air assets. The Japanese were vastly superior to the Allies in the air in any case, but in addition to that, sending out U.S. Army B-17s or P-40s to cooperate with an Anglo-Dutch surface force proved as cumbersome as the relationship between Italian air and surface forces in the Mediterranean. When at an early naval staff meeting Doorman suggested the possibility of cooperation by Allied air forces in a forthcoming operation, it triggered a spontaneous outburst of laughter.

SINGAPORE CAPITULATED on February 15. It was a stunning blow to the British, who even in their darkest moments could not bring themselves to believe that such a defeat was possible. Churchill had ordered that "the battle must be fought to the bitter end at all costs," even insisting that "com-manders and senior officers should die with their troops." It was a measure of the vast demoralization within the British command that General Arthur Percival surrendered a fortified position defended by more than a hundred thousand men to an attacking army of fewer than fifty thousand. Churchill was beside himself.[11]

The Japanese wasted little time in celebration. Even before Singapore fell, four separate Japanese naval task forces were at sea, steaming toward the islands of the Malay Barrier. Three of them were invasion armadas consisting of scores of transports and supply ships escorted by cruisers and destroyers. The fourth was the Kidō Butai.

In order to preempt an attempt by Allied forces to interfere with the invasions, Admiral Yamamoto ordered the Kidō Butai to smash the Allied naval base at Port Darwin on Australia's northern coast. To do that, four of Admiral Nagumo's carriers (*Akagi*, *Kaga*, *Hiryū*, and *Sōryū*) sailed from Davao in the southern Philippines, passed around the eastern end of the Malay Barrier into the Indian Ocean, and just after 6:00 a.m. on February 19 launched 188 planes for a massive air strike at Darwin. In less than two hours, those planes sank eight ships, including the American destroyer *Peary*. The *Peary* had been bombed twice previously while in the Philippines and had survived a harrowing odyssey just to get to Darwin. Now she went down at last, taking eighty-eight men with her. The principal target of the Japanese, however, was the harbor itself, which they utterly wrecked, effectively putting Darwin out of business as a base for ABDA forces. The Japanese also attacked the town of Darwin, which, being built mostly of wood, was all but destroyed in the ensuing fires. The Japanese lost two airplanes.[12]

Even as Nagumo's carriers conducted this raid, the three Japanese invasion fleets approached their targets. The largest of the fleets was the so-called Western Attack Force, commanded by Admiral Takeo Kurita, whose fierce expression masked a scholar's demeanor. Kurita's task force had departed Cam Ranh Bay, in Indochina, ten days earlier, on February 9–10, and steamed almost due south for Sumatra at a leisurely ten knots. It was an impressive armada of nearly a hundred ships that included fifty-six troop-filled transports and supply ships, escorted by three light cruisers and no fewer than twenty-five destroyers, with a separate covering force of heavy cruisers and the small carrier *Ryūjō*, all under Admiral Jisaburō Ozawa.

While en route south, this enormous task force crossed paths with a motley flotilla of vessels escaping from Singapore. Most of the ships were crowded with refugees, but one of them was the small (700-ton) armed river steamer *Li Wo*, commanded by a Royal Navy lieutenant named Thomas Wilkinson.

When he sighted the Japanese invasion force on February 14, Wilkinson impetuously charged into the midst of it and opened fire with his single 4-inch gun. He managed to set one transport on fire and damaged several others before his little vessel was overwhelmed. In a last desperate act, he rammed his crippled steamer into the burning transport. That transport eventually had to be abandoned, but the *Li Wo* sank almost at once, with the loss of seventy-seven men out of her crew of eighty-four, including Wilkinson, who became the latest Royal Navy officer to receive a posthumous Victoria Cross.[13]

Pressed by Helfrich to confront the approaching armada, Doorman put to sea from Surabaya with HMS *Exeter* (the *Houston* was still en route from Darwin), four light cruisers, and ten destroyers. His sortie was nearly as impetuous as Wilkinson's charge. Even without the covering force under Ozawa, the Japanese escorts alone outnumbered him nearly two to one, and like Tom Phillips in the Gulf of Siam, Doorman lacked effective air cover. Indeed, over the next several hours his ships were attacked five times from the air, both by Kate bombers from the *Ryūjō* and by Nell and Betty bombers from Japan's forward airstrips. The bombers scored no hits, though several near misses damaged two of his destroyers and forced them to turn back. Despairing of ever getting close enough to attack the transports, Doorman gave the order to return to port.[14]

The object of Kurita's invasion force was the city of Palembang, in eastern Sumatra, the center of one of the largest and most productive oil fields in the world. In order to prevent the Dutch from sabotaging the refineries as they had done at Balikpapan, the Japanese began the assault by dropping paratroopers directly onto the oil fields. The paratroopers encountered stiff resistance until the arrival of the main Japanese landing force, which quickly seized control and secured the city as well as its oil fields.[15]

At almost the same time, a thousand miles to the east, a much smaller Japanese invasion force targeted the island of Bali, only a few miles east of Java and less than a hundred miles from Doorman's base at Surabaya. Doorman barely had time to refuel his ships before he was out again, seeking to turn back this next assault. He sortied with what he had immediately available: two light cruisers and three destroyers (one Dutch and two American), leaving behind orders for other ships to join him as soon as they

Rear Admiral Karl Doorman led the ABDA Striking Force in a series of battles with Japanese invasion forces in February 1942. Badly outnumbered and with virtually no air cover, his cruiser-destroyer force was repeatedly overmatched.

Netherlands National Archives

were able. The result was the Battle of Badung Strait (February 19–20), a confused and confusing nighttime engagement in which Doorman's ships, though greater in number, got much the worst of it. It was here that the Japanese first demonstrated their superiority in night engagements, as well as the impressive capability of the Type 93 Long Lance torpedo. One Long Lance struck the Dutch destroyer *Piet Hein* and broke her in half. She went down with the loss of sixty-four men, including her captain. Japanese destroyers also shot up the Dutch light cruiser *Tromp*, though she managed to make it back to port under her own power. Doorman's sortie did little to interfere with the landings, and as Doorman's battered force returned to Surabaya, the Japanese consolidated their hold on Bali.[16]

There was more. Only two days later, on February 22, an Allied convoy that included the USS *Langley* departed Fremantle, Australia, and headed for Ceylon. Built as a collier in 1912, then converted into America's first aircraft carrier in 1920, the *Langley* had been converted again into a seaplane tender in 1937. In that capacity, she was now engaged in carrying a cargo of fighter aircraft to reinforce the British garrison in Ceylon. Helfrich, however, who was desperately short of combat aircraft, overrode those orders and instructed her to abandon the convoy and make a dash for Tjilatjap, on Java's southern coast. The confusing Allied chain of command generated a flurry of conflicting orders that kept the *Langley* loitering off

Java's southern coast, and that gave the Japanese time to find her. Just before noon on February 27, nine Betty bombers attacked, and in what was either a remarkable demonstration of skill or blind luck, five of them made direct hits. The *Langley* sank that afternoon, taking all of the onboard aircraft down with her.[17]

THE CENTRAL JAPANESE AMPHIBIOUS THRUST was aimed at Java itself, the linchpin of ABDA defenses and the home of both the Dutch colonial capital, Batavia (now Jakarta), as well as Doorman's naval base at Surabaya. This crucial assignment was the responsibility of what the Japanese called the Eastern Attack Group, consisting of forty-one transports with a close escort of two light cruisers and twelve destroyers under Rear Admiral Shoji Nishimura, and supported by a covering force of ten more cruisers and destroyers under Rear Admiral Takeo Takagi, who followed two hundred miles behind. Though this force was less robust than the one used to seize Palembang, Yamamoto was so confident of its success that he released Nagumo's carrier force from its position south of Java and ordered it to head west into the Indian Ocean for a strike at British assets there.[18]

Yamamoto based that decision on his assumption that the remaining Allied warships at Surabaya were so worn down and demoralized they no longer constituted a serious threat. He was only partly right. Doorman's ships—and their crews—certainly were worn down, but they were not demoralized. In fact, as soon as he learned that yet another enemy fleet was approaching, Doorman put to sea again at dusk on February 26 in an effort to find and attack it. As he steamed to the northwest, he received a signal from Helfrich urging him to "continue your attacks until the enemy is destroyed."[19]

When the sun came up on February 27, however, the only enemy forces in sight were more Japanese bombers. Their repeated attacks did no serious damage, though they kept Doorman's exhausted crews at general quarters all day. Seeing no enemy fleet, Doorman concluded that the sighting report had been in error, and he turned around to return to Surabaya. Helfrich was furious. "Notwithstanding air attack," he radioed, "you are to proceed eastward to search for and attack enemy." That was easy enough for Helfrich to

Fifty-year-old Rear Admiral Takeo Takagi commanded the covering force for the Japanese invasion of the Philippines and the Dutch East Indies. His victory in the Battle of the Java Sea won him a promotion to vice admiral.

U.S. Naval Institute

say back in Surabaya, but as the commander on the scene, Doorman knew what his men could do and what they could not, and rather boldly he radioed Helfrich: "This day the personnel reached the limit of endurance." He continued on his course.[20]

Doorman arrived at the entrance to Surabaya at about two-thirty that afternoon. Even as he was maneuvering to enter the port through the swept channel, however, he received another sighting report, this time a more specific and detailed one: an enemy invasion force of twenty-five transports, two cruisers, and six destroyers was only a few hours away, heading due south for Java. Doorman may have taken a deep breath before deciding to trust it. With no time to meet with his captains, he simply turned around in the entrance channel and signaled the other ships in the squadron: "Follow me. Details later."[21]

Takagi was surprised, though hardly alarmed, by reports from Japanese scout planes that an Allied surface fleet was approaching. Like Yamamoto, Takagi did not think the enemy had much fight left in him, which was why his two heavy cruisers loitered nearly two hundred miles behind the convoy.

Now, however, he directed the forty-one transports to turn north to get out of the way, and ordered the heavy cruisers to increase speed to twenty-eight knots to catch up with the escort group of light cruisers and destroyers.[22]

Having had no time to make any arrangements beyond that quick "Follow me," Doorman's five cruisers were arrayed in a line-ahead formation behind the flagship. Behind the *De Ruyter* were the two heavy cruisers, *Exeter* and *Houston*, which were followed in turn by two light cruisers, the Australian *Perth* and the Dutch *Java*. Three British destroyers scouted ahead, and four American destroyers followed astern. The arrangement was curious because the American destroyers had the greatest number of torpedo tubes, and the fighting thus far had shown that opening a battle with a torpedo attack was more effective, especially at night, than relying on naval guns. On the other hand, Doorman lacked both the time and the communications capability to devise and communicate a more complex battle plan.[23]

The Battle of the Java Sea (February 27, 1942) began just past four o'clock, when lookouts on the leading British destroyers spotted the top-masts of Nishimura's screening force. Almost immediately, Tagaki's two heavy cruisers, *Nachi* and *Haguro*, arrived to tip the balance of power decisively. Each of Takagi's big cruisers had ten 8-inch guns, while the *Exeter* had only six, and the *Houston* only six that worked. That gave the Japanese a twenty-to-twelve advantage in the crucial category of long-range guns. Doorman decided that his best chance was to close the range quickly in order to bring the 6-inch guns on his light cruisers into action. Though his ultimate target was the gaggle of Japanese transports to the northwest, he would have to fight his way through the protecting escorts to get to them.

Both sides opened fire at about four-fifteen. A Japanese destroyer captain recalled that "shells rained all around, raising water pillars on every side." Some of those shell splashes were in vivid colors, since the Allied 8-inch shells included small bags of dye to enable spotters to determine which of the distant shell splashes were theirs and make appropriate adjustments. The *Houston*, for example, used a red dye, and when blood-red shell splashes erupted around the Japanese warships, it startled some of the Japanese crewmen, who wondered if the Americans had developed a new secret weapon.[24]

The turning point came just past five o'clock when an 8-inch shell, probably from the *Haguro*, struck the *Exeter* and penetrated to a boiler. Though it did not initially detonate, the superheated steam in the boiler ignited it, and the ensuing explosion knocked out six of the *Exeter's* eight boilers, cutting her speed to ten knots. To avoid having the *Houston*, directly behind him, collide into his stern, the *Exeter's* captain, Oliver Gordon, ordered an abrupt turn to port. Seeing that maneuver amidst the smoke and confusion of battle, and assuming that he must have missed a signal from the flagship, Captain Albert Rooks of the *Houston* turned to port as well, as did the *Perth* and the *Java* in turn. For several minutes, until he appreciated what had happened, Doorman continued forward in the *De Ruyter* virtually alone.[25]

Takagi next ordered a torpedo attack, and the Japanese sent sixty-four torpedoes streaking toward Doorman's cruisers. Even for the Long Lance, however, the range proved to be too great, and only one of them hit its target, cutting the Dutch destroyer *Kortenaer* in half and sending her quickly to the bottom. Another destroyer, the British *Electra*, a survivor of the battle with the *Bismarck* as well as the sinking of the *Prince of Wales*, was struck by several shells, lost power, and went down with her flag still flying. Doorman sent the badly crippled *Exeter* back to Surabaya, along with an escorting destroyer, cutting the number of 8-inch guns in his squadron from twelve to six. Worse, since the *Exeter* was the only ship in the squadron with radar, Doorman would now be operating blind, especially after dark. In a flurry of orders at 6:15 p.m., he directed the American destroyers to execute a torpedo attack and make smoke to cover a retirement by his cruisers.[26]

In the midst of all this, Allied air support arrived: a dozen attack planes supported by five Brewster Buffalo fighters. Rather than cooperate with Doorman, however, they delivered an independent—and unsuccessful— attack on the Japanese convoy. Takagi, unaware of the dire condition of the Allied squadron, and concerned about the security of his convoy, decided not to pursue Doorman's ships southward.

That might have marked the end of the battle, and certainly Doorman would have been justified in calling it a day. He sent the four American destroyers, which had expended all of their torpedoes and were low on fuel, back to Surabaya. That left him with only two British destroyers (*Jupiter* and *Encounter*) to accompany his four cruisers. Nevertheless, at 9:00 p.m. Doorman started north in a renewed attempt to find the invasion convoy. He had barely set out when *Jupiter* struck a mine and sank, and the *Encounter* stayed by her to pick up survivors. Now Doorman had only the *Houston* and the three light cruisers. Even so, he got his four vessels into line, again signaled, "Follow me," and set off northward. Absent radar, and lacking either a destroyer screen or air cover, he groped forward in the dark like a man with his arms extended in an unlit basement.[27]

At eleven o'clock he found not the convoy but Takagi's two heavy cruisers. Both sides were surprised by this unexpected encounter. The Japanese cruisers were stopped while recovering their search planes. Takagi was so distressed to be caught in such a state that he bit his lip hard enough to draw blood. As soon as the planes were recovered, however, he prepared to engage once again. Amidst the ensuing brisk exchange of fire, he ordered another torpedo attack, and this time the Long Lance missiles proved deadly: first the *Java* and then the *De Ruyter* exploded and went down, each in a matter of minutes. Witnessing it from the Australian cruiser *Perth*, Captain Hector "Hec" Waller found the suddenness of it breathtaking, likening it to the sudden flare of a cigarette lighter in the dark: "a snap and a burst of flame." From the sinking *De Ruyter*, in what may have been his last act on earth, Doorman ordered the *Houston* and the *Perth* not to pick up survivors but to make their way to Batavia, in western Java.[28]

Thus while the crippled *Exeter* limped eastward back to Surabaya, the *Houston* and *Perth* slipped away westward. The victorious Japanese proceeded with the landing operations that would turn Java into a subject province. Doorman's bold sortie had delayed the Japanese landings by only twenty-four hours.

THE FIGHTING WAS NOT OVER. Doorman had gone down with the *De Ruyter*, making Waller, captain of the *Perth*, the senior Allied officer afloat. Though only forty-two, the Australian had already accumulated a distinguished war record, including a key role in the Battle of Cape Matapan (see Chapter 5), and a reputation for unflappability. He would need all his poise over the next twenty-four hours, for he was in a tight spot. His two ships were low on both fuel and ammunition; their crews were on the edge of exhaustion. To save what was left of the command, he would have to get his ships to Tanjong Priok, the naval base near Batavia, refuel, then slip around the western end of Java and head south through the Sunda Strait into the Indian Ocean. From there, if he could avoid Japanese air attacks, he could make his way to Australia. Afterward, Helfrich criticized Waller's decision not to continue the battle, calling it "regrettable" and insisting that Waller had disobeyed his order to "continue attacks till enemy is destroyed." It was an unrealistic and uncharitable criticism.[29]

Both Allied ships arrived in Batavia without further incident on the afternoon of February 28, though it was immediately evident that this was

Australian Navy Captain Hector Waller, photographed here as a captain, commanded a destroyer squadron in the Battle of Cape Matapan (see Chapter 5) and led the remnants of the ABDA Striking Force during the last stages of the Battle of the Java Sea and during the Battle of Sunda Strait.

Australian War Memorial

no safe haven. Japanese bombers had been there, too, and the harbor was littered with wrecked and sunken merchant ships. Even refueling proved difficult, partly because of the damage to the facilities, and partly because the Dutch wanted to hoard their now-scarce fuel oil for Dutch warships. After Waller explained to them that there were no Dutch warships left, the authorities agreed to provide him with the fuel he needed, though there was only enough time to take on a half load.[30]

To avoid Japanese aircraft, Waller left the harbor after dark, shaping a course for the Sunda Straits. As he approached the entrance to the strait at about eleven-fifteen with the *Perth* in the lead, lookouts on the Japanese destroyer *Fubuki* spotted both ships and shadowed them for several miles before anyone in either of the Allied ships realized they were not alone. Far from it. The two Allied cruisers, worn down from battle, low on fuel, and nearly bereft of ammunition, had stumbled into the middle of the Japanese Western Attack Group of over fifty transports and a score of escorts, including six heavy cruisers. Having completed the conquest of eastern Sumatra, the Japanese had crossed the Sunda Strait to land at Banten Bay, on the western tip of Java. Waller may have ruminated wryly on the irony: having searched for more than a week for a Japanese convoy, he had finally found one at the most inauspicious moment. Still, having been sighted by the enemy, there was nothing for it now but to fight it out. At eleven-thirty, Captain Rooks sent the last radio message ever received from the *Houston*: "Enemy forces engaged."[31]

The Battle of the Sunda Strait (February 28, 1942) was another confused night engagement with star shells lighting up the sky, gun flashes on all sides, and torpedoes furrowing the water. The *Perth*'s chief quartermaster remembered it impressionistically: "The glare of searchlights; the flash, blast and roar of [our] own guns; tracer ammunition stitching light across the sky; phosphorescent wakes entangling; ships on fire." It was so confusing that several of the torpedoes launched by Japanese destroyers at the Allied cruisers instead hit their own transports in Banten Bay, where at least two of them were sunk and two more beached themselves to avoid sinking.[32]

Despite that, there was hardly any question of the final outcome. A few minutes into the fight, 8-inch shells struck both Allied ships, the *Perth* at the waterline, the *Houston* on her foredeck. Soon after that, the *Houston* took a hit from a Long Lance torpedo that destroyed the main water feeder in her boilers and cut her speed dramatically. Another torpedo hit the *Perth* and took out her forward engine room. By now, both Allied ships were virtually out of ammunition and resorted to firing practice rounds and illumination flares at the enemy warships. The *Perth* was hit by three more torpedoes in quick succession. Each time Waller responded to the report with a cool "Very good." When the fourth torpedo struck and the *Perth* heeled over sharply to starboard, however, he announced: "Christ! That's torn it. Abandon ship." Soon afterward, the Australian cruiser turned over onto her side and went down bow-first, still making headway.[33]

After that, Rooks turned the *Houston* shoreward, perhaps with the intention of doing as much damage as possible to the transports before he sank, or perhaps to run the big cruiser up onto the beach to give his men a chance to survive. He never got far enough to try either gambit. With fires burning out of control and the ship taking on water, he ordered abandon ship just seconds before he was mortally wounded by shrapnel. The *Houston*'s executive officer, Commander David W. Roberts, countermanded the abandon ship order and tried to carry on the fight, but within minutes he saw the hopelessness of it, and confirmed the order to abandon ship. Like the *Perth*, the *Houston* went down bow-first as men scrambled over the side. Of the 1,087 officers and men on the *Houston*, 721 went down with the ship, including Rooks; 366 others escaped to shore and were captured. In due course, Rooks was posthumously awarded the Medal of Honor.[34]

Unaware of the fate of the *Houston* and *Perth*, the remaining few ships of the ABDA Striking Force in Surabaya made their own escape southward. The four American destroyers Doorman had sent back to Surabaya slipped through Bali Strait, around the eastern end of Java, and made it to Australia. That passage was too shallow for the crippled *Exeter*, so her skipper tried to follow the *Houston* and *Perth* through Sunda Strait. At mid-morning on Sunday, March 1, she was overwhelmed by shellfire and torpedoes from four Japanese heavy cruisers and a destroyer division. Her loss marked the end of ABDA. Helfrich officially resigned that same day, though by then he had no ships left to command. In fact, a full week earlier, Wavell had written

Churchill, "I see little further use for this HQ." The experiment in unified command had lasted just thirty-nine days. It was not the concept of unified command that was flawed; the Western Allies simply lacked the where-withal to stand up to the Japanese onslaught.[35]

THE JAPANESE CONQUEST of the resource-rich Dutch East Indies had proved both faster and less costly than they had dared hope. Indeed, success had come so quickly that the high command was at something of a loss about what to do next. One option, of course, was simply to consolidate their far-flung acquisitions and prepare their defenses so they could hurl back the inevitable Allied counterattack. That had been the governing assumption back when the initial decision was made to embark on the southern campaign. On the other hand, such a course left the initiative to the Westerners, and it seemed foolish not to strike again while the tide of events was so clearly running their way.

Some on the Naval General Staff looked southward. Its chief, Osami Nagano, believed that when the Americans began their inevitable counteroffensive they would use Australia as a base, and that could be preempted by occupying the island continent. The Japanese army, however, was not about to embark on the conquest of another continent when the war in China still festered. Another option was to move westward into the Indian Ocean and occupy British Ceylon. That might provoke an uprising by the native population in India and threaten the British Empire where it was most vulnerable. Once again, however, the Japanese army vetoed the idea. If the army looked anywhere else for new fields to conquer, it was north to the Soviet Union; a Russian collapse still seemed possible despite the recent counterattack by the Red Army outside Moscow.[36]

The army's recalcitrance bred resentment not only within the Naval General Staff in Tokyo but also at Combined Fleet Headquarters on board Yamamoto's flagship in the Inland Sea, where one of his staff officers complained: "We want to invade Ceylon; we are not allowed to! We want to invade Australia; we cannot! We want to attack Hawaii; we cannot do that either! All because the Army will not agree to release the necessary forces." Yamamoto's logistics officer recalled, "Since the Army [and] Navy could not come up with a common agreement of effort on the second phase operations, the Navy looked more and more toward what it could do alone."[37]

Yamamoto did not need army approval for a purely naval raid, and he had already ordered Nagumo and five of his six big carriers (the *Kaga* had hit a reef and needed repair) into the Indian Ocean for a hit-and-run raid on British bases in Ceylon. As a result, even as Japanese forces consolidated their conquests in the Dutch East Indies, Nagumo headed west to strike again.

After the fall of Singapore, the British relocated the base of the Eastern Fleet into the Indian Ocean: to Trincomalee, on Ceylon's northeast coast, and Colombo, on its west coast. They had a substantial fleet there, consisting of four old and slow R-class battleships (*Resolution, Ramillies, Royal Sovereign,* and *Revenge*), plus the even older (though faster) HMS *Warspite,* and two modern carriers—*Indomitable* and *Formidable.* Commanding this fleet was Sir James Somerville, the man who had reluctantly executed the attack on the French at Mers-el-Kébir almost two years before. Alerted by British intelligence of the Japanese approach, and unwilling to be caught in port, Somerville took his fleet to a position southwest of Ceylon in the hope of ambushing the Kidō Butai as it approached and give them what he called "a good crack." He knew he could not slug it out with the Japanese, but he hoped that night torpedo attacks could inflict enough damage to compel Nagumo to withdraw. He expected the Japanese on or about April 1, but when after several more days they didn't arrive, and with his battleships running low on both fuel and water, he sent two heavy cruisers—*Dorsetshire* and *Cornwall*—to Colombo, and pulled the main fleet back to a secret anchorage at Addu Atoll, the southernmost of the Maldive Islands, about six hundred miles southwest of Ceylon.[38]

Nagumo and the Kidō Butai finally showed up on April 5, which was Easter Sunday. That day, more than three hundred Japanese planes struck the British naval base at Colombo. The British commander there, Admiral Geoffrey Layton, ordered out two squadrons of Hawker Hurricane fighter planes—older cousins of the more famous Spitfire—and Fulmar naval fighter planes, a total of forty-two altogether. They fared poorly against the Zeros and the Japanese shot down nineteen of them while losing only seven of their own planes. Layton also dispatched a half dozen Swordfish armed with

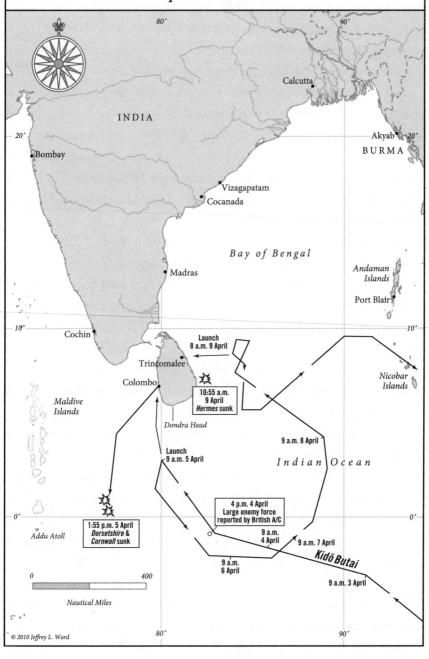

THE *KIDŌ BUTAI* IN THE INDIAN OCEAN
April 3–10, 1942

80°

90°

Calcutta

INDIA

Akyab 20°

BURMA

20°

Bombay

Vizagapatam

Cocanada

Bay of Bengal

Andaman
Islands

Madras

Port Blair

10°

10°

Cochin

Launch
8 a.m. 9 April

Trincomalee

Nicobar
Islands

Colombo

10:55 a.m.
9 April
Hermes sunk

Maldive
Islands

Dondra Head

9 a.m. 8 April

Launch
9 a.m. 5 April

Indian Ocean

4 p.m. 4 April
Large enemy force
reported by British A/C

9 a.m.
4 April

0°

9 a.m. 7 April

0°

1:55 p.m. 5 April
Dorsetshire &
Cornwall sunk

Addu Atoll

Kidō Butai

9 a.m.
6 April

9 a.m. 3 April

0   400

Nautical Miles

80°

90°

© 2010 Jeffrey L. Ward

torpedoes to attack the Japanese ships, but the Stringbags were easy prey for the Zeros and all six were splashed before they got close enough to drop a single torpedo. Meanwhile, the Japanese bombers and torpedo planes sank three British warships—though, as at Pearl Harbor, their principal target, which was Somerville's battleships and carriers, was not there. The Japanese did, however, wreck much of the harbor facilities, as they had at Darwin.[39]

That same afternoon, a Japanese reconnaissance plane spotted the two heavy cruisers Somerville had sent toward Colombo. Nagumo dispatched a strike force of eighty-eight aircraft toward their reported coordinates. The cruisers never had a chance. Like the *Prince of Wales* and *Repulse* the previous December, they had no air cover and were sitting ducks. Hit by ten bombs, the *Dorsetshire* sank in minutes; the *Cornwall*, hit by nine bombs, followed her soon afterward.[40]

The Japanese struck again three days later, on April 9, at Trincomalee. Once again the British fighter planes were brushed aside or sent spinning into the sea by the Zeros. The British also sent nine land-based Blenheim bombers to attack the Japanese carriers, but five of them were shot down, and none managed to land a bomb on target. As a parting shot, the Japanese found and sank the small British aircraft carrier *Hermes*, fleeing southward along Ceylon's east coast with an escort of only a single destroyer.[41]

After that, Somerville sent part of his force to Mombasa, in what was then British East Africa (now Kenya), and took the rest, including his two carriers, north to Bombay (now Mumbai), effectively surrendering the eastern Indian Ocean and the Bay of Bengal to the enemy. "I am convinced," he wrote, "that it is not good policy to take excessive chances with the Eastern Fleet for the sake of Ceylon." In fact, however, Nagumo was done. Having secured Japan's western flank, he turned the Kidō Butai eastward, passed through the Strait of Malacca, which was no longer dominated by the British bastion at Singapore, and returned to the Pacific.[42]

IN FOUR MONTHS, the Japanese had conquered an island empire of more than ten thousand square miles, securing the resource base that they hoped would make them economically self-reliant and militarily invulnerable. They had sunk six Allied capital ships (four in Pearl Harbor, plus the *Prince of Wales* and *Repulse*) and all five cruisers of what had been optimistically named the ABDA Striking Force. They had also destroyed two heavy cruisers and a carrier of Somerville's command, no fewer than seventeen Allied destroyers, and uncounted numbers of freighters and transports. In addition to Malaya and the Dutch East Indies, they occupied Thailand and Burma to the west, and the Bismarck Archipelago to the east. And they had achieved all that with a loss of only four destroyers and a patrol boat. By the end of March 1942, they were masters of a third of the globe. At that moment, their decision to go to war with Britain, Holland, and the United States simultaneously must have seemed nothing less than brilliant.

THE WAR ON TRADE, II

THE EXPANSION OF HOSTILITIES into the Pacific and Indian Oceans turned the European conflict into a world war. It also transformed the war on trade. Even as Admiral Nagumo's carriers bombed British naval facilities in Ceylon, Admiral Jisaburō Ozawa, having completed the conquest of Sumatra and Java, led a powerful surface force spearheaded by five heavy cruisers into the Bay of Bengal to attack British and Allied shipping along the east coast of India between Madras and Calcutta. In five days Ozawa's squadron sank twenty-three merchant vessels displacing 112,312 tons; Japanese submarines sank five more ships displacing 32,404 tons.[1]

The Allies, too, initiated a war on trade. In the Mediterranean, British surface forces conducted active sweeps by cruisers and destroyers out of Malta. In November, two Royal Navy cruisers and two destroyers under the command of Captain William G. Agnew attacked an Italian convoy of seven merchant ships in the Ionian Sea. Agnew's command sank all seven of the merchantmen and three of the escorts. After the slaughter of another convoy a few weeks later, the Italians temporarily canceled night convoys across the Sicilian Narrows. From that point on until the end of the war, the Axis had difficulty keeping Italian and German forces in North Africa supplied.

The war on trade also crossed the Atlantic. For months, Raeder had urged Hitler to allow Dönitz's U-boats to attack the American destroyers that were escorting British convoys to England, and to expand the U-boat hunting grounds into the western Atlantic. Each time, the Führer had turned him down for fear of enlarging the war before the Russians were defeated. On December 9, however, two days after the Pearl Harbor attack, Hitler lifted the restrictions. From now on, all American ships in the North Atlantic and elsewhere were fair game. That same day, Dönitz ordered a U-boat expedition to the eastern coast of the United States.[2]

Finally, the Americans also inaugurated a campaign of submarine warfare against Japanese shipping. There is irony in the fact that although the United States had gone to war with imperial Germany in 1917 ostensibly because of Germany's use of unrestricted submarine warfare, the very first operational order issued from Washington after Pearl Harbor was to "execute unrestricted air and submarine warfare against Japan." In that campaign, the Americans proved as unrelenting in the Pacific as the Germans were in the Atlantic, and as a result of these developments, the war on trade entered a new phase. As 1942 dawned, there was no ocean or sea anywhere on the planet where merchant shipping was free from hazard.[3]

FOR DÖNITZ, the new opportunities in the western Atlantic came just in time, for in the second half of 1941 his U-boats had hit a dry spell. Dönitz blamed it on the German high command (Oberkommando der Wehrmacht, or OKW) in Berlin. From the start, Dönitz had argued that his U-boats should not be used for any other purpose than attacking merchant ships in the North Atlantic. "The most important task of the German Navy," he wrote, "and the task which overshadowed in importance everything else, was the conduct of operations against shipping on Britain's lines of communication across the Atlantic." Yet instead of focusing on this vital effort, OKW regularly sent his U-boats off to conduct subsidiary operations. Some acted as weather stations; others served as escorts for surface units. Dönitz resented these infringements, but the most aggravating interference was the order to send twenty-three U-boats into the Mediterranean. The order was a response to Axis shipping losses to Allied aircraft and submarines out of Malta, which had reached critical levels. In October 1941, fewer than half the ships that set out from Italy with supplies for Rommel's Afrika Korps reached their destination.[4]

The U-boats did good service in the Mediterranean. On November 13, 1941, the U-81 sank the *Ark Royal* with a single torpedo, and eleven days later the U-331 put three torpedoes into the battleship *Barham*, which also sank. Such losses were all the more devastating because on December 19, Italian frogmen, in one of the boldest operations of the war, penetrated the British naval base at Alexandria in Egypt, attached mines to the hulls of the battleships *Queen Elizabeth* and *Valiant*, and blew them up. Though the perpetrators were captured and imprisoned, their daring exploit sent both ships to the bottom. The vessels were later raised, though they were rendered useless for extended periods, one for six months and the other for nine months. That left the Royal Navy temporarily without a single capital ship in the eastern Mediterranean just as the Axis siege of Malta was reaching a critical moment. By March 1942 the British garrison of the beleaguered island was in desperate need of food, fuel, and ammunition, and to supply them, yet another convoy set out from Alexandria on March 20.[5]

That convoy (MW-10) consisted of only three merchant ships and a tanker, but its safe arrival in Malta was so critical that the British committed an exceptionally large escort of three light cruisers, seventeen destroyers, and the cruiser *Carlisle* armed exclusively with anti-air weaponry, all under the command of Philip Vian, who was now a rear admiral. The immense size of the escort was a measure not only of the vital importance of this particular convoy but also of the increase in the availability of escorts for convoy service. Two years before, in the spring of 1940, the Royal Navy had often struggled to find even a single escort to accompany a transatlantic convoy; now it could commit twenty-one of them to protect four vessels.

To intercept the convoy, Admiral Angelo Iachino put to sea with the battleship *Littorio*, at last fully repaired from the Taranto strike, plus two heavy cruisers, a light cruiser, and ten destroyers. The MW-10 convoy also had to contend with the twenty-three U-boats that OKW had sent to the Mediterranean and with German aircraft operating from Sicily. To fend off this three-dimensional assault, Vian coordinated a day-long running fight on March 22 that came to be known as the Second Battle of Sirte (Sirte being the nearby gulf on the coast of Libya). The First Battle of Sirte, back in December, had been a relatively small affair, during which each side attacked a convoy of the other to little effect. This time the Axis were determined to completely destroy the British convoy.

When the attacks began, Vian ordered the four merchant ships to steam for Malta escorted by the *Carlisle* and six Hunt-class destroyers, while he boldly interposed his light cruisers and larger destroyers between the convoy and Iachino's fleet. In a desperate effort to distract the Italians, Vian's ships made smoke and launched torpedoes. The big 15-inch guns of the *Littorio* outranged anything Vian had, and giant shell splashes erupted all around the British cruisers. As Vian recalled, they hit with a loud smack and threw up "columns of water masthead high." For four hours, Vian's light cruisers and destroyers dodged in and out of their own smoke screens, absorbing punishment and firing at moments of opportunity. A torpedo attack bought a brief respite when it forced Iachino to turn away to avoid it. Nevertheless, by the end of the day the Italian heavy ships had damaged all three of Vian's cruisers and six of his destroyers. They did not, however, break through to the transports, and at dusk Iachino called off the attack. While that battle was in progress, German bombers from Sicily attacked the fleeing transports, sinking one of the cargo ships and crippling the tanker so badly it had to be beached. In the end, therefore, only two of the four supply ships arrived safely in Malta's harbor city of Valletta. Those two, however, proved to be just enough to sustain the island's garrison for another few weeks. Though the engagement could hardly be considered a victory, Churchill sent Vian his congratulations.[6]

Malta's fate remained uncertain. Attrition had reduced the number of available fighters on the island to six Hurricanes, and the British were grateful when in April the American aircraft carrier *Wasp* delivered a deck load of Spitfires to Malta's airfields. The *Wasp* repeated the feat in May, which provoked Churchill to quip: "Who said a wasp couldn't sting twice?"[7]

Dönitz was not impressed by these events in the Mediterranean, and continued to insist that sending U-boats there was "a fundamentally wrong policy." The Middle Sea, in his view, was "a mousetrap," not only strategically but also geographically. The prevailing current in the Strait of Gibraltar ran west to east, which meant that while U-boats could ride that current into the Mediterranean, going back out again was slow and tedious, prolonging their exposure to patrolling British aircraft. To add to Dönitz's frustration, OKW ordered several more U-boats to take station off the entrance to Gibraltar, and sent four of them to the coast of Norway.[8]

As a result of these dispositions, by the late summer Dönitz had fewer than two dozen U-boats to commit to the North Atlantic sea-lanes. Moreover, because at any given moment half of them were either en route to or returning from their stations, most of the time he had only eight to twelve of them on patrol, far too few to affect the course of the war.

In part, of course, Dönitz's goal was to prevent the delivery of supplies to Britain. As a 1942 U.S. Navy Training Manual pointed out, the loss of just two small freighters meant losing "42 tanks, 8 six-inch Howitzers, 88 twenty-five pound guns, 40 two-pound guns, 24 armored cars, 50 Bren carriers, 5210 tons of ammunition, 600 rifles, 428 tons of tank supplies, [and] 2000 tons of stores." Quite apart from that, however, Dönitz wanted his U-boats to target the ships themselves—full or empty. Thus the U-boats attacked not only the eastbound (laden) convoys but also the westbound (empty) convoys. This so-called tonnage strategy was at the heart of Germany's war on trade.[9]

The campaign had looked promising in the first half of the year, when the U-boats sank 263 ships with a displacement of nearly 1.5 million tons— about 250,000 tons per month. But in the second half of the year, the numbers fell to only 169 ships displacing 720,000 tons, which worked out to about 120,000 tons per month. Dönitz blamed it on the misallocation of his U-boats by OKW, on the longer summer days, and on the loss of several of his U-boat aces, including Prien, Schepke, and Kretschmer, in March. Even then, however, it seemed to him that the results in the second half of 1941 should have been better. Though he was occasionally able to direct a wolf pack to one or another of the large Allied convoys, it happened much less often. It was almost as if the convoys knew where the U-boats were and maneuvered to avoid them.[10]

In fact, they did.

DÖNITZ'S TACTICS, called *Rudeltaktik* (pack tactics) in German, were utterly dependent on radio communications. In order to receive the initial sighting reports at Kernevel and relay them to other U-boats so they could assemble into a wolf pack, extensive use of wireless communications was essential. The messages were not verbal; they were sent using a telegraph key in a series of dots and dashes. Since all wireless messages were subject to interception, they were routinely encoded.

Though the Allies could not read the messages, there were ways to glean information from them by relying on what was known as traffic analysis (TA). There were several aspects to this. One was simply to monitor the *volume* of transmissions; when the number of radio messages suddenly increased, it suggested that a major operation was in the offing. Another element of traffic analysis was tracking the *origin* of the radio emissions using high-frequency direction finding—HF/DF in the inevitable acronym, or "huff-duff" in the colloquial. This involved tracking the compass bearing of each German radio signal, comparing it with similar data from widely separated stations, and triangulating the results. By 1942, HF/DF units were being placed aboard ship, and that gave the British more data points to track the origin of radio messages. And finally, experienced listeners, many of whom were volunteers in the Women's Royal Navy Service, or WRNS (pronounced "wrens"), could sometimes recognize the characteristic tempo and cadence (the *fist*) of a particular key operator. So many messages originated from Dönitz's headquarters at Kernevel that the eavesdropping Wrens gave nicknames to individual operators whose fist they recognized. Less often, the listeners might recognize the fist of a wireless operator whom they knew to be assigned to a particular U-boat, and combining that information with an HF/DF fix, they could sometimes determine the location of a specific U-boat. It was tedious work, and all too often yielded only fragments of hard intelligence.[11]

Of course, both sides also sought to break through the codes themselves in order to read the *content* of the messages, though that was exponentially harder. The Germans had some early success in breaking the British codes. Even during the battles off Narvik back in the spring of 1940, analysts at the German Naval Intelligence Service (Beobachtungsdienst, commonly known as B-Dienst) were breaking many of the Royal Navy messages. The Germans had scored an intelligence coup in November 1940 when the surface raider *Atlantis* captured the code books on the steamer *Automedon* in the Indian Ocean (see Chapter 6). Soon afterward, B-Dienst was routinely breaking coded messages sent out by Trade Plot to the convoy commanders. Often those messages concerned relatively benign topics such as weather reports, though they occasionally included a suggested course change, which helped reveal the routes of at least some of the convoys.[12]

As for the German message traffic, it was encrypted by one of the most sophisticated encoding devices ever made, which the Allies called the "Enigma machine." Initially marketed (unsuccessfully) for business use in

A photograph of an Enigma machine taken after the war. The three rotors displayed in front fit into the slots behind the keyboard and rotated. In February 1942, the Kriegsmarine added a fourth wheel to their naval Enigma machines. That cost the Allies access to the content of naval messages until March 1943.

U.S. Naval Institute

the 1920s, it attracted German military interest during the 1930s, and by the time war began, each of the German armed services was using a version of the Enigma machine to encode its wireless messages.

The device was deceptively simple in appearance, resembling a type-writer keyboard inside a wooden box. When the operator struck a key, it generated an electrical impulse that passed through three metal rotors on the top of the machine. Each disk had twenty-six possible settings, so the original letter could be changed 17,576 ways ($26 \times 26 \times 26$). Moreover, after each keystroke the disks rotated one or two positions, thus multiplying again the number of possible outcomes. Nor was that all. Plugs similar to those used by telephone operators were arranged in varying patterns on the front of the device. By the time the electrical circuit was completed, the letter initially input by the operator had passed through 160 quintillion—that's 160 followed by eighteen zeros—possible outcomes. The apparently random letters thus generated were then clustered into four-letter groups and sent out by telegraph key. They could be reassembled into a coherent message only if the receiver also had an Enigma machine, knew which disks were in use and in what order, and also knew the settings, which were changed every day.[13]

The story of how the Allies broke the Enigma code is one of the great tales of the Second World War. It started with a brilliant twenty-seven-year-old Polish mathematician named Marian Rejewski, who managed to break through the first layer of secrecy on an early commercial Enigma machine that had been purchased by Polish intelligence in the 1920s. In July 1939, the Poles shared Rejewski's findings with the British, which allowed analysts at what was known as the Government Code and Cypher School (GC&CS) at Bletchley Park, fifty miles northwest of London, to begin working on breaking the system even before the war began.[14]

In that effort, one obvious objective was to capture an intact Enigma machine. In pursuit of that, British commandos targeted and boarded the German armed trawler *Krebs* in March 1941. The captain of the *Krebs* threw his Enigma over the side, though the commandos did manage to seize several spare rotors. Two months later, the capture of the German weather ship *München* yielded a copy of the Enigma key for June. The real breakthrough, however, was the capture of U-110 off Greenland by British destroyers on May 9, 1940. The commander of the U-110 was Kapitänleutnant Fritz-Julius Lemp, the man who had sunk the passenger liner *Athenia* on the first day of the war. Lemp was attacking convoy OB-318 off Greenland when a depth-charge attack damaged his boat's batteries. Seawater mixed with sulfuric acid from the batteries created a poison gas that threatened to asphyxiate the crew, and Lemp had to surface. Before he ordered abandon ship, he directed the crew to open the vents and leave the hatches open to ensure that the U-110 sank. Before it did, however, sailors from the British destroyer *Bulldog* boarded the U-110, closed the vents, and conducted a quick inspection. One member of the boarding party was the *Bulldog*'s telegraphist, Allen O. Long, who entered the sub's radio room and found an intact Enigma machine, including the rotors and the codes for the day. Unscrewing the bolts that held the Enigma to the desk, he and his shipmates formed a human chain to pass it hand to hand to a small boat that carried it back to the *Bulldog*. Because the captured crewmen of the U-110 had been quickly hustled below deck on the *Bulldog*, the British were able to keep secret the fact that they had obtained a working Enigma machine.[15*]

Even before this invaluable acquisition, the team of academics at Bletchley Park, including twenty-eight-year-old Alan Turing, had constructed what they called a "bombe," an early electromechanical computer that could mimic and process Enigma messages—eventually they built several of them. With the insight gained from the captured Enigma, the solutions came faster, though it remained difficult to break a message quickly enough for it to have operational relevance. They kept at it, however, and by the summer of 1941 they were able to read selected messages within thirty-six hours of interception. The fact that they could do so was a secret so closely held that the government created a new category of classification for it. Information thus obtained was called Ultra.[16]

---

* When he saw that the U-110 was not sinking, Lemp desperately swam back toward it, presumably to effect the destruction of its secrets. According to one story, Lemp was shot and killed by the boarding party as he attempted to climb back on board. Many historians have accepted this story, though the British consistently denied it, insisting that Lemp simply drowned.

When the cryptanalysts at Bletchley Park identified a useful piece of Ultra intelligence, they forwarded it to the Operational Intelligence Center (OIC) at Admiralty House, near Pall Mall. There the key figure was Rodger Winn, an attorney in peacetime who, like Franklin Roosevelt, had been badly crippled by polio. He began the war as a volunteer language interpreter, but his uncanny analytical ability earned him a series of swift promotions and an appointment as a Royal Navy commander despite his physical handicap and without attending any of the navy's service schools. By 1941, Winn presided over the Tracking Room, which monitored the location of every ship and (so far as was known) every U-boat in the North Atlantic, and it was he who turned Ultra intercepts into operational orders.[17]

In June 1941 the code breakers at Bletchley Park discovered that Kernevel had ordered ten U-boats to form a reconnaissance line directly athwart the projected route of convoy HX-133. It was the largest number of U-boats Dönitz had yet deployed against a single convoy, and Winn sent a message to the convoy commander to change course while simultaneously ordering escorts from other convoys to join HX-133. The convoy did not escape altogether; six ships were lost out of a total of sixty-four. That was a modest loss, however, especially in light of the fact that the reinforced escort force sank two of the U-boats.[18]

From that moment on, the Battle of the Atlantic entailed not only chaotic and deadly middle-of-the-night confrontations between U-boats and escorts in the North Atlantic but also a clandestine race between German and British code breakers. The Germans decoded British messages to find the convoys, and the British decoded German messages to avoid the wolf packs. The breaking of the Enigma code did not produce a complete reversal of fortune. In September, for example, a wolf pack found and attacked convoy SC-42 off Greenland and sank nineteen ships displacing 73,574 tons, one of the costliest U-boat attacks of the war. It did mean, however, that such encounters became increasingly rare. The German historian Jürgen Rohwer estimates that the rerouting of convoys as a result of Ultra intelligence saved as much as two million tons of Allied shipping during the war.[19]

Code breaking was not the sole explanation for the disappointing results of Dönitz's U-boat war in the second half of 1941. Other factors included the growing number of escorts and the improved efficiency of their commanders and crews, as well as the limited number of U-boats Dönitz had available. Yet breaking the Enigma code played an important, even vital role.

───────────

IN RESPONSE TO THE DISAPPOINTING NUMBERS in the North Atlantic, Dönitz shifted some of his U-boats southward to target the HG convoys from Gibraltar to England. After HG-73 lost ten ships in September despite a robust escort of thirteen destroyers and corvettes, the Admiralty beefed up the escorts for convoy HG-76 in December. This time, in addition to sixteen surface warships, the escort included the small aircraft carrier *Audacity*. The *Audacity* displaced barely 12,000 tons and carried only six airplanes, but she could provide air cover throughout the journey to Liverpool, and by now it had become evident that airplanes were the most efficient weapon against U-boats. Convoy HG-76 left Gibraltar on December 14, one week after the Japanese raid on Pearl Harbor, and came under attack three days later by a wolf pack of seven U-boats. In a running battle that lasted for seven sleepless and harrowing nights, the escorts under the command of Lieutenant Commander Frederic John "Johnny" Walker fended off furious attacks from above and below. In the end, the U-boats managed to sink four merchant ships as well as the *Audacity*. More important, however, Dönitz lost four of the seven attacking U-boats, including the U-567, commanded by another U-boat ace, Engelbert Endrass.[20]

Then, in February 1942, just as it seemed the Allies had finally gained the upper hand in the war on trade, the Kriegsmarine added a fourth wheel to their naval Enigma machines, and the code breakers at Bletchley Park were no longer able to penetrate the text. The cryptanalysts called it the "Great Blackout," and losses to U-boats jumped dramatically from 327,000 tons in January to 476,000 tons in February and 537,000 tons in March. The U-boat crews called this the "Second Happy Time."[21]

Not all of the U-boat success in these months was due to the fact that the British temporarily lost access to Ultra intelligence. Some of it—indeed, much of it—resulted from the expansion of the war on trade into American waters off the Eastern Seaboard.

───────────

DÖNITZ NAMED IT OPERATION PAUKENSCHLAG, which in English translates to "Drumbeat" or "Drumroll." With new U-boats finally becoming available, and with the United States at last an acknowledged enemy, Dönitz envisioned a U-boat campaign along the American coast that would be as dramatic and decisive as the Pearl Harbor attack. There were, of course, serious logistical problems. It was three thousand miles from Lorient to New York City, which made the trip all but prohibitive for the 750-ton Type VII U-boats. On the other hand, Dönitz also had twenty larger (1,100-ton) Type IX U-boats, eleven of them Type IX-C boats that had a theoretical range of more than thirteen thousand miles if they proceeded at a fuel-conserving surface speed of ten knots. On December 9, 1941, the day Hitler unleashed the U-boats for use against American shipping, Dönitz asked OKW to release twelve of them for a campaign in American waters. The German high command allotted him only six, keeping the rest for service off Gibraltar, further annoying an already disgusted Dönitz. Moreover, one of the six boats developed an oil leak, so that in the end, only five of them departed in December to take up positions off the eastern coast of the United States. Dönitz also sent ten of the smaller Type VII boats, packed with extra fuel and supplies, to the waters off Nova Scotia, which was just within their operational range. Those fifteen boats represented a substantial portion of his entire U-boat flotilla.*

Crossing the Atlantic in a surfaced U-boat was harrowing. Peter-Erich Cremer, skipper of the U-333, recalled that "the waves were as high as houses." The boats pitched wildly, banging down on each successive wave with a jarring thump, often knocking crewmen off their feet. They also rolled side to side by as much as 120 degrees. When the seas became so violent as to threaten the safety of the boat, the captain could submerge into the relatively calm waters below the raging surface, but that reduced the boat's speed to about five knots, which dramatically lengthened the transit time

---

* On January 1, 1942, Germany had a total of 259 U-boats. More than half of those, however, were brand-new and still undergoing sea trials or engaged in shakedown cruises. Of the rest, twenty-six were either in the Mediterranean or en route there; six more were stationed off Gibraltar; four were off Norway; and thirty-three were in various stages of refit or repair in the shipyards. That left Dönitz with twenty-two boats for active service in the Atlantic, of which fifteen were dispatched to America.

and used up precious fuel, food, and water supplies. Dönitz wanted all of the boats to begin simultaneous attacks on January 13, and running submerged for any length of time jeopardized meeting that deadline.[22]

Dönitz had ordered all the U-boat captains to avoid attacking ships while en route unless the targets were especially valuable—that is, in excess of 10,000 tons. On January 11, two days before the coordinated assaults were to begin, Richard Hardegen in U-123, one of the big Type IX boats, spotted the British steamer *Cyclops* off Nova Scotia. Judging it to be at least 10,000 tons (actually it was 9,076 tons), he sank it with two torpedoes. News of the sinking arrived the next day in Washington, where the British and Americans were engaged in the strategy conference known as Arcadia. The report triggered a discussion about the best way to protect Allied shipping along the American east coast.[23]

The man at the center of the controversy was the new commander in chief of the U.S. Navy, Admiral Ernest J. King, who had been elevated to that post only two weeks before, on December 30. When he accepted the job, King changed the acronym for his command from CINCUS (Commander in Chief, U.S.), which sounded too much like "sink us," to COMINCH. Technically, King remained subordinate to Harold Stark, who was still the chief of naval operations, though within a few months King would be appointed to that job as well, and for the rest of the war he would wear two hats as both the administrative and operational commander of the U.S. Navy. It was an enormous job, but the tough-minded King embraced it. An apocryphal story that made the rounds in the navy at the time was that upon his appointment he declared, "When they get in trouble they send for the sons of bitches." As for Stark, he was soon dispatched to London to act as the senior U.S. naval commander in Europe. Stark accepted his exile gracefully, aware that, despite his manifest contributions to the alliance, he was the man who had presided over the navy on December 7, and as a result it would be difficult for him to retain the confidence of the nation during the war.[24]

From his very first day in command, King had to orchestrate a two-ocean war with assets that were completely inadequate to the task. Though many of the destroyers authorized by the Two Ocean Navy Act in 1940 had joined the fleet, the major combatants of that program would not become available for at least another year. FDR had ordered the *Yorktown* and eleven destroyers back to the Pacific, but of course that reduced what was available in the Atlantic where King needed a large number of destroyers to provide a robust escort for the American troop convoys to Iceland and Ireland. As a result, when in response to the sinking of the *Cyclops* the British pressed him to establish a convoy system off the American coast, he demurred, arguing that unescorted or minimally escorted convoys were worse than no convoys at all. The British contested that view, insisting that their experience in the North Atlantic showed that even convoys with no escort at all fared better than ships traveling alone. Of course, that calculation may not have applied to coastal convoys, whose route was more predictable than a convoy in the open ocean. In addition, however, King had a second objection that he could not share with the British, which was his suspicion that British advocacy of a coastal convoy system was motivated in part by their desire to integrate all Atlantic convoys into a single organization that would be commanded by a British admiral.[25]

WHILE THE BRITISH AND AMERICANS SQUABBLED, Operation Paukenschlag got under way, though not quite with the kind of devastating impact Dönitz had envisioned. Mainly this was because the five Type IX U-boats did not all manage to get into position by the target date of January 13. Hardegen's U-123 sank the Panamanian tanker *Norness* off Long Island on the fourteenth, but the last of the five boats did not arrive at its assigned position off Cape Hatteras, North Carolina, until the eighteenth.

The Carolina capes constituted a critical choke point for American coastwise trade. In January 1942, 95 percent of the oil pumped from the Louisiana and Texas oil fields made its way to the Eastern Seaboard in tanker ships that necessarily had to pass around Cape Hatteras, where the shoals narrowed the shipping channel to a mere thirty miles. Eventually the United States would shift much of its domestic oil transport to rail cars and pipelines, but when Dönitz's U-boats arrived off Hatteras on January 18, the shipping there was so abundant that upon surfacing, Hardegen was astonished to see "no fewer than twenty steamers, some with their lights on." That night he sank four of them.[26]

In accordance with Dönitz's suggested protocols, the U-boats lay quietly on the bottom of the continental shelf during the daylight hours, surfacing at night to look for passing freighters, and especially tankers. Not only did the targeted ships proceed independently, but many, as Hardegen noted, still had their running lights on, making them irresistible targets. Even those ships proceeding blacked out were often starkly silhouetted against the lights that were still burning on shore, since most cities from Miami to New York did not enforce nighttime blackouts. German U-boat skippers, who had been at war for more than two years, were dumbfounded by such carelessness, and bemused by the sight of car headlights passing along the coastal roads. Peter Cremer, commanding the U-333, recalled that "through the night glasses we could distinguish equally the big hotels and the cheap dives, and read the flickering neon signs." Peering into New York harbor through his binoculars, Hardegen jokingly told his crew that he could see

The British steamer *Empire Thrush*, sunk by the U-203, was one of many Allied ships torpedoed off Cape Hatteras in the first few months of 1942. The water was shallow enough that the vessel's masts and stack remain visible even after she settled on the bottom.

Naval History and Heritage Command

dancers atop the Empire State Building. In such an environment, the U-boats, few as they were, had a field day. In the last two weeks of January, they sank twenty-three ships, thirteen of them tankers. Counting the ships sunk in Canadian waters by the smaller Type VIIs, the U-boats of Operation Paukenschlag dispatched forty-one Allied ships displacing 236,000 tons in just two weeks. The losses were shocking, all the more so in that many of them occurred within sight of the American coastline.[27]

To coordinate what was eventually called the Eastern Sea Frontier, King named Vice Admiral Adolphus Andrews, a 1901 Naval Academy classmate. It was a thankless job. In addition to a dearth of escorts, uncooperative shipping executives, and recalcitrant merchant captains, Andrews got little initial support from the Army Air Forces. Aircraft were especially useful in anti-submarine work because U-boat skippers had learned to crash-dive the moment an airplane—any airplane—appeared on the horizon. King did assign Andrews forty-four of the navy's long-range Catalina flying boats, which were ideally suited to anti-submarine patrol, but that was too few to cover a coastline stretching more than fifteen hundred miles from Nova Scotia to Florida.[28]

Andrews scrambled to find surface escorts to protect the coastwise traffic. He had only a handful of American destroyers plus the cutters of the United States Coast Guard, which Roosevelt placed under control of the navy for the duration of the war. To supplement them, the British sent two dozen coal-burning armed trawlers that had performed well against U-boats in British and Norwegian coastal waters. Small at 170 feet and slow at twelve knots, they were nevertheless equipped with both Asdic and depth charges, and perhaps most important of all, they were manned by experienced Royal Navy crews. One of the trawlers went down with all hands during the stormy transatlantic crossing, and all of them had to go into the yards for repairs after they arrived, but by mid-April they were on duty along the American coast. It was a payback of sorts for the fifty old four-stack destroyers that Roosevelt had sent to Britain in 1940. They didn't look like much, but the Americans had to admit that they did excellent service.[29]

Germany's commitment of U-boats to American waters reached a peak that same April, when a total of thirty-one of them (fourteen Type IXs and seventeen Type VIIs) sank 133 ships displacing 641,053 tons. To deal with these terrifying and strategically significant losses, King released two more destroyers to Andrews, though they, like the others, spent most of their time chasing down all-too-frequent "SSSS" radio calls, only to arrive too late to do anything except pluck survivors from the sea. They made occasional sonar contacts and dropped a prodigious number of depth charges, but in a depressing number of cases the contacts proved to be the sunken hulks of previous U-boat victims.[30]

Andrews tried to jury-rig a solution. One such effort was his attempt to revive Q ships: freighters whose hold was stuffed with kapok or some other buoyant substance, and armed with three-inch guns hidden behind canvas screens. Since the attacking U-boats often surfaced after torpedoing a ship, the idea was that the Q-ship would absorb a torpedo hit, then wait until the U-boat surfaced before dropping the canvas screens and opening fire. Three such ships were prepared and dispatched, but they had no luck. Two of them never encountered a U-boat at all, and the third was sunk by a U-boat despite its kapok cargo and without being able to use its hidden guns.[31]

Another doomed effort was the creation of what became known as the "Hooligan Navy," a group of unarmed civilian fishing vessels and sailing sloops manned by volunteers who agreed to go out and look for U-boats off the coast. The most famous of these volunteers was Ernest Hemingway, who went to sea in his yacht *Pilar* with "a machine gun, a rifle, revolver, and explosives," planning "to throw hand grenades into the conning tower of a U-boat." Despite the eagerness of such volunteers, the best that could be said for this initiative was that it provided some excitement and gratification to a handful of eager volunteers.[32]

There were a few Allied successes: on April 14, the destroyer USS *Roper* sank the U-58, and on May 9, the Coast Guard cutter *Icarus* sank the U-352 off Cape Hatteras. More often, however, the U-boats struck repeatedly and successfully and then melted away into the dark, leaving the sea littered with wreckage and bobbing lifeboats filled with survivors. Tankers were especially at risk, and the loss of so many of them in March and April led the Roosevelt administration to order all tankers to remain in port until some effective countermeasure could be devised.[33]

As an interim step toward a fully developed convoy system, Andrews organized escorts for the dangerous journey around Cape Hatteras. Northbound freighters and tankers gathered at Cape Lookout off Morehead City, North Carolina. There they picked up an escort that took them around Cape Hatteras in a daylight run before dropping them off at Wimble Shoals, twenty or so miles north of the cape. The escorts were a bit like crossing guards walking children across a dangerous intersection.[34]

The U-boats adjusted by moving farther south. By now Dönitz had developed a protocol for refueling the smaller Type VII U-boats at sea, using large 1,600-ton submarine tankers. Officially they were Type XIV U-boats, though virtually everyone called them "*milch* cows." The first of them, U-459, deployed off the American coast in March. They had supplementary fuel tanks that could hold 450 tons of fuel, and they also carried fresh supplies, including an onboard bakery so that the U-boat crews could get fresh bread in mid-patrol. What they did not have was replacement torpedoes. Transferring a 23-foot, 3,300-pound torpedo at sea was virtually impossible, so after a U-boat expended all of its fish, it had to return to France for a new load. The *milch* cows did, however, provide the food and fuel necessary to allow the U-boats to move farther south along the American coast. On May 1, 1942, the veteran U-boat skipper Heinrich Bleichrodt, now commanding the Type IX U-109, sank the British tanker *La Paz* off Miami. Five nights later, Peter Cremer in the U-333 sank three ships in the space of six hours in the Florida Straits. That same month Korvettenkapitän Harro Schacht in the U-507 sank eight ships in six days in the Gulf of Mexico, including the 10,000-ton *Virginia*, sunk in the mouth of Mississippi River. For the second month in a row, losses exceeded 600,000 tons.[35]

The numbers were shocking, so much so that the details were kept secret from the American public. Instead, public reports emphasized that the navy was taking "strong counter-measures" against the U-boats, and in February Secretary of the Navy Frank Knox announced "a very conservative estimate" that at least three U-boats had been sunk and four others damaged. Almost as much press attention was devoted to the far less destructive deployment of nine Japanese submarines off the West Coast from Vancouver to San Diego. Though I-boats on the West Coast sank only five ships displacing

30,000 tons, they created an alarm well out of proportion to their menace. The American public was especially shocked in February when the I-17 lobbed ten shells from her deck gun into an oil refinery near Santa Barbara. Banner headlines the next day announced: "SUBMARINE SHELLS CALIFORNIA OIL PLANT." In the wake of the near panic that this provoked, the Roosevelt administration approved the now-infamous plan to intern Japanese Americans in relocation camps distant from coastal areas.[36]

On the East Coast, the United States Navy finally instituted a full-fledged convoy system in mid-May. North-bound convoys from Key West to Hampton Roads (KN) and southbound convoys to Key West (KS) generally consisted of forty-five or so merchant ships and tankers guarded by seven or eight escorts. Typically, these would consist of two U.S. Navy destroyers, two U.S. Coast Guard cutters, two of the British coal-burning trawlers, and one corvette. The number of sinkings off the American coast declined dramatically, though in part that was because by then the U-boats were prowling the Caribbean.[37]

ON THE EVE OF OPERATION PAUKENSCHLAG, on January 12, 1942, Hitler informed his top commanders that he now believed that Norway was "the zone of destiny." Due in part to a British commando raid on the coast of Norway south of Ålesund on December 27–28, he became convinced that the British were planning a major offensive there. In fact, an invasion of Norway (or more accurately a reinvasion of Norway) was one of Churchill's pet projects that winter, though the British chiefs of staff ultimately blocked it. Unaware of that, Hitler became convinced that "a large-scale Norwegian-Russian offensive" was about to begin. He demanded that the Kriegsmarine concentrate its forces off the Norwegian coast, declaring, "Every ship which is not stationed in Norway is in the wrong place." Soon afterward, OKW sent Dönitz an order to dispatch eight more U-boats to Norway. Norway! Dönitz could hardly believe it. He protested vigorously, but there was no appealing an order from the Führer. Resignedly Dönitz complained to his official war diary that thanks to the interference by Hitler and OKW, "of the sixteen boats in the Atlantic theater of operations... only six were engaged on the German Navy's most important task, the sinking of enemy shipping."[38]

Of course there was enemy shipping off Norway as well, including occasional Allied convoys from Iceland around the North Cape of Norway to Murmansk. It was one of three routes the English-speaking Allies used to supply Russia with desperately needed war materials from the United States, the others being the long route around South Africa to the Indian Ocean and through the Persian Gulf to Iran, and across the Pacific Ocean to Vladivostok. This last route was especially problematical because the convoys had to transit areas under the control of the Imperial Japanese Navy. Yet because the Japanese had reasons of their own to avoid a confrontation, they shut their eyes to the Russian ships transporting cargos of American Lend-Lease goods through Japanese waters. In some cases the ships, often with their running lights on, passed through Tsugura Strait between Hokkaidō and Honshū.[39]

To concentrate Germany's surface fleet off Norway, Hitler instructed Raeder to order the battleship *Tirpitz* from the Baltic to Trondheim, and he insisted that the three large warships still imprisoned in Brest Harbor—the *Scharnhorst, Gneisenau,* and *Prinz Eugen*—be brought back at once from France for service off Norway. Those three ships had sat uselessly in Brest since the previous May, when Raeder's grand scheme of concentrating a large surface force in the Atlantic had sunk along with the *Bismarck.* Since then, they had been bombed regularly and had made no contribution to the war beyond keeping the attention of the Royal Navy and the RAF. That naturally contributed to Hitler's skepticism about the value of surface warships generally, and he demanded that Raeder bring them home.[40]

Raeder was willing enough, and even envisioned using the big ships against the Allied convoys to Russia, and he assumed they would return home through the Iceland-Faroes Gap and around the north of Scotland. Hitler ordered otherwise. They were to come by the shortest route: straight up the English Channel and through the narrows at Dover. Raeder objected, but, as he put it, "Hitler was adamant." It was audacious in the extreme. Not only would the ships have to pass the Royal Navy's principal ports at Plymouth and Portsmouth, but the entire route was clogged with minefields and under nearly constant patrols by British aircraft. Moreover, since the ships must depart Brest at night to ensure secrecy, it meant running through Dover Strait in the daylight.[41]

The sortie began in the middle of the night on February 11–12, and by 8:00 a.m. on the twelfth the three big ships plus six destroyers and ten torpedo boats were steaming eastward off the Bay of the Seine along the coast of France. The British did not sight the flotilla until 10:42 a.m. as it was entering the Dover Strait, and the first air strike by a mere half-dozen Swordfish did not take place until nearly noon. Because Luftwaffe fighters from bases in France provided cover for the German ships, all of the Swordfish were shot down before they could get close enough to launch their torpedoes. A torpedo attack by six British destroyers at 2:30 that afternoon also failed, though soon after that the *Scharnhorst* was temporarily stopped when it hit a mine. Nevertheless, by 4:00 p.m., all three of the German big ships, plus their escorts, were off Rotterdam steaming eastward in excess of thirty knots.[42]

The defense of the Channel was primarily the responsibility of the RAF, and over the next several hours a total of nearly four hundred British planes attacked the German flotilla, both from high altitude with bombs and from wave-top with torpedoes. None of the bombs or torpedoes found a target, however, and the protecting Messerschmitt fighters shot down seventeen of the bombers. In the dark now, and running for home, the *Scharnhorst* hit a second mine at nine-thirty, and she limped into Wilhelmshaven badly hurt but still afloat. The rest of the flotilla made it safely through to Kiel.

The "Channel Dash," as it came to be called, was deeply humiliating to the Royal Navy. As the London *Times* noted, the Germans had succeeded where the Spanish Armada had failed. On the German side of the Channel, the fact that the big ships had survived further eroded Raeder's already weak leverage in dealing with Hitler. Once again, in spite of warnings from the professionals that the Führer's preferred course of action would prove disastrous, it proved not disastrous at all, except to British prestige and morale.[43]

HITLER WAS WRONG, HOWEVER, in his prediction of a major Allied thrust at Norway. Indeed, the Führer's orders to concentrate the German navy off the Norwegian coast were as ill-founded as his conviction that the British would come crawling back to the negotiating table after the fall of France, or his assurance to his generals that the Soviet Union would collapse like a house of cards. Still, the relocation of the *Tirpitz* and a dozen U-boats to the Norwegian coast did create an opportunity for the Kriegsmarine to interfere with the Arctic convoys that were carrying Lend Lease goods to the Soviets. In the first half of 1942 the Arctic Ocean north of Norway became yet another battleground in the global war on trade.

The convoys to Russia around Norway's North Cape had begun in August 1941. Labeled PQ convoys, they were neither as large nor as frequent as the HX or HG convoys to Britain. One difficulty was that such convoys were "in constant competition with shipping requirements" elsewhere, as the U.S. Army's official history put it. They were essential nonetheless, not only to supply the beleaguered Red Army, still bearing the brunt of the land war against the Wehrmacht, but also to allay the suspicions of Josef Stalin that the British and Americans were not simply biding their time while Russians and Germans killed off each other. On average, two convoys of between thirty and forty ships loaded with tanks, planes, and artillery from the United States left Iceland each month for the arduous trek around Norway's North Cape to either Murmansk, on the Barents Sea, or to Archangel, on the White Sea. The voyage was especially difficult in winter, not only because of the challenging weather but also because the more expansive Arctic ice sheet pinched the convoys into a narrow passage above the North Cape. At least the frequent snowstorms often kept the Luftwaffe grounded. As one crewman on the Murmansk run put it, "All hands grew as fond of snow as a small boy with a new sled."[44]

In January 1942, when Churchill and Admiral Tovey learned that the *Tirpitz* had left the Baltic and headed north along the Norwegian coast, they initially feared she might be headed into the Atlantic shipping lanes in a reprise of the *Bismarck*'s sortie the year before. Soon afterward, two of the *Panzerschiffe*—the *Admiral Scheer* and *Lützow* (formerly the *Deutschland*)—arrived at Narvik to pose an additional threat. Over the next several months, Churchill, Tovey, and the officers in Trade Plot all kept a wary eye on the *Tirpitz* and the two pocket battleships in daily anticipation of a sortie.[45]

Like the ships off North Carolina's Cape Hatteras more than four thousand miles away, the ships of the PQ convoys had to round a treacherous headland while under constant threat from U-boats. The similarities ended

The battleship *Tirpitz*, sister ship of the *Bismarck*, seldom fired a gun in anger, yet her very existence kept admirals at Whitehall awake at night. Raeder sought to exploit her status as a one-ship fleet-in-being, though Hitler saw only that she seldom achieved anything tangible.

U.S. Naval Institute

there, however. Unlike shipping along the American eastern coastline, the PQ convoys had to battle the ferocious weather north of the Arctic Circle where conditions were the worst in twenty-five years. And because the North Cape (unlike Hatteras) was in enemy hands, they also faced a threat from land-based aircraft. Whereas airplanes off Cape Hatteras were a welcome sight to the merchant ships, airplanes off Norway posed a greater danger than the U-boats. Now, added to those perils, was the lurking specter of German capital ships.[46]

The *Tirpitz* did sortie twice in March, and each time it did, Tovey took the Home Fleet out to confront her. Amidst the ice and fog of the Arctic Sea, however, the *Tirpitz* never found the convoys, and Tovey never found the *Tirpitz*. He came close once, thanks to the code breakers at Bletchley Park. On March 9, a tip from OIC prompted Tovey to order an attack on the *Tirpitz* by a dozen Albacore torpedo bombers from the carrier *Victorious*.

None of them scored a hit, however, and the *Tirpitz* returned to port undamaged. Throughout the rest of March and into April, Churchill urged near-continuous air strikes against the *Tirpitz* in her lair at Trondheim, insisting that her destruction would be worth the loss of a hundred aircraft and five hundred men. None of the air strikes succeeded in damaging the big battleship, however, much less destroying it, and it continued to pose a latent threat to the periodic PQ convoys that had to thread their way around the North Cape to Murmansk while fending off both U-boats and bombers.[47]

THESE WERE THE CIRCUMSTANCES when convoy PQ-17 set out from Hvalfjord in Iceland on June 27 bound for the White Sea port of Archangel. Composed of thirty-four merchant ships, the convoy had a substantial, even imposing escort consisting of six destroyers, four corvettes, two anti-air cruisers, four armed minesweepers, and two submarines, all under Royal Navy Captain Jack Broome. In addition, however, Tovey himself put to sea with a covering force of two battleships—his flagship *Duke of York* and (for the first time) an American battleship, the brand-new USS *Washington*—plus two cruisers, a carrier, and fourteen more destroyers.[48]

Though Hitler had placed severe restrictions on the use of the Kriegsmarine's big ships since the loss of the *Bismarck*, Raeder longed for a chance to use them against the North Cape convoys. In pursuit of that goal, he got Hitler's permission to move the *Tirpitz* and the heavy cruiser *Hipper* north from Trondheim to Vestfjord near Narvik, and to order the pocket battleships *Admiral Scheer* and *Lützow* to Altenfjord at the very tip of the North Cape, where the *Tirpitz* and *Hipper* would eventually join them. Hitler made it clear, however, that they were not to sortie unless Raeder could verify that the British had no aircraft carriers within striking distance. The *Lützow* ran aground during the tortuous coastal passage, but the other big ships arrived at Altenfjord in early July. There they were directly on the flank of the PQ convoys.[49]

At noon on July 4, 1942, PQ-17 was steaming eastward almost due north of Altenfjord, more than halfway to its destination, when a long-range German patrol plane spotted it and broadcast its location. The American destroyer *Wainwright*, equipped with fire-control radar, kept the plane at a respectful distance, but the radio reports got through. Soon afterward, twenty-six Heinkel 111 bombers arrived and conducted a torpedo attack. One ship, the *Christopher Newport*, was hit and had to be abandoned. An hour later a second air attack claimed two more victims. Such losses were considered acceptable, however, and the convoy plodded onward. Broome, the escort commander, was grateful for the *Wainwright*'s support and blinkered the American cruiser a message: "Was the original Fourth of July as noisy as this?"[50]

Far more important messages were being sent by the Germans that day, and the cryptanalysts at Bletchley Park were breaking them as fast as they could. Already at 2:40 that morning, OIC had informed Tovey that unusually heavy radio traffic suggested an imminent operation by German heavy units. Then, eighteen hours later, the cryptanalysts broke a message ordering the authorities at Altenfjord to top off the fuel tanks of the big warships for immediate service. The message was passed quickly from Bletchley Park to OIC, and by nine o'clock that night, the First Sea Lord, Dudley Pound, was reading it. The implication was unmistakable: the *Tirpitz* and the two pocket battleships, perhaps with the cruiser *Hipper*, were preparing to descend upon PQ-17. By then, Tovey's big ships, including the aircraft carrier *Victorious*, had turned back for home, and the cruisers and destroyers providing close support would be helpless against the German big ships. The naval staff agonized over what to do. The vice chief of staff, Sir Henry Moore, recalled that Pound listened to the discussion with his eyes closed. There were no good options, but Pound reasoned that at the very least the cruisers should be sent out of harm's way. At 9:11 he ordered them to withdraw westward "at high speed." Twelve minutes later he sent an even more consequential message to Broome: "Owing to threat from surface ships convoy is to disperse and proceed to Russian ports." Less than a minute later, he repeated the order more succinctly: "Convoy is to scatter."[51]

The swift arrival of these alarming messages, one after the other, created a sense of urgency on board the convoy flagship HMS *Keppel*. Broome later wrote that Pound's signal was like "an electric shock." Its classification of

SECRET, MOST IMMEDIATE, and the timing of the two messages, less than a minute apart, left the impression that the arrival of the *Tirpitz* was imminent, that her masts were likely to appear over the horizon at any moment. Broome necessarily obeyed the order, a decision he regretted for the rest of his life, and directed the merchant captains to make their separate ways to a Russian port.[52]

With the merchant ships proceeding independently, they became vulnerable to attacks from both above and below—indeed, they were all but helpless. As an officer on the American freighter *Ironclad* put it, it was "like shooting fish in a rain barrel." The long July days allowed the Luftwaffe to patrol widely over the Barents Sea to track down the fleeing ships, and over the next twenty-four hours, twelve of the convoy ships were sunk, half by aircraft and half by U-boats. A handful of the ships fled northward into the pack ice, painted themselves white as camouflage, and eventually made their circuitous way into Archangel. Twenty-three ships, however, were lost, and with them went 430 tanks, 210 bombers, 3,550 vehicles, and 100,000 tons of munitions. Lost, too, were 153 crewmen. Many more survived, though they experienced harrowing journeys in small boats amidst the drifting ice before being rescued. That same week, the returning (empty) convoy from Russia to Iceland (QP-13) ran into a minefield and lost four more ships. These losses were so disastrous that the Allies canceled the next several North Cape convoys. The Russians protested passionately, and the decision fed the existing skepticism within the Kremlin about Allied commitment.[53]

The massacre of PQ-17 in July 1942 was part of a global pattern, for by then, Allied and neutral ships were being sunk in unprecedented numbers worldwide. Only days before, Italian surface forces under Iachino and German aircraft from Sicily had savaged two more convoys to Malta, one from Gibraltar and one from Alexandria, in what the Italians dubbed the Battle of Pantelleria. In one of the few clear-cut Italian victories over the Royal Navy, the British lost two destroyers sunk and two cruisers and three destroyers badly damaged. Only two cargo ships got through to Valletta. Elsewhere, the story was much the same. From the North Cape of Norway to the Caribbean Sea, Dönitz's U-boats, despite their small numbers, inflicted grievous losses on the Allies. In both May and June, Allied shipping losses exceeded 600,000 tons. Adding the losses to German and Italian aircraft and mines, global Allied losses in June surpassed a truly frightening 850,000 tons. It was all but indisputable that in midsummer 1942, the Axis powers were winning the war on trade.[54]

PART III

WATERSHED

The first half of 1942 had been harrowing for the Allies. The Japanese had conducted a five-month rampage through the Pacific and Indian Oceans without suffering a single reverse; Italian and German forces had incapacitated every Royal Navy capital ship in the eastern Mediterranean and strained the supply lifeline to Malta to its breaking point; Allied shipping losses in the Atlantic, especially along the eastern coastline of the United States and in the Caribbean, were unsustainable; and the destruction of PQ-17 in the Barents Sea temporarily halted North Cape convoys to the Soviet Union, where, despite a successful counterattack outside Moscow, the Red Army still confronted nearly two hundred Axis divisions.

The Western press put the best light it could on the circumstances, but so dark were Allied prospects that British and American leaders looked urgently for some way to strike back, if for no other purpose than to boost morale at home. That was a principal motive behind the American decision to undertake a high-risk and strategically questionable bombing raid against Japan in April, and Churchill's decision to assault the seaport city of Dieppe, on the coast of occupied France, in

August. In between those events, the U.S. Navy confronted the Imperial Japanese Navy in two milestone defensive engagements in the Pacific that underscored the emergence of carrier-borne aircraft as the dominant weapon of naval warfare. By the end of the year, the Anglo-American forces managed to scrape together the wherewithal to initiate the first strategic counteroffensives of the war: on the island of Guadalcanal in the Pacific, and on the coast of North Africa in the Atlantic.

It is mainly in hindsight that these events emerge as a kind of watershed, for neither of them inflicted a mortal or even serious wound on the Axis powers. Rather, their importance lay in the fact that they demonstrated to friend and foe alike that the Allies had survived the initial hammer blows of 1940–41 and could now contemplate taking the initiative. By the end of 1942, the growing resilience of the Red Army on the Eastern Front and the promise of nearly unlimited material resources from the United States made the prospects of an Allied victory, if not yet bright, then at least not entirely bleak. It became possible to believe that in time the combination of British grit, Russian manpower, and American industrial productivity could someday overwhelm the Axis.

But not yet. There were more than three years of war to come—of destruction and disappointment, of hopes kindled and extinguished, of human loss and misery—before the final triumph. As Churchill put it in a speech in November 1942: "This is not the end. It is not even the beginning of the end. But it is, perhaps, the end of the beginning."

CHAPTER 13

STEMMING THE TIDE

O N JANUARY 31, 1942, U.S. Navy Captain Donald Duncan, Ernie King's aviation officer, climbed aboard the newest of America's aircraft carriers, the USS *Hornet*, anchored off Norfolk, Virginia. Because the carrier *Saratoga* had been torpedoed by a Japanese submarine twenty days before and compelled to go to the West Coast for repairs, the *Hornet* was now one of only four full-sized U.S. Navy carriers available for duty. The Americans did have two smaller carriers (*Ranger* and *Wasp*) in the Atlantic—in a few weeks, *Wasp* would begin ferrying Spitfire fighters from Britain to besieged Malta in the Mediterranean. In the Pacific, however, there was only the *Yorktown*, her sister ship *Enterprise*, and the larger but older *Lexington*—the "Lady Lex."

After Duncan performed the traditional ceremony of saluting first the *Hornet's* flag and then the officer of the deck, the man who greeted him was the ship's captain, fifty-five-year-old Marc "Pete" Mitscher, a pale, gaunt, indeed almost cadaverous individual who covered his bald head with a cus-tomized baseball cap that had an oversized bill to protect his sun-ravaged skin from further damage. Mitscher was a veteran pilot who had earned his gold wings back in 1916 as U.S. naval aviator number 33. After welcoming Duncan aboard, Mitscher led him to his cabin, and once they were seated, Duncan came straight to the point: "Can you put a loaded B-25 in the air on a normal deck run?" Mitscher answered with a question: "How many B-25s?" Duncan responded immediately, "Fifteen."

Mitscher took his time before answering. He studied the large wooden spotting board with its outline of the *Hornet's* flight deck, and checked the specs on the army's B-25 Mitchell bomber, which had a 67-foot wingspan. The flight deck of the *Hornet* was 86 feet wide, so that was no problem. On the other hand, the Mitchells were too big to fit on the ship's elevators, which meant they could not be lowered to the hangar deck. Putting fifteen of them on the flight deck would leave little room for takeoffs, and while thus encumbered the *Hornet* would be unable to perform normal flight operations. Still, after running the calculations through his head, Mitscher told Duncan, "Yes it can be done."[1]

FROM ALMOST THE VERY DAY of Pearl Harbor, Franklin Roosevelt had sought to find some way to strike back at Japan, not to inflict a strategic defeat—that, he knew, was months if not years away—but to revive the morale of the American public. Japan had bombed the United States, or at least an important U.S. facility; there must be some way for the United States to bomb Japan. He considered flying American bombers from airfields in China, but getting the planes into China was a daunting logistical problem, and in any case it would take so long as to miss the moment. Sending one or more of the nation's few and valuable aircraft carriers near enough to bomb Japan with conventional carrier planes involved too much risk, since the carriers would have to loiter off the Japanese coast to recover the planes afterward. It was a navy captain named Seth Low who came up with the idea of flying land-based bombers off a carrier deck, then landing them on airfields in China while the carriers steamed for home.[2]

The commander and guiding hand for the project was U.S. Army Lieutenant Colonel James H. Doolittle, known universally as "Jimmy," a former boxer, test pilot for the army, and demonstration pilot for the Shell Oil Company. When the war broke out, Doolittle returned to active duty and was appointed to the staff of General Henry H. Arnold, head of the U.S. Army Air Forces. Once Duncan reported that it was indeed possible to fly B-25 bombers off a carrier deck, Doolittle took over the project, assembling a group of B-25 plane crews at Eglin Field in Florida. He told them that they had been selected for a top-secret and very dangerous mission and that he wanted only volunteers. Naturally, everyone volunteered. Officially, they did not know their objective, but some concluded rather quickly that it probably involved carrier takeoffs, since they received their training from a navy lieutenant named Hank Miller and it consisted mostly of practicing short takeoffs in as little as 250 feet of runway.[3]

Doolittle had been candid about the danger to the plane crews, but the mission was dangerous in other ways, too. Because the *Hornet* would not be able to fly combat air patrol (CAP) over the task force during the long Pacific Ocean transit, a second carrier would have to accompany her. That meant that two carriers—fully half of America's entire carrier force—would be committed to what was essentially a morale-boosting mission. The American commander of the Pacific theater, Admiral Chester Nimitz, was dubious about making such a commitment, but he

American Admiral Chester Nimitz arrived in Pearl Harbor on Christmas Day in 1941 and remained in command of the Pacific Ocean Area for the duration of the war. His quiet dignity and apparent serenity masked a willingness to make bold decisions.

Naval History and Heritage Command

knew better than to get in the way of a project that emanated from the White House.

Nimitz was a low-key commander who conducted himself with a quiet reserve. Many who dealt with him in his Pearl Harbor headquarters were slightly unnerved by the cool gaze of his pale blue eyes. Unlike Churchill, who exercised authority as a birthright, or Roosevelt, who sought to jolly his visitors with bonhomie, Nimitz listened quietly, assessed the circumstances, then made his decision. Those decisions, however, could be surprisingly bold, for his soft-spoken demeanor masked a fierce determination. Upon receipt of the proposal to bomb Japan with two carriers, he sent for Rear Admiral William F. Halsey, commander of the task force that was built around the USS *Enterprise*. Nimitz asked Halsey if he thought the plan could work. "They'll need a lot of luck," Halsey replied. "Are you willing to take them out there?" Nimitz asked. Halsey did not hesitate: "Yes I am." "Good," Nimitz replied, "it's all yours."[4]

Meanwhile, the *Hornet* left Norfolk in February, steamed south to the Caribbean, through the Panama Canal, and then up the Pacific coast to Alameda, in San Francisco Bay, where she arrived on March 20. The B-25s, having flown across the country from Florida, taxied down to the pier and were lifted aboard by crane. The big two-engine bombers looked incongruous on the *Hornet*'s flight deck, but they fit. In fact, Lieutenant Miller, the navy pilot who had trained the army flyers, suggested adding one more plane—a sixteenth—which he offered to fly off the *Hornet* personally once the carrier was at sea to demonstrate that it could be done. Mitscher agreed, and so when the *Hornet* passed under the Golden Gate Bridge into the Pacific on April 2, there were sixteen bombers on her deck. Rather than fly off as a demonstration, however, the sixteenth plane stayed on board and took part in the raid on Japan.[5]

Accompanied by two cruisers, four destroyers, and an oiler, the *Hornet* task force steamed west toward Hawaii and a rendezvous with Halsey's *Enterprise* on April 12. (That same week in the Indian Ocean, Japanese carriers were completing their destruction of British naval bases in Ceylon.) With planes from the *Enterprise* flying cover, the unified two-carrier task force continued west across the Pacific. Five days later, on April 17, the

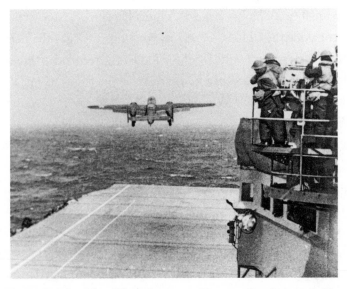

A Mitchell B-25 bomber lifts off from the carrier *Hornet* on April 18, 1942. Though the seas appear relatively calm in this photograph, the weather was unsettled and the launch precarious.

Naval History and Heritage Command

accompanying tanker topped off the carriers and cruisers and the big ships began a high-speed run toward the target. That night, however, Japanese picket boats, placed well out to sea for just such a contingency, managed to get off a sighting report to Tokyo before they were sunk by the cruiser *Nashville*. That convinced Halsey and Doolittle that they should not wait. Though they were still a hundred miles from the desired launch position, a klaxon sounded on board the *Hornet* and a voice called out: "Army pilots man your planes."[6]

The launch was difficult. The seas were rough and the *Hornet* pitched so dramatically that the signal officer, tethered to the deck by a lifeline, timed the takeoffs to coincide with the carrier's swooping rise and fall. Despite the difficulties, all sixteen of the planes took off successfully, circled the ship once, then headed west. They did not form up into a group, as that would take more time and waste fuel; instead, they headed off independently.[7]

Each plane carried only four 500-pound bombs, and they attacked five different cities. As a result, the damage they wrought was more symbolic than strategic. Moreover, due partly to the early takeoff, none of the sixteen planes made it to a Chinese airfield, as initially planned. Most crash-landed in China or along the Chinese coast after running out of gas, their crews bailing out into the dark; six of the Doolittle Raiders were killed in those crashes. One plane landed in Vladivostok, where, since the Russians remained officially neutral in the Pacific War, both the plane and the crew were interned by the Soviet Government. Eight of the Doolittle Raiders were captured by the Japanese. Of those eight, three were executed, one died in prison, and four survived the war as POWs. The rest, including Doolittle, eventually made it safely back to the United States, where Roosevelt awarded him a Medal of Honor in a White House ceremony.[8]

In the wake of the attack, the Japanese claimed that the American bombers had targeted schools and hospitals, though few outside Japan took such claims seriously. On the whole, the raid had exactly the effect that Roosevelt had sought: it was a tonic for American public opinion and an embarrassment to the Japanese. Yamamoto was shamed that although the Imperial Palace was not targeted, the very presence of American bombers over Japan had put the emperor's life at risk.[9]

NIMITZ HAD WORRIED about devoting half of his carrier force to the Doolittle Raid, which left him with only two carriers to cover the rest of the Pacific Ocean, and his concern appeared justified when in mid-April he learned that the Japanese were planning another major offensive in the South Pacific. The news came to him from a group of American code breakers at what was called Station Hypo in Hawaii, a group that was fully as consequential to the Pacific War as the British team at Bletchley Park was to the Battle of the Atlantic.

The operational code of the Imperial Japanese Navy, known as JN-25b, did not depend on a mechanical device for encryption like the German Enigma, but it had nevertheless resisted all efforts to break it until after the Pearl Harbor attack. For that, Nimitz's chief cryptanalyst, Lieutenant Commander Joseph Rochefort, could never fully forgive himself. It was hardly his fault. For one thing, transcriptions of the Japanese *diplomatic* message traffic, code-named Purple, that were being read in Washington were not shared with the command in Pearl Harbor. Rochefort later wondered if access to those messages might have aided him in his effort to crack the operational code. Then, too, the naval intelligence command in Washington (Op-20-G) repeatedly changed Rochefort's orders about where he should focus his efforts. As a result, Rochefort had no opportunity to develop a long-range strategy against any of Japan's specialized codes. In spite of that, the fact that he had not been able to prevent or to predict the raid on December 7 motivated him to work almost literally around the clock, seeking hints about future Japanese initiatives.[10]

On April 5, three days before Halsey and the *Enterprise* left Pearl Harbor to join the *Hornet* en route to Tokyo, Rochefort was working on an intercepted message that had been sent from Yamamoto's Combined Fleet headquarters in the Inland Sea to the aircraft carrier *Kaga*, which was undergoing repairs at Sasebo. Rochefort had already determined the four-letter code for "invasion group," and now he saw that code used in close association with the letters "RZP." Because the Japanese had previously used those letters to refer to Port Moresby, on the south coast of New Guinea, Rochefort suspected at once that Port Moresby was the target of the next Japanese invasion.[11]

Rochefort called Commander Edwin Layton, Nimitz's intelligence officer, and told him he had "a hot one." Layton arranged a meeting with the admiral, and Rochefort laid out his case. Nimitz was convinced. But with two of his carriers halfway to Tokyo and a third, the *Lexington*, in the yards at Pearl Harbor having her 8-inch guns removed to make room for more anti-air batteries, it was not clear what he could do about it. Moreover, there was skepticism in Washington about the reliability of Rochefort's analysis. The director of naval communications, Rear Admiral Joseph Redman, and his younger brother Captain John Redman worried that Rochefort's predictions were based more on guesswork than on analysis. That was true enough, though it was informed guesswork. Nimitz decided to trust his intelligence team, and he got permission from King to send the *Lexington* to join the *Yorktown* in the Coral Sea off the eastern tip of New Guinea to see if they could intercept the Japanese invasion force. He placed both carriers, collectively designated as Task Force 17, under the command of Rear Admiral Frank Jack Fletcher. A 1906 academy graduate (one year after

Nimitz, and five years after King), Fletcher was a surface warfare officer whom circumstance had placed in command of carrier forces. He was a sailor's sailor: open-faced, competent, and straightforward.[12]

Despite the skepticism in Washington, Rochefort's analysis was spot-on. The Japanese high command had indeed targeted Port Moresby as their next conquest, and rather than fight their way over the crest of the Owen Stanley Mountains, which ran the length of New Guinea, they decided to conduct an end run around the eastern tip of the island to attack Port Moresby from the sea. Preliminary to that main thrust, they also planned to seize the tiny island of Tulagi, in the Solomon Islands, as a seaplane base to keep track of American activity in the Coral Sea. Following that, the task force committed to Tulagi would help screen the Port Moresby invasion group. Two of Japan's big carriers, *Shōkaku* and *Zuikaku*, would provide distant cover for both operations, but only after delivering planes to the Japanese base at Rabaul, at the northern tip of New Britain, five hundred miles north of Port Moresby. By thus loading up the various task groups with a number of secondary objectives, Japanese planners overlooked Mahan's dictum that a key to naval success was the concentration of force.[13]

As the various elements of the Japanese fleet got under way in early May, Fletcher's *Yorktown* group, having replenished at Samoa, received a report from an Australian scout plane of a Japanese invasion force headed for Tulagi. Fletcher sped northward to attack it, and in a series of air assaults on May 4, American bombers and torpedo planes damaged several Japanese ships in the harbor there, though by then much of the invasion force had already withdrawn. After recovering his planes, Fletcher turned the *Yorktown* southward again to rendezvous with the *Lexington*, and after both carriers refueled from the tanker *Neosho*, they headed west into the Coral Sea.[14]

Even as the Americans attacked the shipping at Tulagi, Admiral Takeo Takagi was entering the Coral Sea with the carriers *Shōkaku* and *Zuikaku*. Rather than steam due south from the Japanese base at Truk, in the Carolines, Takagi had directed his two carriers around the eastern end of the Solomon Islands, so by May 6 he was actually coming up *behind* Fletcher's Task Force 17. In a nautical form of blindman's bluff, neither of the opposing commanders was aware of the other, even though at one

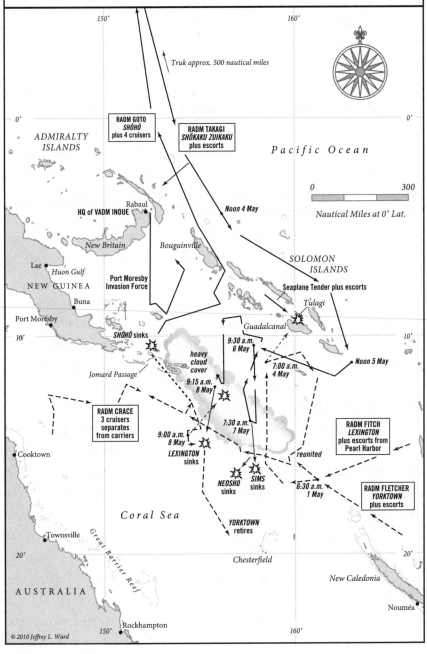

THE BATTLE OF THE CORAL SEA
May 7–8, 1942

150° 160°

Truk approx. 500 nautical miles

RADM GOTO
SHŌHŌ
plus 4 cruisers

RADM TAKAGI
SHŌKAKU ZUIKAKU
plus escorts

0° 0°

ADMIRALTY
ISLANDS

Pacific Ocean

Noon 4 May

0   300

Nautical Miles at 0° Lat.

Rabaul
HQ of VADM INOUE

New Britain

Bougainville

SOLOMON
ISLANDS

Lae
Huon Gulf
NEW GUINEA

Port Moresby Invasion Force

Seaplane Tender plus escorts

Buna

Tulagi

Port Moresby

Guadalcanal

10° 10°

SHŌHŌ sinks

9:30 a.m.
6 May

heavy cloud cover

7:00 a.m.
4 May

Noon 5 May

Jomard Passage

9:15 a.m.
8 May

RADM CRACE
3 cruisers
separates
from carriers

7:30 a.m.
7 May

RADM FITCH
LEXINGTON
plus escorts from
Pearl Harbor

9:00 a.m.
8 May

Cooktown

LEXINGTON
sinks

reunited

NEOSHO
sinks

SIMS
sinks

6:30 a.m.
1 May

RADM FLETCHER
YORKTOWN
plus escorts

Coral Sea

YORKTOWN
retires

Townsville

Great Barrier Reef

20° 20°

Chesterfield

New Caledonia

AUSTRALIA

Nouméa

© 2010 Jeffrey L. Ward

150° Rockhampton 160°

point they passed within seventy miles of each other. Takagi (like Nimitz) was a former submarine officer and more recently had commanded cruiser forces, including the one that had virtually annihilated Doorman's ABDA command in the Battle of the Java Sea two months before. As a result, he delegated air operations to the commander of the Fifth Carrier Division and his close friend, Rear Admiral Chūichi Hara, a large, stout man whose nickname in the fleet was "King Kong."[15]

Before dawn on May 7, both sides launched search planes. Though none of them found the enemy's main force, one plane from the *Yorktown* did sight elements of the Port Moresby invasion group, including two cruisers and four destroyers, off the eastern tip of New Guinea. Instead of reporting two *cruisers*, however, the American radio operator used the wrong code key and reported two *carriers*. That electrifying message led Fletcher to order a full air strike from both of his carriers, and by ten-fifteen that morning, the Americans had ninety-three planes in the air heading toward the reported coordinates.[16]

By the time Fletcher learned about the glitch in the radio transmission, it was too late to recall the strike, but providentially, another report, this one from a U.S. Army search plane, put a Japanese carrier only twenty miles away from the initial target coordinates. Fletcher broke radio silence to vector the attack planes to the new target, which proved to be the small light carrier *Shōhō* accompanying the invasion force. Assailed by ninety American aircraft, the *Shōhō* was overwhelmed. Pilots from the *Lexington* claimed five bomb hits and nine torpedo hits, and those from the *Yorktown* claimed fourteen bomb hits and ten torpedo hits. Even allowing for inflated damage reports from enthusiastic pilots, the *Shōhō* was virtually blown to pieces. Out of a crew of 736, only 204 men survived. It was the first Japanese carrier lost during the Pacific War—the first important combatant of any kind—and Lieutenant Commander Robert Dixon, leading the *Lexington's* scout bombers, radioed the subsequently famous report: "Scratch one flattop."[17]

The Japanese, too, sent a strike force toward a false sighting that morning. At 7:22 a.m., a Japanese scout plane reported a carrier and a cruiser within striking distance, and like Fletcher, Hara launched a full air strike

The Japanese light carrier *Shōhō* under attack and on fire during the Battle of the Coral Sea on May 7, 1942. Overwhelmed by air groups from two U.S. carriers, the *Shōhō* went down with the loss of 532 of her crew. She was the first major Japanese combatant lost in the war.

U.S. National Archives photo no. 80-G-17026

from both of his carriers toward the reported coordinates. What the scout pilot had seen, however, was the oiler *Neosho* and her escorting destroyer USS *Sims*. Just as the Americans had obliterated the *Shōhō*, Japanese pilots overwhelmed both American ships, sinking the *Sims* and punishing the *Neosho* so badly that her burning wreckage stayed afloat only because of her half-empty fuel tanks.[18]

The air attacks of May 7 were only the preliminary skirmish. The next day scout planes from each side finally sighted the other's carriers, and at almost the same moment, the Americans and the Japanese launched full deckloads of attack planes toward the other's position—the planes even passed one another en route to their targets. Arriving first, the Americans encountered ferocious opposition from Japanese Zeros flying CAP. An American pilot recalled, "It was an incredible scramble. People yelling over the radio, mixed up, and you never knew who was on top of whom." Amidst the chaos, and harassed by the Zeros, the torpedo planes scored no hits. The dive-bombers, however, plunging almost straight down from fourteen thousand feet, put three 1,000-pound bombs onto the *Shōkaku*, utterly wrecking her flight deck, though she managed to stay afloat. The *Zuikaku*, obscured by dense cloud cover, escaped entirely.[19]

Meanwhile, Japanese planes were attacking Task Force 17. The well-trained Japanese aviators, most of them petty officers and warrant officers, conducted an "anvil attack" on the American carriers, coming in from both sides simultaneously to make it difficult for the carriers to avoid the torpedoes. The big flattops maneuvered furiously in an effort to comb the torpedoes, but the *Lexington* in particular, built atop a heavy battlecruiser hull, was slow to turn. Her skipper, Frederick Sherman, recalled that "it took 30 to 40 seconds just to put the rudder hard over," and even then, the big ship turned "majestically and ponderously." Within the first few minutes the *Lexington* was hit by two bombs and two torpedoes. Down in the engine room, machinist Gustave Sembritzky felt them. As he later recalled, "When a bomb hits the ship, it just sort of shakes it. And if a torpedo hits, it lifts it up. You can tell the difference."[20]

Fires raged throughout the *Lexington*, and she heeled over to a seven-degree list. Damage control teams got the fires under control and counter-flooding brought her back to an even keel so that she could recover the planes returning from their attack on the Japanese carriers. Then at 12:47 a huge internal explosion from the ruptured fuel tanks blew a giant hole in the flight deck and sent the elevator platform, weighing several tons, spinning up into the air before it came down with a loud crash on top of an airplane. Another internal explosion an hour later made it obvious that the ship was doomed. Sherman reluctantly ordered abandon ship, and when everyone was clear, an American destroyer, the USS *Phelps*, sent the burning wreck to the bottom with five torpedoes.[21]

The *Yorktown*, too, was hit, though not fatally. Frantic maneuvering allowed her to dodge at least eight torpedoes, but she was repeatedly shaken by near misses from bombs that damaged her hull below the waterline. One landed directly on her flight deck and penetrated deep into her engine spaces before exploding. Sixty-six men were killed, the lights went out, and three of the ship's six boilers had to be secured. Though the *Yorktown* stayed afloat, she now trailed a long black oil slick from leaking fuel tanks.[22]

In the aftermath of the fighting on May 8, Fletcher briefly considered a second strike, but a sober assessment of his remaining assets convinced him to call it a day. Takagi and Hara, too, pulled back from the fight. Most consequential of all was that Admiral Shigeyoshi Inoue, who commanded the overall operation from his headquarters at Rabaul, ordered the invasion force to retire northward. It was the first time in the war that the Japanese failed to achieve their military objective, and as it happened, they never did take Port Moresby. Maps in future textbooks on World War II would depict the furthest advance of Japanese conquests stopping just short of Port Moresby. Though no one knew it at the time, the Imperial Japanese Navy had reached the limit of its conquests.

Based on the reports of their pilots, the Japanese believed they had sunk both of the American carriers, and the domestic press in Japan trumpeted another triumph by the Imperial Japanese Navy, one more step on the inevitable march to victory. Privately, however, Yamamoto was disappointed that Hara had not followed up on his tactical victory to ensure that both carriers had in fact been destroyed, and he was distraught that Inoue had called off the invasion. He went so far as to radio Inoue, in what was clearly a formal rebuke, to ask "the reason for issuing such an order [to retire] when further advance and attack were needed."[23]

The Americans, too, inflated their achievement in the Coral Sea. Headlines in the *New York Times* insisted that American bombers had sunk no fewer than seventeen Japanese warships, including "the certain destruction of two aircraft carriers, one heavy cruiser, and six destroyers." The papers were initially silent, however, about American losses, reporting only that they were "comparatively light." In fact, American losses in the Coral Sea were heavier than those of the Japanese, and the loss of the *Lexington* in particular, representing as it did one-quarter of the nation's available strike force in the Pacific, was especially worrisome. At the moment, however, the public was hungry for good news, and the Navy Department did not discourage the national celebration.[24]

THE BATTLE OF THE CORAL SEA had other consequences not appreciated at the time. Though the damage to the *Shōkaku* was only marginally worse than the wounds inflicted on the *Yorktown*, the Japanese decided to send her into the yards for a full refit, while the Americans, and Chester Nimitz in particular, decided that the *Yorktown* should be patched up quickly at Pearl Harbor, taking whatever shortcuts were necessary to get her swiftly back into fighting order. Nimitz insisted on the quick turnaround because Rochefort had brought him another piece of critical information. On the very day the *Lexington* went down in the Coral Sea, Rochefort and his team intercepted a coded message that indicated the creation of a new Japanese battle force, consisting of Japan's four other large carriers and two of her fast battleships, plus a large number of escorts. The target of this armada was something designated in the message as "AF," which Rochefort believed was the tiny atoll of Midway, eleven hundred miles northwest of Pearl Harbor.

Once again, Rochefort's administrative bosses in Washington were skeptical. If his assessment was wrong, they noted, the next Japanese blow could fall on American Samoa, New Caledonia, or even the American West Coast. Rochefort was confident in his assessment, and to prove it he orchestrated a subterfuge. He sent a message to Midway by subterranean cable, requesting American authorities there to send a radio message back to Hawaii stating that their salt water evaporators had broken down. Then he waited. As he expected, the Japanese intercepted the message, and soon afterward the Americans at Station Hypo were reading a Japanese message stating that "AF" was short of drinking water.[25]

By the middle of May, the Hypo team had compiled dozens of small bits of information from scores of Japanese radio transmissions. Rochefort pieced them together until he was satisfied that he had a fairly clear idea of Japanese intentions. The enemy, he told Nimitz, would attack and attempt to occupy Midway Atoll with a force spearheaded by four or possibly five carriers, and they would do so in the last few days of May or the first week of June.[26]

It was not entirely clear, however, what Nimitz could or should do with the information. The *Saratoga* was still undergoing a refit on the West Coast, the *Lexington* was gone, and the damaged *Yorktown* was limping back toward Pearl Harbor, trailing a ten-mile-long oil slick. The only other American carriers in the Pacific—the *Enterprise* and *Hornet*—were still returning from the Doolittle Raid and would not arrive in Pearl Harbor until May 25. Even if they got back in time and Nimitz sent them out to defend Midway, they would face at least twice as many Japanese carriers plus two battleships. Given that, Rochefort's report created a dilemma for Nimitz. Since the overarching Allied strategy was to defeat Germany first, one option—clearly the safest—was to keep his only two undamaged carriers out of harm's way.

Nimitz saw it differently. Rejecting the conservative strategy, he calculated that if the *Yorktown*'s hull could be repaired quickly, he could replenish her devastated air group with planes and pilots from the absent *Saratoga*. That would give him three operational carriers, and the airfield at Midway would constitute a fourth: if Midway could not maneuver, neither could it be sunk. That made it four airplane platforms against four, and Nimitz had the advantage of the advance information that Rochefort's team had provided. From the very start, the cool and calculating Nimitz determined to resist the Japanese offensive; he would turn the tables on the attackers and send at least some of their carriers to the bottom.[27]

There was, however, one more wrinkle. When the *Enterprise* and *Hornet* steamed into Pearl Harbor on May 25, Nimitz found Halsey so haggard and worn down that he immediately ordered him to the hospital. There Halsey was found to have a severe case of shingles, and the doctors declared him unfit for duty. Nimitz asked him who should command his two carriers in the coming battle, and without hesitation Halsey named Rear Admiral Raymond A. Spruance, the commander of his cruiser-destroyer screen. The calm and courtly Spruance had a satisfactory combat record. The problem was that, like Fletcher, he was a surface warfare officer who had never worn the gold wings of a naval aviator. Thus in the most important carrier battle of the war to date, the American carriers would be under the operational direction of two non-aviator surface warfare officers.[28]

After a quick replenishment and refueling, the *Hornet* and *Enterprise* headed back out to sea on May 28. *Yorktown* followed the next day with some of the repair parties still on board, the bright lights of their acetylene torches visible from shore as she passed through the ship channel. Over the next several days, the three American carriers and their escorts steamed northward to a preselected rendezvous 325 miles north of Midway designated as "Point Luck." It was, quite literally, the last place the Japanese would look for them. Weeks before, during one of the war games that the

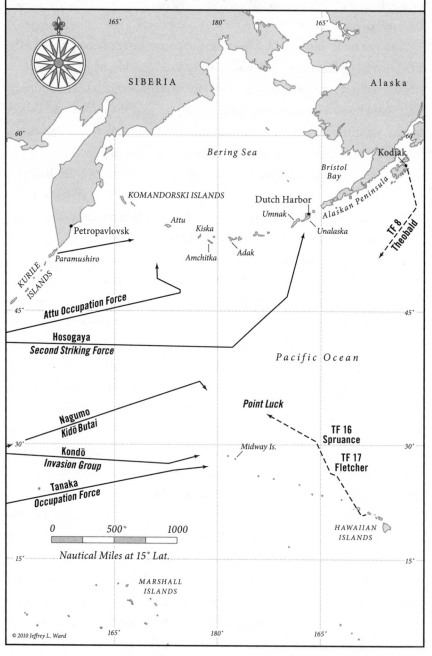

FLEET MOVEMENTS PRIOR TO THE BATTLE OF MIDWAY
June 3–5, 1942

165°   180°   165°

SIBERIA

Alaska

60°   60°

Bering Sea

Kodiak

Bristol
Bay

KOMANDORSKI ISLANDS

Dutch Harbor

Petropavlovsk

Attu

Umnak

Alaskan Peninsula

Unalaska

TF 8
Theobald

Kiska

Paramushiro

Amchitka   Adak

KURILE
ISLANDS

45°   45°

Attu Occupation Force

Hosogaya
Second Striking Force

Pacific Ocean

Nagumo
Kidō Butai

Point Luck

TF 16
Spruance

30°   30°

Kondō
Invasion Group

Midway Is.

TF 17
Fletcher

Tanaka
Occupation Force

0   500   1000

HAWAIIAN
ISLANDS

Nautical Miles at 15° Lat.

15°   15°

MARSHALL
ISLANDS

© 2010 Jeffrey L. Ward   165°   180°   165°

Japanese had conducted for the coming battle, the officer who had been assigned the role of the American commander had placed the Blue Force carriers very near the spot now designated as Point Luck. The referee of the exercise, Yamamoto's chief of staff Matome Ugaki, overruled the move, declaring that it was utterly illogical that the United States would put its carriers in such a place.[29]

Yamamoto's primary objective in authorizing—indeed, insisting on—the Midway operation was his determination to sink the American aircraft carriers that had escaped the raid on Pearl Harbor. The attack on Midway was the bait to draw them out from their base so they could be sunk in deep water. The destruction of the American carriers would solidify Japanese naval superiority in the Pacific and give Japan time to consolidate her conquests. Because he believed the Americans had only two functioning carriers, he did not think it necessary to send all six of Japan's big carriers. That was why the wounded *Shōkaku* was kept out of the operation. More problematically, the undamaged *Zuikaku* was also held back largely because so many of her planes had been lost in the Coral Sea. The Japanese might have done what the Americans did with the *Yorktown* and used air squadrons from other vessels to fill out the *Zuikaku*'s complement, but it not only seemed unnecessary, it violated the Japanese sense of order. Consequently, the Japanese steamed toward Midway with only four carriers, all of them under the command of Vice Admiral Chūichi Nagumo, who had led the Kidō Butai in its attack on Pearl Harbor.[30]

Nagumo's four carriers constituted only one of four different task forces that the Japanese committed to the operation. What was called an "invasion force" of two battleships, four cruisers, eight destroyers, and a light carrier under Vice Admiral Nobutake Kondō sailed separately, as did a "close support group" of four more heavy cruisers and a "main body" of three more battleships, including the giant *Yamato* with Yamamoto himself on board. Even more questionable was the Japanese decision to dispatch a fifth force to occupy two tiny islands in the Aleutians. Often described as a diversionary attack for the assault on Midway, the occupation of Attu and Kiska Islands was instead part of the Japanese effort to seize and maintain a defensive perimeter for their Pacific empire. Whatever the value of possessing a few isolated outposts in the Aleutians, that campaign might reasonably have been postponed until after the Midway operation was completed. Once again, however, the Japanese did not consider it necessary.

Meanwhile, thanks to the advance notice won them by the code breakers, the Americans maintained a continuous air search north and west of Midway by long-range PBY Catalina flying boats. On June 3, the same morning that Japanese planes bombed Dutch Harbor in Alaska twenty-five hundred miles to the north, one of the PBY pilots, Ensign Jewell "Jack" Reid, radioed the startling report: "Sighted main body." His follow-up report, however, revealed that the force he had seen consisted of "one small carrier, one seaplane tender, two battleships, several cruisers, [and] several destroyers." It was not, therefore, the "main body," but Kondō's "invasion force." Back at Pearl Harbor, Nimitz recognized that, and sent a cautionary message to Fletcher and Spruance: "That is not, repeat not, the enemy striking force," he radioed. "That is the landing force. The striking force will hit from the northwest at daylight tomorrow."[31]

HE WAS EXACTLY RIGHT. The Japanese opened the battle at dawn on June 4 with an air strike against the American airfield on Midway. When the Japanese bombers arrived, however, the pilots found the airfield bare of planes. The Marine fighters, mostly older Brewster Buffalos, were already in the air to challenge the attackers, and the American bombers were en route toward the Japanese carriers, whose position had been reported at five-thirty that morning by another PBY pilot, Howard Ady. As a result, though the Japanese Zeros shot down most of the American fighters, and Japanese bombers severely mauled the facilities on the island, the flight commander, Lieutenant Joichi Tomonaga, reported back to Nagumo that a second air attack would be necessary to neutralize the airfield.[32]

That created a dilemma for Nagumo. Tomonaga had led half of Nagumo's total complement of airplanes to attack Midway, and after those planes departed, Nagumo prepared the other half, armed with anti-ship ordnance, for the expected strike against the American carriers. So far, however, no American carriers had been sighted, and here was Tomonaga requesting a second strike on Midway. As Nagumo mulled this over, the American bombers from Midway arrived overhead. The Zeros flying CAP shot down most of them, and the Americans did no damage to the Japanese ships. Still, their presence underscored the reality that the Midway airfield had not been neutralized. Nagumo therefore ordered that the planes down on the hangar deck be re-armed with explosive ordnance for a second attack on the island.[33]

In the midst of the shift of ordnance, Nagumo received a sighting report from one of the six floatplanes he had sent out that morning to look for the American carriers. Its pilot reported seeing ten enemy surface ships north of Midway. The pilot did not specify what kind of ships they were, however, and Nagumo ordered him to clarify his report. While he waited for that, he ordered a temporary halt to the transfer of ordnance. If any of these ships was a carrier, he would strike it immediately. After an anxious ten minutes, the pilot reported that the ships consisted of five cruisers and five destroyers. Nagumo ordered the transfer of ordnance to continue. He might have asked himself why there were ten surface ships more than three hundred miles north of Midway, for it was too strong a force to be a routine patrol and too weak to be a strike force. It made sense only if they were there to protect a carrier. And, in fact, they were. What the scout plane pilot had spotted was the screen of Frank Jack Fletcher's *Yorktown* group, though he had somehow failed to see the *Yorktown* itself. Nagumo found that out another ten minutes later when the pilot sent in an amended report: "Enemy force [is] accompanied by what appears to be an aircraft carrier."[34]

That changed everything, and Nagumo now had to decide what to do with this startling information. He could order the anti-ship ordnance put back on the planes and prepare an immediate attack on this American carrier. That, after all, was his primary mission. The problem was that by now, Tomonaga's planes were returning from the strike on Midway and they needed to land. So, too, did the Zeros that had been flying CAP all morning and were running low on fuel. Nagumo could not recover and launch planes at the same time; he had to choose. Because he did not like doing things by halves, he decided to recover Tomonaga's planes as well as the circling Zeros, then refuel and rearm all of them for a coordinated strike on the

American carrier—or perhaps carriers. All that would take time, of course, but Nagumo believed he had time enough.[35]

He didn't. His carriers successfully recovered the planes returning from Midway and launched replacement Zeros to fly CAP, but the scrambling crews down on the hangar deck were still in the midst of shifting ordnance when attack aircraft from the American carriers arrived over the Kidō Butai. The first of them, arriving at 9:18, were fifteen TBD Devastator torpedo planes from the *Hornet*.

———

THE AMERICAN CARRIERS had begun launching planes at seven that morning, with the *Enterprise* and *Hornet* launching first. It took nearly an hour for all of their planes to get airborne and assemble into formation, and at seven forty-five Spruance, concerned about the loss of time, ordered the bombers that were already aloft not to wait for the torpedo planes. Consequently, the dive-bomber squadrons flew off toward the target at twenty thousand feet, leaving the late-launching Devastators to make their way to the target separately. As it happened, however, the slower torpedo planes, flying at just fifteen hundred feet, took a more direct course to the target and arrived ahead of the bombers. The first to arrive were the fifteen planes of Torpedo Squadron 8 from the *Hornet*, and the account of their flight path remains one of the enduring mysteries of the Battle of Midway.[36]

The commander of the *Hornet*'s torpedo squadron was Lieutenant Commander John C. Waldron, a conscientious and self-confident aviator who was particularly proud of his Native American heritage. Waldron had calculated his own course to the reported coordinates of the enemy carriers, and he was surprised when, once airborne, the *Hornet*'s air group commander, Stanhope Ring, led them not to the southwest as Waldron had calculated, but almost due west. Breaking radio silence, Waldron raised Ring on the radio to protest, but Ring told him to keep quiet and stay with the group. Instead, Waldron peeled off toward the southwest, taking his whole squadron with him. As it happened, Waldron was correct about the location of the enemy, but his willfulness meant that his squadron arrived over the Kidō Butai alone, unassisted by fighter cover and without the cooperation of dive-bombers.[37]

The protocols for the American TBD Devastator torpedo planes were similar to those used by the British Swordfish and Albacores: they had to approach the target low and slow in order to drop their torpedoes. That made them vulnerable to the agile Zeros. The rear-seat gunners in Waldron's squadron did their best to fend them off, but the Zeros were too fast and too nimble, and of course the Devastators had to hold a steady line in order to launch their weapons. One by one, the Japanese shot down all fifteen planes of Waldron's squadron, killing all of the pilots and gunners except for Ensign George Gay, the squadron navigator, who crawled out of his sinking plane and inflated his life vest.[38]

Only minutes later, the torpedo bombers from *Enterprise* and *Yorktown* arrived, and they, too, were overwhelmed by the Zeros. Of forty-one torpedo bombers launched by the American carriers that morning, only four made it back to their ships. And despite that horrific sacrifice, none of them managed to hit an enemy ship with a torpedo. Counting the bombers from Midway, the Americans had by now sent ninety-four airplanes to attack the Japanese. All but a handful had been shot down, and none of them had managed to land either a bomb or a torpedo on any Japanese ship. At 10:20 in the morning on June 4, 1942, Nagumo had reason to believe he was winning the battle. To complete the victory, he needed to finish the transfer of ordnance down on the hangar deck, bring his planes up to the flight deck, and send them off to destroy the American carriers.

None of Nagumo's vessels had radar, so it was one of the many lookouts on board the flagship *Akagi* who pointed skyward at 10:22 a.m. and screamed out, "Kyukoka"—dive-bombers.[39]

THE PRINCIPAL STRIKE WEAPON of U.S. Navy carrier forces was the SBD Dauntless dive-bomber. It was a sturdier and more capable plane than the Japanese Val and carried a heavier bomb load. It had a two-man crew: a pilot in the front seat, almost always an officer, and an enlisted radioman/gunner in the back seat. Unlike the torpedo planes, the Dauntless dive-bombers came in high at fifteen to twenty thousand feet, and they dove down, preferably from out of the sun, at a seventy-degree angle, releasing their bomb at about 1,500 feet before pulling out.[40]

The dive-bombers from *Enterprise* and *Hornet* had launched at the same time that morning, though they flew in different directions. While the planes from the *Enterprise* (and later the *Yorktown*) flew to the southwest, the bombers and fighters from the *Hornet*, as noted above, flew westward on a course of 265 degrees. As a result, all of the planes from the *Hornet* except Waldron's torpedo bombers missed the enemy carriers entirely. Ring did not fly this course on his own reckoning; almost certainly his guidance came from Pete Mitscher, the most senior U.S. aviator officer present, who relied on the morning reconnaissance report and intelligence estimates to conclude that two of the four Japanese carriers were operating eighty to a hundred miles behind the others. It was not an unreasonable deduction, for the Japanese had indeed split their forces into several groups, but that morning all four of the carriers were operating together. As a result, Ring and the *Hornet* Air Group flew off to the west and out of the battle in what is sometimes called "the flight to nowhere."[41]

If Ring and the *Hornet*'s dive-bombers flew too far north, those from the *Enterprise* under Lieutenant Commander Clarence Wade McClusky flew too far to the south. That was primarily because Nagumo had turned north at 9:17, while McClusky's planes were already en route. As a result, when McClusky arrived at the coordinates he had calculated, he saw only empty ocean. Though he and his pilots had already consumed more than half their fuel, he began a standard box search. In the midst of it, he espied a lone Japanese destroyer heading northward at thirty knots, creating a bright white bow wave on the blue sea. McClusky calculated that the destroyer's skipper was speeding to catch up with the main body, which in fact he was, and McClusky led his bombers in that direction. At 10:20 a.m. he found the Kidō Butai.

Most of McClusky's bombers attacked the biggest of the Japanese carriers, the giant *Kaga*. Unmolested by the Zeros, which had descended to low altitudes to shoot down the American torpedo planes, the American dive-bombers plunged downward en masse to hit the *Kaga* with several bombs in quick succession, igniting the ordnance that was stacked on her hangar deck, as well as the aviation fuel being used to top off the tanks of her aircraft. Explosions rippled along the *Kaga*'s lengthy hangar deck, and within minutes she was a burning, smoking wreck.[42]

Commander Clarence Wade McClusky poses on the wing of an F4F Wildcat fighter in August 1943. At Midway, McClusky led the bombing squadron from *Enterprise.* His decision to turn north after spotting a Japanese destroyer heading in that direction proved decisive. McClusky is wearing the aviator's forest-green navy uniform.

Naval History and Heritage Command

Three of McClusky's planes, led by the thirty-two-year-old Lieutenant Richard Best, bypassed the *Kaga* and attacked Nagumo's flagship, *Akagi.* Each of Best's wingmen scored near misses that did severe underwater damage to the *Agaki,* but it was Best's 1,000-pound bomb hitting her square amidships that was the kill shot. That bomb penetrated to the hangar deck and exploded among eighteen Kate torpedo bombers fully loaded with ordnance and filled with volatile aviation fuel. As on the *Kaga,* a cascading series of secondary explosions created a firestorm. Ordinarily a carrier could survive a single bomb hit—in the Coral Sea the *Shōkaku* had survived three of them—but the particular circumstances made this single strike fatal. Within minutes, two of Japan's biggest and best carriers had been damaged beyond recovery.[43]

Nor was that all. Even as McClusky and Best pushed over to dive on their targets, the dive-bombers of Max Leslie's squadron from the *Yorktown* also arrived. Though the *Yorktown* planes had launched later that morning, they had not had to search for the Kidō Butai as McClusky had done, and they arrived at almost the same moment he did, coming in from the northeast rather than from the south, to target the carrier *Sōryū*. The first bomb struck square on the *Sōryū*'s forward elevator, and a second plunged through her flight deck and exploded in her engine spaces. The *Sōryū* became, in Leslie's words, "an inferno of flame." Within a period of only five to eight minutes, American dive-bombers had destroyed three of Japan's frontline carriers, exactly half of the big carriers in her entire navy.[44]

The Japanese struck back. With only one operational carrier left, they nevertheless launched an attack on the *Yorktown*. Lieutenant Michio Kobayashi led the attack with eighteen dive-bombers, protected by six Zeros, and despite furious opposition from the *Yorktown*'s fighters and heavy AA fire, they put three bombs onto her flight deck. One bomb had been enough to doom the *Akagi*, but the *Yorktown* managed to survive three of them. There were three reasons. One was that the Americans had radar, which warned them of the incoming bombers and allowed the *Yorktown*'s crew to prepare for the attack by securing the fuel lines and launching fighters. Another was that the Japanese Vals carried only a 250-kilogram (551-pound) bomb instead of the 1,000-pound bombs carried by the bigger American Dauntlesses. The third reason was the efficiency of the *Yorktown*'s damage control teams. Given their commitment to offensive tactics, the Japanese spent less time and energy on damage control protocols than the Americans, and swift and efficient damage control saved the *Yorktown*.

That afternoon, the Japanese conducted a second attack on the *Yorktown*, this one by ten Kate torpedo planes—virtually all they had left. The flight commander was Lieutenant Tomonaga, who had led the morning attack on Midway Atoll. Even before he left the *Hiryu* to attack the *Yorktown*, Tomonaga knew he would not be coming back. His left wing tank had been punctured earlier in the fighting, and he had only enough gas for a one-way trip. As he approached the *Yorktown*, his plane was hit several times by American fighter planes. With his plane on fire, Tomonaga nevertheless held it steady long enough to launch his torpedo before he crashed into the sea.[45]

Tomonaga's was one of two torpedoes that hit the *Yorktown*, blowing a huge hole in her side and knocking out her emergency generator. The big flattop heeled over in a 26-degree list and Captain Elliott Buckmaster reluctantly ordered abandon ship. Even then, the big carrier stubbornly refused to sink, and the next day Buckmaster took volunteers back aboard to see if she could be salvaged. The coup de grâce came from a Japanese submarine. On the afternoon of June 5, as the *Yorktown* was being towed back to Pearl, Lieutenant Commander Yahachi Tanabe, in the I-68, crept in through her destroyer screen and put three more torpedoes into her. That proved too much, and the *Yorktown* finally succumbed.[46]

By then, the Americans had sunk the fourth Japanese carrier, the *Hiryū*. A squadron of dive-bombers from *Enterprise*, joined by several now-orphaned bombers from *Yorktown*, hit the *Hiryū* just past five o'clock on that eventful June 4. Four bombs landed in the middle of her flight deck, and the entire midsection of the ship was obliterated. Like the other three carriers of the Kidō Butai, she was smashed beyond recovery. The loss of four carriers in one day was a devastating blow to the Japanese navy. Almost as disastrous was the loss of 110 Japanese pilots and air crew, most of them from the *Hiryū*.[47]

The Battle of Midway was one of the most consequential naval engagements in world history, ranking alongside Salamis, Trafalgar, and Tsushima as both tactically decisive and strategically influential. The Imperial Japanese Navy remained a dangerous foe after June 4, 1942, but her mobile striking force, the Kidō Butai, which had dominated the Pacific for six months, had been reduced to only two carriers: *Shōkaku* and *Zuikaku*. In those critical five minutes between 10:22 and 10:27 on the morning of June 4, 1942, the strategic initiative in the Pacific theater passed from the Japanese to the Americans and their allies.

CHAPTER 14

TWO BELEAGUERED ISLANDS

N THE SUMMER OF 1942, much of the world's attention was riveted on the Soviet Union, where more than two million German soldiers—80 percent of the German army—and a million more from Hungary, Romania, and other of Hitler's willing and unwilling allies confronted more than five million soldiers of the Red Army along a thousand-mile front from the Baltic to the Black Sea. In this land confrontation, naval forces played only a small role.

The Finns, who had lost territory to the Soviet Union in the so-called Winter War (1939–40), saw an opportunity to reclaim it by siding with Germany against the Russians, though they remained officially neutral otherwise. Though there was never a formal alliance between Germany and Finland, German warships used Helsinki as a base, and that helped them dominate the Baltic. The Russians also had a substantial naval presence in the Baltic with what they called the Red Banner Fleet, which included two battleships and two heavy cruisers. At one point the Germans sent the *Tirpitz* into the Baltic to prevent those ships from escaping to neutral Sweden.

The Russians, however, had no intention of escaping. Instead, they kept their battleships in the Baltic to add their heavy guns to the defense of Leningrad. When German panzers approached the city on September 8, 1941, they were temporarily halted by long-range fire from the 12-inch guns on the battleship *Marat* (formerly the *Petropavlovsk*). On September 23, the Germans sent dive-bombers to take her out, and the Stukas hit her with two 1,000-pound bombs. The *Marat* sank in Kronstadt harbor, but her rear turrets remained above water and they continued to fire in defense of the city throughout a two-and-a-half-year siege. Elsewhere in the Baltic, in the Gulf of Finland, and further south in the Black Sea, the Russians relied heavily on mine-laying operations.[1]

The campaign in Russia entered a new phase on December 6 (the day before the Japanese attacked Pearl Harbor), when Marshal Georgy Zhukov directed a surprise counterattack outside Moscow that pushed the Wehrmacht several hundred miles westward and strained German logistics to the breaking point. Perhaps in consequence of that, and to replenish his dwindling supplies of critical raw materials for the 1942 summer campaign, Hitler ordered his armies to turn south into the Caucasus to gain access to that region's oil and wheat. In June (as American bombers wrecked the Kidō Butai at Midway), two German armies (the Fourth and the Sixth) spearheaded an invasion of the Caucasus, and in July they assailed the city of Stalingrad.

In conjunction with that drive, Hitler approved a plan long advocated by Raeder for a simultaneous thrust through the Mediterranean to Egypt. If successful, the entire Middle East region would be enveloped by a giant pincer movement. To achieve it, however, Rommel's Afrika Korps needed a more reliable supply route across the Mediterranean, and what stood in the way of that secure supply line was the British island outpost of Malta. To neutralize this troublesome Allied base, German bombers accelerated their air campaign against the island. By July, Malta was in danger of being battered and starved into submission, and its capitulation would open the way for the Axis conquest of the entire Mediterranean region.[2]

At the same time, half a world away, another island became the focus of Allied, and especially American, interest. Geographically, Guadalcanal was very nearly the opposite of Malta: large, sparsely populated, and virtually blanketed by a tropical rain forest. Yet in August 1942 these two islands—Malta and Guadalcanal—became precarious Allied outposts assailed by nearly continuous Axis assaults by both sea and air. Their survival as Allied assets depended entirely on the ability of Western naval forces to keep them supplied, and given the scarcity of Allied shipping as well as the ferocity of Axis attacks, for several months it was not at all clear that they could do so.

THERE IS NO CANAL on Guadalcanal Island. Like other islands in the South Pacific, from New Britain to the Bismarck archipelago, Guadalcanal got its name from a European "discoverer," in this case the Spaniard Pedro de Ortega Valencia, who in 1568 named it after his hometown in Seville. Despite the tribute, Guadalcanal bore no physical resemblance to Seville. With an average year-round temperature of 87 degrees, and rain that fell 197 days a year, it was choked by thick foliage that began only a few feet from the water's edge and covered the entire island, clinging even to the steep slopes and ravines of the mountains that rose more than seven thousand feet into clouds that obscured their peaks. Between the massive trees, a web of liana vines, razor-edged kunai grass, and bamboo constituted a nearly impenetrable jungle that hosted a wide variety of birds, snakes, lizards, and rodents—some as big as cats. Ninety miles long, it was populated in 1942 by several thousand Melanesians who survived by hunting and fishing, as well as by a few score Europeans who managed the copra and coconut plantations on its north shore, the only part of the island flat enough to sustain such cultivation.

Guadalcanal was one of seven large islands that, along with scores of smaller ones, made up the Solomon Islands. Before the war, the Solomons had been a British protectorate, and English officials had exercised a loose dominion over them from the tiny island of Tulagi, twenty miles north of Guadalcanal, where they established an administrative headquarters as well as the requisite officers' club, golf course, and cricket pitch. The Japanese chased them out of that enclave in early May 1942 and established a seaplane base there just prior to the Battle of the Coral Sea. The strategic importance of Tulagi, of Guadalcanal, and of the Solomons generally was that aircraft operating from there could patrol, and potentially dominate, the vital sea-lanes between Hawaii and Australia. That was why the Japanese had seized Tulagi in the first place, and in June, after the Battle of Midway, they decided to construct an airfield on Guadalcanal as well.[3]

On July 6, a dozen Japanese ships arrived off Guadalcanal's north coast and began unloading construction equipment including a hundred trucks, six road-rollers, and a pair of narrow-gauge railroad engines plus track and some hopper cars. From his jungle retreat high above the beach, British coast watcher Martin Clemens sent the news by radio to Townsville, Australia, and from there it was quickly forwarded to the Americans. By the end of the day (which was actually July 5 east of the International Date Line) it was being read by Admiral King in Washington.[4]

Even before the American victory at Midway, King had sought some way to push back against the Japanese onslaught in the Pacific, and he was particularly concerned about the Solomon Islands. After the Japanese seized Tulagi, he ordered Nimitz to plan an operation to recapture it and to seize the nearby Santa Cruz Islands as well. Now with the news from Guadalcanal, he shifted his focus to that island.

King's eagerness to go on the offensive, however, was hampered not only by the virtual destruction of the American battle fleet in Pearl Harbor but also by the Anglo-American agreement made back in January 1941 to give priority to the defeat of Germany while remaining largely on the defensive in the Pacific. The news from Guadalcanal offered King a way around this last impediment, for he argued that preventing the Japanese from completing an airfield was in effect a *defensive* measure that would not violate the Germany-first policy.

King had a second problem, however, which was that Guadalcanal was not within the navy's command theater. After the collapse of ABDA at the end of February, the British, Dutch, and Australians formally relinquished responsibility for the war in the Pacific to the Americans, and on April 18 (the same day Doolittle's bombers struck at Tokyo) the American Joint Chiefs of Staff created two separate commands there: the Southwest Pacific Area (SoWesPac) under MacArthur, and the Pacific Ocean Area (POA) under Nimitz. The Solomon Islands fell inside MacArthur's zone along with Australia, the Dutch East Indies, New Guinea, and the Philippines. Now King wanted that line moved so that Guadalcanal came within the navy's zone of operations. He noted that he had not objected to giving the U.S. Army the lead in the European war, but it was evident to him that operations in the Pacific should be—indeed must be—primarily naval. MacArthur objected, accusing King and the navy of seeking to take over the war in the Pacific altogether and relegate the army—*his* army—to the role of providing occupation troops for captured enemy territory.[5]

George Marshall brokered the dispute. King got his immediate objective: the line of demarcation was moved one degree to the west to put Guadalcanal just within the navy's command theater. In return, King agreed that MacArthur's forces would have full responsibility for subsequent moves in the Solomons, including the campaign to capture the Japanese citadel at Rabaul. Meanwhile, Marshall insisted that each service was to provide "every available support" to the other. In effect, he told them to find a way to work together and get along.[6]

Having won the administrative battle (for now), King announced an accelerated timetable for the operation. Once the Japanese airfield on Guadalcanal became operational, it would give them air superiority over the invasion beaches. To ensure that did not happen, King set a target of August 1, 1942—only three weeks away—for the invasion. It was stunningly ambitious, and in the eyes of many unrealistic. All the components of a complex amphibious assault—a landing force, the ships to carry them, other ships to escort them, plus the fuel, supplies, and the ammunition to sustain them—had to be found, gathered, organized, and delivered in a shockingly short time. That would be daunting under any circumstances, but especially so in mid-1942 due to the acute shortage of transports. Though the assault was endowed with the code name Operation Watchtower, colloquially it came to be called Operation Shoestring.[7]

Neither King nor Nimitz would exercise operational command. That job went to Vice Admiral Robert Ghormley, the man Roosevelt had sent to London back in 1940 to work with the British and who had spent two years in what was essentially a diplomatic post. Now Ghormley flew halfway around the world to take up a job that could hardly have been more different, establishing his headquarters at Nouméa, New Caledonia. His three opera-tional commanders did not quite constitute a team. The assault force of a single reinforced U.S. Marine Corps division—about nineteen thousand men—was commanded by Major General Alexander A. Vandegrift, whose quiet Virginia drawl and cheerful disposition (his nickname was Sunny Jim) belied his ferocity as a combat warrior who had more than thirty years' expe-rience in the so-called Banana Wars, from Nicaragua to Haiti. To carry Vandegrift's men to the beach, the U.S. Navy scraped together twenty-two transport and supply ships and put them under the command of Rear Admiral Richmond Kelly Turner, a brusque and egocentric gunnery special-ist whose most recent assignment had been as a member of King's staff. In fact, Turner's take-no-prisoners personality mirrored King's command style. A contemporary recalled that Turner was "intolerant of mistakes and bitter in his denunciations of the offender." The third component of the invasion was the covering force of three aircraft carriers—the Midway veteran *Enterprise*, the now-repaired *Saratoga*, and the smaller *Wasp*, newly arrived from the Atlantic—all under the command of Frank Jack Fletcher.[8]

That Fletcher was to lead the carrier force worried King. Like Churchill, King had a single yardstick to measure his seagoing commanders, which was unrelenting aggressive intensity, and he doubted that Fletcher met that

Though he was a surface line officer (colloquially a "black shoe"), Frank Jack Fletcher commanded the American carrier force at both Coral Sea and Midway. Like MacArthur, Fletcher smoked corncob pipes, which he had sent to him by the dozen from his native Iowa.

Naval History and Heritage Command

standard. King had been displeased in March when Fletcher had taken his task force back to Nouméa to refuel and resupply instead of continuing with an offensive. On that occasion, King had radioed him that he did not understand why "you are retiring from enemy vicinity in order to provision." King's doubts grew following the Battle of the Coral Sea after Fletcher decided not to send his destroyers to conduct a night attack on the Japanese carriers. Whatever the wisdom of either decision, King wondered if Fletcher had a warrior's instinct. Nimitz defended Fletcher, writing King that Fletcher was "an excellent, seagoing, fighting naval officer and I wish to retain him as task force commander." King left him in command of the carrier task force for the Guadalcanal operation, though he remained skeptical.[9]

If King was uncertain about Fletcher's ferocity, Fletcher was dubious about the timetable that King had foisted on him. He was particularly concerned about the prospect of having his carriers tethered to Guadalcanal for an extended period. It was crucial, he believed, that his carriers retain freedom of movement so they could react to a Japanese counteroffensive. Consequently, at a meeting on board his flagship *Saratoga* on July 27, Fletcher told Turner and Vandegrift that he planned to keep his carriers near the beachhead for only two days. Both men vigorously protested; Turner insisted that he needed five days to unload his transports, and Vandegrift wanted air cover for his Marines ashore until the airfield on the island could be captured and made operational. Grudgingly Fletcher agreed to stay for three days, though he continued to believe that his primary job was the security of his own carrier force. Turner and Vandegrift didn't like it, but unless Ghormley intervened, there was little they could do about it.[10]

The initial phase of this first American counteroffensive of the war was characterized by remarkable good fortune for the invaders. A heavy cloud cover obscured the approach of Turner's invasion fleet from Japanese scout planes, and when the Marines splashed ashore on August 7, they achieved complete tactical surprise. The outnumbered Japanese, most of them construction troops, fled into the jungle. The next day, the Marines overran the still-unfinished airfield and staked out a security perimeter. It remained to be seen if they could hold the enclave they had seized.

WHEN JAPANESE AUTHORITIES AT RABAUL learned that an American force had landed on Guadalcanal Island, their reaction was swift. From the first, the overall Japanese strategic blueprint for the war had been to seize the resource base they needed, erect a strong defensive perimeter, and then defy the inevitable effort by the Americans and their allies to reclaim it. Now that the Americans had made their first move, the commander of the Eleventh Air Fleet, Vice Admiral Nishizo Tsukahara, ordered the planes at Rabaul to "destroy the enemy force." Within three hours of the initial American landings, twenty-seven dual-engine Betty bombers escorted by eighteen long-range Zero fighters began taking off from Rabaul. As they were en route to their target, the Australian coast watcher Paul Mason spotted them and radioed a warning: "24 bombers headed yours."[11]

The principal target of those bombers was Turner's transport and supply vessels anchored off the invasion sites: nineteen of them at Guadalcanal, and five more off Tulagi. Those ships had no heavy guns, but they carried an impressive array of anti-aircraft weaponry, and they had support from a strong surface escort group of cruisers and destroyers. Alerted by Mason's warning, Turner's ships went to general quarters and got under way, and when the Bettys arrived, the maneuvering transports proved elusive targets. Dangerous, too, since they put up a daunting volume of anti-aircraft fire. A witness on one of the American cruisers recalled that "the sky was one black mass, the exploding shells overlapping their patterns." Under such circumstances, the bombers were wildly inaccurate, dropping most of their ordnance harmlessly into the sea.[12]

The bombers also had to contend with fighters from the American carriers, and by the end of the raid, the Japanese had lost fourteen Bettys and two Zeros, while the Americans lost nine Wildcats, plus five more that were badly shot up and not likely to fly again. The Japanese attacked again later in the day, this time with torpedo bombers, but they were no more successful than the high-level bombers. Despite that, the surviving Japanese pilots, in the way of pilots everywhere, dramatically overestimated their effectiveness, claiming the destruction of seven cruisers, two destroyers, and three transports. In fact, they had damaged only two vessels: the transport *Elliott* (which later sank) and a destroyer.[13]

The air battles, however, had two other important consequences. One was that while they were still in progress, Fletcher received a report that in addition to the Bettys and Zeros, the Japanese assault planes included nine Type 99 Val dive-bombers, planes that nearly always flew from carriers. The Wildcats splashed all nine of them, but their presence suggested the possibility that a Japanese carrier was operating nearby. In fact, the Vals had been sent from Rabaul on a one-way mission, with orders to deliver their bombs and then ditch in the water near the seaplane tender *Akitsushima*, which was at Shortland Island, though of course Fletcher didn't know that. The other consequence of the air raids was that the inflated damage reports by the Japanese pilots convinced the Japanese high command that Turner's invasion fleet had been all but wrecked. That assumption would play an important role the next night.[14]

Because the transports had gotten under way to fight off the air attacks, the timetable for unloading supplies to the beachhead was somewhat delayed. Nevertheless, by nightfall on D-Day (August 7), Allied prospects were most encouraging.* In a message to Ghormley (a message that was copied by Fletcher), Turner reported "all troops ashore" with "no opposition," and he notified Ghormley that he planned to send off most of the transport fleet the next morning, August 8.[15]

That led Fletcher to conclude that he had fulfilled his mission of covering the landing, and at 6:00 p.m. on August 8 he sent his own message to Ghormley with copies to Turner and Vandegrift asking permission to withdraw, listing low fuel reserves and the loss of more than twenty planes as relevant factors. Ghormley, who was still at Nouméa, did not respond for more than nine hours, though when he did, at three-thirty in the morning on August 9, he approved Fletcher's request. By then, however, a great deal had changed in the waters north and west of the Guadalcanal beachhead.[16]

When Turner received his copy of Fletcher's request to withdraw, he was furious. He later characterized Fletcher's departure as nothing less than "deser-

---

* Since the end of the Second World War, it has become customary to use the term "D-Day" to refer to the Allied landing in Normandy on June 6, 1944. In fact, however, that term was used throughout the war (and is used still) to indicate the date on which any major operation begins, and "H-hour" refers to the moment the assault begins.

tion," and he used even harsher words in private. At the moment, however, his most immediate concern was how to readjust the unloading timetable. He had already decided to send off the empty transports the next morning. Now he had to decide whether he should also send off those cargo ships that had not yet fully unloaded, or if he should risk leaving them off the beach for one more day without air cover. That depended in part on what the Marines needed ashore, and rather than query Vandegrift by radio, he summoned him to a meeting that night on board his flagship, the attack transport *McCawley*.[17]

Turner also invited British Rear Admiral Victor Crutchley, who commanded the cruiser-destroyer force guarding the surface approach to the invasion beach. The sandy-haired, full-bearded Crutchley had been seconded to the Australian navy only weeks before. A holder of the Victoria Cross, which he had won as a junior officer in the First World War, he had

Rear Admiral Richmond Kelly Turner (in foreground) and Marine Corps Major General Alexander A. Vandegrift examine a map together on board Turner's flagship, the attack transport *McCawley*, during the Guadalcanal campaign.

U.S. National Archives photo no. 80-CF-112-4-63

also commanded the battleship *Warspite* during its intrepid sortie into Narvik Harbor (see Chapter 3). If Fletcher's job was to fend off Japanese carrier attacks and provide air cover, Crutchley's assignment was to defend the beachhead from a surface attack. To do that, this British admiral had command of eight cruisers—five American and three Australian—which he divided into three groups.

Crutchley assigned to himself the most likely enemy approach route: the ten-mile-wide passage between Cape Esperance, at the western tip of Guadalcanal, and the rounded hump of Savo Island. There Crutchley placed three of his six heavy cruisers: the Australian *Canberra*, the American *Chicago*, and his own flagship, the *Australia*. In case the Japanese tried to approach the beachhead by swinging around to the north of Savo Island, Crutchley put his other three heavy cruisers there under U.S. Navy Captain Frederick Riefkohl, who had the distinction of being the first Puerto Rican–born American to graduate from the Naval Academy. For each cruiser group, Crutchley positioned a picket destroyer westward of the cruisers to provide advance warning. His remaining two cruisers—the American anti-aircraft cruiser *San Juan* and the Australian light cruiser *Hobart*, both under the command of American Rear Admiral Norman Scott—patrolled the presumably less dangerous waters east of the beachhead.

Afterward, critics found fault with Crutchley's dispositions, asking rhetorically if he should "have combined the strength of his six heavy cruisers in one formation." Whatever the merits of that, Crutchley made another decision that night that was at least as questionable. When he received Turner's summons to a conference, he decided that rather than take a ship's boat or even a destroyer to the meeting, he would steam there in his flagship, leaving Captain Howard Bode of the *Chicago* in temporary command of the first cruiser group, now reduced from three ships to two. Worse, he did not inform Riefkohl that he was leaving the area.[18]

What none of the Allied commanders knew was that even as Crutchley headed eastward in the *Australia* for the meeting with Turner, and while Fletcher waited for a reply from Ghormley about his request to withdraw, a large Japanese surface force was closing on Guadalcanal Island from the west.

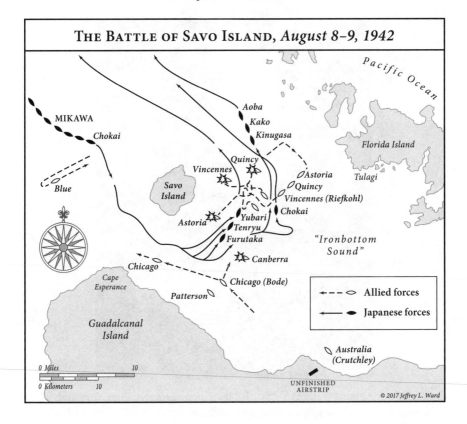

THE COMMANDER OF THAT SURFACE FORCE was Vice Admiral Gunichi Mikawa, who led the Japanese Eighth Fleet, established at Rabaul just weeks before. Aggressive by nature, Mikawa was spurred to action by the defiant last report from the Japanese defenders at Tulagi: "We will defend our positions to the death," which they did. That report arrived in Rabaul at 6:05 that morning and by eight o'clock Mikawa had issued orders to concentrate a surface force of five heavy cruisers, two light cruisers, and one destroyer at Rabaul. At noon he sent off a battle plan to navy chief of staff Osami Nagano in Tokyo asking permission to sortie. Nagano's initial reaction to Mikawa's request was that such a precipitous attack was dangerous, even "reckless." In the end, however, he left the decision to the local commander, and by two-thirty that afternoon, Mikawa was at sea heading southeastward at twenty-four knots.[19]

Japanese Rear Admiral Gunichi Mikawa led the group of seven cruisers from Rabaul that assaulted the Allied covering force off Guadalcanal in the Battle of Savo Island, August 8–9, 1942.

Naval History and Heritage Command

Fifty-three years old in 1942 (he would turn fifty-four later that month), Mikawa had commanded the battleship group that had accompanied Nagumo to Pearl Harbor, as well as the battleship screen of the Kidō Butai during its rampage in the Indian Ocean and its demise in the Battle of Midway. Indeed, his experience at Midway, where he had witnessed the devastating effect of American dive-bombers, made him especially sensitive to the threat posed by the American carriers. En route to his target, he twice broke radio silence to ask Rabaul for news of the whereabouts of those carriers, though Rabaul was no better informed than he was.[20]

Late in the afternoon a long-range Hudson patrol plane, part of MacArthur's command from Milne Bay, passed overhead, and Mikawa temporarily changed course from east to north in an effort to confuse the pilot about his intentions. He needn't have worried. The pilot inaccurately identified Mikawa's force as consisting of three cruisers, three destroyers, and two seaplane carriers. Not only was the report inaccurate, it was delayed more than nine hours in transmission—a casualty of the cumbersome divided command structure in the Southwest Pacific. Perhaps because of that, the patrol force of Catalinas and B-17s under Rear Admiral John S. McCain at Nouméa did not conduct a follow-up search, an oversight that Turner later called "a masterful failure of air reconnaissance." As a result, the American surface forces north and south of Savo Island had no forewarning of Mikawa's approach.[21]

It was pitch dark at forty minutes past midnight early on the morning of August 9 when Mikawa's cruisers, with his flagship *Chokai* in the lead, entered the passage between Guadalcanal and Savo Island. There was no moon that night, though Mikawa's chief of staff, Toshikazu Ohmae, recalled that "visibility was if anything too good." The American destroyer *Blue*, placed in that exact spot to provide an early warning of just such a threat as this, had its radar in active mode, but it was an SC (air search) radar, and false returns from the land on both sides of the channel interfered with the readings. The *Chokai* had no radar at all, but sharp-eyed lookouts on board espied the *Blue* conducting its patrol across the channel entrance. Mikawa reduced speed and waited to see if he would be discovered. Ohmae later recalled that "all breathing seemed to stop" on the bridge as everyone watched the *Blue* silently steam past, then reverse course and move away. "Breathing became more normal again" on the *Chokai*, and Mikawa increased speed to thirty knots. At 1:36 he sighted the Allied cruisers *Chicago* and *Canberra*.[22]

On the *Chicago*, the first indication Bode had that an enemy might be near came at 1:45 when the destroyer *Patterson* radioed the message: "Warning, warning. Strange ships entering harbor." The *Patterson* also launched star shells to illuminate the intruder. On the American cruisers, however, such warnings were inconclusive, and like Admiral Cattaneo at Cape Matapan, Bode learned that an enemy force was virtually upon him only when large-caliber shells began throwing up huge geysers around his ship.[23]

Even before he opened fire, Mikawa had ordered his ships to launch full salvos of Long Lance torpedoes. Ohmae recalled the sound they made "smacking the water one by one." Thus, even as the first enemy shells began landing around him, Bode also received multiple reports of torpedoes in the water, and he ordered the *Chicago* hard to port to comb their track. Several torpedoes missed, passing within yards, but one of them blew off the ship's bow, though the *Chicago* was still able to maneuver. Perhaps forgetting that Crutchley's absence made him the senior officer present, Bode neglected to send out a contact report and instead focused on maneuvering his own ship. In the confusion of the moment, he continued heading west for several minutes, and the wounded *Chicago* steamed off virtually out of the battle. The official account subsequently prepared by the Office of Naval Intelligence declared, "It appears that the *Chicago* had not yet sized up the situation." Less charitably, a crewman on board recalled that "there was mass confusion on the bridge as nobody had any idea what was happening." The *Chicago*'s wayward course allowed Mikawa's cruisers to concentrate their fire on the Australian *Canberra*, which took twenty-four shell hits in less than four minutes. With *Chicago* steaming away and the *Canberra* a burning and sinking wreck, Mikawa turned north, swinging counterclockwise around Savo Island, to assail Riefkohl's three cruisers.[24]

Bode's failure to send out a contact report meant that Riefkohl's ships were fully as surprised as the *Chicago* and *Canberra* had been. Arriving amidst the northern group, Mikawa lit up his searchlight and used it as a pointer. Like a bright white finger in the night, it illuminated one American ship after another as if to say: "Here . . . fire on this ship." The cruiser *Astoria* was the first victim. An early salvo started a fire in her airplane hangar and the bright flames in the dark night provided the Japanese with a vivid target. Pounded by successive hits from 8-inch shells, she lost power and was dead in the water. Captain Samuel Moore's *Quincy* was next. Caught in a deadly crossfire, the *Quincy* was shot to pieces before her main battery guns could be trained on the foe. Moore himself was an early victim when a shell hit the bridge, leaving it "a shambles of dead bodies." In his last order, the mortally wounded Moore told the helmsman to try to ground the crippled vessel on Savo Island to prevent her from sinking. That gambit failed, and when a torpedo hit the *Quincy's* magazine, in the words of one survivor, she "literally leaped out of the ocean." She sank at 2:35.[25]

Riefkohl's flagship, the *Vincennes*, was also sinking. Unable to get off a contact report because an early hit on the bridge knocked out his communications, Riefkohl found his ship hit both by heavy shells and "two or three torpedoes" within only a few minutes, and he ordered abandon ship at 2:14. The *Astoria* stayed afloat throughout the night, though she rolled over and sank the next day.[26]

BY THEN MIKAWA WAS LONG GONE. He might have continued on after savaging the Allied surface force, and turned his heavy guns on the Allied transports. He had plenty of ammunition left, but his ships had expended all of their torpedoes, which the Japanese considered their primary offensive weapon. His most pressing concern, however, was that it would take him several hours to re-form his dispersed squadron in order to attack the transports, and by then the sun would be up. Dawn would bring American carrier planes swarming down on him and, as he wrote later, he "would meet the fate our carriers had suffered at Midway." Besides, hadn't the pilots from the earlier bombing mission reported that they had already eliminated most of the ships in the invasion force? Concluding that he had accomplished what he set out to do, he ordered a withdrawal to the northwest at 2:25 a.m. in order to get beyond aircraft range by daylight.[27]

At that moment, the American carriers that Mikawa so feared were still in their covering position south of Guadalcanal, but because neither Bode nor Riefkohl had reported that a battle was in progress, Fletcher did not learn of it until three-fifteen, when he heard from Turner that the *Chicago* had been hit by a torpedo and that the *Canberra* was on fire. Fletcher forwarded that news to Ghormley, but it did not change Ghormley's affirmative response to Fletcher's earlier request for permission to withdraw, which came in at three-thirty. An hour later, as Mikawa fled westward, Fletcher retired eastward to the refueling rendezvous. Though Turner subsequently blamed Fletcher for the disaster at Savo Island, the American carriers did not begin their withdrawal until the battle was over, and it was Mikawa's fear of those carriers that saved Turner's transport fleet from almost certain destruction.[28]

The Battle of Savo Island was a humiliating defeat for the Allies. With the exception of Pearl Harbor, it was the worst defeat in the history of the United States Navy. It was so bad that, like the Japanese authorities after Midway, the American government kept the outcome an official secret. Based on the official navy briefings, the *New York Times* reported on August 18: "An attempt by Japanese warships to hamper our landing operations…was thwarted. The Japanese surface force was intercepted by our warships and compelled to retreat before it could take under fire our transports and cargo vessels." While technically accurate, it was also deliberately misleading. The navy was so concerned about the public response, it kept the survivors of the sunken cruisers in virtual quarantine, and it was two months before the American government acknowledged the disaster.[29]

In the aftermath of the battle there was much faultfinding and finger-pointing. Eventually, at King's direction, the U.S. Navy conducted an investigation led by Admiral Arthur J. Hepburn, a former commander of the U.S. Fleet. His report was not issued until the following spring, and in it he cited a long list of errors, including an inadequate air search, poor communications, and not being sufficiently "battle minded." Though Turner was the senior officer present, he was perceived more as victim than as culprit. Perhaps in the interest of Allied harmony, Crutchley, who had raced back to the scene of the battle just as it ended, also escaped blame. With uncharacteristic empathy, King later concluded that "both [men] found themselves in awkward positions and both did their best with the means at their disposal." King and Hepburn were far less sympathetic with Fletcher and with Captain Bode, whom Hepburn found guilty of "culpable inefficiency." A few days after the report was made public, Bode shot himself, becoming the final Allied casualty of the battle.[30]

As Hepburn's report indicated, American errors of omission and commission had contributed to the outcome, though it is important to acknowledge that the battle was not merely an Allied defeat; it was also a Japanese victory. The ships and crews of Mikawa's command were prepared, alert, disciplined, efficient, and ultimately successful. Japan had entered the war in the firm belief that its ships, planes, and especially its trained warriors were qualitatively superior to those of the United States. The outcome of the Battle of Savo Island suggested that such confidence was not entirely misplaced.*

If there was a silver lining for the Allies in this abject defeat, it was that Turner's transports remained largely unscathed. Those ships represented nearly half of all the large transport shipping available to the Americans in 1942. If, instead of racing back toward Rabaul, Mikawa had pressed on to sink or damage a significant number of them, it would have jeopardized not only the Guadalcanal operation but Allied operations worldwide. Even with the transports intact, the Marines on Guadalcanal were in a precarious position. If they were to keep their foothold on the island, the Allies would have to maintain a steady stream of reinforcements and supplies across a disputed sea. In that respect, their circumstance was not significantly different from that of the besieged British garrison on Malta, in the Mediterranean.

BOTH PHYSICALLY AND CULTURALLY, Malta was quite different from Guadalcanal. Consisting of two islands (Malta and Gozo) that together covered only 122 square miles, it was one-twentieth the size of Guadalcanal, yet with more than 270,000 residents it had many times the population. If a rain forest was the signature feature of Guadalcanal, the dominant characteristic of Malta's summer was the nearly ubiquitous dust. For more than 250 years, beginning in 1530, the two small islands had been the homeland of the Knights of St. John, a crusading order that had been granted sovereignty over the islands by Charles V of Spain as "a buttress to the power of Islam." That era ended with the island's conquest by Napoleon in 1798, and

---

* In the aftermath of the Battle of Gettysburg during the American Civil War, disappointed Confederate leaders sought explanations for their defeat. The potential culprits were all southern generals: some blamed Jeb Stuart, whose cavalry failed to provide Robert E. Lee with the intelligence reports he needed; some blamed Richard Ewell for failing to take Cemetery Hill on the first day of battle; still others blamed James Longstreet for delaying the attack on the second day. When he was asked who was most to blame, George Pickett allegedly replied: "I always thought the Yankees had something to do with it."

French oversight ended with Britain's victory in the Napoleonic Wars in 1815. Since then, it had been an outpost of the British Empire, its location and excellent harbor at Valletta making it nearly as important to British interests in the Mediterranean as Gibraltar or Suez. It had been an object of Italian ambitions from the moment Il Duce declared war in 1940, and in 1942 it remained in a state of virtual siege. For most of two years, the Royal Navy had been compelled to run regular supply convoys to the island, many of which had triggered naval skirmishes and, as noted in Chapter 5, a few full-scale battles.[31]

Ships and planes from Malta were more than an annoyance to the Axis; they seriously depleted the convoys of food and fuel from Naples to North Africa on which Rommel depended to carry on his war against the British in Egypt. Raeder believed that "these communication lines would never be completely secure until we eliminated the British wasp nest at Malta." To protect the convoys, Hitler sent Luftwaffe General Albert Kesselring with a substantial reinforcement of German aircraft to Sardinia and Sicily. Kesselring disliked using warplanes to escort convoys, which he considered passive and defensive, and his preferred option was to seize Malta itself. He developed a plan, Operation Hercules, to do exactly that, but he never pulled the trigger. For one thing, the appalling casualties sustained by German paratroopers in Crete made Kesselring chary of trying something similar in Malta. As the historian Gerhard Weinberg put it, "The unsuccessful defense of Crete successfully defended Malta." Then, too, Hitler was preoccupied with the war in the East, the Italians were less than enthusiastic, and the opportunity passed.[32]

Denied his preferred strategy, Kesselring sought to neutralize Malta by destroying its harbor and airfields with a massive bombing campaign. In April 1942 alone, his bombers dropped 6,700 tons of ordnance on the tiny island, more than fell on London during the whole of 1940. On April 14, the raids began at six-thirty in the morning and lasted until eight that night—the longest single alert of the entire war. The population retreated into caves and tunnels. A visiting American admiral confessed that he "was not prepared for the complete devastation which met my eyes." He marveled that "the city of Valletta itself was a mass of rubble, with much of the population living in underground caves." Due to the nearly constant air raids, anti-aircraft gunners had to ration their ammunition. Spitfire and Hurricane fighters flew from Malta's cratered airfield to fend off the attackers, but the island was so low on fuel reserves that local commanders became reluctant to order the planes into the air for fear of running out of gasoline altogether.[33]

The erosion of Malta's military assets allowed the Axis convoys to proceed largely unhindered. Axis convoy losses declined from over 60 percent in October 1941 to less than 5 percent in March 1942. Thus bolstered, Rommel resumed the offensive in North Africa and captured the British citadel of Tobruk on June 21. More than thirty thousand British and Commonwealth soldiers were taken prisoner; for British arms, it was the greatest catastrophe of the war since the fall of Singapore.[34]

Meanwhile, Malta itself appeared to be on the brink of capitulation. Its cities and towns, and especially the seaport of Valletta, had been reduced to rubble, and food had become scarce as fewer and fewer ships arrived with essential supplies. In June, only two supply ships made it through. British submarines delivered small quantities of powdered milk, medicine, and some anti-air ammunition, but not enough to sustain the island's population or its garrison. Citizens survived on a ration of six ounces of meat and one ounce of rice *per week*. As the island's deputy governor, Sir Edward Jackson, put it, "Our security depends, more than anything else, on the time for which our bread will last." Air Vice Marshal Keith Park, commanding the air assets on Malta, reported in July that he had less than seven weeks of fuel remaining. If he did not receive a resupply within that time frame, he reported, Malta must surrender.[35]

In London, the Admiralty authorized a rescue mission dubbed Operation Pedestal. The same week that the American invasion convoy approached Guadalcanal in the South Pacific and Hitler's legions closed in on the oil fields in the Caucasus, the British assembled a convoy of fourteen supply ships in the Clyde Estuary in Scotland. The ships were loaded with a mixed cargo of food and fuel, including 1,500 tons of aviation gas in each ship, so that the loss of one or even several of them would still ensure the delivery of a balanced cargo. The exception was the American oil tanker *Ohio*, built, owned, and operated by the Texaco Oil Company. As Park had reported, fuel was critical to Malta's survival, and Churchill made a personal appeal to Roosevelt to include the *Ohio* in the convoy. Roosevelt agreed. He and the British were willing for the ship's original crew to remain on board, but King would not hear of it. If the British wanted the ship, he insisted, they should provide their own crew. In consequence of that, while the *Ohio* was in Glasgow, the American crew filed off her and a British crew filed aboard. Her new skipper was a thirty-nine-year-old British civilian merchant marine captain named Dudley W. Mason. He and his men knew that the *Ohio* was the one essential element in the entire convoy, for without the delivery of gasoline to Malta, the Spitfires and Hurricanes would be grounded and the island rendered virtually defenseless.[36]

Once all the transport ships—including the *Ohio*—put to sea on August 2, they were surrounded by the largest escort force ever assembled for convoy protection. The escort force under Vice Admiral Neville Syfret eventually included two battleships, four aircraft carriers, seven light cruisers, and no fewer than thirty-two destroyers, with the escorts outnumbering the cargo ships more than three to one.* In effect, the Royal Navy committed most of the Home Fleet to the protection of this convoy, leaving behind only two battleships to watch the North Sea and the Baltic, where the *Tirpitz* still posed a potential threat. Dropping the usual convoy designations, this one was dubbed a WS convoy (Winston Special) in honor of the prime minister. On August 10 (the day after Mikawa sank four Allied cruisers off Savo Island), the convoy passed through the Strait of Gibraltar bound for Malta.[37]

FOR THE NEXT FIVE DAYS, as the convoy zigzagged eastward at fifteen knots, it was assailed from above, from below, and on the surface. Surface attacks were limited by Italian fuel oil shortages, so most of the danger came from the more than five hundred bombers and torpedo planes of the Second Fliegerkorps, based in Sicily and Sardinia, as well as from German and Italian submarines.

---

* The carrier *Indomitable* joined the escort group en route. When it did, it marked the first time the Royal Navy deployed five aircraft carriers in a single operation.

The carrier HMS *Eagle* was the first victim. On the morning of August 11 south of Majorca, Captain Edmund Rushbrooke had just ordered the *Eagle* to turn into the wind to launch long-range Spitfires to reinforce Malta's fighter squadrons when Kapitänleutnant Helmut Rosenbaum in the U-73 slipped between two of the escorting destroyers and fired a spread of four torpedoes at her. In rapid succession, four large explosions erupted along the side of the carrier, and she began listing heavily to port, men and planes on her flight deck sliding sideways into the sea. Witnesses on the nearby *Indomitable* watched helplessly as the *Eagle* rolled over and "disappeared into the cloud of smoke and steam," sinking in less than eight minutes with a loss of 231 men, some of whom were killed by the concussion of numerous depth charges dropped by the British destroyers in a vain attempt to find and sink the U-boat.[38]

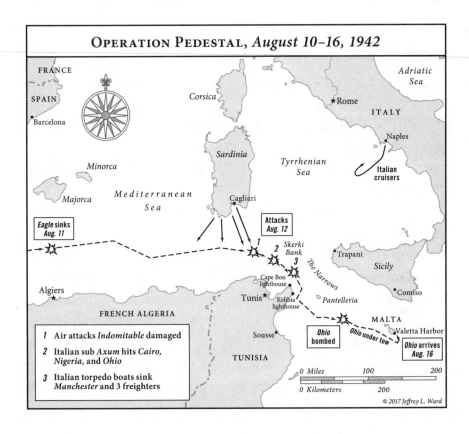

OPERATION PEDESTAL, *August 10–16, 1942*

1 Air attacks *Indomitable* damaged

2 Italian sub *Axum* hits *Cairo*, *Nigeria*, and *Ohio*

3 Italian torpedo boats sink *Manchester* and 3 freighters

© 2017 Jeffrey L. Ward

The attacks resumed that night, this time from above. There were 540 operational Axis aircraft on Sicily and Sardinia, and at dusk German and Italian dive-bombers, level bombers, and torpedo bombers attacked the convoy. Other planes dropped mines in front of the convoy's track, and for the first time in the war they employed Italian torpedo mines, called *moto-bombe*. Dropped by parachute in front of the convoy, they circled errati-cally, creating an unpredictable menace. For most of the raids, British air search radar identified the inbound bogies and launched fighters to inter-cept them. As the roiling air battle moved closer to the convoy, the escorts and transports, all of which had been fitted with new 20 mm Oerlikon AA guns, threw up an extraordinary amount of ordnance. A witness recalled seeing "tracers screaming across the sky in all directions, and overhead liter-ally thousands of black puffs of bursting shells." Even the 16-inch guns of the battleships were loaded with shrapnel and fired skyward. Because the gunners fired at anything that flew, several of the British fighter planes were hit by friendly fire.[39]

The attackers focused on the carrier *Indomitable*, and three bombs hit her flight deck. One witness thought she "looked like an old-fashioned sar-dine can with the lid rolled back." True to her name, she managed to stay afloat, and even recovered her planes that night, though because the land-ing lights had been destroyed and the senior flight officer killed, the second flight officer had to direct the landings onto the damaged deck with "a flash-light in each hand and one in his mouth." Detached from the convoy, the *Indomitable* headed back to Gibraltar with a destroyer escort.[40]

Axis submarines were active, too, though British use of both radar and Asdic made their job difficult. Thanks to his new Type 271 radar set, Lieutenant Commander Peter Gretton in the destroyer *Wolverine* surprised the Italian submarine *Dagabur* on the surface and, eager to pounce on the sub before it could dive, rammed it at full speed. It was fatal to the *Dagabar*, but it also smashed up thirty feet of the *Wolverine's* bow. Only hours later, another destroyer, HMS *Ithuriel*, duplicated *Wolverine's* feat, ramming the *Cobalto*. On both occasions, however, the ramming destroyer was com-pelled to withdraw from the convoy and return to Gibraltar for repairs. That annoyed Syfret, who saw his destroyer screen slowly diminishing. It was especially worrisome because at seven o'clock that evening (August 12) the battleships and carriers turned back to Gibraltar as planned, leaving escort duties to the light cruisers and destroyers under Rear Admiral Harold Burrough.[41]

Five Italian submarines had formed a line across the narrows between Cape Bon, at the northern tip of Tunisia, and the toe of Sicily. One of them, the *Axum*, commanded by Tenente di Vascello (Lieutenant) Renato Ferrini, fired a particularly consequential spread of torpedoes that scored hits on three different ships. One so damaged the light cruiser *Cairo* that she had to be abandoned. Another hit the light cruiser *Nigeria*, which was Burrough's flagship. Though she stayed afloat, Burrough had to transfer his flag to a destroyer so the *Nigeria* could be sent limping back to Gibraltar with a three-destroyer escort, thus further eroding Burrough's combat strength. The third of Ferrini's torpedoes, the most consequential of all, hit the *Ohio*, opening a twenty-seven-by-twenty-four-foot hole in her side and flooding several compartments. The explosion blew out the tanker's boiler fires and wrecked both her steering and her gyrocompass. She lay dead in the water with more Axis bombers en route.[42]

Captain Mason thought the *Ohio* was doomed and ordered the crew to muster at their boat stations for evacuation. Instead, the engineers got the boilers relit and the engines working, though she now lagged significantly behind the rest of the convoy. Perhaps because of that, the next air attack overlooked her to focus on other ships, especially the cargo ships. A direct hit on the ammunition ship *Clan Ferguson* triggered an enormous explosion and she disappeared in "a mushroom of smoke and flame." Another bomb struck the transport *Waimarana* and detonated her volatile cargo of aviation fuel. Like the *Clan Ferguson*, she virtually disintegrated. A third transport, the *Deucalion*, already damaged in an earlier raid, sank as well.[43]

Night brought a respite from the bombers but introduced a new peril. Only a few miles north of Cape Bon, twenty-two Italian and two German motor torpedo boats conducted a swarm attack. With the Allied ships separated after maneuvering individually during the air attacks, the torpedo boats targeted them one by one. Two of the Italian *motosiluranti* (MS) boats (MS-16 and MS-22) boldly closed to within fifty yards of the cruiser

Manchester to fire their torpedoes. One malfunctioned, but the other struck the cruiser and flooded her engine room, leaving her dead in the water. Though her crew fought to save her, she eventually had to be scuttled. Other motor torpedo boats focused on the transports, sinking four and crippling a fifth.[44]

By midmorning on August 14, only four merchant ships, plus the limping *Ohio*, remained with the badly depleted convoy. Moreover, battle damage and the need to send off destroyers to escort cripples back to Gibraltar or to conduct searches for survivors had reduced the convoy escort to only two light cruisers and six destroyers. At that moment, Burrough learned that six Italian cruisers were approaching from the north.

In Rome, Admiral Riccardi could not send out Italy's battleships to confront the convoy because there was simply not fuel enough for them to make the round trip. He did, however, authorize a sortie by three heavy and three light cruisers under Admiral Alberto Da Zara, though he worried about air cover for Da Zara's ships. The Regia Aeronautica had proved unreliable during past sorties, and the Germans had become leery of committing Luftwaffe assets to support what they considered the "ridiculous demands" of the Supermarina. The absence of air support became especially worrisome after several British scout aircraft from Malta dropped flares to illuminate Da Zara's cruisers and sent out uncoded radio messages supposedly vectoring a large formation of attack aircraft to their position. It was a bluff. There was no such formation—at the time Malta had only fifteen attack planes available, none of which could be spared for the cruisers. It was Mussolini himself who decided to recall the cruisers, and Da Zara had no option but to comply. En route back to their ports, they were attacked by British submarines, and two of them were damaged. It was, as the German representative on the Italian Naval Staff put it, "a useless waste of fighting power."[45]

Despite this narrow escape, the convoy remained in dire peril. There was still more than a hundred miles to go, and more German bombers on the way. This time the bombers focused on the crippled *Ohio*. Several near misses buckled her hull plates below the water, and one bomber, shot down by the AA fire, crashed into her superstructure. The plane, a Junkers 88, did not explode, but pieces of her fuselage stayed there, hung up in the *Ohio*'s upper works, an incongruous ornament straddling her bridge. Not long afterward, another bomb penetrated the *Ohio*'s deck near the stern and exploded in her engine room. Entirely without power now, and riding dangerously low in the water, the *Ohio* was taken in tow by the destroyer *Penn*, though even that proved difficult because the weight of the *Ohio*'s flooded compartments made her sluggish and unwieldy. As the *Penn* took the strain of the tow, the *Ohio* yawed off sharply to starboard, so the destroyer was essentially pulling her sideways. The strain proved too much and the ten-inch manila hawser, the largest the *Penn* had, parted with a loud snap.[46]

Meanwhile, the bombers returned. Again, bombs fell all around the *Ohio*, near misses sending fountains of water over her deck. One landed fair on her midsection and broke her back, as her stern bent out at an angle from the rest of her hull. It was evident to the naked eye that she was sinking. Even so, the escorts resumed their effort to tow her, this time with one vessel towing and another tied up alongside to minimize her tendency to yaw. By doing so, they were eventually able to work up to five knots. Twice the *Ohio*'s civilian crew was ordered to abandon ship before being ordered back on board again when it appeared that she might stay afloat after all. One escort commander, recalling the criticism that had been directed at the Royal Navy for abandoning PQ-17 in the Barents Sea the month before, insisted that he would stay by the convoy "as long as there is a [single] merchant ship afloat."[47]

The towline parted again, and this time both destroyers came alongside. Lashing themselves to port and starboard, they acted like water wings to keep the *Ohio* afloat as they nudged her forward. With her decks awash and her back broken, with no engine, no steering, and no compass, the *Ohio* somehow stayed afloat throughout the night of August 14–15, creeping along with agonizing slowness toward Malta. At 7:55 on the morning of August 15, with Captain Mason and his crew staggering from exhaustion and bleary-eyed from lack of sleep, the *Ohio* gingerly entered the channel to Valletta harbor. As she rounded the last bend, waving and cheering crowds lined the waterfront, and a brass band played "Rule Britannia."[48]

Of the fourteen cargo ships that had set out from Britain two weeks before, only five—including the *Ohio*—made it through to Malta. En route,

The tanker *Ohio*, her decks awash, is almost literally carried into Valletta Harbor by her escorting destroyers. Though much of the Pedestal convoy was destroyed, the *Ohio's* arrival in Malta allowed the British outpost to hold on for a few more weeks.

Naval History and Heritage Command

the Royal Navy lost one aircraft carrier sunk and another badly damaged, two cruisers sunk and two more damaged, one destroyer sunk, and major and minor damage to a half dozen others. Nine transports had been sunk as well, and the *Ohio*, too, once her priceless cargo had been discharged, was towed out to sea and consigned to deep water, her mission accomplished. Such losses were horrifying—far worse than the loss of four cruisers off Savo Island or even the slaughter of PQ-17 the month before. Yet the arrival of that handful of ships allowed Malta to hold out for another nine weeks. It could hardly be called a victory, though Churchill sent his personal congratulations. It was, after all, precisely the kind of heroic defiance of the odds that appealed to the romantic Churchill. Subsequently, the men of the *Ohio's* crew received fourteen medals, including the George Cross for her skipper, Dudley Mason, an award created by George VI to recognize extraordinary heroism by British civilians.[49]

IN THE FIRST HALF OF AUGUST 1942, at both Guadalcanal in the Pacific and near Malta in the Mediterranean, Allied naval forces suffered stunning tactical reverses. Yet neither confrontation gained any strategic advantage for the Axis. Mikawa's decision to get beyond range of the American carriers before dawn saved Turner's transport fleet off Guadalcanal and allowed the Americans to retain their toehold on the island. In the six months that followed, the campaign for Guadalcanal turned into an agonizing meat grinder that sapped Japanese strength and inflicted losses that neither the nation nor her navy could sustain.

Similarly, the grim determination of the British escorts to press on with the Operation Pedestal convoy to Malta despite incessant air and sea attacks managed to deliver enough supplies to Malta to enable that outpost to remain a thorn in the side of the Axis, especially to Axis convoys from Italy to Africa. When Rommel began his ground offensive at the end of the month, he was stopped short in no small part because of his lack of fuel reserves, and that laid the groundwork for an eventual British counterattack.[50]

In hindsight, it is possible to see the naval engagements near Savo Island in the Pacific and near Malta in the Mediterranean during the late summer of 1942 as moments when, despite tactical successes, the Axis powers fell just short of achieving strategic victories. In both engagements, the Axis proved that they could make the world's oceans a dangerous place for Allied shipping, though that was about to change. The outpouring of new construction from American shipyards was only months away, and it would dramatically reshape the war at sea.

CHAPTER 15

A TWO-OCEAN WAR

G ERMANY FIRST. It was literally the first strategic decision made by the British and Americans, formally embraced in January 1941, and confirmed at the Arcadia conference a year later after the United States was finally and fully in the war. By then, the logic of that decision was even more compelling, since German armies had driven deep inside the Soviet Union and, despite Zhukov's counterattack in December, it was by no means certain that the Russians could hold out. And yet, amidst the worldwide pressures during 1942, the Germany-first strategy, though honored in principle, was all but abandoned in practice.

In part this was because the threats were ubiquitous: not only along the Eastern Front but also in the Pacific, the Mediterranean, Burma, and China, and of course in the ongoing war against the U-boats. As a result, the Western Allies remained in a largely reactive mode for much of 1942. In addition, however, there was the stark reality that the Anglo-American forces simply lacked the wherewithal to conduct an early offensive against Nazi Germany. It would be many more months, if not years, before a meaningful number of

American combat divisions would be ready to face the Wehrmacht. And even if the men could be found, there was not enough shipping to carry them across the Atlantic to England, keep them supplied, and then sealift them across the English Channel to an invasion beach. The Royal Navy had suffered terrible shipping losses—especially in transports and destroyers—at Narvik, at Dunkirk, in the evacuation from Crete, and during Operation Pedestal. As for the Americans, the products of the 1940 Two-Ocean Navy Act would not be coming off the building ways until early in 1943, and in both the Atlantic and the Pacific, the shortage of shipping was an inescapable bottleneck.[1]

Another difficulty was that the Americans and the British did not necessarily share the same priorities. The Americans, brash, impatient, and angered by the attack on Pearl Harbor, were eager to take action—to do something and do it quickly. The British, who had been at war for more than two years, took a longer view. Though the broad strokes of Anglo-American strategy depended heavily on input from the heads of government, the details—that place where the devil resided—had to be worked out by what was known as the Combined Chiefs of Staff (CCS), a permanent working committee of senior officers that met regularly in Washington. All members of the American Joint Chiefs were members of the Combined Chiefs, as were senior representatives of the British Army, the Royal Navy, and the Royal Air Force. In the regular meetings of the Combined Chiefs, the American instinct for a swift counterblow collided with the British preference for a more calculated approach.

Within that body, the foremost champion of an early offensive in Europe was George Marshall. The American army chief of staff was realistic enough to see that a 1942 invasion of Nazi-occupied France was not practical except in an emergency such as the imminent collapse of the Red Army (for which he prepared a contingency plan called Sledgehammer). Even absent an emergency, however, Marshall argued that American manpower and military equipment should be sent to England as fast as possible in order to build up resources there for a full-scale invasion of France in the spring of 1943. The difficulty was that doing so meant sending scarce manpower and war materials to Britain to bide their time for a year or more while they were desperately needed elsewhere—indeed everywhere.[2]

Roosevelt knew that the American public would not tolerate waiting until 1943 to strike back—that was the main reason he had ordered the Doolittle Raid against Japan in April. In his view, the Allies must undertake some kind of offensive against Germany before the end of 1942 or he would be unable to resist the pressure, not only from King and the U.S. Navy but also from the public at large, to turn the full force of American power (such as it was) on the Japanese. Then, too, Roosevelt had all but promised Stalin's foreign minister, Vyacheslav Molotov, that the West would open a second front against Germany sometime in 1942.

The British declared themselves fully committed to Marshall's invasion plan, but they vividly recalled the horrific bloodletting in the trenches from 1914 to 1917, which the Americans had mostly missed. And, of course, British arms had been driven ignominiously from Dunkirk just two years earlier. Those experiences made them less than eager to jump back onto the Continent until the odds had shifted in their favor. For his part, Churchill hoped that the naval blockade of Germany, continuous aerial bombing, and peripheral raids on the European coast would eventually weaken Nazi resilience to the point that an invasion—whenever it occurred—would be largely a matter of picking up the pieces of a shattered empire.[3]

In support of that vision, Churchill authorized a number of pinprick assaults against the coast of Nazi-dominated Europe in 1942. In March, British commandos piloted HMS *Campbeltown* (formerly USS Buchanan), packed with explosives, into the dry dock at St. Nazaire, on the French coast. The objective was to wreck the dock so that it could not be used by the *Tirpitz*. The raid accomplished its mission, though of the 622 volunteers who executed it, two-thirds were killed or wounded. In May, British forces seized French Madagascar to forestall a German plan to establish U-boat bases there for a campaign against Allied convoys to Russia via the Persian Gulf. Another, even more ambitious raid took place on August 19 (four days after the Operation Pedestal convoy arrived in Malta), when five thousand mostly Canadian soldiers landed at Dieppe, halfway between Calais and Normandy. That raid ended in disaster, with nearly a thousand Canadians killed and two thousand captured. The experience seemed to confirm that the English-speaking Allies were simply not ready for a serious thrust onto the Continent.[4]

Churchill suggested that if something *had* to be done in 1942, that something should be an Allied invasion of French North Africa. Though Vichy France was technically neutral, Churchill hoped that seizing its North African colonies would effectively surround the Nazi empire in Europe, and perhaps encourage the French to rejoin the conflict. Then, too, a campaign into North Africa would commit American troops to the Mediterranean theater, where Britain had great strategic interests. Marshall pushed back against this proposal, at one point even suggesting that the United States abandon the Germany-first protocol altogether and go on the offensive in the Pacific. Roosevelt rejected that suggestion and insisted that Marshall find "a specific and definite theater where our ground and sea forces can operate against German ground forces in 1942." On July 27 (the same day Fletcher, Turner, and Vandegrift met on board the *Saratoga* to discuss the invasion of Guadalcanal), Marshall met with his British counterpart in London to hammer out a strategy. In the end, Marshall gave way to both political pressure and logistical realities, and the British and American Combined Chiefs of Staff approved a plan to invade French North Africa in the first week of November. Its code name was Operation Torch.[5]

Assuming the invasion was successful, Torch would get Allied forces into the European theater before the end of the year, though it fell well short of establishing a second front that would take pressure off the Red Army. It did not, for example, fulfill Roosevelt's goal of operating against German ground forces because in the fall of 1942 there were no Germans in French North Africa.

Moreover, even this modest initiative against a putative neutral could prove difficult to execute because of the logistical challenges, which were exacerbated by the simultaneous need to sustain the U.S. Marines on Guadalcanal. For the Marines to keep their precarious foothold on that jungle outpost, they would have to be significantly reinforced and resupplied on a regular basis by convoys and their escorts. These two imperatives—the perceived political need to execute a major landing in North Africa and the logistical necessity to keep Guadalcanal supplied—meant that despite a formal commitment to the Germany-first principle, the British and Americans found themselves fighting a de facto two-front war, one in which sealift capability was both the essential component and the principal weakness.

———————

WHILE PLANNING FOR TORCH CONTINUED in the Atlantic Theater, both the Americans and the Japanese frantically shuttled reinforcements to Guadalcanal in the South Pacific—the Americans by day, the Japanese by night. The Americans expanded and reinforced their perimeter around the initial landing beach, and the Japanese reinforced their position on the western end of the island. In between, most of the island remained a kind of no-man's-land of thick jungle. The scarcity of transports remained a central problem for both sides, a fact that compelled them to adjust their strategic planning elsewhere. The Japanese canceled plans for further initiatives in the Indian Ocean, and the Americans, despite the demands of Operation Torch, kept all of Turner's transports in the Pacific and even shifted the *Wasp* there to beef up Fletcher's carrier force. In that way, Guadalcanal had a significant impact on the global war as well as in the South Pacific.[6]

A key factor in the campaign was American air superiority. Though the American enclave remained relatively small, it included the unfinished Japanese airstrip. The Americans completed it and named it Henderson Field after a Marine major who had been killed in the Battle of Midway. On August 20, American combat planes—flown by Marine pilots—landed there to establish a permanent air presence. Since the code word for Guadalcanal was "Cactus," these planes came to be known as the Cactus Air Force. In an effort to blunt the impact of these airplanes, the Japanese conducted regular night air attacks on the American beachhead and especially on Henderson Field, though they proved more of a nuisance than a serious threat. To at least one Marine pilot it seemed that "every night some God damn Jap bomber would come down" and drop a few bombs on or near the airfield, then fly off again.[7]

It was the threat of the planes in the Cactus Air Force that compelled the Japanese to deliver their own reinforcements to Guadalcanal by night. They did so, for the most part, with destroyers, cramming each of them with two hundred soldiers for the six-hundred-mile run from Rabaul to Cape Esperance, at the western end of Guadalcanal. The destroyer crews disliked

Henderson Field on Guadalcanal photographed from the air. Begun by the Japanese and completed by the Americans, it proved critical to the American effort to maintain a foothold on Guadalcanal during the summer and fall of 1942. Ironbottom Sound is visible in the distance beyond the rows of banana palms.

U.S. National Archives photo no. 80-G-12216

being used as transports. As one staff officer put it, "We are more a freighter convoy than a fighting squadron these days." No doubt the soldiers, too, were unhappy about being crowded onto a narrow destroyer, where seasickness was rampant. But Japan was also desperately short of transports, which in any case could make only about ten to twelve knots, whereas the destroyers could reach thirty or more. To avoid attacks by the Cactus Air

Force, the destroyers timed their departure from Rabaul so that they entered the two-hundred-mile air envelope from Henderson Field just past nightfall. Then they made a high-speed run to the island in the dark, dropped off their by now miserable passengers, and then dashed back again to get beyond that two-hundred-mile limit before dawn. They did this with such regularity that the Marines on the island referred to these runs as the "Tokyo Express."[8]

Among the first Japanese reinforcements brought to the island was a battalion of 916 men under Colonel Kiyonao Ichiki. Rather than wait for support, Ichiki foolishly ordered a night ground attack on the Marines' perimeter on August 21. His force was not only defeated, it was virtually annihilated, an outcome that sobered the Japanese theater commanders at Rabaul. Admiral Yamamoto moved his flagship, the giant *Yamato,* to Truk in the Carolines on August 28, and from there he ordered Operation KA, a far larger reinforcement effort designed to deliver to Guadalcanal the fifty-eight hundred soldiers that had initially been slotted to occupy Midway had the battle gone according to plan. Yamamoto directed Admiral Nagumo's carrier force to cover the convoy, and that decision led to the third major carrier battle of the Pacific War.[9]

Characteristically, the Japanese plan for delivering their reinforcements was complex, even elaborate. The troop convoy itself consisted of one transport and four older destroyers, all crammed with soldiers, escorted by the 2nd Destroyer Division, commanded by Rear Admiral Raizo Tanaka, known for his competence and stoic imperturbability. To cover the convoy and its escort, Chūichi "King Kong" Hara led a diversionary group consisting of the light carrier *Ryūjō* plus a light cruiser and two destroyers. Behind them was a surface force of six cruisers under Nobutake Kondō followed by another, larger surface force of battleships and heavy cruisers under Hiroaki Abe, and then finally the main carrier force under Nagumo. As at Midway, these forces were so dispersed as to make it difficult for them to provide mutual support.

To oppose them, Fletcher had three carriers, though in an effort to ensure that they were all kept well fueled, he rotated them one at a time back to Nouméa to top off their tanks, so that much of the time he had only two carriers available for combat. This week it was the *Wasp*'s turn to refuel, and she had left for Nouméa the day before. Fletcher also had a substantial surface force that included the new battleship *North Carolina* and three heavy cruisers. The *North Carolina* carried nine 16-inch guns, but, more important for Fletcher, she also bristled with scores of new anti-aircraft guns.[10]

The ensuing confrontation, dubbed the Battle of the Eastern Solomons, took place in the last week of August, and was very nearly a clone of the Battle of the Coral Sea the previous May. As in that earlier battle, planes from the big fleet carriers on each side spent most of the first day looking for one another. An American PBY found and reported the location of Hara's *Ryūjō* just past 9:00 a.m., though the report never made it to Fletcher's carriers. Fletcher did get a report of two light cruisers and a destroyer from his own search planes, but he was looking for bigger game. In the Coral Sea, he had committed his entire strike force to attack what turned out to be the small carrier *Shōhō*. This time he waited several hours to make sure there weren't more important targets in the area. In the interim, Hara dispatched a strike force of six bombers and fifteen fighters from the *Ryūjō* to attack Henderson Field. It was his undoing, not only because it left the *Ryūjō* with just nine fighters to protect the task force but also, and mainly, because the planes showed up on the *Saratoga*'s radar, which alerted Fletcher to the presence of a carrier. Since he had heard nothing from his other scouts, at 1:40 Fletcher ordered an air strike against the *Ryūjō*.[11]

The thirty-eight planes Fletcher sent caught the *Ryūjō* with its remaining fighters still on the flight deck. Even as she belatedly turned into the wind to launch, the Americans overwhelmed her, hitting her with four 1,000-pound bombs and one torpedo, without losing a single plane. A witness on a nearby Japanese destroyer recalled that "*Ryūjō*, no longer resembling a ship, was a huge stove, full of holes which belched eerie red flames." She sank later that night (though the Allies did not know that for certain until a year later). Those of the *Ryūjō*'s planes that survived the strike on Henderson Field, which did minimal damage, either flew to Buka, halfway to Rabaul, or ditched in the water, with most of the pilots picked up by the escorting destroyers.[12]

Meanwhile, just past two o'clock, Nagumo on the *Shōkaku* received a sighting report of the American carriers from his search planes, and he launched an attack of his own. American radar again proved invaluable when, a little after four o'clock, it detected the first wave of inbound Japanese planes—twenty-seven Val dive-bombers and ten Zeros—while they were still a hundred miles out. The Americans launched every plane they had, increasing the CAP to fifty-three Wildcats and sending the bombers off to attack Nagumo's carriers.

The high sky and bright sun made for ideal attack conditions. The American air defense was less effective than it might have been because the pilots exercised little radio discipline, cluttering up the circuit with calls such as "Look out" and "Two bogies on your left," giving the fighter director on the *Enterprise* trouble coordinating the defense. The Wildcats splashed several of the Vals before they got close enough to release their bombs, though enough of them fought their way through the heavy AA fire from the *North Carolina* to put three bombs on the *Enterprise* in quick succession. As one crewman on the *Enterprise* recalled, "We were blowed up pretty good." Damage control parties kept the ship afloat, and within half an hour she was able to recover airplanes, though Fletcher had no choice but to order her back to Pearl Harbor for repairs. Luckily for the Americans, the second wave of Japanese bombers never found the American ships at all and returned to their own carriers still bearing their ordnance.[13]

As daylight faded, Fletcher had both a crippled *Enterprise* and orders from Admiral Ghormley in Nouméa to "fuel your task force as soon as possible." Rather than continue the battle, therefore, he decided to retire southward. It was the right decision, for Abe's surface force of two battleships and ten heavy cruisers was steaming for him at twenty-five knots. Still, it was precisely the kind of decision that was sure to provoke King's ire, and Fletcher knew it. According to Fletcher's intelligence officer, Lieutenant Gil Slonim, Fletcher collapsed into a chair and said: "Boys, I'm going to get two dispatches tonight, one from Admiral Nimitz telling me what a wonderful job we did, and one from King saying, 'Why in hell didn't you use your destroyers and make [night] torpedo attacks?' and by God, they'll both be right."[14]

In addition to the *Ryūjō*, the Japanese had lost thirty-three carrier planes in the exchange, and in yet another echo of the Battle of the Coral Sea, that was enough to convince Nagumo to withdraw northward. The troop convoy under Tanaka held on toward Guadalcanal for several more hours, though late that afternoon it was attacked by planes of the Cactus Air Force. One of the American planes landed a bomb on the foredeck of Tanaka's flagship, the light cruiser *Jintsu*, and another hit the transport *Kinryu Maru*, carrying a thousand soldiers. Soon after that, several army B-17s attacked. In a rare example of successful bombing from above ten thousand feet, one bomb landed square on the destroyer *Mutsuki*, breaking her in half and sending her to the bottom. After that, Tanaka got orders to reverse course and head north.[15]

As in the Coral Sea, it was a drawn battle. The Japanese lost the *Ryūjō*, the *Mutsuki*, a troopship, and those thirty-three planes. The Americans lost seventeen planes and temporary use of the *Enterprise*. More important, the engagement convinced the Japanese to cancel the landings on Guadalcanal. Back in May, the Americans had trumpeted the Battle of the Coral Sea as a victory because it had led the Japanese to call off their invasion of Port Moresby. This time, despite similar results, King decided that the Battle of the Eastern Solomons was a disappointment, and that it was due to Fletcher's timidity. In part, King's displeasure was based on the claims of American pilots who reported destroying eighty Japanese planes, more than double the actual number. If accurate, it would mean that the Japanese had been stripped of much of their offensive potential and Fletcher could have renewed the attack on the carriers with relative impunity, though he still would have had to deal with Abe's surface force.

By now Fletcher had commanded U.S. carrier forces in three major battles—the Coral Sea, Midway, and the Solomon Islands. The only clear-cut victory of the three was Midway, and King gave most of the credit for that to Spruance. Up to now, Nimitz had defended Fletcher, but King's patience was exhausted, and he sought a reason to replace Fletcher with a more aggressive commander. He found it five days later, on August 31, when a Japanese submarine put a torpedo into the *Saratoga*, compelling her to return to Pearl Harbor along with the *Enterprise* for repairs. King used the opportunity to give Fletcher a shore assignment, and he never com-manded at sea again.[16]

The temporary loss of the *Saratoga* left the newly arrived *Hornet* and the *Wasp* the only two operational American carriers in the South Pacific, though it helped that before the *Saratoga* departed for Pearl many of her planes flew to Henderson Field to bolster the Cactus Air Force. Like Midway three months before, Guadalcanal itself became a vital airplane platform to aug-ment the carriers. On September 1, the Marines on Guadalcanal received another important reinforcement with the arrival of the first unit of the Naval Construction Battalions, the "Seabees," who kept Henderson Field in working order despite the regular Japanese air raids. As the historian John Costello has noted, "Keeping the airstrip open so that the American planes could operate was as crucial to the mounting pace of the battle for Guadalcanal as the Marines defending their positions."[17]

The Cactus Air Force became even more critical two weeks later. On the morning of September 15, Commander Takaichi Kinashi in the submarine I-19 was electrified to spot an American convoy of six troop transports headed for Guadalcanal. They were carrying the 7th Marine Regiment, and, given the value of that human cargo, they were escorted by both of America's remaining aircraft carriers plus a battleship and several cruisers and destroy-ers. Kinashi fired a spread of six torpedoes at the nearest carrier. In what was arguably the most devastating torpedo salvo of the war, one torpedo hit the battleship *North Carolina*, one hit the destroyer *O'Brien*, and three hit the carrier *Wasp*. The torpedo that hit the *North Carolina* struck below her armored belt and opened a huge hole in her port side. Almost at once she heeled over to a five-degree list, though effective counterflooding set her back to an even keel and she was able to maintain speed. The *O'Brien*, too, stayed afloat, though she subsequently foundered while making her way back to Pearl Harbor for repairs.

As for the *Wasp*, two direct hits and one glancing blow by the big Type 95 torpedoes ignited multiple fires on board, and in a replication of the Japanese experience at Midway, those fires triggered a number of second-ary explosions among the ammunition and aviation fuel on the *Wasp*'s hangar deck. Despite valiant damage control efforts, it was soon evident that

The American carrier USS *Wasp* in her death throes after being hit by three torpedoes fired from the Japanese submarine I-19 on September 15, 1942. Torpedoes from the same salvo crippled the battleship *North Carolina* and sank the destroyer *O'Brien*.

U.S. National Archives photo no. 80-G-16331

the big carrier had been mortally wounded, and Captain Forrest P. Sherman ordered abandon ship.*

The reinforcement convoy made it to Guadalcanal, where the arrival of the 7th Regiment greatly strengthened Vandegrift's command. That same convoy also delivered 147 vehicles and 400 drums of aviation fuel for the Cactus Air Force. The loss of the *Wasp*, however, left the *Hornet* as the only fully operational U.S. carrier in the Pacific.[18]

IT WAS NO BETTER IN THE ATLANTIC, where the sole carrier in the American maritime arsenal was the undersized USS *Ranger*. Combined with British carrier losses in the Mediterranean during Pedestal, the prospect of

---

* Forrest Sherman was not related to Frederick C. "Ted" Sherman, who commanded the *Lexington* when it was sunk in the Battle of the Coral Sea.

providing sufficient air cover for Torch became problematical. In fact, the Allies had difficulty scraping together shipping of all types for the forthcoming invasion: troopships to carry soldiers to the beachhead, cargo ships to carry their equipment and supplies, escorts to protect them during the transit, and the specialized amphibious vessels needed to carry the men and their equipment to the invasion beaches and sustain them there. As Mark Clark, the American deputy commander of Operation Torch, put it, there was "a continual crisis over shipping space and frequent changes in plans had to be made in order to overcome what was always a shortage of vessels." Difficult and contentious as it had been, making the decision to go into North Africa was the easy part; actually doing it posed daunting logistical challenges.[19]

Perhaps as a consolation prize for having lost the strategic argument, the commander of Operation Torch was an American: Marshall's former planning officer, Dwight D. Eisenhower. Ike, as he was universally known, was appointed to the command on August 6 (the day before U.S. Marines splashed ashore on Guadalcanal), and he presided over a complex administrative puzzle involving an infinite number of logistical details. His job also required the diplomatic sensitivity necessary to ensure that British and American forces worked together more or less harmoniously. Eisenhower was an unproven combat leader—he had never led soldiers in a battle—but he was a deft manager of personalities, and his determination to subordinate national ambitions to the overall objective was critical.[20]

The naval commander for Torch was Admiral Sir Andrew Cunningham. Once the toast of the Royal Navy for his audacious and successful attack on Taranto in 1940 and his victory at Cape Matapan in 1941, Cunningham had lost favor with Churchill; the prime minister had soured on him after the disastrous evacuation from Crete and sent him off to Washington to serve on the staff of the Combined Chiefs. Meanwhile, the Mediterranean command went to Henry Harwood, hero of the battle with the *Graf Spee*. Alas, Harwood also failed to live up to Churchill's expectations, and so now Cunningham was back. Cunningham's deputy for the Torch operation was Sir Bertram Ramsay, who had orchestrated the evacuation from Dunkirk.[21]

The Allies' material shortages, especially in shipping, compelled them to improvise. The British had three full-sized aircraft carriers and three smaller ones to cover their assigned targets, but the Americans had only the *Ranger*. To supplement her, they constructed flight decks atop four oilers and redesignated them as auxiliary carriers. Significantly smaller than regular carriers, and lacking a hangar deck, they could still embark thirty planes each, though all of them had to be carried on the flight deck.

Troop transports were another problem. What few landing ships the British possessed had been lost at Narvik and Dunkirk, and many of the American transports were half a world away, running supplies into Guadalcanal. It was a zero-sum game: ships needed for one undertaking necessarily had to come from someplace else. As the official British history of the campaign puts it, "The transports, store-ships, and auxiliaries of all sorts which had to be taken out of circulation seriously upset the Allied shipping programme throughout the world." The Allies cobbled together what they could. To carry soldiers to North Africa, they relied heavily on prewar cruise ships; the British even commandeered ferryboats from the Glasgow-Belfast run. Similarly, American civilian cargo vessels metamorphosed into "attack transports." In effect, the invasion fleets for Torch were jury-rigged (as the Americans put it); in the British idiom, they were "lash-ups."[22]

Of course, the packed troopships and laden cargo vessels required a substantial escort in order to cross the several thousand miles of hostile ocean to the invasion beaches, and that, too, meant withdrawing forces from other theaters. Britain could escort its contingent only by relying heavily on the Home Fleet, as it had for Pedestal, committing three battleships (*Duke of York*, *Nelson*, and *Rodney*), the battlecruiser *Renown*, five cruisers, and all five of the Royal Navy's aircraft carriers plus thirty-one destroyers. To obtain them, the Royal Navy reduced the escorts for the transatlantic convoys and suspended convoys to Russia altogether. The escorts for the American troopships, which would sail directly to North Africa from the East Coast of the United States, included three battleships (*Massachusetts*, *New York*, and *Texas*), seven cruisers, and thirty-eight destroyers. More destroyers would have been desirable, but in the late summer of 1942, destroyers were in demand everywhere, including the Solomon Islands.[23]

Once the troopships and cargo vessels arrived at the target beaches, there was the additional problem of getting the men, their equipment, and their vehicles from the transports to the beach. The Marines who had landed at Guadalcanal had benefited from years of practice landings during the 1930s, and their assault on Guadalcanal had been almost routine; they merely had to climb over the sides of their landing boats and wade ashore. The assault in North Africa, however, would involve soldiers, not Marines, and on a much larger scale. To get them from ship to shore, they would have to climb down rope or chain nets from the transports into small plywood boats that would carry them several miles to the beach.

The vessels needed to accomplish that were also in short supply. The British version of this type of small landing boat was called "landing craft, assault" (LCA), and the American version was called "landing craft, personnel" (LCP). Each was capable of carrying thirty-six soldiers at a time, and their navy crewmen were to shuttle back and forth between ship and shore until the landing force was established. Because the American LCPs had been designed and built by Andrew Jackson Higgins, nearly everyone called them Higgins boats (a practice that will be followed here). Later in the war, both the British and American versions would have armored drop-front bows that would enable the soldiers to run directly from the boat out onto the beach, but the early models were simply rectangular plywood boxes with a motor on the back, and when they ground up onto the sand, the men, each of them carrying between sixty and ninety pounds of gear plus their rifle, had to climb out over the sides into waist-deep water before making their way to the beach, as the Marines had done at Guadalcanal.[24]

Getting armored vehicles ashore was a bigger problem. The campaigns in France and Flanders in 1940 had demonstrated that ground combat in the Second World War meant the use of armored vehicles, specifically tanks. Getting tanks from ship to shore was a far more difficult problem than carrying soldiers. The British had experimented with tank-carrying ships that were converted from shallow-draft oil tankers used on Venezuela's Lake Maracaibo. Like so many innovations, this one had originated in the fertile mind of the prime minister, and the vessels were dubbed "Winstons" (smaller versions were called "Winettes"). What made them distinctive was their massive bow doors, which opened like a giant cupboard. After running up as close to the beach as they could get, they opened their big bow doors and deployed a long ramp. In theory, tanks and trucks could then drive out from their commodious hold directly onto the beach. The concept was certainly valid, as later models of such ships demonstrated. The early versions, however, were cumbersome and difficult to unload, and they had proved disappointing, and nearly disastrous, during the ill-fated raid on Dieppe.[25]

The Americans attacked the problem differently, appropriating a large cargo ship, the *Seatrain New Jersey*, that had been designed to carry railroad cars from New York to Cuba, and modifying it to carry tanks. She was not a true amphibious ship, however, since her deep V-shaped hull did not allow her to steam up onto a beach, and she could unload her cargo of tanks only if she had access to a working harbor.

Carriers, battleships, cruisers, troopships, cargo ships, destroyers, and landing craft: altogether, the British and Americans employed nearly six hundred ships, plus the small Higgins boats, to execute this first major strategic counteroffensive of the war. From the start, the commanders had to scramble to find the manpower, the equipment, and especially the shipping to make it happen. The nickname "Operation Shoestring" that had been used to describe the Guadalcanal landing might just as easily have been applied to Torch.

———

AS EISENHOWER AND HIS TEAM struggled to put together the various components of the North African invasion force, the race to pour more troops into Guadalcanal continued. The Tokyo Express remained persistent, and by October it had delivered more than twenty thousand men plus their equipment to the island. The Americans were also building up their forces. In the second week of October they added the U.S. Army's 164th Infantry Regiment, a National Guard unit that was part of the Americal Division. It was escorted to the island by two heavy and two light cruisers plus five destroyers, dubbed Task Force 64, under Rear Admiral Norman Scott.[26]

While that convoy was en route, the Japanese dispatched their own reinforcement convoy from Rabaul, this one consisting of two fully loaded seaplane carriers, *Nisshin* and *Chitose*, with a circular screen of six destroyers. As usual, the ships proceeded at a leisurely fifteen knots until they hit the invisible line two hundred miles from Henderson Field, at which point they increased speed to twenty-five knots for the run into the island. At ten-thirty that morning, however, a patrolling B-17 spotted the convoy and reported its location and course. Armed with that report, Scott's Task Force 64,

American Rear Admiral Norman Scott (left) and Japanese Rear Admiral Arimoto Goto (right) clashed in the Battle of Cape Esperance on October 11-12, 1942. At night, in unsettled weather, the combat was marked by errors on both sides, though American possession of radar gave them a tremendous advantage.

U.S. Naval Institute

having safely delivered the Americal Division to Guadalcanal, headed north to intercept it.

The fifty-three-year-old Scott was aware of the enemy's prowess in night fighting, but if the sighting report from the B-17 was accurate, he also knew that he had clear superiority over this foe. Two other factors were on his side as well. One was that all of his ships now had radar, though only two of them, the light cruisers *Boise* and *Helena*, had the new SG radar with the now-familiar rotating dish capable of providing both range and bearing to surface contacts and displaying them on a maplike PPI (plan position indicator) scope. The other advantage Scott had was surprise. Unlike Savo Island, this time it would be the Americans who were seeking battle and the Japanese who would be caught unawares. Scott had missed the Battle of

Savo Island because he had commanded the two cruisers of the eastern force, the side away from the action, and that may have contributed to his determination to avenge the humiliation of that defeat. Armed with the sighting report, Scott rounded the western end of Guadalcanal and headed north, determined to ambush the Japanese convoy.[27]

What Scott did not know was that several hours behind the Japanese reinforcement convoy was a second Japanese force, consisting of three heavy cruisers, all of them veterans of the Battle of Savo Island, plus two destroyers, all under the command of Rear Admiral Aritomo Gotō, himself a veteran of Savo Island. Gotō's force had a different mission than the reinforcement group. His assignment was to bombard Henderson Field.

It was a dark night with no moon and, thanks to a heavy cloud cover, no stars. Scott's ships, proceeding in a single column, were blacked out. Intermittent rain showers swept over the ships, and the only visibility came from an occasional flicker of distant lightning. At fifteen minutes to midnight, as the American ships neared Savo Island, Scott ordered a course reversal to recross the passage between Savo Island and Cape Esperance. When he gave the execute order, the lead destroyer dutifully put its helm over and was followed in turn by the next two, each ship turning at the same point to maintain the line-ahead formation. The officer conning the flagship *San Francisco*, however, put the helm over at once, and the *Boise*, just astern of her, followed in her track. That error meant that the three lead destroyers were now somewhere off to the starboard from the main body. Scott, trying to reassemble his formation, confirmed it by the short-range TBS (talk between ships) radio: "Are you taking station ahead?" he queried the destroyers.* The response was, "Affirmative. Coming up on your starboard side." Thus when the *Helena* and *Boise* each reported a strong radar contact to starboard, Scott assumed it was his own three destroyers.[28]

It was not. The SG radar sets on the light cruisers had picked up not the three American destroyers, nor the supply convoy that Scott was seeking. Instead, the blips were the ships of Gotō's heavy cruisers. Though they were

---

* A low-powered very-high-frequency (VHF) radio system, TBS messages could be sent only to recipients who were within line of sight-about 25 miles. This prevented opposition forces from intercepting or even receiving them.

unaware of it, this was a priceless opportunity for the Americans because Gotō, having no radar at all, had no idea the Americans were there. The gun crews on the American light cruisers loaded their main batteries, trained their guns out to starboard, and waited for the order to commence firing. The radio talker on the *Helena* contacted the flagship repeatedly to request permission to fire. Scott, however, was still uncertain of the location of those three destroyers, and did not respond. In the end, it was a communications glitch that triggered the battle.

Prior to the implementation of the oral TBS system, the Morse code signal to open fire had been "dot-dash-dot"—the letter *R* or "Roger." When the *Helena*'s radio talker repeated his request for permission to fire, he used this abbreviated form, asking simply: "Interrogatory Roger," in effect, "Can we open fire?" When the radio talker on the flagship acknowledged the query by saying "Roger," it was interpreted as an affirmative reply, and immediately the fifteen 6-inch guns on the *Helena* opened up. When they did, every other American ship opened fire as well, even the flagship.[29]

Scott was horrified. He feared that his cruisers were firing on his own destroyers, and he frantically ordered a cease-fire. Amidst the cacophony of the barrage, only the guns on his own ship were stilled. Scott had to repeat the order several times before the firing finally died out.[30]

The targets were, in fact, Gotō's cruisers, which were several thousand yards beyond the American destroyers. Quite by accident, Scott's battle line had crossed the bows of Gotō's force as it entered the passage between Cape Esperance and Savo Island—the same waters where Mikawa had won his victory two months before. Gotō was as horrified as Scott. He believed that he was under fire by the Japanese reinforcement group that he knew to be ahead of him. He flashed a signal to identify himself, furious at the fools who were firing into their own ships—or so he thought. "Stupid idiots!" he muttered. They were his last words. All nine of the 8-inch shells from the *San Francisco*'s second salvo struck Gotō's flagship, *Aoba*, and the Japanese admiral became an early casualty.[31]

Scott's cease-fire order very nearly threw away the huge advantage that fortune had offered him, but he soon confirmed the location of the American destroyers, and four minutes after ordering a cease-fire, he ordered the guns to recommence firing. Navy veteran Charles Cook described the firing sequence: "There was a clatter of loading trays and the sharp, musical ring of shells driven firmly into their seats by the power rammers. Powder bags were shoved in quickly behind the shells, trays pulled back, breech blocks swung closed." When all the turrets reported ready, a warning buzzer sounded twice, then once, and the ship's fire director pressed the trigger. Stabs of orange flame burst from the muzzles, and thousands of pounds of armor-piercing ordnance flew into the night.[32]

The gun turrets on the American light cruisers could fire ten salvos per minute. With all five turrets engaged, the *Helena* and *Boise* together could fire three hundred 6-inch shells every minute. Stunned as they were by this onslaught, the Japanese soon recovered, and their fire, too, was accurate. Several Japanese shells hit the light cruiser *Boise*, including one 8-inch shell that struck her forward turret and started fires that threatened to reach the forward magazine. Fortuitously, other shells punched holes in her side and flooded that magazine. Two of the wayward American destroyers that had so worried Scott were caught in no-man's-land and hit by both American and Japanese shells, forcing them to retire quickly from the battle. By then, several of the Japanese ships were on fire, and it was clear that they were overmatched by a superior force. Within thirty minutes of the first shots, the Japanese were fleeing back up the Slot with their mortally wounded admiral.[33]

This Battle of Cape Esperance (October 11, 1942) was a reversal of what had happened two months earlier at Savo Island, when Mikawa's squadron had surprised the Allies. This time, thanks mainly to American radar, it was the Japanese who were surprised and the Americans who were ready at their stations when the battle opened. Despite these advantages, the Americans did not inflict the kind of one-sided defeat on their opponent that Mikawa had done. Scott reported sinking four cruisers and two destroyers, though in fact only one, the *Furutaka*, actually sank, along with the destroyer *Fubuki*. Gotō's flagship, the *Aoba*, though it was hit no less than forty times, somehow managed to remain afloat and make her way back to Rabaul under her own power. Moreover, just as Mikawa had failed to interfere with the American transports after Savo Island, Scott never found the

Japanese reinforcement group—his initial target, which successfully landed its men and supplies on Guadalcanal. Finally, after midnight, two Japanese battleships, *Kongo* and *Haruna*, bombarded Henderson Field with 14-inch shells, wrecking and damaging so many planes of the Cactus Air Force that at dawn only eleven of them were combat ready. As Samuel Eliot Morison put it in 1949, "Savo Island was a victory for the Japanese but the American transports were not touched; Cape Esperance was an American victory but the Japanese accomplished their main object."[34]

ONE WEEK LATER, on October 18, Vice Admiral William Halsey was in Nouméa on an inspection and familiarization tour when he received a message from Nimitz that he was to relieve Ghormley and assume command of U.S. naval forces in the South Pacific. "Jesus Christ and General Jackson!" Halsey exclaimed. "This is the hottest potato they have ever handed me." In Washington and in Pearl Harbor, U.S. Navy leadership had concluded that the cautious and careful Ghormley, effective as he had been as a diplomat, simply lacked the aggressive temperament needed in a theater commander. Nimitz asked King for permission to relieve him, and King agreed.[35]

In the words of his most recent biographer, Bill Halsey was "flamboyant, superstitious, and sentimental." His reputation in the fleet for bold action was such that the appointment by itself had a powerful morale-boosting effect on the whole theater. Upon hearing the news, the Marines on Guadalcanal jumped out of their foxholes and began celebrating. Aware that he had been elevated to this post to infuse aggressiveness into the campaign, Halsey ordered Rear Admiral Thomas J. Kinkaid, now in command of the *Hornet*, and George D. Murray, in the repaired *Enterprise*, to make a sweep to the north and east of the Santa Cruz Islands. It was certainly bold, perhaps even reckless, and signaled a new direction in American strategy. Halsey also ordered Rear Admiral Willis Lee, in command of the surface warships of Task Force 64, which now included the new battleship *Washington*, to steam up the Slot and try to interfere with the Tokyo Express. Rather than await events, Halsey was determined to take the initiative.[36]

The Japanese were also planning a new campaign, one in which the army and navy were to work together—at least theoretically. The accumulated

When Admiral William F. Halsey Jr. got unexpected orders to take command of the South Pacific, he knew that King and Nimitz expected him to be more aggressive than his predecessor.

U.S. National Archives photo no. 80-G-205279

ground forces brought down from Rabaul by the Tokyo Express now numbered more than twenty-two thousand men, and the Japanese plan was for those forces to capture Henderson Field, thus neutralizing the Cactus Air Force, while Japanese naval forces fended off interference by the U.S. Navy. Once Henderson Field was in Japanese hands, planes from the Japanese carriers would land there to secure air superiority. The ships the Japanese assigned to this mission constituted the most impressive naval armada of the war since Midway. The "advance force" under Nabutake Kondō included two battleships (*Kongo* and *Haruna*), four heavy cruisers, and the new carrier *Jun'yō*, which, though smaller than the big fleet carriers, still carried forty-five planes. The "striking force" under Nagumo included both of the big carriers (*Shōkaku* and *Zuikaku*) plus the smaller *Zuihō*. Altogether, the Japanese could put 194 planes in the air, 57 more than the Americans, and the Japanese were also stronger in battleships and cruisers.[37]

Yamamoto grew annoyed as this mighty armada milled about north of Guadalcanal while he waited to hear from the army that it had captured Henderson Field. He warned his army counterparts that unless it happened soon, his ships would have to retire in order to refuel. Army commanders assured him that Henderson Field would be taken that very night, and the attack began at 9:30 p.m. on October 24 during a driving rainstorm. The U.S. Marines defending the airfield, a battalion of about seven hundred men under Lieutenant Colonel Lewis B. "Chesty" Puller, fought off repeated assaults by a full division of Japanese soldiers. In the thick jungle and heavy rainfall, the fighting was confused, and in the midst of it, the Japanese operations officer, Colonel Hiroshi Matsumoto, reported incorrectly that Henderson Field was in Japanese hands. Rabaul forwarded that message to the fleet, and the Japanese navy began to close on the island. The captain of the *Zuihō*, Sueo Ōbayashi, sent fourteen Zeros and several bombers to Guadalcanal to land on the captured airstrip, and the pilots were astonished when they were met by a swarm of Marine fighters, who shot all of them down. When Halsey learned that a major Japanese naval force was closing on Guadalcanal, he sent a terse order to his carrier force: "STRIKE, REPEAT, STRIKE."[38]

The engagement that ensued, called the Battle of the Santa Cruz Islands by the Americans and the Battle of the South Pacific by the Japanese, took place on October 26–27, 1942. In what was by now a familiar scenario, scout planes from each side found and reported the location of the enemy flattops, and the opposing commanders launched strike forces toward the reported coordinates. The Americans drew first blood when one of the scout planes, piloted by Lieutenant Stockton B. Strong, dropped a 500-pound bomb on the small carrier *Zuihō*, which disabled her flight deck and rendered her incapable of further flight operations.

For the main attack, the efficient Japanese crews got their planes into the air first, though the Americans were only twenty minutes behind them. As in the Coral Sea, the opposing attack formations actually passed each other en route to their targets. As they did, nine Zeros peeled out of formation to attack the American bombers, shooting down three of the torpedo planes and damaging a fourth before the Wildcats drove them off.[39]

The Americans operated their two carriers in separate task forces, and because the *Enterprise* was partially obscured by a rain squall, the Japanese focused their attack on the *Hornet*. Despite a curtain of AA fire from four cruisers and six destroyers, the determined Val pilots pushed through the flak and put three bombs onto the American carrier. One pilot, his plane crippled by AA fire, deliberately crashed into the *Hornet*, spreading burning

This photograph, taken during the Battle of the Santa Cruz Islands (October 26, 1942), depicts the moment just seconds before a crippled Val dive-bomber (directly above the ship's island) smashed into the *Hornet's* flight deck.

U.S. National Archives photo no. 80-G-33947

aviation fuel across her flight deck. Later, a crippled Val smashed into the *Hornet's* forward five-inch gun galley and came to rest in the elevator pit.* That was not the fatal blow, however, which came from the Kate torpedo bombers. Conducting a classic anvil attack from two directions at once, the Japanese put two torpedoes into the *Hornet*. With that, the big carrier lost power and was dead in the water. Subsequently, while the heavy cruiser *Northampton* attempted to tow her to safety, another flight of torpedo

---

* Often cited as early kamikaze attacks, these suicidal crashes were not yet part of Japanese battle tactics. Rather, they were spontaneous decisions made by men who calculated that their planes were too badly crippled to make it back to their carriers and decided to do the most damage they could before dying. The deliberate use of suicide planes did not become Japanese policy until October 1944 and not fully embraced until the spring of 1945 (see Chapter 27).

planes arrived, and though eight of them were splashed, the ninth put a third torpedo into the *Hornet*'s starboard side. As that plane swooped low over the *Hornet*'s deck, it was riddled with AA fire and burst into flames. Hit by three bombs, three torpedoes, and two aircraft, the *Hornet* had to be abandoned. Two of Kondō's destroyers, arriving later, finally sent her to the bottom with more torpedoes.[40]

Meanwhile, the *Hornet* pilots, unaware that their own ship was dying, obtained some measure of revenge when they put three 1,000-pound bombs onto the flight deck of the *Shōkaku*. The big carrier stayed afloat, but her flight deck was ruined, and like the *Zuihō*, she retired from the battle.[41]

Nearly two hundred miles to the south, the Japanese attack planes shifted their attention to the *Enterprise*. The circle of escorts around the *Enterprise* included the new battleship *South Dakota*, which put up an astounding volume of radar-directed AA fire and accounted for several of the more than thirty Japanese planes shot down. The surviving Japanese pilots, however, put three bombs onto the *Enterprise*, though no torpedoes, which very likely saved her from sharing the *Hornet*'s fate. Like the *Shōkaku*, she continued to float, but she could no longer fight.[42]

Halsey, famous for his bellicosity and eager to fulfill the expectations of his bosses, had sent his only two carriers to duel a superior enemy force, and they had been roughly handled. The *Hornet* was gone, and while the *Enterprise* remained afloat, her smashed forward deck elevator was stuck in place, which dramatically reduced her efficiency. Admiral Thomas Kinkaid, who commanded the task group, was unwilling to lower it, fearing that if it then failed to return to deck level, it would render the ship incapable of flight operations. Until the *Enterprise* could be repaired, the Americans would have no operational aircraft carriers at all in the Pacific Ocean. The goal for which Yamamoto had crafted the Midway operation had finally been realized.[43]

THE JAPANESE CELEBRATED what they called the Battle of the South Pacific as another great victory by the Imperial Japanese Navy. Their enthusiastic pilots reported sinking four aircraft carriers and three battleships, and even if Yamamoto discounted such inflated claims, the Japanese press announced it as fact. Of course, the Japanese had suffered, too. Both the

Zuihō and the *Shōkaku* would live to fight another day, but they were knocked out of the war until they could be repaired, and in the case of the *Shōkaku*, that took a full nine months. Even more serious was the loss of Japanese aircraft: ninety-seven of them were shot down that day, and 148 pilots and air crewmen were lost with them, including precisely half of dive-bomber crews and 40 percent of torpedo bomber crews. The Americans had also suffered severe aircraft losses—a total of eighty-one planes—but not only could the Americans replace those planes more easily, they also recovered most of their invaluable aircrews. For the Japanese, the losses in planes and especially pilots were beginning to accumulate, and they were losses the country could not afford. Not to be overlooked was the critical fact that despite a major effort by both the Japanese army and navy, Guadalcanal and its airfield remained in American hands. Once again, a Japanese tactical victory had failed to secure the strategic objective.[44]

There was one more battle casualty. Chūichi Nagumo, who had commanded the Kidō Butai in all of its engagements from Pearl Harbor to the Solomons, was worn down and worn out. Yamamoto had given him an opportunity to redeem himself after the Midway disaster, and he had, winning two tactical victories in the Eastern Solomons. Neither victory, however, had brought strategic success, and now, like Frank Jack Fletcher, he was consigned to shore duty, replaced by the six-foot-seven-inch Admiral Jisaburō Ozawa.

Finally, underscoring the global character of the naval war, the same week that American and Japanese pilots ravaged each other's carrier forces in the Pacific, twenty-eight American transports, filled with more than thirty-three thousand soldiers and escorted by an armada of cruisers and destroyers, departed Norfolk, Virginia, to begin a four-thousand-mile journey across the Atlantic to French Morocco to initiate Operation Torch.

CHAPTER 16

THE TIPPING POINT

IN THE THIRD WEEK OF OCTOBER 1942, as Japanese and American pilots dueled near the Santa Cruz Islands and Allied invasion convoys from Scotland and the United States converged on North Africa, General Bernard Law Montgomery, commanding the British Eighth Army in Egypt, ordered a ground attack on Erwin Rommel's forces at El Alamein. He could do so thanks mainly to overwhelming superiority in equipment and material, much of it made available to him via convoys from the United States. To reach him, those convoys traced a twenty-thousand-mile route across the South Atlantic to Cape Town, up through the Indian Ocean to the Red Sea, and then through the Suez Canal to Alexandria. In September and October alone, they delivered more than a quarter of a million tons of military stores plus 18,480 vehicles. Among them were 318 Sherman tanks that Roosevelt had promised to Churchill after the fall of Tobruk. That raised British tank strength to over a thousand; Rommel had less than half that.[1]

The Axis could not match the Allied buildup because British naval and air forces from Malta, guided by Ultra intercepts, continued their persistent and devastating attacks on Rommel's supply convoys from Italy. In September the British sank 30 percent of all Axis ships in those convoys; in October it was more than 40 percent. That was more than double the rate of Allied losses to U-boats in the North Atlantic, and in consequence Rommel was short of almost everything, not only tanks but ammunition and especially gasoline—in October, the loss rate among Axis oil tankers was more than 60 percent. As a result, Montgomery's strengthened army pounded the outnumbered Germans at El Alamein for most of two weeks, eventually winning a signal victory—indeed, the first major British victory of the war against a German army. That victory made Montgomery a viscount, but it would not have been possible without Allied sealift.[2]

Sealift was also the key to Operation Torch. Even as the fighting played out in the Egyptian desert, more than a hundred Allied transport and cargo ships and nearly as many escorts, all under the command of Royal Navy Vice Admiral Neville Syfret, sailed for French North Africa in ten separate convoys from Scapa Flow and ports in Scotland. To deceive the Germans and avoid the U-boats, they steamed westward out to mid-ocean before they turned southeast toward Gibraltar. A U-boat did sight one of the convoys on October 26, and Karl Dönitz vectored five U-boats toward it, though they never found it. A wolf pack did find and attack a different convoy (SL-125) bound from Sierra Leone to Liverpool. During the five days from October 27 to 31, ten U-boats sank thirteen Allied ships from that convoy and damaged seven others. The carnage had a silver lining, however, in that it diverted German attention away from the even more valuable Torch convoys. Later, some speculated that SL-125 had been deliberately sacrificed to distract the Germans. That was not the case, though it filled that function nonetheless.[3]

After passing through the Strait of Gibraltar, the British invasion convoys assembled into two groups: one bound for Oran, 266 miles inside the Mediterranean, and the other for Algiers, another 200 miles further east. The British had argued for a landing even deeper into the Mediterranean— at Bône, near the Tunisian border—but the Americans were uncomfortable with that. As it was, the Allied landings were spread out across a seven-hundred-mile front from Safi, on the Atlantic coast, all the way to Algiers.

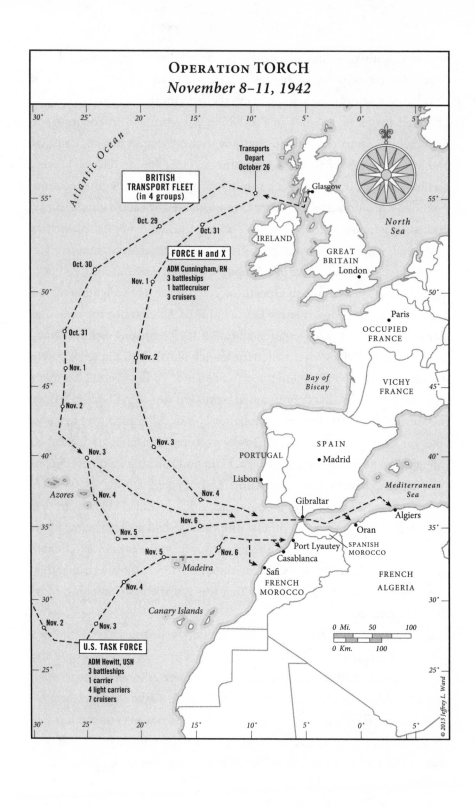

OPERATION TORCH
November 8–11, 1942

Atlantic Ocean

Transports
Depart
October 26

**BRITISH
TRANSPORT FLEET
(in 4 groups)**

Glasgow

Oct. 29

Oct. 31

*North
Sea*

IRELAND

FORCE H and X

ADM Cunningham, RN
3 battleships
1 battlecruiser
3 cruisers

Oct. 30

Nov. 1

GREAT
BRITAIN

London

Oct. 31

Nov. 1

Nov. 2

Paris

OCCUPIED
FRANCE

Nov. 2

*Bay of
Biscay*

VICHY
FRANCE

Nov. 3

Nov. 3

SPAIN

Nov. 4

PORTUGAL

Madrid

*Mediterranean
Sea*

Azores

Nov. 4

Nov. 4

Lisbon

Gibraltar

Algiers

Nov. 6

Nov. 5

Nov. 6

Oran

Nov. 5

Nov. 6

Port Lyautey

SPANISH
MOROCCO

Nov. 4

Madeira

Casablanca

Safi

FRENCH
MOROCCO

FRENCH
ALGERIA

Nov. 2

Nov. 3

Canary Islands

U.S. TASK FORCE

ADM Hewitt, USN
3 battleships
1 carrier
4 light carriers
7 cruisers

0 Mi.   50   100

0 Km.   100

© 2013 *Jeffrey L. Ward*

The commander of the convoy bound for Oran was Commodore Thomas Hope Troubridge, many of whose forebears had been Royal Navy admirals (the first of them, also named Thomas, had fought alongside Nelson at the Battle of Cape St. Vincent in 1797). The slightly larger convoy bound for Algiers was led by Vice Admiral Sir Harold Burrough, who had commanded the Operation Pedestal convoy during its harrowing journey to Malta less than three months before.

As the British ships ran through the Straits of Gibraltar, Spanish observers noted their passage and forwarded the information to the Axis. Nine German and twenty-one Italian submarines prepared to intercept them. The Italians assumed that this was another reinforcement convoy for Malta, a speculation the British encouraged by maintaining a course for that island until they were almost due north of their actual targets, then abruptly turning south. That subterfuge led the Italians to concentrate most of their boats in the narrows between Cape Bon and Sicily and allowed the invasion convoys to avoid them altogether. The German U-boats did their best to interfere with the Allied convoys, but the strength of the escorts deflected them.[4]

Nor did the Axis command the skies as they had during Pedestal. In addition to the planes on the Royal Navy carriers, the British had 350 aircraft at Gibraltar, many of which had been shipped in crates from the United States and assembled on the tarmac on Gibraltar's single airstrip. Nevertheless, it was a German air attack from Sardinia that drew first blood on November 7 when a Heinkel 111 torpedoed the American troop transport *Thomas Stone*, part of Burrough's convoy bound for Algiers. The torpedo exploded near the engine room and broke the transport's propeller shaft. The *Thomas Stone* was dead in the water and unable to continue. Burroughs left the River class frigate *Spey* to stand by her and pressed on with the rest of the invasion convoy.[5]

The commander of the American soldiers embarked on the *Thomas Stone* was Major Walter M. Oakes, and he was determined not to be left behind. He convinced the ship's captain, Olton R. Bennehoff, to lower the twenty-four Higgins boats and allow his men to make their way to the landing beach 160 miles away, escorted by the *Spey*. Oakes's enthusiasm was commendable, but the decision was foolish. Higgins boats were not made for such an extended voyage, and they found it impossible to stay together at night in a challenging sea. Soon enough they began shipping water, and several broke down. As the boats foundered one by one, the accompanying *Spey* took the men on board until the 1,400-ton vessel was all but swamped. Oakes and his men eventually got to Algiers more than fifteen hours late.[6]

While the British invasion convoys approached the landing beaches, intense negotiations were taking place ashore. The American consul general in Algiers, Robert Murphy, sought to convince French officials in North Africa to welcome the invaders as liberators. Instead, he very nearly gave the game away. Early on November 8, Murphy went to see the French army commander in Algeria, General Alphonse Juin, to tell him of the imminent landing by (he claimed) half a million men. Juin was a proud nationalist who had lost his right arm in combat in World War I and therefore saluted with his left. Torn between his sworn duty and his sense of history, he insisted that he must first consult with Admiral Jean François Darlan, commander of the French navy, who had recently arrived in Algiers with his wife to visit their son, who had been stricken with polio. When Darlan arrived at Juin's home, it seemed to him that the Americans were behaving much as the British had done at Mers-el-Kébir: attacking a neutral nation without provocation. He did agree, however, to consult with Marshal Pétain. By then, Pétain had received a message from Roosevelt claiming that because Germany and Italy were about to invade North Africa, the United States was forced to intervene to protect the French. That fooled no one, and Pierre Laval, Pétain's pro-German deputy, crafted a formal answer: "France and her honor are at stake. We are attacked; we will defend ourselves."[7]

The first Allied units to confront French resistance consisted of American and British commandos who had volunteered to steal into the harbors at both Oran and Algiers in the predawn darkness and secure the port facilities. The Allies hoped to effect this stealth mission unnoticed. Yet when the two small ships carrying the commandos entered Oran harbor, sirens wailed, searchlights pierced the darkness, and the French batteries opened fire. Of the 393 commandos who landed, 189 were killed outright and another 157 were wounded—a casualty rate of 88 percent.[8]

French naval forces also launched a counterattack. Rear Admiral André Georges Rioult ordered out the only three destroyers he had that were combat ready, and, as Troubridge put it, they charged out of port "with a bravery worthy of a better cause." Almost immediately, one of them, the *Tramontane*, was struck by several 6-inch shells from the British light cruiser *Aurora*. The *Aurora's* captain, William G. Agnew, then closed to within three thousand yards and pounded the *Tramontane* until she was sinking. The other French destroyers launched torpedoes and engaged in a running fight with the British fleet before one of them was forced aground. The third turned back. A second sortie on November 9 proved equally futile. Rioult had the last word, however. Once it became evident that the Anglo-American landings were likely to succeed, he ordered crews on the remaining French ships to scuttle their vessels in the harbor. That not only clogged the waterfront with wrecks but deprived the Allies of thirteen large transport ships at a time when shipping was at a premium.[9]

Allied attempts to seize the port facilities at Algiers fared no better. If the results were less horrific than at Oran, it was only because one of the two ships assigned to the mission failed to get into the harbor at all. The other did. After three tries, HMS *Broke* successfully landed its embarked American commandos, though within hours they were surrounded by French colonial troops and forced to surrender. The crippled *Broke* was towed out to sea and later sank.[10]

For the main landings at Algiers, the Allies avoided the proximate and accessible (but also predictable) beach near the city and landed instead at more remote beaches to the east and west. There was confusion and disorder as several units landed on the wrong beaches and became intermingled. The fragile landing craft suffered more from the elements than from enemy fire. At Sidi Ferruch, west of the city, where the American units landed, 98 of 104 landing boats were wrecked in the course of the operation. That might have proved disastrous had the French been unified in their resistance. As it was, local reactions varied widely. One group of British commandos encountered fierce resistance as they sought to seize a coastal battery, while a dozen miles away an American unit was greeted with cries of "Vive les américains!" One factor in this mixed response was French concern that if they openly welcomed the Anglo-American forces and the incursion proved to be only a raid like Dieppe, the Germans would return afterward and exact fearful revenge. Once it was clear that the Allies had come to stay, Darlan authorized Juin to negotiate a local cease-fire with the American ground commander, Major General Charles Ryder.[11]

Darlan continued to weigh his options. Though he remained distrustful of the British, he did not want to be on the wrong side of history, and late on November 10 he ordered French forces throughout North Africa to cease opposition. Two days later, he openly aligned himself with the Allies in exchange for their agreement that he would command French forces in North Africa as "high commissioner."[12]

MEANWHILE, ALONG THE ATLANTIC COAST in French Morocco, the Americans were having a difficult time of it. The British had argued against landing there at all, pointing out that success in Algiers would cut off Morocco in any case. The Americans, however, were leery of sticking their heads into the cul-de-sac of the Mediterranean and had stipulated that at least some of the landings must take place on the Atlantic coast. Roosevelt had personally insisted on it.[13]

The invasion convoys for this landing originated not in Britain but on the East Coast of the United States, thirty-eight hundred miles from the target beaches. It was the first transatlantic amphibious assault since Cortés invaded Mexico in 1519. The American convoy, officially dubbed Task Force 34, was under the command of Rear Admiral H. Kent Hewitt, whose easygoing manner and disheveled appearance belied an incisive and analytical mind.

Once all the various elements of the American invasion armada rendezvoused off Norfolk on October 25, the transports and cargo vessels formed up into nine columns with the ships following one another at one-thousand-yard intervals. Like the British, the Americans committed a large escort to the troop transports, including three battleships, seven cruisers, and thirty-eight destroyers, plus the *Ranger* and the four auxiliary carriers that had been converted from oilers. Altogether, the formation covered some six hundred square miles of ocean. And also like the British, the Americans took an indirect course to the target beaches, feinting southward toward the bulge of Africa before turning northeast to close in on French Morocco from the southwest. As a result of that, and some luck, the convoy was undisturbed by U-boats and arrived off the Moroccan beaches intact and on time.[14]

Once there, however, American readiness to conduct a large-scale amphibious landing faced a stern test. Before dawn on November 8, the American transports dropped anchor off Fédala, fifteen miles north of Casablanca, and began hoisting out the Higgins boats. Soon the soldiers were climbing down into them on chain or rope nets thrown over the side. As at Algiers, there was more than a little confusion and delay. It took longer than scheduled to fill the boats, and even after they were on their way, the U.S. Navy coxswains who drove them often headed for the wrong beach. The only coastal reconnaissance the Allies had conducted prior to the landings was to examine the target beaches through submarine peri-scopes, and the vague maps that resulted failed to give the coxswains a clear understanding of the terrain.[15]

The landings themselves were unopposed, which was just as well because the surf at Fédala was heavier than expected. When the men scrambled out of the boats, many were knocked off their feet by the oversized waves, and loaded as they were with heavy gear, some never regained their footing and drowned in water that was only three or four feet deep. The surf also played havoc with the plywood Higgins boats. As at Sidi Ferruch, near Algiers, the big waves threw the boats into one another or pushed them so far up onto the beach they could not retract and had to be abandoned. Even so, the Americans managed to get most of their men and equipment ashore, and by the end of the first day, there were 7,750 GIs on the beach.[16]

As in Algiers, efforts to convince the French that their best interest lay in welcoming the Americans bumped up against concepts of duty and honor. The French had a significant naval presence in Casablanca harbor, includ-ing the still-unfinished battleship *Jean Bart*. Though the *Jean Bart* had only one working turret, it housed four 15-inch guns, and they fired nine salvos at the American warships offshore, a group that included the battleship *Massachusetts* and heavy cruisers *Tuscaloosa* and *Wichita*. Planes from the

A photograph of the unfinished French battleship *Jean Bart* in Casablanca harbor taken four days after the Americans captured the city. The bomb damage on her starboard side was inflicted by planes from the *Ranger*. A 16-inch shell from the *Massachusetts* also wrecked her only working turret. Note the torpedo nets in place off her port side.

U.S. National Archives photo no. 80-G-31605

Ranger sought to neutralize the *Jean Bart*, but the decisive blow was a well-aimed 16-inch shell from the *Massachusetts* that struck near the *Jean Bart*'s turret and jammed it in place, rendering it inoperable.[17]

That was not the end of the naval fighting. Rear Admiral Gervais de Lafond, unwilling to be trapped in port, led seven destroyers, joined later by a light cruiser, in a sortie. Once clear of the harbor, they sought to escape by heading north along the coast, a course that took them directly toward the American landing force at Fédala. De Lafond became an early casualty when he was wounded by a strafing attack conducted by Wildcat fighters from the *Ranger*. The French destroyers were also targeted by American warships off Casablanca, and as they neared Fédala, the American cruisers *Augusta* and *Brooklyn*, guarding the landing force, joined in the fight. Samuel Eliot Morison, who was on board the *Brooklyn* that morning, exercised some poetic license in writing that the American ships "went tearing into action like a pack of dogs unleashed."[18]

It was mostly a one-sided action. After a 16-inch shell from the *Massachusetts* struck the destroyer *Fougueux*, she sank within minutes; another severely damaged de Lafond's flagship, *Milan*. The French pressed on, making smoke to disguise their movements, and managed to sink one of

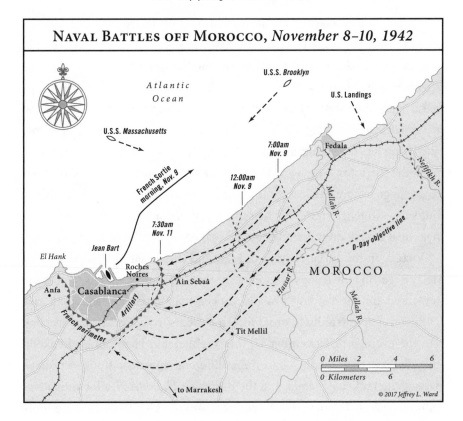

NAVAL BATTLES OFF MOROCCO, *November 8–10, 1942*

the landing ships, but they were badly overmatched. Hit repeatedly, several of the French vessels were forced aground to avoid sinking, and soon only the destroyer *L'Alcyon* remained. She focused on picking up survivors. In all, the French lost more than eight hundred killed and a thousand wounded. The great tragedy, of course, was that except as a salve to honor, it was entirely unnecessary. Justifying it later, a French admiral wrote that the navy "suffered its martyrdom purely because of those higher values without which no country can continue to exist—loyalty, discipline, patriotism, respect for national unity."[19]

For their part, the Americans suffered only minor damage to two cruisers and more serious damage to the destroyer *Ludlow*. On the other hand, the Americans had also expended much of their ammunition, which was a serious concern at the end of a thirty-eight-hundred-mile supply line.[20]

Major General George S. Patton, who was on board Hewitt's flagship, *Augusta*, and preparing to go ashore when the French sortie began, had to endure the passive role of spectator during the naval engagement, and he spent part of the morning writing a letter to his wife. "We have been in a naval battle since 0800," he wrote, "and it is still going on." He found his first naval battle exhilarating. He noted that the American ships were "all firing and going like hell in big zig-zags." During the battle, repeated concussions from the *Augusta*'s 8-inch guns wrecked the small boat Patton had planned to use to go ashore. He lost some of his personal equipment in that mishap, but successfully retrieved his ivory-handled pistols. Not long afterward, a near miss from a French artillery shell soaked him with seawater.[21]

Victory in the surface action did not end the threat from seaward. The delay in getting the troops ashore meant that the transports and cargo ships remained off the landing beaches longer than intended, and that gave Dönitz the opportunity to order fifteen U-boats to the Moroccan beaches. On the evening of November 11, Fregattenkapitän Heinz-Ehler Beuke in the U-173 fired torpedoes into three different ships: the transport *Joseph Hewes*, the tanker *Winooski*, and the destroyer *Hambleton*, all within a ten-minute period. The next day, torpedoes from the U-130 struck three more troopships, all of which sank. By then the ships had discharged their priceless human cargo, but it was another blow to scarce Allied shipping. Later that same day (ironically, Armistice Day), as Patton's ground forces neared Casablanca, news arrived of Darlan's order for a cease-fire, and by November 12, the Allies had secured their foothold in both Algeria and Morocco.[22]

Seizing the beaches, however, was only the first step. To make the invasion strategically meaningful, the Allies needed to consolidate their foothold and advance eastward into Tunisia. That meant building up their forces and sustaining them with a virtually continuous stream of reinforcements and supplies over a long and precarious ocean route. Of course, as soon as the news of the Allied landings reached Rome and Berlin, the Axis, too, began to rush men and supplies into North Africa, mostly by air. As at Guadalcanal, though on a larger scale, the opponents engaged in a race to see which side could build up its forces in the combat area to gain a decisive advantage.[23]

IN THAT RACE, geography seemed to favor the Axis. After all, it was only 170 nautical miles from Sicily to Tunis across the Mediterranean narrows, whereas the Allies had to bring men and material from England or the United States. Yet strained as Allied sealift was, Axis maritime capabilities were even more limited. The need to sustain their forces in Crete, Sicily, and Sardinia, as well as in North Africa, required more shipping in the Mediterranean than the Axis had. And the British in Malta continued to interfere with that shipping. Because the Germans had insisted that the Italians adopt the Enigma machine for their naval communications, Bletchley Park was breaking Italian messages as well as German ones, and that allowed British planes, submarines, and surface ships to find and attack their convoys.

Fuel remained a serious problem for the Axis. From virtually the first days of the war, the Italians had never had quite enough of it to keep their fleet active. It required 50,000 tons of fuel per month just to keep the convoys to North Africa going, and in August 1942, Italian oil reserves totaled only 12,100 tons. That left little for the Regia Marina or for delivery to Rommel's hard-pressed ground forces. Aware of the situation, the Allies focused their attacks on Axis tankers. The sinking of the Italian *Giordani* and her cargo of 8,800 tons of fuel oil on November 21 was an especially heavy blow for Rommel. Facing Montgomery's Eighth Army to the east and Eisenhower's Anglo-American forces to the west, Rommel had to fight a two-front war with barely enough fuel to keep his panzers mobile.[24]

One option for the Axis was to pull Rommel's forces out of Africa altogether, an outcome that, given the logistical situation, appeared all but inevitable. Raeder, however, wanted to maintain a presence in North Africa as long as possible, to prevent the Allies from regaining free transit of the Mediterranean. As he told Hitler on November 17, "The presence of our forces in Tunisia prevents enemy success, since passage through the Mediterranean is denied him." As long as the Axis controlled the narrows between Sicily and Tunisia, the Allies would be compelled to send their supplies to the Middle East via the long route around the Cape of Good Hope.[25]

Kesselring also wanted to hold North Africa, and he believed his Luftwaffe could compensate for the weakness in shipping. Only hours after the Allied landings began, troop-carrying Junkers-52 transport planes from Sicily and Sardinia began an airlift into Tunisia, and soon they were bringing in an average of 750 men per day, though many of the planes were withdrawn after only a few weeks in order to fly supplies to the German Sixth Army, trapped in Stalingrad. In addition to the Junkers, the Axis employed gigantic six-engine Messerschmitt 323 aircraft, the largest transport planes in the world, to bring light tanks and trucks to North Africa. The airlift allowed the Axis to establish a military presence in Tunisia quickly. In the long run, however, airlift could never compete with sealift. The Messerschmitt 323 had a capacity of twenty tons, but one such plane would have to make two hundred round trips, burning up tons of aviation fuel, to match the capacity of a single transport ship.[26]

To bolster their supply effort, the Germans employed what were called *Kriegstransporters* or KT boats: small, armed transport vessels displacing 850 tons each (about the size of British corvettes) that could make the run from Sicily to Tunisia at a modest fourteen knots, usually by night. Even

A giant Messerschmitt-323 lands in North Africa. Though they were the largest transport aircraft of the war, these planes could not compensate for insufficient Axis sealift capability.

Bundesarchiv

more creative were several score of the so-called Siebel ferries, named after their designer, Fritz Siebel, and built initially for the planned invasion of England. They were so small they could be disassembled and shipped south by railroad from the Channel to the Mediterranean. They consisted of two bridging pontoons supporting a flat deck, which technically made them catamarans, though such a designation hardly seemed suitable for such squat, ugly vessels. Still, each of them could carry fifty to a hundred tons of cargo or one heavy vehicle (truck or tank) and a score of soldiers. The Italians also employed destroyers as transports. Like the Japanese at Guadalcanal, Italian destroyers made swift nighttime runs from Sicily to Tunis, though such high-speed runs exacerbated the persistent fuel problem. Nevertheless, by the end of the month, the Axis had landed five full divisions in Tunisia, three German and two Italian.[27]

The Axis convoys were subject to Allied interdiction, of course, and on December 2, three Royal Navy light cruisers, guided by Ultra intelligence, intercepted an Italian convoy of four transports. The British sank one of the escorts and all four of the supply ships, one of which was a troopship that went down with the loss of more than two thousand Axis soldiers.[28]

In dramatic contrast, Allied convoys from the United States arrived in North Africa at regular intervals thanks in part to the effective suppression of the U-boat menace. The first of the supply convoys left New York on November 2, while the invasion convoy was still en route, and it arrived on November 18 with thirty thousand more troops and 161,000 tons of supplies. After that, convoys arrived regularly: on December 1, 24, and 30, and at roughly four-week intervals thereafter. Fast convoys filled with troops alternated with slow convoys loaded with supplies. However, the commitment of so many ships to a single purpose meant that compromises had to be made elsewhere. In particular, it meant fewer convoys to England, and a dramatic reduction in the convoys to the Soviet Union, though a trickle of supplies continued to get through to the Russians via the Persian Gulf and then overland through Iran. Still, having been promised a genuine second front in 1942, Stalin was unimpressed with the Allied seizure of French colonies in Africa, especially since it also led to a reduction in supplies for the Red Army.[29]

Eisenhower had hoped to "rush eastward without delay" after the initial landings and capture Tunisia, especially the port of Tunis. It didn't happen. Airfields had to be built or repaired; American troops and equipment that had landed in Morocco had to be transferred to Algeria along a lengthy single-track railroad. By the time the Allied landing force had been reorganized into a field army, the winter rains had set in. Instead of a swift coup de main, therefore, the campaign for North Africa turned into a lengthy slog.[30]

With the Allies slowed by rain and Rommel handicapped by logistical problems, the winter campaign in North Africa stalled. In February, Rommel sought to gain the initiative by attacking the Americans and their French allies at the Kasserine Pass through the Atlas Mountains. The inexperience of the Americans was laid bare as Rommel's armored units drove them some fifty miles to the west, yet his tactical success did not yield a strategic breakthrough, for he lacked the material wherewithal to follow up his victory.

ANOTHER ALLIED DISAPPOINTMENT was the final disposition of the French fleet. One of the reasons Hitler had allowed France to retain at least a modicum of independence under the Vichy regime—the so-called Free Zone—was his fear that if he occupied all of France, the French navy would openly side with the Allies. Under the terms of the 1940 agreement, therefore, the High Seas Fleet at Toulon remained under Vichy control, though it was also mostly confined to harbor. When the Allies moved into North Africa and Darlan joined them, however, an infuriated Hitler ordered the Wehrmacht to occupy the Free Zone and to seize control of the fleet at Toulon, which he planned to turn over to the Italians.

The man on the spot was Admiral Gabriel Auphan, who became head of the French navy after Darlan changed sides. While Auphan was at least willing to consider joining Darlan, Admiral Jean de Laborde, who commanded the High Seas Fleet at Toulon, was both anti-British and loyal to the Vichy regime, and he refused to act without specific orders from Pétain. Though he insisted that he would not surrender his fleet to the Germans, neither was he willing to join hands with perfidious Albion. By late November, however, it was clear that those were the only options left to him. On November 27, as the German 7th Panzer Division closed in on the Toulon

Navy Base, de Laborde ordered the crews on the French warships to scuttle their vessels. Just hours before the Germans arrived, three French battleships, seven cruisers, and fifteen destroyers went to the bottom, along with more than fifty smaller vessels. Just as the Germans had scuttled their fleet in 1919 to prevent it from being turned over to the British, so now did the French scuttle their principal fleet to prevent it from being seized by the Germans. As Maxime Weygand, a French general, wrote after the war, "The Navy amputated one of its limbs, but saved its soul."[31]

Elsewhere, the Allies and the French succeeded in reaching a more amicable agreement. At Casablanca, Admiral Félix Michelier was particularly cooperative. His primary objective was to repair his damaged warships, especially the battleship *Jean Bart*, so they could reenter the war as Allied partners. Roosevelt was willing to go further and pay the salaries of the French officers and men as if they were in the U.S. Navy. Michelier declined that offer, asking only for material support for the ships, most of which transited the Atlantic to be refitted in American yards. The Allies urged Admiral Godfroy, whose squadron at Alexandria had been effectively mothballed since 1940, to follow suit. Godfroy was wary. He had heard nothing from Pétain, he was uncertain of Allied plans, and he was suspicious of Charles de Gaulle, whom he disliked and distrusted. For the moment, he and his ships remained where they were.[32]

Back in 1940, Darlan had pledged to Churchill that no matter what else happened, the French fleet would never be turned over to the Germans. For all Darlan's subsequent service to Vichy, his collaboration with Hitler's government, and his opportunistic volte-face in 1942, that pledge, at least, was fulfilled. In the end, though, Darlan's shape-shifting did him little good. On Christmas Eve, a twenty-year-old Frenchman who advocated reestablishment of the monarchy assassinated him.

TEN THOUSAND MILES AWAY, the Americans and Japanese continued their race to reinforce Guadalcanal. In the South Pacific as well as in the Mediterranean, nervous and seasick young men in combat fatigues crowded into steel ships that carried them to battlefronts, though instead of a desert they disembarked into a jungle. Here, too, the Axis had far greater problems with sealift than did the Allies. The Tokyo Express maintained its regular nighttime runs to Guadalcanal, though the use of destroyers as transports to deliver men and supplies was absurdly inefficient. A single troopship could carry twenty times the number of men as a destroyer. Delivering cargo from a destroyer was even more problematic. As the destroyer approached the beach, the crew threw sealed drums filled with supplies over the side in the hope that the current would carry them ashore where Japanese soldiers could find and recover them.[33]

Appreciating the inefficiency of such a protocol, Yamamoto decided to up the ante by dispatching a major convoy of eleven troop transports filled with thirty thousand men. To cover it, he also sent a force nearly as large as the armada the British and Americans had used to invade North Africa. In addition to the twelve destroyers accompanying the troopships, the Japanese committed a covering force under Vice Admiral Kondō that consisted of four battleships, three heavy and three light cruisers, and twenty-one destroyers, plus a support force of four more heavy cruisers under Rear Admiral Mikawa. The only carrier involved was the smaller Jun'yō, but since the Americans had only the crippled Enterprise, the Japanese had the upper hand in the air as well—or they would have if they could neutralize the American airfield on Guadalcanal. To do that, the plan was for two of Kondō's battleships to bombard Henderson Field with their 14-inch guns. That would keep the Cactus Air Force grounded while the troopships offloaded their men near Cape Esperance.[34]

Alerted to the Japanese plan by the cryptanalysts at Station Hypo in Hawaii, Halsey dispatched a reinforcement of his own to Guadalcanal. On November 9 (as American troops were going ashore in Morocco), seven transports carrying six thousand men, half of them from the 182nd Infantry Regiment, sailed for Guadalcanal from the New Hebrides Islands and New Caledonia. The transports arrived safely, and Kelly Turner, who was also alerted to the approach of Kondō's armada, organized the escorts from that convoy into a strike force to confront the approaching Japanese. It was a tall order. The American surface force, commanded by newly arrived Rear Admiral Daniel J. Callaghan, consisted of two heavy cruisers, three light cruisers, and eight destroyers. It would be badly overmatched by Kondō's battleships.[35]

A posed photograph of Captain Daniel J. Callaghan in his dress whites on the bridge wing of the heavy cruiser *San Francisco*, near the spot where he was killed by a 14-inch shell from the Japanese battleship *Hiei* during the naval Battle of Guadalcanal on November 13, 1942.

U.S. National Archives photo no. 80-G-20824

Then there was Callaghan. A striking figure with white hair, he had served as Roosevelt's naval aide and then as Ghormley's chief of staff. Eager to make his mark as a combat officer, he had asked to be relieved from administrative duties in order to command at sea. It was a commendable instinct, but Callaghan had no battle experience in the waters around Guadalcanal, and he superseded the well-respected Norman Scott, who had won the Battle of Cape Esperance. With Callaghan's arrival, Scott was relegated to riding the light cruiser *Atlanta*. Officially, he was second in command, but operationally he had no responsibilities at all. On the evening of November 12 (the day the Americans secured Casablanca), Callaghan set out from Lunga Point on Guadalcanal to confront the approaching Japanese. He knew he could not slug it out with enemy battleships; his best hope was to inflict enough damage on them to convince them to call off the bombardment. It was not quite a forlorn hope, but nearly so.

As Callaghan headed north, Hiroaki Abe headed south with two of Kondō's battleships—*Hiei* and *Kirishima*—and an escort of a light cruiser and eleven destroyers. Abe was a torpedo specialist who had been promoted to vice admiral just eleven days before, despite a reputation in the service for being cautious—some thought excessively so. Still, a shore bombardment mission at night called for little audacity or innovation. As Abe's force approached Guadalcanal late on November 12, his ships were enveloped by a tropical storm with rain so heavy the Japanese ships lost sight of one another. That and some last-minute maneuvering disordered the Japanese formation. Of course, rain was no barrier to American radar, and at 1:30 in the morning on Friday, November 13, the new SG radar on the *Helena* revealed the presence of the enemy ships fourteen miles away.[36]

With the Americans steaming north at twenty knots and the Japanese coming south at eighteen knots, the range closed swiftly, and it was duly reported by the radarman on the *Helena*: ten thousand yards... six thousand yards... four thousand yards! Eager torpedomen in the American destroyers and gunners in the cruisers waited for the order to open fire, but it didn't come. Radar was so new in the U.S. fleet that officers such as Callaghan, who were unfamiliar with its capabilities, were hesitant to rely on it. Since he did not have a clear mental picture of the circumstances, he simply continued toward the enemy force without issuing any orders at all. As a result, he threw away the advantage of surprise.[37]

With the rain clearing, a lookout on Abe's flagship, *Hiei*, reported, "Four black objects ahead... look like warships. Five degrees to starboard." Five degrees! That was almost dead ahead! According to a witness, Abe covered his face with his hands. His first order was to replace the explosive ordnance that had already been loaded into the guns for the shore bombardment mission with armor-piercing projectiles for use against ships. That led to what an observer called a "stampede" down in the magazines as crewmen frantically sought to change out the ordnance. Like Nagumo's carriers at Midway, the Japanese battleships were rendered briefly vulnerable with both kinds of ordnance stacked up near the lifts. Yet the Americans continued to hold their fire as the two fleets closed rapidly.[38]

Finally, at only two thousand yards, the Japanese warships snapped on their searchlights, and vessels on both sides maneuvered frantically, either to avoid a collision or to gain a better angle. The two fleets bled into each other and lost cohesion almost at once. Rather than forming clear battle lines, the ships were intermingled; as Samuel Eliot Morison later put it, they were "like minnows in a bucket." The executive officer of the American destroyer *O'Bannon* later wrote, "No man can adequately describe the shock and terror and tremendousness of a great naval battle fought at close range in the dead of night." Edward N. Parker, leading the American battle line in the destroyer *Cushing*, likened it to "a barroom brawl with the lights out." Belatedly, Callaghan tried to impose order on the chaos by ordering "odd" ships to fire to starboard and "even" ships to port. But with the column already out of order, that only brought more confusion as each skipper tried to figure out if his ship was odd or even. The captain of the destroyer *Aaron Ward* recalled "firing every gun that would bear [and] launching torpedoes port and starboard." On the *Helena* the commands came in a brisk, if confusing, sequence: "Full speed ahead! Fire to starboard! Shift target! Get the one on our port bow; he's firing on us! Full speed astern."[39]

The unusual circumstances put several of the smaller ships close alongside the battleships. One officer on the *Helena* remembered, "We were so close that when the fire started you could actually see the Japanese aboard their ships." Indeed, they were so close, the big guns on Abe's flagship could not be depressed enough to fire on the smaller American ships, and the American torpedoes aimed at the *Hiei* did not have sufficient run time to arm themselves and merely bounced off her side. Still, the *Helena* and the four leading American destroyers pumped several hundred 5- and 6-inch shells into the *Hiei*. The destroyer *Laffey* even employed her 20 mm machine guns, which raked the bridge of the *Hiei*, killing Abe's chief of staff and severely wounding Abe himself. The big battleship was in no danger of sinking from such an assault, but her steering and fire-control systems were knocked out, her upper works were shattered, and fires in her superstructure made her a visible target for the bigger American ships, including Callaghan's flagship, *San Francisco*.[40]

Amidst the chaos, there were multiple friendly fire incidents. An officer on the *Helena* sought "to find a target and shoot, and hope it is the enemy." Often it was not. The captain of the heavy cruiser *Portland*, Laurence Du Bose, recalled, "In the confused picture of burning and milling ships it became impossible to distinguish friend from foe." The *Atlanta* was soon caught in a crossfire between the opposing flagships and became an early victim. Callaghan quickly ordered, "Cease fire own ships!"—an order that was ignored by every ship except the *San Francisco*. Hit by two torpedoes as well as shells from both sides, the *Atlanta* was wrecked beyond saving, and among the many killed was Norman Scott. The *San Francisco* was next. Four of *Hiei*'s 14-inch shells smashed into her bridge, killing nearly everyone there, including Callaghan.* With both numbers and greater throw weight, the Japanese quickly gained the upper hand. In only a few minutes, the cruisers *Portland* and *Juneau* were torpedoed, and the destroyers *Sterett* and *Laffey* were set afire; the *Laffey* blew up in a spectacular explosion when the fires reached her magazine. The entire battle lasted just thirty-four minutes. Of the American warships, only the light cruiser *Helena* and the destroyer *Fletcher* remained relatively unscathed.[41]

It was perhaps inevitable that Callaghan's squadron of cruisers and destroyers would be roughly handled by Abe's larger force, but the ferocity of the American attack on the *Hiei* convinced the wounded Abe to call off the bombardment of Henderson Field and withdraw. Like Mikawa after the Battle of Savo Island, he gave up the game too soon. With every American warship except the *Helena* badly crippled, he might have sent the undamaged battleship *Kirishima* ahead to fulfill its mission with little risk. Had it rendered Henderson Field unusable and kept the Cactus Air Force grounded, it might have saved Abe's command. Instead, Abe exercised the caution for which he was known; he transferred his flag to a cruiser and headed north. The crippled *Hiei*, able to make only about five knots, lagged behind, and when the sun came up on that Friday the thirteenth, planes from the Cactus Air Force found her limping along still inside their two-hundred-mile operational range. Nearly two years before, land-based Japanese planes had sunk the British battleship *Prince of Wales* in the Gulf of Siam. Now the tactical circumstances were reversed, and after repeated attacks by torpedo bombers from Guadalcanal and high-level B-17s from Espiritu Santo in the New Hebrides, the 36,600-ton *Hiei* went to the bottom.[42]

---

* In tribute to their martyrdom, both Scott and Callaghan were posthumously awarded the Medal of Honor.

Yamamoto was furious and relieved Abe of his command by radio even before he returned to port. When Abe reported himself aboard the *Yamato* at Truk four days later, his face still swathed in bandages, he told Yamamoto's chief of staff he wished he had gone down with his ship.[43]

As for the American ships, those that were still afloat were badly shattered. In an effort to salvage as many of them as possible, the cripples were sent off toward Espiritu Santo for repairs. While they were en route there, Commander Yokota Minoru in the I-26, the same submarine that had damaged the *Saratoga* back in August, fired a torpedo at the *San Francisco*. It missed its intended target and struck the light cruiser *Juneau*. It may have detonated in the *Juneau*'s magazine, for the resulting explosion blew the ship to pieces. A witness recalled seeing "a tower of smoke that shot skyward as though spewed from a volcano." To Americans on the other ships, it seemed impossible that anyone could have survived. The senior officer present, Captain Gilbert Hoover on the *Helena*, felt he could not risk the other ships by stopping to search for survivors, so after reporting the coordinates, he continued on to Espiritu Santo. By the time a rescue place arrived several days later, only ten men of the *Juneau*'s original crew of 660 were left alive. Among the killed were the subsequently famous five Sullivan brothers.[44]

IT WAS NOT OVER. Though the bombardment mission had failed to neutralize Henderson Field, Rear Admiral Tanaka's transport force continued toward Guadalcanal. The American land-based bombers assailed it with everything they had. Tanaka later remembered the "bombs wobbling down from high-flying B-17s" and the dive-bombers "releasing bombs and pulling out barely in time." He lost six of his transports to that onslaught, but, tenacious as ever, he pressed on with the remaining four. To cover them, Yamamoto ordered Kondō to take the wounded *Kirishima* and two heavy cruisers (*Atago* and *Takao*) to attempt another strike at Henderson Field.[45]

Forewarned again by radio intercepts decoded in Pearl Harbor, Halsey had few arrows left in his quiver to respond to this new threat. After the virtual destruction of Callaghan's force, he felt he had no choice but to commit his two battleships, *Washington* and *South Dakota*. He pulled them from the screen of the still-crippled *Enterprise* south of the island and sent them into the fight with a four-destroyer escort. The commander of this top-heavy task force was Vice Admiral Willis Lee. Despite poor eyesight, for which he wore owlish wire-rimmed glasses, Lee was a crack shot who had won five gold medals for shooting at the 1920 Olympics. Unsurprisingly, gunnery was his specialty, and he had made a particular study of how to employ the new radar-directed gunfire system on the *Washington*. If Callaghan had failed to take advantage of radar, Lee was eager to test its full capabilities.[46]

The battle did not begin well for the Americans. Just before midnight on November 13, Lee's four destroyers ran into their Japanese counterparts. One of the American destroyers was sunk outright and two more sank later from battle damage. Nearly as bad, one of Lee's two battleships, the *South Dakota*, suffered an electrical power failure and was unable to use her big guns. Silhouetted in front of the burning destroyers, she became a target for every ship in Kondō's command. Riddled by 5-inch and 14-inch shells, she was saved from destruction mainly because she somehow managed to avoid all of the thirty-four Long Lance torpedoes launched in her direction.[47]

As the *South Dakota* absorbed the fury of Kondō's big ships, Willis Lee in the *Washington* readied his flagship's main battery. The radar plotting

Rear Admiral Willis "Ching" Lee got his academy nickname from his supposedly Chinese-sounding name. Photographed here on the bridge wing of his flagship, the fast battleship *Washington*, Lee was a crack shot with a rifle and pistol and among the first to employ radar-directed gunfire in battle.

U.S. Naval institute

team fed the pertinent information to the ship's Mark 8 fire-control system. With each 16-inch shell weighing 2,700 pounds, a single salvo from either battleship's main battery sent more than twelve tons of armor-piercing ordnance toward its foe. When the *South Dakota* fired its first broadside, the concussion was so great it knocked sailors off their feet and the muzzle blast set fire to the ship's scout planes. The second salvo blew the planes over the side entirely. Fired from a range of only eighty-five hundred yards (less than five miles), the 16-inch projectiles were murderous. Shells from the *Washington's* first two salvos struck the *Kirishima's* radio room, her forward turrets, and her steering and machinery spaces. Altogether more than twenty 16-inch shells struck the Japanese battleship in only a few minutes. With hundreds dead and fires burning out of control, Kondō's flagship listed badly and lost speed, unable to maneuver. She continued to fire, but all her salvos went high, and the *Washington* remained undamaged. Kondō called upon the light cruiser *Nagara* to tow the *Kirishima*, but the battleship was too badly wounded to remain afloat and she went down at 3:25 a.m. on November 15.[48]

Like Abe, Kondō suffered the consequences of Yamamoto's disappointment. Given Kondō's stature within the Imperial Japanese Navy as a former president of the Naval Staff College and chief of staff for the Combined Fleet, he could not be summarily dismissed. Instead he was relegated to the command of a single ship at Truk.

THE LOSS OF TWO BATTLESHIPS within barely twenty-four hours was a sobering wake-up call for the Japanese, and a decisive turning point in the Guadalcanal campaign. Two weeks later, Raizo Tanaka won a decisive victory over an American cruiser-destroyer force in the Battle of Tassafaronga—yet another night surface engagement in the waters between Guadalcanal and Savo Island, now almost universally known as Ironbottom Sound for all the ships that were sunk there. Despite that, Yamamoto and the Naval General Staff decided to cut their losses. Guadalcanal had become a magnet, pulling in far too many resources for a far longer period than anyone had imagined. Back in August when the campaign began, Colonel Kiyonao Ichiki had expected to destroy the American enclave on Guadalcanal with nine hundred men; a month later, Major General Kawaguchi had hurled six thousand men at the Marine defenders of Bloody Ridge; by November, the Japanese had thirty thousand men on the island. Yet American ground strength more than kept pace, for by then the Americans had more than forty thousand men on the island. In December, the Japanese high command decided that enough was enough. In a series of carefully staged withdrawals, the Japanese ground forces pulled back from their lines around the American enclave and began a systematic evacuation—Operation KE. By February 7, they were gone. For all the heroic courage and sacrifice of the men on both sides who fought for six months in appalling conditions, the key to eventual Allied success was superior sealift protected by land-based air power.[49]

NOVEMBER 1942 WAS A WATERSHED MOMENT in the history of the Second World War. Allied landings in North Africa and American success in the waters around Guadalcanal were tangible evidence that the balance had begun to tip in favor of the Allies in both theaters. The sinking of the *Kirishima* was particularly symbolic. Willis Lee's employment of radar-directed gunfire all but erased the edge the Japanese had previously demonstrated in nighttime naval engagements due to their training and superior optics. It suggested that emerging technology was outpacing even the most inspirational bravery. In addition to underestimating American resilience and industrial productivity, the Japanese had also failed to account for American ingenuity in the development of new and technologically sophisticated weaponry.

CHAPTER 17

THE WAR ON TRADE, III

T HE FALL OF 1942 was also a tipping point in the global war on trade, for it marked the moment when the Allies gained and kept the upper hand in the U-boat war. It hardly seemed so at first. In October the U-boats sank eighty-nine Allied ships displacing 583,690 tons—including fifteen ships from a single convoy (SC-107)—and in November the total reached a staggering 126 ships displacing more than 800,000 tons. Churchill wrote to FDR that "the spectacle of all these splendid ships being built, sent to sea crammed with priceless food and munitions, and being sunk—three or four every day—torments me day and night."[1]

Torment and anguish were unavoidable by-products of the war on trade. A dozen years before, at the London Conference of 1930, Henry Stimson, then the American secretary of state and now Roosevelt's secretary of war, had declared, "The use of the submarine revolted the conscience of the world." He predicted that regardless of whatever rules were adopted for its use, "those who employ the submarine will be under strong temptation, perhaps irresistible temptation, to use it in the way which is most effective for immediate purposes," which was the ruthless destruction of unarmed merchant ships. His prescience was validated by the ensuing conflict, and periodically a specific incident illuminated the particular peril of submarine warfare. One such incident occurred in mid-September 1942.[2]

That month, Dönitz sent several of the large Type IX U-boats toward the Cape of Good Hope to interdict British shipping to and from the Middle East. En route to that hunting ground, on September 12, *Korvettenkapitän* Werner Hartenstein in the U-156 espied the large (19,650-ton) liner *Laconia* just south of Sierra Leone. The *Laconia* was a former British luxury liner that had been converted into a troop transport to carry soldiers to the Middle East battlefields. Hartenstein tracked her for several hours while waiting for dark, and just past 8:00 p.m., he fired two torpedoes at her. Both found their target. As Hartenstein circled the stricken vessel, he noted that due to her pronounced list, she had trouble launching her lifeboats, and that hundreds of people were leaping into the water. Some of them shouted for help—*in Italian*. After pulling several of them on board, Hartenstein was horrified to discover that the ship had been carrying 1,800 Italian prisoners of war, nominally his allies, from the battlefields of Egypt to Britain. He decided to rescue as many of them as he could and radioed Dönitz at Kernevel asking him to send more U-boats to his coordinates to help. Dönitz did so, and a number of survivors were eventually pulled aboard other U-boats as well as the U-156. By then Hartenstein had fished more than four hundred people from the sea, most of them Italian but also some Englishmen and Poles, including a number of women and children. He took as many as he could on board and placed the others in lifeboats, which he towed behind him in a long string like a child's pull toy. On his own authority he broadcast a message in English announcing his intention to rescue the survivors and pledging not to attack any Allied ship that arrived to assist.[3]

The Allies heard the message but suspected that it was a trap, and in any case Hartenstein's offer was immediately disavowed in Berlin. Dönitz requested assistance from the Vichy French—then still technically neutral—who sent a rescue ship from Dakar. Before it arrived, however, an American bomber from Ascension Island found the U-156 on the surface, and despite the presence of a large white banner bearing a red cross that Hartenstein had erected on the sub's foredeck, it attacked. One bomb fell among the lifeboats trailing astern, killing some of their occupants and spilling others into the sea. The U-156 was wounded but survived. Hartenstein cut loose the lifeboats, gave up on further rescue efforts, and fled the scene. A thousand Italian POWs died, as did another six hundred passengers and crew.[4]

For Dönitz, the lesson of this tragedy was that Hartenstein had been foolish to risk his boat in order to save survivors. Despite previous orders to ignore survivors, many U-boat captains had routinely sought to ensure that people in lifeboats had food and water, and sometimes provided a course to the nearest land. Now Dönitz issued new and more explicit guidance. In what came to be called the *Laconia* Order, he directed that "any attempt to save the survivors of sunken ships, fishing them out of the sea [or] putting them in lifeboats," was to be discontinued. That included "the handing over of food and water." "Be harsh," he ordered, "having in mind that the enemy takes no regard of women and children in his bombing attacks on German cities."[5]*

Hartenstein, the U-156, and the other boats assigned to the South African station proceeded on their mission and collectively sank twenty-seven ships off the Cape of Good Hope. Dönitz was pleased and considered the foray "a complete success." Indeed, the 802,160 tons of shipping sunk in November 1942 made it the most successful month of the war so far for the U-boats, triggering Churchill's distraught letter to Roosevelt quoted above. Dönitz, however, was disappointed that of the 126 Allied ships sunk that month, only twenty-nine of them were from the vital HX and SC convoys, which were now using New York rather than Halifax as a western terminus. He remained convinced that the decisive theater in the war on trade was the North Atlantic, and to cut that lifeline he needed both more U-boats and a free hand to deploy them where they could have the maximum

---

* After the war, this order of September 17, 1942, became a centerpiece of the case against Dönitz at the Nuremberg Trials. Though the court found him guilty of "waging a war of aggression," he was found not guilty of "crimes against humanity" due largely to written testimony from Chester Nimitz that American submarine skippers also declined to rescue passengers or crewmen from ships they had sunk.

impact. He didn't know it, but he was about to get his chance, and ironically it was a failure by the Kriegsmarine to intercept a convoy that created the opportunity.[6]

THE CONVOY WAS JW-51B. After the British and Americans secured their foothold in North Africa, they resumed the North Cape convoys to Russia, which, except for a single effort in September, had been suspended following the slaughter of PQ-17 the previous July. The new convoys sailed from Loch Ewe in Scotland rather than from Iceland, and the designation changed from PQ to JW, with the numbers starting at 51. Thus the first of the renewed convoys was JW-51, which sailed in two groups, labeled 51A and 51B, in December. The first group of sixteen ships encountered no opposition at all and arrived safely at Murmansk on Christmas Day. The second group (JW-51B) consisted of fourteen merchant ships with a close escort of six destroyers and five smaller ships plus a covering force of two British light cruisers (*Sheffield* and *Jamaica*). This time the Germans discovered it and dispatched a surface force into the Barents Sea to intercept it.

The attacking force consisted of the heavy cruiser *Hipper* and the pocket battleship *Lützow* plus six destroyers. It was a strong enough force to encourage a belief in Berlin that the convoy would be destroyed altogether. Instead, though the *Hipper* sank the destroyer *Achates* and the minesweeper *Bramble*, a bold defense by the other destroyers and a counterattack by the two British light cruisers, one of which put a shell into the *Hipper*'s engine room, led the Germans to call off the fight and withdraw. All fourteen of the ships in the Allied convoy arrived safely at Murmansk on January 6. When that news arrived in Berlin, Hitler was infuriated. Here was yet another humiliating performance by Erich Raeder's large, expensive, and apparently altogether useless surface warships.[7]

Hitler's misgivings about Raeder and his partiality for battleships and cruisers had been growing for months. His doubts were encouraged by both Göring and Josef Goebbels. Göring complained that the Luftwaffe was too often asked to fly protective cover for the big ships, a requirement that in his view wasted fuel and hobbled the air arm; Goebbels complained that the Kriegsmarine often released its own press reports without going through the

Propaganda Ministry. Amidst these criticisms, the failure of the attack on the North Cape convoy on New Year's Eve was the last straw, and Hitler gave way to one of his furious rants.[8]

The recipient of the tirade was Theodor Krancke, who had commanded the *Admiral Scheer* during its lengthy commerce raiding cruise back in 1940. Krancke had the bad luck to be the naval officer on duty when news arrived that *Hipper* and *Lützow* had ignominiously withdrawn without doing any damage to the convoy. Summoned to Hitler's office, Krancke stood silently at attention as the Führer insisted that the Kriegsmarine was a national disgrace. Hitler declared that he was going to scrap the navy altogether, send the guns ashore, and use the men for submarine duty. Krancke had the temerity to suggest that to do so would hand the British their greatest victory of the war without their having to make any effort to achieve it. Hitler was unmoved. He summoned Raeder to give him the new orders, but Raeder pleaded illness, very likely hoping that after a few days the Führer would calm down.[9]

He didn't. Five days later, at Eagle's Nest, near Berchtesgaden, Hitler treated Raeder to a reprise of the tirade he had delivered to Krancke—Raeder called it a dressing-down. In an hour-long lecture on world history and naval strategy, Hitler told Raeder that the navy was no more than a burden on other forces. "Light naval forces have been doing most of the fighting," he said. "Whenever the larger ships put out to sea, light forces have to accompany them. It is not the large ships which protect the small, but rather the reverse." Raeder was particularly stung by Hitler's claim that the navy had forgotten how to fight—that once committed to action, naval forces had too often failed to see the battle through to a decision and had instead meekly withdrawn. The big ships, Hitler insisted, had outlived their usefulness. Like the cavalry, they no longer had a meaningful purpose in modern war. He told Raeder to prepare a plan to retire all the big ships and to suggest where their guns might be placed on shore.[10]

Raeder immediately tendered his resignation. He had offered to resign twice before, and each time Hitler had talked him out of it. Not this time. The sixty-six-year-old Raeder suggested that his replacement should be either Admiral Rolf Carls or Dönitz. Since Carls, like Raeder, was a battleship man, Hitler chose the commander of the U-boat force to head the Kriegsmarine. At last Dönitz would be able to implement the kind of anti-shipping strategy he had long advocated.[11]*

BACK WHEN THE WAR BEGAN, Dönitz had asserted that with three hundred U-boats he could bring Britain to her knees. Such a number would allow him to keep one hundred U-boats on active patrol in the Atlantic while the other two hundred trained, replenished, or were in transit. By January 1943, when he took command of the navy, the Kriegsmarine did have three hundred U-boats, many of them newer boats that were technologically superior to those Dönitz had deployed in 1940. Moreover, the technicians had finally resolved the torpedo problem, and they had made other improvements as well, including the development of what were called *Federapparat Torpedoes* (FAT) that executed an unpredictable meandering course back and forth across the path of a convoy.

On the other hand, too few of those three hundred U-boats were committed to the Atlantic sea-lanes. Many of them (too many, in Dönitz's view) were in the Arctic, the Mediterranean, or the Baltic, leaving him with only about fifty to sixty boats for the North Atlantic. In addition, the heavy losses of U-boats during 1942 meant that many of the newer boats were commanded by relative novices, young men in their twenties, and had crews composed of raw recruits with little or no training. The skipper of the U-353, Wolfgang Römer, lamented that 80 percent of his crew consisted of teenage neophytes on their first deployment. It was with this force that Dönitz anticipated a final showdown with the Allied convoys in the spring and summer of 1943.[12]

The Allies also prepared for a showdown. On March 1, admirals from three English-speaking countries met in Washington to divide up responsibilities in the Battle of the Atlantic. They agreed that the British and Canadians would have primary responsibility for the North Atlantic convoys while the Americans handled the Western Hemisphere and the Central

---

* Dönitz was able to talk Hitler out of decommissioning all of the big ships, though no more of them were built and new construction priorities focused almost exclusively on the U-boats. See Chapter 20.

Atlantic (Norfolk to North Africa) convoys. The Allies, too, had made a number of technological advances. Virtually all the escorts now had improved sonar/Asdic capability; more important, many of them also had the new Type 271 radar sets with the circular PPI scope that gave both range and bearing to a surface contact. That allowed any escort so equipped to "see" in the dark, and all but erased the advantage the U-boats had previously had in night surface attacks.

Another Allied innovation was something called a Hedgehog. Heretofore, depth-charging a U-boat meant passing over the top of it and rolling barrel-shaped depth charges off a rack on the stern. The Hedgehog was a mortar that sat on the ship's foredeck and fired a pattern of two dozen 65-pound

Sailors load 65-pound depth charges onto a hedgehog launcher. With a 35-pound torpex warhead that detonated on contact, one hit was enough to sink a submarine. Because the hedgehog canisters fired forward, the escorts were able to take the initiative when confronting a submarine.

Naval History and Heritage Command

depth charges out in front of the ship and off to both sides in an elliptical pattern. (The name derived from the spiky appearance of the empty mortar rack after the bombs had been fired.) Finally, the increased availability of aircraft contributed significantly to trade defense. Radar-equipped Catalina seaplanes, British Sunderlands, and American B-24 Liberators, operating mostly from Iceland, gave the convoys eyes in the air. Soon many of these planes would also carry new air-launched torpedoes with acoustic homing devices capable of following the sounds of a U-boat's propellers underwater.[13]

Poor weather was a factor for both sides, though it affected the U-boats more than the convoys. Sailors on the merchant ships might curse the high seas and freezing spray as they battled their way across the North Atlantic, but the much smaller U-boats struggled merely to stay afloat in the towering seas. Dönitz complained to his war diary in January 1943 that "the elements seemed to rage in uncontrolled fury," and one U-boat commander wrote that the "mountainous seas" turned the U-boats into "bobbing steel cockleshells." The officers, shackled by safety lines to the railing on the tiny bridge of their conning towers, could not navigate because the clouds obscured the stars, and the lookouts could barely see past the huge waves. As Dönitz noted later, "Under such conditions only meager success could be achieved."[14]

And meager success was what they got. After sinking twenty-three ships in December 1942, including thirteen from ONS-154 at the end of the month, the U-boats sank only eight ships in all of January. They did better in February, sinking thirty-five ships, including fourteen from the west-bound (and therefore empty) convoy ON-166. But there was little cheering in Kernevel afterward, because the Allied escort, consisting of two American Coast Guard cutters and six destroyers (four Canadian, one British, and one Polish) sank three of the U-boats. That ratio of loss—one U-boat per 4.6 cargo ships—was not sustainable. At that exchange rate, sinking 120 Allied ships monthly—the number Dönitz believed necessary to ensure victory—would mean the loss of twenty-six U-boats per month as well, and Dönitz had only forty-seven in the North Atlantic. Not until March, with the weather moderating at last, did the U-boats achieve success. It came against eastbound convoy HX-229.[15]

HX-229 was a fast convoy that sailed from New York on March 8 with forty merchant ships. It was initially accompanied by a local escort, which was relieved on March 14 by a mid-ocean escort force of four destroyers and a corvette. German code breakers at B-Dienst intercepted a message regarding her course and speed, and on March 15, Heinz Walkerling in the U-91 found it and reported the coordinates to Kernevel. Dönitz sent not one but three wolf packs to intercept it. Moreover, by the time they arrived, HX-229 had overtaken a slow convoy (SC-122) of sixty ships that had left New York on March 5. That meant that as the wolf packs closed in, there were a hundred Allied merchant ships within 150 miles of one another, guarded by a combined total of fourteen escorts. Looking to annihilate this abundance of targets, Dönitz sent every U-boat within reach—a total of thirty-seven in all—toward the two convoys.[16]

The crews on the ships of HX-229 already had their hands full with the sea conditions. The vessels labored northeastward, pitching heavily due to a following sea that lifted their sterns and plunged them forward and downward in an endless and dizzying sequence. Occasionally a ship had a wave break over the stern, a phenomenon called being "pooped," and she would be inundated by tons of water rushing forward along the deck. Then on March 16, the U-boat attacks began. Just past midnight under a nearly full moon, a junior officer spotted "two streaks of greasy light, parallel, moving fast, coming in at an angle." There was hardly time to sound the alarm, and he watched helplessly while gripping the rail: "In one instant there were the tracks, in another a great shattering crash."[17]

Once begun, the attacks continued all night, explosions erupting periodically along the sides of the merchantmen, and by dawn the U-boats had sunk ten ships displacing 77,500 tons. The next day, the Allies sent additional escorts to join the convoy as well as a number of long-range bombers from Iceland. Throughout that St. Patrick's Day, the escorts pursued elusive contacts, dropping depth charges on suspected U-boats and flinging Hedgehog bombs into the sea to keep the wolves at bay. Two of the U-boats raced ahead to take up a submerged position in advance of the convoys and sank two more ships as the convoy approached. Airplanes from Iceland deterred more daytime attacks, but Dönitz was relentless. Ignore the planes, he ordered, and "pursue at top speed." The carnage resumed after dark and raged unceasing for three days and nights. By the time Dönitz called it off on March 19, his U-boats had sunk twenty-two ships displacing 146,500 tons and paid for it with the loss of only a single U-boat. It was, Dönitz wrote, "the greatest success that we had so far scored against a convoy."[18]

For the whole of that month, the U-boats claimed a total of eighty-four ships displacing more than 500,000 tons. Adding the losses from other theaters, the worldwide total came to an alarming total of 635,000 tons. Some worried that the Germans were on the brink of a strategic breakthrough. Dönitz also hoped that the slaughter of HX-229/SC-122 marked a turning point in the war on trade. Instead of a harbinger of things to come, however, it proved to be the apex of the U-boat campaign. Over the next two months, in spite of greatly improved weather conditions, the number of ships sunk by U-boats in the North Atlantic declined to thirty-two in April and to only six in May.[19]

There were several reasons for it. In addition to the Type 271 radar and the Hedgehog, the British and Americans added two new ship types to convoy defense that spring. One was a new class of small auxiliary aircraft carriers. Built initially atop freighter hulls, these "baby flattops" provided air cover for the convoys throughout the crossing, or at least they did so when the weather permitted. The small carriers embarked only 18–20 of planes, but they were newer U.S.-made Avenger torpedo planes, that carried depth charges. The first of the small escort carriers, the USS *Bogue*, was commissioned in September 1942, joined the fleet in February 1943, and made her first convoy deployment with HX-228 in March. Others soon joined her, and by May it had become almost routine to have an auxiliary carrier as part of a convoy escort. This dramatically changed the dynamics of convoy defense. As Herbert Werner, commander of the U-230, wrote in his classic memoir *Iron Coffins*, "The idea of a convoy with its own air defense smashed our basic concept of U-boat warfare."[20]

The other new convoy defense vessel was something called a destroyer escort (DE), a kind of mini destroyer, the first of which, USS *Bayntun*, was launched in late June 1942 and transferred to the Royal Navy in January 1943. At 1,360 tons, they were smaller than full-sized American destroyers,

Destroyer escorts, such as the USS *Breeman* (DE-104), seen here, were only marginally larger than British corvettes. Note the open bridge and the two 3-inch guns. The United States built several classes of these small, handy vessels for escort and anti-submarine duty, and many of them ended up in British or French service.

U.S. Naval Institute

though larger than British corvettes. Armed with 3-inch guns, they were hopelessly underarmed for any kind of surface action, but with sonar, radar, depth charge racks, and a Hedgehog, they were eminently suitable for the anti-submarine mission. Eventually the United States built more than five hundred of these small, handy vessels, seventy-eight of which were handed over to the Royal Navy, which called them "frigates." They became a staple of convoy protection throughout 1943 and to the end of the war.

Important as both of these new ship types were to convoy defense, they were not as decisive as the breakthrough that was achieved on March 19—the last day of the battle for convoy HX-229/SC-122—because it was on that date that cryptanalysts at Bletchley Park regained access to the naval Enigma codes. After the Germans added a fourth wheel to the naval Enigma back in February 1942, the Allies had lost the ability to decipher the content of Dönitz's message traffic. Now, thirteen months later, they again began reading those critical messages. That allowed the coordinators in Trade Plot to monitor the location of U-boats and route the convoys away from them.

Dönitz was aware that the convoys were somehow maneuvering to avoid his U-boats, but since B-Dienst assured him that the Enigma codes were unbreakable, he concluded that the British and Americans were using long-range airborne radar to track his wolf packs. He believed that allowed them, as he put it, "to find the U-boat formations with sufficient precision to permit his convoys to take evasive action." In fact, though neither side knew it, both the British *and* the Germans were reading each other's message traffic, a circumstance that led to what historian Clay Blair called "a gigantic game of naval chess." Dönitz directed the wolf packs to the convoys, and the British rerouted the convoys to avoid them. In that chess game, the Allies generally prevailed.[21]

ALL OF THESE FACTORS were evident in the convoy battles that took place in early May. Two in particular are worth noting. One was ONS-5, a westbound (empty) and slow convoy of forty-two merchant ships guarded by eight British and Canadian escorts. It plodded westward, zigzagging at seven and a half knots through frigid weather and past small icebergs. On April 28, the U-650 spotted and reported it to Kernevel, and Dönitz vectored fourteen U-boats toward it. The U-boat skippers anticipated success as a force 10 gale kept Allied airplanes grounded. The U-boats attacked in pairs and in threes to both port and starboard throughout the night of April 28–29, yet none of them broke through the convoy defense, and only a single ship was lost. For two more days the slow convoy headed westward with the U-boats dogging its flanks. The continuing bad weather kept Allied planes on the ground, but it also made it difficult for the U-boats to get into position. Then luck turned against the Allies. Dönitz had placed another group of U-boats farther west to intercept a different convoy, and on May 4 ONS-5 blundered into it.

That night the convoy was attacked by no fewer than forty-three U-boats—the largest concentration of U-boats in the whole of the war. For once they actually outnumbered the ships in the convoy, and that night they sank six ships. A crewman on the U.S. tanker *Sapelo* watched as two torpedoes streaked past the bow of his ship, missing by mere yards. They continued on and exploded against a ship in the next column. Hit twice within seconds, she went down swiftly, leaving only "one lonely raft turning slowly in a circle of dirty water."[22]

Dönitz ordered the U-boats to finish off the convoy altogether before it entered the umbrella of Allied air cover from Newfoundland. They did their best, making twenty-five separate attacks on the night of May 5, but they were stymied by a thick fog that cut visibility to near zero. Thanks to radar, the Allied ships could see through the fog, while the U-boats remained blind. That enabled the escorts to go on the offensive. The destroyer *Vidette* used her Hedgehog to sink the U-125; the *Oribi* rammed and sank the U-531; the sloop *Pelican* depth-charged and destroyed the U-438. And so it went. In his after-action report, the escort commander, Captain Peter Gretton of the Royal Navy, noted, "All ships showed dash and initiative. No ship required to be told what to do and signals were distinguished both by their brevity and their wit." By morning the escorts had sunk six U-boats and inflicted serious damage on seven others without losing a single merchant ship. Dönitz called off the attack. The final tally was thirteen Allied ships sunk against seven U-boats lost (one by aircraft from Newfoundland) and seven more badly damaged. Having committed more than forty U-boats to the destruction of a slow and weakly defended convoy, the Germans had nevertheless suffered a major defeat.[23]

Two weeks later, the outcome of an attack on eastbound SC-130 proved even more decisive. This time, Dönitz vectored twenty-five U-boats toward this slow convoy of thirty-seven ships guarded by eight escorts, and despite repeated attacks over two days (May 19–20) not a single merchant ship was lost, and the escorts sank three U-boats and damaged a fourth. One of the U-boats that went down with all hands was the brand-new U-954, whose first watch officer was nineteen-year-old Peter Dönitz, the admiral's son.[24]

The utter failure of the attack on SC-130 convinced the heartbroken Dönitz that the North Atlantic convoys had become too well defended for his U-boats to achieve any strategic success. Taken together, the convoy battles of May 1943 had cost him forty-one U-boats as well as their crews, and proved, in his words, "the overwhelming superiority achieved by the enemy defence." He ordered the U-boats to abandon the North Atlantic and redeploy southward. When he issued those orders, he fully intended to resume the contest in the North Atlantic at some future point, but when he looked back on it years later, it was clear to him that "we had lost the Battle of the Atlantic."[25]

—————

THOUGH HE DID NOT KNOW IT, Dönitz had actually lost it well before that, due to circumstances that had nothing to do with the events in the North Atlantic. Peter Gretton, the Royal Navy officer who commanded the escort forces for both ONS-5 and SC-130, attributed the Allied victories over the U-boats to several factors—intelligence, technology, and air cover among them—as well as the "skill and courage [shown] by the escorts." That was true enough, though the "skill and courage" of the U-boat crews were equally evident. In addition to all that, however, there was another factor in the war on trade that ultimately proved more decisive. That factor was shipbuilding.[26]

Dönitz himself acknowledged it. "The submarine war will be a failure," he told Hitler in April 1943, "if we do not sink more ships than the enemy is able to build." That in the end proved the key, for in the late fall of 1942, the Allies, and specifically the Americans, began launching new merchant ships faster than the U-boats could sink them. It was a cruel calculation, for it not only discounted a dispiriting loss of material and supplies in the east-bound convoys but also overlooked the pain and suffering of their crews, doomed to drift about the frigid North Atlantic on their tiny rafts or life-boats until they were rescued or, far too often, until they died of thirst, star-vation, or exposure. Still, as long as the Allies could build ships faster than the Axis could sink them, Dönitz could never break the Allied supply line.[27]

Only five days after the war had begun, on September 8, 1939, Roosevelt had declared a "limited national emergency" to justify an expanded ship-building program. Two years later, on May 27, 1941, he declared an "*unlimited* national emergency" in order to commence what he called "the largest armament production we have ever undertaken." After the United States was fully in the war, he created a War Shipping Administration, headed by Rear Admiral Emory Scott Land, and ordered him to ramp up ship construction dramatically. The president challenged Land to produce 5 million tons of new shipping in 1942 and 7 million tons in 1943. It was extraordinarily ambitious. The latter figure worked out to 583,000 tons of new shipping every month; only three times during the entire war did the U-boats manage to sink that much in a month. Some experts believed that such a construction goal was unrealistic, even absurd, yet Roosevelt soon raised the bar again. In February 1942, George Marshall wrote the president to warn him that unless shipping production was increased further, it would be impossible to carry to Britain the men and equipment necessary for an eventual invasion of occupied France. Marshall explained that it took 144,000 tons of shipping to move a single infantry division, and twice as much if it was an armored division. To send 750,000 men to England, therefore, would require an additional eighteen ships every month beyond what was currently scheduled. Spurred by that, FDR notified Land that he now wanted 9 million tons of new shipping in 1942 and 15 million tons in 1943. The latter figure worked out to 1.25 *million* tons of new shipping per month, a total the U-boats could never hope to destroy. As a British historian later noted, "America's shipbuilding programme almost defies belief."[28]

A key to achieving these daunting goals was standardization. Before the war, building a ship was like building a skyscraper: they were designed and constructed individually, each one a unique accomplishment. That ended with the president's declaration of an "unlimited national emergency" in May 1941. After that, ships were standardized to a national model so that they could be assembled the way Henry Ford built cars, in mass production. One set of blueprints yielded hundreds of hulls; component parts were mass-produced at factories around the country and shipped by rail to the building yards; welding replaced rivets. The transport ship that would become the most famous of the war was developed from a British design for a vessel that was 440 feet long, capable of carrying 10,000 tons of cargo, and able to steam at eleven knots. They were not beautiful ships—indeed, their unofficial working name was Ugly Ducklings. It was mainly for public relations that they were renamed Liberty Ships.[29]

In an effort to meet Roosevelt's goal, Land signed contracts with a number of builders who invested heavily (with government support) in dozens of new shipyards, most of them with six or more building ways per yard. New workers were hired by the tens of thousands, including men who had

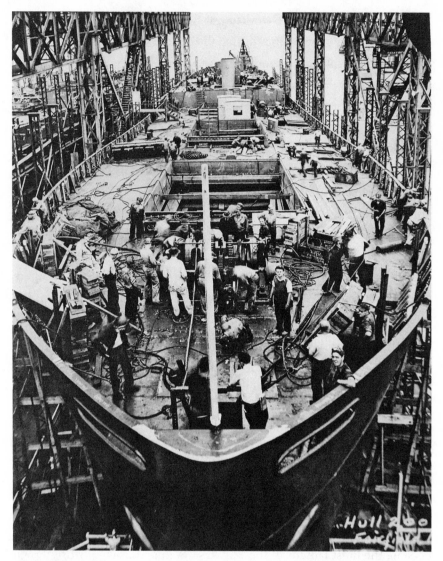

A Liberty ship under construction at the Fairfield Bethlehem Shipyard in Baltimore. The keel of this particular vessel, the SS *Bret Harte*, was laid on April 19, 1942, and she was launched forty days later, on May 29. She survived the war intact and was scrapped in 1963.

Naval History and Heritage Command

been rated 4-F and thus were ineligible for military service, as well as large numbers of women. There was some resistance to the latter; the shipbuilding trades had long been dominated by a male-only culture. Necessity, however, wrought a social revolution, and soon the shipyards had their version of Rosie the Riveter in "Wendy the Welder." By 1944, 20 percent of all shipyard workers were women.[30]

Once the infrastructure was in place, production increased dramatically. Long strings of rail cars brought raw materials to the shipyards, where the steel was initially housed in storage sheds. The historian of the wartime shipbuilding program, Frederic C. Lane, described the subsequent process. The steel plate, he wrote, "first went to storage racks, then to the fabrication shop to be cut and bent. From the fabrication shop, it passed to an assembly building in which sections weighing 10 to 20 tons were welded together. These sections were then piled on the skids or platens at the head of the ways or were there welded into larger sections weighting, normally, up to 45 tons. Thence they were put into their place in the hulls."[31]

This assembly-line process greatly accelerated the production of new ships. In January 1942, producing a Liberty Ship from keel-laying to launch took 250 days; by December, it took less than fifty days. In November, the Robert E. Peary was launched after only four days, fifteen hours, and twenty-nine minutes, though that was mainly a publicity stunt. Nevertheless, at scores of shipyards and hundreds of building ways on both coasts, a frenetic pace of construction went on twenty-four hours a day in three shifts. The result was an unprecedented, indeed previously unimaginable outpouring of new shipping. In December 1942, a month in which Dönitz's U-boats sank just over 400,000 tons, American yards produced more than 1 million tons of new shipping for the first time. After that, they surpassed 1 million tons nearly every month, and from that point on, no matter what Dönitz's U-boats did, they could never get ahead of that production curve (see graph).[32]

Along with the resilience of the Red Army on the Eastern Front, American industrial productivity was the single most determinative element in the eventual Allied victory in World War II. That said, the American industrial juggernaut was not infinite, and there was fierce competition among the various programs for the raw materials needed to produce the planes, the tanks, and particularly the ships needed to secure that victory. All ships, of every kind, required the same materials: electric motors, welding rods, generators, reduction gears, bearings, pumps, and especially steel plate. If all or

Allied Shipping Losses vs. Construction of New Ships, *1942–1944*

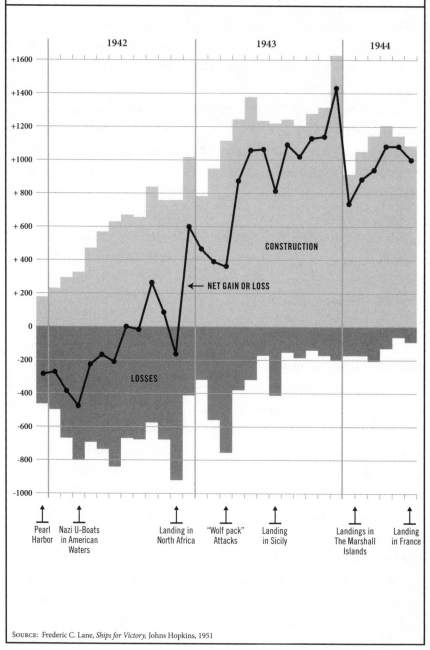

Source: Frederic C. Lane, *Ships for Victory*, Johns Hopkins, 1951

most of these vital components were committed to the construction of new transports, it necessarily meant cutbacks in the other types of ships being built, including warships. As American secretary of the navy Frank Knox noted, "It does us little good to produce one hundred cargo ships a month if we do not produce enough escort vessels during that month to enable us to protect them when they go to sea." Churchill agreed, writing Roosevelt to urge "the maximum construction of escort vessels." An analysis of shipping losses showed that convoys with nine escorts had 25 percent fewer losses than convoys with six escorts. In effect, each additional escort built saved two merchant ships from destruction, or as Ernie King put it, "one ship saved was worth two ships sunk." That led to escorts getting a higher priority than cargo ships in the American construction process, though squabbling continued throughout the war about what ships ought to have first access to which materials.[33]

Despite those disagreements, the ability of the Americans to produce ships of all kinds—transports and escorts, carriers and cruisers, landing ships and landing craft—and to do so in unprecedented numbers was decisive both in the war on trade and in the war effort generally.

ANOTHER WAR ON TRADE took place in the Pacific. That same spring of 1943, as U-boat successes declined in the Atlantic and American shipbuilding accelerated, the American submarine war on Japanese trade also entered a new phase. Though the Americans had begun unrestricted submarine warfare on the first day of the war, the early results had been disappointing. Due to the immensity of the Pacific theater, American submarines were larger than their German counterparts, with greater range and better seakeeping capability. The problem was that the Americans had relatively few of them—only fifty-five of the large fleet boats, plus another eighteen of the older and smaller S-class boats* that had been built in the 1920s—roughly

---

* The American S-boats were roughly the size and configuration of the German Type VIIc U-boats, and like them were identified only by a number (e.g., S-37, S-38) while the larger fleet boats had individual names, many of them reflecting their marine element (e.g., *Archerfish, Sealion, Albacore*). Small as they were, the S-boats did good service. An S-boat (the S-44) sank the Japanese cruiser *Kako* as it returned from the Battle of Savo Island on August 8, 1942.

the same number that Dönitz had had back in 1939 when the European war began. In addition to having relatively few boats, the Americans also had too few torpedoes. They had been forced to abandon more than 230 of them in the first weeks of the war, when they hurriedly evacuated the Cavite Navy Yard near Manila, and the stockpile in the States was small. Moreover, getting them from the United States out to the Pacific added one more requirement for the country's overburdened transports. That led to a directive from Washington to conserve torpedoes, suggesting that instead of a full spread of three or four torpedoes, skippers should fire them individually, one at a time, though most skippers ignored that advice.[34]

More consequential was the fact that the torpedoes the Americans did have often failed to detonate. As one submarine veteran put it, "There wasn't but one thing wrong with them—they didn't work." Like German torpedoes in 1940, the American Mark XIV torpedoes ran too deep—eleven feet deeper than the settings indicated, which meant that as they passed under the hull of their targets, their magnetic triggers did not come near enough to the hull to detonate. Worse, some torpedoes ran an erratic course, veering off unpredictably or even turning in a circle to head back toward the submarine that had fired it. Sub skippers returned from their patrols furious that after traveling as much as three thousand miles to their cruising ground, finding and carefully stalking a target, and getting into position for a shot, they then watched helplessly as their torpedoes exploded prematurely, passed under the target and kept going, or even bounced harmlessly off the ship's side. In a few cases, a torpedo embedded itself in the target's hull and just stuck there. More than one Japanese ship arrived back in port with an unexploded American torpedo protruding from its hull.[35]

It was especially infuriating when a torpedo failure provoked a terrifying counterattack, as often happened. On August 14, 1942, Commander Charles "Weary" Wilkins, conducting a patrol off Honshu in the Narwhal, fired a torpedo that spontaneously exploded only twelve seconds after it left the tube. That alerted the Japanese escort ships, several of which immediately counterattacked. The escorts, aided by Japanese aircraft, collectively dropped a total of 124 depth charges on the Narwhal, an experience so unnerving that one of the crew went "berserk" and had to be restrained. The Narwhal survived the onslaught, and after it returned to port, Wilkins added his complaints about faulty torpedoes to those of other skippers. The technicians at the Bureau of Ordnance (BuOrd) were skeptical, if not dismissive, and attributed all the failures to poor shooting. As one angry submarine veteran put it, their attitude was: "Don't complain about faulty torpedoes until you can prove that rightful blame does not lie with your own personnel." It took more than a year to overcome the bureaucratic resistance and for the technical problems to be identified and resolved.[36]

Another factor contributing to the disappointing results was that American submarine skippers were initially directed to focus their attacks on Japanese warships. The official U.S. submarine doctrine promulgated in 1939 was that "the primary task of the submarine is to attack enemy heavy ships...a battleship, a battlecruiser, or an aircraft carrier." One can imagine what Dönitz would have made of such a directive. He knew that conducting submarine warfare against an island power meant targeting its cargo ships and especially its tankers. That was particularly true in the Pacific, for it was Japan's desperate need for oil that had convinced her to begin the war in the first place. Yet for many months American submarines chased after the big warships rather than the more pedestrian *marus* (merchant ships) and tankers. The Americans also used many of their scarce submarines to conduct what Dönitz would have considered auxiliary, even frivolous, missions: landing or picking up raiding parties or transporting supplies. Eventually these priorities were changed, but in the first year of the Pacific War they inhibited the effectiveness of the American submarine force.[37]

There were few large-scale convoy battles in the Pacific like those that characterized the Battle of the Atlantic. For one thing, Japanese merchant ships did not travel in large protected convoys. Though troop transports were heavily escorted, Japanese merchant ships generally steamed independently, or in groups of two or three often guarded by a single destroyer, though a tanker might have two or even three escorts. Nor were there any American wolf packs because U.S. subs were individual predators. "You were given a geographical area," one skipper recalled, "and you could sink any ship that got in there." Though later in the war, as submarines became more plentiful, two or three of them might cooperate in groups called "wolf packs" in conscious imitation of the Germans, throughout 1942 and into 1943, most boats operated independently.[38]

In theory, all of the American submarine officers and crewmen were volunteers, though many had volunteered in the traditional navy way. One sub veteran recalled that when he reported for basic training early in the war, "we were asked if we wanted to go to Torpedo School. No one wanted to volunteer for Torpedo School. He told us that it was too bad. You get your sea-bags and your duffle bags packed because you are going to Keyport, Washington at six o'clock in the morning." Later, the submarine service adopted more rigorous standards. Living in a submarine for sixty days at a time not only was physically taxing but put a strain on crew dynamics. "There wasn't much space," David B. Bell, the skipper of the *Cuttlefish*, recalled. "It was like living inside a Swiss watch." Given the close quarters on long patrols, it was essential that the men had even temperaments and were not prone to panic. "If you showed any sign of nervousness," one crewman reported, such as tapping the table with your fingers, "you were automatically turned down. You had to be pretty mellow."[39]

While on patrol, the American submarines maneuvered on the surface with lookouts fore and aft on the sub's small conning tower amidships. Equipped with Bausch and Lomb binoculars, the lookouts scanned the horizon constantly. In order to ensure that they could scramble back inside quickly in case the sub needed to dive, they sometimes failed to secure their safety lines. That was risky in a conning tower fifteen feet above a rolling sea. When operating in enemy territory, specifically whenever they were within five hundred miles of an enemy base, the subs generally stayed submerged during the daytime (as German U-boats did off Cape Hatteras), surfacing at night to recharge their batteries and search for prey. During prolonged periods submerged, sometimes as long as twenty hours, the boat took on what one veteran described as "the peculiar submarine smell of diesel fuel, cigarette smoke, cooking odors, paint, and human aroma." When the boat finally surfaced after dark, "my, did that fresh air smell sweet." That was often when the evening meal would be served. "At night when we surfaced, we'd have a big pot of oatmeal or something like that," a crewman recalled.

"That was because we were saving battery juice. When we dove in the morning, we had a full meal and that was our one big meal of the day."[40]

Conditions were spartan. There were few heads and no showers. Even on newer boats that did have showers, they were often secured for the duration of the patrol to save fresh water. Crewmen took baths when they could in a two-and-a-half-gallon bucket. The bunks, colloquially called "racks," were arranged between the torpedoes or stacked six levels high along the bulkhead with eight inches of space between them. The top bunks were the most desirable. When a veteran rotated out of a boat and a new recruit came on board, each person moved up one level and the new recruit got the bottom bunk. There were fewer racks on board than crewmen, so everyone except the officers hot-bunked: the man coming in from watch took the rack of the man who had just gotten up to begin his watch. When the men fell into bed, they generally did so wearing the clothes they had worn all day. "The only thing you took off was your shoes," one recalled. In the smaller S-boats, there was not even a mess table. The men picked up their chow from the cook in the galley and sat in a corner somewhere to eat. As on the German U-boats, military protocol was honored mostly in the breach. Officers might wander among the crewmen in their skivvy shorts and T-shirts. "They weren't all hung up on all of the military formality," a veteran recalled. "We saluted and everything, but no one got punished if you didn't."[41]

Like the U-boats in the Atlantic, the Americans made no serious effort to rescue or provision survivors from any of the ships they sunk. "You just felt sorry for them," one skipper recalled later, "but that's as far as you could go." Nor, in spite of a deep-seated racial animosity toward the Japanese, did they always seek to finish off survivors in the water, though there were exceptions. One of the most notorious occurred in January 1943.[42]

On January 26, on only his tenth day in command of the submarine *Wahoo*, Commander Dudley "Mush" Morton boldly stole into Wewak Harbor on the north coast of New Guinea and sank a Japanese destroyer with a down-the-throat shot, hitting it head-on as it charged toward him. Morton successfully extricated the *Wahoo* from Wewak, and the next day he encountered a Japanese convoy of four ships. He sank all four of them,

Lieutenant Commander Dudley "Mush" Morton (at right) with his executive officer, Lieutenant Richard H. O'Kane, on the conning tower of the submarine *Wahoo* in February 1943.

U.S. National Archives photo no. 80-G-35725

one of which was the *Buyo Maru,* a troop transport filled with soldiers. Morton cleared the scene, but after the four ships had all gone down, he returned to find the area crowded with twenty or so lifeboats filled with survivors. Grimly he ordered, "Battle stations. Man both guns." His executive officer, Richard H. O'Kane, looked questioningly at him, which provoked this explanation: "Dick, the army bombards strategic areas, and the air corps uses area-bombing.... Both bring civilian casualties. Now without any other casualties, I will prevent these soldiers from getting ashore, for every one who does can mean an American life." Morton ordered the boat's 4-inch gun crew to fire into the largest of the lifeboats, and when that provoked return fire, he ordered all the guns to open fire. For most of an hour, machine guns on the *Wahoo* swept the area, "like fire hoses cleaning a street," as O'Kane put it. When all the lifeboats had been shattered, Morton ordered cease fire. What he did not know was that in addition to 600 Japanese soldiers, the *Buyo Maru* had also been carrying 500 British and Indian prisoners of war, 195 of whom were also killed. Instead of a backlash, however,

Morton and the *Wahoo* received a "well done" from Nimitz and "congratulations" from Halsey for a successful patrol. Morton received the Navy Cross for gallantry, and the *Wahoo* received a Presidential Unit Citation for "destroying one transport *and their personnel*."[43]*

After forty to sixty days, depending on how long it took to expend their torpedoes, the American submarines returned to their bases and reported the results of their patrol. Often, especially in the early months, there was little to report. Some claimed the destruction of one or two ships, most often small *marus* displacing an average of only about 4,000 tons each. Even then, subsequent investigation often revealed that their estimates were too high. While some skippers had successful patrols, notably Morton in *Wahoo*, Lieutenant Commander Frank W. Fenno in *Trout*, and Lieutenant Commander Charles C. Kirkpatrick in *Triton*, the overall record of American submarines in 1942 was a disappointment. In the first six months of the year, American subs sank only fifty-six ships, many of them small minesweepers, with a total displacement of 216,150 tons, an average of only 36,000 tons a month, barely a tenth of what Dönitz's U-boats were doing in the Atlantic. The numbers improved slightly in the second half of the year, a result of the experience gained by the officers and their crews. From July to December 1942, American submarines sank 105 ships displacing 397,700 tons (66,000 tons per month), though of the ten fleet submarines that left Pearl Harbor in October 1942, eight returned having sunk no ships at all. Because of new ship construction, the net loss to Japanese shipping during the year was only 89,000 tons. As the historian Clay Blair has noted, it was "a figure so slight as to be meaningless."[44]

Early in 1943, however, the American war on Japanese trade reached a watershed moment of its own. One aspect of it was the arrival of Charles Lockwood as the new Commander of Submarines in the South Pacific

---

* Though officially lauded at the time, Morton's decision to machine-gun survivors in the water remained controversial within the service and very likely prevented him from receiving the Medal of Honor. After the war, a German U-boat skipper, Kapitänleutnant Heinz-Wilhelm Eck, was tried, convicted, and executed for destroying rafts and lifeboats from a ship he had sunk, in order to disguise the location of the attack. Morton did not face a postwar investigation, for he was killed in October 1943, when the *Wahoo* was sunk in the Sea of Japan.

(COMSUBPAC). Initially, American Pacific submarines had been under the command of Rear Admiral Robert H. English, who was killed in a plane crash in January 1943, after which Lockwood assumed command. A popular leader who was called "Uncle Charlie" by the sub crews, Lockwood took their complaints about torpedo performance seriously. (He entitled the first chapter of his postwar memoir "Damn the Torpedoes.") Lockwood personally supervised new torpedo tests, and brought the results to the attention of what one submarine skipper called "the desk-bound moguls in Washington." Even then there was resistance from the technical experts, but eventually Nimitz (himself an old submarine hand) ordered the skippers to deactivate the magnetic proximity fuses and rely exclusively on the contact triggers.[45]

Unfortunately, there was a problem with the contact fuses, too. When a Mark XIV torpedo hit a ship flush on its side, the impact often crushed the firing pin, so the warhead did not detonate. In one extreme case in July 1943, Commander Dan Daspit in the submarine *Tinosa* hit a Japanese whale factory ship eleven times: eleven hits, no explosions. Lockwood later reported that when Daspit returned to Pearl Harbor, "Dan was so furious as to be practically speechless." Lockwood ordered more tests and discovered that the firing pins worked best when they struck the target at an angle of less than 45 degrees. Until new firing pins could be designed and installed, he advised his skippers to fire torpedoes at an acute angle to the target.[46]

Another cause of improved submarine performance in 1943 was that more and newer boats were joining the fleet. Whereas the Americans had only 47 submarines on active patrols in February of that year, three months later, in May, there were 107. Many of them were newer *Gato*-class submarines that, unlike the smaller German boats, had both air-conditioning and refrigerated food storage, making them much more accommodating for their crew of eighty men, especially on long patrols. The result of these improvements was immediately evident. The twenty-four boats that put to sea in April 1943 sank a total of twenty-six Japanese ships displacing 121,800 tons, a significant increase over previous months.[47]

THIS REVITALIZATION of the American submarine force occurred simultaneously with the deterioration of U-boat effectiveness in the Atlantic. In

April and May 1943, Dönitz lost no fewer than fifty-eight U-boats world-wide, fifty-three of them in the Atlantic. The loss of so many U-boats and their continued lack of success against Allied convoys forced him to admit that "victory over the two maritime powers could not be achieved" with U-boats. He even considered giving up the U-boat war altogether. "I had to make up my mind," he wrote later, "whether to withdraw the boats from all areas and call off the U-boat war, or let them continue operations in some suitably modified form." In the end, he decided that there was no alternative but to play it out, no matter how hopeless it seemed. In the aftermath of the failed attacks on ONS-5 and SC-130 in May, he told Hitler, "The U-boat war must be continued even if the goal can no longer be obtained, because the enemy forces it absorbs are extraordinarily large." Hitler agreed: "There is absolutely no question of abandoning the U-boat war," he decreed, for it was "better than defending myself first on the coasts of Europe." It was an utterly bankrupt calculation: young and largely inexperienced U-boat crews must keep going to sea, many of them never to return, and the transports must continue to be targeted and sunk, not because it might affect the outcome of the war, or even its trajectory, but because it kept Allied shipping, escorts, and airplanes occupied. Of course, given the torrent of newly constructed ships and planes coming from American slipways and factories, it was unlikely to make any strategic difference anyway.[48]

As Dönitz's war on Allied trade began its slow but inexorable ebb in the spring of 1943, the American war on Japanese trade began its equally inexorable rise. The American submarine campaign had not yet become a flood, though that would come, and eventually it would constitute a tsunami.

PART IV

ALLIED COUNTERATTACK

Early in 1943 the Allies seized the initiative. The last Japanese soldiers evacuated Guadalcanal in February; that same month the starving remnants of the German Sixth Army surrendered at Stalingrad; and the North African campaign came to an end in May, when a quarter of a million Italian and German soldiers capitulated in Tunisia. Even at the time, Admiral Andrew Browne Cunningham mused, "The months of April and May, 1943, will probably be chosen by historians as the period when the pendulum swung." Collectively, these events changed the character of the war and allowed the Allies to consider—and to argue about—what to do next.

From the start, all three of the major Allied partners had agreed that Germany was the primary foe. This had never been an issue for the Russians, whose very survival had been hanging in the balance since the German invasion in June 1941. Of necessity they had focused all of their effort and energy on that struggle while remaining neutral in the war with Japan. It was more problematic for the British and Americans, who continued to endorse the Germany-first strategy in principle, but who confronted a global war on multiple fronts. In addition, the Western Allies still lacked the trained manpower, the weaponry, and especially the sealift capacity to make a direct assault on the Wehrmacht in Europe, which was why they had landed instead in North Africa. After the Torch landings, the Mediterranean—like Guadalcanal—had become a logistical black hole, absorbing manpower and resources so voraciously that it was soon evident that a 1943 invasion of Europe was equally impossible. Meanwhile, the Americans continued their advance against the Japanese in the South Pacific, no longer pretending that the movements were defensive in character.

At the same time, the war in Europe reached new heights—or depths—of violence. In July, the German army sought to regain the initiative on the Eastern Front with a massive pincer movement (Operation Citadel) carried out by eight hundred thousand men and three thousand tanks. The Russians counterattacked in August with two million men and eight thousand tanks. For their part, the English-speaking Allies ramped up the bombing campaign with Operation Gomorrah, a massive aerial attack on the city of Hamburg. For a full week (July 24–31), British and American long-range bombers dropped nine thousand tons of bombs, leaving more than forty-two thousand dead and wrecking much of the city, including the Blohm and Voss shipyard where the Bismarck had been built. And it must never be forgotten that even as all this took place hundreds of thousands of men, women, and children were being systematically murdered in the Nazi death camps.

At sea, the Anglo-American forces took the offensive both in the Mediterranean and in the South Pacific. The geography of those theaters compelled the Allies to conduct a number of amphibious assaults: crossing the Mediterranean from Tunisia to Sicily in Operation Husky, and climbing the ladder of the Solomon Islands in Operation Cartwheel. In all these efforts, a common thread, and logistical bottleneck, was the unrelenting demand for amphibious landing ships.

CHAPTER 18

AIRPLANES AND CONVOYS

BACK IN THE FIRST DAYS OF THE PACIFIC WAR, the destruction of HMS *Prince of Wales* in the Gulf of Siam by land-based Japanese aircraft demonstrated the lethal effectiveness of airplanes against surface warships maneuvering without air cover. The lesson was confirmed during the prolonged campaign for Guadalcanal, when American possession of Henderson Field and the presence of the Cactus Air Force proved critical in foiling the Tokyo Express. Air superiority proved crucial again in the spring of 1943 when, after the Japanese evacuation of Guadalcanal, the campaign in the South Pacific entered a new phase.

The Japanese had known from the day of Pearl Harbor that the Americans would eventually launch a counteroffensive, and their plan to defeat it was to wear out the attackers by forcing them to assault numerous strong points within their network of island bases all across the South Pacific. The Japanese accepted the likelihood that the Americans would win some tactical victories in such a campaign, but they also believed that the feckless Yankees would soon tire of their losses and agree to a negotiated end to the war. After the loss of Guadalcanal, therefore, they sought to reinforce many of those forward bases, one of which was the northern New Guinea port city of Lae, already under pressure from a force of Australians at Wau, only fifty miles inland. In January 1943, the Japanese sent a strongly escorted convoy of three transports carrying four thousand soldiers from Rabaul to Lae, and in February, Admiral Yamamoto approved the dispatch of another, even larger convoy. This time, eight transports carrying six thousand soldiers would be escorted by eight destroyers under Rear Admiral Masatomi Kimura, whose luxuriant walrus mustache gave him an incongruous resemblance to Sir Herbert Kitchener, the British Army officer whose face stared out challengingly from thousands of recruiting posters during World War I. The convoy would have top cover by Zero fighters, but Kimura also hoped that the unsettled weather forecast for the Bismarck Sea would provide its own cover for his flotilla, though it would certainly add to the discomfort of the soldiers, packed into the transports like sardines.[1]

Bad weather, however, was no impediment to the American code breakers. By now Station Hypo had grown exponentially and would soon be rechristened the Joint Intelligence Center Pacific Ocean Area (JICPOA in the inevitable acronym), with more than a thousand workers. That dramatically improved the number of messages the Americans could intercept and the speed at which those messages could be broken. In February 1943, the code breakers read enough of the Japanese message traffic to send an alert about the reinforcement of Lae to American Major General George Kenney, commanding MacArthur's air forces at Milne Bay on the eastern tip of New Guinea. Kenney ordered American and Australian bombers to intercept the convoy. On March 1, the heavy cloud cover that Kimura had counted on hid the convoy from Allied search planes, but they found it the next day and one of them landed a bomb on the troop transport *Kyokusei Maru,* loaded with twelve hundred soldiers plus two thousand cubic meters of munitions. The bomb detonated the munitions, and the explosion sent the *Kyokusei Maru* to the bottom. Two of the escorting Japanese destroyers picked up 875 survivors and sped off ahead of the convoy to deliver them to Lae. As it turned out, they were the lucky ones.[2]

The next day, March 3, Kenney sent more than a hundred bombers out to finish off the convoy, and the main battle began amidst clearing skies around 10:00 a.m. By then the Japanese ships had entered the Huon Gulf and were only a few dozen miles from their goal. Though the nearly five thousand men on the transports could see the coast of New Guinea on the southern horizon, none of them would reach it.

In this air assault, the Allies employed a new tactic known as "skip-bombing." Flying just above wave height, specially modified B-25C Mitchell bombers released bombs equipped with a five-second delay fuse so that, like a rock thrown across a still lake, they skipped across the surface until they struck the side of the target. Using this protocol, the pilots claimed seventeen hits out of thirty-seven bombs dropped. A horrified Japanese sailor on one of the escort ships watched the disintegration of the transport ships as the Allied planes savaged them: "Their masts tumbled down, their bridges blew to pieces, the ammunition they were carrying was hit, and whole ships blew up."[3]

Meanwhile, the bigger, high-flying B-17 Flying Fortresses dropped their bombs from twenty thousand feet. Though hitting ships from altitude was rare, two bombs struck the *Aiyo Maru*, one of which penetrated to her boiler and exploded. The destroyer *Arashio* stopped to pick up survivors, and soon her deck was crammed with more than five hundred of them. The soldiers' respite was temporary, however. The American Mitchell bombers had been fitted with eight forward-firing .50 caliber machine guns, and they conducted repeated strafing runs on the *Arashio*. Reiji Masuda recalled the onslaught: "Bullet fragments and shrapnel made it look like a beehive. All the steam pipes burst. The ship became boiling hot." The *Arashio*'s rudder jammed and, unable to steer, she collided with another destroyer. The Japanese soldiers who had just been rescued from the *Aiyo Maru* abandoned ship for the second time. As they clambered into lifeboats and barges, the American bombers strafed them, too. Masada remembered, "We tried to abandon ship, but planes flying almost as low as the masts sprayed us with machine-guns." The justification Kenny later offered for shooting survivors in the water was that with the New Guinea coast so close, the lifeboats might still carry the soldiers to their destination, where they would fight and kill Americans or Australians. Nevertheless, strafing survivors

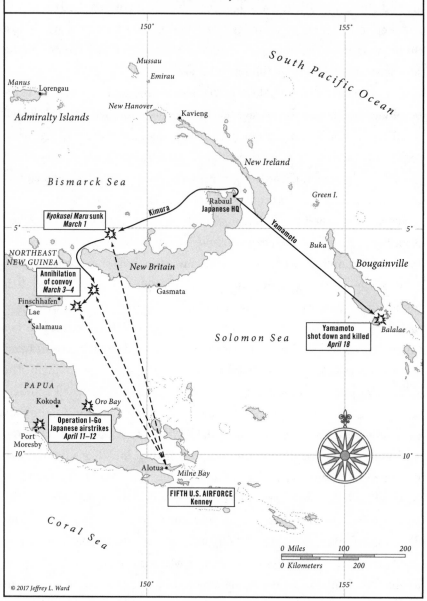

BATTLE OF THE BISMARCK SEA
March 1–4, 1943

150°

155°

Mussau

Emirau

Manus

Lorengau

New Hanover

Kavieng

Admiralty Islands

South Pacific Ocean

New Ireland

Green I.

Bismarck Sea

Rabaul
Japanese HQ

Kimura

Yamamoto

Buka

5°

**Kyokusei Maru sunk
March 1**

5°

*NORTHEAST
NEW GUINEA*

New Britain

Bougainville

**Annihilation
of convoy
March 3–4**

Gasmata

Finschhafen

Lae

Salamaua

Solomon Sea

**Yamamoto
shot down and killed
*April 18***

Balalae

PAPUA

Kokoda

Oro Bay

**Operation I-Go
Japanese airstrikes
*April 11–12***

Port
Moresby

10°

10°

Alotua

Milne Bay

FIFTH U.S. AIRFORCE
Kenney

Coral Sea

0 Miles   100   200

0 Kilometers   200

© 2017 Jeffrey L. Ward

150°

155°

in the water, like "Mush" Morton's destruction of lifeboats two months before, was another example of how the violence of war blurred the lines of humane behavior.[4]

There was more. When Zero fighters flying cover over the convoy shot down Army Lieutenant Woodrow Wilson Moore's B-17, he and his eleven-man crew bailed out. As they drifted seaward in their parachutes, they were machine-gunned in the air by three Zeros. To the outraged Americans, this was somehow worse than targeting survivors in lifeboats, and news of it spread quickly through the squadron. At their morning briefing the next day, the American pilots were encouraged to hit anything that floated. On March 4, as the American bombers flew low over a sea now littered with men clinging to rafts and wreckage, they opened fire, killing uncounted hundreds. Some of the pilots were simply angry. "I wanted...to kill every Japanese son of a bitch I could find," one declared. Others found it "distasteful" but did it out of a sense of duty. Kenney himself remarked simply, "The Jap asks no quarter and expects none." After the planes departed, a squadron of American PT boats arrived to complete what Samuel Eliot Morison called "the sickening business of killing survivors in boats, rafts, or wreckage." There was no inquiry into such behavior, either at the time or later; it was how the war was now being fought.[5]

By nightfall on March 4, all eight of the Japanese transports had been sunk, plus four of the eight destroyers. Only those 875 survivors from the *Kyokusei Maru* made it to Lae; another 1,400 were carried back to Rabaul by the surviving destroyers; and Japanese submarines rescued a few hundred more. A handful washed up on nearby islands, where they were hunted down and killed by Australian patrols. The rest, more than three thousand, perished at sea. For their part, the Americans lost six airplanes and thirteen men, including the crew of Moore's B-17. The Americans christened this destruction of a troop convoy the Battle of the Bismarck Sea. Though hardly a battle in the conventional sense, it demonstrated once again that surface ships proceeding without substantial air cover constituted a vulnerable, even defenseless target.[6]

IT WAS A LESSON AVAILABLE TO BOTH SIDES, and in the wake of these events, Yamamoto decided to use Japanese airpower to blunt the anticipated

American offensive. From his headquarters on board the new super-battle-ship *Musashi*, anchored at Truk, in the Caroline Islands, he authorized Operation I-Go, a massive air attack on Allied forward positions in the South Pacific. He was skeptical that the land-based Nell and Betty bombers could inflict a strategically significant blow on their own. His chief of staff, Matome Ugaki, no doubt reflected his boss's prejudices when he wrote in his diary, "We cannot expect much of the land-based air force partly because of a passive atmosphere among them." It was to stiffen this "passive atmosphere" that Yamamoto insisted on adding the carrier air groups to the strike force. The Japanese carrier commander, Jisaburō Ozawa, was reluctant to strip the carriers of their planes for such a mission, but Yamamoto insisted that it was necessary in order to have a meaningful impact on the Americans. To oversee the air offensive, both Yamamoto and Ozawa flew to Rabaul on April 3. Though outwardly hopeful, Yamamoto was also realistic. There was more than a hint of fatalism in Ugaki's diary entry that day: "If and when this attempt fails to achieve a satisfactory result, there will be no hope of future success in this area."[7]

To conduct the attacks, Yamamoto had a total of 350 aircraft. It was a significantly larger force than the one Kenney had used to destroy the convoy to Lae, but there were several important differences between the air forces of the two sides. One was that due to heavy losses of experienced Japanese pilots during the campaign so far, this new attack would be carried out mostly by novices. Ugaki noted that of sixty pilots in one fighter group, forty-four had no experience flying the type of aircraft assigned to them. Another difference was that many of the Japanese pilots were in questionable health, suffering from dengue fever, diarrhea, and especially malaria. The historian Bruce Gamble calculated that "fully 95 percent of the soldiers, sailors, and airmen at Rabaul suffered at least one bout of malaria during their deployment." Still, Yamamoto had few other weapons to hand.[8]

Operation I-Go got under way before dawn on April 7 when 177 planes took off from the airfields at Rabaul—67 bombers escorted by 110 Zeros—to attack the thirty-one Allied ships that Japanese reconnaissance planes had reported present off Guadalcanal. It was the largest Japanese air attack since Pearl Harbor. Alerted by the code breakers and by radar, the Americans were ready for them. Thanks to the Seabees, there were now three airstrips on Guadalcanal, and from them the Americans launched seventy-six fighters to intercept the attackers. The American planes shot down twelve Zeros and nine Vals. One Wildcat pilot, Marine First Lieutenant James E. Swett, personally shot down seven Vals, an accomplishment for which he was later awarded the Medal of Honor. Despite such determined opposition, the Japanese pilots fought through the intercept and attacked the shipping at both Tulagi and Guadalcanal. After they returned to Rabaul, they reported sinking ten transports, a cruiser, and a destroyer.[9]

By now, theater commanders on both sides knew that damage reports from pilots had to be taken with a grain or two of salt, and the actual Allied losses were significantly less: two transports, an American destroyer, and a corvette of the New Zealand navy. Nevertheless, Yamamoto doubled down on the strategy, sending ninety-four planes to hit Oro Bay, on the north coast of New Guinea, on April 11, then 174 planes to attack Port Moresby on April 12, and 188 planes to attack Milne Bay on April 14. For Yamamoto, who had been an early champion of the strategic importance of aircraft carriers, the decision to employ specially trained and increasingly scarce carrier pilots to attack static bases rather than preserve them for a future carrier battle is curious. The British historian Stephen Roskill concludes that it was "a good example of the misuse of air power."[10]

Despite the meager results, Yamamoto officially declared Operation I-Go a success. Though personally skeptical of the pilots' inflated damage reports, he forwarded them without comment to Tokyo, where the newspapers reported another triumph by Japanese arms and the emperor expressed his satisfaction. Yamamoto knew, however, that the raids had failed to inflict the kind of damage that would significantly retard or even delay the forthcoming American offensive. There was no alternative now but to fall back on the strategy espoused by the Japanese army of defending each of the Empire's outposts so fiercely that even as they fell one by one, the losses the Americans suffered in capturing them would erode their will to continue the war. To bolster the morale of the doomed men who would be asked to execute this strategy by selling their lives dearly, Yamamoto decided to visit these advance bases personally to assure them that they were not forgotten. The first leg of his tour would take him to Balalae, a small island that hosted a Japanese air base at the southeastern tip of Bougainville.*

ON WEDNESDAY, APRIL 14, U.S. Marine Lieutenant Colonel Alva Lasswell was working in the basement of the fleet radio unit at Pearl Harbor when he suddenly jumped out of his chair and yelled, "We've hit the jackpot!" In his hands was a partially decrypted message that appeared to be the travel itinerary for the commander in chief of the Japanese Navy. After Lasswell's outburst, others in the cryptanalytic team rushed to help him crack the rest of the message, and as the pieces fell into place, they learned that Yamamoto would depart Rabaul at 6:00 a.m. on April 18 in a medium attack plane, probably a Betty, escorted by six Zero fighters. He would arrive at Balalae at 8:00 a.m., make a short tour of the facility, visit the sick and wounded, and depart again at 11:00 for the next leg of his trip. Reading the message, one of the American cryptanalysts muttered, "I hope we get the S.O.B."[11]

Commander Edwin Layton immediately took the decrypted message to Admiral Nimitz. According to Layton, Nimitz read it, looked up, and asked, "Do we try to get him?" There were arguments against it. For one thing, the distance from Henderson Field to Bougainville was nearly four hundred miles, beyond the capability of even the longest-range American fighter. The only plane that might attempt it was the Army's P-38 Lightning, instantly recognizable by its unique twin fuselage, and it could make the flight only if it was equipped with supplementary fuel tanks. Even more problematic was the possibility that the sudden appearance of an American fighter squadron so far from its base and exactly where the Japanese naval commander in chief was scheduled to appear could lead the Japanese to suspect that the Americans had broken their operational code. If that hap-

---

* Balalae was the scene of yet another war atrocity. After the fall of Singapore, the Japanese transported more than five hundred British POWs there to build the airfield. After the airfield was completed, the Japanese lined up the POWs and executed all five hundred of them.

pened, they would change the code and the Allies would be deprived of an invaluable intelligence source. Was killing Yamamoto that important? And finally, there was the moral issue. Men died in combat every day, but to target a specific individual like this seemed more like an assassination. Did the United States want to do that?[12]

Nimitz decided that killing Yamamoto was a legitimate military operation and that the benefits outweighed the risks.* Quite apart from the revenge factor (Americans were aware that Yamamoto had been the architect of the attack on Pearl Harbor), there was the likelihood that Yamamoto's death would be a severe blow to both Japanese morale and operational effectiveness.

Nimitz sent the order to Halsey, who passed it on to Marc Mitscher, now commanding what had been the Cactus Air Force, and endowed now with the more formal name Air Command Solomons (AirSols). On April 17 Mitscher met with a score of U.S. Army P-38 pilots on Guadalcanal. The pilots were curious about the specificity of the prediction that Yamamoto would arrive at Balalae precisely at 8:00 a.m. Even if he did, they wondered, would it be better to shoot down his plane as he arrived or to ambush him on the ground after he landed? In the end, it was decided to shoot down his plane and hope that he was killed in the crash. Eighteen P-38 fighters under the command of Major John W. Mitchell took off that night from the Guadalcanal airfields, and after flying all night, they were in position off Bougainville at 7:25 the next morning.[13]

Yamamoto was right on time. Upon spotting the Japanese formation, the P-38 pilots dropped their external fuel tanks and broke into two groups. Mitchell took all but four of the planes up to altitude, to take on the Zeros

---

* After the war, a story emerged that Nimitz had queried Washington about the legal and moral ramifications of a targeted attack on Yamamoto, and that navy secretary Frank Knox met with President Roosevelt in a midnight meeting to discuss it. According to this tale, it was Roosevelt himself who decided to kill Yamamoto. If so, there is no credible record of it: no record of Nimitz's query, of a meeting between Knox and Roosevelt, or of orders from Washington. Of course, it is possible that all such orders were destroyed, but a more likely conclusion is that Nimitz made the decision on his own.

that everyone expected would be arriving at any moment from the nearby Japanese air base at Kahili, and Captain Thomas G. Lanphier led the other four toward the two bombers, which immediately separated: one flying inland over Bougainville, the other heading out to sea. Lanphier and his wingman, Lieutenant Rex T. Barber, pursued the one heading inland. Lanphier fended off the covering Zeros while Barber went for the bomber. He fired into its tail section, and Barber watched as "its rudder and a good portion of its vertical fin came off." The Betty then cartwheeled into the jungle and exploded.[14]

Barber then turned and sped after the other bomber. After all, there was no way to know which of the planes held Yamamoto as a passenger. The P-38 pilots, including Barber, chased the second Betty out over the sea, where it flew so low its props made waves on the surface. Several of the American pilots concentrated on the pursuing Zeros, and again it was Barber, along with Lieutenant Besby Holmes, who got a clear shot at the bomber. Both men opened with their .50 caliber machine guns as well as their 20 mm cannons. Holmes could both see and hear the shells hitting the bomber's fuselage, but the Betty refused to go down. "Blow up dammit!" he screamed. "What do I have to do?" Finally, "a huge puff of smoke, followed by an orange flame, burst from the right engine cowling," and the Betty crashed into the sea. Watching from above, Mitchell radioed: "Mission accomplished. Everybody, get your ass home."[15]

Afterward, the Americans made a point of announcing that an Australian coast watcher had reported a group of Japanese planes flying the length of Bougainville, and that his report had prompted the decision to send a fighter squadron to attack it. The cover story stood up, and the Japanese did not change their code.

As it happened, Yamamoto had been in the first bomber, the one that crashed in the jungle, and almost certainly he was already dead when the plane went down, for when the Japanese recovered his body he had a .50 caliber machine gun wound through his head. Ugaki had been in the second plane that crashed into the sea, and despite serious wounds, he lived, though he never quite forgave himself for surviving when his beloved commander had not. The Japanese kept the news of Yamamoto's death secret for more than a month. When it was finally made public, on May 22, the government reported that his body had been found sitting upright with his gloved hand on his sword hilt. His ashes were returned to Tokyo, and on June 5 the government staged an elaborate state funeral at which he was posthumously honored with the highest decorations in the gift of the Japanese and German governments. It was a measure of the cultural differences between them that the Japanese decoration was the Order of the Chrysanthemum, while the German medal bore the title of Knight's Cross of the Iron Cross with Oak Leaves and Swords.[16]

Yamamoto's replacement in command of the Combined Fleet was Admiral Mineichi Koga, a colorless battleship man who had spent much of his career in administrative positions and on the Naval General Staff. He flew out to Truk and occupied the cabin that had been Yamamoto's on board the *Musashi*. Initially Koga toyed with the idea of seeking another major fleet engagement, but of necessity he soon adopted the more realistic strategy of conserving his naval assets in the hope of inflicting a major defeat on the Americans when they neared the Philippines. It is unlikely that Yamamoto, had he lived, would have been able to do much else, for heavy Japanese losses of ships, planes, and especially pilots during the

Admiral Mineichi Koga assumed command of the Japanese Combined Fleet after Yamamoto's death in April 1943. Though eager to achieve the elusive "decisive battle" with the Americans, he was realistic enough to appreciate that the heavy losses endured during the Solomons Islands campaign made that impossible.

U.S. National Archives photo no. 80-G-35135

extended fighting for Guadalcanal had already changed the trajectory of the war in the South Pacific. Still, Yamamoto's funeral, one year and one day after the Battle of Midway, was a symbolic milestone, one that underscored the fact that the initiative in the Pacific had passed fully and irrevocably to the Americans.

———

ALLIED AIR SUPERIORITY was also a key factor in resolving the campaign in North Africa. There, Rommel's command had a new title: it was now Army Group Afrika, consisting of the German Fifth Panzer Army plus the Italian First Army. Despite the expansive title, Rommel and his army were in a tight spot. Montgomery's British Eighth Army was advancing from the east, while the Americans were approaching from the west. As noted in Chapter 16, Rommel sought to regain the initiative with an attack on the Americans at Kasserine Pass in February 1943, though he lacked the logistic support needed to follow up his initial success. Instead he turned to confront the British Eighth Army, hoping to forestall an attack from that quarter. His preemptive assault was unsuccessful, and by March he was squeezed into an ever-shrinking enclave around Tunis and Bizerte, where he found it increasingly difficult to keep his outnumbered forces supplied.

The initial German buildup in response to the Torch landings had relied heavily on airlift, but while an airlift could bring in the personnel, it could not carry the supplies necessary to sustain them. Only ships could do that. Of the 144,000 tons of ammunition and supplies the Axis sent into North Africa in January and February 1943, less than 6 percent of it (8,000 tons) came by air, and the rest had to cross the waist of the Mediterranean by sea; the flow of those supplies shrank dramatically as the Allies struck relentlessly at the Axis convoys by sea and by air. Axis sealift capability was strained to the breaking point by the need to support not only Rommel's men in North Africa but also German forces in Albania, in Greece, on the Greek islands, and even in the Crimea via the Black Sea. There simply was not enough Axis shipping to do all that. The German chief of supply and transport estimated that it would require 140,000 tons of supplies a month to sustain Axis forces in Africa, yet in February arriving supplies totaled less than half of that: only 64,000 tons; in March it was 43,000 tons, and in

April 29,000. The Germans continued to send additional men into Tunisia, adding thirty thousand more in March, but they could neither feed them nor fuel their vehicles.[17]

Indeed, Axis supply ships put to sea at all only at their peril. On March 7, the day after Rommel's abortive counterattack on Montgomery (and three days after Kenney's bombers destroyed the Japanese troop convoy in the Bismarck Sea), American B-25 Mitchell bombers, escorted by fourteen fighters, found an Italian convoy northeast of Cape Bon and sank all three of the cargo vessels plus an escort. Five days later, a squadron of British Beaufort fighters wrecked the tanker *Sterope*, carrying four thousand tons of precious fuel oil. The tanker remained afloat, but she had to limp into Palermo harbor, on Sicily's north coast, and never made it to Tunisia. Royal Navy submarines and surface ships operating from Malta swept up what the airplanes missed. Of the thirty-six ships lost by the Axis in the Mediterranean in March, Allied aircraft dispatched eighteen of them, and submarines accounted for sixteen more. Admiral Cunningham expressed amazement that "Italian seamen continued to operate their ships in the face of the dangers that beset them."[18]

Meanwhile, Allied heavy bombers hammered the ports where the ships were loaded and unloaded. Occasionally, a vessel that survived the perilous journey from Naples or Palermo was destroyed by Allied bombers as it attempted to offload its cargo in Tunis or Bizerte. By the end of March, the Italian merchant marine had been utterly devastated, and the few ships that were left often had to delay sailing due to the fuel shortage. Lacking transports, the Italians (like the Japanese at Guadalcanal) used destroyers and destroyer escorts to carry both men and supplies from Italy to Africa—at least two destroyers made thirteen consecutive round trips from Naples to Tunis. But the price was steep: thirteen Italian destroyers were lost while engaged in this duty. The extent of Axis desperation was evident in an exchange Dönitz had with Admiral Riccardi during a visit to Rome in mid-May. Dönitz suggested that "if there are not enough small vessels [to transport supplies], submarines will have to be used." For a man who had long insisted that submarines must not be used for any other purpose than sinking Allied shipping, this was a stunning assertion, and Riccardi was incredulous.

"To transport supplies?" he queried. "Yes," Dönitz replied, adding that "cruisers, too, must frequently make fast trips with supplies."[19]

They did, but it was not enough. In March, Italian soldiers in North Africa began to beg food from their German allies, and by April the Germans, too, were surviving hand-to-mouth. Almost as bad, their vehicles had enough fuel to travel only about forty miles, which rendered them largely immobile. Rommel's once-feared Afrika Korps had become effectively impotent.

Aware that his position in North Africa was untenable, on March 9 Rommel flew to Berlin to convince Hitler to change course. Hitler was unmovable, characteristically insisting that the forces in North Africa must fight to the last man and the last bullet. Rather than send Rommel back to oversee that denouement, however, Hitler instead ordered him to remain in Berlin and gave to General Hans-Jürgen von Arnim the thankless job of commanding the doomed forces in North Africa.

Von Arnim sought to make up for the lack of shipping by relying even more on air transport. In April, the Germans flew two hundred planes a day from Italy and Sicily into Tunisia. He employed twenty-one of the giant six-engine Me-323 transport planes as flying tankers, loading each of them with ten tons of fuel. On their first such flight on April 22, they were assailed by a swarm of British and American fighters that shot down sixteen of them. Given their cargo, they exploded spectacularly and fell into the sea burning like torches. Even had the airlift succeeded, however, it would not have been enough to solve von Arnim's fuel problem.[20]

Unaware that Hitler had ordered the soldiers of von Arnim's army to die in place, the Allies assumed that they would try to escape to fight another day. To ensure that did not happen, Cunningham ordered Operation Retribution, stationing destroyers on the escape route between Tunis and Sicily with orders to "sink, burn, and destroy. Let nothing pass." Nothing did. On May 13, von Arnim accepted the inevitable and surrendered his entire command of a quarter of a million German and Italian soldiers. Von Arnim himself spent the rest of the war in, of all places, Camp Clinton, Mississippi. In a meeting with Riccardi on May 12, Dönitz stated bluntly that "we . . . were defeated because our supply system failed."[21]

It had taken the Americans six months to push the Japanese from Guadalcanal, and it took the Anglo-American forces (along with the newly constituted Free French Army) six months to drive the Axis from Africa. To be sure, the fight for North Africa involved larger armies and greater casualties—seven thousand Americans fell on Guadalcanal, while more than seventy thousand Allied soldiers fell in North Africa.* A common factor, however, was that each campaign had depended heavily on sealift, and in both theaters it was Allied superiority in this key aspect of war production that had led to victory.[22]

American success on Guadalcanal and in North Africa turned the momentum of the war in the favor of the Allies in both theaters. The victory in North Africa also reopened the critical line of sea communications from Gibraltar to Suez. On May 17 an Allied convoy left Gibraltar and arrived in Alexandria nine days later without loss. With both of these campaigns now resolved, the pressing question for the Allies was where to go next.

IT WAS TO DISCUSS THAT QUESTION that the English-speaking Allies met in January while the North African campaign was still in progress. Convening at a small hotel near Casablanca in Morocco, Roosevelt, Churchill, and their advisors managed a number of successes. One was the contrived entente they imposed on the rival leaders of the Free French movement, Henri Giraud and Charles de Gaulle. Along with the death of Admiral Darlan the month before, the "shotgun wedding" of Giraud and de Gaulle cleared the way for French forces to join with the British and Americans for the rest of the North African campaign. By June, even Admiral Godfroy's naval squadron at Alexandria, effectively mothballed for nearly a full year, got under way and joined the Allied cause. It was also at Casablanca that Roosevelt publicly announced that the Allies would accept nothing less than the unconditional surrender of the Axis powers. His declaration provoked controversy both at the time and later, with critics suggesting

---

* The lead role taken by British forces in the campaign was reflected in the casualty rates. The British suffered 38,000 killed, wounded, and missing, while the French and Americans each suffered nearly identical losses of about 19,500 each.

that such a demand could undermine efforts inside the Nazi empire to over-throw their leaders and seek a negotiated peace. Whatever the merits of that criticism, a decision with more immediate consequences was the one Allied planners made to continue with the offensive in the Mediterranean by con-ducting a major amphibious assault on the island of Sicily: Operation Husky.[23]

This was a change from the assumption that once North Africa had been pacified, the Allies would focus on building up their forces in Britain for a cross-Channel invasion of German-occupied France. It had already become evident that a 1943 invasion of France was not possible, and the Americans therefore acquiesced to the British view that it was more pragmatic to employ the half million Allied soldiers already in North Africa to invade Sicily rather than to try to find the thousands of ships needed to carry them

Franklin Roosevelt and Winston Churchill look over some papers during a photo session at the Casablanca Conference in January 1943. Behind FDR are Ernest J. King and George C. Marshall. To Marshall's left is Admiral Dudley Pound. The vice admiral at right is Louis Mountbatten.

Naval History and Heritage Command

to England. Even so, it was a disappointment to the Americans, and sure to infuriate Josef Stalin. While the Red Army continued to carry the lion's share of the fight against the German army, the Anglo-American forces decided to target an Italian island in the Mediterranean. Churchill liked to talk about southern Europe as "the soft underbelly" of the Axis empire, but by invading Sicily the Allies were, as Ike's naval aide Harry Butcher put it, "only nibbling at the navel of the underbelly."[24]

The British had initially championed an invasion of Sardinia, which could have been a stepping-stone into southern France, but Sicily was closer and less likely to become another magnet for Allied resources. Still, Sardinia did play a curious role of its own in the Allied invasion plan. British Lieutenant Commander Ewen Montagu concocted a scheme to mislead the Axis into believing that either Sardinia, Greece, or both were next on the Allied target list. To do that, his team prepared identification papers for a mythical officer named William Martin, supposedly a major in the Royal Marines. Obtaining the body of a recently deceased Welshman, they fitted his corpse with a uniform, placed ID papers in his pocket, and handcuffed a sealed briefcase to his wrist. The briefcase contained false but official-looking correspondence that made oblique references to a forthcoming Allied invasion of Sardinia. The body was then dumped into the sea off Cadiz, Spain, near where a PBY Catalina had recently gone down. The body washed ashore in Spain, where Spanish authorities carefully extracted the papers from the briefcase, copied them, and turned the copies over to the Germans before carefully replacing the originals in the briefcase and releasing the body to the British embassy. The copies made their way all the way to Hitler, who was convinced of their genuineness. Though a study by the Italian Supermarina declared unequivocally that "the next Allied objective will be to take Sicily," Hitler insisted they were bound for Sardinia and the Peloponnesus. In the end, the Axis spread their reinforcements between both islands as well as Corsica.[25]

Roosevelt and Churchill met again in May only days after von Arnim surrendered his army. At that meeting, held in Washington and christened the Trident Conference, Churchill sought to build on the diplomatic triumph he had won at Casablanca by arguing that after Sicily was occupied, the Anglo-American forces should continue the campaign in the Mediterranean by invading Italy and knocking her out of the war. This time, Roosevelt and the Americans pushed back. The usually equable Marshall snapped that rather than knocking Italy out of the war, they should focus on "knocking Germany out of the war." King expressed concern that a move into Italy would create "a vacuum into which our forces would be sucked," as they had been in North Africa, though he might have noted that Guadalcanal had also proved to be just such a vacuum. This time, the Americans demanded a specific commitment from Churchill for a cross-Channel invasion in the spring of 1944. The fact that the Americans were now producing by far the lion's share of military goods for all of the Allied powers gave Roosevelt and Marshall great leverage in the discussions, and in the end Churchill felt compelled to pledge his support of an Anglo-American invasion of northern France on May 1, 1944.[26]

As for Italy, the heads of government decided that since so much depended on how successful Operation Husky was, it would be best to leave the decision about invading the Italian boot to the Allied theater commander, Dwight D. Eisenhower.[27]

CHAPTER 19

HUSKY

SICILY IS THE LARGEST ISLAND IN THE MEDITERRANEAN SEA. Shaped like a triangle, or like a pyramid leaning precariously to the right, its strategic importance derived from its position guarding the aptly named Sicilian Narrows. Its southwestern corner is less than a hundred miles from Cape Bon in Africa, and its northern apex points to the toe of Italy, less than two miles away across the Strait of Messina. The Allies might have sought to land near the tip of the pyramid in order to cut the Axis defenders off from the mainland and bag the whole lot. That would have been the bold move, but Allied planners were not feeling especially bold after the lengthy campaign in North Africa. Instead, the plan developed by what was called Task Force 141 (the room number at the Hotel St. Georges in Algiers where the team met) was to make a number of widely separated landings on both sides of the pyramid: the British near Catania on the east, and the Americans near Palermo on the west. The planners chose this option partly because Messina was beyond the range of Allied fighter planes from North Africa.

Dwight Eisenhower remained focused on the campaign for Tunisia and played almost no role in the planning process, essentially rubber-stamping the work that emerged. Ike's great strength as an Allied commander was his deft management of people. He was an adjudicator and a negotiator who could resolve—or at least minimize—nationalist disputes and soothe the personal quarrels of touchy army, navy, and air force commanders. It was just as well, for not everyone was pleased with the plan that Task Group 141 presented.[1]

Andrew Browne Cunningham, who had recently returned to the Mediterranean to replace Harry Harwood as overall naval commander, liked it, mainly because it called for the early seizure of Axis airfields and because it included the capture of Palermo, which had a useful harbor. Army commanders, however, found the plan both cumbersome and even dangerous, since it would put Allied ground forces on opposite sides of the island separated by a hundred miles of difficult countryside. Montgomery was especially critical, calling the plan "a dog's breakfast." He insisted on a more concentrated assault against the southeast corner of the pyramid, with the British landing on the eastern side near Avola, and the Americans on the southern side in the Gulf of Gela. A Canadian division would assault the beaches in between, near Pachino. Montgomery's plan scrapped the seizure of Palermo entirely.

Though Montgomery was subordinate to General Harold Alexander, the Allied ground commander, as well as to Eisenhower, he was nevertheless entirely comfortable presenting them with what amounted to an ultimatum. His plan, he told them, "is the only possible way" to conduct the invasion. "If we carry out the existing plan," he declared, "it will fail [while] the plan put forward by me will succeed." In his mind, the American and Canadian landings would provide a shield to protect the left flank of his own Eighth Army so that it (and he) could be the spear that thrust northward toward Messina. Though the American army had made impressive progress since its humiliation at Kasserine Pass in February, many Britons—Montgomery among them—continued to conceive of American soldiers as useful mainly in supporting roles and that when it came to hard fighting against German units only British soldiers could be counted on. He won the

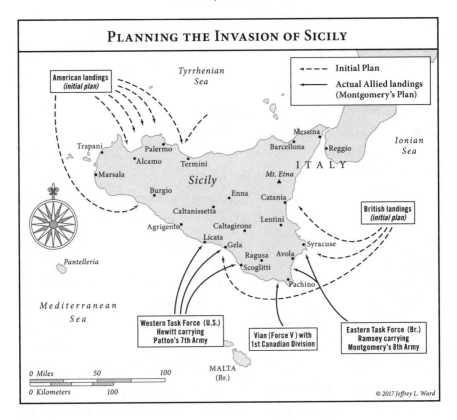

PLANNING THE INVASION OF SICILY

- - - - Initial Plan

──────► Actual Allied landings (Montgomery's Plan)

American landings *(initial plan)*

British landings *(initial plan)*

Tyrrhenian Sea

Ionian Sea

Messina
Barcellona
Reggio
Trapani
Palermo
Alcamo
Termini
ITALY
Marsala
Mt. Etna
Sicily
Burgio
Enna
Catania
Caltanissetta
Lentini
Agrigento
Caltagirone
Licata
Gela
Syracuse
Ragusa
Avola
Scoglitti
Pantelleria
Pachino

Mediterranean Sea

Western Task Force (U.S.) Hewitt carrying Patton's 7th Army

Vian (Force V) with 1st Canadian Division

Eastern Task Force (Br.) Ramsey carrying Montgomery's 8th Army

0 Miles   50   100

MALTA (Br.)

0 Kilometers   100

© 2017 Jeffrey L. Ward

argument but made few friends in the process. Cunningham complained to Pound: "I am afraid Montgomery is a bit of a nuisance; he seems to think that all he has to do is say what is to be done and everyone will dance to the tune of his piping." Fed up by the squabbling during one meeting, Cunningham declared, "If the Army can't agree, let them do the show alone."[2]

Cunningham's gibe underscored the obvious fact that the army—or, more properly, the armies—could *not* "do the show alone." As Hitler had learned in first planning and then scrapping Operation Sea Lion back in 1940, naval forces were the key element in any amphibious operation. As the slow asphyxiation of the Afrika Korps in Tunisia had proved, no army, however splendid or well led, could last long without logistical support from the sea. For the invasion of Sicily the first step involved bringing the tools of war from Britain and the United States to the several embarkation ports in North Africa through a literal gauntlet of Axis U-boats and aircraft.

The air threat was particularly menacing. Though the Regia Aeronautica was largely toothless by now, the Germans had accumulated nearly a thousand combat airplanes in Sardinia, Corsica, and Sicily, all of which were certain to attack Allied convoys heading for the embarkation ports.[3]

The Allied assault on Sicily—Operation Husky—involved seven Allied divisions: 160,000 men, 14,000 vehicles, 600 tanks, and 1,800 artillery pieces, plus food, fuel, and ammunition. To carry such an expedition to a hostile coast and sustain it there, the Allied naval force that was assembled dwarfed all previous invasions, including the Allied landings in North Africa. Altogether, some 2,590 ships, plus hundreds of small landing boats, would take part. Most of the vessels were American and British, though the armada also included ships from Belgium, the Netherlands, Greece, Norway, and Poland. It was the largest naval force ever assembled.[4]

Cunningham presided over all of it. He had been granted a fifth star in January and was now an Admiral of the Fleet (the same rank held by Dudley Pound and King George VI). That gave him one more star than Eisenhower, though he fully accepted Ike's command authority. As he had said during the campaign for North Africa, "We count it a privilege to follow in his train." Of course, Cunningham could not "command" his extensive naval force the way, for example, Admiral Lord Nelson had commanded at Trafalgar in 1805 or as Admiral of the Fleet Sir John Jellicoe had commanded at Jutland in 1916. Like Eisenhower, his job was to coordinate the hundreds of component parts, and he did so initially from his room in the St. Georges Hotel in Algiers. (The American naval commander, H. Kent Hewitt, now a vice admiral, had the room next door.) During the actual invasion, both Cunningham and Eisenhower went to Malta and occupied a bombproof headquarters in a tunnel under the harbor that was infested with sand fleas. For an old sea dog like Cunningham, it was stifling.[5]

On July 1, nine days before the invasion, Cunningham dispatched a covering force (dubbed Force H) of four battleships and two carriers eastward, partly as a diversion, partly in the hope of drawing out what was left of the Italian battle fleet. The Italians were not tempted. Quite apart from the persistent fuel shortage, a June 5 Allied air raid against the Italian naval base at La Spezia, 250 miles north of Rome, had damaged three of Italy's remaining battleships, and the Regia Marina had only three smaller battleships and five light cruisers that were operational. Moreover, having employed (and lost) so many destroyers in attempting to supply Axis forces in Tunisia, the Italians had only ten working destroyers to escort them. In addition, some elements in the Italian high command were already looking toward possible peace negotiations with the Allies and sought to preserve as much of the fleet as possible for bargaining leverage.

There were a handful of Italian submarines and a half dozen German U-boats in the Mediterranean, and they did their best to interfere with the gathering Allied armada. On June 22, the U-593 sank two American cargo ships, and a week later U-375 sank three transports of Admiral Philip Vian's Force V as it steamed from Gibraltar to Malta with the First Canadian Division. Though the loss of life was minimal, the Canadians lost much of their artillery. The Allies struck back, and over the next several weeks British and American escorts sank a total of thirteen Axis submarines— nine Italian and four German—greatly reducing the submarine threat.[6]

While Cunningham presided from Malta, operational command of the ships in the invasion force devolved upon two others: Bertram Ramsay, the hero of Dunkirk, led the eastern (British) task force, carrying Montgomery's Eighth Army, and Hewitt who had orchestrated the landings in Morocco, led the western (American) task force, carrying Patton's Seventh Army. Like Cunningham, Hewitt was concerned about the revised invasion plan. Without the early seizure of Palermo, he would have to sustain and supply Patton's three divisions over the beach. That meant landing supplies, food, fuel, and ammunition for seventy-five thousand men onto a beach without access to piers or heavy cranes. It was a daunting prospect, and that it was possible at all was thanks largely to an entirely new type of vessel whose very existence constituted a revolution in ship design and amphibious warfare.

EIGHT MONTHS EARLIER in North Africa, the Allies had relied on whatever vessels they could scrape together, including car ferries and passenger liners, for the Torch landings. The results had been sobering. As American Major General Lucian Truscott had noted, the landings were "a hit-or-miss affair that would have spelled disaster against a well-armed enemy intent upon resistance." Chaotic as it was to land the soldiers, an even more serious problem had been the offloading of jeeps, trucks, and especially tanks. As the British had learned at Dieppe, landing tanks onto a hostile beach was extraordinarily difficult. Those experiences led British and American ship designers to create vessels to fulfill that function. The result was the emergence of an entire family of specialized amphibious ships, each of which was routinely identified by an acronym.[7]

The largest and most important of them was the "landing ship, tank," or LST. Large, slow, and ungainly, LSTs were designed specifically to solve the problem of landing large numbers of heavy tanks on an enemy beach. Previously, that task had been the duty of a much smaller vessel called a "landing craft, mechanized" (LCM) or Mike boat, often referred to as a "tank lighter." While an LCM could carry one thirty-three-ton Sherman tank, it was self-evident that depositing tanks one at a time onto a defended beach was unlikely to overwhelm a determined enemy. By contrast, one LST could accommodate twenty Sherman tanks or thirty two-and-a-half-ton trucks (the famous "deuce and a half") in its cavernous hold, plus another thirty to forty jeeps or artillery pieces on its weather deck. Moreover, despite their great size, the LSTs had a flat bottom (as one veteran noted, they were "shaped like a bathtub") and could push right up onto the sand of the invasion beach. There they opened massive bow doors and deployed a short ramp, and the tanks and trucks could then drive out onto the beach. After discharging their cargoes, the LSTs closed their bow doors and retracted from the beach by using a powerful winch on the stern that hauled in on an anchor that had been dropped offshore. As Churchill himself noted, the LST "became the foundation of all our future amphibious operations."[8]

Before the war was over, the United States would build more than a thousand LSTs, but in April and May 1943, when the Allies assembled the plan for the invasion of Sicily, there were fewer than two hundred of them, and many of those were still undergoing sea trials. As a result, the invasion groups for Operation Husky sought to maximize each LST to its fullest capacity. During one pre-invasion exercise, Allied planners loaded one with

450 men, all of their equipment, and no fewer than ninety-four vehicles to see if it could still operate. It could.[9]

Another new amphibious ship was a smaller tank carrier that the British called a "tank landing craft" (TLC) and the Americans a "landing craft, tank" (LCT).* Half the length of an LST, and displacing only a third the tonnage, an LCT could carry up to five tanks or trucks in its open-air hold. These sturdy amphibs were especially useful for bringing tanks ashore during the first several waves, when it was too dangerous to expose the large, scarce, and expensive LSTs to shore-based artillery fire.

To carry the men ashore, the Allies would again rely heavily on the small landing boats, officially LCAs (British) or LCVPs (American), often (and herein) called Higgins boats. The newest versions had an armored drop-front bow so that the men did not have to climb out over the sides to get to

LST-77 landing M-4 Sherman tanks. Note the Higgins boats suspended from davits on her starboard side.

U.S. National Archives photo no. SC 189668

---

* Officially any vessel displacing more than 200 tons was a ship while vessels displacing less than 200 tons were craft. This rule of thumb was not universally applied, however, since both LCTs and LCIs displaced more than 500 tons but were still called craft.

LCT-410 loaded with ambulance trucks and jeeps heads for a beach in 1943.

U.S. Naval Institute

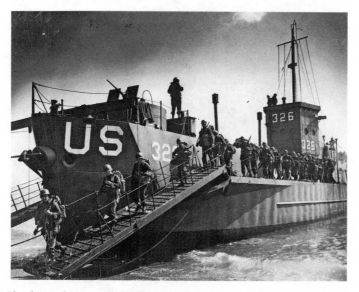

LCI-326 landing infantry. Called "Elsies" by their crewmen, these ships could embark two hundred soldiers at a time, though no vehicles.

U.S. Coast Guard

the beach. Small, cheap, and almost literally disposable, the Higgins boats were ideal for the first several assault waves, though in order to build up troop numbers quickly during subsequent waves, the Allies also had a larger troop carrier called a "landing craft, infantry" (LCI), which their crews affectionately called an LC or "Elsie." The most common type was an LCI(L), the second L standing for "large." Significantly bigger than the Higgins boats, an LCI(L) could carry up to two hundred soldiers at a time. They did not carry any vehicles, as they had no bow doors. After pushing up onto the beach, they deployed two narrow ramps, one on either side of the bow, and the embarked soldiers charged down those ramps onto the beach. Armed with only four 20 mm guns and mostly unarmored, an LCI was all but help-less against hostile shore fire, but it was indispensable for bringing in large numbers of infantry.[10]

The most creative of the new amphibious craft was something endowed with the awkward acronym DUKW, but which virtually everyone called "ducks." These were essentially amphibious trucks, thirty-one feet long

A DUKW amphibious truck carries a cargo of medical supplies ashore. (The cartons are marked "Stored Blood.") A variety of other amphibious ships, including LSTs, LCTs, and LSIs, can be seen in the distance.

U.S. National Archives photo no. SC 429012

and weighing six tons each, that could be loaded up with supplies—often ammunition—and drive off the ramp of an LST from several miles off-shore, chug to the beach at six knots under their own power, and then, like a true amphibian, crawl up onto the sand and keep going.[11]

Collectively, these new vessels were a game changer. Only a few years before, attacking from the sea meant that soldiers had to climb into whale-boats or other small craft, motor through the surf to the beach, clamber out over the thwarts, and charge the defenders with rifles. The development of these new specialized landing ships and landing craft redefined the character of amphibious warfare.

───────────

THE PROCESS OF EMBARKING the men, vehicles, and equipment into all these various ships was complex. The seven divisions (three British, three American, and one Canadian) that took part in the initial assault on Sicily departed from six different Mediterranean ports, and one assault force (Vian's Force V, with the Canadian First Division) came all the way from Scotland. The supplies and equipment had to be distributed with great care, not only among the various fleets but also among the individual ships, to ensure that no one vessel was indispensable. Moreover, each ship had to be combat-loaded; the items certain to be in immediate demand (weapons and ammunition) were loaded last so they could be unloaded first. The ships themselves then had to be marshaled into specific convoys, their routes plotted, and their exact speed carefully calculated so that, as Cunningham put it, "they arrived at their final destination at the right time and in the right order." Getting all the men and material to the appropriate loading port, stowing everything on board, and organizing the ships into flotillas to assault twenty-six different landing beaches from six different ports was an extraordinarily challenging administrative puzzle. As Cunningham put it in his memoir, "The complications were endless."[12]

As this was both a joint and a combined operation, communication and collaboration between the various services was essential. It helped that the Royal Navy was primarily responsible for carrying British men and equipment, while the U.S. Navy carried Americans, though there were exceptions. Hewitt's command included thirty-seven Royal Navy ships, and Ramsay's command had twenty-five American Liberty Ships. Though everyone spoke the same language (more or less), misunderstandings and disagreements—between the army and navy, between the army and the air forces, and between the navy and the air forces—occurred every day. One common difficulty was that the generals kept adding new requirements to the ships' manifests. At one point, Rear Admiral Alan Kirk, who commanded one of the American naval task forces, explained to his opposite number in the army, Major General Troy Middleton, "You must remember, these ships have *not* got rubber sides. You can't stretch them beyond a certain point."[13]

One example of the kind of misunderstandings that emerged occurred within the task force assigned to carry the twenty-seven thousand Americans of Major General Lucian Truscott's 3rd Division to the beach at Licata, on the south coast of Sicily. The ships were under the command of Rear Admiral Richard L. Conolly, and in general Conolly and Truscott got on quite well, but there was one hiccup during the loading process. Truscott noted on the map that the ground beyond the invasion beach was mountainous, with few roads, and he decided that it would be useful to have some pack animals to help carry his division's equipment through the rugged terrain. He therefore ordered that eight or ten burros should be loaded onto each of the LCIs in Conolly's flotilla.[14]

When Conolly learned about it, he was outraged. An Annapolis graduate, he could hardly believe that Truscott was seriously suggesting that he should carry army mules in his navy ships. Conolly had previously served under Halsey in the Pacific and more recently on King's staff in Washington, and given those leadership examples, it is not surprising that he reacted immediately and directly. Calling Truscott on the secure phone line, he read him the riot act. "You have loaded a bunch of damn mules on my ships," he thundered over the phone. "And you have done it without saying a word to me!" Truscott tried to pacify him: "If I have failed to mention it to you, it is simply an oversight which I deeply regret." Conolly was having none of it. "I will be the laughing stock of the Navy," he said. "I won't stand for it." Truscott agreed to remove the burros, but he also pushed back: "You don't want them on your ships. I am going to have them off. But what I am wondering now is what I shall do tomorrow if you should object to carrying infantry mortars, or tanks, or any other item of equipment which the Navy does not usually transport." As Truscott remembered the incident, there was a full minute of silence on the other end of the phone before Conolly spoke again. "Dammit, General," he said, "you are right. We will carry the goddam mules and anything else you want carried." In the end, the burros proved useful in the difficult terrain of the Sicilian mountains. To the credit of both men, this was the only source of disagreement between them, and Truscott later wrote in his memoir, "No Army commander ever had a Navy opposite number more able than Admiral Conolly."[15]

Cooperation with the air forces was less harmonious. British Air Marshal Sir Arthur Tedder, who took over as Mediterranean Air Commander in February, achieved something of a miracle by integrating the Royal Air Force and U.S. Army Air Forces into a single command for the campaign. Moreover, the Allies would have overwhelming air superiority, with upward of four thousand aircraft of all types in the theater. On the other hand, both Tedder and his American counterpart, Carl "Tooey" Spaatz, were determined to maintain their administrative independence. Unwilling to become mere adjuncts to the army or navy, they insisted that it was not necessary for them to coordinate with either service, for their job was to rid the skies of enemy planes; once they achieved that, the Allied forces could proceed on their missions with impunity. Hewitt lamented that requests for air support had to be submitted to air force headquarters for consideration, and even then there was no assurance they would be met. He bemoaned the fact that "the air show is to be run entirely independently." Kirk wished that "we had our own air under our own control," and Rear Admiral John Lesslie Hall Jr., who commanded the landing force for Gela, was even more outspoken: "In my opinion any system that doesn't let the fellow who's responsible for winning the battle either ashore or afloat have the aircraft under his command is just like a man trying to fight without his right hand." Patton, who was the overall commander of the American invasion force, begged Hewitt to add at least one aircraft carrier to the American assault armada. "You can get your Navy planes to do anything you want," he wrote to Hewitt, "but we can't get the Air Force to do a goddam thing!"[16] In the end, the only American "carrier" in the invasion force was a modified LST on which the crew erected an ersatz flight deck so that two tiny single-seat Piper Cubs could conduct reconnaissance.

JUST PRIOR TO THE INVASION, the Allies seized the small Italian islands of Pantelleria and Lampedusa, which sat athwart the intended invasion route. After being bombed for nineteen consecutive days, the seven thousand dispirited Italian soldiers on those islands surrendered before the first Allied troops came ashore. That cleared the way for the invasion convoys to assemble west of Malta on July 9. Another preliminary move was the dropping of paratroopers and glider troops behind the beaches. Due largely to high winds and poor visibility, most of the gliders missed their landing zones, and fully half of them landed in the sea.* One utterly confused glider pilot made it onto solid ground in what he thought was Sicily, only to discover that he had landed on Malta, fifty miles to the south.[17]

The ships, too, suffered from what Hewitt called "extremely adverse weather conditions." With waves cresting at twelve feet, green water cascaded over the bows of many of the landing ships, especially the smaller LCTs and LCIs. Under such conditions, some of the ships could make only two and a half knots, which put the whole operation behind schedule. The soldiers on board suffered miserably. Truscott remembered that "every craft was loaded with sea sick, sea weary, and thoroughly drenched soldiers." Many of the officers and men recalled the fate of the Spanish Armada in 1588, undone less by the enemy than by the Channel storms. An anxious Eisenhower considered a postponement but, assured that such storms frequently blew themselves out quickly, and concerned that a postponement would only add more confusion, decided to stick to the schedule. The ships

---

* The unwillingness of the Allied air forces to fully integrate with the army or navy yielded tragic consequences. Although a key element of the campaign was a paratroop and glider drop behind the beaches, the air staff did not provide naval commanders with timely, detailed information about the flight paths the planes would use. Cunningham warned that without such information his ships might open fire on the unarmed air transports. On the night of July 11, nervous gunners on the Allied ships opened fire and shot down twenty-three of the transports, killing sixty airmen and eighty-one paratroopers, including Brigadier General Charles L. Keerans Jr. The historian Carlo D'Este has called this "one of the worst examples of inter-service cooperation of the war."

struggled forward to the rendezvous position and arrived off their assigned beaches a few minutes after midnight on July 9–10.[18]

The three American task forces (code-named Joss, Dime, and Cent) each carried a reinforced U.S. Army division, and they targeted locations along the southern coast of Sicily in the Gulf of Gela, while the Royal Navy task forces (designated Acid and Bark) carried British divisions to beaches on the eastern side of the island.* Force V under Vian brought the Canadian First Division all the way from the Clyde Estuary in Scotland to a beach near the Cape Passaro headland, on the southeast corner of the Sicilian triangle.

Two of the six landings were shore-to-shore operations in which fully loaded landing craft steamed from the port of embarkation directly to the landing beach. Conolly's Task Force Joss, assigned to land on beaches near the small village of Licata, was one of these. Truscott's men and their vehicles loaded up in Bizerte (burros and all) onto thirty-eight LSTs, fifty-four LCIs, and eighty LCTs and crossed the Mediterranean in two convoys escorted by cruisers and destroyers accompanied by minesweepers and patrol craft—276 ships altogether.[19]

Most of the landings, however, were ship-to-shore operations, in which men and equipment were carried across the waist of the Mediterranean in large transports, then disembarked into Higgins boats for the final run ashore. On some ships, the men climbed into the landing boats while they were still suspended alongside and then were lowered into the water. In the volatile sea, the fully loaded landing craft swung alarmingly out and back again during the descent. A British officer of the 51st Highland Division recalled the experience: "Down, down we went, towards the swirling waves; every now and then our steel landing-craft, weighing some fourteen tons, would thud and crash against the ship's hull. Then, with a splash, we were in the water, rising and falling in an alarming manner." On one of the American LSTs, a davit broke while the men were climbing aboard, and the entire boatload was dumped into the water. Nine men died.[20]

---

* The origin of these particular code names is not clear. Hewitt himself later wrote, "I have never learned the genesis of strange code names JOSS, DIME, and CENT, assigned by the Supreme staff planners."

On most of the transports and LSTs, however, the landing boats were lowered empty and the men climbed down into them on rope nets. That, too, proved challenging, especially in an unsteady sea in pitch darkness with each man carrying two canteens of water, a gas mask, several days of K-rations, and extra ammunition, as well as a rifle. The small boats along-side rose and fell wildly as the men groped their way down the slippery rope ladders in the dark. Mistiming the final jump could, and did, result in severe bruising and the occasional broken leg. On the American transport *Jefferson*, some of the manila rope ladders broke, not once but several times, each time spilling men into the water or leaving them hanging on a broken net.[21]

The weather had already played havoc with the schedule, and there was another long wait now as the men who loaded first had to circle, sometimes for hours, until all the boats were filled and assembled into assault waves. Jack Belden, a combat journalist going ashore in the second wave, recalled, "We went into a circle, going round and round in the shadow of our fleet till, certain that every boat was present, we broke out of the circle formation and headed in a line" toward the beach. To describe that journey, Belden (perhaps armed with a thesaurus) wrote that the boat "pitched, rolled, swayed, bucked, jerked from side to side, spanked up and down, undulated, careened, and insanely danced on the throbbing, pulsing, hissing sea." As H-hour passed, the admirals became nervous. Vian impatiently blinkered a signal: "Will your assault ever start?"[22]

Finally at about 4:30 a.m., about an hour behind schedule, the first soldiers hit the beach. By now the quarter moon had set, and dawn was still a half hour away. The shoreline was barely perceptible as a slightly darker shadow on the dark sea. The only light came from the red tracers of machine guns on the high ground behind the beach. There were few losses from this desultory fire, though at Licata the LCI-1 was disabled, lost steerageway, and broached stern-first on the sand. Undaunted, the embarked soldiers scrambled over the stern and dropped onto the beach while navy gunners on the ship returned the fire of the machine guns. Overall, resistance was light and the landings mostly routine—or as routine as an amphibious landing under fire on an unfamiliar shore in pitch darkness can be.[23]

Twenty miles to the west, at Gela, Task Force Dime under Rear Admiral Hall landed the men of the American 1st Division, already famous as the "Fighting First," or the "Big Red One" for their bright red shoulder patches. The Allies had hoped to use the pier at Gela to disembark, but the Italians had blown it up, which meant that all the men and equipment had to land on the beaches. Several miles beyond that, Task Force Cent under Rear Admiral Kirk landed the men of Major General Middleton's 45th Division near Scoglitti. There, a number of the landing craft grounded on unmarked sandbars while they were still a hundred yards or more off the beach, forcing the men to climb over the sides of their Higgins boats and trudge to the beach through three to five feet of water. Despite that mishap, the Americans suffered more from confusion and uncertainty than from enemy fire. One soldier recalled that one group of Italians manning a machine gun position only 150 yards from the beach "simply refused to fire on us and allowed themselves to be captured."[24]

The British beaches on the east side of the island were in the lee of the Pachino Peninsula, where the weather was less intrusive, though even there the men in several of the LCTs had to bail almost continuously to keep their craft afloat. As on the American beaches, confusion was a more serious obstacle than the defenders. Some of the troop transports had anchored six miles farther offshore than planned, making the long trip to the beach in the Higgins boats even longer. In the dark, many of the small landing boats got lost and headed for the wrong beach. Units became intermingled, and efforts to sort it all out ashore often added only more confusion.

British Rear Admiral Rhoderick McGrigor commanded the ships that landed the 5th and 50th Divisions under Lieutenant General Miles Dempsey on several beaches in a ten-mile stretch between Syracuse and Avola, while Thomas Troubridge, who had supervised the landings at Oran the previous November, commanded Force Bark, which landed the 51st Highland Division further south at Pachino. Cruisers and destroyers supported all these landings, and the Canadians, arriving just on the other side of the headland from Pachino, received additional support from an odd-looking vessel the British called a "monitor." HMS *Roberts* was essentially a light cruiser with a gigantic and incongruous-looking 15-inch gun turret on her foredeck. She fired those enormous shells toward the Pachino airfield, which was the Canadians' first-day objective.[25]

After the Higgins boats and LCIs brought the men ashore, the LCTs began landing the first tanks. A few of the tank carriers hung up on the sandbars, and the bigger LSTs had even more trouble. Several grounded well off the beach—too far for the heavy tanks. In anticipation of that, some of the LSTs carried steel pontoons that could be hooked together to form a floating causeway. While effective, it was also slow and tedious, and the tanks and self-propelled artillery pieces were consequently delayed. Against more serious resistance, that might have proved disastrous.[26]

In this early phase of the battle, the greatest danger came from Axis aircraft, which began to assail the invasion fleet while it was still dark, and continued to do so throughout the morning. The gunners on the ships fired blindly into the black sky, "aiming" their guns at the sound of the propellers. Having been promised robust Allied air support, many of the gunners accompanied their AA fire with angry curses about the absence of their own air forces, most of which were busy bombing Axis airfields. The American destroyer *Maddox* was an early victim, when just past sunrise a Stuka dive-bomber landed a bomb on her stern that penetrated to her magazine, where it exploded; she went down in less than two minutes. The Germans also sank the *Talumba* off Syracuse, though the British hospital ship was clearly marked, and late that afternoon an Me-109, attacking out of the setting sun, put a bomb into the fully packed LST-313 just as it was pushing up onto the beach, turning it into "a raging inferno and deathtrap." The next afternoon, a Junkers 88 landed a bomb on the Liberty ship *Robert Rowan*, which was carrying a full load of ammunition, producing a spectacular explosion. None of this, however, halted the landing process.[27]

Other problems did slow the landings. One was land mines on the beaches, which disabled a number of bulldozers trying to carve a road inland. Elsewhere, the beach sand was so soft that many of the wheeled vehicles could not find purchase. To deal with that, the Allies had brought long rolls of steel mesh to create pathways for the trucks and jeeps, though this also created a bottleneck for unloading. Finally, while most of the men and vehicles made it safely ashore, they were not necessarily on the beach

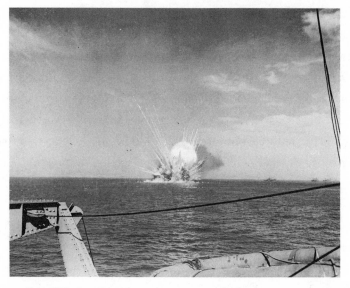

The Liberty Ship SS *Robert Rowan*, carrying a cargo of ammunition, explodes off Gela Beach after being hit by a bomb from a Junkers 88 on July 11, 1943.

Naval History and Heritage Command

that had been assigned to them. Navy beachmasters did their best to direct the ships to their landing positions, army officers supervised the unloading, and other army officers directed traffic on the beach—occasionally at cross purposes. By the afternoon, the beaches had become so crowded that vessels in later waves seeking a place to land occasionally gave up and returned to the transports. A combat journalist arriving on a beach near Gela saw "abandoned trucks, overturned jeeps and smashed boats, and on the sands there were blown-up cars, a tank with its tread off, heaps of bedding rolls and baggage with soldiers sitting on them waiting for transportation, mechanics struggling over broken-down vehicles, and supply troops gathering up broken-open boxes of rations." It looked confusing, and it was. Yet somehow it all got sorted out, and by midday the men, tanks, and trucks were moving inland.[28]

THERE WERE SIX AXIS DIVISIONS IN SICILY—two German and four Italian—a total of nearly 250,000 men, though only one of the Italian divisions was battle-ready. Rather than defend the island at the shoreline, the Axis plan was to wait until it was evident exactly where the Allies were making their main assault, then launch a concerted counterattack to drive them back into the sea. That attack began the next morning at eight o'clock when the Hermann Göring Division launched a three-pronged assault on the American landing beach east of Gela. Spearheaded by heavy Tiger tanks, the attack posed a serious threat, in part because the American tanks had been delayed, and because many of the Allied anti-tank guns had been destroyed in the explosion of LST-313. The crisis came around eleven o'clock when the German tanks reached the coastal highway, less than two miles from the beach, and threatened to cut the American salient in half. A report from the front line back to 1st Division headquarters put the matter succinctly: "Situation critical. We are being overrun by tanks."[29]

It was naval gunfire that saved the day for the Allies. Four American destroyers—*Beatty, Cowie, Laub,* and *Tillman*—closed on the beach and opened fire, sending 1,176 rounds of rapid-fire 5-inch shells at the German tanks. The light cruiser USS *Boise* also joined the fight. After her mauling in the Battle of Cape Esperance the previous October, the *Boise* had limped all the way back to Philadelphia for a refit that took five months. She left there on June 8, and now, only a month later, she was off the beach at Gela, halfway around the world from Guadalcanal, firing 6-inch airburst shells into German infantry formations. The Allied ships had to suspend fire briefly when the opposing forces on land became so intermingled that the navy gunners could not distinguish friend from foe. By early afternoon, newly arrived Allied tanks joined the fight, in some cases driving straight from the landing ships into the battle. By two o'clock, the Germans began to withdraw and the assault petered out. A colonel in the Hermann Göring Division subsequently reported that "naval gunfire forced us to withdraw."[30]

In addition to direct fire (that is, shooting at targets they could see), the navy also engaged in indirect fire (shooting at targets they could *not* see). Two factors made this possible in the summer of 1943. One was the development of more effective radar systems that allowed ships to maintain a continuous and accurate track of their position. The other was the preparation of gridded maps and charts that enabled spotters on land to communicate to the naval gunners off shore precisely where the enemy targets were. On the cruisers and destroyers, data about the bearing and range to the target were fed into a mechanical computer, which aligned those data with the ship's speed and course to keep the fire-control director on target. Up to now, army commanders had been skeptical of the value of naval gunfire once the soldiers had left the beach. Before the invasion, army planners had told Hewitt that "naval gunfire is not designed for land bombardment." The events of July 11, 1943, totally discredited that assumption.[31]

The second Axis counterattack, this one west of Gela, came from the Italian Livorno Division, and it, too, was spearheaded by tanks. Patton, who had just come ashore from Hewitt's command ship, *Monrovia*, saw a column of Italian tanks advancing toward him from the high ground behind the beach. Turning to his naval aide, he told the young ensign, "If you can connect with your Goddam Navy, tell them for God's sake to drop some shell fire on the road." The ensign radioed the coordinates to the cruisers and destroyers, and within minutes 5-inch and 6-inch shells began landing among the tanks. The shells came from two destroyers—*Shubrick* and *Jeffers*—as well as the light cruisers *Savannah* and, again, the *Boise*. With five turrets of three guns each, the light cruisers could fire fifteen rounds every six seconds. That yielded a storm of more than a thousand rounds of 6-inch shells in less than five minutes and practically annihilated the Italian column. Afterward, artists on the *Boise* added the silhouettes of Italian tanks to those of Japanese ships and aircraft painted on her superstructure. Even Patton was impressed, noting in his war diary, "The naval gunfire support...has been outstanding."[32]

In fact, it was decisive. Hewitt asserted that "the cruisers really saved the day," though it was Eisenhower who offered the most comprehensive analysis: "Naval gunfire was so devastating in its effectiveness as to dispose finally any doubts that naval guns are suitable for shore bombardment." An old tank commander himself, Eisenhower went so far as to say, "The fire power of vessels assigned to gunfire support exceeded that of the artillery landed in the assaults, and...permitted a greater concentration of fire than artillery could achieve in the early stages."[33]

WITH THE BEACHES SECURED, the Allies began to advance inland. The British headed north along the east coast of Sicily to confront the main strength of the German defenders, soon reinforced by additional units rushed over from Italy. At Catania, the battleship *Warspite* and the light cruiser *Euryalus* supported the British ground attack, but instead of exploiting this resource further, Montgomery sought to outflank the German defenders by executing a maneuver through the rugged interior of Sicily. In North Africa, his execution of a "left hook" through the desert had proved decisive, but a similar move here dramatically slowed his advance.

For their part, the Americans headed west, capturing the ancient city of Agrigento and its nearby harbor at Porto Empedocle. Eager to pursue the enemy and to enlarge the role of his Seventh Army, Patton flew back to North Africa to ask the Allied ground commander, General Harold Alexander, for permission to expand his initial assignment. Alexander, a benign and gentlemanly officer of the old school, disliked confrontations and gave way at once before Patton's impetuous request. Thus unleashed, Patton and the Americans rounded the western corner of the Sicilian triangle and headed up the west coast to Palermo, which fell on July 22. By now, most Italians were thoroughly sick of the war, and as Patton toured the city he was greeted by cries of "Down with Mussolini!" and "Long live America!" Allied bombs and the retreating Germans had wrecked most of the harbor facilities at Palermo; the explosion of an ammunition ship in the harbor had created a tidal wave that lifted two oceangoing freighters right out of the water and deposited them on the quay. Nevertheless, the Allies had the port functioning again within a week.[34]

Meanwhile, Patton, who conceived of the campaign in Sicily as a competition with the British, raced eastward toward Messina. To get around enemy strong points, instead of turning the landward flank as Montgomery sought to do, he employed amphibious landings to turn the seaward flank, and American LSTs landed a tank force behind the Axis defensive line north of Palermo. German forces launched a counterattack, and once again naval gunfire was decisive in routing it. An American journalist on the scene recorded the words of a GI who was grateful for the support. "The good old navy," he said. "Jesus, there ain't nothin' like navy guns." Cunningham agreed, describing Patton's use of amphibious end runs as "a striking example of the proper use of sea power."[35]

The crucial role played by Allied naval forces in the conquest of Sicily was diluted somewhat by the fact that most of the German troops managed to escape across the Strait of Messina before they could be captured. Though 100,000 Italians were taken prisoner, most of them happy to be out of the war, more than 60,000 Italians and 55,000 Germans, plus 9,789 vehicles and fifty-one tanks, made their way across the narrow strait to Italy. Kapitän zur See Gustav von Liebenstein employed an ersatz fleet of ferries and transports in a daylight maneuver as daring and dramatic as the British evacuation of Crete or the Japanese evacuation of Guadalcanal. British motor torpedo boats and Allied air forces made a half-hearted attempt to interdict this traffic, but with little success. Still, Sicily was now in Allied hands, and that had an immediate and dramatic strategic and political impact. On July 24, the Fascist Grand Council in Rome voted no confidence in Mussolini, and the next day King Victor Emmanuel III removed him from office, placing him under de facto arrest and naming Pietro Badoglio as his successor.[36]

CHAPTER 20

TWILIGHT OF TWO NAVIES

A LMOST FROM THE DAY HE DECLARED WAR, Benito Mussolini had planned to use a nearly intact Italian fleet as leverage in the negotiations that he thought might begin soon after the fall of France. Instead, the conflict expanded into a war of attrition—and exhaustion—that cost him a significant portion of that fleet plus all of Italy's African colonies, most of its merchant marine, and now Sicily, too. By then, Mussolini himself was gone, replaced by Pietro Badoglio, a former army chief of staff, who (like Mussolini) continued to wear a uniform as the head of government. Though Badoglio announced publicly that Italy would adhere to the Axis alliance, almost at once he sought to open a channel to the Allies to discuss an armistice. He did not want to surrender; he wanted to change sides. The timing, however, would have to be perfect: he was unwilling to jump into the Allied camp until Anglo-American armies were in a position to protect his country from German reprisal. It would be a delicate maneuver, and, as events would prove, he did not have quite the political dexterity or the necessary leverage to carry it off.

Gone, too, was Arturo Riccardi, the admiral who had led the Regia Marina after December 1940 and who was tied too closely to the Mussolini regime to keep his job. His replacement was Admiral Raffaele de Courten, a former deputy chief of Staff who had no close ties to Mussolini, though he was German on his mother's side and spoke the language flawlessly. Perhaps because of that, or simply to keep his cards close to his vest, Badoglio did not inform De Courten of his clandestine efforts to switch sides.

At first Badoglio hoped the Vatican might act as an intermediary in his dealings with the Allies. That initiative had not progressed very far, however, when it became evident that the Anglo-American forces were actively preparing an invasion of the Italian mainland.

Back in May at the Trident Conference, Churchill had energetically campaigned for such a move, though at the time the conferees had postponed the decision. Now with Sicily overrun, they chose to go ahead with the invasion, which was code-named Operation Avalanche. That added a new sense of urgency to Badoglio's efforts and provoked a decision by Brigadier General Giuseppe Castellano to take matters into his own hands.[1]

Castellano resented the condescending way the Germans treated him and all other Italian officers. He had played a minor role in toppling Mussolini, and now he obtained permission from Badoglio to approach the Allies directly. Traveling incognito to Madrid, he presented himself at the British embassy, where he suggested that Italy was willing to join the Allies. News of his proposal was quickly forwarded to London and Washington, where there was some initial skepticism. Roosevelt thought it best to treat the approach as an offer to surrender and let Eisenhower handle it. Churchill was initially reluctant to delegate the negotiations to "the general commanding in the field," though in the end he agreed to let Eisenhower "deal with any Italian authority which can deliver the goods."[2]

Eisenhower sent his deputy, Major General Walter Bedell "Beetle" Smith, disguised as a British businessman, to meet with Castellano in Lisbon, instructing him that he should make no promises and tell the Italians that their only option was to surrender unconditionally and, in Eisenhower's words, "depend upon the decency and sense of justice of the Allied governments."[3]

In Lisbon, Smith made it clear to Castellano that he was there as a military man to accept an Italian surrender, not to negotiate. On the other hand, he did have several specific demands, one of which was that "the Italian government must, at the hour of the Armistice, order the Italian Fleet and as much of their merchant shipping as possible to put to sea for Allied ports," and in particular that "no Italian warships are to be allowed to fall into German hands." Castellano protested mildly, noting that the language "implied the *surrender* of the fleet" while his purpose was not to capitulate so much as to join the Allies in the war against Nazi Germany. Smith stood firm, insisting, "The subject under discussion must be considered a military capitulation and not any arrangement for the participation of Italy in the war on our side." Castellano also expressed concern about the requirement that Italian warships sail to an Allied port given that it was possible, he told Smith, that at least some of the ships did not have enough fuel to make it to one.[4]

De Courten, who commanded the navy in question, was unaware of any of this. He and his officers were still making plans for the Squadra Navale, the main Italian fleet at La Spezia in the Ligurian Sea near Genoa, to confront the Allied invasion armada that was gathering in several North African ports as well as at Palermo in Sicily. He knew that when the fleet left on that mission, it would be the last gasp of the Regia Marina, for not only would the Italians be hopelessly overmatched, but there was the inescapable fact that the ships had enough fuel for only one last fleet action.[5]

De Courten was not the only one being kept in the dark. For obvious reasons, Badoglio also kept the pending agreement secret from the Germans, though they had already begun to suspect his fidelity. Even before Castellano went to Madrid, Hitler told Dönitz that the Italians were stalling, "biding their time in order to come to terms with the Anglo-Saxons before an open break." Though he had felt no compunction invading the Soviet Union while it was still a German ally, Hitler professed to be "disgusted" that "the Italian government is double-crossing us." Dönitz suggested that under such circumstances, the Italian navy should be brought "under German leadership" as soon as possible. He proposed replacing the current leaders of the Regia Marina with "a new command with a good

German staff," even naming a few of the younger Italian admirals who might be persuaded to cooperate. Hitler agreed, and ordered two initiatives. One was a mission to rescue Mussolini, who was being held as a prisoner by the Badoglio government, and the other (Operation Achse) was a scheme for Rommel's command to surround and disarm Italian military units and to seize the warships at La Spezia upon forty-eight hours' notice.[6]

Unaware that his navy was the object of secret plotting by both sides, De Courten continued to organize a final, desperate sortie against the Allied invasion fleet. On August 6, he notified Dönitz of his intention to confront the Allied invaders with a force of three battleships, as many light cruisers, and eight destroyers. Dönitz took De Courten at his word, telling Hitler that the Italian navy was "probably not informed about any political intrigues and is co-operating with us in good faith." Hitler was skeptical, telling Dönitz that his "intuition" told him that the Italians were planning "treason."[7]

That was true enough, though in Rome Badoglio sought more assurances from the Allies before inking the deal. He wanted the Allies to land a substantial force in mainland Italy *before* Italy came over to their side. In particular, he wanted a strong Allied force to protect Rome from German retribution. He instructed Castellano to insist on both things when he met again with Beetle Smith at Palermo on August 31.

Smith refused to make any commitments. The Allies had made their plans, he told Castellano, and they were not subject to modification at the behest of the Italian government. Nor would Smith share those plans. Castellano then asked if, rather than steam to an Allied port, the Italian fleet might go instead to La Maddalena, an Italian naval facility off the north coast of Sardinia. Again the answer was no. In effect, Smith told him: here is the deal, take it or leave it. Castellano contacted Badoglio on a secure line to ask him. Terrified as he was of German retribution, Badoglio badly wanted a deal, and he authorized Castellano to sign the agreement.[8*]

---

* The negotiations were complicated by two additional factors. One was that the limited time frame led to the signing of a "short form" agreement that did not include specifics on many issues. The other was the arrival of a second Italian negotiator, General Giacomo Zanussi, who opened his own dialogue with the Allies. All this left room for subsequent disagreement and accusations of duplicity by both sides.

MATTERS CAME TO A HEAD during the first week of September. At 4:00 a.m. on September 3—the fourth anniversary of Britain's declaration of war—British forces crossed the Strait of Messina to land on the toe of Italy against negligible opposition. That same afternoon, Badoglio called De Courten into his office to tell him that "His Majesty has decided to ne- gotiate for an armistice." That was less than fully candid, of course, for an agreement had already been concluded, one that included a clause requir- ing "Italian warships of all descriptions, auxiliaries and transports" to be "as- sembled as directed in ports to be specified by the Allied Commander-in- Chief," and for "all Italian merchant shipping" to be turned over to the Allies in good condition. Not only did Badoglio withhold that information from his navy chief, but he ordered him not to tell anyone else, even his own chief of staff, Admiral Luigi Sansonetti, that negotiations were being considered.[9]

Three days later, Badoglio called De Courten into his office again, this time to tell him that the deal had been struck; an armistice would be announced sometime between the tenth and fifteenth of the month. He handed De Courten a copy of "Promemoria No. 1," which outlined his orders in case of an attempted German takeover. Those orders authorized the Regia Marina to defend itself against German naval forces, but they also specified that De Courten was not to share that information with any of his officers, who were at that moment preparing to sortie against the Allied invasion armada, which was already at sea.[10]

De Courten was understandably furious that the government had bar- gained away his fleet without consulting or even informing him, and he delivered a stiff formal protest to General Vittorio Ambrosio, head of the Italian Joint Chiefs (Comando Supremo). In an effort to mollify him, Ambrosio suggested that he could still send the fleet to La Maddalena in Sardinia even though Smith had explicitly rejected that alternative. De Courten remained embittered, but he was a professional who felt, in the words of a fellow officer, that "the Navy . . . could only comply with the deci- sions made."[11]

Compliance would have to wait, however, until the matter was made public, for until then De Courten was bound by secrecy. Badoglio had told him that the public announcement would be made on September 11, the night before the expected Allied invasion on the twelfth. That was the date Castellano had surmised based on the few hints Smith had dropped, and he had passed it on to Badoglio as fact. It therefore came as a surprise to everyone on the evening of September 8 when, in a radio address broadcast from North Africa, Eisenhower announced the armistice. "The Italian Government," Eisenhower read in his flat midwestern accent, "had surrendered its armed forces unconditionally.... Hostilities between the armed forces of the United Nations and those of Italy terminate at once."[12]

The announcement was a blockbuster even for those few who were expecting it. Badoglio thought he had until the twelfth to prepare his government. He also thought that an Allied division would land in Rome to secure the city from German reprisal either before or soon after the announcement. In fact, the Allies had planned such a landing by the 82nd Airborne Division, but they called it off at the last moment when American Brigadier General Maxwell Taylor, on a secret mission to Rome, radioed back that in his view Italian units would not be able to secure the airfields where the Americans were supposed to land, and that in any case a single American division could not hold Rome against the German forces arrayed nearby.[13]

According to the agreement, Badoglio was supposed to confirm the armistice with a radio announcement of his own soon after Eisenhower's. Now that the moment had come, however, Badoglio hesitated. He felt that the Allies had not been forthcoming with him by refusing to name the date or location of the invasion or landing a force to hold Rome. Then, too, during the past week, the arrival of tens of thousands of German troops under Rommel made it evident that if he *did* confirm the armistice, Rommel's forces would effectively take over the country, or at least the northern two-thirds of it. Under these circumstances, Badoglio lost his nerve. He sent a cable to Eisenhower claiming that the disposition and strength of the German forces near Rome made it impossible "to accept an immediate armistice."[14]

Eisenhower's response was immediate and unequivocal. "I do not accept your message," he wired back. "Failure now on your part to carry out the full obligations of the signed agreement will have the most serious consequences for your country." It now seemed possible that a disavowal of the armistice could put Italy at war with *both* Germany and the Allies. In the end, it was King Victor Emmanuel who decided: it was too late to change sides again, he said, and he instructed Badoglio to make the announcement, which he did at 7:45—one hour late. The only orders issued to Italy's armed forces were vague instructions to defend themselves if the Germans attacked. With that, both Badoglio and the king left Rome for Brindisi, a port city on the heel of the Italian boot, near Taranto. Absent clear leadership from the top, and short of fuel, ammunition, and in some cases even shoes, the Italian army, which might have provided significant help to the Allied invaders, remained passive and inert. Many soldiers, assuming their war was over, simply threw down their arms and went home.[15]

Badoglio's announcement caught all of the Italian uniformed services flat-footed. At Regia Marina headquarters, De Courten's chief of operations was incredulous. "I do not believe it!" he shouted. "Can it be possible, that we know nothing about it, even as our battleships are getting ready to leave for Salerno?" As he spoke, the phone rang. It was Sansonetti calling to tell him that it was true. The fleet was to sortie as planned, but not for battle—instead, it was to sail to North Africa for internment, and it should do so at once before the Germans had a chance to seize the ships.[16]

Italian naval officers had only moments to determine a course of action. According to the armistice terms, they were to put to sea immediately: the ships at La Spezia for a rendezvous with an Allied fleet near Bône, on the North African coast, and those at Taranto for Malta. Some Italian officers recoiled at such orders and announced that, rather than turn their ships over to the British, they would prefer to scuttle them, as the French had done.

At La Spezia, Admiral Carlo Bergamini, who had succeeded Iachino in command of the Squadra Navale, called his officers together to convince them otherwise. "This is not what we imagined," he told them, "but this is the course by which we must now steer..., because what counts in the history of a people is not dreams and hopes...but the consciousness of duty carried out to the bitter end." He ordered the ships to prepare for sea, and discipline held. Three battleships, including Bergamini's flagship, the new 46,000-ton *Roma*, plus six light cruisers and eight destroyers all got up steam. As they got under way near midnight, Rommel's soldiers were entering the

Admiral Carlo Bergamini bore the politically and morally awkward responsibility of turning the Squadra Navale over to the Anglo-American forces in September 1943.

Courtesy of Alamy

outskirts of the city. They arrived at the harbor to find that the quarry had flown.[17]

Dawn found Bergamini's flotilla, augmented by three more cruisers from Genoa, heading south along the west coast of Corsica. His course suggested that he still planned to head for La Maddalena, though if so, that option disappeared when he learned that German forces had occupied the city and its harbor in response to Badoglio's radio announcement. There was nothing for it now but to steam on to meet the British off North Africa.

Though Bergamini's force was a powerful one, it lacked air cover. The Regia Aeronautica had literally ceased to function, and Allied air forces were busy covering the invasion beaches south of Salerno. When German bombers arrived overhead at about eleven o'clock that morning, the Italians initially fought them off. That afternoon the planes were back, and this time they carried a new, and until now secret, weapon: the FX-1400 guided bomb, popularly known as the "Fritz X." Launched from several miles away, beyond the range of a ship's anti-aircraft fire, these flying bombs with a six-hundred-pound warhead could be guided to the target by radio commands from an operator in the bomber. They were, in effect, air-launched guided missiles. One of them hit the *Roma* near her forward magazine and set the ship afire. After twenty minutes, the fire reached the magazine. A witness on the cruiser *Attilio Regolo* remembered the explosion so vividly he described it in the present tense: "Terrible yellow-red flame bursts out and envelops all the bow part of the beautiful ship, while a gigantic pillar of smoke climbs up to several hundred of metres into the air and thousands of pieces of iron blown up now continue to fall into the sea." The brand-new *Roma*, which had never been in a battle or even fired her guns in anger, sank quickly. Bergamini, who had carried out his duty "to the bitter end" as promised, was one of more than thirteen hundred killed. The *Italia* and two of the cruisers were also hit, though not fatally, and they continued on with the rest of the flotilla to their rendezvous off North Africa, where a British squadron escorted them into Bizerte. In a nod to *The Decline and Fall of the Roman Empire*, the code name for the British reception and escort of the surrendered Italian fleet was Operation Gibbon.[18]

The squadron at Taranto under Admiral Alberto Da Zara, composed of the battleships *Andrea Doria* and *Caio Duilio* plus two cruisers and a

The Italian battleship *Roma* photographed not long after her launch in 1942. The flagship of Admiral Bergamini's Squadra Navale, she never had an opportunity to fire any of her nine 15-inch guns in battle before being sunk by a "Fritz X" guided bomb on September 9, 1943, while en route to North Africa to intern herself to the British.

Naval History and Heritage Command

destroyer, also got under way that night, heading for Malta. There was a tense moment outside the harbor when the outbound Italian squadron passed an inbound British task force of two battleships and several cruisers, carrying the British 1st Airborne Division to the occupation of Taranto. As Samuel Eliot Morison put it, "One trigger-happy gun pointer on either side might have set off a minor Jutland." Instead, the two fleets steamed past each other without incident: one headed for conquest, the other for internment.[19]

Several of Italy's smaller warships made their own way to Allied ports; a handful found their way to Freetown, Sierra Leone. Not all of them got away, however, for many lacked the fuel to put to sea and others simply refused to go. Most of those were scuttled by their crews to prevent them from being seized by the Germans. The Germans were furious, both at the escape of the main fleet and at the "treachery," as they saw it, of those who scuttled their ships. They arrested the captains of all the ships that were sabotaged and summarily executed them by firing squad.[20]

It was not quite the end of the war for the ships of the Regia Marina, at least one of which had a curious subsequent history. The officers and men of the *Giulio Cesare* resented having to turn their ship over to the British, and en route to Malta they effected what amounted to a mutiny, seizing control of the ship with the intention of sinking her in deep water. They relented only after the captain solemnly pledged that he would not allow the British to take possession of the ship under any circumstances. He was able to keep that promise, though it was a near thing. As part of their ongoing effort to placate Stalin, the Allies had promised the Soviets an Italian battleship, a cruiser, and eight destroyers as their share of the spoils of war. Churchill felt obligated to satisfy Stalin on this issue if he could, but he was also reluctant to betray his newest ally. He therefore offered to give Stalin a British battleship, the *Royal Sovereign*, and Roosevelt agreed to contribute an American cruiser. The eight destroyers, Churchill told Stalin, would be sent after the D-Day landings. Stalin agreed to the substitution, and the *Giulio Cesare* remained under the Italian flag. (The story does not end there. In 1949, the Russians returned the borrowed *Royal Sovereign* to Britain and laid claim to the *Giulio Cesare*. This time they got it, and it served five years in the Soviet Navy as the *Novorossiysk*. In the middle of the night on October 28–29, 1955, she exploded and capsized in Sevastopol, likely the victim of an unswept German mine. Her destruction spawned a persistent legend that Italian navy frogmen had destroyed her to redeem the honor of the Regia Marina.)

Most of the Italian cruisers and destroyers, still under their Italian officers and still flying the Italian flag, joined the Allied fleet in the Mediterranean, where they served out the war along with ships from Belgium, France, Greece, Holland, Norway, and Poland, as well as the United States and Britain. The Germans did secure a few of the Italian warships that never left their harbors, including the heavy cruisers *Bolzano* and *Gorizia*. (A year later, on the night of June 21, 1944, British and Italian frogmen boldly stole into Spezia Harbor and sank both of them.) An additional benefit for the Allies was the bloodless acquisition of two of Italy's best harbors, at Taranto and Brindisi, the latter city now the de facto capital of Badoglio's government. De Courten joined the king and Badoglio at Brindisi on September 12.

That same day, German special forces conducted a spectacular rescue of Mussolini from a remote ski lodge on a mountain peak in the Apennines. Hitler set the former Il Duce up in the small northern Italian town of Salò, on Lake Garda, as the head of what was called the Italian Social Republic.

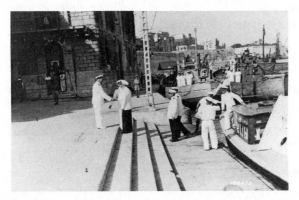

In accordance with the surrender agreement, Italian Admiral Alberto da Zara and his staff (in dark slacks) arrive at the Customs House in Valletta Harbor in Malta on September 10, 1943.

U.S. National Archives photo no. SC 188573

As a result, there were now two Italian governments: one at Brindisi, headed by King Victor Emmanuel and backed by Allied arms, and one at Salò, headed by Mussolini and supported by the German army.[21]

An epilogue to this drama took place on September 29 in Valletta harbor, in Malta. There, on the deck of the battleship HMS *Nelson*, and surrounded by the rubble of the city that had been bombed by both Germans and Italians for most of three years, Badoglio and Eisenhower, both in uniform, formally signed the Instrument of Surrender, though the full terms were kept secret until after the war as a salve to Italian sensibilities. Witnesses to the ceremony included both De Courten and Cunningham, but not Castellano, whose actions had done much to lead to this moment. Two weeks later, on October 13, the Badoglio government at Brindisi formally declared war on Germany.

BY THEN THE ALLIES HAD SECURED THEIR FOOTHOLD on the Italian mainland, though it had not been easy. The Combined Chiefs of Staff in Washington were chary of creating another magnet for manpower and resources in the Mediterranean, and they deliberately limited Eisenhower's assets for Operation Avalanche. He was to have a total of twenty-seven divisions, but only with the stipulation that after the landing, and within no more than two months, he was to send seven of them to England as part of the buildup for the invasion of northern France in the spring. As for naval forces, he was to have only those ships already in the Mediterranean. That was not a problem in terms of warships, for, with the Regia Marina neutralized, the Allies had unchallenged supremacy at sea. The difficulty was with the landing ships and landing craft. The loss of so many of them during the invasion of Sicily left Eisenhower with a small margin of error for the invasion of Italy. At Quebec, the Combined Chiefs acknowledged that "landing ships and craft will…be the bottleneck limiting the full scope of assault in approved operations."[22]

Like Husky, Avalanche was an Anglo-American operation, with the British seizing a beach just below Salerno and the Americans a beach fifteen miles further south, near the ancient Greek city of Paestum. Hewitt commanded the 627 transports and amphibious ships, and Royal Navy Vice

Admiral Sir Algernon Willis commanded the covering force of four battleships, two carriers, and twenty destroyers. En route to the landing beaches, the embarked soldiers all heard Eisenhower's announcement, played over the ships' loudspeakers, reporting that the Italians had surrendered "unconditionally." There was cheering and celebrating throughout the fleet, and Hewitt worried that it "had a bad psychological effect on some of the troops, who got the idea that they were going to be able to walk ashore unopposed." Admiral Hall, commanding the covering force for the American beaches, recalled seeing some soldiers toss away their grenade belts assuming they would no longer be necessary. Their officers knew better. The practical result of the agreement was that instead of discouraged Italians, the invaders would now confront battle-hardened Germans.[23]

Rommel executed Operation Achse—essentially a German takeover of Italian military assets—immediately after Badoglio's radio announcement, and it made him the de facto military commander of northern Italy. Luftwaffe General Albert Kesselring established effective control of southern Italy. Though Hitler initially had no plans to defend the southern half of the Italian boot, Kesselring was convinced it could be done, and at the very least, he wanted to keep open the roads past Salerno and Naples so that the 26th Panzer Division could evacuate Calabria in the Italian toe. Hitler agreed, and Kesselring gave the assignment of holding Salerno to the newly constituted Tenth Army under General Heinrich von Vietinghoff, a veteran of the Russian front, who, in a tribute to the Führer, sported a little brush mustache.[24]

The beach at Salerno is a thirty-mile-long crescent of sand and shingle twenty miles south of Naples. Allied planners had considered landing further north, closer to Rome, but as in Sicily, they did not want to go beyond the reach of land-based Allied fighters. American General Mark Clark exercised overall command, and despite earnest pleading from Hewitt, he decided against a preliminary air or naval bombardment in the hope of catching the enemy by surprise. It was a mistake, for the Germans were not surprised, and the lack of a preliminary bombardment meant that Vietinghoff's soldiers were ready and waiting. At one point, as American landing craft neared the beach on September 9, a loudspeaker on shore announced in perfect English: "Come on in and give up. We have you covered."[25]

It was no idle boast. As the first wave of Americans hit the beach, they encountered fire from heavy tanks, machine guns, and mobile 88 mm artillery pieces. The 88s in particular proved perilous, and as at Gela, Allied destroyers and light cruisers closed the shore to challenge them. Off the American beach at Paestum, the light cruisers *Philadelphia* and *Savannah* were especially active. The *Philadelphia* broke up a counterattack by thirty-five German tanks, destroying seven of them and sending the rest fleeing back into the hills; the *Savannah* fired 645 rounds of 6-inch shells in response to eleven separate requests for direct fire support. The Royal Navy monitor *Abercrombie* hurled her 15-inch shells at the German artillery in the hills until she struck a mine and had to retire. In spite of all this, the fighting ashore was fierce and Allied progress slow. One GI was overheard muttering, "Maybe it would be better for us to fight without an armistice."[26]

The 88s were a problem at the northern beach, too, and Royal Navy Commodore Geoffrey Oliver, whom Cunningham characterized as "calm, imperturbable, and completely optimistic," sent the destroyers *Laforey*, *Loyal*, *Tartar*, and *Nubian* shoreward to take them on. The *Nubian* repulsed one German tank attack almost single-handedly. Several smaller Hunt-class destroyers also joined the fight, and even Admiral Conolly got into the act. As a rear admiral, Conolly was senior to Oliver, though he had agreed to serve under him during the landing. Noting a particularly active German artillery position, and unable to raise the destroyers on the radio, Conolly ordered his command ship, the USS *Biscayne*, which had two 5-inch guns, to close on the beach and take it under fire. That earned him the nickname "Close-in Conolly," a moniker that followed him for the rest of his life.[27]

Once again, air support was more problematic. Salerno had been chosen because it was within reach of Allied land-based fighters, yet because of the long flight time from Sicily, Tedder said he could provide only nine long-range fighters over the beachhead at any given time. For that reason, Cunningham had requested the addition of several of the small American-built escort carriers that had been transferred to the Royal Navy under Lend-Lease. Pound authorized sending four of them under Philip Vian, all of them named as if they were riding to hounds: *Stalker*, *Hunter*, *Attacker*, and *Battler*, plus the aircraft repair ship *Unicorn*. Each carried eighteen Seafire fighters, naval versions of the more famous Spitfire.* During the first three days of the invasion, they flew a total of 713 sorties over the beach, and though half of them were lost, they provided the bulk of the air support for the troops until landing strips could be seized ashore.[28]

On the beaches, the fighting was, as Eisenhower reported to Marshall, "touch and go." A combined Ranger unit under American Lieutenant Colonel William O. Darby seized the rugged Sorrento Peninsula, north of Salerno, but Vietinghoff's Germans stubbornly held the high ground beyond the beach, and their artillery kept the invaders pinned down inside that deadly amphitheater. The twin landing beaches were too far apart for mutual support, and at one point Clark seriously considered consolidating them by evacuating one or the other, though the commanders who would have to execute such a perilous move talked him out of it. Hewitt told Clark that beaching a loaded LST and then emptying it was vastly easier than beaching an empty LST, loading it up, and then trying to retract. Instead, covered by a thick smoke screen laid by Allied destroyers, the transports and LSTs continued to shuttle in men, supplies, and ammunition to both beaches. Some of the smoke got sucked into the ventilation intakes of the LSTs and triggered coughing spasms among the embarked soldiers.[29]

The Germans struck back at the transports and especially the gunfire support ships with the small, swift E-boats (one of which sank an American destroyer on September 10), though the greatest danger continued to come from German aircraft, many of them armed with the new radio-controlled bombs. One such bomb hit the *Savannah* on September 11, damaging her so badly she had to be towed to Malta, eventually making her way back to the United States for extensive repairs. Another hit the British cruiser *Uganda*, the bomb penetrating through all seven decks and exploding under her hull. She, too, limped off to Malta under tow. Other ships suffered damage from near-misses. The Germans also bombed two hospital ships, one of

---

* Because of the short flight decks on the escort carriers, many of the Seafires were damaged upon landing because they rocked forward at the end of the deck run, which bent the tips of their propeller blades. The solution was to cut nine inches off the end of each blade. That slightly reduced their top speed but enabled them to land without incident.

An unidentified U.S. Navy destroyer, photographed from the deck of the light cruiser *Philadelphia*, lays a smoke screen off the beachhead at Salerno during the invasion. The *Philadelphia* played an important role at Salerno, breaking up a German tank attack on September 9.

U.S. National Archives photo no. 80-G-83243

which sank. The losses among the gunfire support ships were so great that there was a real possibility the troops ashore would not be able to hold their positions. With laconic understatement, Hewitt noted, "The situation ashore and afloat was far from favorable."[30]

Encouraged by the slackening fire from offshore, Vietinghoff ordered a ground attack on September 12 that was designed to split the Allied enclave in half. The panzers advanced down the valley of the Sele River and came within two miles of the beach before they were repelled by artillery ashore aided by the naval gunfire. In his after-action report, Cunningham claimed primacy for the ships, asserting, "It was the Naval gunfire, incessant in effect, that held the ring when there was danger of the enemy breaking through to the beaches."[31]

Concerned by the losses offshore, Hewitt asked Cunningham for some battleships. Cunningham sent him the *Valiant* and the "grand old lady" *Warspite*, whose 15-inch guns blasted the German gun positions in the hills. Even then, the Allied invasion might have been stillborn but for Rommel's conviction that the main defensive effort should be made further north. Because of that, he declined to send additional divisions to Kesselring, and on September 16 (the day after *Valiant* and *Warspite* arrived) the Germans pulled back from the hills, effectively giving up the fight for the beach. Kesselring reported to Berlin that it was necessary to fall back in order "to evade the effective shelling from warships." That same day, two radio-guided bombs hit the *Warspite*, which was towed to Malta with a five-destroyer escort.[32]

Released from their beachfront enclave, Allied ground forces moved north to capture Naples, yet because the Germans had thoroughly sabotaged the harbors at both Salerno and Naples, Allied reinforcements and supplies had to continue to come in over the beach via the amphibians. Cunningham described the beach at Salerno as an "ants' nest" with "streams of boats and landing-craft passing to and fro between the ships and the shore." Over the ensuing three weeks, a nearly constant rotation of LSTs, LCIs, and LCTs delivered 225,000 men, 34,000 vehicles, and 118,000 tons of supplies over the beaches.[33]

Axis resistance at Salerno was more robust than any of the Allied planners had foreseen, and the key to eventual Allied success both there and throughout the Mediterranean was unchallenged control of the sea. Though German planes employing the new FX-1400 guided bombs caused serious problems, the Allies were able to maintain enough naval gunfire from the sea to protect the troops ashore, and enough sealift capability to keep them supplied both during the invasion and over the ensuing days and weeks. The Luftwaffe was not toothless, however, as became evident on December 2 when 105 German Junkers 88 bombers attacked Allied ships anchored at Bari, sixty miles north of Brindisi on the Adriatic coast, and sank twenty-seven Allied transport and supply ships. It was the greatest Allied maritime loss of the war.*

---

* One of the Allied victims at Bari was the Liberty ship *John Harvey*, which was carrying a cargo of mustard gas bombs, sent there as a contingency in case the Germans resorted to gas warfare. When the *John Harvey* was hit, the released mustard gas caused more than six hundred friendly casualties. The Allies naturally sought to keep the incident a secret, including the very existence of mustard gas bombs, but there were so many casualties that the U.S. Chiefs of Staff were forced to acknowledge the circumstances in February 1944.

In Sicily the successful Allied landings had led to a swift conquest of the island. Not so this time. The Allies had their foothold, but the campaign for Italy would grind on for another year and a half. As George Marshall had feared, the decision to invade the Italian boot created another black hole for Allied men and resources as well as for the scarce, valuable, and essential landing ships. That would have a dramatic effect on Allied planning for the rest of the war.

THERE WERE THIRTY DEGREES OF LATITUDE and forty degrees of temperature difference between the beaches at Salerno and the fjords of northern Norway, where the last concentration of Axis capital ships was berthed at Altenfjord, near the North Cape. Back in January when Hitler had replaced Erich Raeder with Karl Dönitz, he had ordered the scrapping of Raeder's beloved surface fleet. "Large ships are a thing of the past," he had declared, and the *Gneisenau*, *Hipper*, *Leipzig*, and other large warships were decommissioned, their guns removed, and their crews sent to other duties. Yet despite a lifelong commitment to U-boats, Dönitz talked Hitler out of eliminating the surface navy altogether, and in the fall of 1943, three ships in particular constituted what naval strategists called a "fleet in being" at Altenfjord. They were the battleship *Tirpitz* (sister ship of the *Bismarck*), the oversized battlecruiser *Scharnhorst*, and the venerable *Lützow*, laid down back in 1929 as the *Deutschland*. They seldom left port, but their very existence compelled the Royal Navy to maintain a superior force in the North Sea to keep an eye on them.[34]

Then on September 6 (the same day Badoglio informed De Courten of the pending agreement with the Allies), all three ships, along with ten destroyers, left Altenfjord to conduct the first major sortie by the Kriegsmarine in fourteen months. Their objective was Spitsbergen, an ice-covered and nearly barren Norwegian outpost half way between the Arctic Circle and the North Pole. Spitsbergen had a coal mine and a weather station but was otherwise an unimposing target. Very likely, Dönitz ordered the raid simply to remind the Allies that there still was a Kriegsmarine without having to put the ships in any serious jeopardy. The Germans smashed up the coal mine and the weather station and returned to their base at Altenfjord on September 10.[35]

The next day, six British midget submarines, called X-craft in the Royal Navy, left Loch Cairnbawn in Scotland under tow by conventional subs. Only forty-eight feet long with a five-and-a-half foot beam, the X-craft each had a crew of four—all of them volunteers. They carried no torpedoes; their only weapon was a pair of detachable two-thousand-pound mines that they could deposit underneath the hull of an enemy ship. It took them ten days to reach Altenfjord under tow, and two of them were lost en route. By then, only one of the three German ships was still at her berth. The *Lützow* had been sent back to Germany for repairs and would remain in the Baltic as a training ship for the rest of the war. The fact that the *Lützow* was able to make it from the North Cape to the Baltic without being intercepted and destroyed led to considerable frustration and finger-pointing in Whitehall. Nor was the *Scharnhorst* in her anchorage. Her commanding officer, Captain Friedrich Hüffmeier, disappointed by the ship's poor marksmanship during the bombardment of Spitsbergen, had taken her out for gunnery drills. The *Tirpitz*, however, was still anchored in Kaa Fjord, a small appendage of Altenfjord.[36]

In the middle of the night on September 22, 1943, lookouts on the big German battleship spotted "a long, black submarine-like object" alongside. It was too close to bring any of the ship's guns to bear, so the Germans opened up on it with small arms and hand grenades. The "submarine-like object" was the X-6, which was forced to the surface by the German onslaught, and her four-man crew taken prisoner, though not before her skipper, Lieutenant Donald Cameron, jettisoned her mines. The British prisoners were taken below and provided with hot coffee and schnapps. Several of the German crewmen who spoke English complimented them on their boldness, though one noted that the Englishmen seemed to be frequently checking their watches. Meanwhile, another of the mini subs, the X-7, actually collided with the *Tirpitz* while submerged, then passed underneath it and successfully planted both of her mines under her hull.[37]

At 8:12, two giant explosions, less than a second apart, rocked the *Tirpitz*. According to a witness, "the whole ship heaved several f[ee]t out of the water and bounced down again with a slight list." Despite a giant hole in her bottom, the *Tirpitz* did not sink, largely because her captain, Hans Meyer, had ordered the closing of her watertight doors immediately after sighting the X-6. The damage, however, was significant. One of the massive gun turrets on the *Tirpitz* was lifted off its bearings and smashed down again, wrecking the mechanism. And the ship's turbine engine had been shaken from its bed. The X-7, which was responsible for the damage, was attempting to leave Kaa Fjord when it got entangled in the torpedo nets and had to surface. Her commander, Lieutenant Basil Place, immediately looked toward the *Tirpitz* to see if it had sunk. When he saw her still afloat, he pronounced it "tiresome." He and his crew were also taken prisoner aboard the German battleship, where their captors were significantly less hospitable than before.[38]

The *Tirpitz* could not be fully repaired in Norway, where there was no crane large enough to lift the damaged turret. On the other hand, if she tried to make it back to Germany, it would be a fraught and dangerous trip, and would cede the North Sea to the British. Hitler and Dönitz therefore decided to leave her where she was, mainly to keep the British guessing about her seaworthiness. Back in London, it was not immediately evident how badly the *Tirpitz* had been hurt, though from decrypted messages culled from Ultra they learned that she would be out of service for at least six months. That made the *Scharnhorst* the only operational German capital ship in the North Sea.[39]*

THAT SAME FALL, the Royal Navy got a new command structure. Back in May, Churchill had appointed Admiral Sir Bruce Fraser to command the Home Fleet. Churchill had lost confidence in John Tovey, not only for a perceived lack of aggressiveness (his usual criticism) but also because Tovey had been impertinent enough to question the effectiveness of strategic bombing, a program that Churchill still hoped could win the war, obviating the need to invade the Continent. That led Churchill to brand Tovey as "a stubborn and obstinate man," and to exile him to a new job as

---

* In the spring, the British struck the *Tirpitz* again, this time with aircraft. On April 3, 1944, Barracuda bombers hit the battleship with fourteen bombs, three of them weighing sixteen hundred pounds. The *Tirpitz* never again put to sea as a functioning warship.

commander at The Nore, at the mouth of the Thames, in charge of coastal defense. A few months later, Churchill offered Fraser the navy's top job as First Sea Lord. It had become increasingly evident that Pound's failing health would not allow him to continue in the job, and he submitted his resignation in October.* Fraser declined the appointment and urged Churchill to appoint Andrew Cunningham, who was significantly senior and much beloved throughout the Navy. "I believe I have the confidence of my own fleet," Fraser told the prime minister, "Cunningham has that of the whole Navy." Remarking that Fraser's attitude did him credit, Churchill elevated Cunningham to the top job. Ironically, it was another Cunningham, Admiral Sir John Cunningham (no relation), who took over A. B. Cunningham's command in the Mediterranean.[40]

That fall Churchill reinstituted the North Cape convoys. The neutralization of the *Tirpitz* had removed a serious surface threat, and with the coming of winter, the shorter days meant there was almost no daylight in the Arctic Sea; even at midday there were only a few hours of weak twilight. That would limit enemy air strikes, though the Luftwaffe was not the threat it once had been because most of the squadrons had been pulled out of Norway to fight the Russians. The U-boats were also limited during the Arctic winter by the fierce weather, which made it all but impossible for the small 750-ton submarines to operate effectively on the surface.

The immediate impetus to restart the convoys, however, was Stalin's persistent complaining, which had become so confrontational recently as to verge on rude taunts. Stalin no doubt treated his lackeys that way, but it was a poor tactic to employ with Churchill. The prime minister informed the Russian leader that the supply convoys were not an Allied obligation, but rather a symbol of Anglo-American resolve. Stalin's response to that was so offensive that Churchill refused to receive his message officially, handing it back to the Russian ambassador. Still, given that the Red Army continued to bear the brunt of the land war, it was clearly good strategy to keep it well supplied.[41]

---

* Pound lived for only a few more weeks, suffering a massive stroke in October, and dying, fittingly, on Trafalgar Day: October 21, 1943.

The first of the renewed convoys (JW-54A) got under way from Loch Ewe, on the west coast of Scotland, on November 15. It consisted of nineteen transports escorted by nine destroyers, a corvette, and a minesweeper. In addition to the close escort, Fraser also went to sea with a substantial part of the Home Fleet in case the *Scharnhorst* tried to interfere. It did not, and the first two convoys, entirely unmolested, arrived safely at Murmansk.[42]

Once again, Hitler was infuriated. Increasingly frustrated by the sustained progress being made by the Red Army in the East, the Führer was desperate to cut off its supplies. During a meeting at Berchtesgaden on December 20, he asked Dönitz what could be done about it. Like many of Hitler's lieutenants, Dönitz was eager to bring the Führer news of a success, especially a naval success. If the *Scharnhorst* could dash out of Altenfjord, rough up an Allied convoy, and get back safely, Hitler would look more favorably on the navy. With such a sortie in mind, Dönitz promised Hitler that "the *Scharnhorst* and destroyers of the task force will attack the next Allied convoy headed from England for Russia via the northern route."[43]

Two days later, on December 22, a German reconnaissance aircraft spotted and reported the third of the Allied winter convoys (JW-55B), and Dönitz ordered the northern force commander, Admiral Erich Bey, to prepare the *Scharnhorst* for sea. The orders reflected both Dönitz's eagerness to accomplish something against the convoys and his concern not to lose his last operational capital ship. He told Bey, "The opportunity must be seized [and] *Scharnhorst*'s superior firepower affords the best chance of success." At the same time, however, he emphasized that the *Scharnhorst* should not be put at risk. "If a superior enemy is encountered," he wrote, "you are to disengage."[44]

Bey interrupted the crew's Christmas dinner to put to sea with the *Scharnhorst* and five destroyers just before 8:00 p.m. on December 25. He was soon heading north at twenty-five knots, though the sea conditions were such that his destroyers could barely keep up as their bows crashed through the oversized waves. In the subzero temperatures, the sea spray froze instantly on the gun barrels and the upper works of all the ships until they resembled fantastic ice castles.

This photo of the main battery guns of the *Scharnhorst* covered in ice was taken in the Baltic in 1939–40, and only hints at the kind of conditions that prevailed near the North Cape during the Christmas battle of 1943.

Naval History and Heritage Command

As he headed north, Bey did not know that in addition to the convoy and its escort, two other Royal Navy surface forces were also at sea on that Christmas night. One of them, approaching from the east, consisted of three cruisers and several destroyers under Vice Admiral Robert Burnett, who was covering the returning (empty) ships of the first two winter convoys. The other, approaching from the west, was Fraser's covering force, which included the battleship *Duke of York*. The unsuspecting Bey was at the center of a triangle of converging enemy forces.[45]

At midnight, the heavy weather forced Bey to reduce speed. His destroyers were not only falling hopelessly behind, they were in peril of swamping, and Bey broke radio silence to report it. Perhaps he hoped that Dönitz would order a recall. If so, he was disappointed. Dönitz replied: "If destroyers cannot keep at sea, possibility of *Scharnhorst* completing task alone . . . should be considered," and added unhelpfully, "Decision rests with Admiral commanding." Combined with the earlier order to break contact on the "appearance of strong enemy force," Bey's orders seemed to be that Bey should press the issue forcefully, alone if necessary, but that he should not risk his ship, and that the responsibility was entirely his.[46]

The code breakers at Bletchley Park intercepted Bey's message to Dönitz, and only three hours later, just before four in the morning, Admiralty House was able to inform Fraser that the *Scharnhorst* was at sea and heading north toward the convoy. Fraser decided to break radio silence himself to order the convoy to turn northward, away from the *Scharnhorst*, and he simultaneously ordered his own force, including the battleship *Duke of York*, to increase speed from nineteen to twenty-four knots. Even at that speed, he was unlikely to catch the *Scharnhorst* unless Burnett's cruiser group could somehow slow her down.[47]

To do that, Burnett had one heavy cruiser, the *Norfolk*, which had played a key role in the pursuit of the *Bismarck* three years earlier, plus two light cruisers. Leaving the westbound convoy in the care of the destroyers, he charged toward the most likely position of the *Scharnhorst*, and at 8:40 a.m. on December 26, the radar on his flagship, the light cruiser *Belfast*, reported a contact. Twenty minutes later, a lookout on the *Sheffield* called out, "Enemy in sight." At 9:30, Burnett opened fire.[48]

Bey was caught completely by surprise. Though Fraser had broken radio silence, the Germans at B-Dienst had failed to intercept it. The atrocious weather kept German reconnaissance planes grounded, and though the *Scharnhorst* had radar of her own, it was based on prewar technology and had limited range; on top of that, one of the two sets was not working. Now ambushed by Burnett's three cruisers, Bey's immediate instinct was to turn away, though the *Norfolk* got in two quick hits with her 8-inch guns, one of which destroyed the antennas of the *Scharnhorst*'s only working radar set. Bey might have stayed and fought it out. Though the British had three ships to his one, the *Scharnhorst* had bigger guns and thicker armor. Indeed, the balance of power was very similar to what Hans Langsdorff and the *Graf Spee* had faced at the river Plate back in the first months of the war, and Bey was certainly aware that Langsdorff had been posthumously criticized for not fighting it out on that occasion. On the other hand, he also knew that the convoy was his main objective and that Dönitz had warned him not to risk his ship. So he turned away and pursued a course to loop around Burnett and back toward the convoy.[49]

Burnett let him go. He did not have the speed to pursue the *Scharnhorst* in any case, and he suspected (correctly) that Bey was looking for the convoy. Burnett therefore headed directly toward the convoy, traversing the chord of Bey's arc, hoping and expecting to regain contact. Just over two hours later, he did. Again Burnett opened fire, and this time the *Scharnhorst* fought back, inflicting serious damage on the *Norfolk*, disabling one of her turrets. Even so, despairing of finding the convoy in the midst of a force 8 gale, faced by three enemy ships, and separated from his destroyers, Bey decided to retire.[50]

It was too late. Bey's maneuver northward to avoid Burnett's cruisers had given Fraser the time he needed to close the distance with the *Duke of York*, and that afternoon at 4:17, already full dark in the Arctic winter, he made radar contact with the *Scharnhorst*. Bey had no idea that a British battleship was in the vicinity, and he was therefore surprised for the second time that day when at 4:40, star shells burst overhead to illuminate him. Fifteen minutes later, the *Duke of York* opened fire. Laconically but ominously, Bey reported to Berlin, "Am in action with a battleship."[51]

Speed was now Bey's only defense, for the *Scharnhorst* was faster than the *Duke of York*. Even as he began to pull away, however, three 14-inch shells from the *Duke of York* found their mark. One hit the *Scharnhorst*'s number one boiler room, cutting a critical steam pipe and reducing her speed to ten knots. Though the engineers managed to reroute the ruptured pipe and get the battlecruiser back up to twenty-two knots, the opportunity to escape had passed. The interim allowed several British and one Norwegian destroyer to get close enough to fire torpedoes, at least a few of which struck home. A gun layer on the British destroyer *Savage* recalled "how beautiful the *Scharnhorst* looked—all silver in the cold arctic light." In spite of that, the big ship was doomed, and Bey knew it. He sent a radio message that consciously or unconsciously echoed the one sent by Günther Lütjens as the *Bismarck* was sinking: "We shall fight to the last shell. Hail to the Führer."[52]

As the *Scharnhorst* slowed to only five knots, the *Duke of York* pounded her with 14-inch shells. Fraser's flag lieutenant, Vernon Merry, watched it. "Every time a salvo landed," he wrote, "there was this great gust of flame roaring up into the air, just as though we were prodding a huge fire with a poker." Fraser ordered the cruisers and destroyers to attack with torpedoes, and a total of fifty-six of them were unleashed with perhaps eight or ten of them hitting home. For nearly two hours the *Scharnhorst* absorbed this punishment. A few of her guns continued to fire, though with little effect, until at 6:20 p.m. she ceased firing altogether. At 7:45, her stern rose up out of the sea, her propellers still turning slowly, and she went down bow first. Of her crew of 1,968, only thirty-six survived. With her went the last remnants of Raeder's surface navy. For all practical purposes, both the Italian and German surface navies—the Regia Marina and the Kriegsmarine—had ceased to exist.[53]

CHAPTER 21

BREAKING THE SHIELD

A S THE GERMAN AND ITALIAN NAVIES came to grief in 1943, the still-dangerous Imperial Japanese Navy confronted its own grim prospects. The steady attrition of ships and planes during the lengthy Guadalcanal campaign had put the Japanese navy on a perceptible downward trajectory even as the American Pacific Fleet expanded almost daily. As if to underscore that, on June 1, 1943, the brand-new aircraft carrier *Essex*, first of an eventual twenty-four of her class, steamed into Pearl Harbor. Her air group consisted of more than ninety aircraft, all of them of the newest type: F6F Hellcat and F4U Corsair fighters, SB2C Helldiver bombers, and TBF Avenger Torpedo bombers, each larger, faster, and more efficient than their predecessors, and significantly advanced beyond their Japanese counterparts. Whereas the Zero had been the premier fighter in the Pacific in 1941, the new Hellcat was faster, more heavily armed, and better armored. Their pilots loved them, one gushing that "the Hellcat was a perfect carrier plane." Two more *Essex*-class carriers joined the fleet over the next two months, and by the end of the year there would be six of them in the Pacific, two of which were named to honor the *Lexington* and *Yorktown*, lost in the Battles of Coral Sea and Midway. It was a source of frustration to the Japanese that they believed they had sunk the *Yorktown* in the Coral Sea in May 1942, then had to do it again at Midway in June. Now, phoenix-like, here was yet another newer and larger *Yorktown* to take her place.[1]*

Another problem for the Japanese in 1943 was that they found themselves badly overextended. Having seized their far-flung maritime empire with relative ease in 1942, they now found it difficult to supply the garrisons of their distant outposts. Among the most precarious were two islands at the tail end of the Aleutian archipelago, Attu and Kiska, which they had captured during the campaign that had ended so disastrously at Midway. The twenty-six hundred or so Japanese soldiers consigned to those forlorn outposts were so isolated they might as well have been in an American POW camp. Indeed, they would have made a greater contribution to Japan's war effort had they been actual POWs, since in that case the United States would have been responsible for supplying and feeding them. As it was, they added one more burden to Japan's strained sealift capability.

To interdict the Japanese convoys to Attu and Kiska, the Americans sent several submarines and a surface force of two cruisers and four destroyers under Rear Admiral Charles H. McMorris (who bore the nickname "Socrates" or simply "Soc" in tribute to his academic prowess at the academy). On March 26, 1943, radar operators on McMorris's flagship, the light cruiser *Richmond*, reported two large transports, two light cruisers, and a destroyer near the Komandorski Islands just west of Attu, and McMorris turned toward them. In fact, however, the two "transports" were actually heavy cruisers, a fact that became evident only when the ships were within sight. Appreciating that he was overmatched, McMorris turned to the

---

* The existence of two carriers both named *Yorktown* still causes confusion for students of the war. After the *Yorktown* (CV-5) was sunk at Midway, a carrier then under construction and prospectively named the *Bonhomme Richard* in honor of John Paul Jones's flagship during the American Revolution, was instead christened *Yorktown*, though of course it had a different hull number, CV-10. That is the ship that floats still, and is open to visitors at Patriot's Point near Charleston, South Carolina.

southwest and increased speed to twenty-five knots. The Japanese commander, Vice Admiral Bushirō Hosogaya, set out in pursuit.

In a running fight that lasted most of four hours, Hosogaya concentrated his fire on the American heavy cruiser *Salt Lake City*, which after being hit several times began listing and slowed to a stop. McMorris managed to conceal her plight by having his destroyers lay down a heavy smoke screen. The Japanese launched torpedoes, but they all missed, and because Hosogaya mistook American shell splashes for near misses by unseen (and nonexistent) bombers, he decided to call off the pursuit. The Americans counted this Battle of the Komandorski Islands as a victory because the supply convoy that Hosogaya had been protecting turned back, and because McMorris's ships escaped further injury. The admirals in Tokyo agreed and removed Hosogaya from his command.[2]

Two months later, amidst dense fog and bitter cold, an American task force that included three older battleships, all repaired Pearl Harbor survivors, covered an American landing on Attu, and after several weeks of bitter fighting in horrible conditions, the Americans recaptured the island from a hungry and demoralized garrison. Soon afterward, the Japanese abandoned Kiska as well.

FOUR THOUSAND MILES ALMOST DUE SOUTH, American and Australian forces began parallel and complementary advances that summer in the South Pacific, a campaign rather exuberantly code-named Cartwheel. Conditions there could not have been more different from those off the Aleutians. It was, as one American sailor put it, "wickedly hot." On U.S. warships, men went about their duties in their undershirts—or less—while "swimming in sweat." Afternoon thundershowers added to the humidity without significantly moderating the temperature. Sailors avoided going below except to eat, and when they did, "everybody was soaking before he finished." Nor was there any respite at night, for, as one officer recalled, "the steel plates retained the tropical heat of the day...and made it almost unbearably hot below decks." Rather than try to sleep in their racks, many slept topside using kapok life preservers as pillows. As the skipper of one American destroyer put it, "We could not get dry. We could not keep cool. And there was no rest."[3]

The campaign in the South Pacific took place on two fronts. One was an American drive northwestward from Guadalcanal through the Solomon Islands chain, and the other was an Allied advance along the north coast of New Guinea. The ultimate target of both offensives was the Japanese citadel of Rabaul, located at the northern tip of New Britain. The principal Japanese base in the South Pacific, Rabaul was host to four all-weather airfields as well as a superb harbor created by a defunct and submerged volcano caldera. Despite the Germany-first principle, the Anglo-American forces were now openly on the offensive everywhere: in the Mediterranean, in New Guinea, in the Solomon Islands, and soon in the Central Pacific as well— indeed, almost everywhere *except* northern Europe, a circumstance of which Stalin took particular note.

The dual advance in the South Pacific was complicated by the awkward Allied command structure. Though King had managed to wrest control of the Guadalcanal campaign from MacArthur back in the summer of 1942, both of the twin thrusts toward Rabaul in 1943 were incontrovertibly within MacArthur's command zone.

Douglas MacArthur was then, and remains today, a lightning rod for both admirers and critics. The son of U.S. Army General Arthur MacArthur, who had been awarded the Medal of Honor for his heroism on Missionary Ridge during the Civil War, the younger MacArthur had been something of a celebrity even during his cadet days at West Point, where he had graduated first in the class of 1903. During the First World War he had performed brilliantly, returning from the war in 1919 as a thirty-nine-year-old brigadier general with two Distinguished Service Crosses and no fewer than seven Silver Stars. He became West Point superintendent, and then in 1930, at the age of fifty, he became the U.S. Army chief of staff. Despite that glittering service record, his defense of the Philippines in December 1941 was surprisingly inept and ultimately unsuccessful. In March 1942, Roosevelt ordered him to quit the Philippines and go to Australia, presumably to lead an Allied counterattack. The president also endowed him with a Medal of Honor, doing so primarily to provide the American public with a hero at a dark moment. If MacArthur's Medal of Honor in 1942 was almost entirely a public relations maneuver, it might fairly be argued that his service in the First World War had justified it.[4]

MacArthur also had a special relationship with the Philippines. In part this was because his father had served there as military governor, and also because Douglas spent his first active duty tour there as a young second lieutenant. Then in the 1920s, the younger MacArthur returned to the Philippines as commander of the military District of Manila, a largely social and political assignment where his cultivation of Filipino society was viewed with suspicion by some American officials.

Then there was the man himself. In addition to his obvious intellectual gifts, MacArthur's personal demeanor included an all-too-evident self-regard that put off many of his contemporaries. He seemed ever conscious of himself as a historical figure, and frequently behaved, even in private, as if he were declaiming from a stage, pacing back and forth and gesturing theatrically with his corncob pipe. He discounted, even disparaged, the

American General Douglas MacArthur surveys the terrain on Los Negros Island in the Admiralty Islands in February 1944. MacArthur was a larger-than-life figure in the Pacific War who attracted both admirers and critics. The figure behind him is his aide Col. Lloyd Lehrabas.

U.S. National Archives photo no. SC 187355

opinions of others, and saw criticism as less disagreement than treason. As the historian Max Hastings put it, "MacArthur's belief that his critics were not merely wrong, but evil, verged on derangement." These characteristics repelled many of the men he had to work with, including King and Nimitz. MacArthur had an astonishing memory, a deep knowledge of history, and a quick and incisive mind. It remained to be seen, however, if he also possessed the diplomatic sensitivity to orchestrate the land, air, and sea forces of several countries, a skill so evident in his former aide Dwight Eisenhower.[5]

MacArthur exercised command authority over all Allied forces in his theater, including Australian and New Zealand units as well as American army and navy forces. Significantly, he also had "strategic control" of Halsey's South Pacific Forces. What that meant was that although Halsey remained officially within Nimitz's chain of command, he was subject to MacArthur's direction whenever he operated within the Southwest Pacific Area. For Operation Cartwheel, Halsey would supervise the advance through the Solomon Islands while MacArthur directed the advance up the coast of New Guinea. It was therefore essential to Allied success that the two men work together amicably, and given their strong, even dominant personalities, it was by no means certain they could do so. In February 1943 Halsey wrote to Nimitz in one of his weekly informal letters that MacArthur was "a self-advertising Son of a Bitch." Two months later, Halsey flew to Brisbane, where the two men met for the first time.[6]

Perhaps surprisingly, they hit it off at once. Halsey later wrote, "I have seldom seen a man who makes a quicker, stronger, more favorable impression.... Five minutes after I reported, I felt as if we were lifelong friends." MacArthur felt the same. More than with any other subordinate, MacArthur gave Halsey unusual freedom of action and occasionally even deferred to him. For example, several months later, Nimitz wired King to suggest that since Navy Seabees were constructing an advance naval base for Halsey's fleet on Manus Island, at the northern edge of the Bismarck Sea, administrative control of that base should be transferred from MacArthur to the navy. King passed the request on to Marshall, and Marshall sent it down the army chain of command to MacArthur. Sensitive to what he considered a professional slight, MacArthur summoned Halsey to his headquarters. There, surrounded by his staff, he explained why Manus Island should remain in his own command orbit. He spoke eloquently and at length (as he often did), and at the end of his disquisition, as Halsey remembered it later, he "pointed his pipe stem at me and demanded, 'Am I not right, Bill?'" To which Halsey replied, "No, sir!" There was an audible gasp from the members of MacArthur's staff. Not only did Halsey disagree, but he went on to assert that by removing administrative control from the authorities on site, MacArthur would be "hampering the war effort." They discussed the issue for hours, and renewed their conversation the next day. Finally MacArthur smiled and said, "You win, Bill." MacArthur may have been genuinely persuaded, or he may have simply admired Halsey's willingness to defend his position. Whatever the cause, the two men managed to work amicably together during the ensuing campaign.[7]

Japanese command relationships in the South Pacific were more institutional. The army generals in Tokyo, now in full control of the government, dominated strategic decision-making in all theaters of the war, including the Pacific. It was the army that mandated the "New Operational Policy" of defending individual strong points to the last man in order to wear down, and eventually wear out, the attackers. Admiral Koga still hoped to fight and win a decisive battle at sea, but as he saw no opportunity to do so, he directed Vice Admiral Jin'ichi Kusaka at Rabaul to adhere to the army's blueprint and defend every outpost to the death. Despite the many reversals suffered since Midway, Japanese leaders continued to believe—or at least to hope—that the deathless spirit of *yamato-damashii* would eventually triumph over American wealth and numbers. As General Harukichi Hyakutake, commander of the Japanese Seventeenth Army, put it, "The battle plan is to resist the enemy's material strength with perseverance, while at the same time displaying our spiritual strength."[8]

THE SOLOMON ISLANDS GROUP is often likened to a ladder because the parallel lines of islands suggest a ladder's twin rails. The Cartwheel operational plan called for Halsey's forces to climb that ladder from Guadalcanal to Bougainville by conducting a series of amphibious landings on the intervening islands, which had exotic names such as Rendova, Kolombangara, and Vella Lavella. Meanwhile, MacArthur's forces—Australian as well as American—would assault Japanese positions along the north coast of New Guinea, at places with equally exotic names, such as Lae, Buna, Gona, Salamaua, and (somewhat incongruously) Finschhafen.

To catalogue these campaigns fully and faithfully would require a detailed account of every Allied landing, every Japanese counterattack, every night surface action, and every bitterly contested yard of jungle, and even then it would fail to do justice to either the events or the participants. Many of the operations, however—and especially the naval battles— followed a common pattern. First, because the Americans could select their targets from a score or more of possible invasion sites, they often faced relatively modest initial opposition on the beach. Soon enough, however, and

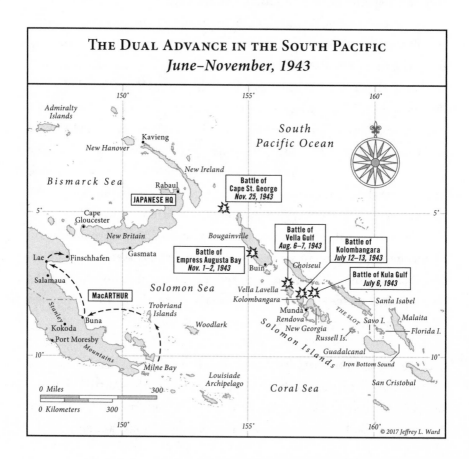

THE DUAL ADVANCE IN THE SOUTH PACIFIC
June–November, 1943

© 2017 Jeffrey L. Ward

often within hours, the Japanese reacted: first with air assaults, then with a naval surface force, and finally with overland attacks through the jungle. The moment the Allies stepped ashore, they knew that a Japanese counterpunch was only a matter of time, and usually not very much time. Since the moment of greatest danger to the invaders was when the big landing ships were unloading, a lot depended on how quickly the transport and amphibious ships could get in, unload, and get out.

As in Sicily, those ships included a number of the new LSTs. Despite their designation as "landing ship, tank," the LSTs involved in Operation Cartwheel carried fewer tanks than crates of supplies, since tanks were less central to combat in the rain forests of the Solomon Islands. When the LSTs ground up onto the target beach, supply-laden trucks rolled off the ramps, drove to a suitable site to unload, then returned for a second load, and a third. After the first few invasions, this protocol was improved further by embarking pre-loaded trailers—as many as thirty of them—on the LSTs, plus several trucks. Upon landing, the trucks hauled the first of the trailers off the ship, parked them ashore to be unloaded later, then returned for more trailers. As a result, the unloading of the supply ships, and especially the LSTs, was greatly accelerated. A year earlier at Guadalcanal, Richmond Kelly Turner had demanded five days to unload his transports. Now they could be unloaded in a single day, though even that was not always fast enough to avoid the first Japanese air strikes.[9]

After the air strikes, the next threat came from the sea. From Rabaul, Kusaka dispatched convoys consisting of destroyer-transports crammed with troops to reinforce the threatened area, as well as a combat force of cruisers and destroyers to attack the American invasion flotilla. If they were not as regular or predictable as in 1942, the Allies nevertheless continued to refer to these resupply convoys as the "Tokyo Express." Inevitably, the Allied covering forces challenged these sorties, and that led to a series of furious middle-of-the-night naval battles in the waters around the Solomon Islands during the summer and fall of 1943. In the pitch darkness, the combat was often confusing, even to those who directed it, and it was occasionally unclear, even afterward, what exactly had happened. One veteran described it as "one big game of hide and seek."[10]

The template for these engagements was established in the first week of July 1943. That week (as Allied soldiers stormed ashore in Sicily), American soldiers and Marines executed Operation Toenails by landing on several islands in the New Georgia group, just north of Guadalcanal: Vangunu to the south and Rendova to the west, as well as New Georgia itself, home to the principal Japanese base at Munda. Alerted to these landings, Kusaka immediately dispatched planes to attack the invaders, plus a reinforcement convoy of six transport-destroyers filled with twenty-six hundred soldiers escorted by four more destroyers, all under the command of Rear Admiral Teruo Akiyama. American scout planes spotted the convoy en route and flashed a warning to Halsey, who ordered three light cruisers and four destroyers under Rear Admiral Walden Ainsworth, then headed for refueling and a refit, to reverse course and intercept it.[11]

In this, as in all of the naval actions that summer, the combat pitted American radar-controlled gunfire against the Japanese Long Lance torpedoes. By now virtually all of the American warships had radar, and the user-friendly PPI scopes were grouped together in what was initially called "radar plot," often located one level down from the bridge. It was Nimitz who proposed formalizing this practice by creating a Combat Operations Center to receive and evaluate information from all sources, including radar. By mid-1943 its name had been changed to Combat Information Center (CIC), the name it bears today. Such a facility not only allowed American commanders to "see in the dark" but provided them with an electronic overview of the tactical picture even when the visibility from the bridge was near zero. The Japanese had radar only on their biggest ships and continued to rely mainly on their night optics, though all their combatants, even the destroyer-transports, carried the deadly Long Lance torpedo, which was still the most dangerous and effective ship-killing weapon of the war.[12]

The confrontation between Akiyama's reinforcement convoy and Ainsworth's surface force took place in the early morning hours of July 6 in what has gone down in history as the Battle of Kula Gulf. A low cloud cover blotted out the moon and stars, making it pitch black, and the sea, in the words of one participant, was "rough and ugly." Thanks to their radar, the Americans got in the first blow, firing from six miles away before either side could actually see the other. Since each of the American light cruisers could fire ten rounds a minute, together they could shoot 450 shells every sixty seconds. The Japanese called them 6-inch machine guns.[13]

After firing more than two thousand rounds in five minutes, Ainsworth thought the Japanese must be "practically obliterated." In fact, only two Japanese destroyers were sunk by the American onslaught, though one of them was the *Niizuki*, with Akiyama on board. Even as she went down, taking Akiyama with her, a score or more of Japanese torpedoes were already in the water, streaking toward the American ships at forty-nine knots. Aboard the *St. Louis*, an American war correspondent watched "a thick white finger coming straight at us like a chalk line drawn across a blackboard." The torpedo exploded against the side of the *St. Louis*, though she remained afloat. The *Helena* was less fortunate. One torpedo took off her bow, and two others struck almost simultaneously amidships. The cruiser "leaped into the air and dropped again," her back broken. Her bow and stern jackknifed upward, and the order to abandon ship came just thirteen minutes later.* Though each side had drawn blood in this confrontation, the Japanese managed to fulfill their mission by landing the twenty-six hundred embarked soldiers on Kolombangara.[14]

Six days later, the Battle of Kolombangara (July 12–13) followed a similar script. Once again, American radar-controlled gunfire gave the Allies an early advantage that was swiftly eliminated when Long Lance torpedoes struck two of the Allied cruisers, *Honolulu* and *Leander*, plus the destroyer *Gwin*. The cruisers managed to stay afloat, though they were out of action for months; the *Gwin* had to be scuttled. In the confusion of another night battle, each side reported inflicting more damage on the enemy than was actually the case. As Samuel Eliot Morison put it, "Each side found consolation for its own losses in imaginary damage inflicted on the enemy."[15]

---

* One hundred and sixty eight of the *Helena*'s crew of nearly 900 men died. The rest endured a lengthy ordeal. The American destroyers *Nicholas* and *Radford* initially picked up 275 of them, but they broke off rescue operations to pursue nearby Japanese warships. Several hundred more spent several days paddling and pushing their rafts and lifeboats to nearby islands, where they were aided by Australian coast watchers and eventually rescued.

The Americans did much better three weeks later in the Battle of Vella Gulf (August 6–7), when Captain Frederick Moosbrugger with six American destroyers took on a Japanese force of four destroyers and sank three of them without suffering a loss. Even so, most of these engagements could be labeled Japanese victories, mainly because even though both sides suffered losses, the Japanese succeeded in landing reinforcements for the ground war. On the other hand, as noted above, the Americans could replace their battle losses, while the Japanese could not.*

IT TOOK 32,000 U.S. ARMY SOLDIERS and 1,700 U.S. Marines five weeks to capture Munda from 5,000 Japanese defenders, and in the process the Americans lost nearly 1,200 killed and more than twice as many wounded. This, of course, was precisely the scenario the Japanese had forecast for the war in the South Pacific, and it made Halsey "wary of another slugging match," as he put it. The next rung of the ladder was the well-fortified island of Kolombangara, held by 10,000 Japanese. Nimitz and Halsey discussed skipping it altogether and jumping past it to Vella Lavella, which was occupied by only about 250 Japanese. Such a move not only would avoid a direct confrontation with another powerful Japanese army but would cut that army off from further support and leave it in a strategic backwater to "wither on the vine," as MacArthur put it. If successful, this new protocol of "hitting 'em where they ain't," to use baseball lingo, would completely invalidate the Japanese strategic plan to compel the Americans to absorb unacceptable losses on island after island as they advanced. It was one of the most important strategic decisions of the Pacific war.[16]

The idea was not a new one, and had been a key element in a number of Naval War College studies before the war. Several individuals have been credited with applying it to Cartwheel, including MacArthur, who claimed responsibility for it in his memoirs, though in fact he initially opposed it

---

* Among the many small engagements during this extended campaign was one in which the Japanese destroyer *Amagiri* cut an American PT boat in half. This relatively minor confrontation might have been overlooked by history entirely if the commander of PT-109 had not been Lieutenant (j.g.) and future president John F. Kennedy, who managed to save most of his crew.

and was a late convert to the idea. The burden of evidence suggests that the individual most responsible for the practice of bypassing heavily fortified objectives was Halsey's deputy commander, Rear Admiral Theodore S. Wilkinson, a former director of naval intelligence, who took over the amphibious forces from Kelly Turner on July 15.

One month later, on August 15, three LSTs and twelve LCTs under Wilkinson landed forty-six hundred Americans on Vella Lavella. There was no initial opposition, though, as always, the Japanese quickly responded with their usual air attack. Over the next three weeks the Seabees constructed an airfield on Vella Lavella that effectively isolated Kolombangara from Rabaul. As a result, the Japanese evacuated Kolombangara at the end of September, surrendering it without a single Allied soldier ever having to set foot on it.[17]

MacArthur's American-Australian forces employed a similar protocol in their campaign along the New Guinea coast. In August, Australian troops under General Thomas Blamey approached Lae overland through the jungle, and in September American amphibious ships under Rear Admiral Daniel E. Barbey carried another seventy-eight hundred Australian troops to a landing beach west of the Japanese position. It was the first amphibious operation involving Australian soldiers since the ill-fated campaign at Gallipoli in 1915. MacArthur also sent seventeen hundred American paratroopers to seize an abandoned jungle airstrip, and Lae was virtually surrounded. On September 8 (the same day British and American forces landed at Salerno) U.S. Navy ships bombarded Lae from seaward while Allied ground troops converged overland from both east and west. To avoid being enveloped, the Japanese evacuated the town, giving it up without a battle, as they had Kolombangara.[18]

Finschhafen was next. Again Blamey's Australians advanced overland while Barbey's amphibs, escorted by ten destroyers, carried four thousand more Australians to a beach five miles north of the Japanese base. The Japanese counterattacked on October 17, but, aided by Australian "Matilda" tanks landed by the LSTs, the Australians fought them off and the Allies secured the town, eventually turning it into a major base for the next leap westward.[19]

BOUGAINVILLE WAS THE LARGEST of the Solomon Islands and the closest of the large islands to Rabaul. It was too big to bypass altogether, though

the Allies did succeed in bypassing its strong points. The Japanese anticipated that the Allied attack would occur somewhere on the southern coast
of Bougainville near Buin, which had an excellent harbor, or at nearby
Kahili Airfield, the largest on the island, and they positioned most of their
forty thousand troops there. Instead, the Allies targeted a remote site on the
western side of the island at Empress Augusta Bay. There was no harbor or
airfield there, but there were also few Japanese (only about 270 combat
troops), and the Americans calculated that once they had seized a foothold,
they could build their own airfield, as they had on Vella Lavella. The dense
jungle on Bougainville would protect their enclave from a swift Japanese
counterattack; the same jungle might well prevent the Americans from expanding their foothold to secure the rest of the island, but that was not their
goal. In fact, the Allies never did capture the rest of Bougainville, and there
were Japanese soldiers at both Buin and Kahili still awaiting an attack when
the war ended nearly two years later.[20]

Given that Empress Augusta Bay was only about 210 miles from the
Japanese airfields at Rabaul, the invaders knew they would be subject to a
swift air attack. To minimize that threat, Kenney's bombers carried out a
series of preemptive air strikes against Rabaul throughout the month of
October, including a massive 349-plane raid on October 12. Simultaneously,
planes from AirSols (Air Command Solomons), now commanded by Army
Major General Nathan Twining, struck Japanese airfields on Bougainville,
including Kahili and Balalae, where Yamamoto had been headed when he
was shot down back in April. Even Halsey's carriers got into the act, as air
groups from the *Saratoga* and the new *Independence*-class light carrier
Princeton also bombed the airfields. Altogether in the two weeks prior to
the invasion, Allied planes conducted no fewer than sixty air raids against
Japanese installations and airfields. At the same time, an American surface
force of light cruisers (Task Force 39) under Rear Admiral Aaron Merrill
shelled Japanese positions on Buka, just north of Bougainville. All this
activity not only suppressed Japanese airpower but also disguised the eventual Allied target.[21]

The invasion of Bougainville began on November 1 when the 3rd Marine
Division splashed ashore near Cape Torokina in Empress Augusta Bay,

with the Army's 37th Division joining them a week later. Though enemy resistance was minimal, the daunting geography proved a dangerous foe. The best available American charts of the area dated from 1841 and proved to be as much as eight miles in error. On one occasion when a skipper asked his navigation officer their current location on the chart, the crisp answer was, "About three miles inland, sir." American radar again proved its worth as conning officers navigated the coastline by watching the PPI scopes.[22]

Leery of exposing the scarce and valuable LSTs to airstrikes from Rabaul, the Allies held them back from this invasion, loading the troops instead onto eight transports and consigning their supplies to four cargo ships, all escorted by two destroyer divisions. As usual, the Higgins boats went in first, though many of them broached in the high surf and steep beach gradients; no fewer than sixty-four had to be abandoned along with twenty-two of the Mike boats (LCMs). Utterly surprised, the Japanese nevertheless responded quickly, sending fifty planes from Rabaul that same morning and a hundred more in the afternoon. The raids did little damage, though they slowed the unloading of the supply ships.[23]

As usual, a Japanese surface attack was not far behind. Koga ordered Kusaka to send out a force of two recently arrived heavy cruisers (*Myōkō* and *Haguro*) plus two light cruisers and six destroyers, all under Vice Admiral Sentarō Ōmori. Until recently, Ōmori had been an instructor at the Torpedo School and had never been in a naval battle. Before setting out, he gave his captains a pep talk to express his faith in them, insisting, "I believe we shall win." His skippers were less sure. As they left the briefing, one destroyer captain told another, "Let's be prepared for a swim and take along plenty of shark repellant." In no mood for black humor, the other captain replied grimly, "Japan will topple if Bougainville falls."[24]

Ōmori headed south that very afternoon intending to strike after dark and duplicate Mikawa's feat at Savo Island, though he resolved that, unlike Mikawa, he would not overlook the American transports. He did not know that there *were* no American transports on the landing beach, for Wilkinson had sent all of them off at dusk with orders to return the next day. Nor, thanks to Allied air surveillance, would Ōmori be able to spring a surprise on the Allies, as Mikawa had done. From intercepted radio messages,

Ōmori knew that radar-equipped American search planes had found and reported him. He continued south nonetheless.[25]

The opposing forces collided in another middle-of-the-night battle at 2:30 a.m. on November 2. Heavy cloud cover and a steady drizzle reduced visibility to less than three miles, though of course that was no barrier to American radar. For the Japanese, it was like a blind man fighting a sighted opponent. The first salvo from the American cruisers crashed into the light cruiser *Sendai* at 2:45, and a witness on the destroyer *Shigure* was astonished that the Americans could strike with such "fantastic precision." A year earlier, in the Battle of Savo Island, the Japanese had ruled the night. No more. Captain Tameichi Hara noted ruefully and accurately that "enemy radar had wrested from the Japanese Navy its former supremacy in night action."[26]

Another Japanese problem was that Ōmori never fully grasped the tactical situation. Because of the astonishing accuracy of American gunfire, he believed the range between the two forces was less than it actually was, and most of the Japanese shells fell short, though three Japanese 8-inch shells did hit the American cruiser *Denver*, forcing her to retire. Amidst the confusion, the heavy cruiser *Myōkō* collided with the destroyer *Hatsukaze*, clipping off the destroyer's bow. There was confusion on the American side, too. The destroyer *Thatcher* sideswiped the *Spence* and both ships suffered serious damage. That was not the end of the *Spence*'s bad luck. With the American radar scopes showing pips all over the sea, it was difficult to distinguish friend from foe, and Captain Arleigh Burke, commanding one of Merrill's two destroyer divisions, opened fire on what he thought was a crippled Japanese destroyer. Almost at once, Captain Bernard L. Austin on the *Spence* jumped on the short-range TBS radio to holler: "Cease firing! Cease firing! Goddammit, that's me!" A chastened Burke asked: "Were you hit?" to which Austin replied, "Negative, but they aren't all here yet." Burke replied, "Sorry but you'll have to excuse the next four salvos as they are already on their way." Luckily, they all missed.[27]

After an hour, and still uncertain about what had happened or was happening, Ōmori reversed course and headed back to Rabaul. There would be no second Savo Island, nor did the Japanese succeed in landing their reinforcement convoy. Burke's destroyers pursued Ōmori for some distance until Merrill recalled them. He was eager to put his task force in a defensive formation before sunrise brought the inevitable daylight attack by Japanese aircraft. Sure enough, at 8:00 a.m. a hundred planes from Rabaul approached his formation. They did only superficial damage, however, and Merrill was able to retire for refueling and replenishment. At Rabaul, Ōmori was relieved of his command.[28]

THOUGH DISAPPOINTED by the results of the Battle of Empress Augusta Bay, Koga nevertheless decided to raise the stakes. From Truk, he sent a more powerful surface force to Rabaul for another try. It consisted of seven heavy cruisers and one light cruiser, all commanded by the battle-hardened Vice Admiral Takeo Kurita. Notified of the buildup by a patrolling B-24, Halsey feared that he did not have sufficient strength to repel it, and later described the moment as "the most desperate emergency that confronted me in my entire term as ComSoPac." He decided to preempt Kurita's surface attack with an air strike by the carriers Saratoga and Princeton. On November 5, the two flattops sent ninety-seven aircraft, virtually every plane that would fly, toward Rabaul. They could do so because AirSols pledged to provide the CAP for the carriers. The American carrier planes did not sink any of Kurita's ships, but they severely damaged four of the heavy cruisers and two light cruisers at a cost of only ten planes. The Japanese postponed the planned sortie, and in the end it never materialized.[29]

Japanese aircraft at Rabaul did launch a retaliatory strike against the American carriers, but all they found was an LCI gunship and a PT boat. Both were damaged, though neither was sunk. Even so, the pilots returned to announce that they had sunk two American aircraft carriers and two heavy cruisers. Though pilots on both sides continued to exaggerate the impact of their efforts, Samuel Eliot Morison speculated that this was "probably the biggest feat of lying in the entire Pacific war." Such exaggerated reports had a greater impact on the Japanese than on the Americans, for while American strategic decision-makers generally assumed that most damage reports were inflated, the Japanese high command too often took such claims seriously— even literally—and based their subsequent planning on them.[30]

A pilot's-eye view of the American air raid on Japanese shipping in Simpson Harbor at Rabaul on November 5, 1943. Note the burning Japanese cruiser at right.

U.S. National Archives photo no. 80-G-89104

Halsey followed up the November 5 air strike with another one six days later, when two brand-new *Essex*-class carriers plus the smaller *Independence* joined the *Saratoga* and *Princeton* in a series of raids on Rabaul. It was another measure, if one were needed, of mounting American naval superiority.

For the rest of November, the Allies kept the pressure on. Allied bombs pummeled the base virtually every day, and to at least one Japanese pilot at Rabaul, "the endless days and nights became a nightmare." Allied surface ships also got into the act. On November 25 (Thanksgiving Day in the United States), five destroyers under Arleigh Burke ambushed a convoy of five Japanese destroyer-transports returning to Rabaul from landing reinforcements on Buka. In what became known as the Battle of Cape St. George,

Burke's destroyers sank three of them.* The incessant attacks so reduced Rabaul's military assets that the necessity, or even the desirability, of capturing it at all was brought into question. For his part, MacArthur remained eager to seize Rabaul and argued that its excellent harbor and four all-weather airfields made it essential to subsequent operations. At the Quebec Conference, however, the Combined Chiefs overruled him and declared that Rabaul, like Kolombangara and southern Bougainville, should be bypassed. MacArthur was mollified by the news that the next Allied objective in his theater would be a landing on Mindanao in the Philippines.[31]

In January 1944, the Allies began yet another sustained bombing campaign against Rabaul, hitting the harbor and the airfields so regularly that the Japanese withdrew the rest of their combat vessels from the harbor. Fewer and fewer planes rose up to contest the attacks, and on February 20, the Japanese withdrew the last of their combat aircraft as well. There were still a hundred thousand Japanese servicemen at Rabaul, but they spent most of their time digging tunnels to protect themselves from the constant bombing while suffering from hunger and malaria. One witness likened the now isolated defenders of Rabaul to "living corpses, bereft of spiritual and physical strength." They were still there when the war ended.[32]

WELL BEFORE THAT DENOUEMENT, the Allies initiated a third offensive in the Pacific. Ever since the 1920s, the dominant feature and central theme of all U.S. Navy planning at the War College and elsewhere had been a grand offensive directly across the Central Pacific that would culminate in a showdown battle with the Japanese somewhere in the Philippine Sea. That vision had to be shelved during the first two years of war because the United

---

* It was during this operation that Burke reported his ships as "proceeding at 31 knots." The message struck Halsey as humorous because Burke had previously ended most of his dispatches with the comment that he was "proceeding at 30 knots" as a subtle protest about the fact that his ships, officially capable of thirty-five knots, could make only thirty knots because of their need for a refit. Now he indicated that he had managed to squeeze one more knot out of them, and Halsey teased him about it, referring to him subsequently in dispatches as "31-Knot Burke," a nickname that stuck with him for the rest of his life, including during his term as chief of naval operations in the 1950s.

States, like the other Allied powers, had been rocked back on its heels after the initial Axis onslaught. Now, having seized the initiative, and bolstered by the outpouring of new vessels from American shipyards, King believed it was time to resuscitate it. The British were dubious, fearing that this was another detour from the Germany-first strategy, which was already severely compromised. At the Quebec Conference, as King argued heatedly for an offensive in the Central Pacific, Sir James Somerville blurted out, "Come on Ernie, you know you are talking bullshit!" King, whose language was as colorful as anyone's, responded in kind.[33]

Another skeptic was MacArthur, who insisted that embarking on a new campaign in the Central Pacific while the one in the South Pacific was still in progress was foolish at best, and potentially disastrous. For one thing, it violated the strategic principle that a military commander should never divide his forces in the face of an enemy, though of course in some ways the Allies had already done that by conducting simultaneous campaigns in the Solomons and New Guinea. Now that the Solomons had been conquered and Rabaul neutralized, MacArthur believed the stage had been set for an invasion of the Philippines, and he had no doubt who should command it. "Give me central direction of the war in the Pacific," he wrote to Secretary of War Stimson. "Don't let the Navy's pride of position and ignorance continue this great tragedy." His plea fell on deaf ears. Instead, the Joint Chiefs proposed to remove Halsey's South Pacific Force and the First Marine Division from MacArthur's theater and send both to the Central Pacific for a new thrust that would become the main effort in the Pacific, essentially relegating MacArthur and his command to a secondary theater.[34]

MacArthur smelled a rat. He believed that King promoted the Central Pacific Drive largely to undermine the army, and him in particular. He even suspected Roosevelt of trying to sabotage the South Pacific campaign for fear that a triumphant MacArthur would mount a 1944 presidential campaign against him. He was particularly angered by the news that he would lose the 1st Marine Division, which had fought in his theater since Guadalcanal. To assuage him, the Joint Chiefs allowed MacArthur to keep that unit, and to compensate Nimitz, Marshall gave him control of the army's 27th Division.[35]

It was not just a fight over resources. King was frustrated by MacArthur's careful step-by-step (King might have said inch-by-inch) advance, and envisioned instead a campaign of giant leaps—six or eight hundred miles at a time—across the mid-Pacific. He noted that a Central Pacific campaign was a more direct path to Japan, as well as a more healthful environment for the men, and that it created the opportunity for a confrontation with the main Japanese fleet that could yield a decisive victory. Finally, the seizure of islands closer to Japan could lead to a strategic bombing campaign against Japanese cities. Of course, there were logistical difficulties. All previous Allied invasions, in the Mediterranean as well as in the Pacific, had taken place within the protective envelope of friendly airfields. By contrast, the Gilbert Islands—the first target in the new offensive—were more than seven hundred miles from the closest Allied airfield. The invaders would have to take their own air cover with them.

What made that possible was the influx of those new-construction American warships, and especially aircraft carriers, to the Pacific theater. Just as American shipyards produced transports, cargo ships, and escorts faster than the German U-boats could sink them in the Atlantic, they also produced battleships, cruisers, and aircraft carriers faster than the Japanese could destroy them in the Pacific. In addition to the new *Essex*-class carriers, the Americans also converted nine cruiser hulls already under construction into *Independence*-class light carriers.

The new ships were manned by tens of thousands of new recruits, many of them right out of navy boot camp. One officer described them as "clerks, haberdashers, soda jerkers, bell hops, high-school athletes, and farm boys." Seventy percent of them had never been to sea before. Such a dramatic increase in the size and capability of the American Pacific fleet was unprecedented. In November 1943, Secretary of the Navy Frank Knox announced that since the first of the year, the United States had added no fewer than 419 new combatants to the fleet, including forty new aircraft carriers, though that number included the so-called baby flattops. Given those circumstances, the decision of the Joint Chiefs to open a new front in the Pacific War, while certainly bold, was neither as foolish as the British believed nor as nefarious as MacArthur suggested.[36]

To conduct it, Nimitz activated a new fleet organization in August. Halsey retained command of naval forces in the South Pacific to complete the neutralization of Rabaul, but for the drive through the Central Pacific Nimitz authorized what was initially designated as Task Force 50, then renamed the Central Pacific Force, and finally christened the Fifth Fleet. It was an enormous command, boasting twelve battleships (five of them the new fast battleships) and nine fleet carriers plus eleven smaller carriers, twelve cruisers, and thirty-seven large transports and amphibious ships. It was the largest combat fleet the United States had ever assembled, and in terms of naval airpower the greatest armada in history. To command it, Nimitz selected Vice Admiral Raymond Spruance.[37]

A gaunt figure, Spruance was a reserved, contemplative, even cerebral commander who displayed none of the dash or flair of either Bull Halsey or Douglas MacArthur. Thomas B. Buell, Spruance's principal biographer, entitled his book *The Quiet Warrior,* and an interviewer likened Spruance's demeanor to that of "a soft-spoken university professor." Since the Battle of Midway nearly two years earlier, Spruance had served as Nimitz's chief of staff. Nimitz valued and admired Spruance's work ethic and calm efficiency, and he was initially reluctant to release him for sea duty, though he eventually

Admiral Raymond A. Spruance (left, in pith helmet) and Marine Lieutenant General Holland M. Smith (right) teamed up for much of the Central Pacific drive that began at Tarawa in November 1943. In this photo, taken on Saipan in July 1944, Smith seems to belie his nickname, "Howling Mad."

U.S. National Archives photo no. 80-G-287225

relented and informed Spruance that his new assignment as commander of the Central Pacific Force was to invade the Gilbert Islands in November.[38]

THE GILBERT ISLANDS consist of sixteen coral atolls scattered across 420 square miles of ocean bisected by the equator. Like the atolls and islands of the other chains in that region of the Pacific, the Gilberts are tiny—hence the region's name, Micronesia. Originally they had been larger volcanic islands with colonies of coral growth around their periphery. Over the centuries, as the volcanoes grew dormant and the islands subsided, the coral skeletons remained in place and formed giant circular reefs called atolls around a central lagoon. Some of the reefs barely broke the surface of the water; others grew small islands just large enough to support sparse vegetation. One of the atolls in the Gilberts, Tarawa, hosted several such islands, on one of which, Betio, the Japanese had constructed an airstrip that became operational in January 1943. Betio Island was so small—less than one square mile—that the airstrip practically filled it. From ten thousand feet it suggested an oversized aircraft carrier with a tail that had somehow sprouted palm trees around its periphery. Despite its small size, it was defended by more than twenty-six hundred *rikusentai* or Special Naval Landing Forces, the Japanese equivalent of U.S. Marines, plus another twenty-two hundred construction troops. It was also strongly fortified, and the garrison's commander, Rear Admiral Keiji Shibazaki, told his men that a million men fighting for a hundred years could not take it.[39]

Several circumstances made the American assault on Tarawa different from previous invasions. Until now, the objective of all amphibious operations had been to secure a foothold that could be reinforced in order to conduct a subsequent campaign into the hinterland. This time, the great distance of the Gilberts from the closest Allied base meant that all of the men, including their equipment and supplies, had to be embarked in the initial invasion fleet. A foothold would not be sufficient; the invaders had to seize the whole of the island on the first try or fail entirely. Melodramatic as it sounds, the invaders had to conquer or die.[40]

Another critical factor was the presence of a coral reef, a kind of shelf just below the surface that extended out from the island to a distance of four

Betio Island in Tarawa Atoll was so small that its airstrip very nearly filled the island. The coral reef that caused so much difficulty to the attackers is clearly evident in this aerial photograph.

U.S. National Archives photo no. 80-G-83771

hundred to eight hundred yards. Even at high tide, there might be only three or four feet of water over this shelf. That meant that LSTs could not carry men or equipment into the beach; even a loaded Higgins boat drew three and a half feet. Aware of that, the American commander of the V Amphibious Corps, Marine Major General Holland M. Smith,* wanted to use specialized landing craft known as a "landing vehicle, tracked" (LVT), commonly called an "amphtrack" or an "alligator." These vessels had tank-like treads fitted with small paddles, which meant they could swim in the water (at six knots) and crawl across a coral reef (at ten miles per hour). They could carry twenty men at a time but, lacking a bow ramp, could not carry either vehicles or artillery pieces. Smith had to overcome navy skepticism about their utility, telling Kelly Turner that he would refuse to attempt the invasion without them. Turner gave way, but Smith managed to assemble only 125 of them for the assault. There were no others closer than San Diego and not enough time or available shipping to get them to the South Pacific. Smith decided to use amphtracks for the first three waves, then

---

* There were three General Smiths involved in Operation Galvanic, a fact that occasionally causes confusion. Marine Major General Holland M. Smith was the overall commander of the V Corps, which included both the 2nd Marine Division of Major General Julian M. Smith, which assaulted Betio, and the 27th Army Division of Major General Ralph C. Smith, which assaulted Makin.

simply hope that subsequent waves of men in Higgins boats could somehow manage to get across the reef. The men of the 2nd Marine Division, most of them veterans of Guadalcanal, were warned that there was a 50-50 chance they might have to wade to shore.[41]

The assault began on November 20, only three weeks after the landing on Bougainville. Smith promised his Marines that the island would be subjected to "the greatest concentration of aerial bombardment and naval gunfire in the history of warfare." The naval commander, Rear Admiral Harry Hill, used the battleship *Maryland* as his flagship, and she opened the bombardment a few minutes after 5:00 a.m. The concussion from the initial salvo immediately knocked out all the communications on board, which made Hill and the embarked Marine commander, Major General Julian Smith, essentially observers, since they were now cut off from their commands.[42]

Despite a muzzle velocity of twenty-six hundred feet per second, the 16-inch shells from the *Maryland* seemed to travel through the predawn twilight in a slow arc, reminding one witness of "an easily lobbed tennis ball." Within seconds of the initial salvo every other ship in the fleet opened fire as well: battleships, cruisers, and even destroyers all plastered the island incessantly for most of an hour. Then the ships lifted fire and, after a short delay, the carrier planes came in to drop hundreds of tons of bombs on the island, after which the ships opened up again. With so much ordnance hurled onto so small a space in so short a time, many observers assumed that the Japanese garrison must have been obliterated. *Time* correspondent Robert Sherrod recalled thinking, "Surely no mortal men could live through such a destroying power." On the receiving end of the bombardment, Japanese soldier Kiyoski Ota recalled it as "a frightening and horrifying experience! It went on and on without ceasing."[43]

In fact, however, for all its sound and fury, the preliminary bombardment did far less damage than Sherrod, Ota, or anyone else assumed. For one thing, the Japanese fortifications were more substantial and resilient than the Americans had anticipated, and another factor was that the naval gunners and pilots tended to target the island itself rather than specific installations. As one U.S. Marine put it, "Where the Navy gunnery officers make their mistake is in assuming that land targets are like ships—when you hit a ship it sinks and all is lost, but on land you've got to get direct hits." The naval gunfire destroyed one Japanese 8-inch gun, and it wiped out Shibazaki's communications system, but it left much of the Japanese defenses intact.[44]

The first wave of landing craft, all of them tracked LVTs, crawled across the coral reef toward the shore at eight-thirty. The Japanese held their fire until the alligators were less than half a mile away, then opened with deadly efficiency. The LVTs pressed on, though they took a beating from the Japanese artillery, and by the end of the day only 35 of the original 132 remained operational. When the fourth wave, consisting of Higgins boats, headed shoreward, the Navy coxswains found that most of the boats could not surmount the reef. A neap tide, which occurs when the sun and the moon are at right angles to the earth, had lowered the water level over the coral shelf to only a few feet, and the Higgins boats could go no further. The Marines climbed out over the sides of the boats and began to wade ashore from as far as four hundred yards away, all while under fire from dozens of well-sited machine guns. One Marine recalled that the bullets hitting the water around him sounded like "a sheet of rain." Some units suffered over

U.S. Navy landing craft filled with Marines head for the beaches on Betio Island as destroyers (in middle distance) pound Japanese positions. Despite the preliminary bombardment, Japanese defenses proved far more resilient than the Americans believed possible and U.S. casualties were sobering.

U.S. Naval Institute

70 percent casualties before they ever reached the beach. Getting the 37 mm artillery pieces ashore was even more challenging. The Marines had to manhandle them out of the Higgins boats and Mike boats, then drag them shoreward by brute force. The guns bounced and rolled along the uneven coral shelf with excruciating slowness while a dozen or more Marines hauled on the towropes.* When one man fell, another took his place.[45]

Somehow enough men and guns got ashore to secure a foothold, and over the next three days, as they were reinforced and resupplied, they gradually pushed their way forward. Naval gunfire support was helpful, especially on the lagoon side of the island, where two destroyers, *Ringgold* and *Dashiell*, fired six hundred rounds of 5-inch shells into the Japanese positions from only a thousand yards off the beach. Responding to call fire requests was difficult, however, because communication between ship and shore was haphazard, and fighting was at such close quarters that the lines were intermingled. Nevertheless, the Marines, who eventually numbered more than twenty thousand, slowly drove the Japanese defenders back into a small corner of the island. From his bombproof headquarters, Shibazaki sent his last message: "Everyone is attempting a final charge.... May Japan exist 10,000 years." By the time the battle ended, after seventy-six hours, only 17 of the 4,800 Japanese defenders on the island were taken alive.[46]

The Americans, too, suffered heavy casualties: more than a thousand were killed and three thousand wounded. The Americans had secured their objective, but the cost had been far beyond any of the pre-invasion projections. The losses on Guadalcanal had been greater, but the slaughter on Tarawa took place in three days instead of six months, and in less than one square mile.

Makin Island fell as well, though with far less cost to the invaders (64 killed, 120 wounded). H. M. Smith was disgusted with what he considered the slow pace of the army forces under Ralph Smith. Had Ralph Smith been a Marine, H. M. Smith later wrote, "I would have relieved him of his command on the spot." The delay gave Japanese submarines the opportunity to find the invasion fleet, and on November 23, the I-175 put a torpedo into

---

* The Marines had anticipated that some of the artillery pieces might have to be dragged ashore underwater, and to test their durability they had subjected several of them to a lengthy submersion beforehand to ensure that they would still fire.

the brand-new escort carrier *Liscome Bay*. The torpedo detonated below the ship's bomb magazine and the *Liscome Bay* simply evaporated. A witness on a nearby destroyer recalled: "She just went *whoom*—an orange ball of flame." Out of her crew of 917 men, only 272 survived.[47]

At both Munda on New Georgia Island and at Tarawa in the Gilberts, the Allies won important victories. Just as the Japanese had forecast, however, those victories had come at a heavy cost. Japanese losses were greater, to be sure, but the Japanese still doubted that the Yankees had the will or the strength of character to continue making such sacrifices. Many more "victories" like Tarawa, they reassured one another, would surely convince the Americans to agree to a negotiated settlement.

Indeed, there was significant political fallout in the United States in response to the casualties at Tarawa. The *New York Times* noted that the Marines "have paid the stiffest price in human life per square yard that was ever exacted in the history of the corps." MacArthur called the whole operation "a tragic and unnecessary massacre of American lives," and renewed his plea to be given overall command in the Pacific. Members of Congress called for an investigation. A newsreel produced by United Films played in American theaters, and despite the martial music and triumphalist narration, it could not disguise the heavy cost the Americans had incurred in taking so tiny an island. Even more influential was a color film entitled *With the Marines at Tarawa*. Based on footage shot on the island by the Marines themselves, edited by Warner Brothers, it included haunting scenes of dead Americans on the beach and was so graphic that many in the government wanted to withhold it from the public, though Roosevelt decided that it should be released. It later won an Academy Award for Best Documentary Short Subject. Horrifying it might have been, but instead of prompting calls for peace, it provoked demands for retribution.[48]

BY THE END OF 1943, as horrific fighting continued along the Russian front and in Italy, Allied forces in the Pacific had pierced the Japanese defensive shield: first in the North Pacific at Attu, then in the South Pacific at Rabaul, and now in the Central Pacific at Tarawa. Though the Japanese had made the invaders pay a heavy price, it failed to erode Allied determination. It was still more than three thousand miles from Tarawa to Tokyo Bay, but by the end of 1943 the Allies had taken the first steps.

CHAPTER 22

LARGE SLOW TARGET

S AILORS IN ALL NAVIES ARE NOTORIOUSLY IRREVERENT. They poke fun at their officers, at the absurdities of military protocol, at their food, and, as if whistling in the dark, at almost any prospect of danger or death. British crews on auxiliary merchant cruisers joked that the acronym AMC actually stood for "Admiralty-made coffins"; German U-boat crews routinely referred to their boats as "iron coffins"; and American sailors on the vessels called "landing ships, tank" claimed that LST actually stood for "large slow target."

They were not wrong. At over three hundred feet in length, LSTs were indeed large, and, with a maximum speed of ten knots, slow as well. Moreover, their demonstrated importance in amphibious landings made them prime targets. LST sailors also lampooned the sailing qualities of their clumsy vessels. With their blunt bows (which one LST sailor called "a horrible snow-shovel snout that cannot cut the water"), shallow draft, and flat bottoms, they were remarkably poor sailors, thumping down jarringly on every wave. Even in the relatively mild waters of the Mediterranean, they induced nearly universal seasickness not only among the embarked soldiers but also among the crew. As an LST veteran recalled, the ships "stank of diesel oil, backed-up toilets, and vomit."[1]

For all that, by 1944 LSTs had emerged as the essential component in Allied amphibious landings from the Mediterranean to the Central Pacific, and operational commanders found them useful for all sorts of other missions, from transporting personnel and vehicles to afloat stowage. The problem was that there were not enough of them. Despite America's astonishing industrial productivity, circumstances conspired to create a shortage of these unattractive but essential vessels at a critical moment in the war. In 1942, the War Production Board, established by Roosevelt to supervise war mobilization, had made LSTs the highest priority in the American wartime construction program. Soon after Operation Torch, however, when it became clear that a cross-Channel invasion of northern France was simply not possible in 1943, and with the Battle of the Atlantic reaching its climax, the board elevated destroyer escorts to the highest priority and dropped LST construction to twelfth place, behind minesweepers.[2]

It was the right decision at the time because the new escorts helped turn the tide in the Battle of the Atlantic (see Chapter 17). Then in the late spring of 1943, with the U-boat menace under control if not entirely suppressed, the Allies sought to reinvigorate the LST program. Four of the American shipyards that had been reconfigured to build destroyers were ordered to shift back to the construction of Liberty ships and LSTs. Retooling a ship-yard, however, is not a matter of simply throwing a switch. More than thirty thousand parts went into the construction of an LST, and recreating such a lengthy supply chain took time. In addition, the LST construction program necessarily competed with other accession programs. All those new *Essex*- and *Independence*-class carriers being sent to the Pacific required many of the same components as the LSTs. In particular, there was fierce competition for steel plate, needed not only for ship construction but also for tanks, airplanes, and indeed almost all weapons of twentieth-century warfare. The American industrial juggernaut was awesome and unprecedented, but it was not infinite, and by late 1943 a shortage of LSTs had become the single greatest impediment to the fulfillment of Allied ambitions.[3]

An LST is launched into the Ohio River from one of the "cornfield" shipyards in the American Midwest—this one is the Neville Island Shipyard on the Ohio River below Pittsburgh. From there, the new LSTs sailed downriver to Algiers, across from New Orleans, to be fitted out.

U. S. Naval Institute

Most LSTs were constructed at so-called cornfield shipyards along the Ohio and Illinois Rivers. Collectively, these shipyards produced an average of twenty-four new LSTs each month. Impressive as that was, it fell well short the need. Kent Hewitt had employed ninety LSTs in the invasion of Salerno; both Nimitz and MacArthur needed at least that many more in the Pacific; and casting a giant shadow over all theaters was the pending invasion of northern France—Operation Overlord—officially scheduled for May 1, 1944, which called for 230 LSTs. As the New Year began, such a goal was a mere chimera on the distant horizon. In the Mediterranean, in the Pacific, and in the English Channel, operational commanders clamored for more LSTs, and there simply weren't enough of them.[4]

That forced the Allied decision-makers to prioritize competing demands. A few operations were canceled altogether. For many months the Americans had pushed for an invasion of Burma in order to open the supply road to Chiang Kai-shek's Chinese army, which continued to hold down more than a million Japanese soldiers. The British had never been enthusiastic about the operation, however, and now it was eliminated so that the fifteen LSTs allocated to it could be employed elsewhere. The Combined Chiefs in Washington also hoped that LSTs could be shared between competing theaters. The distance between the Pacific Theater and the English Channel was too great, but the Mediterranean was near enough to England that it seemed plausible that the LSTs that had been used to invade Sicily and Salerno could participate in Overlord. It was not an unreasonable expectation, but for a variety of reasons, it did not happen.[5]

HITLER HAD NOT PLANNED to defend southern Italy at all, in part because it was obvious that any defensive position on the lower half of the peninsula could be easily outflanked by sea. He had been so impressed with Kesselring's strong stand at Salerno, however, that he changed his mind. In addition, Dönitz convinced him that the Allies wanted Italy "as a bridge to the Balkans," and that it was therefore important to hold out there as long as possible. Hitler agreed. He recalled Rommel from Italy, sending him to France, and elevated Kesselring to command in the Italian boot. Kesselring established a strong defensive position some fifty miles north of Naples that ran across the width of Italy from Ortona, on the Adriatic, to the Gulf of Gaeta, on the Tyrrhenian Sea. Like the Western Front in 1915–16, its precise location accommodated the shifting fortunes of war, and its several versions had various names: the Winter Line, the Hitler Line, and, most often, the Gustav Line. It consisted of a string of pillboxes, bunkers, and minefields anchored on the small Italian town of Cassino, which was overlooked by a Benedictine abbey known as Monte Cassino. When the Allies collided with this heavily fortified position after their breakout from Salerno in September, they came to an abrupt halt. Almost at once the idea of outflanking the Gustav Line with an amphibious end run became a prominent element of Allied planning.[6]

The problem was that a landing behind the Gustav Line required the use of those very LSTs that were scheduled to go to England for Overlord. Of course, if it could be done quickly, the LSTs might be able to do both,

THE BATTLE FOR ITALY

though that would work only if the LSTs could be released after the initial landing. Eisenhower, who was scheduled to go to England himself in a few weeks to assume command of the cross-Channel invasion, thought such an end run was worth consideration. He asked the Combined Chiefs for permission to keep fifty-six British and twelve American LSTs (sixty-eight total) in the Mediterranean until January 15, 1944. That would enable him to land one Allied division at Anzio, seventy miles behind the Gustav Line, which, in conjunction with a breakthrough by Mark Clark's Fifth Army near Cassino, would overthrow Kesselring's defenses. The plan had a short life, however, for it soon became evident that a swift Allied breakthrough at Cassino was unlikely, and the idea was shelved.[7]

It was Churchill who revived it. At the Tehran Conference that winter (November 28–December 1), where Churchill, Roosevelt, and Stalin met face-to-face for the first time, the British prime minister argued passionately for extending the campaign in the Mediterranean to Rome and beyond.* His pleas met stern and unyielding opposition from both the Americans and the Russians, who saw it as yet another effort by the British to delay or postpone the cross-Channel invasion. Churchill was undeterred. He found the stalemate at Cassino "scandalous" and continued to hope that he could somehow engineer a decisive Allied victory in Italy. He even imagined that a dramatic success there might make the Normandy landings unnecessary.[8]

Churchill's ability to influence military operations in the Mediterranean was greatly strengthened in January 1944 when Eisenhower departed for England to command Overlord, leaving the theater in the hands of an all-British command team. Field Marshal Henry Maitland Wilson (called "Jumbo" in tribute to his girth) took over as theater commander; Harold Alexander remained in command of the ground forces; and Sir John Cunningham (no relation to Andrew Cunningham) commanded the naval forces. Moreover, Churchill himself remained in the theater after the Tehran Conference. That he did so was more a product of chance than of intrigue. The conference had so exhausted him that he contracted pneumonia, and on his doctor's orders he remained in North Africa, first at Tunis and then at Marrakech, to recover. That put him on the spot to attend, and even to dominate, planning sessions for the Mediterranean.†

---

* En route to the conference, Roosevelt rode the new battleship *Iowa*. On November 14, some six hundred miles off the Virginia coast, he was topside in his wheelchair watching a gunnery exercise when an announcement blared out over the 1MC, the shipboard public address system: "Torpedo in the water. This is no drill." Far from being concerned, Roosevelt's reaction was to tell his valet, "Arthur! Arthur! Take me over to the starboard rail. I want to watch the torpedo!" It was not from a German U-boat but from an American destroyer, the USS *William D. Porter*, which accidentally launched it directly toward the *Iowa* during the exercise. The *Iowa*'s captain maneuvered to avoid it, and the torpedo exploded harmlessly. The guilty torpedoman on the *William D. Porter* was subsequently sentenced to fourteen years' hard labor, but FDR intervened, ordering that no one was to be punished for the mishap.

† Roosevelt, too, fell ill after returning from Tehran and was under the weather for several months. His illness was officially diagnosed as the flu by his White House physician, Admiral Ross T. McIntyre, though other doctors correctly suspected "malignant hypertension," a precursor of the heart disease that would later kill him.

The decisive meeting took place in Tunis on Christmas Day 1943. (Thirty-five hundred miles almost due north, Erich Bey and the *Scharnhorst* were preparing to leave Altenfjord on their final and fatal sortie.) At the meeting in Tunis, the eloquent Churchill beguiled his military command-ers with a vision of the inevitable success that would result from outflank-ing the Gustav Line by sea, a move that Churchill, whose vocabulary had not been enriched by American football terms, called not an "end run" but a "cat's paw." It would so threaten the German supply line, he insisted, that Kesselring would have to respond in one of two ways: either he must weaken his defenses at Cassino to protect his supply line, in which case Allied armies would smash through the Gustav Line, or he must retreat entirely. Whereas Eisenhower had considered a breakthrough at Cassino an essen-tial component of a landing at Anzio, Churchill's vision was that the landing itself would open the road to Rome. To ensure its success, the landing force was expanded from one division to two.[9]

Of course, that also meant keeping more LSTs in the Mediterranean and keeping them there for a longer period, but Churchill did not see this as a serious problem. Impatient as he was with logistical details, Churchill argued that this was a mere inconvenience. As Henry Stimson put it in his diary, Churchill had "a mind which revolts against the hard facts of logis-tics." In addition, however, Churchill noted that because the ships and the crews of the LSTs in the Mediterranean were veterans of previous landings at Sicily and Salerno, they did not need the kind of training and rehearsals that the new LSTs coming from America required. Because of that, he insisted that the sixty-eight or so LSTs required to land a flanking force at Anzio could remain in the Mediterranean an extra month, until February 15, and still get back to England in time for the cross-Channel invasion in May. After obtaining the approval of the Mediterranean commanders, Churchill successfully sold his vision to both Roosevelt and the Combined Chiefs.[10]

To make it work, timing was critical. The landing at Anzio was set for January 20, and the LSTs would have to depart for England no later than three weeks after that. That should have been a sufficient margin of error, and it likely would have been if Kesselring had behaved as Churchill pre-dicted. Churchill was confident that the battle would be decided "in a week or ten days," though some of his operational commanders were less sure. Alexander wrote him that it would be unconscionable to leave two divisions marooned on the Italian coast without support from the sea, and he insisted that fourteen of the LSTs must stay behind under any circumstances "for maintenance." For his part, Cunningham told Churchill that the operation was "fraught with great risks," to which Churchill replied: "Without risk there is no honor."[11]

To command the Anzio invasion, the Combined Chiefs appointed a pair of Americans: Major General John P. Lucas would command the ground forces, and Rear Admiral Frank J. Lowry, a veteran of both Coral Sea and Midway, commanded the naval force. (Richard Conolly, who might have led the invasion flotilla, went to the Pacific to participate in the Central Pacific Drive.) Lowry had a fleet of seventy LSTs, plus ninety-six LCIs and thirty-nine LCTs, escorted by five cruisers and two dozen destroyers, plus the usual assortment of minesweepers and sub chasers.[12]

Lucas harbored substantial doubts about the operation. In his diary he likened the forthcoming encounter to the Battle of the Little Bighorn, with himself in the role of Custer. He thought "the whole affair has a strong odor of Gallipoli," which, of course, had been another of Churchill's enthusiasms.[13]

UNLIKE THE LANDINGS AT SALERNO, the Allies achieved complete surprise at Anzio, and the initial landings were virtually unopposed. By midmorning, all of the first day's objectives had been seized and the Allies held an enclave fifteen miles wide and seven miles deep. In a decision that has been much criticized since, Lucas did not immediately advance inland, either northward toward Rome or eastward to the Alban Hills to cut the roads that led to the German defenses at Cassino. Given the absence of strong opposition, he might have done so, though it is unlikely he could have sustained himself very long in either foray. He might well have been cut off altogether and destroyed. Besides, his orders indicated that his primary assignment was to establish a strong beachhead, the very existence of which, he was assured, would compel the Germans to fall back. Because of that, Lucas established a strong perimeter and focused on getting the

Allied troops wade ashore from LCI-281 on Anzio beach on January 22, 1944. Though the landing caught the Germans by surprise, it did not compel the Axis to fall back from the Gustav Line, and the Allied enclave at Anzio became a liability requiring constant resupply and reinforcement.

U.S. National Archives photo no. SC 185796

harbor at Anzio into a state of repair to receive more men and supplies. By the end of the first day, the LSTs and transports had successfully landed thirty-six thousand men and thirty-two hundred vehicles at Anzio with few casualties.[14]

Surprised as he was, Kesselring did not for a moment consider a retreat. He believed he could both hold the Gustav Line *and* pin down the Allies at Anzio. Rather than withdraw forces from Cassino, he brought two reserve divisions from Rome and summoned additional forces from Yugoslavia and France. Within days he had concentrated elements of eight divisions around the Allied enclave without weakening his forces on the Gustav Line. Mark Clark's Fifth Army hammered away at that line, but with little success, and as a result there was no link-up between Clark's army and Lucas's two divisions at Anzio. The Germans thus held an interior position between two Allied fronts and were able to choose where to defend and where to attack.[15]

Kesselring decided to attack Lucas. On the last day of January, he sent columns of tanks and infantry against the Allied enclave (which Hitler called an "abscess") in an effort to drive the invaders back into the sea. The Allied lines bent under these sustained attacks, but they did not break. In addition to hard fighting ashore, one reason was that the LSTs and the other supply ships brought in a continuous flow of reinforcements and supplies.

Throughout February, convoys of LSTs left Naples every day carrying rein-forcements as well as trucks loaded with food, supplies, and ammunition. When they arrived at Anzio, the men disembarked and the loaded trucks drove ashore. Other trucks filled with Allied wounded and Axis POWs took their place, and the LSTs headed back to Naples to repeat the process. The LST crews labored around the clock. They were either loading, unload-ing, or under way virtually all the time, and during much of that time they were also under air attack. Theodore Wyman, the first lieutenant on LST-197, recalled, "We were so damnably tired that we just didn't have time to be bothered about being tired." It was so hectic that the LSTs soon began sending ashore crewmen afflicted with "combat fatigue" and "shell shock," the terms then used to describe post-traumatic stress disorder. After the war, Wyman asserted that of the five operations they participated in from North Africa to Normandy, "it was the Anzio campaign that took the most out of us." Yet the supplies got through, and because they did, the Allies at Anzio held on.[16]

Of course, holding on had never been the objective. Churchill was frus-trated and distraught that his cat's paw had failed to open the road to Rome. An operation that was supposed to end the stalemate and enable Allied sol-diers to charge up the Italian boot had instead turned into another bloody battle of attrition. He later wrote, in a much quoted passage, "I had hoped that we were hurling a wild cat on to the shore, but all we got was a stranded whale." He consoled himself with the thought that it was not all in vain because the bitter fighting at Anzio at least tied down large numbers of Germans. To the British army representative on the Combined Chiefs in Washington he wrote that "even a battle of attrition is better than standing by and watching the Russians fight," and he reported to the House of Commons that the Allied initiative at Anzio occupied large numbers of Germans who otherwise would be employed elsewhere, an obvious reference to the Eastern Front. Of course, if the fighting at Anzio occupied German troops, it also occupied Allied troops. As the historian Martin Blumenson put it, "Exactly who was holding whom was never quite clear."[17]

Then, too, in addition to the heavy cost in human life (the combined casualties from both sides eventually exceeded eighty thousand), the prolonged fighting at Anzio also wrecked the carefully planned reassignment of LSTs to the English Channel. When Eisenhower arrived in England to take up his new assignment as Supreme Allied Commander, he already knew that LSTs would be a critical problem, even without the added pressure of sustaining the Anzio beachhead. British Major General Frederick Morgan, who had led the team that compiled the original plan for Overlord, had based all his calculations on a three-division assault, mainly because he had been told by the Combined Chiefs that there would be sufficient sealift for only three divisions. From the start, however, Eisenhower knew that three divisions would not be enough to break through the Atlantic Wall. After all, he had used seven divisions to invade Sicily. He therefore directed that the plan be rewritten to accommodate a five-division sea assault plus two airborne divisions. That meant a dramatic expansion of landing craft, and in particular the essential LSTs. On January 23, the day after Lucas's two divisions went ashore at Anzio, Eisenhower wrote the Joint Chiefs in Washington to insist that in addition to the 230 LSTs, 250 LCIs, and 900 LCTs that Morgan had called for in the original plan, he needed 271 more landing ships and landing craft, including 47 of the vital but scarce LSTs.[18]

In receipt of this startling information, the Joint Chiefs responded with barely disguised skepticism. They asked him to document "the basis you used in arriving at the additional resources required." They wanted to know how many landing craft he had. What was their capacity? What was his justification for needing more? The Supreme Allied Commander might have replied testily to such an enquiry, but Eisenhower's famous patience and diplomacy led him to respond with a careful item-by-item reply, and he allowed the numbers to speak for themselves. The current number of LSTs in England, he reported, was 173. If he added the LSTs that were expected to arrive from America between January and May (twenty-five per month if there were no losses en route), it would give him 248 on D-Day. Because several would be used as command ships and fighter-director ships, he would have almost exactly the 230 that Morgan had calculated as necessary for a three-division assault. But it was clearly not enough to carry five divisions across the Channel and sustain them there.[19]

Grudgingly accepting Eisenhower's math, the Joint and Combined Chiefs sought some way to direct LSTs to England from other theaters. The initial plan to transfer them from the Mediterranean was frustrated by the crisis at Anzio, and Eisenhower suggested that perhaps the LSTs there could be replaced by attack transports so the LSTs could be sent to England for Overlord. The Joint Chiefs (very likely prompted by King) had a different suggestion. They proposed sending twenty-six brand-new LSTs from America to the Mediterranean if Jumbo Wilson agreed to send twenty-six of those he now had to England. Quite reasonably, Wilson wondered why it would not be easier simply to send the twenty-six new LSTs directly to England. Only then did the Joint Chiefs reveal that the new LSTs in question were still on the building ways and would not be available until the end of May. That would make them too late for Overlord. As far as Wilson was concerned, it also made them too late for the defenders of Anzio.[20]

Another complication was that at Tehran, Churchill, Roosevelt, and Stalin had agreed to mount a two-division assault of southern France— Operation Anvil—simultaneous with the invasion of Normandy. The Americans had suggested it in the first place as a way to rein in Churchill's enthusiasm for other, more tangential adventures, such as his proposal to invade the island of Rhodes. At Tehran, however, Stalin had surprised everyone by expressing great enthusiasm for a landing in southern France. As he saw it, the Normandy hammer would slam down on the Mediterranean anvil. To execute it, however, the Allies needed another eighty or ninety LSTs, and where would they come from? The fifteen or so that had been withdrawn from the canceled invasion of Burma would help, but they were not enough, especially given the circumstances at Anzio. As Churchill noted, "Everything turned on landing-craft, which held for some weeks all our strategy in the tightest ligature. What with the rigid date prescribed for 'Overlord' and the movement, repair, and refitting of less than a hundred of these small vessels, all plans were in a straitjacket."[21]

The solution was twofold. First the date for Overlord was postponed by a month, from the first week of May to the first week of June. That would provide American shipyards one more month to build as many LSTs as possible. As Eisenhower wrote to Marshall, "One extra month of landing craft production, including LSTs, should help a lot." It would still not be enough, however. In addition to delaying Overlord, the Allies were also compelled to cancel or at least postpone Anvil. Ike was disappointed by that. "It looks like ANVIL is doomed," he wrote in his diary. "I hate this." Still, there was no escaping the numbers. Without the additional LSTs that had been earmarked for Anvil, Eisenhower would not have enough to sustain the invasion force at Normandy. He wrote to Marshall that while there would be enough LSTs for the first three tides, after that "we will have no *repeat no* LSTs reaching the beaches after the morning of D plus 1 until the morning of D plus 4." In other words, the Allied invasion force would be stranded on the Normandy beaches for three days without the means to reinforce, supply, or (God forbid) evacuate. That was obviously unacceptable, and so Eisenhower reluctantly acknowledged the reality that Anvil had to be postponed.[22]

Anzio and Anvil were not the only complications. As far as Eisenhower was concerned, the war in the Pacific was "absorbing far too much of our limited resources in landing craft." Again finding an outlet for his frustration in his diary, he complained that despite the Germany-first strategy, a policy that all parties had accepted from the beginning, an American offensive was going full blast in the Pacific, even as he had to scramble for the necessary sealift to carry out the most important operation of the entire war. "We are fighting two wars at once," he wrote, "which is wrong."[23]

AS IF TO UNDERSCORE THAT, eight days after Churchill's cat's paw landed at Anzio, elements of Raymond Spruance's Fifth Fleet, including forty LSTs, conducted large-scale amphibious landings in the Marshall Islands—the second step in the Central Pacific Drive.

A group of thirty-two coral atolls, the Marshall Islands sprawl over more than four hundred thousand square miles of ocean. In about the middle of them was Kwajalein, the largest atoll in the world, whose central lagoon was more than sixty miles long and twenty miles wide. From fifteen thousand feet, the atoll resembled a silver necklace hastily discarded onto a blue carpet after a night of revelry. Like most atolls, this one boasted a number of small islands—tiny beads on the necklace—some of which were large enough to host significant military facilities. The three most important of them were Kwajalein Island, at the southern tip of the atoll, and the twin islands of Roi and Namur, at its northern end.[24]

After the bloodletting on Betio, the Allies were concerned that Kwajalein, which was more than six hundred miles northwest of Tarawa, might prove even more costly. Not only was it larger, but the Japanese had been there far longer. Whereas the Japanese had seized Betio Island only in January 1942, they had occupied the Marshall Islands since the 1920s under a League of Nations mandate. According to Article 22 of that mandate, Japan was prohibited from fortifying those islands, a restriction confirmed by the 1922 Naval Arms Limitation Agreement. Nevertheless, the Americans assumed (correctly) that Japan had ignored those restrictions and had fortified the islands anyway. Aware of that, virtually every member of Nimitz's staff urged that the next offensive should be against one of the outer islands in the Marshalls group rather than the main Japanese base at Kwajalein. Nimitz overruled them, for he believed that the lessons learned at Tarawa could be effectively applied at Kwajalein.[25]

One of those lessons was the importance of a prolonged and well-directed preliminary bombardment. It was self-evident that the bombardment of Betio had been a failure. The official Marine Corps history of the war noted that "a greater weight of metal was hurled into each square foot of Betio Island than had rained down on any previous amphibious objective." And yet when the invaders went ashore, the defenders were ready and waiting. This time, rather than simply blast the island with high explosives, individual ships were assigned specific targets with the responsibility of neutralizing those targets before the landings began. To ensure they could do so, American forces conducted rehearsals on the island of Kahoolawe, a small (nine miles by five miles) uninhabited piece of volcanic rock in the Hawaiian chain. There U.S. Marines built coconut-log and concrete pillboxes similar to those found on Tarawa, and the crews of the battleships and cruisers practiced shelling them and then inspecting the results. The Marine historian Robert Heinl estimated that Kahoolawe was "the most shot-at island in the Pacific."[26]

A group of LVTs (amtracks, amphtracks, or alligators) heads toward the beach with a dozen embarked Marines. Some LVTs also carried a 37 mm gun, which made them amphibious light tanks.

Collection of James E. Bailey, Naval History and Heritage Command

A second lesson was the obvious need for more of the tracked alligators (LVTs) to allow the soldiers and Marines to get across the coral reef without having to wade ashore. After Tarawa, the War Production Board doubled the number of LVTs under construction from a planned 2,055 to more than 4,000. Many of them were armored and redesigned to carry 37 mm guns, essentially making them amphibious light tanks; they were rechristened LVT(A)s. With such vehicles, the soldiers and Marines could crawl across the reef under the cover of their own amphibious artillery. Of course, the construction of two thousand more LVTs added to the demands being made on an already challenged shipbuilding industry.[27]

At Pearl Harbor, the new LVTs were loaded inside the LSTs. Eighteen of them fit into an LST's cavernous tank deck, and an equal number could be craned up onto the weather deck. Once the LSTs arrived at Kwajalein, they could steam up to within five or six miles of the target beach, open their bow doors, and launch the LVTs into the sea, with each LVT carrying twenty soldiers or Marines. After the first eighteen were afloat, the LVTs on the weather deck could then be lowered to the tank deck by elevator to follow them in a second wave. Twenty of the LSTs belonged to Kelly Turner's Southern Task Force for the invasion of Kwajalein Island, and eighteen more were entrusted to Richard "Close-in" Conolly, recently arrived from the Mediterranean, for the invasion of the twin islands of Roi and Namur. Two more were used as command and gunfire-control ships.

Most of the LSTs were brand-new, rushed from their Ohio River building yards down the Mississippi to New Orleans, where they were fitted out, then through the Panama Canal and up to San Diego, where they arrived only days before departing for Pearl Harbor. The men who made up their crews were brand-new as well, most of them straight out of boot camp, and the long voyage from New Orleans to the mid-Pacific constituted their only sea experience. Some engaged in a practice landing on San Clemente Island on January 2–3. That rehearsal exposed several alarming weaknesses in the protocols for launching the LVTs, but the tight schedule precluded additional exercises. On at least one LST, only one man in the entire crew had ever even seen an LVT lowered down a ship's elevator to the tank deck.[28]

The invasion of Kwajalein took place on January 31 (the same day that Kesselring began his counterattack against the Anzio beachhead). As in almost any amphibious assault, there were unforeseen problems and delays. One was the choppy sea state, which triggered a decision to send the LSTs into the much calmer lagoon before launching the LVTs. After the LSTs had launched the first wave of eighteen LVTs, those vessels circled while the LVTs on the weather deck were lowered one by one to the tank deck to join them. That process took far longer than anticipated. On one LST, the elevator stuck fast and left nine of the LVTs sitting uselessly on the weather deck. And of course there were the usual delays as the LVTs organized themselves into waves for the assault. Despite all that, the landings on Kwajalein were far more successful than those at Tarawa. The official army history concluded that the ship-to-shore movement was "conducted expeditiously and without [a] serious hitch."[29]

That was not quite true. After landing the first wave of soldiers (on Kwajalein) and Marines (on Roi and Namur), the tracked LVTs were supposed to return to their LSTs for a second load. Some of the returning LVTs could not find their mother ships, and others ran out of gas on their way back. In something of an understatement, the official Marine Corps historians wrote that the LSTs and LVTs "did not cooperate as well as they should have." Amidst the confusion, many of the men assigned to later waves had to rely on the Higgins boats after all. In the end, it turned out not to matter. The defenders had been so shattered by the lengthy and accurate pre-invasion bombardment that the survivors were dazed and disoriented. On Kwajalein Island, only a single palm tree remained standing. The Marines on Roi and Namur seized their objectives within a day; the soldiers of the army's 7th Division needed until February 4 to subdue Kwajalein (a source of annoyance to Holland Smith, who thought the army, as usual, displayed undue caution). Still, in both cases, the islands were secured more swiftly and with fewer casualties than the planners had calculated.[30]

Indeed, the swift conquest led Nimitz to accelerate his schedule and seize the island of Eniwetok, at the western end of the atoll, as well. That was accomplished two weeks later, on February 17, with relatively light losses. For all practical purposes, the Americans had seized control of the Marshall Islands.

ONE REASON FOR SUCH STARTLING SUCCESS was American domination of the air, made possible by what was called the Fast Carrier Task Force—officially Task Force 58, commanded by Marc Mitscher, now a vice admiral. Spruance, who was fully aware of Mitscher's problematic performance at Midway—ordering the "flight to nowhere"—was initially dubious about giving him the command, but Admiral John Towers, head of the Bureau of Aeronautics, championed Mitscher's cause and Spruance acceded to the appointment. It turned out to be inspired. Task Force 58 consisted of no fewer than twelve aircraft carriers, six of them the big *Essex*-class carriers with ninety or more aircraft each. Altogether, the carriers of TF 58 boasted more than seven hundred airplanes. Accompanied by the new fast battleships, heavy cruisers, and forty destroyers, it was the most powerful naval striking force ever assembled. For the Marshalls Operation, it was broken into four task groups of three carriers each that roamed the Central Pacific at will, attacking and destroying Japanese planes in the air and on the ground. So devastating were these attacks that by February 4, when Kwajalein was declared secure, the American pilots had literally run out of targets. In consequence of that, no Allied vessel experienced a single air attack during the operation, a dramatic contrast with the landings at Salerno and Anzio.[31]

Admiral Koga dared not come out to challenge this overwhelming naval power. Even the Kidō Butai at its height would have been no match for Task Force 58, and because Koga had followed Yamamoto's lead in using his carrier air groups to aid in the defense of Rabaul, his carriers had far less than their full complement of aircraft. Sending his battleships and heavy cruisers to sea without robust air cover would have been suicidal. Then, too, the Japanese defense strategy was to hoard its resources for the final battle. Only when the Americans penetrated the inner circle of Japanese defenses would the Imperial Japanese Navy commit its carriers and battleships.

That moment was closer than anyone in Tokyo or at Truk suspected. The American conquest of the Marshall Islands had been so swift and one-sided that it encouraged Nimitz and the Joint Chiefs to consider bypassing Koga's main base at Truk altogether. It seemed a bold move at the time, for Truk had been the principal Japanese base in the Central Pacific since 1942. In fact, however, it was not nearly as well fortified as the Americans thought, for the Japanese had never quite believed the Americans would get that far. Now that they had, Nimitz and Spruance concluded that the Fifth Fleet could leap past it nearly fifteen hundred miles, all the way to Saipan in the Marianas.[32]

MEANWHILE, IN ITALY, Kesselring launched a final all-out assault on the Anzio beachhead on February 18, the day after Eniwetok fell. There were now seven Allied divisions inside that crowded beachhead, yet the assault by the German Tenth Army was so furious that Mark Clark briefly considered ordering an evacuation. It never came to that. The German attack eventually petered out, and having shot his bolt, Kesselring abandoned the idea of driving the invaders into the sea, though of course neither Clark nor Lucas knew that. A week later, Lucas himself was gone. On February 25, American Major General Lucian Truscott replaced him in command at Anzio, though that did not significantly affect the now static situation.

The change occurred nearly three months later. As Eisenhower had suspected from the start, success at Anzio came only after a breakthrough on the Gustav Line. In a genuinely Allied effort, American, British, and Canadian units hammered the Gustav Line near the main highway to Rome while the French Expeditionary Force under General Alphonse Juin achieved a key breakthrough to their right, and the Polish Second Corps under Lieutenant General Wladyslaw Anders seized Monte Cassino, raising the Polish flag over the ruins of the abbey on May 17. These assaults restored fluidity to the tactical situation, and five days later Truscott orchestrated a breakout from Anzio, driving inland to capture the strategically significant town of Cisterna. Clark had a chance to trap the retreating German Tenth Army, but he was so obsessed with capturing Rome, he let the Germans go in order to win the race to Italy's capital.

On June 4, elements of three American divisions (the 3rd, 85th, and 88th) entered Rome. Clark had worked hard to ensure that American (and not British) units entered the city first, and he cherished his moment of triumph as the city's population spilled out into the streets on June 5 to cheer the Americans, welcoming them as liberators. It was a heady moment, and generated oversized headlines in the *New York Times*: "ROME CAPTURED INTACT." Clark's moment of triumph did not last. The headline the next day read: "ALLIED ARMIES LAND IN FRANCE."[33]

PART V

RECKONING

The separate and independent decisions made in 1941 by Adolf Hitler in Berlin and the Japanese warlords in Tokyo to hurl their military forces at the Soviet Union and the United States will forever rank as among the most self-destructive acts in history. By 1944, the extent of their folly had become fully evident. In Europe, the Red Army, more than three million strong, drove the Germans back to the borders of Poland and Romania, and Anglo-American forces prepared to invade occupied France; in the Pacific, the American Fifth Fleet was poised to break through the inner ring of Japan's defenses in the Marianas.

For more than two years, the Red Army had shouldered the burden of the land war in Europe while the English-speaking Allies suppressed the U-boats at sea, stanched the Japanese offensive in the Pacific, and asserted control over the Mediterranean. Suspicious by nature, Stalin had grown more so as the British and Americans declined to open a genuine second front against the Wehrmacht. He had watched with barely concealed scorn as the Anglo-American forces invaded first French North Africa, then Sicily, then Italy, and the Americans prosecuted not one but two offensives in the Pacific. Despite the official policy of defeating Germany first, the Americans had invaded Guadalcanal before North Africa, and launched Cartwheel before Husky. Even in the summer of 1944, as the British and Americans at last prepared to breach Hitler's vaunted Atlantic Wall in Normandy, U.S. forces also initiated new offensives in the Pacific.

It was a measure of how dominant Allied material superiority had become that the Americans could even consider conducting a new campaign in the Pacific at virtually the same moment they were preparing to assail the Normandy coast. The American industrial giant had started slowly, and for more than a year a shortage of shipping had constituted a crippling impediment to major operations. Now, however, American factories and shipyards were operating at full flood, and their products poured into the operational theaters. Nor was the Allied advantage measured only in terms of quantity. In 1941 German tanks and aircraft had been qualitatively superior to Allied weaponry; Japanese warplanes and torpedoes had been the best in the world. By 1944 that was no longer true.

Given those circumstances, the final outcome of the war, though still a full year away, could hardly be doubted. That reality bred desperation in both Germany and Japan, a desperation exemplified by the German decision to push the "Final Solution" to its horrific conclusion, and by the Japanese adoption of "body crash" tactics in the Pacific. Meanwhile, at Los Alamos, in the hills above Santa Fe, New Mexico, and elsewhere scientists worked at secret laboratories to develop a weapon of such destructive power it could hardly be imagined. Having sown the wind, the Axis powers were about to reap the whirlwind.

CHAPTER 23

D-DAY

I N JANUARY 1944, the same month that Allied soldiers went ashore at Anzio, more than one and a half million American, British, and Canadian soldiers in southern England began rehearsing for a full-scale invasion of German-occupied France. Here, at last, was the second front that Stalin had been demanding for more than two years. Though the code name for it was Operation Overlord, the naval and maritime element, including the crossing and the landings themselves, was christened Operation Neptune. While Eisenhower commanded Overlord, Admiral Sir Bertram Ramsay, the hero of Dunkirk who had been Cunningham's deputy for Torch and led the Eastern (British) task force during the invasion of Sicily, presided over Neptune. In that capacity, he commanded the greatest assembly of shipping in world history.

Ramsay arrived in England in October 1943, well ahead of Eisenhower, and established his headquarters at Southwick House near Portsmouth, a stately Georgian mansion being used as the Royal Navy's navigation school. After Ramsay moved in, his staff erected a giant wall map of the English

Channel depicting all the ports in southern England where Allied troops were congregating, as well as the target beaches in Normandy where the Allies would land. Having choreographed the massive evacuation of the continent at Dunkirk in 1940, Ramsay would now have the satisfaction of overseeing the Allied reentry four years later. To do it, he had to move an entire Allied army—indeed, two armies—as well as the necessary equipment and vehicles across the Channel, provide naval gunfire support for the landings, then keep the invaders reinforced and supplied during the days, weeks, or months it took to secure and expand their foothold.[1]

The rehearsals for D-Day took place all along the English coast, from the Bristol Channel on the west to the Thames estuary on the east. To accommodate the Americans, the British government made available 141,000 acres of English coastline in Devon and Cornwall. Here the Americans established what was called the American Army Battle School near Slapton Sands, a picturesque beach a few miles west of Dartmouth, where the British naval academy was located. Several factors besides its location made it nearly ideal for the rehearsals. Like the target beaches across the Channel, Slapton Sands was composed of shingle: billions of small wave-polished black and gray pebbles. Moreover, the rolling countryside behind Slapton Sands, crisscrossed by hedgerows between green fields, was superficially similar to the *bocage* country behind the landing beaches in Normandy. After evacuating the civilian population from the region, the Americans moved in, and week after week, first by battalions, then by regiments, and finally by divisions, they conducted practice landings at Slapton Sands and elsewhere. "We loaded and unloaded various troops and equipment time after time," an LST crewman recalled. "We were never sure if each practice might be the real thing." In the spring, as the days lengthened and the weather warmed, the number of available LSTs at last neared the target figure, and the rehearsals grew larger and more complex.[2]

One of them, in mid-April, was dubbed Exercise Tiger. It involved Force U, the naval element of the invasion group for Utah Beach, which was commanded by American Rear Admiral Don Moon. The plan was to land the bulk of Major General J. Lawton Collins's VII Corps at Slapton Sands under the cover of naval gunfire, and from there, the soldiers would advance inland to "capture" the town of Oakhampton. Eisenhower and Ramsay wanted the exercise to be as realistic as possible, and to create the conditions the invaders were likely to encounter on Utah Beach, Allied engineers placed two lines of steel tetrahedra and barbed wire on the shingle. They even planted live mines.[3]

Moon's task force for the practice landing included twenty-one LSTs, twenty-eight LCI(L)s, and sixty-five LCTs, plus nearly a hundred smaller vessels and the usual escort of warships. The ships would leave Plymouth in two waves, steam out into the middle of the Channel overnight, and then turn back toward the English coast to land the embarked soldiers at dawn, just as they would six weeks later in Normandy.

It got off to a bad start. One of the LST flotillas in the first wave was late to the rendezvous, and Moon postponed the landing until it arrived. Not everyone got the word. As a result, when some of the loaded Higgins boats began heading for the beach in accordance with the original schedule, they found themselves bracketed by "preliminary" naval gunfire from the cruisers and destroyers. Though it was quickly straightened out, it was an ill omen.[4]

The second wave of eight fully loaded LSTs departed Plymouth at 10:00 p.m. on April 27. There was the usual confusion as the ships jostled about in the dark to exit the harbor and find their place in the formation. In the midst of it, the British destroyer Scimitar, one of two escorts assigned to the convoy, collided with an American landing craft and had to be pulled from the operation, leaving only the Flower-class corvette Azalea as an escort. Entirely coincidentally, Theodor Krancke, former captain of the Admiral Scheer and now commanding the E-Boat flotilla at Cherbourg, ordered out nine German Schnellbooten for a routine patrol of the Channel.[5]

The eight American LSTs were approaching Lyme Bay a few minutes past 1:00 a.m. on April 28 when a crewman on LST-507 heard what he described as "a scraping and dragging noise" under the ship. Unrecognized at the time, in hindsight it is evident that it was a German torpedo passing just under the hull. The skipper of the 507, Lieutenant J. S. Swarts, sounded general quarters, though most of the sailors who dutifully headed for their combat stations assumed that this was simply part of the exercise—there had been so many of them. Minutes later, bright green tracer rounds from the E-boats lit up the darkness, and at 2:07 a.m. a torpedo exploded against the hull.[6]

The expansive cargo bays on the LSTs meant that there were few watertight bulkheads that could be closed off to limit flooding, and the 507 began to sink even as fires raged among the parked vehicles on the tank deck. Lieutenant (j.g.) Gene Eckstam, the ship's doctor, looked into the cargo bay to see "a huge, roaring blast furnace" as the tanks and trucks, all of them with full gas tanks, caught fire and exploded one by one. As Eckstam remembered it, "Trucks were burning; gasoline was burning; and small-arms ammunition was exploding." He could hear the screams of men being consumed by the flames. He knew there was nothing he could do for them; smoke inhalation would soon overcome any who were still alive. "So I closed the hatches into the tank deck and dogged them tightly shut."[7]

The 507 was not the only victim. Only eleven minutes later, two torpedoes hit the LST-531 in quick succession. She went down in only six minutes, taking most of her crew and many of the embarked soldiers with her. Those not trapped inside leaped into the frigid water of the English Channel.

Ten miles ahead of the convoy, Royal Navy Commander George C. Geddes, in the *Azalea*, reversed course and sped back to the scene of the disaster. Assuming that a German U-boat was the culprit, he slowed down and activated his Asdic. There were no contacts. He hesitated to fire star shells into the night to illuminate the scene for fear of exposing the remaining LSTs, all of which now headed for shore as fast as they could. By then, the E-boats were already speeding back to their lair at Cherbourg.

The final toll was two LSTs sunk and two damaged, one so badly that it would never put to sea again. The death toll was sobering: 198 sailors and 441 soldiers died. That was more, as it happened, than were killed during the actual landings on Utah Beach six weeks later. Eisenhower insisted that the entire event be kept secret. Not only would it advertise to the Germans how successful their sortie had been, it would be a crushing blow to Allied morale on the eve of the invasion.[8]

In addition, however, Eisenhower and Ramsay were almost as concerned about the loss of those three LSTs. The margin of safety in terms of available

During Exercise Tiger off Slapton Sands in April 1944, German E-boats sank two fully loaded American LSTs and badly damaged LST-289, seen here. The loss of life was heavy, and the loss of three LSTs threatened the timetable for the D-Day landings.

U.S. National Archives photo no. 80-G-283500

LSTs was so narrow that the loss of three of them threatened the viability of the operation. Eisenhower immediately asked for replacement LSTs from America. King told him that there were none to spare, and even if there were, they could not possibly get there in time. King wired Cunningham in the Mediterranean to suggest that he send three LSTs to Eisenhower, promising to replace them with new LSTs as soon as they were available. Once again, the Allies were forced to shift naval assets from theater to theater.[9]

THE DISASTER IN LYME BAY did not derail the schedule. On May 28, Ramsay sent an order to all naval commands: "Carry out Operation Neptune." Thousands of vessels got under way: battleships and cruisers for the naval gunfire support mission left ports in Northern Ireland and Scotland while landing ships and landing craft began loading at ports from Falmouth in Cornwall to Newhaven in East Sussex. On land, long columns of trucks carrying soldiers in full kit made their way in an endless stream along the narrow roads of southern England toward the coast. All the complex pieces of a giant military puzzle moved as if directed by a single impulse, as in fact they were.[10]

The soldiers gathered at scores of Channel ports where engineers had constructed concrete beaches called "hards." On these hards, the smaller landing ships could beach themselves and load tanks, trucks, jeeps, and other vehicles directly from shore without the need for a pier or heavy cranes. Some of the big LSTs also nosed up to the hards, though most remained anchored out in the harbor, where the soldiers and equipment were shuttled out to them.[11]

At Plymouth, the men of Collins's VII Corps loaded up into the 865 ships of Moon's Force U. Further east, at Weymouth and Portland, men of Major General Charles Huebner's Big Red One, veterans of the landing at Gela in Sicily and now designated for Omaha Beach, boarded the ships of Rear Admiral John L. "Jimmy" Hall. Still further east at Southampton and Portsmouth, men of the Second British Army, commanded by Lieutenant General Miles Dempsey, boarded the ships of Force S (Rear Admiral George Talbot) and Force G (Rear Admiral Cyril Douglas-Pennant), which would carry them to Sword and Gold Beaches while men of the Canadian First Division embarked on the ships of Force J for Juno Beach, commanded by Commodore Sir Geoffrey Oliver, a veteran of the landings in Sicily and Salerno.[12]

The loading process was deliberate but continuous. The specific load of every ship had been carefully worked out in the detailed planning documents, and quartermasters armed with clipboards checked off every item as vehicles backed gingerly into place aboard the landing ships. Once there, they were tied down so that they would not shift about during the crossing. Men lugging sixty-pound packs and carrying nine-pound Garand M-1 rifles marched aboard, and they, too, were counted one by one. Once the load was certified as complete and accurate, the skipper of the landing ships

A group of LSTs loads an artillery unit at Brixham, near Dartmouth, on June 1, 1944. Of the five LSTs seen here, one (LST-499 at left center) was destroyed by a German mine on June 8.

U.S. Naval Institute

ordered the ramp closed and the vessel retracted from the hard to anchor out in the harbor. As soon as it did, another took its place and the process continued. This went on at 171 embarkation sites for five days.[13]

D-Day was June 5. Originally scheduled for the first week of May, it had been postponed in order to obtain another month's worth of new-construction LSTs. To meet that deadline, the landing ships did not depart all at once. To effect a simultaneous rendezvous, those farthest away put to sea first, with some departing on June 3. As they ventured into the Channel, it was evident that it was going to be a rough crossing. Sea spray cascaded over the thwarts of the smaller ships and sloshed about the deck; men began throwing up over the side even before the ships cleared the harbor. Then it began to rain. Eisenhower met with his team of commanders at Ramsay's headquarters at Southwick House, where the staff meteorologist, Group Captain James M. Stagg, reported that the weather was likely to get much worse before it got any better. Similar circumstances had characterized the invasion of Sicily, and on that occasion Eisenhower had decided to stick with the original schedule. This time he decided it was necessary to postpone the invasion for twenty-four hours.[14]

That was easier said than done. More than a thousand ships were already at sea and they all had to be rerouted back into port. Ramsay called his task group commanders to ask if they could hold up. They could. In the detailed planning, nearly every contingency had been considered, including this one. A designated code phrase ("One Mike Post") went out over the short-range, high-frequency TBS network, and the ships adjusted accordingly. One group of amphibs from Moon's Force U was already beyond the range of the TBS, and Ramsay had to send a destroyer steaming at flank speed to find the ships and bring them back.

Eisenhower's command team met again at 4:00 a.m. on June 5. The weather had improved a bit, though it was still quite rough out in the Channel. Nevertheless, Stagg reported that it was likely to improve the next day, and Ike made his decision. "OK," he said. "We'll go."[15]

ALL THAT AFTERNOON AND EVENING, thousands of ships from ports in England, Wales, Scotland, and Northern Ireland steamed for the rendezvous site in the middle of the English Channel, twenty miles south of the Isle of Wight. Officially, the rendezvous was designated as Area Zebra, but almost everyone called it Piccadilly Circus after the notoriously congested traffic circle in central London. Among the ships that gathered there were 284 warships from more than half a dozen countries, including Canada, France, Holland, Norway, and Poland, though most of them were British or American. There were also nearly two thousand amphibious ships, including 311 of the precious LSTs. It was an eclectic assemblage. Some vessels were exotic creations, such as the monitors carrying 15-inch guns, LCTs that had been altered to carry racks of sixty-pound rockets, command ships with an untidy array of electronic antennae, and raftlike vessels called rhino ferries, used to shuttle vehicles and equipment from the LSTs to the beach. Counting the hundreds of Higgins boats, they totaled more than six thousand vessels. Of all the impressions veterans recalled in the years afterward, the most enduring and ubiquitous was the vista of "thousands and thousands of ships of all classes stretched from horizon to horizon."[16]

Just before midnight, the Allied ships at Area Zebra began to move southward, steaming toward the French coast through swept channels. It was still several hours before dawn when they arrived off the French coast, and the soldiers on the transports lined up at the rails to climb gingerly down the rope ladders into the Higgins boats. As the boats filled with their allotted number, they cast off and motored away to circle nearby as other boats took their place alongside. Not all the men embarked at once—only those designated for the first several waves. The invasion of France, like those of Sicily and Italy, would be accomplished not by a single rush shoreward but by a continuous series of landings fifteen or twenty minutes apart, lasting all day, and indeed for several days and even weeks afterward.[17]

To the soldiers in the tossing Higgins boats, the circling seemed endless, and some had to endure it for three hours or more. Men puked over the side or, unable to raise themselves over the high thwart, threw up onto their boot tops. Soon most of the boats were redolent with a noxious combination of diesel fumes, cordite from the naval gunfire, and *mal de mer*. Finally, at about 4:00 a.m., with just a hint of light appearing along the eastern horizon, the boats formed up into a line abreast and headed for shore, still four miles away and indistinct in the predawn darkness. H-hour—the moment they were expected to touch the beach—was 6:30 a.m. for the Americans and 7:30 for the British and Canadians. The time disparity was necessary because the gentle gradient of the British and Canadian beaches meant that, despite a rising tide, there would not be enough water at Gold, Juno, and Sword Beaches for the landing craft to reach the shore until 7:25.[18]

In the Pacific, at Tarawa and elsewhere, the Americans had learned that a short naval bombardment, no matter how intense, often failed to disable or even damage the carefully prepared shore defenses. That lesson had been applied at Kwajalein and Eniwetok, where the bombardments had been both longer and more carefully orchestrated; months later, the naval bombardments at Iwo Jima and Okinawa would last for several days. Lengthy bombardments were possible in the Pacific because once the Americans surrounded an island and cut it off, the Japanese were unable to reinforce it. That was not the case on the coast of France, where a prolonged

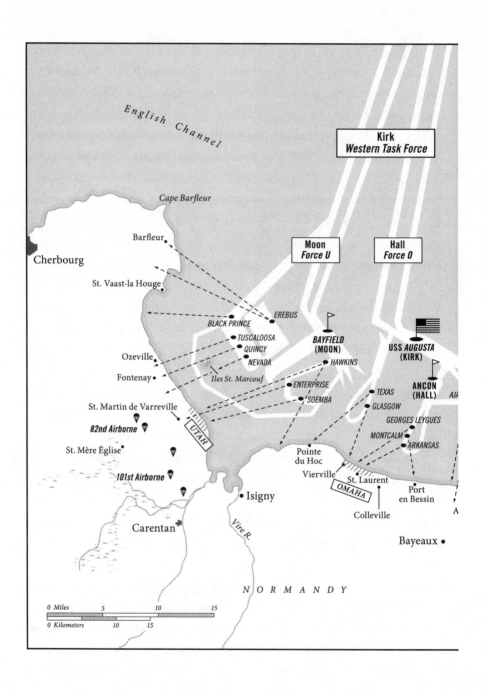

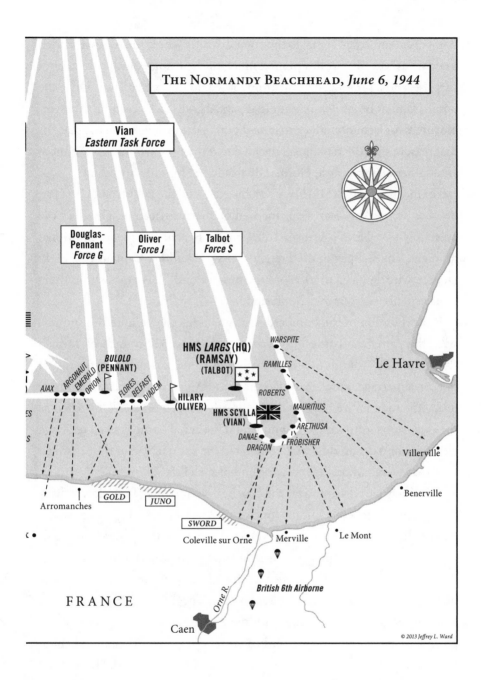

THE NORMANDY BEACHHEAD, *June 6, 1944*

Vian
Eastern Task Force

Douglas-
Pennant
Force G

Oliver
Force J

Talbot
Force S

WARSPITE

HMS *LARGS* (HQ)
(RAMSAY)
(TALBOT)

RAMILLES

Le Havre

BULOLO
(PENNANT)

AJAX ARGONAUT EMERALD ORION FLORES BELFAST DIADEM

ROBERTS

HILARY
(OLIVER)

HMS SCYLLA
(VIAN)

MAURITIUS

ARETHUSA

DANAE

FROBISHER

DRAGON

Villerville

GOLD

JUNO

Arromanches

Beneville

SWORD

Coleville sur Orne

Merville

Le Mont

FRANCE

Orne R.

British 6th Airborne

Caen

© 2013 Jeffrey L. Ward

bombardment would signal to the enemy exactly where the Allies intended to come ashore. The Allies pinned much of their hope on the element of surprise, and a prolonged bombardment would throw that away. Once the bombardment began, every hour that passed gave the Nazis time to assemble forces for a counterattack that might drive the invaders into the sea. For that reason, the Allied planners decided that the pre-invasion naval gunfire and the aerial bombing at Normandy would last for only one hour.

For the most part, Royal Navy warships targeted the British and Canadian beaches, while American ships focused on the American beaches. For the crews on two French cruisers off Omaha Beach, it was an emotional moment. The skipper of the French cruiser *Montcalm*, Captain E. J. H. L. Deprez, who flew a giant tricolor flag, mused aloud, "It is a monstrous thing to have to fire on your own homeland."[19]

If the duration of the bombardment was brief, the volume was impressive. The American battleship *Nevada* alone fired 337 rounds of 14-inch shells and 2,693 rounds of 5-inch shells onto Omaha Beach. In the midst of this naval barrage, more than two thousand Allied bombers arrived overhead. The men in the Higgins boats, already headed for shore, watched as the explosions from the naval gunfire and the aerial bombs generated huge clouds of smoke and dust that obliterated the shoreline, and they thanked God they were not on the receiving end of such fury.

The heavy cloud cover over the beaches—remnants of the slowly dissipating storm—severely diluted the impact of the air raid. Flying above the clouds, the pilots and bombardiers had to estimate where to drop, and, fearing to drop early lest their bombs land among friendly landing ships, they deposited much of their ordnance too far inland, cratering the countryside but hardly affecting the beach defenses at all. For their part, the battleships and cruisers continued to fire until mere seconds before the first of the Higgins boats ground up onto the beaches at 6:40, only ten minutes behind schedule. The ramps dropped, the navy coxswains hollered, "Everybody out!" and the soldiers staggered out into a maelstrom of violence.[20]

OF THE FIVE TARGET BEACHES, it was Omaha that proved most hazardous. One reason was geography. As at Salerno, Omaha Beach occupied a shallow bowl overlooked by enemy forces on high bluffs behind the beach and on both flanks. And unlike Salerno, the defenders had spent months placing their guns in hardened sites, some of them constructed of thirteen inches or more of reinforced concrete, and most of them cleverly camouflaged. Another factor was one that was unknown to the Allies despite intense pre-invasion reconnaissance: by sheer chance, the Germans had recently sent an additional division, the 352nd, to Omaha Beach for training.

The invading Allied infantrymen had been told that the naval gunfire and aerial bombing would knock out most of the enemy positions, but that proved not to be the case, and almost at once the men were pinned down on the beach with nowhere to go. Many of the Higgins boats and LCTs that had carried them ashore were wrecked on the beach or smashed by the German artillery, and soon the beachfront was littered with wrecked and burning landing boats and landing craft. Coxswains in subsequent waves looked in vain for an open piece of beach where they could land. Within an hour it was clear that the invasion of Omaha Beach had stalled.[21]

What saved the day for the Allies was a handful of British and American destroyers. Officially, the primary assignment of the destroyers during the landing was to screen the invasion fleet from U-boats and E-boats, but in this crisis they were recalled from that duty and sent to provide close-in gunfire support to the men on the beach, as they had at Gela and Salerno. Admiral Carleton Bryant on the battleship *Texas* radioed a general message to nearby destroyers: "Get on them, men! Get on them! They are raising hell with the men on the beach, and we can't have any more of that. We must stop it."[22]

They did. Most of the destroyers were from American Destroyer Squadron (DesRon) 18, commanded by Captain Harry Sanders, joined by several Royal Navy destroyers. Spurred to action by the call for help, and eager to get into the fray, they dashed shoreward with such enthusiasm that some observers feared they would run aground on the gently sloping beach. Most took up positions only eight hundred to a thousand yards from the surf, where there was only an inch or two of water under their keels. They were so close, many were hit by rifle bullets. Nevertheless, for most of an hour and a half, from nine o'clock until past ten-thirty, they stayed there and fired thousands of 5-inch rounds into the German positions behind the beach. Despite pre-invasion orders not to use more than half of their ammunition in case of emergencies, the skippers decided that this *was* an emergency, and they fired off nearly everything they had. The USS *Carmick* was stocked with 1,500 shells for her 5-inch guns and fired 1,127 of them in less than an hour. Brass shell casings cascaded to the deck and accumulated into great piles as the gun barrels glowed cherry red and had to be hosed down to keep them firing.[23]

At first the destroyer skippers had to speculate about appropriate targets. Poor visibility due to smoke and dust, effective German camouflage, and inadequate radio communication with the shore compelled the gunners to search for "targets of opportunity." The American gunners scanned for tell-tale puffs of smoke, but because the Germans used smokeless powder, the search was mostly in vain. On one occasion, the skipper of the *Carmick*, Robert Beer, saw that the few Allied tanks that had made it to the beach were shooting at a specific area on the bluffs, and he ordered the gunners on his ship to follow suit. After a flurry of 5-inch shells smashed into the site, the tanks redirected their fire elsewhere, and again the *Carmick* followed suit. "It was evident," Beer observed in his report, "that the Army was using tank fire in [the] hope that the support vessels would see the target and take it under fire." Though the lengthy plan for Operation Neptune had sought to cover every contingency, this was not a product of planning or protocol, but of men innovating on the spot.[24]

Around noon, the destroyers finally established reliable radio contact with the spotters ashore. After that, they responded to calls for both direct and indirect fire support. Area fire by the heavy guns of the Allied battleships and cruisers had failed to knock out the German gun positions, but the cumulative effect of aimed fire from the smaller 5-inch guns on the destroyers began to take them out one by one. That allowed the men pinned down on the beach to rise and work their way to the base of the coastal cliffs. Then they began to climb. This was not how it had been drawn up in the planning documents, yet the soldiers took the battle into their own hands and scrambled their way to the top. By late afternoon, though the beach was not yet fully secure, it had become evident that the invaders would not be driven into the sea.[25]

CARRYING THE MEN AND THEIR EQUIPMENT TO THE BEACH and supporting them with naval gunfire were two of the three key roles played by Allied naval forces in the invasion of Europe. The third was sustaining them there. The Allies put a total of 132,450 men ashore on D-Day, but impressive as that was, it was obviously not enough to conquer Europe. Many thousands more—eventually millions—would have to join them. In addition, the ships had to land thousands of tanks, trucks, and jeeps, and of course food for the men and fuel for the vehicles. Not to be forgotten were the French citizens of Normandy, now largely homeless and bereft of food and supplies as well. They also had to be sustained. In short, the several weeks after D-Day were as much of a strain on Allied sealift as the invasion itself.[26]

For the first few days much of the equipment had to be ferried ashore by the smaller landing craft or the raftlike rhino ferries because the beach remained too dangerous to risk the scarce and valuable LSTs. Though some LSTs got ashore on Utah Beach on June 6, it was not until June 10 that Omaha Beach was deemed sufficiently secure to send the big LSTs all the way to the beach. That greatly accelerated the buildup. In what amounted to a shuttle service, LSTs pushed up onto one or another of the invasion beaches, offloaded their cargoes, then retracted to head back across the Channel for another load. As just one example, LST-543 discharged her cargo on D-Day, returned across the Channel to load up again at Southampton the next night, then crossed the Channel again to offload at Normandy on the eighth. She repeated this routine on the tenth, the thirteenth, and the fifteenth. Given a top speed of ten knots, this meant that her crew was loading, unloading, or under way virtually around the clock for at least two full weeks. Nor was that unusual. Some LSTs made as many as fifty Channel crossings in the weeks after the initial landings. As with the LSTs that had supplied the beachhead at Anzio, the only rest any of the crew got was if they happened to be off duty while the ship was under way so they could fall into their racks for some much-needed sleep.[27]

British and American LSTs unload vehicles and cargo on Omaha Beach in June 1944. The absence of a working port, plus storm damage to the artificial harbor (Mulberry), made the LSTs essential to the success of the invasion. The barrage balloons were to prevent enemy aircraft from strafing the beach.

U.S. National Archives photo no. 80-G-46817

Even the LSTs could not supply a continental army of several hundred thousand men over the beach for the long term. To do that, the Allies needed a port, and the port they had in mind was Cherbourg, one of the Allies' initial military objectives. The Allies seized it on June 29, though the Germans, with ruthless efficiency, had destroyed the harbor so thoroughly it would be at least a month before it could be used. The Allies had anticipated that, however, and only a few days after the D-Day landings, they began to assemble the prefabricated elements of two massive artificial harbors off the invasion beaches: one at Omaha Beach and one at Gold Beach.

So much money, time, and resources had gone into preparing the component parts of these artificial harbors—called Mulberries—that they have been accorded a special place in D-Day mythology. Conventional wisdom is that the Allied invasion would not have been successful without them. The facts suggest otherwise. The official tabulation of offloaded supplies demonstrates that the Mulberries did not significantly increase the amount of goods brought ashore beyond what the LSTs had managed to do in the three days before the artificial harbors became operational. In addition, one of the two Mulberries was wrecked by a Channel storm only two days after it was completed, and the surviving Mulberry proved only marginally more efficient than the LSTs on the beach. In Normandy, as at Anzio, it was the LSTs that sustained and very likely saved the invasion.[28]

To confront the unprecedented Allied armada, the Germans had only four destroyers, thirty E-boats, and nine torpedo boats. In this crisis, they activated their "individual combat weapons," consisting of manned torpedoes similar to the *motoscafo turismos* that the Italians had employed so successfully in the Mediterranean. They also used something called a *Sprengboot*, a remote-control vessel filled with explosives that could be guided to a target by radio signals. The Germans had high hopes for these special weapons, but none of them proved particularly effective and after only a few days they abandoned them.[29]

Dönitz committed his U-boats. The newest of them boasted significant improvements, including the addition of a *schnorchel*, essentially a breathing tube atop a U-boat's conning tower that brought fresh air into a submerged boat so that it could use its diesel engines underwater, greatly enhancing their capability. In spite of that, the thirty *schnorchel*-equipped U-boats that Donitz sent to attack Allied shipping in the Channel succeeded in sinking only twenty-one ships over three months, and twenty of those thirty U-boats were lost. Dönitz acknowledged that "these operations had no decisive effect upon the enemy's build-up," yet, grasping at straws, he declared them "satisfactory" because they "hampered" the Allied effort.[30]

One month after the landings, in the first week of July, the one millionth Allied soldier landed in France, and two days after that, George Patton arrived to take command of the newly constituted American Third Army. On July 25, the Allied armies burst out of their continental enclave to begin Operation Cobra, racing across the French countryside toward Paris.

Two weeks later, Allied forces conducted Operation Anvil on the southern coast of France, the operation that had been delayed for a month in order to ensure a sufficiency of LSTs for Normandy. On August 15, Kent Hewitt's task force covered the landing of Lucian Truscott's VI U.S. Corps on the French Riviera. Thirteen hundred Allied planes bombed the three targeted beaches—Alpha, Delta, and Camel—between Cannes and Toulon, followed by a robust naval bombardment, and at 8:00 a.m. the Allies landed. The landings themselves proved almost anticlimactic, for the Axis forces there consisted mostly of reluctant conscript troops from Poland and Czechoslovakia, many of whom were willing to welcome the Allies as liberators. In the aftermath of the landings, an American division drove northward up the Rhône Valley while a French division headed west along the coast to liberate Marseilles. Ten days later, Allied forces advancing from Normandy and Brittany liberated Paris, fifty-five days ahead of schedule.

THE WAR IN EUROPE WAS NOT OVER, and there would be more hard fighting that winter in the Ardennes, but it had clearly entered a new phase. In that new phase, the principal role of Allied naval forces was twofold: first, to act as the guardian of the vital maritime supply lines, and second, to serve as on-call artillery support for the armies ashore. In the two months between the D-Day landings and the fall of Paris, Royal Navy warships, including the veteran *Warspite*, conducted more than 750 bombardment missions against targets ashore, firing 58,621 rounds of naval ordnance. Dönitz sought to challenge Allied command of the Channel with both U-boats and E-boats, but those vessels that made it into the Channel at all found themselves constantly on the defensive.[31]

Royal Navy warships also assisted in the capture of Le Havre in September, though as at Cherbourg, when the Allies occupied the city the harbor they found it so wrecked by German demolitions as to be unusable. Ramsay told Eisenhower that he could not keep the armies supplied without access to the port of Antwerp, and Eisenhower informed Montgomery that it was "absolutely imperative...to capture the approaches to Antwerp." Monty, however, was obsessed with his plan to get quickly across the Rhine— Operation Market Garden—and delegated the capture of Antwerp to the Canadians with orders to "push on quickly."[32]

The Allies seized Antwerp on September 4. Dönitz had ordered that the harbor facilities be demolished, but as he put it later, the Allies "came too fast." The problem was that the city and its priceless harbor would be useless unless the Allies could also gain possession of the Scheldt Estuary that connected Antwerp to the North Sea. Heavy coastal batteries made a direct naval assault all but impossible, though a land attack was nearly as daunting since the Germans had also heavily fortified the overland approaches. Moreover, here, as elsewhere, Hitler had ordered the defenders of the Scheldt to fight to the last man.[33]

To seize this crucial gateway, men of the Third Canadian Division first assaulted the so-called "Breskens Pocket" on the south bank of the Scheldt. They crossed the heavily-defended Leopold Canal in assault craft, then effectively outflanked the German position by crossing an arm of the Scheldt in tracked armored vehicles called Buffalos, British cousins to the LVTs used by the U.S. Marines at Saipan. These small-scale amphibious crossings did not ensure success. The Germans had flooded the land beyond the canals, and Allied bombing added to the disorder by wrecking many of the dikes, turning the land into a treacly mess. The Canadians advanced yard-by-yard through that mess against ferocious resistance. Further east, other Canadian units fought their way up a narrow causeway onto South Beveland Island in the face of concentrated heavy artillery.[34]

While the Canadians clawed their way forward through the mud, "Force T," under the command of Royal Navy Captain Anthony F. Pugsley, conducted more conventional amphibious landings on two beaches on the seaward side of Walcheren Island. As in Normandy, aerial bombing failed to take out the German positions, especially after a thick fog grounded the aerial spotters, and once again, the Allied naval barrage was too brief. But also as in Normandy, the gallant sacrifice of the close-in escort ships proved critical. Though nine of the Allied support ships were sunk and eleven others damaged, they drew the fire of the German batteries and enabled the LCTs and LCIs to bring enough troops ashore to wrest key defensive positions from the defenders. Even then, Antwerp Harbor remained inaccessible until Allied minesweepers could clear the Scheldt Estuary of German mines.[35]

Costly as it was, the capture of Walcheren in November opened Antwerp to shipping and dramatically eased the Allied supply problem. That success led some to hope that the war could be over by the end of the year.

CHAPTER 24

SEEKING THE DECISIVE BATTLE

T HE INVASION OF NORMANDY, central as it was, was not the only D-Day in June 1944. Just nine days after Allied soldiers landed in France, two divisions of U.S. Marines splashed ashore on the island of Saipan in the Marianas, seventy-five hundred miles away in the mid-Pacific. That the Allies could mount two major invasions on opposite sides of the world only nine days apart underscored both the global character of the war as well as the depth of Allied resources. The landing in Saipan also triggered one of the largest naval battles of the Second World War: the Battle of the Philippine Sea.

The Philippine Sea is less an enclosed body of water than a label attached to a portion of the western Pacific. It is bounded on the west by the Philippine Islands and to the east by the Mariana Islands chain, fifteen hundred miles away. For two decades and more, both the Americans and the Japanese had assumed that in any future war between them the outcome would hinge on a decisive fleet engagement somewhere in the western Pacific, and most likely in the Philippine Sea. That assumption influenced their prewar strategic planning, their war games, and their annual naval exercises. The Battle of Midway notwithstanding, both sides continued to believe that the truly decisive battle—the one that would determine the outcome of the war—was still to come, and that it was likely to occur within the bounds of the Philippine Sea.

The fifteen islands that make up the Marianas chain run in a 450-mile north-south arc across the central Pacific halfway between Japan and New Guinea. The American decision to target them was driven by two factors. One was that Guam, the largest of the Marianas, had been an American possession before the war and the first U.S. territory captured by the Japanese back in December 1941. Far more important, however, was the fact that from the Marianas American long-range B-29 Superfortress bombers could reach the Japanese home islands—even Tokyo itself. Three of the fifteen islands were large enough to host military bases, and the northernmost of them—the one closest to Japan—was Saipan. It was there the Americans planned to conduct their initial landings, and once the island was in American hands, the Seabees could build airfields that would allow the new B-29s to conduct the kind of bombing campaign against Japan that the Allies had been inflicting on Germany for most of two years.[1]

The Marianas had great significance for the Japanese, too. To them the islands constituted the last geographical barrier—the last defensible position—before the home islands. Moreover, the thought that American bombers could range at will over Japanese cities, thereby putting the life of the emperor at risk, was intolerable. Ever since the Allies had bypassed Rabaul, Japanese policy had been to conserve the fleet. Now, with the Americans threatening to penetrate the inner ring of their defenses, the moment had come to commit the fleet to battle. If the Americans assailed the Marianas, Admiral Koga planned to sortie with the fleet and engage them in "a decisive battle with full strength."[2]

He never got the chance, for on the last day of March he was killed when his plane went down in a typhoon. His replacement was Admiral Soemu Toyoda, a man of nondescript appearance (the historian John Prados suggests that "he looked more like a railroad conductor than a fighting admiral") and who, as the former chief of naval procurement, had virtually no combat experience. Nevertheless, the strategy remained the same: if the Americans attacked the Marianas, the Japanese would commit the fleet to battle. As Toyoda put it, "We must achieve our objectives by crushing with one stroke the nucleus of the great enemy concentration of forces...in one decisive battle."[3]

The Americans also looked forward to such a battle. Though the character of that much-anticipated confrontation changed over time from a Jutland-like battleship slugfest to a carrier engagement at long range, the idea of a decisive battle was as deeply embedded in the culture of the U.S. Navy as it was in that of the Imperial Japanese Navy. As the two sides entered the critical phase of the Pacific War, each assumed that sooner or later it would come down to an all-or-nothing confrontation in the Philippine Sea.

THE AMERICAN BUILDUP for the invasion of Saipan (code-named Operation Forager) occurred simultaneously with preparations for Overlord; measured by firepower, the Saipan invasion fleet was even larger than the one devoted to Normandy. Raymond Spruance commanded the overall invasion force that included Pete Mitscher's powerful Task Force 58, which by now consisted of fifteen carriers, seven battleships, eleven cruisers, and eighty-six destroyers. It would provide cover for an invasion force that included fifty-six attack transports and eighty-four LSTs carrying 127,571 soldiers and Marines. The employment of eighty-four LSTs in the Pacific at a time when Eisenhower was scrambling for just one or two more for Normandy was powerful evidence that the Germany-first principle had been virtually abandoned.[4]

The invasion of Saipan also required a much *longer* sealift than at Normandy. While the invasion forces for Neptune-Overlord had to leap fifty or a hundred miles across the English Channel, many of the transports and amphibious ships loaded up at Pearl Harbor, more than thirty-five hundred miles from the target beach. For Neptune-Overlord, the LSTs could, and did, shuttle reinforcements and supplies to the beaches in a near-constant rotation for weeks after the initial landings. For Saipan, by contrast, the men, the equipment, the supplies, and the ammunition all had to cross the broad Pacific in a single giant stride. Eisenhower had warned Marshall that a shortage of LSTs at Normandy could mean that his invasion force might be stranded on the beach for as long as three days without resupply. By design, the men who invaded Saipan would be stranded there for three *months* before significant reinforcements or supplies could reach them, though of course the Japanese, too, would have to fight the battle with what they had on hand, since Saipan would be virtually cut off from support.

Like the men who invaded Normandy, the would-be invaders of Saipan first had to load the landing ships and landing craft; it was hard work, and dangerous, too. On May 17, as work parties were off-loading 4.2-inch mortar ammunition from LST-353 in Pearl Harbor, one of the mortar rounds detonated. The explosion ignited nearby barrels of gasoline, and the entire ship went up in a thunderous fireball, setting off a number of explosions on nearby ships. A witness recalled that "whole jeeps, parts of ships, guns, equipment, shrapnel, fragments of metal, all rained down on the waters of West Loch." Before it was over, 168 men were dead, and six LSTs and three LCTs had been completely destroyed. It was just nineteen days after the loss of three LSTs off Slapton Sands in the English Channel. To replace the lost vessels, eight LSTs were transferred from MacArthur's command. No doubt Ike wished it had been that easy for him.[5]

The Saipan invasion force departed Pearl Harbor during the last three days of May. While en route, the tedium was broken by a not altogether unexpected announcement: "Now hear this. The invasion of France has started. Supreme Headquarters announced that the landings to date have been successful. That is all." The news provoked loud and sustained cheering, and no doubt boosted the morale of those who were about to conduct their own D-Day.[6]

To meet the approaching threat, the Japanese fleet commander, Jisaburō Ozawa, had a significant strike force available; despite recent losses, the Imperial Japanese Navy remained the third-most-powerful sea force in the world. Ozawa planned to sortie with five full-sized carriers, one of which was the brand-new *Taiho*, commissioned only two months before and the only Japanese carrier with an armored flight deck. He also had four smaller carriers, and collectively those eight flattops could put 473 planes in the air.

Many of those planes were sleek new Yokosuka D4Y dive bombers, which the Americans code-named "Judys," and Nakajima B6N torpedo planes, which the Americans called "Jills." On paper it was a force more powerful than the one that had struck at Pearl Harbor back in December 1941.

On the other hand, most of those new planes would be flown by relative novices. Japan's carrier pilots had been the best in the world in 1941, but since then far too many had been lost in combat. Unlike the Americans, who sent their best pilots back to the United States to train new pilots, the Japanese kept theirs on the front line until there were few of them left. The new men, some of them teenagers, were eager enough; they simply lacked experience.[7]

Ozawa also had operational control of a powerful surface force under Yamamoto's former chief of staff, Matome Ugaki, that included both of Japan's super-battleships—*Yamato* and *Musashi*. Back in the 1930s when they were laid down, the Japanese had hoped that these giant warships would be their trump cards in the Pacific War, yet so far neither of them had fired their guns in earnest. Here at last was the decisive engagement for which they had been designed.

Besides untrained pilots, another problem Ozawa had was a shortage of fuel. Though the Japanese had successfully seized the oil fields of South Asia back in the glory days of 1942, by 1944 oil was scarcer than ever. For the most part this was due to American submarines, which savaged the Japanese tanker fleet, sinking twenty-one tankers in the first five months of 1944. Before departing for battle, Ozawa's ships topped off their tanks with unrefined crude oil right out of the ground. It would get them where they needed to go, but such fuel was volatile to handle and tended to foul the boilers. It demonstrated just how close to the edge the Japanese operated in mid-1944.[8]

One advantage that Ozawa did have was that because Japanese airplanes lacked both armor and self-sealing fuel tanks, they were much lighter than their American counterparts. While that made their planes—and the pilots who flew them—particularly vulnerable, it also gave them a longer range than American aircraft. They could launch from three hundred miles out, conduct an attack on the American carriers, land on Guam to rearm and refuel, and then bomb the Americans again on their way back to their own ships, all while the Japanese carriers stayed outside the range of the American planes. Ozawa also counted on support from land-based aircraft on both Guam and Saipan; Combined Fleet headquarters assured him that planes from Guam would sink a third of the American carriers before the battle even began. But the Americans had worried about that, too, and so Mitscher's carriers had conducted a series of devastating pre-invasion raids on Guam's airfields. Ozawa was unaware of this, and as he approached Saipan, he believed there were as many as 450 Japanese aircraft in the Marianas ready to support him. Instead, by the time he arrived there were fewer than fifty.[9]

OZAWA'S CARRIER FORCE left its base at Tawi Tawi south of the Philippines on June 13. American submarines had noted the concentration of Japanese surface forces there, and Admiral Ozawa's ships had barely cleared the harbor when the American submarine *Redfin* reported their departure to Spruance. Ozawa's carriers headed north, passed through the Philippine archipelago, and on June 15 emerged into the Philippine Sea, where they were spotted by another U.S. sub, the *Flying Fish*. Only an hour later, another American submarine, the *Seahorse*, reported the approach of Ugaki's surface force from the south.[10]

In receipt of these sighting reports, Spruance knew that the Japanese had dispatched at least two major fleets in his direction. Aware of their predilection for complex battle plans, he wondered if one of the two—very likely the carrier force—was intended as a decoy to draw off his main battle fleet so that the surface force coming up from the south could slip in behind it and attack the American transports. Two days later on June 17, the submarine *Cavalla* sent in another sighting report: at least fifteen large warships were approaching from the west. Fifteen. Spruance had to wonder, where were the rest? Was this part of Ozawa's force, or Ugaki's? In fact, the two fleets had merged, but, unaware of that, Spruance tried to second-guess his opponent. If he were Ozawa, Spruance told his flag secretary, Charles Barber, he would try to "take out the transports," which would deprive American ground forces of their supplies and support. "I'd split my forces," he mused, use the carriers to draw off the American warships, "and send some of my fast ships to deal with the transports." Believing that his primary job was protection of the beachhead, Spruance kept the older battleships near Saipan for fire support, and ordered Mitscher's carriers plus Willis Lee's fast battleships to an interception point 180 miles west of Saipan, specifically instructing Mitscher to "cover Saipan and our forces engaged in that operation."[11]

The advantage of such dispositions was that they kept the American carriers within supporting distance of the hard-pressed Marines on the beach. The disadvantage, as far as Mitscher was concerned, was that those orders effectively tethered his carriers to Saipan. One of the country's first navy pilots, Mitscher believed that carriers were offensive weapons, and he wanted to use them to attack the approaching Japanese. He had missed his opportunity to participate in the destruction of the enemy carrier force at Midway when he had sent his air group in the wrong direction; now he feared he would be denied a second chance due to Spruance's misunderstanding of carrier tactics—indeed, the very purpose of aircraft carriers. Here was an opportunity to achieve the decisive fleet victory that navy planners had contemplated since the 1920s. It was galling to him—and to his aviators—that they were being held back from that destiny by what they perceived to be the caution of a hidebound battleship admiral.[12]

Another factor affecting Spruance's decision was that neither he nor Willis Lee was eager for a night action with the Japanese. Though improvements in American radar had greatly reduced the advantage the Japanese had previously enjoyed in night engagements, Spruance instructed Mitscher that while his carriers could advance westward toward Ozawa during the day, they must turn around and head eastward at night to ensure that the enemy did not slip past them in the dark. Mitscher protested those orders, blinking a message asking Spruance to reconsider. The response was terse: "We will proceed with my original orders."[13]

Before dawn on June 19, Ozawa sent out forty-three scout planes to search for the Americans. Though several of them were intercepted by patrolling Hellcats, at 7:30 a.m. one of them found and reported the location of Mitscher's task force, 160 miles due west of Saipan. The range from Ozawa's carriers—380 miles—was too great for a plane with an ordnance package to make a round trip, but since Ozawa believed his planes could

BATTLE OF THE PHILIPPINE SEA, *June 19–21, 1944*
(Great Marianas Turkey Shoot)

30° 120°   125°   130°   135°   140°   145° 30°

CHINA

East China Sea

RYUKYU IS.

Okinawa

BONIN
ISLANDS

Iwo Jima

25° 25°

Formosa

Luzon Strait

MARIANA
ISLANDS

20° 20°

PHILIPPINES

Luzon

U.S. air strike
Jan. 20

Mitscher TF58
15 carriers
plus screen

200 Miles from Saipan

Saipan

Manila

Ozawa enters
Philippine Sea
June 15 reported
by Flying Fish

Hiyo sunk

Tinian

15° 15°

Rota

Guam

Philippine

Cebu

Shōkaku sunk

Taiho sunk

area of
air battle

rendezvous

Sea

Yap

10° 10°

Sulu Sea

Mindanao

Peleliu

PALAU IS.

Pacific Ocean

Ugaki's
surface force incl.
Yamato & Musashi

Tawi Tawi

Ozawa departs
June 13 reported
by Redfin

5° 5°

Borneo

Celebes Sea

MacArthur's
Advance

Halmehera

EQUATOR

0° Batjan 0°

Molucca Sea

Schouten Is.

Biak captured
May 1944

Celebes

Vogelkop
Peninsula

Hollandia captured
May 1944

Buru

Ceram

5° NEW GUINEA 5°

Banda Sea

Lae

Port Moresby

10° 120°   125°   130°   135°   140°   145° 10°

© 2017 Jeffrey L. Ward

land on Guam afterward, he launched anyway. The distance was unquestionably too great for the heavier American planes, and Mitscher again asked Spruance if he could head west to close the enemy. Spruance blinked back, "Change proposed does not appear advisable." He reminded Mitscher that an "end run by other fast ones [enemy ships] remains a possibility." When that message arrived on Mitscher's flagship, one of Mitscher's staff officers responded by throwing his cap onto the deck and stomping on it.[14]

The morning of June 19 dawned with clear blue skies and virtually unlimited visibility. An American sailor on one of the screening ships recalled that it was "as lovely a day as one could wish to see." (On that same day seventy-five hundred miles away in the English Channel, a ferocious storm was smashing up the artificial harbors off Omaha and Gold Beaches.) Just before 10:00 a.m., American radar identified a large number of "bogeys" approaching from the west. Mitscher recalled the planes over Guam with the radio call "Hey, Rube," and ordered 140 more fighter planes into the air. The Hellcats flew westward to intercept the attackers while the bombers and torpedo planes headed east to get out of the way. Lieutenant Joseph R. Eggert on the *Lexington* coordinated the fighter directors on all of the carriers, who used radar to vector the pilots out toward the approaching Japanese. One of the pilots from the *Lexington*, Lieutenant (j.g.) Alex Vraciu, thought he sensed an unusual edge of excitement in Eggert's voice that morning; staring out his windscreen in the direction of the reported contact, he saw "a large rambling mass of at least fifty enemy planes" heading directly toward him. There were actually sixty-nine of them. Instead of sending all his planes at once, Ozawa had decided to send them in waves about an hour apart. Using the universal call for sighting the enemy, Vraciu radioed "Tally ho!" to his squadron mates, and set upon the intruders.[15]*

---

* The old fox-hunting cry of "Tally ho!" was used by pilots in both the American and British navies (and air forces as well) to signal that the enemy had been sighted. The use of "Hey Rube" as a recall signal was particular to the U.S. Navy. It was first employed in early 1942 when fighter pilots flying CAP over the first USS *Lexington* strayed too far from the carrier to pursue fleeing Japanese planes. To recall them to their primary duty, the radioman on the *Lexington* (perhaps an old circus hand) used the phrase that was employed in circuses and carnivals to call for support from his fellow carnies. After that, "Hey Rube" became universal shorthand for recalling pilots to the carrier.

American sailors watch as planes from Mitscher's Task Force 58 take on inbound Japanese bombers during the Battle of the Philippine Sea on June 19, 1944.

U.S. Naval Institute

Watching the air battle from the surface ships, American sailors had front-row seats to an extraordinary vista. As a rule, airplane contrails do not appear below thirty thousand feet, but some unusual atmospheric condition made them distinctly visible on June 19. Against that clear blue sky, long white streaks stretched out behind the inbound Japanese planes, and more streaks trailed out behind the American planes heading to meet them. The streaks came together fifty miles out from the task force and blended into a frenzy of loops and circles. A witness recalled that the contrails "formed crisscrossing white arcs against the azure sky."[16]

The Americans had twice as many planes as the Japanese and more experienced pilots to fly them, and it began to tell immediately, as Japanese bombers and torpedo planes started to break up and fall into the sea. One American pilot recalled that "the sky appeared to be full of smoke and pieces of planes." The surviving Japanese pressed on, with the Hellcats pursuing them until they came within the envelope of the AA fire from the ships in the screen. At that point, the Hellcats peeled off and left the attackers to the gunners below. On the destroyer *Twining*, the gunnery officer recalled that "the sky was full of them." His ship and every other vessel in the screen opened up with rapid-fire ordnance of every caliber, putting up "a solid curtain of steel" that claimed more Japanese bombers. Of the sixty-nine

Japanese planes in that first wave, only one got close enough to put a bomb onto the battleship *South Dakota*. None got through to the carriers.[17]

Most of the credit for that belonged to the American pilots. Commander David McCampbell, who led the air group on the *Essex*, personally shot down five planes; Vraciu himself shot down six. As he flew back across the scene of the air battle "with smoke still hanging in the air," Vraciu recalled seeing "flaming oil slicks in the water," stretching "in a pattern thirty-five miles long."[18]

There was another, larger Japanese attack later that morning, and two more that afternoon. Only a few planes succeeded in getting through the swarm of Hellcat fighters and the curtain of AA fire. One managed to land a bomb close alongside the *Bunker Hill*, though it did no serious damage and the carrier continued to conduct flight operations. By the time the long day was over, the Japanese had lost 358 airplanes, along with most of their pilots and aircrews. Counting the planes the Americans had downed over Guam, Japanese aircraft losses exceeded 400. The Americans lost thirty-three. Moreover, despite the Japanese sacrifice, no American ship had suffered any important damage. The battle was so one-sided that after landing back on the *Lexington*, Lieutenant (j.g.) Ziggy Neff, an avid hunter in civilian life, told his squadron commander, Paul Buie, "It was just like a turkey shoot." Buie included that in his report, and the name stuck. To the aviators who fought it, the Battle of the Philippine Sea would ever after be known as the Great Marianas Turkey Shoot.[19]

THOUGH PLEASED BY THE PROWESS OF HIS PILOTS, Mitscher remained disappointed to have been denied a chance to go after the enemy carriers. He did not know it yet, but the Japanese carrier force had already suffered a heavy blow. At 8:10 that morning, before the air attacks even began, Commander J. W. Blanchard in the American submarine *Albacore* succeeded in hitting the brand-new *Taiho* with a single torpedo.* The well-armored

---

* The *Taiho* might have suffered a second hit but for the action of Warrant Officer Sakio Komatsu. After launching from the *Taiho*, he saw the wake of a torpedo headed directly for his ship. He swung his plane around and crashed it into the torpedo, detonating it prematurely.

Taiho seemed to shrug it off, barely slowing down, and she continued to launch planes. Deep inside her, however, gasoline vapors from ruptured aviation fuel tanks began to seep through the deck spaces. Meanwhile, another American sub commander, Herman Kossler on the *Cavalla*, got the Pearl Harbor veteran *Shōkaku* in his sights and, from only twelve hundred yards, fired a spread of six torpedoes. Three of them hit, and they triggered a number of secondary explosions among the torpedo planes being fueled on her hangar deck. At 1:30, with the fires out of control, Captain Takisaburo Matsobara ordered abandon ship. The *Shōkaku* went down bow first, her stern rising nearly vertically before she plunged under the sea, taking more than twelve hundred men with her. Only half an hour later, the gasoline fumes released by the earlier hit on the *Taiho* ignited in a massive explosion, and that carrier, too, went down. Ozawa, who had been using *Taiho* as his flagship, transferred to the heavy cruiser *Haguro*. Even without any attacks from the air, Ozawa had lost two of his biggest and most powerful carriers.[20]

Mitscher, however, remained frustrated by being shackled (as he saw it) to Saipan. Finally on June 20, with the Japanese in full retreat, Spruance cut the tether and released Mitscher to go find them. It took longer than Mitscher had hoped. With the wind out of the east, he had been forced to steam in that direction, away from the enemy, throughout the air battle on the nineteenth in order to launch and recover planes. As a result, by the time he turned around to pursue the enemy, his ships were more than a hundred miles east of where they had started. It took four hours just to recover that lost ground, and it was late in the afternoon when he at last got a solid sighting report from one of his scout planes. The enemy carriers, the pilot reported, were 275 miles away—a bit too far for the American bombers. Or was it? Mitscher calculated that if his own carriers steamed at full speed westward while his planes conducted the strike, the return flight would be significantly shorter and most of his planes could get back safely. As he wrote later in his action report, he thought this might be the last chance to destroy the Japanese strike force "once and for all." He hesitated only about ten minutes before deciding to launch. After the first deckload was in the air, the scout plane pilot sent in an amended report, indicating that the Japanese carriers were farther away than he initially reported—more than 330 miles. Mitscher did not recall the strike force, though he did hold back the second deckload.[21]

The 216 American planes caught up with the Japanese at dusk. In the fading light, guided in part by the winking flashes of Japanese AA fire, the Americans swooped to the attack, easily repelling the few fighters Ozawa had left. They sank the light carrier *Hiyo*, and damaged the *Zuikaku* and several other vessels. Stripped now of all but a handful of aircraft, the surviving Japanese carriers continued their retreat back to their home islands.

The American pilots, however, still had to get back to their carriers, and given the distance they had flown already, that was problematic. The American pilots grouped up and headed eastward, most of them flying at seven thousand feet, their best altitude for conserving fuel, and watched as the needles on their fuel gauges settled lower and lower. En route, many of the engines on the planes coughed, sputtered, and stopped—out of gas. The pilots used their short-range radios to announce their circumstances, providing their call sign and locations in a perfunctory way, then one after another they landed in the water. The rest continued their flight eastward.[22]

Marc "Pete" Mitscher waits, cigarette in hand, on the open bridge wing of the USS *Lexington* for the pilots to return from the strike on Ozawa's carriers on June 20, 1944.

U.S. National Archives photo no. 80-G-236867

Mitscher waited on the bridge wing of the *Lexington*, chain-smoking and occasionally rubbing his chin as daylight faded. He had known when he gave the order to launch that the pilots would have difficulty getting back, and that many would not get back at all. If they did, they would not have fuel enough to search for the carriers in the dark with the ships blacked out as they always were at night. Aware of that, when the first returning planes showed up on radar, he radioed a message over the TBS: "Bald Eagle, this is Blue Jacket himself. Turn on the lights." In addition to their running lights, each of the carriers and the screening cruisers aimed their giant thirty-inch spotlights straight up into the night sky as beacons to the returning pilots. Had any Japanese submarines been nearby, it was like announcing, "Here we are."[23]

Mitscher's decision to turn on the lights—much celebrated then and since among aviators—was neither spontaneous nor unprecedented. Spruance, too, had ordered the lights turned on to recover planes returning from the last stages of the Battle of Midway. Even so, Mitscher's decision has resonated in the years since. He also passed the word that pilots should not attempt to locate their own carriers, but land on whatever flattop was closest. Some landed with so little gas, they could not taxi forward and had to be man-handled out of the way to clear the deck for the next plane. Many didn't make it at all and ditched in the water within sight of the carriers. The pilots of those planes, and those who had been forced to ditch much farther away, inflated their tiny life rafts and waited. Some rafted up into small groups. The next morning, American destroyers following the track of the air attack, recovered 143 of the 177 men who had been forced down for lack of fuel.[24]

The Battle of the Philippine Sea (or the Great Marianas Turkey Shoot) was an overwhelming American victory. If it did not play out exactly the way American planners had imagined when they had gamed it out at the Naval War College in the 1930s, it was decisive nonetheless. The Japanese lost three carriers, including their newest and largest, and more than four hundred airplanes. The Americans themselves lost no ships and just over a hundred planes, most of them on the long return flight from the attack on the Japanese carriers. More important, the Japanese also lost several hundred pilots, while the Americans lost only twenty. Carriers without airplanes or trained pilots offered little threat to American mastery of the sea.

The Japanese knew how disastrous the battle had been. As Ugaki noted in his diary, "The result of the decisive battle on which we staked so much was extremely miserable."[25]

Even so, Mitscher remained unhappy. He was frustrated that the remaining Japanese carriers had escaped, and he never fully forgave Spruance for refusing to allow him to go on the attack on June 19, especially after it became evident that there never had been a second Japanese force planning an end run. Even Nimitz, who greatly admired Spruance, wrote wistfully about what might have been. In his action summary for June he wrote, "It may be argued" that if Spruance had allowed Mitscher's force to steam toward the enemy, "a decisive fleet air action could have been fought, the Japanese fleet destroyed, and the end of the war hastened." Such views would cast a long shadow over subsequent events.[26]

ASHORE ON SAIPAN, THE FIGHTING WAS INTENSE. The 2nd and 4th U.S. Marine Divisions had landed on June 15, and the U.S. Army's 27th Division joined them soon afterward as the Americans pushed inland against unrelenting resistance. As on other Pacific islands, the Japanese defenders often preferred suicide to surrender. On July 6, the Japanese commander on Saipan, Admiral Nagumo, the man who had led the Kidō Butai in the attack on Pearl Harbor as well as at Midway, shot himself. Four days later, Lieutenant General Yoshitsugu Saitō disemboweled himself in a ritual suicide, his adjutant dutifully shooting him in the head afterward. Either by example or by compulsion, similar fanaticism spread to the civilian population. Japanese army leaders had told the resident civilians that if they were captured, the Americans would torture them to death, and in consequence, civilians who hid in caves during the fighting refused to come out when entreated to do so by the Americans, choosing instead to blow themselves up with grenades. The greatest tragedy, witnessed by hundreds of horrified Americans, was a mass suicide that took place atop the eight-hundred-foot-high cliff at Marpi Point at the northernmost end of the island. With their backs to the sea and the Americans closing in, whole families committed suicide, either blowing themselves up with grenades or leaping to their deaths from the cliff. Fathers threw their children over the edge, watched their wives jump, and then followed them over the cliff. Shocking as it was, it was the logical consequence of the intense propaganda by which the Japanese government sustained the passionate nationalism of the war years.[27]

Tojo, too, was a casualty of the campaign. Already under attack by critics, his failure to hold Saipan undermined his authority and he was forced from office on July 18, replaced by another general, Kuniaki Koiso. Admiral Shimada also lost his job as navy minister and was replaced by Mitsumasa Yonai, a former prime minister who had opposed the Tripartite Pact back in 1940. Officially at least, the focus of the new regime was a recommitment to the war effort, though unofficially the new ministers began to look for a way out. Koiso indulged a fantasy that it was still possible for Japan to come to terms with the British and Americans, and he toyed with the idea of sending a peace mission to a neutral country such as Sweden or Switzerland, though he decided that Japan would obtain better terms if he waited until after a victorious battle.[28]

June 1944 might well be labeled the decisive month of the entire Second World War. In the Philippine Sea as well as on the coast of Normandy, the Allies burst through defensive barriers, and the Axis powers would never fully recover. Overwhelming material superiority in naval power and sealift allowed the Allies to conduct both of these major offensives virtually simultaneously. Two years earlier, in North Africa and on Guadalcanal, the Allies had breached the outer perimeter of the Axis empires. Now in June 1944, they had kicked in the front door.

ON JULY 26, THIRTY-SEVEN DAYS AFTER American carrier pilots annihilated Japanese naval air power in the Philippine Sea, the heavy cruiser *Baltimore* rounded Diamond Head off Waikiki Beach, steamed past the Honolulu waterfront, and turned into the entrance channel to Pearl Harbor. The fact that President Roosevelt was on board was supposed to be a closely held secret, yet somehow the word had spread and American warships inside the great naval base were decked out with oversized flags while men lined the rails to cheer their commander in chief. That the United States could send its head of state on such a voyage demonstrated its complete domination of the eastern Pacific.

Roosevelt had made the five-thousand-mile trip for several reasons. Ostensibly, his purpose was to meet with his two Pacific commanders, Douglas MacArthur and Chester Nimitz, in order to determine the next step in the Pacific offensive. In addition, however, Roosevelt enjoyed getting away from the White House and he especially relished ocean voyages on Navy warships. Back in 1935, during his first term as president, he had made this same journey in the cruiser *Houston*, now resting at the bottom of Sunda Strait. A third reason for the trip was that Roosevelt knew the political value of being seen with his successful Pacific commanders. Nominated by his party for a fourth term as president while en route, he was acutely aware that photographs of him conferring with Nimitz and MacArthur on board a warship in Pearl Harbor would be helpful in the campaign. MacArthur found the whole event distasteful. Indeed, he was initially reluctant to come at all, referring to it as "a picture-taking junket," and had to be ordered to make the trip.[29]

The business of their meetings focused on Pacific strategy. Having penetrated the inner defenses of the Japanese Empire, the Americans were now in a position to block Japan from the essential resources of the South Pacific. That could be accomplished by seizing either the island of Formosa or the Philippines. The American chief of naval operations, Ernie King, strongly preferred Formosa. It was, after all, a single island, albeit a large one, as opposed to the more than seven thousand islands that made up the Philippine archipelago. Then, too, from Formosa, the United States could more easily supply their Chinese allies on the mainland. Dutifully arguing the navy's position, Nimitz suggested that the Philippines could be bypassed and cut off as Rabaul and Truk had been.

MacArthur found that suggestion not only unwise but immoral. Liberating the Philippines, he argued, was "a great national obligation." Back in 1942, he had famously pledged that he would return to the Philippines, and he warned now that if America failed to fulfill that pledge, Asians would never trust the word of the United States again. He reminded the president that there were thirty-seven hundred American POWs in the Philippines, and hinted darkly that they would remember being bypassed. Roosevelt found such arguments compelling; he knew that liberation was good politics. In

A smiling Franklin Roosevelt sits between his two grim-faced theater commanders, Douglas MacArthur (left) and Chester Nimitz (right), on the deck of the cruiser *Baltimore* in Pearl Harbor on July 26, 1944.

Naval History and Heritage Command

the end, however, he left the final decision to the Joint Chiefs. They voted for the Philippines, and orders were drafted for an invasion with a proposed D-Day of December 20, 1944.[30]

One complicating factor for the Americans was that their planned assault on the Philippines would involve the coordinated efforts of both Nimitz and MacArthur, and that resulted in a problematical chain of command. MacArthur had overall authority over the invasion, including control of Vice Admiral Thomas Kinkaid's Seventh Fleet. The precise role of the Third Fleet, however, was less clear.

The Third Fleet was essentially the Fifth Fleet with a new name. After the seizure of the Marianas, Spruance and his staff returned to Pearl Harbor to work up new plans while Halsey and his staff took over the Big Blue Fleet for the Philippine operation. When he did, Spruance's Fifth Fleet became Halsey's Third Fleet. Halsey likened it to a stagecoach, though instead of keeping the drivers and changing the horses, the drivers changed places while the horses remained in the traces. Not all of the top admirals rotated out; Pete Mitscher kept command of the fast carrier task force, though Task Force 58 now became Task Force 38.[31]

The Seventh Fleet was not affected by this switching of drivers. Often called "MacArthur's Navy," Kinkaid's command included ships from both the American and Australian navies, though American vessels were far more numerous. Back in March 1943, MacArthur had expressed his unhappiness with the incumbent fleet commander, Rear Admiral Arthur S. Carpender, and King had appointed Kinkaid to replace him. That had created a bit of a kerfuffle since by agreement the Australian government was to have a say in deciding who commanded the American-Australian naval force. Uncharacteristically, King backpedaled, telling Australian prime minister John Curtin that Kinkaid's appointment was merely a nomination and subject to Curtin's approval. Having made his point, Curtin decided that Kinkaid would do. The incident highlighted the fact that Kinkaid occupied a precarious political perch: he was responsible to King in Washington, to MacArthur in Brisbane, and to Curtin in Canberra, yet he remained outside the chain of command that included Halsey and Nimitz.[32]

His Seventh Fleet consisted mostly of amphibious and transport ships, including many borrowed from the Fifth/Third Fleet for the Philippine campaign. Kinkaid also had six older battleships—five of them Pearl Harbor survivors—under Rear Admiral Jesse Oldendorf.* Given their indifferent speed, their assignment during the invasion was naval gunfire support. Kinkaid had none of the big fleet carriers, though he did have eighteen small "jeep" carriers to provide air support over the beachhead. These "baby flattops" resembled their Brobdingnagian cousins with the characteristic

---

* Technically, Rear Admiral George L. Weyler commanded the six battleships, though Oldendorf exercised overall authority over the surface warships from the heavy cruiser *Louisville*.

profile of a rectangular flight deck and an island amidships, except that they were much smaller (at 8,000–10,000 tons), considerably slower (at eighteen knots), and virtually unarmored, having only enough steel, as one crewman noted, "to keep the water out." For ordnance they had a single 5-inch gun aft, almost as an afterthought. Each carried twenty to thirty aircraft, mostly modified Avenger bombers and FM-2 Wildcat fighters, updated versions of the F4F. Built to protect convoys or cover a beachhead, they were not designed for combat at sea.[33]

One problem was that the lines of authority affecting Kinkaid and Halsey never merged. Kinkaid reported to MacArthur, who reported to Marshall, who reported to the secretary of war, who reported to the president; Halsey reported to Nimitz, who reported to King, who reported to the secretary of the navy, who reported to the president. Though the two fleets were expected to cooperate, there was no common commander closer than Washington. Moreover, to ensure that Nimitz did not attempt to usurp his authority, MacArthur forbade Kinkaid from communicating with Nimitz directly and stipulated that communications between the two fleets—that is, between Halsey and Kinkaid—had to pass through the communications center at Manus, in the Admiralty Islands. That helped keep MacArthur and his staff in the loop, though it also added about two hours to the time it took for messages to pass from one fleet to the other. That would prove not only cumbersome but nearly disastrous.[34]

Another factor was Halsey's conviction that Spruance had erred when he ordered Mitscher's carriers to remain by the beachhead during the Battle of the Philippine Sea. Though Halsey and Spruance were close friends, Halsey believed that Spruance had bungled a historic opportunity. To ensure that it would not happen again, he prevailed on Nimitz to amend his orders for the Philippine campaign to make the destruction of the enemy main fleet his primary objective. The key sentence read: "In case opportunity for destruction of [a] major portion of the enemy fleet is offered or can be created, such destruction becomes the primary task." Thus did the perception of a lost opportunity in the Philippine Sea and the irresistible lure of the decisive battle, itself a legacy of two decades of American planning and war gaming, put their mark on both the attitude and the orders that Halsey took with him into the campaign.[35]

———————

THE JAPANESE, TOO, MADE PLANS. Despite the near-destruction of their naval air arm in the Philippine Sea, they still possessed a powerful surface navy that included the giant battleships *Yamato* and *Musashi*, plus a half dozen other battleships, fifteen heavy cruisers, and a significant destroyer force armed with the always dangerous Long Lance torpedoes.

Two particular weaknesses limited the capability of this surface navy. One was the lack of air cover. Ever since the destruction of the *Prince of Wales* in the first month of the Pacific War, it had been evident that even the most powerful battleship could not survive a concerted air attack without air cover, and by the fall of 1944 the Japanese could no longer provide it. Land-based Japanese air had been eviscerated by American raids through-out the first half of 1944, and of course the naval air arm had been all but annihilated in the Philippine Sea. Of the six carriers that had attacked Pearl Harbor, only one—the *Zuikaku*—still floated. The Japanese made strenu-ous efforts to replenish their carrier force, completing and launching the brand-new *Taiho* in April, only to have her sunk two months later in June. A similar effort went into the conversion of what was initially to have been a third super-battleship, the *Shinano*, which the Japanese began to convert into a carrier after the Battle of Midway. Throughout 1944, dockyard work-ers labored in a near frenzy to complete her in time for the Philippine cam-paign, though even had they succeeded in doing so, the Japanese lacked the planes and trained pilots needed to make her or any carrier a legitimate weapon of war. The Japanese also boosted airplane production, though it barely kept up with losses.[36]

The other problem was fuel. Like the Italians, the Japanese simply lacked the oil needed to keep their ships at sea and their planes in the air. Japan's shortage of trained pilots was due not only to the losses they had suffered in battle but also to the fact that there wasn't enough aviation fuel for the trainees to log the hours they needed to become proficient. By late 1944, the only place the Japanese had ready access to fuel was near the Sumatran oil fields they had captured back in 1942. For that reason, the bulk of Japan's still-powerful surface navy, commanded by the experienced and reliable Takeo Kurita, was anchored in Lingga Roads, off the northern coast of Sumatra near Palembang. That force became the centerpiece of the Japanese plan to confront the American thrust at the Philippines.[37]

Labeled Operation Sho-Go (Victory Operation), the plan replicated almost exactly what Spruance had suspected the Japanese of attempting during the fight for the Marianas. A decoy force coming from the north would attempt to draw the main American battle fleet away from the landing beaches, while Kurita's surface force sneaked in behind it to annihilate the invasion armada. The decoy was Ozawa's carrier force—or what was left of it. A pale shadow of the once mighty Kidō Butai that had struck at Pearl Harbor not quite three years before, Ozawa's force consisted of the *Zuikaku*, three smaller carriers (*Zuihō*, *Chitose*, and *Chiyoda*), and two curious vessels that might be called "hermaphrodite carriers": battleships that had been modified to accommodate an abbreviated flight deck aft. Those short flight decks allowed the modified battleships to launch planes, though not to recover them. The very existence of such vessels was additional proof that carriers had supplanted battleships as the principal weapon of naval warfare. Technically, then, there were six airplane carriers in what the Americans subsequently labeled the "Northern Force," though collectively those ships hosted barely a hundred operational aircraft. Neither of the two hermaphrodite carriers had any airplanes at all. In any confrontation with Mitscher's Task Force 38, or even any one element of it, Ozawa would be hopelessly overmatched and very likely annihilated. His assignment, however, was not to fight but to attract the attention of the Americans and lure them northward, and he stoically accepted that duty.[38]

Assuming that Ozawa succeeded in his role as bait, the hammer blow against the Americans would be struck by Kurita's surface force of battleships and cruisers at Lingga Roads. Dubbed the "Center Force" by the Americans, Kurita's command had no carriers at all, though he did have the *Yamato* and *Musashi* plus five other battleships and ten heavy cruisers. By any measure, it was a substantial, even daunting combat force. While Ozawa distracted the American carriers, Kurita would thread his way through the Philippine archipelago and fall upon the invasion fleet. Specifically, his orders enjoined him to "advance through San Bernardino Strait and annihilate the enemy invasion force."[39]

The Japanese expected the Americans to target either Mindanao, the large southern island that included the Japanese naval base at Davao, or Luzon, the largest and northernmost of the Philippine islands and host to the capital city, Manila. Instead, the Americans selected Leyte, one of a half dozen moderately sized islands between the two larger ones. Leyte's eastern shore had excellent landing beaches and level terrain where new airfields could be built, as well as an enormous offshore anchorage protected by the islands of Samar to the north and Dinagat to the south. The body of water off the landing beaches was Leyte Gulf.

THOUGH KURITA'S FORCE WAS THE KEY to the entire operation, Kurita himself wondered what he could accomplish against the Americans in Leyte Gulf. His orders called for him to "rush forward and destroy the enemy transports on the water *before they disembark their troops.*" It was evident to him, however, that by the time he steamed the sixteen hundred miles from Lingga Roads to the landing beaches, the American transports and supply ships surely would have landed the troops and their cargos, and he would have only empty transports to sink. Such an assignment ran up against the Japanese warrior culture. For the Japanese, as for the Americans, two decades of planning the decisive battle had codified the view that the destruction of the enemy's combat warships was the very purpose of a navy. Kurita's own conviction, expressed by his chief of staff, Tomiji Koyanagi, was that "it would be foolish to sink emptied transports at the cost of our great surface force." In his view, "top priority should be given to engaging the carrier striking force of the enemy." It was hardly a unique viewpoint; virtually every Japanese naval officer believed that sinking American warships was the ultimate goal of warfare at sea, just as American naval officers sought to target Japanese warships.[40]

Given that, it is both noteworthy and curious that Toyoda ordered Kurita to focus on the transports. A possible explanation lies in the political transformation that had taken place in Tokyo in the aftermath of the fall of Saipan. Tojo's resignation on July 18 and the elevation of Admiral Yonai to head the Navy Ministry suggest that the Japanese government may have begun to look for alternatives to outright victory. Toyoda himself had been an opponent of the decision to go to war with the Americans. Now it appeared that his instinct had been correct and that complete victory was no longer possible, if it ever had been. Of course, no one in Tokyo could admit that publicly, but Yonai and Toyoda may have hoped that prolonging the war would provide time to find an honorable alternative to surrender. Sinking the American transport fleet would not help Japan win the war, but it would almost certainly delay the American invasion, challenge American resolve, and buy time for Japan's leaders to seek some kind of settlement. If that was the objective behind Toyoda's orders, he did not explain it to the operational commanders, and in any case such a strategy ran up against the zealous commitment within the Imperial Japanese Navy to the doctrine of the decisive battle. Sacrificing one's life while attacking a carrier force was glorious; doing so while sinking empty transports, regardless of the political objective, was not only inglorious, it was ignoble.

On August 10, Toyoda's chief of operations, Captain Shigenori Kami, met in Manila with Kurita's chief of staff, Tomiji Koyanagi, to discuss the details of Operation Sho-Go. At that meeting, Koyanagi asked Kami directly what Kurita's force should do if it got the chance to engage American warships, especially the carriers. Kami's response was strikingly similar to what Nimitz had told Halsey: if the opportunity presented itself, Kurita should make the American carriers his primary objective. That guidance was confirmed ten days later by Operations Order #87: the targets of Japanese warships were to be aircraft carriers, battleships, and troop transports, in that order. In the Imperial Japanese Navy, as in the United States Navy—to Kurita as to Halsey—the pull of the decisive battle was irresistible. For both men that meant sinking the enemy's carriers. Each would soon have an opportunity to fulfill that vision.[41]

CHAPTER 25

LEYTE GULF

HALSEY TOOK COMMAND of the Big Blue Fleet on August 24, 1944, breaking his flag on the new fast battleship *New Jersey*. A week later, the *New Jersey* sailed from Pearl Harbor for the western Pacific, where it accompanied Mitscher's carriers on a series of raids against Japanese bases. By now, the Americans cruised the western Pacific almost at will. Mitscher's task force boasted seventeen carriers with more than a thousand aircraft, and it was sustained by a fleet of service ships, including tenders, repair ships, even floating dry docks. Fuel posed no difficulty because the United States remained the world's foremost producer of oil. Commercial tankers brought refined oil from the West Coast of the United States to a nine-million-barrel storage facility in Hawaii. From there, navy oilers carried it to what amounted to a floating tank farm at Ulithi Atoll, in the Caroline Islands, halfway between the Marinas and the Philippines—an enormous maritime gas station in the western Pacific.[1]

During the September carrier raids, fewer Japanese planes rose up to contest the Americans than either Halsey or Mitscher had anticipated, and the feeble resistance encouraged Halsey to suggest to Nimitz that the invasion date for the Philippines could be moved up from December to October. Nimitz forwarded the recommendation to the Allied Combined Chiefs who were meeting in Quebec, and after obtaining MacArthur's approval, D-Day for the Philippine invasion was advanced from December 20 to October 20.

While Nimitz approved the accelerated timetable, he was loath to cancel another project that was already under way: the capture of the island of Peleliu, in the Palau Group of islands, some six hundred miles east of the Philippines. The American Joint Chiefs had considered capture of this island necessary to prevent planes there from interfering with the Philippine invasion force. In fact, Japanese airpower on Peleliu was too weak to pose a serious threat to either Kinkaid or Halsey, but since preliminary operations had already begun and a recall would look like a defeat, Nimitz allowed it to continue. It was one of his few errors of the war.

The Marines went ashore on Peleliu on September 15. The landings were difficult and the casualties substantial. Nevertheless, the Marines advanced inland and within three days they had secured the critical airstrip. That, however, proved only the beginning. Geologically, the island of Peleliu was dominated by a series of limestone ridges honeycombed with caves and tunnels that were impervious to aerial bombing or naval gunfire. The ten thousand Japanese defenders withdrew into those caves, determined to make the Americans pay in blood for every yard of soil. Amid temperatures that occasionally exceeded 115 degrees, men of the 1st Marine Division, soon reinforced by the U.S. Army's 81st Division, had to go into the caves and take out the defenders one at a time. It took ten weeks for the Americans to clear the island, and they did so only at a great cost to both sides. Virtually all ten thousand Japanese defenders were killed—only two hundred were taken alive. American losses, while lighter, were nevertheless painful: a thousand killed and five thousand wounded—greater than the losses at Tarawa.[2]

AS THE FIGHTING ON PELELIU played out to its sanguineous conclusion, two enormous American invasion armadas headed for Leyte, one departing from Manus, in the Admiralties, and the other from Hollandia, on New

Guinea. That movement triggered the Battle of Leyte Gulf, the largest naval battle in history. It was so complex and geographically dispersed that many historians have chosen to portray it as four separate engagements. While such an approach helps to clarify the events in each confrontation, it also obscures their interconnectedness, because each was part of a single enormous and sprawling tapestry of violence spanning nearly one hundred thousand square miles.[3]

U. S. Army soldiers began landing on the eastern beaches of Leyte on the morning of October 20 while MacArthur watched from the deck of the light cruiser *Nashville*. All around him, spread out across the expanse of Leyte Gulf, were hundreds of ships of the Seventh Fleet: attack transports, cargo ships, LSTs, LCIs, and a new vessel called a "landing ship, medium" (LSM) that was larger (and also faster) than an LCT, though still smaller than an LST. A half dozen battleships and as many cruisers provided gunfire support, and further east, out beyond the entrance to the gulf, were eighteen small jeep carriers and their escorting destroyers, organized into three groups of six carriers, each group identified by its radio call sign: "Taffy One," "Taffy Two," and "Taffy Three."[4]

The landings proceeded in textbook fashion. The only difficulty was that the shallow gradient of the beach meant that the LSTs could not come all the way up onto the sand to unload, and the Seabees built ramps out into the gulf so that the LSTs could land their cargos.[5]

That afternoon, MacArthur fulfilled the pledge he had made two and a half years before. He and Philippine president Sergio Osmeña climbed down into a Higgins boat that carried them from the *Nashville* to the beach. They strode ashore through knee-deep water for the benefit of the cameras. Then, stepping up to a microphone, MacArthur announced in his dramatic baritone: "People of the Philippines, I have returned." He urged the citizens of the islands to rise up and strike their oppressors. "For your homes and hearths, strike! For future generations of your sons and daughters, strike! In the name of your sacred dead, strike!" After a short inspection tour of the beach, he paused to write a letter to Roosevelt "from the beach near Tacloban." Then he returned to the *Nashville*. The landings continued, and by nightfall the Americans had four infantry divisions and 107,000 tons of supplies on Leyte.[6]

That same afternoon, twenty-six hundred miles to the north, Ozawa's decoy carrier force left Kure in the Inland Sea, passed out through the Bungo Channel between Kyushu and Shikoku, and turned south. Ozawa did not expect to be coming back. He knew that his job was to attract the attention of the Americans and lure them northward, and he later acknowledged that he expected "complete destruction." Ironically, although Ozawa actually *wanted* to be found by the Americans, the three U.S. submarines that had been watching the exit from the Inland Sea had departed two days before to conduct war patrols, and Ozawa's ships slipped out unseen. For three days they steamed southward without the Americans being any the wiser.[7]

As Ozawa's carriers headed south, Kurita's battleships and cruisers left Lingga Roads and headed northeast toward Brunei Bay on the coast of Borneo. There, while his ships topped off their fuel tanks, Kurita met with his captains to go over the mission. Only now, with the operation already under way, did Kurita decide to split his command, detaching a portion of it for a separate and complementary assault on Leyte Gulf from the south. The idea had originated with Toyoda's chief of staff, Admiral Ryūnosuke Kusaka, in Tokyo, though Kusaka left the final decision up to Kurita. At Brunei, Kurita informed his captains that while the main attack force would use San Bernardino Strait and strike the Americans from the north, a separate "Southern Force" consisting of two elderly battleships, *Yamashiro* and *Fuso*, plus the veteran cruiser *Mogami* and four destroyers, all commanded by Admiral Shōji Nishimura, would approach Leyte Gulf from the south via Surigao Strait. It would be a classic double envelopment with the Americans caught in the middle.*

Kurita embraced this plan for several reasons. In addition to the hint from Kusaka and the fact that a double envelopment was an elegant maneuver, he was very likely happy to rid himself of two old and slow battleships, both of which had been laid down before the First World War. Moreover, given the weakness of Nishimura's command, it is possible that Kurita conceived

---

* The Japanese added another surface force of three cruisers and seven destroyers under Admiral Kiyohide Shima to the Southern Force at the last moment, though Shima never did catch up with Nishimura, and his ships played no meaningful role in the subsequent battle.

A ferocious-looking Admiral Takeo Kurita in his formal Imperial Japanese Navy photograph. Kurita's actions during the Battle of Leyte Gulf were controversial at the time and have seemed enigmatic ever since.

Naval History and Heritage Command

of it less as a complementary attack than as a second decoy. During the battle for Saipan in June, the Naval General Staff had considered sending the *Yamashiro* and the *Fuso* on what amounted to a suicide mission—to run themselves aground on the Saipan beaches and act as stationary batteries. The mission was cancelled after Ozawa's defeat, but that it had been considered at all suggests that both ships were presumed to be expendable.[8]

Another topic of discussion on Kurita's flagship that day was Toyoda's unpopular order to focus on the American transports. That assignment was no more attractive to Kurita's captains than it was to Kurita himself. As one put it, "We do not mind death, but if the final effort of our great navy is to be an attack on a cluster of empty freighters, surely admirals Tōgō and Yamamoto would weep in their graves." To encourage them, Kurita told them that he believed that the "Imperial General Headquarters is giving us a glorious opportunity." It was altogether possible, he said, that they might confront the American carrier fleet. "What man can say that there is no chance for our fleet to turn the tide of war in a decisive battle? We shall have a chance to meet our enemies. *We shall engage his task forces.*" The captains leapt to their feet, shouting, "Banzai!"[9]

At dawn on October 22, Kurita's battleships and cruisers began pulling up their anchors. One by one they eased out to sea, then they assembled into cruising formation and headed north. Later that day, Nishimura's two old battleships and their consorts also put to sea. In the entire thousand-mile length of the Philippines, there were only two navigable channels that allowed deep-draft ships to approach Leyte Gulf from the west: San Bernardino Strait, which Kurita would use, and Surigao Strait, which Nishimura would use. The Americans were sure to be keeping an eye on both passages, and it was therefore only a matter of time before they discovered the approaching Japanese.

———

JUST PAST MIDNIGHT, in the first minutes of October 23, two American submarines, *Darter* and *Dace*, were cruising together on the surface to recharge their batteries in the tricky waters north of the island of Palawan, where scores of shoals made navigation hazardous. When a blip appeared on the *Darter's* radarscope, her captain, Commander David H. McClintock, called across to Commander Bladen Claggett on the *Dace*: "We have a radar contact. Let's go!"[10]

The character of that contact became evident as the subs tracked it, and McClintock sent a sighting report up the chain of command: "Many ships including 3 probable BBs [battleships], 08-28 N, 116-30 E. Course 040. Speed 18. Chasing." He might have been "chasing," but given that his own top speed was also about eighteen knots, it was unlikely that he could actually overtake any of Kurita's ships. Just then, however, Kurita ordered his ships to reduce speed to fifteen knots to transit the dangerous waters of the Palawan Passage, and McClintock shouted, "We have them now!" The two American subs raced ahead to take up ambush positions and wait for dawn.[11]

At 5:30 a.m., with just enough light to recognize "dim shapes from the bridge," McClintock submerged to periscope depth and fired a full spread of six torpedoes at the nearest warship, which, as it happened, was Kurita's flagship, the heavy cruiser *Atago*. While McClintock maneuvered to bring his stern tubes to bear, he heard five distinct explosions. Whipping his periscope around, he saw what he described as "the sight of a lifetime." So close that her image filled his periscope lens, McClintock saw that the *Atago* "was a mass of billowing smoke... Bright orange flames shot out from the side along the main deck from the bow to the after turret." As he watched, the bow of the big cruiser dipped forward and she plunged downward, still making headway. Though McClintock guessed that there were "few if any survivors," there were, in fact, more than six hundred survivors, including Kurita himself, who was plucked from the sea by a destroyer and transferred to the battleship *Yamato*.[12]

The American subs were not done yet. Within seconds, four torpedoes from the *Darter*'s stern tubes hit the heavy cruiser *Takeo*. Then the *Dace* struck, hitting the heavy cruiser *Maya* with four more. One of the *Dace*'s torpedoes detonated the *Maya*'s magazine, and the big cruiser exploded and went down in less than four minutes. On the *Dace* Claggett heard "crunching" and "heavy rumbling" sounds as she broke apart. It was, he reported, "the most gruesome sound I have ever heard." After that, the two American subs crash-dived and rigged for silent running as the escorting Japanese destroyers swarmed after them. The men on the *Dace* could hear the high-speed whir of destroyer propellers overhead and tracked them with their eyes as the sound passed from bow to stern. "The suspense," Claggett wrote, "was worse than the depth charging," especially since none of the depth charges came close enough to do any damage.[13]

Both the *Atago* and the *Maya* sank; the *Takao* was so badly crippled Kurita sent her limping back to Brunei with a two-destroyer escort.* Thus even before Kurita reached the Philippines, his force had been reduced by three cruisers and two destroyers. Nearly as important to the forthcoming contest were the several sighting messages sent in by *Darter* and *Dace*. By six-thirty that morning, Halsey knew that Kurita was at sea, that he had several battleships and heavy cruisers, and that he was on a course that would take him across the Sibuyan Sea toward San Bernardino Strait. Within minutes of receiving that report, Halsey ordered search planes to fan out over the Sibuyan Sea to look for him.

———

THEY FOUND HIM just past 8:00 a.m., when a search plane from the *Intrepid*, part of Gerald Bogan's carrier group operating off San Bernardino Strait, reported five battleships, nine cruisers, and thirteen destroyers

---

* McClintock sought to finish off the crippled *Takao*, though in trying to obtain a firing position, he ran the *Darter* hard aground on Bombay Shoal. Despite desperate efforts, his crew could not get her off the shoal and her crew evacuated to the *Dace*.

entering the Sibuyan Sea. Within minutes, Halsey ordered an attack by planes from the *Intrepid* and *Cabot*, doing so characteristically in a brief and succinct order: "STRIKE! REPEAT, STRIKE!" Technically, Halsey ought to have directed Mitscher to deliver that order, since Mitscher commanded the carrier task force. Given Halsey's temperament, however, it is not surprising that he effectively bypassed Mitscher and gave the order himself. What Mitscher thought of it is not recorded.[14]

At almost the same moment, three hundred miles to the south, a dozen scout bombers from Ralph Davison's carrier group found and reported Nishimura's Southern Force in the Sulu Sea. After sending in their report, the scout bombers attacked and inflicted meaningful damage on both of Nishimura's battleships, especially the *Fuso*, which was hit twice: once near the number two turret and once on the quarterdeck. The obvious irony was that while Ozawa's decoy carriers steamed southward still undiscovered, the Americans found the main attack forces rather quickly.[15]

Kurita had hoped to have air cover from land-based aircraft as he threaded his way through the Philippines, a hope that proved entirely unfounded for two reasons. One was that the Japanese had squandered most of their land-based aircraft ten days earlier, losing nearly five hundred of them off Formosa in a futile attempt to fend off more air strikes from Halsey's carriers. The second reason was that the planners in Tokyo believed that a better use of their scarce air assets was to attack Halsey's carriers, thus providing Kurita with what they called "indirect support." Consequently, as Kurita entered the Sibuyan Sea, only four friendly aircraft circled over his ships.[16]

The Japanese focused their air strikes on the northernmost of Halsey's carrier groups, which belonged to Rear Admiral Frederick Sherman. Most of the attackers fell victim almost at once to the American Hellcats. David McCampbell, who had shot down five Japanese planes during one sortie in the Battle of the Philippine Sea, this time shot down *nine* Zeros in a single flight, a record that was unmatched in the war and for which he later received the Medal of Honor. The Americans did not shoot down all the Japanese planes, however. Just before ten o'clock, a lone Judy flew out of low-lying clouds toward the light carrier *Princeton* and placed a single bomb very near the center of her flight deck. That bomb penetrated to the hangar

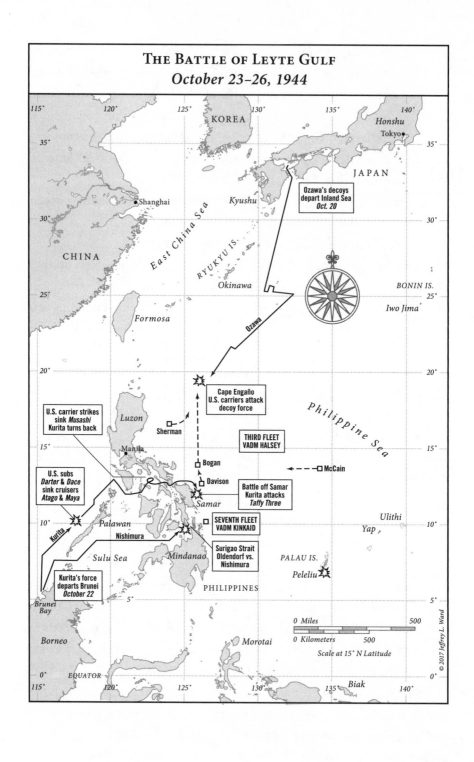

THE BATTLE OF LEYTE GULF
October 23–26, 1944

KOREA

Honshu

Tokyo•

JAPAN

Ozawa's decoys
depart Inland Sea
Oct. 20

Shanghai•

East China Sea

Kyushu

CHINA

RYUKYU IS.

BONIN IS.

Okinawa

Iwo Jima•

Formosa

Ozawa

Philippine Sea

Cape Engaño
U.S. carriers attack
decoy force

U.S. carrier strikes
sink *Musashi*
Kurita turns back

Luzon

☐
Sherman

THIRD FLEET
VADM HALSEY

Manila•

☐ Bogan

☐ McCain

U.S. subs
Darter & *Dace*
sink cruisers
Atago & *Maya*

☐ Davison

Battle off Samar
Kurita attacks
Taffy Three

Ulithi

Samar

Kurita

Palawan

☐

SEVENTH FLEET
VADM KINKAID

Yap ,

Nishimura

PALAU IS.

Sulu Sea

Mindanao

Surigao Strait
Oldendorf vs.
Nishimura

Peleliu ☆

Kurita's force
departs Brunei
October 22

PHILIPPINES

*Brunei
Bay*

Borneo

Morotai

0 Miles   500

0 Kilometers   500

Scale at 15° N Latitude

EQUATOR

Biak

© 2017 Jeffrey L. Ward

deck and exploded among six torpedo planes that were being refueled, triggering several secondary explosions. It was evident at once that the *Princeton* was in trouble. The cruiser *Birmingham* came alongside to help, and was herself badly damaged when the *Princeton*'s after magazine exploded. The crews of both ships fought heroically to try to save the *Princeton*, but it proved a losing battle.[17]

While the *Princeton* burned, American planes from Bogan's and Davison's carrier groups attacked Kurita's force in the Sibuyan Sea. Quickly dispatching Kurita's weak CAP, they executed several bombing and torpedo attacks on most of Kurita's ships. The heavy cruiser *Myōkō* was an early victim; badly crippled, she dropped out of formation and limped westward. Subsequent waves of American planes focused on the two big battleships, especially the *Musashi*. Though American accuracy was indifferent, there were so many planes attacking that the big battleship was hit repeatedly with both bombs and torpedoes—American pilots later claimed a total of seventeen bomb hits and twenty torpedo hits. No ship could survive such abuse, and it was soon evident that this "unsinkable" battleship was doomed. Throughout the attacks, Kurita doggedly maintained his eastward course despite his frustration with the lack of friendly air cover. There was a hint of criticism in his radio report to Tokyo that "we are being subjected to repeated enemy carrier-based air attacks." Koyanagi, who was on board the *Yamato* with his

This photo, taken from an American bomber, shows the Japanese super-battleship *Musashi* under attack in the Sibuyan Sea on October 24, 1944. Hit by more than a dozen bombs and as many torpedoes, she sank that night.

U.S. National Archives photo no. 80-G-281766

boss, later wrote, "We had expected air attacks, but this day's were almost enough to discourage us." It was evident, Koyanagi wrote, that "if we pushed on into the narrow [San Bernardino] strait and the raids continued, our force would be wiped out."[18]

By three-thirty, Kurita had had enough. He ordered his fleet to reverse course and head west. He did not intend it as a permanent retirement; he simply wanted to gain respite from the relentless air attacks. He sent a message to Toyoda in Tokyo, explaining that he planned "to retire temporarily beyond range of hostile planes," perhaps hoping that such a message might trigger more support from land-based Japanese planes.[19]

Only then, at four-forty in the afternoon, with the sun already low in the sky, did an American scout plane from the *Lexington* report the startling news that a Japanese force of "four carriers, two light cruisers, [and] five destroyers" was three hundred miles to the north off Luzon's Cape Engaño. Ozawa had been found at last. The news reached Halsey on the *New Jersey* at about five-thirty, hard on the heels of the report that Kurita had reversed course. With one enemy force apparently defeated, Halsey quickly decided to go after the carriers. As he explained it later, he believed that Kurita's Center Force "had suffered so much topside damage, especially in its guns and fire control instruments, that it…could be left to Kinkaid." In Halsey's view, Kinkaid's Seventh Fleet had primary responsibility for protecting the invasion force, leaving his own command free to seek out and destroy the enemy's main fleet. Here was the opportunity that Mitscher had been denied in the Philippine Sea.

Halsey walked into flag plot on the *New Jersey*, pointed to a spot on the chart, and announced, "Here's where we're going." Addressing his chief of staff, Robert B. "Mick" Carney, he gave the fateful order: "Mick, start them north."[20]

It was up to Carney to turn that brief command into instructions for the various elements of Halsey's Third Fleet, and over the next hour, a series of orders went out from the *New Jersey* by both TBS and radio. Bogan and Davison, whose carriers had been conducting the attacks on Kurita, were to recover their planes and head due north (course 000). En route they would join with Ted Sherman's group, which had spent the day fighting off the

Japanese air attacks that had claimed the *Princeton*. The fourth carrier group, that of Rear Admiral John S. McCain, which Halsey had sent to Ulithi to refuel, was to join the other three "at best speed." Though Kinkaid was not in Halsey's chain of command, a message went out to him as well simply to keep him informed: "Central force heavily damaged according to strike reports. Am proceeding north with 3 groups to attack carrier force at dawn."[21]

There were several difficulties with that message. One was that due to the communication protocols that required messages between the two fleets to pass through Manus, it did not reach Kinkaid for several hours. Quite apart from that, however, was the ambiguity of the message itself. Did the fact that "3 groups" were heading north mean that a fourth group was remaining behind to cover the Seventh Fleet's northern flank? If so, which group: McCain's carriers or Lee's battleships? The battleships were not mentioned at all, and therein lay a problem.[22]

Five hours earlier, at 3:12 that afternoon, Halsey had sent out a message creating a surface unit to be designated as Task Force 34. It would consist of four of Lee's fast battleships, including Halsey's flagship *New Jersey*, two heavy and three light cruisers, and nineteen destroyers. If Kurita's ships, which were at that time still heading determinedly east, managed to get through San Bernardino Strait, this was the force that would confront them. Halsey addressed the message to Lee on his flagship, *Washington*, and to each of the ships captains involved, with copies to Nimitz in Pearl Harbor and King in Washington. It was not, however, addressed to Kinkaid, who, in Halsey's view, did not have a need to know. Kinkaid's radio room received it nonetheless, decoded it, and sent it up to the bridge. Based on it, Kinkaid concluded that this surface force—Task Force 34—would cover his northern flank by defending San Bernardino Strait. A few hours later, Halsey clarified that order with another message indicating that Task Force 34 would be formed only "when directed by me." That second message, however, was sent by the short-range TBS radio, which meant that it never reached Kinkaid—or Nimitz, or King. It simply never occurred to Halsey that Kinkaid needed to be informed of his plans and movements.

Now, more than five hours later, the newest message from Halsey, which *was* addressed to Kinkaid, stated that "3 groups" were heading north. That confirmed Kinkaid in the belief that Task Force 34 remained behind, leaving him free to focus on Nishimura's force in the Sulu Sea. Accordingly, Kinkaid ordered Rear Admiral Jesse Oldendorf to "prepare for [a] night engagement" in Surigao Strait.[23]

In fact, however, when Halsey ordered Carney to "start them north," he meant everything: the carriers, the battleships, the escorts, the whole of Task Force 38—sixty-five ships altogether. He did not even leave a picket destroyer behind to watch San Bernardino Strait. Determined to annihilate the Japanese carrier force, he wanted Lee's battleships available to finish off any cripples that the air strikes left afloat. [24]

Even at the time, several key players tried to suggest to Halsey that it was a mistake to leave San Bernardino Strait unguarded, especially because even as Halsey's forces steamed northward, night-flying American patrol planes reported that Kurita had reversed course again and was once more heading east. Equally alarming, the Japanese had turned on the navigation lights marking the ship channel through the strait. From the *Washington*, Lee twice blinked Halsey a message suggesting that his battleships should be left behind to guard the strait. Each time, the only response he got from the flagship was a "roger," meaning "message received." Bogan also sent a message to Halsey using TBS radio to note that Kurita had reversed course and that the navigation lights in San Bernardino Strait had been turned on—a message that was intended to be suggestive as well as informative. The response from the flagship sounded exasperated: "Yes, yes, we have that information." Captain Mike Cheek, head of the Third Fleet intelligence group on the *New Jersey*, told Carney that his analysis of captured Japanese plans suggested that the carriers were decoys and that the greater danger came from the surface force. Carney told him that Halsey had gone to sleep and could not be disturbed. Mitscher, too, went to bed as soon as the carrier force had settled on its northward course, no doubt to be alert for the anticipated dawn strike. His chief of staff, Arleigh Burke, woke him up to tell him about the navigation lights and to urge him to tell Halsey about it. Mitscher asked if the flagship had that information; assured that it did, Mitscher said, "If he wants my advice he'll ask for it," and with that he turned over and went back to sleep.[25]

The Japanese were also sending messages that evening. Kurita's 4:00 p.m. dispatch, reporting that he was turning around "temporarily," had taken some time to reach Tokyo. When it did, Toyoda responded that Kurita should resume the attack regardless of the circumstances or the consequences: "With confidence in heavenly guidance," Toyoda radioed, "the entire force will attack." In fact, Kurita had already turned back eastward again even before he received that message. The American air strikes had stopped, and at 5:14 he turned around. His detour had wreaked havoc with the timetable, however, and he now informed Tokyo—and Nishimura—that he would not arrive in Leyte Gulf until about eleven the next morning.[26]

Nishimura, who had also received Toyoda's order to attack "with heavenly guidance," responded: "It is my plan to charge into Leyte Gulf, at 0440 hours [4:40 a.m.] on the 25th." That was seven hours ahead of Kurita, which of course made a simultaneous double envelopment impossible. He might have tried to postpone his arrival to match Kurita's, which would also have allowed the cruiser-destroyer force of Kiyohide Shima to overtake him, adding to his hitting power. Nishimura decided against it. To do so would mean circling slowly in the Sulu Sea for seven hours, a prime target for American submarines and aircraft, and Shima's presence might prove awkward. The two men did not like each other, and since both of them were vice admirals, there might be some uncertainty about who was in charge. Nishimura decided to press on ahead and accept the consequences. Whatever the initial intention had been for his separate command, it was evident now that he was engaged in what the Japanese called a "special attack." In a last message to both Toyoda and Kurita, he reported, "We proceed to Leyte for *gyokusai*," a term that literally meant "shattered jewel" and figuratively denoted a suicide attack.[27]

WHILE HALSEY HEADED NORTH, Oldendorf summoned his captains on board the flagship *Louisville* to plan a night battle against Nishimura. Since Surigao Strait was the only approach to Leyte Gulf from the south, it would necessarily funnel the Japanese into a predictable course, and that allowed Oldendorf to lay a trap. He positioned his battleships and heavy cruisers across the northern end of the strait and stationed his destroyers along its sides. Below them near the entrance to the strait were thirty-nine PT boats under the tactical command of Lieutenant Commander Robert A. Leeson. Oldendorf did not expect much of this mosquito fleet aside from spotting and reporting, but they did carry torpedoes and might find a chance to use them. As a result of these dispositions, Nishimura would have to run a gauntlet of American PT boats and destroyers even before his two battle-ships confronted the six battleships under Oldendorf.[28]

Unaware that Nishimura had already decided that he was sailing to his doom, Oldendorf's "one anxiety," as he wrote later, "was that the enemy would not keep coming"—that Nishimura would appreciate the extent of his peril and withdraw. A secondary concern was the ammunition on his battleships. Because his ships had put to sea for a shore bombardment mission, their maga-zines were stocked primarily with high explosive (HE) ordnance rather than armor-piercing (AP) shells for use against ships. Two of Oldendorf's ships (*Maryland* and *West Virginia*) had 16-inch guns, but they had only 440 rounds of AP shells between them. Oldendorf therefore told his captains to hold their fire until the enemy was within twenty thousand yards.[29]

Nishimura entered Surigao Strait just past midnight on October 24–25. At almost the same moment, Kurita exited San Bernardino Strait. Their experiences could not have been more different. Nishimura encountered a swarm of American PT boats, which attacked him in groups of three. Their torpedoes did no damage, though they compelled the Japanese to maneu-ver to avoid them, and their reports kept Oldendorf apprised of Nishimura's progress.

As for Kurita, far to the north, when his ships emerged from San Bernardino Strait, they found nothing at all. Kurita was astonished. He had ordered everyone to battle stations in anticipation of a severe fight with the American fleet, yet as his ships steamed out into the Philippine Sea, there was only dark and empty ocean. Dumbfounded, he turned south along the coast of Samar and headed for the American landing beaches on Leyte.

Nishimura, meanwhile, continued northward into Surigao Strait, slap-ping away the PT boats like so many annoying gnats. At around 2:00 a.m., his ships encountered the first of the American destroyers. They belonged to Destroyer Squadron 54, commanded by Captain Jesse Coward, and their torpedoes proved much more efficient. One of them hit the already wounded *Fuso* and flooded her boiler rooms. The big ship slowed, took on a pronounced list to starboard, and veered out of line. Another hit the *Yamashiro*, and three torpedoes struck Japanese destroyers—two of them hitting the *Yamagumo* almost simultaneously, so she "simply exploded." Not yet halfway through the strait, Nishimura had lost more than half his force. He pressed grimly on.[30]

At three-thirty, Nishimura's remaining vessels entered the arc of fire from Oldendorf's heavy ships. The American cruisers fired first, flinging more than three thousand rounds toward the oncoming warships. Then the battleships opened up. Three of them had the new Mark 8 fire-control system, and their salvos were deadly accurate. Shells from the eight 16-inch guns on the *West Virginia*, each of them weighing twenty-seven hundred pounds, passed almost directly over Oldendorf's flagship *Louisville*, sounding, Oldendorf wrote later, "like a train of boxcars passing over a high trestle." The shortage of AP ammunition proved irrelevant, since after only eighteen minutes there was nothing left for the Americans to shoot at. The *Fuso* sank first, her hull spiraling downward as if she were trying to corkscrew herself into the sea. The *Yamashiro* stayed afloat a little longer, still heading toward the American battle line as she sank, rolling over to port and plunging downward. Of the thirty-five hundred men on the two battleships, virtually all died; just twenty survived.[31]

The cruiser *Mogami* remained afloat, though she, too, was badly damaged. Both her captain and her executive officer had been killed, leaving the senior gunnery officer in command. With her rudder out, he tried to navigate the crippled ship back down the strait maneuvering on engines alone. While doing so, he collided with the heavy cruiser *Nachi*, flagship of Kiyohide Shima, whose force of cruisers and destroyers was coming north at thirty knots to support Nishimura. After that, both Shima and the wounded *Mogami* retired southward. Oldendorf led a pursuit by his cruisers and they punished the *Mogami* with ten to twenty more shell hits, though she remained stubbornly afloat until the next day, when she finally sank. Nishimura's Southern Force had been virtually annihilated. Of the seven ships in his strike force, only the destroyer *Shigure*, herself badly crippled, escaped destruction. It was her captain, Commander Shigeru Nishino, who sent the news to Toyoda: "All ships except *Shigure* went down under gunfire and torpedo attack."[32]

That same morning, more than five hundred miles to the north, Mitscher was preparing to launch full-deckload strikes at Ozawa's decoy force. Four hours earlier, at 2:55 a.m., while American torpedoes were smashing into Nishimura's battleships, Halsey had finally formed Task Force 34, doing so not to watch San Bernardino Strait—it was far too late for that—but to steam out in front of the carriers so they would be within gun range to mop up the wreckage of the Japanese fleet after the carrier planes were done with them. Now, just as the first of his bombers were heading off to strike those carriers, Halsey received a message that Kinkaid had sent him hours earlier, notifying him of the progress of Oldendorf's fight with Nishimura. In it, almost as an afterthought, Kinkaid asked, "Is TF34 guarding San Bernardino Strait?" Halsey was surprised. Why should Kinkaid think that? Why should he even *know* about Task Force 34? But he answered the query: "Negative. Task Force 34 is with carrier groups engaging enemy carrier force." It was the first hint Kinkaid got that San Bernardino Strait had been left unguarded.[33]

ALL THAT NIGHT, while Nishimura was being annihilated in Surigao Strait and Halsey was planning a dawn airstrike against Ozawa, Kurita's battleships and cruisers steamed southward along the east coast of Samar. Radar swept the empty sea and lookouts peered eagerly but fruitlessly into the darkness. Even after the sun rose at 6:27, there was no enemy in sight—nothing but a message from Nishino reporting that Nishimura's group had been annihilated. The previous afternoon, while he was still in the Sibuyan Sea, Kurita had received a report from a Japanese float plane that there were twelve American carriers southeast of Leyte Gulf, which he naturally assumed was Halsey's fleet, and from the moment he had exited San Bernardino Strait he had been expecting to encounter them. Then, just a few minutes before 7:00 a.m., lookouts reported ships on the horizon. Kurita grabbed his binoculars, and there they were: American aircraft carriers and their escorts. As he had promised his captains at Brunei Bay, they would have an opportunity to fight an American carrier force after all. He flashed an exultant message to Toyoda: "By heaven-sent opportunity, we are dashing to attack the enemy carriers." Eager to seize the moment, he dispensed with a battle plan and simply ordered "general attack."[34]

The ships espied by Kurita's lookouts that morning were not, of course, Halsey's big carriers, which were five hundred miles to the north attacking Ozawa. They were the jeep carriers of Rear Admiral Clifton Sprague's Taffy Three, northernmost of the three escort carrier groups off Leyte Gulf. South of it and over the horizon was Taffy Two, commanded by Rear Admiral Felix Stump, and beyond that was Taffy One, commanded by Thomas L. Sprague, the overall escort group commander. (Though the two Spragues had been classmates at the Academy, they were not related.) Those three Taffy groups were now all that stood between Kurita and the Seventh Fleet transports inside Leyte Gulf.

Sprague was a Naval Academy graduate who had earned the nickname "Ziggy" for his habit of zigzagging down the corridors of Bancroft Hall like a broken-field runner. A career naval aviator, he had made the first catapult launch and the first arrested landing on the old *Yorktown* back in 1936. He had also commanded the seaplane tender *Tangier* in Pearl Harbor during the Japanese attack in 1941. Yet before October 25, 1944, his greatest claim to fame may have been that his wife was the sister of F. Scott Fitzgerald, though his wife

An apprehensive-looking Clifton "Ziggy" Sprague on the bridge of his flagship, the escort carrier USS *Fanshaw Bay*. This photo is from the battle off Okinawa in April 1945, but it captures the tension on board the *Fanshaw Bay* on October 25, 1944.

U.S. National Archives photo no. 80-G-371327

and her famous brother had been estranged for some time. On this historic morning, Sprague had no idea that a major Japanese surface force was nearby. At 6:46 he was on the bridge of his flagship, *Fanshaw Bay*, watching the launch of the dawn submarine patrol when the radar room reported a contact. One minute later, a search plane from the *St. Lô* made an astonishing sighting report: "Enemy surface force of four battleships, four heavy cruisers, two light cruisers, and ten to twelve destroyers sighted twenty miles northwest of your task group and closing in on you at thirty knots." Twenty miles! That was virtually within gun range. It was so improbable that Sprague ordered the pilot to look again: "Air plot, tell him to check his identification." The pilot dove down for another look and reported, "I can see the pagoda masts, and I see the biggest red meatball flag I ever saw flying on the biggest battleship I ever saw." With that, Sprague issued two orders in quick succession. The first was for all of his carriers to turn immediately into the wind and "launch everything"; the second was for the destroyer escorts to make smoke and carry out a torpedo attack. Then he got on the radio to call for help.[35]

Down in Surigao Strait, Kinkaid was jolted from his celebration of Oldendorf's victory by Sprague's radio call, and at 7:07 he sent an urgent message to Halsey: his escort carriers were under attack. Given the mandated routing through Manus, the message did not arrive on the *New Jersey* until 8:22.[36]

In the meantime, the destroyers of Taffy Three sped toward the Japanese heavy ships—a pack of whippets charging a herd of elephants. One of the destroyers, USS *Johnston*, did not even wait for Sprague's order. Her skipper, Commander Ernest E. Evans, headed directly for the heavy cruiser *Kumano* as soon as it edged over the horizon. The *Johnston* was only a year old and 80 percent of her crew were on their first deployment, though Evans had done all he could to bring them up to the mark. The men had taken to calling their ship "GQ Johnny" because of Evans's tendency to send them regularly to general quarters. It paid off now. Like Sprague, Evans issued several orders in rapid sequence: "All hands to general quarters . . . All engines ahead flank. Commence making smoke and stand by for a torpedo attack. Left full rudder." The *Johnston*'s gunnery officer, Lieutenant Robert Hagen, recalled later, "We felt like David without a slingshot." Not far

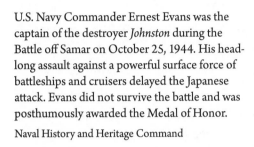

U.S. Navy Commander Ernest Evans was the captain of the destroyer *Johnston* during the Battle off Samar on October 25, 1944. His head-long assault against a powerful surface force of battleships and cruisers delayed the Japanese attack. Evans did not survive the battle and was posthumously awarded the Medal of Honor.

Naval History and Heritage Command

behind the *Johnston* were the destroyers *Hoel* and *Heermann* followed by the destroyer escort *Samuel B. Roberts*. All four charged the Japanese fleet, launching torpedoes and generating smoke while firing their 5-inch guns.[37]

At least some of the American torpedoes found their mark, and even those that did not slowed the Japanese advance by forcing them to maneuver to avoid them, giving the American carriers a chance to get their planes aloft. All that time, however, the Japanese were also firing. Some of their heavy armor-piercing shells passed right through the thin-skinned American ships without exploding, though enough of them did explode to cause severe damage. Three 14-inch shells struck the *Johnston* in quick succession. It was, Hagen recalled, "like a puppy being smacked by a truck." Somehow the *Johnston* remained afloat, though she had to maneuver on one engine without either compass or radar. Despite that, and the fact that she had expended all her torpedoes, she remained in the fight using only her two forward 5-inch guns. The other escorts were also hit—the men on the *Hoel* counted forty shell hits in all, and the *Roberts* was hit by "a salvo of 5-inch shells in the engineering spaces" that ripped open the steam lines and scalded the men of the engineering gang. Both the *Hoel* and *Roberts* sank, and soon enough the *Johnston*, too, succumbed. With his last order, Evans directed the crew to abandon ship, and the men on the *Johnston* leapt into the sea. As they floated in their life jackets, they looked up apprehensively as a Japanese destroyer passed nearby, wondering if they were about to be machine-gunned in the water, since such behavior by both sides had now become almost routine in the Pacific War. Instead, as the destroyer passed, they were astonished to see a Japanese officer on the bridge saluting them.[38]

While the destroyers of Taffy Three hurled themselves sacrificially at the Japanese, aircraft from Sprague's carriers also attacked. The planes were mostly older Avengers and Wildcats intended to conduct CAP, anti-submarine patrols, and to support the troops ashore—they were not equipped for a fight against armored warships. The Wildcats had only their .50 caliber machine guns. An FM-2 Wildcat had only about thirty seconds' worth of ammunition, and the pilots expended that quickly. Even after their ammunition was gone, however, some of them continued to conduct dry runs on the Japanese ships, essentially buzzing the bridges of battleships and cruisers, hoping to create the impression that they were still under attack. Lieutenant Paul B. Garrison, a Wildcat pilot from the *Kitkun Bay*, strafed the Japanese battleships ten times, then made ten more strafing runs with no ammunition.[39]

All naval battles contain an element of chaos, but the Battle of Leyte Gulf was particularly chaotic, especially for a daytime confrontation. Kurita's unstructured charge and Sprague's hurried counterattack meant that ships on both sides maneuvered independently, occasionally getting into one another's way. With heavy smoke, intermittent rain squalls, torpedoes in the water, and planes overhead, neither commander had a clear sense of the battle. Kurita still believed he was facing the big carriers of Halsey's fleet, and it was evident that several of them had been hit. The *Kalinin Bay* was hit fifteen times, though she somehow stayed afloat. The *Gambier Bay* was less fortunate and became the first aircraft carrier sunk by surface gunfire since HMS *Glorious* had gone down in the North Sea back in 1940.[40]

All this time, both Sprague and Kinkaid continued to send out radio calls for help, each slightly more alarming than the last. Twenty minutes after his initial report to Halsey that Sprague was under attack, Kinkaid sent him another: "Request Lee proceed at top speed to cover Leyte; request immediate strike by fast carriers." Then, ten minutes later, another: "Situation

critical. Battleships and fast carrier strike wanted to prevent enemy penetrating Leyte Gulf." And finally, in uncoded plain English: "Where is Lee?
Send Lee."[41]

Halsey received the first of Kinkaid's calls for help at 8:22, when the battle off Leyte Gulf was at its peak. By then, his planes were in the midst of
conducting the first strike against Ozawa's carriers, and Halsey was too far
away to respond in any case. His first thought, he claimed later, was to wonder "how Kinkaid had let 'Ziggy' Sprague get caught like this." He still
believed that covering the beachhead was entirely Kinkaid's responsibility,
insisting in his postwar memoir, "It was not my job to protect the Seventh
Fleet," even though MacArthur had reminded him that "full support by
Third Fleet" of the invasion force was both "essential and paramount."
Halsey did order McCain's carrier group, still approaching from Ulithi, to
change course and head west, though McCain was 335 miles away and
unlikely to get there in time. What he did *not* do was detach Lee's fast battleships. Had he sent them at once they would almost certainly have reached
San Bernardino Strait in time to trap Kurita on the eastern side of the
Philippines, but Halsey remained focused on what they could do against
crippled Japanese carriers. On the bridge of the *New Jersey*, he muttered
aloud to no one in particular, "When I get my teeth into something, I hate
to let go."[42]

Halsey and Kinkaid were not the only ones listening in on the radio net
that morning. More than five thousand miles away in Pearl Harbor, Nimitz
also noted the increasingly plaintive calls for help from Kinkaid and Sprague.
He wondered how Kurita had gotten through San Bernardino Strait undetected; like Kinkaid, he assumed that Task Force 34 had been left behind to
guard the strait. He did not want to interfere with a fleet commander in the
middle of a battle, but he thought he could at least ask him a question. With
some diffidence, he agreed to send Halsey a short query, with copies to
Kinkaid and King, that read simply, "Where is Task Force 34?"

Throughout the war, all naval communications were routinely encumbered with what was called "padding" at the beginning and the end of each
message to make decryption by the enemy more difficult. To ensure that
the padding was not included as part of the message, it was separated from

the text by a double consonant so that the radioman on the receiving end could delete it before delivering it to the recipient. The message that went out from Pearl Harbor to Halsey that morning read:

TURKEY TROTS TO WATER GG FROM CINCPAC ACTION COM THIRD FLEET INFO COMINCH CTF SEVENTY-SEVEN X WHERE IS RPT WHERE IS TASK FORCE THIRTY FOUR RR THE WORLD WONDERS.[43]

On this day, however, the radioman on the *New Jersey* thought the terminal padding sounded like part of the message and he failed to delete it before it was delivered to Halsey on the bridge of the *New Jersey*. In a calmer moment Halsey might have noticed the telltale "RR" in front of "THE WORLD WONDERS," but he was in the middle of what he hoped would be the decisive naval battle of the war and more than a little on edge due to the repeated cries for help from Kinkaid. When he read Nimitz's message, he exploded. He wrote later that it was "as if I had been struck in the face." He threw the message to the deck and stomped on it. According to a witness, he shouted, "What right does Chester have to send me a God-damned message like that?" Carney grabbed him by the shoulders. "Stop it!" Carney yelled. "What the hell's the matter with you? Pull yourself together!"[44]

Halsey did not issue any new orders right away. Instead, he and Carney left the bridge and went down to Halsey's flag quarters, where they stayed for more than an hour. No one knows what happened during that hour as Halsey's fleet continued northward, away from Leyte Gulf, at twenty-five knots. When he returned to the bridge at 11:15, he ordered Lee's battleships to turn around. Of course, it took another hour for Lee's ships to make up the distance they had traveled northward while Halsey was in his flag quarters.[45]

Because the battleships would need air cover, Halsey also ordered Bogan's carrier group to go with them. The other two carrier groups he left behind with Mitscher to finish off Ozawa. In what was labeled the Battle of Cape Engaño, Mitscher's two carrier groups sank all four of Ozawa's decoy carriers, matching the tally of the Battle of Midway. One of those carriers was the *Zuikaku*, the last of the six that had attacked Pearl Harbor three years before. The hybrid battleships *Ise* and *Hyuga*, a light cruiser, and a handful of destroyers got away.

═══════════════════

SO DID KURITA. Despite the confusion and the loss of two of his cruisers, by nine o'clock Kurita had reason to believe that he was doing rather well after two hours of combat. The captains of the *Kongo*, *Yamato*, and *Haguro* each reported sinking an American *Enterprise*-class carrier, and the lookouts and gunners reported the *Fletcher*-class destroyers they had sunk as *Baltimore*-class cruisers. Such claims are more comprehensible in consideration of the fact that until this moment virtually all of the confrontations between American and Japanese surface ships had occurred at night. No one on Kurita's ships had ever seen an American carrier or cruiser in the daytime. Based on these reports, Kurita concluded that he had sunk three or four fleet carriers, as many cruisers, and three destroyers—essentially wrecking one of Halsey's carrier groups. In addition, he had intercepted the panicky American radio calls for immediate support and concluded that a second American carrier force was north of him and approaching. That was technically true, but those ships were still hundreds of miles away and were neither a threat nor a realistic potential target. Still, with his ships spread out over a thirty-mile front, he sought to bring order out of the existing chaos, and so at 9:11, though still under active air attack, he ordered them to regroup. They had no sooner begun to do so when he lost two more of his heavy cruisers. Between 9:18 and 9:25, American aircraft mortally wounded both the *Chikuma* and *Chokai*. Kurita still had four battleships, but he was down to only two heavy cruisers.[46]

For the next hour and a half, from 9:15 to 10:45, Kurita maneuvered erratically. A definitive explanation for his conduct is impossible at this remove. He may have been exhausted and confused, behaving, as Lincoln said of General William S. Rosecrans in 1863, "like a duck hit on the head." After the war, he acknowledged to an interviewer, "My mind was extremely fatigued," and he told Captain Tameichi Hara of his "sheer physical exhaustion." Or he may have been looking for that other American carrier group. In any case, at 11:20—at virtually the same moment that Halsey ordered Lee's battleships to head south—he reported to Toyoda that he was about to execute "the planned penetration of Leyte Gulf," and he turned southwest. Almost immediately, however, he got a sighting report—which subsequently proved false—that an American carrier group was only a short distance away to the north. In his action report, Kurita wrote that rather than enter Leyte Gulf, from which it seemed likely that most of the American transports would have fled by now anyway, it seemed "wiser" to strike this new enemy carrier force. "Having so determined," he wrote, "we turned northward." After the war, Koyanagi stated explicitly, "We proceeded northward in search of the [other] enemy carrier groups."[47]

Watching them depart, Ziggy Sprague was incredulous, later admitting, "I could not believe my eyes." That morning when Kurita's big ships had first appeared, Sprague had not expected his command to last fifteen minutes. Now, four hours later, the enemy was giving up the fight. A signalman on his flagship, his sense of humor undamaged by four hours of violence, exclaimed, "God damn it boys, they're getting away!"[48]

Kurita's decision to turn north when he appeared to be on the verge of victory baffled witnesses at the time, and has confounded historians since. Both Kurita and his chief of staff insisted that he was setting out in pursuit of more American carriers. If so, it was a desperate long shot, for even if there was such a force near enough for him to engage it, which was mostly speculative, he would have to get close enough to it in broad daylight to use his big guns before their planes found and sank him. Still, the explanation fits both Kurita's character and the culture of the Imperial Japanese Navy—and of the U.S. Navy, too, for that matter. Both Halsey and Kurita were products of a professional ethos that emphasized the importance of the decisive battle; both were disciples of Alfred Thayer Mahan; and both were obsessed with the destruction of the enemy's carrier force. Kurita had never fully embraced the mission of sinking empty transports, and Halsey had never accepted the fact that he was responsible for protecting them. In Kurita's only postwar interview, he told a journalist, "The destruction of enemy aircraft carriers was a kind of obsession with me, and I fell victim to it." Halsey might have said the same.[49]

That afternoon, as Kurita steamed northward seeking a phantom American carrier force, he was attacked by long-range planes from McCain's task group. He found no carriers, however, and when he reached San Bernardino Strait at 9:40 that night, he directed his remaining ships into it. The leading battleships of Task Force 34 arrived there just over two hours later, highlighting the importance of the two hours that had been lost while Halsey in his flag cabin with Mick Carney tried to determine how to respond to the crisis. McCain's aircraft attacked Kurita's ships as they recrossed the Sibuyan Sea, and the *Yamato* in particular was heavily damaged. Kurita arrived back at Brunei Bay on October 28 with exactly half the number of ships he had set out with six days earlier.

There was an epilogue. Even as the Battle off Samar was ending, Japanese commanders in the Philippines dispatched the first squadrons of "special attack" or "kamikaze" aircraft. On the morning of October 25, while Taffy Three fought desperately against Kurita's heavy ships, three Japanese suicide pilots smashed their planes into American jeep carriers: the *Santee*, the *Suwannee*, and the *St. Lô*. Crews on the first two managed to contain the damage, but on the *St. Lô*, the bomb on the kamikaze plane exploded on the hangar deck, igniting fires that spread quickly. The *St. Lô* sank not long after the *Gambier Bay*.[50]

THE BATTLE OF LEYTE GULF was the largest naval engagement in history and, despite the escape of part of Kurita's surface force and Halsey's frustration that he had not been able to destroy all of Ozawa's force, it was an overwhelming American victory. The Americans lost the light carrier *Princeton*, two escort carriers, two destroyers, and one destroyer escort; the Japanese lost four carriers, three battleships, six heavy cruisers, four light cruisers, and thirteen destroyers. It was beyond devastating. As Koyanagi acknowledged, those losses "spelled the collapse of our Navy as an effective fighting force."[51]

In the aftermath of the battle, both Halsey and Kurita were haunted by their missed opportunities, though Kurita did not learn until after the war was over just how close he had come to a breakthrough, or that instead of Halsey's big carriers, he had battled a group of small escort carriers. Both men became the object of criticism from their peers, some of it quite bitter, yet their superiors supported them. Privately Nimitz expressed annoyance that Halsey had left San Bernardino Strait unguarded, but officially both he and King sanctioned his every move, and Halsey retained command of the Big Blue Fleet. As for Kurita, some of the criticism aimed at him was so bitter, the Naval General Staff reassigned him to command the Naval Academy at Etajima to protect him from assassination.

Whatever the operational lessons of the Battle of Leyte Gulf—about unity of command, clear communication channels, and keeping everyone apprised of the big picture—its strategic consequences were self-evident: the Imperial Japanese Navy had been effectively destroyed. Rather than delay the end of the war, as Toyoda and others had hoped, the Battle of Leyte Gulf hastened it.

CHAPTER 26

THE NOOSE TIGHTENS

T HE DESTRUCTION OF THREE HEAVY CRUISERS by *Darter* and *Dace* in the Palawan Passage early on October 23 was only one example of the critical role played by American submarines during the fight for the Philippines, and indeed throughout the Pacific War. On that same day in the Formosa Strait, Richard O'Kane in the submarine *Tang* sank three freighters and a transport from a Japanese convoy. Less than twenty-four hours later he sank two more freighters from a different convoy. Several of those ships carried crated airplanes and aviation gas for the planes that Kurita had hoped would provide cover for his transit of the Sibuyan Sea. Their loss reflects the indirect impact that American submarines had on the war at large. Without the supplies, equipment, and especially the fuel needed to conduct military operations, the Japanese army and navy as well as their air forces were increasingly paralyzed.[1]

Submarine patrols were dangerous. O'Kane fired his twenty-fourth and last torpedo just past midnight on October 24–25. It was only a few yards clear of the tube when it suddenly broke to the surface, turned sharply left, and circled back toward the *Tang*. O'Kane ordered left full rudder, but it was too late. It struck the *Tang* in the after torpedo room and the sub went down in mere seconds. O'Kane himself was one of only nine survivors. All nine were picked up by a Japanese patrol boat and spent the rest of the war in a prisoner-of-war camp.[2]

Collectively, submarines such as the *Tang* had a powerful strategic impact on the Japanese war economy. Early in the war they had been mostly a nuisance, but by 1944 an average of between forty and fifty American subs patrolled the western Pacific at any given moment, and they threatened to shut down the Japanese economy altogether. About a hundred of them operated out of Pearl Harbor, which required a long run to their hunting grounds, often including a fuel stop at Midway or Guam. Another forty were based in Australia: either on its west coast at Fremantle or its east coast at Brisbane. Charles Lockwood commanded the boats out of Brisbane, and Ralph Waldo Christie those out of Fremantle. Both men were loyal champions of the skippers under their command. It was Lockwood who had been largely responsible for getting the experts in Washington to take seriously the complaints about malfunctioning torpedoes. For his part, Christie liked to meet returning submarines on the docks at Fremantle to congratulate them and hand out medals. That had a positive impact on the morale of the submarine crews, but it got him into trouble with Kinkaid, since Christie did not have the authority to issue medals. Eventually the two admirals were at such loggerheads that Kinkaid asked that Christie be relieved. In November 1944, Christie left to command the Puget Sound Navy Yard and was replaced by Rear Admiral James Fife.[3]

The new *Balao*-class American submarines benefited from a number of improvements over earlier versions. For one thing, they were larger—at 1,500 tons, they were twice the size of a German Type VII U-boat, and larger than many destroyer escorts. (The *Samuel L. Roberts*, sunk at Leyte Gulf, displaced only 1,350 tons.) They had thicker, stronger steel on their pressure hulls, which enabled them to dive to three hundred, four hundred, even five hundred feet; O'Kane once took the *Tang* down to six hundred feet. They had both air search (SC) and surface search (SG) radar, night periscopes that allowed them to see better in the dark while submerged,

Baleo-class submarines such as the USS *Tang*, shown here off Mare Island Navy Yard in December 1943, were larger and more efficient than their predecessors, and collectively they devastated Japanese shipping during 1944.

Naval History and Heritage Command

and even an acoustical torpedo (called a "Cutie") that homed in on the sound of a ship's propellers.[4]

Submarine service remained a hardship. Even the new, larger boats were crowded, the patrols lengthy (usually forty-five to sixty days or until the torpedoes were expended), and the most mundane activities remained complicated. Here, for example, are the directions that were posted next to the toilet on a *Balao*-class sub: "Shut the bowl flapper valve, flood the bowl with sea water through the sea and stop valves, and then shut both valves. After using the toilet, operate the flapper valve to empty the contents of the bowl into the expulsion chamber, then shut the flapper valve. Charge the volume tank until the pressure is 10 pounds higher than the sea pressure. Open the gate and plug valves on the discharge line and operate the rocker valve to discharge the contents of the expulsion chamber overboard." Failure to follow these instructions precisely could result in a repellent mess.[5]

In spite of such inconveniences, the quality of life on American submarines was greatly improved by 1944. Occasional showers were now possible, and rations were dramatically better. The captain of one sub reported that "our freezer was filled with boned meats—including steaks, roasts, chops, and hamburgers. The baker was up at 0300 each day to prepare fresh breads, rolls, cakes, and cookies." On most subs, there was an "open door policy" that allowed crewmen to help themselves to cold cuts and sandwiches as well as fresh coffee around the clock. A number of boats had self-service Coca-Cola machines, which one skipper called "a real morale booster." Periodically, the crews might gather in the forward torpedo room to watch a movie. Such luxuries were unimaginable to the crews of Germany's "iron coffins," or, indeed, those of Japanese or British submarines.[6]

For the first two years of the war, the older, smaller American subs had ventured forth individually. By 1944, however, there were enough of them that they generally operated in groups of three or occasionally four. Officially, these were called coordinated attack groups (CAGs), but in imitation of the Kriegsmarine, virtually everyone referred to them as "wolf packs." Most of these packs were named somewhat fancifully in honor of the senior officer, with monikers such as Park's Pirates for Captain Lew Parks, Hydeman's Hellcats for Commander Earl T. Hydeman, and Burt's Brooms for Captain Burt Klakring.[7]

The new American subs were also more efficient. The torpedo problems had been largely solved (though the loss of the Tang showed that some problems remained), and the number of Japanese ships sunk increased dramatically. Whereas in 1942, American submarines sank a total of 612,039 tons of shipping, in 1944 they destroyed 2,388,709 tons, nearly four times as much. If that was less than the tonnage claimed by Dönitz's more numerous U-boats back in the "happy time" of 1942, as a percentage of Japanese shipping it was far greater. In 1941 the Japanese had nearly 6.4 million tons of merchant shipping. Despite adding 3.5 million more during the war—nearly half of it in 1944—by the end of that year there was less than 2.5 million tons left. The Japanese merchant marine was steadily disappearing because Japan could not do what the United States did: build ships as fast or faster than its enemy could sink them.[8]

Another reason for American success was that Japanese anti-submarine warfare was not particularly effective. Japanese escorts had both sonar and depth charges, but their crews were less efficient in using them than the British in the Atlantic or the Americans in the Pacific. It was not uncommon for American subs to endure prolonged depth charge attacks with little or no damage. On one occasion, the *Balao*-class submarine *Batfish* fired several torpedoes into a convoy, then went deep and stayed down for more than twelve hours while Japanese destroyers dropped hundreds of depth charges near her "one right after the other." None of them came close enough to do any damage. When the air inside the sub began to get stale, the skipper of the *Batfish*, Lieutenant Commander Wayne Merrill, decided it would be better to die fighting on the surface than to stay under and suffocate. The *Batfish* surfaced into a thick fogbank and simply crept away. Of course, having to lie quiet and endure a depth-charge attack, even an unsuccessful one, was psychologically draining. The repeated concussions often shattered lightbulbs and loosened the cork lining on the bulkheads; still, as long as the pressure hull held, the boat survived. Japanese inefficiency in depth-charge attacks is especially curious since they were extraordinarily efficient in most other areas of naval warfare. The explanation may be at least partly cultural. Valuing the offense over the defense, Japanese destroyermen worked harder at perfecting torpedo attacks than they did at the more pedantic job of escorting lumbering merchant ships or pinpointing the location of unseen American submarines.[9]

In addition to the gradual depletion of the number of Japanese ships, those that survived became increasingly inefficient. One reason was a shortage of cargo handlers. By 1944, conscription had swept up most experienced longshoremen into the armed forces and Japan was compelled to rely on dock workers rounded up from the regions they had conquered— Filipinos, Koreans, and Chinese—as well as Japanese women and even American prisoners of war. Such workers were inexperienced, and many of them were less than enthusiastic in their labor, so efficiency suffered. Another problem was Japanese reluctance to embrace convoys. They did not put a convoy system in place until late in 1943, and convoys did not become routine until the spring of 1944. Even then, there were so few escorts that convoys were delayed, sometimes for weeks, for lack of an escort vessel. In such circumstances, it seemed wiser to send out ships individually, especially through what were assumed to be safe areas. The problem was that by 1944 there were no safe areas. The Japanese were shocked in October 1943 when "Mush" Morton led a three-submarine wolf pack into the Sea of Japan and sank a troop transport in what the Japanese considered "the emperor's bathtub." It was little consolation that Morton's boat, the *Wahoo*, was itself sunk a few days later as it attempted to exit the Sea of Japan.[10]

The devastation of Japan's shipping affected every aspect of her war effort. Coal imports dropped from 24 million tons in 1941 to 8.3 million tons in 1944; iron ore from 4.8 million tons to 1 million tons. Oil imports fell by 48 percent between 1943 and 1944, and fell even further after the loss of the Philippines. Japan's endangered tankers lay inshore during the day and ventured to sea only at night, steaming blacked out until dawn, then heading for shore again. The seas were dangerous everywhere. In May 1944, an American sub sank Japan's largest tanker, the 17,000-ton *Nisshin Maru*, in the South China Sea, where the Japanese believed their shipping was safe. In December, on his inaugural patrol as skipper of the *Flasher*, George Grider sank four tankers displacing 10,000 tons each. The tankers, very likely filled with volatile crude oil from Java or Borneo, "disintegrated with the explosions." It was so spectacular a sight that Grider allowed his crewmen to come topside two at a time to watch them burn. Only a few days later, the *Flasher* sank three more tankers off Indochina. As a result of such attacks, oil became so scarce that the Japanese began fueling their ships with soybean oil. They confiscated the rice crops of Indochina, causing widespread starvation, in order to turn the rice into biofuel. In effect, American submarines were doing to Japan what German U-boats had failed to do to Great Britain: starve it of the essential tools of war.[11]

By late 1944 Japan was running out of ships altogether. In the last two months of the year, Japanese ship losses actually declined from more than 250,000 tons a month to about 100,000 tons a month, not because American submarines had become less efficient but because fewer and fewer Japanese ships put to sea at all. Lacking sufficient transports and tankers, the Japanese (like the Italians in 1943) turned to using submarines and barges—even rafts—as supply vessels. By the end of the year, American subs were literally running out of targets.[12]

Neither Lockwood nor Christie (and later Fife) attempted the kind of close coordination of their submarines that Dönitz had done in the Atlantic. They did, however, occasionally pass on a piece of Ultra intelligence to the wolf pack skippers. In November, for example, the code breakers learned that the Japanese planned to transfer the 23rd Infantry Division from China to the Philippines. Given the high value of such a convoy, it had an especially strong escort, consisting of the aircraft carrier *Jun'yō* plus six destroyers. Tipped off by the code breakers, Lockwood vectored two wolf pack groups—six boats altogether—to the coordinates, and over three days in mid-November they sank two of the troop transports, three freighters, and put three torpedoes into the *Jun'yō*. That, too, was a measure of the kind of impact the submarines had on the Pacific War. It was one less division that MacArthur's soldiers had to confront on Luzon.[13]

IN ADDITION TO THE INTERDICTION OF SHIPPING, American submarines also rescued U.S. aircrews from bombers that were forced down over the ocean. This became especially critical in the last week of November 1944, when the United States began a concentrated bombing program of Japan's home islands from Saipan, using new long-range B-29s. These remarkable airplanes, the largest operational aircraft of the Second World War, could carry ten tons of bombs forty-two hundred miles at thirty thousand feet, and because they were completely pressurized, the eleven-man crew could forgo oxygen masks. Air Force leaders believed that with such a weapon they could win the war without the need for costly invasions.[14]

At first, the United States tried bombing Japan from Chinese airfields with what was labeled the XX Bomber Command but getting the bombs and especially the fuel "over the hump" of the Himalayas from India proved such a logistical impediment the planes managed only one mission a week. It was far more efficient to fly from Saipan, and once the airfields there were completed the newly created XXI Bomber Command began a sustained bombing offensive against Japanese cities.[15]

The first attack occurred on November 24, when more than a hundred B-29s took off from Saipan for Tokyo. Even for the B-29s, the round-trip flight of three thousand miles was challenging. It was all but inevitable that

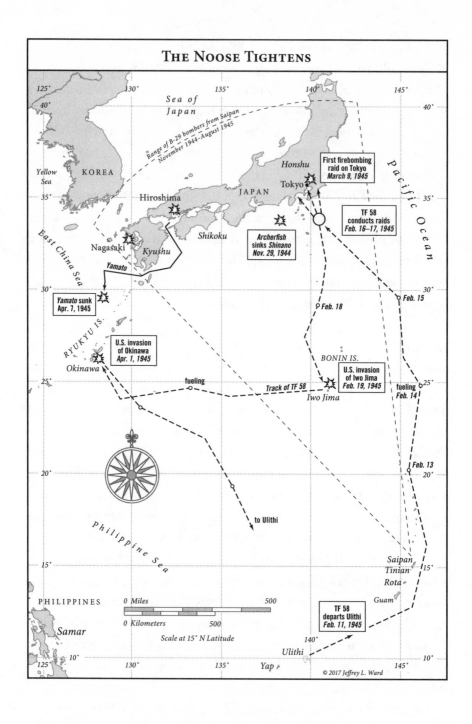

THE NOOSE TIGHTENS

Sea of Japan

Range of B-29 bombers from Saipan November 1944–August 1945

KOREA

Yellow Sea

Honshu

First firebombing raid on Tokyo
March 9, 1945

Tokyo

Hiroshima

JAPAN

TF 58 conducts raids
Feb. 16–17, 1945

Pacific Ocean

Nagasaki

Kyushu

Shikoku

Archerfish sinks *Shinano*
Nov. 29, 1944

Yamato

East China Sea

Yamato sunk
Apr. 7, 1945

Feb. 18

Feb. 15

RYUKYU IS.

U.S. invasion of Okinawa
Apr. 1, 1945

Okinawa

BONIN IS.

U.S. invasion of Iwo Jima
Feb. 19, 1945

fueling

Track of TF 58

Iwo Jima

fueling
Feb. 14

Feb. 13

Philippine Sea

to Ulithi

Saipan
Tinian
Rota

PHILIPPINES

0 Miles   500

Guam

TF 58 departs Ulithi
Feb. 11, 1945

Samar

0 Kilometers   500

Scale at 15° N Latitude

140°

Ulithi

Yap

© 2017 Jeffrey L. Ward

some of them would have engine difficulty; others were crippled by Japanese air defenses. When that happened, the bombers had to land in the ocean, and it was to rescue the crews of those planes that American submarines were pre-positioned off Japan's east coast. One of the boats assigned to that duty for the initial series of raids in November was the *Balao*-class submarine *Archerfish*.[16]

The *Archerfish* was a new boat, just over a year old. Though she had made four previous Pacific patrols, she had yet to sink a ship. Her skipper, Commander Joseph Enright, hoped to change that, though his chances of doing so seemed unlikely as long as his boat remained on rescue duty. As it happened, the *Archerfish* had no opportunity to rescue any aircrews during the first few raids, and there was no raid on November 28, so Enright was released to make an independent patrol. The problem was that his radar had broken down. All afternoon he repeatedly called down from the conning tower to ask how the repairs were going. Finally at eight-thirty that night, the engineer reported that the radar was once again functioning. Eighteen minutes later it registered a contact.[17]

Enright picked up his binoculars and stared in the direction of the reported contact but saw nothing. In a few minutes, however, a lookout with younger eyes than his reported "a long, low, bump on the horizon," and soon Enright saw it too. It was a large vessel escorted by a destroyer, and it was approaching. Enright speculated that it was likely a tanker—a prime target. He quickly calculated his approach: he would let the escort pass, then speed toward the tanker to fire a full spread. While he was envisioning that scenario, the lookout spoke again: "That ship looks like an aircraft carrier."[18]

BACK IN APRIL 1940, amid tight security, the Japanese laid the keel of a new battleship in Yokosuka Shipyard on the southern rim of Tokyo Harbor. The ship was to be the third of Japan's oversize battleships—a sister ship to the *Yamato* and *Musashi*. Work progressed at a modest pace even after the war began until the debacle at Midway. At that point, the Naval General Staff decided that the ship under construction should be converted into an oversize carrier. Her hull was reconfigured to accommodate a heavily armored flight deck to protect her from the 1,000-pound bombs of the American dive-bombers that had proved so devastating at Midway. Indeed, the ship's 17,000 tons of armor made up nearly a third of her displacement tonnage. Like so many ships before her, from the *Titanic* to the *Bismarck*, she was declared "unsinkable." Initially scheduled for completion in February 1945, the timetable was accelerated after the loss of three more carriers in the Battle of the Philippine Sea. There was some hope that she could be completed in time for the Sho Operation, though an accident in the building yard quashed that. Launched on November 11, she was commissioned eight days later as the *Shinano*.[19]

Displacing 71,890 tons when fully loaded, the *Shinano* was the largest aircraft carrier ever built, a distinction she retained until 1961 when the U.S. Navy commissioned the nuclear-powered *Enterprise*. Having invested so much in her, Japanese authorities were horrified on November 24 when long-range American bombers appeared over Tokyo on the initial raid by the XXI Bomber Command. The Japanese high command decided that it was essential to get the *Shinano* away from Tokyo Bay as soon as possible. Four hundred miles to the south in the Inland Sea she would be better protected

The Japanese super-carrier *Shinano*, sunk by the *Archerfish*, was in commission for so short a time that few photographs of her exist. This sketch by Japanese artist Shizuo Fukui was made after the war. Though the *Archerfish* sank only one ship on her patrol, measured by total tonnage it was the most successful patrol of the entire war.

Naval History and Heritage Command

and her crew could conduct flight operations to make her combat-ready. Consequently, even though only half of her boilers were on line and many of her watertight doors were still uninstalled, her captain, Toshio Abe, received orders to go to sea at once. Abe dutifully took the *Shinano* out of Tokyo harbor one hour after sunset on November 28 with a four-destroyer escort. Two and a half hours later, the *Archerfish* picked her up on radar.[20]

Enright could hardly believe it. He had once before had an opportunity to target an aircraft carrier when he had commanded the *Dace* during her first patrol back in 1943. On that occasion the carrier had gotten away, and Enright was determined it should not happen twice. This carrier was coming south but would pass him at a range of nine miles. He needed to get closer. *Archerfish* had a top speed of nineteen knots on the surface, and in normal circumstances a carrier could simply run away from a submarine. Enright decided to parallel her track as best he could and hope that her next course change would bring her within range. Operating on only six of her twelve boilers, the *Shinano* was making twenty knots, and when one of the six working boilers malfunctioned she slowed to eighteen knots. That allowed Enright and the *Archerfish* to keep pace with her nine miles to starboard.[21]

At 3:00 a.m. on November 29, Abe ordered the *Shinano* and her escorts to turn west, toward the coast. It was the opportunity Enright had been waiting for, and at 3:17 he fired six torpedoes. For an attack on a carrier torpedoes would ordinarily be set to run at a depth of twenty-five to thirty feet, but Enright thought if he hit the big carrier higher up on her hull, it could make her top-heavy and more likely to capsize. He ordered the torpedoes set to run at only ten feet. That decision doomed the *Shinano*, because the torpedoes struck just above her armored blisters. As the *Archerfish* submerged, Enright thought he heard six explosions, though in fact only four of his torpedoes hit. It was enough. Tons of seawater rushed into the *Shinano*'s hull, and almost at once she took on a fifteen-degree list to starboard. With many of the watertight doors not yet installed, the flooding spread quickly. The ship's list increased to twenty-five degrees, then thirty. Too late, Abe steered for the coast, hoping to run the *Shinano* aground in shallow water, where she might be recovered and repaired. He didn't make it, and the *Shinano* sank just past ten-thirty the next morning. She had been in commission only ten days, and at sea for only sixteen and a half hours.[22]*

WHILE AMERICAN SUBS devastated the Japanese merchant marine and U.S. Army Air Force (AAF) bombers attacked their cities, MacArthur continued his conquest of the Philippines. After Leyte, his next target was the island of Mindoro, which he planned to use as a staging area for the main event: the invasion of Luzon and the capture of Manila. Once again, Halsey's Third Fleet was to support the landings, and sensitized by the debacle of what pundits were calling "Bull's Run" during the Battle of Leyte Gulf, Halsey was determined to provide full support. To do so, he had to counter the new kamikaze threat. Between October 29 and November 1, kamikazes hit four of his carriers—the *Intrepid, Franklin, Belleau Wood,* and *Lexington.* None of the four was lost, though two of them had to go to Puget Sound for extensive repairs. To deal with this new threat, Halsey changed the proportion of aircraft types on the carriers, reducing the number of bombers and torpedo planes in order to expand the number of fighters, not only to shoot down the suicide planes as they approached but also to blanket the Japanese airfields on Mindoro and Luzon and keep the kamikazes from getting off the ground in the first place.[23]

MacArthur's invasion of Mindoro began on December 15. (That same day, half a world away, German ground forces in the dark shadows of the Ardennes Forest prepared to launch the offensive subsequently known as the Battle of the Bulge—Hitler's last desperate effort to regain the initiative in the European War.) Halsey's carriers had been continuously at sea for almost four months, and in addition to the normal wear and tear on both men and machines, Halsey had to pay attention to the fuel and supply needs of his ships. The big American carriers could steam for twenty thousand

---

* U.S. Navy authorities initially declined to credit Enright and the *Archerfish* with sinking an aircraft carrier. The very existence of the *Shinano* was so secret that even the code breakers were unaware of her. The navy credited Enright with a tanker, then with a light carrier, and only much later acknowledged that he had sunk a full-size, even oversize carrier. That brought him a belated Navy Cross. Though the *Archerfish* sank only one ship on her patrol, measured by total tonnage it was the most successful patrol of the entire war.

miles or more without refueling, but the smaller destroyers and destroyer escorts burned up fuel like race cars and had to be resupplied frequently. They often refueled from the bigger ships, but eventually the big ships, too, needed fuel, and that meant a rendezvous with a tanker group from the fleet base at Ulithi. Before delivering an air strike on Mindoro that he had planned for December 19, Halsey ordered a fleet refueling at a rendezvous east of the Philippine Islands for December 17.[24]

May to December was typhoon season in the southern Pacific, so it was not unusual that a storm began to develop south of Guam on December 15. It tracked slowly westward across the width of the Philippine Sea, growing in intensity. The weather expert (called an "aerologist") on Halsey's flagship, *New Jersey*, was George F. Kosco. He noted the unsettled weather, but lacking the kind of satellite views familiar to modern forecasters, he could not accurately predict its track and did not anticipate anything out of the ordinary. On December 15, the barometer on the *New Jersey* stood at a fairly normal 29.88 inches with winds at twenty-three knots.[25]

Halsey was not the kind of man to be deterred by unsettled weather, and with some of his destroyers down to only 15 percent of fuel capacity—a dangerous level—he decided to go ahead with the rendezvous as planned. In order to avoid the rough weather, he moved the rendezvous site to a position 180 miles further south. He did not know that by doing so he was moving directly into the path of the approaching storm, which had grown into a full-fledged typhoon.

On the day that the refueling was scheduled to begin, it was evident that the weather would not allow it. The waves were so huge they threatened even the big carriers. "We had waves come up over the flight deck," a crewman on the *Enterprise* recalled. "I don't know how we stayed afloat." It was much worse for the smaller ships, which were tossed around like toys in a bathtub. The captain of the 1,700-ton USS *Dewey*, Commander Raymond Calhoun, recalled that his ship "was corkscrewing and writhing like a wounded animal." The wind grew in intensity until it surpassed a hundred knots. At that speed, the sea spray acted like a sandblaster, peeling paint off the exterior bulkheads. Those who ventured out into the elements found that the spray literally ripped the skin from their faces. Halsey felt compelled to try to refuel anyway; if the destroyers ran dry, they would be completely helpless. He concluded that "we had to try it, not only for MacArthur's sake but for ours." In receipt of those orders, Calhoun wondered "how in the hell the fleet commander could think that fueling was possible." It wasn't. The barometer on the *Dewey* plunged to 27.30 inches, the lowest recording ever made by a navy ship to that date. Accepting reality, Halsey postponed the refueling.[26]

The destroyers now faced the very real possibility of running out of fuel altogether, and, desperate to escape the storm, Halsey issued a new fleet course westward, inadvertently prolonging the fleet's exposure by moving with the storm. While he cannot be blamed for being ignorant of the storm's track, he erred by keeping the fleet on a prescribed course too long before releasing the skippers to maneuver independently to save themselves.* It was already too late for three of the ships: the destroyers *Hull*, *Monaghan*, and *Spence* all sank, with heavy loss of life. Two carriers (*Cowpens* and *Monterey*) were severely damaged when airplanes on their hangar decks broke loose from their constraints, smashed into one another, and burst into flames even as towering seas crashed into the ships from the outside. Two hundred planes were destroyed and twenty-five ships damaged, seven of them severely. Seven hundred and ninety men lost their lives.[27]

By the time the storm finally abated, the ships of the fleet were "scattered all over that part of the Pacific Ocean," as one officer recalled. They reconnected slowly and were eventually able to refuel. Halsey was eager to return to Mindoro to conduct the planned air strike, but it was evident that most of the ships were in no condition to do so, and he directed them to Ulithi for repairs. Less than two months after his controversial performance in the Battle of Leyte Gulf, Halsey again faced both official and public criticism for his decision-making during what has ever since been known as "Halsey's Typhoon."[28]

---

* Some destroyer skippers broke from the prescribed fleet course anyway, believing it was necessary to save their ships. That issue was at the center of Herman Wouk's fictional *Caine Mutiny*. In the novel, the captain of the destroyer-minesweeper USS *Caine*, Philip Francis Queeg, insists on keeping the ship on the designated fleet course despite the ferocity of the typhoon. The "mutiny" occurs when the ship's executive officer, Stephen Maryk, relieves him in order to maneuver independently.

At Ulithi, the Navy held a court of inquiry, and Nimitz himself flew out from Pearl Harbor to witness it and to manage the fallout. At the hearing, Halsey testified that he had had "no warning" of the coming storm, which was true enough, though the court did suggest that he might have launched planes to conduct a weather search while en route to the refueling rendezvous. For his part, Nimitz was not entirely uncritical, but his goal was to put this catastrophe behind him and get on with the war. He acknowledged that Halsey had made mistakes, but insisted that they "were errors of judgment committed under stress of war operations and stemming from a commendable desire to meet military commitments." King concurred. In his endorsement, he wrote that although "primary responsibility" for the damage lay with Halsey, no further action was necessary. Others in the fleet were less certain. In a postwar oral history, Gerald Bogan, who commanded one of Halsey's carrier groups, concluded that the main problem was Halsey's unwillingness to adjust his behavior to the dictates of reality. It was, Bogan insisted, "just plain, goddam stubbornness."[29]

A month later, in a move long scheduled and entirely separate from the events of the typhoon, Halsey turned the Big Blue Fleet back over to Spruance; the Third Fleet again became the Fifth Fleet, and Task Force 38 again became Task Force 58. In five months under Halsey's direction, that fleet had sunk ninety Japanese warships, a million tons of shipping, and destroyed more than seven thousand enemy airplanes. Halsey's tenure in command had been controversial, yet despite the criticism he received from "Bull's Run" and "Halsey's Typhoon," his reputation as a fierce and dogged warrior of the sea—the George S. Patton of the Navy—remained intact.[30]

MEANWHILE, THE AMERICAN BOMBING CAMPAIGN against Japan's home islands continued and, in fact, accelerated. Its primary purpose was to wreck the Japanese war industry and particularly its aircraft-manufacturing capability, though Allied planners also assumed that prolonged bombing would erode civilian morale. In addition to all that, however, the champions of a postwar independent American air force were also eager to demonstrate the efficacy of strategic bombing. To do that they were counting heavily on the new B-29 bombers. Like Dönitz, who insisted that his

U-boats should not be used for any other purpose than sinking Allied merchant ships in the North Atlantic, General Henry "Hap" Arnold insisted that his new B-29 bombers must not be used for anything other than strategic bombing. He did not want them diverted to providing tactical support for naval or amphibious operations, and to ensure it he prevailed upon the Joint Chiefs to stipulate that the XXI Bomber Command on Saipan would not be subject to the authority of the theater commander—that it would function as a separate and independent command. Of course, the bombers still had to rely on the navy for material support. Each B-29 required 6,400 gallons of aviation fuel and eight tons of bombs per flight, and it required more than one hundred ships in nearly constant rotation to supply it. Navy authorities complained that the air force's demand for more parts, more bombs, and more fuel strained the navy's sealift capacity. For their part, the aircrews complained that navy personnel had better food, better quarters, even hot showers. After comparing his own circumstances to his naval peers, a nineteen-year-old gunner in the 6th Bomb Group wrote his family, "I was sorry that I had not joined the Navy." Army Air Force commanders grumbled that "the Navy always treated us rather like stepchildren."[31]

In addition to logistic difficulties and interservice quarreling, the bombing program also struggled with a doctrinal conundrum. Arnold and the other champions of strategic bombing believed they had a war-winning secret weapon in the Norden bombsight, which, in theory at least, could put a bomb not just on a specific city but on a particular building. In Europe, while the British RAF focused on area bombing of German cities at night, the Americans flew daytime raids in order to target specific objectives, such as the German ball bearing factory at Schweinfurt, or the Romanian oil refinery at Ploesti. These daytime attacks were costly in terms of lost planes and aircrews and in the end proved less effective than the planners had hoped—though that was not fully evident until after the war.

Consistent with these protocols, when the B-29s began attacking Japan's home islands in November of 1944, they did so in daytime raids, dropping their bombs from thirty thousand feet. Precision proved elusive from such a height. For one thing, the nearly constant cloud cover over Japan during the winter months obscured the bombardier's vision, and as one B-29 commander noted, "even with the Norden bombsight, the bombardier still had to see the target." Another problem was that from thirty thousand feet the high winds that prevailed over Japan blew the bombs, even heavy bombs, all over the place. Despite the commitment of more planes and more bombs, the results during the first several months of the campaign were disappointing. As one group commander confided to his diary in February 1945, the raids were "a pretty complete failure." That was not only an operational disappointment but also a political disaster. The United States had spent $4 billion on the B-29 program—more than it spent on the Manhattan Project—and for the champions of strategic bombing it was imperative that the planes be successful.[32]

Seeking to improve their indifferent performance, AAF leaders suggested adding long-range fighter escorts to the bombing raids, though it was unclear how the presence of fighters would improve bombing accuracy. No fighter could fly the fifteen-hundred-mile round trip from Saipan to Tokyo, but halfway in between was the small island of Iwo Jima in the Bonin Islands, and from there, a P-51 Mustang could just make it to Japan and back. King later wrote that the "sole importance" of Iwo Jima to the Americans was to improve "the performance of the long range aircraft of the Army Air Corps." After the fact, it was also argued that the island was useful as an emergency landing field for wounded B-29s returning from the raids.[33]

The idea of seizing Iwo Jima did not originate with the Army Air Force. Long before the B-29 raids even began, Spruance had argued that capturing both Iwo Jima and Okinawa was a desirable alternative to attacking Formosa, which remained King's preferred option. King believed that seizing Formosa would cut Japan off entirely from her essential imports and starve her into surrender, making an invasion of the home islands unnecessary. Concerned that Formosa was too large, army commanders agreed with Spruance that Okinawa was a better option. With the army and navy divided, Arnold's support for Iwo Jima tipped the balance, and "after considerable discussion," the Joint Chiefs approved a plan (Operation Detachment) to invade and occupy Iwo Jima in February 1945, both as a warm-up for Okinawa and to provide fighter escorts for the B-29s.[34]

The Japanese anticipated that Iwo Jima could become an American objective, and they reinforced the garrison there until there were more than twenty thousand men on the island. There might have been more, but American submarines played a role here, too, by attacking the reinforcement convoys. A wolf pack of five subs (called Mac's Mops, after Commander Barney McMahon) patrolled the sea between Japan and the Bonins and sank several troop transports. After the *Sterlett* sank a small transport off Iwo Jima, she surfaced in the midst of the survivors. Recalling it later, a crewman on the *Sterlett* explained, "What we did then a lot of people wouldn't approve of, but when you hate, you hate real bad, you know. So we did what we thought we had to do."[35]

Iwo Jima was one of the bloodiest battles of the Pacific War, claiming a combined total of more than forty-five thousand casualties, and that horrific cost led to much after-the-fact second-guessing about the campaign.* One controversy concerned Spruance's decision to order a carrier strike against Japan's home islands simultaneous with the invasion. At Saipan, Spruance had tethered Mitscher's carriers to the beachhead, a decision the naval aviation community had bitterly criticized. Now, eight months later, he unleashed Mitscher's TF 58 from the invasion force and sent it off to attack Japanese cities, Tokyo in particular. His objective was to keep Japanese planes—especially the kamikazes—from interfering with the landings. In addition, however, he also saw the raids as an opportunity to achieve what the B-29s had so far failed to do: destroy Japanese airpower at its source—the factories. The week after the first disappointing B-29 raids in November, he wrote to Admiral John Hoover to suggest that "we should stop fighting the products of the Jap aircraft factories on the perimeter, and

---

* There is some uncertainty about the final casualty toll. The official U.S. Marine Corps numbers are 5,875 killed, including those who died subsequently of their wounds, plus another 17,272 wounded, for a total of 23,157. These numbers, however, represent losses only through mid-March, when the island was declared secured. Subsequent "mopping-up" operations raise the totals to 6,821 killed and 19,217 wounded, a total of 26,038. Japanese records are missing, and the numbers are necessarily an estimate, but most experts cite 18,000 to 19,000 killed and another 1,083 taken prisoner. Iwo Jima was the only battle in the Pacific War where American casualties exceeded those of the Japanese.

take our carrier air in to the center to knock out the factories themselves." This, of course, was usurping the Army Air Force's mission, but Spruance insisted that "we cannot afford to await the outcome of bombing 'with precision instruments' from 30,000 feet," his quotation marks acting as a kind of verbal eye roll. In addition to the carriers, Spruance also took the fleet's battleship-cruiser force, including his flagship, *Indianapolis*, in order to provide the carriers with additional AA support. The carrier raids were inhibited by dreadful weather over the target, though American pilots claimed the destruction of more than five hundred Japanese aircraft while losing only sixty of their own. Of course, the raids also kept the carriers and the fast battleships away from the landing beaches on Iwo Jima until D-Day.[36]

Another controversy concerned the relatively short preliminary naval gunfire support at Iwo Jima. The number of ships available for the bombardment mission was reduced because the new fast battleships accompanied Mitscher's carriers; in addition, those that were available got orders to fire for only three days. The Marines, again commanded by Holland Smith, had asked for ten days. When told that was not possible, they asked for four. That, too, was denied. There were two reasons for this. The first was that Spruance feared that if the bombardment of Iwo Jima began before the carrier strikes were under way, the Japanese would be able to send aircraft from the home islands—including kamikazes—to attack the invasion flotilla.

A second reason the navy rejected a more extended bombardment of Iwo Jima was a concern that it would use up much of the fleet's available high-explosive ammunition. With MacArthur's campaign in the Philippines still ongoing and the invasion of Okinawa looming, an extended bombardment of Iwo Jima would almost certainly require a long trek back to Ulithi to resupply, and that would throw off the whole schedule. In addition, because American B-24s from Saipan bombed Iwo Jima for seventy-four consecutive days, it was believed that this would more than compensate for a shortened naval bombardment. Planes from Saipan dropped a total of sixty-eight hundred tons of bombs on Iwo Jima in those seventy-four days, most of it from high altitude, and ships fired more than twenty thousand rounds of 8-inch and 5-inch ordnance. Nevertheless, it became evident

LSM-238 disembarks men and equipment on the black sand beach of Iwo Jima. This photograph, taken several days after the initial landings, gives some sense of the size of the American invasion armada.

Naval History and Heritage Command

almost the moment the Marines set foot ashore that all this had failed to knock out the Japanese defenses.[37]

Given the horrors of the ensuing campaign, it is tempting to cite these decisions as not only unfortunate but callous. Afterward, the Marines accused both the air forces and the navy of inadequate support. It is unlikely, however, that a more focused aerial bombing or a longer period of naval gunfire would have made a great deal of difference; the real source of the heavy American casualties on Iwo Jima was the resiliency of Japanese defenses and the tactics of the Japanese army commander, Lieutenant General Tadamichi Kuribayashi. As on Peleliu, the Japanese on Iwo Jima were dug deep into underground caves and connecting tunnels that were all but impervious to either bombs or shellfire. Each position had to be taken on the ground at close range with hand grenades and flamethrowers.

Moreover, instead of mounting the kind of passionate but hopeless banzai charges that had characterized Japanese tactics on other Pacific islands, Kuribayashi ordered his men to remain in their subterranean fortifications and compel the Marines to come and get them. That was why the battle for Iwo Jima lasted so long and cost so much. On this, as on so many issues, Admiral Morison deserves the final word: "There is no reason to believe that ten or even thirty days of naval and air pounding would have had much more effect on the defenses than the bombardment that was delivered."[38]

Iwo Jima was another Marine Corps battle, as testified to by the famous photo by Joe Rosenthal of the flag-raising on Mount Suribachi and by the monument in Arlington, Virginia. Yet the navy's role was critical. The escort carriers of the invasion fleet conducted spotting and attack missions in support of the men on the ground, and the big carriers of TF 58, back from their raid on Tokyo, launched nearly continuous air strikes. Late in the afternoon on February 21 the carrier *Saratoga* was providing CAP over the island when six hostile planes approached out of the clouds. At least four of them were kamikazes. Two were splashed just short of the carrier, though their bombs exploded close alongside and caused significant damage. Two others successfully crashed into the flattop, one to port and one to starboard. The *Saratoga* stayed afloat, but she was out of action for three months. The next night, a single kamikaze crashed into the escort carrier *Bismarck Sea*, igniting several secondary explosions, and the *Bismarck Sea* sank quickly with the loss of 218 men. Japanese airpower had been eviscerated, but its special attack units remained dangerous.[39]

ON JANUARY 20, 1945—the day Franklin Roosevelt took the oath of office for a fourth term as president—Major General Curtis LeMay arrived in Saipan to take over the 21st Bomber Command. After attempting several more unsuccessful high-altitude daylight raids, LeMay decided that "this high-altitude stuff was strictly for the birds." He may have been inspired by the impact of a devastating air raid on Dresden, Germany, on the night of February 13–14. In that raid, 805 Allied bombers dropped 1,478 tons of high explosives and 1,182 tons of incendiaries. The incendiaries triggered a firestorm that laid waste much of the city and killed perhaps sixty thousand people. Aware that Japanese houses, which were built largely of wood and paper, were highly flammable, LeMay concluded that his B-29s could also employ incendiaries. On March 7, while the fighting for Iwo Jima was still ongoing, he called his group commanders into his office and told them that he was changing the game. Instead of attacking in daytime from thirty thousand feet with high explosives, the next attack would be conducted at night from low level with incendiaries. The goal, he said, was "to burn the place to the ground."[40]

The very next night, 346 B-29s took off from Guam and Saipan for a massive raid against Tokyo. Flying at only five thousand feet, the planes scattered half a million 6-pound M-69 canisters filled with napalm over much of the downtown area. Each canister trailed a three-foot-long streamer to orient the impact fuse downward; to one observer they looked like "a silver curtain" falling. When the canisters hit the rooftops of homes and buildings they exploded and spread burning napalm up to thirty feet in all directions. The ensuing firestorm spread rapidly as flames towered thousands of feet into the air. In one night, fire destroyed over a third of the city—some sixteen square miles. A hundred thousand people were killed; a million were left homeless. In the words of the lead pilot, it was "probably the most destructive blow ever delivered by aircraft," and it marked a new chapter in the air war against Japan.[41]

Over the next three weeks, the B-29s delivered firebomb attacks against several more Japanese cities, including Nagoya, Osaka, and Kobe. With the planes coming in low and at night, fighter escorts were unnecessary because the Japanese did not have effective night fighters. LeMay even had the machine guns on the B-29s removed so the planes could carry more incendiaries. That meant that even before Iwo Jima was secured, the principal justification for attacking the island in the first place had been overtaken by events. Back in January, LeMay had told Spruance, "Without Iwo Jima I couldn't bomb Japan effectively." He very likely believed it when he said it, though it turned out not to have been true.[42]

In the months and years that followed, both the U.S. Navy and the Army Air Force rationalized the losses endured on Iwo Jima by citing its value as an emergency landing field. Eventually, B-29s made a total of 2,251 landings on the island, and because each plane had a crew of eleven, it was suggested that the American occupation of Iwo Jima saved the lives of some 24,000 airmen. Even the Marines embraced this view, in part, perhaps, because it validated their sacrifice; it is a human instinct to rationalize decisions that cannot be undone. In fact, however, fighter escorts on Iwo Jima played virtually no role in protecting the B-29s. Those that made the flight had orders simply to strafe targets of opportunity. In addition, more than 80 percent of the B-29 landings on the island were planned fuel stops rather than genuine emergencies. The number of air crewmen whose lives were saved by American possession of Iwo Jima may approach one or even two thousand, but it was significantly less than the 6,821 lives lost in capturing it.[43]

The firebombing of Japan's major cities was apocalyptic. The postwar Strategic Bombing Survey concluded that "some 40 percent of the built up area of the 66 cities attacked was destroyed. Approximately 30 percent of the entire urban population of Japan lost their homes and many their possessions." The impact that such devastation had on Japan's wartime economy is less clear. At the time, the AAF insisted that destruction of the "housing units" of factory workers weakened Japanese industry. Yet most of the industries in the areas that were destroyed by firebombing had ceased to function long before the raids began because American submarines had halted the delivery of most raw materials. A factory without access to raw materials is just a building. Several of the air strikes directed at Japan's petroleum resources, for example, hit refineries that were no longer functioning and tank farms that were empty. The historian Mark Parillo put it anatomically: "The submarine had stopped Japan's industrial heart from beating by severing its arteries and it did so well before the bomber ruptured the organ." Given that, the B-29 firebombing raids that began in March 1945 and continued almost without interruption for the rest of the war were less strategic bombing than terror bombing.[44]

Wars are brutal. For eight years, beginning with the China Incident in 1937, which marked the genesis of what became the Second World War, the Japanese had practiced unrestrained, often purposelessly cruel violence against their foes, indiscriminately executing prisoners and even using civilians for bayonet practice. In Europe, the carnage on the Eastern Front was cataclysmic, and the Nazi regime orchestrated the organized murder of millions. By 1945, in both the submarine war and the air war, the Allies had embraced a worldview in which anything that brought the war more quickly to an end was not only justifiable but necessary—even commendable. When news of the firebomb raid on Tokyo reached the American press, the *New York Times* reported triumphantly that "the heart of Tokyo is gone," and quoted Curtis LeMay's declaration that "if the war is shortened by a single day the attack will have served its purpose."[45]

CHAPTER 27

DENOUEMENT

HITLER HAD GAMBLED EVERYTHING on what the allies, and the Americans in particular, called the Battle of the Bulge; after that plan collapsed in January 1945, Germany lay open to invasion from the west. That same month, four million Russian infantry spearheaded by nine thousand tanks launched a massive assault from the east. Hitler had rejected reports of a Soviet buildup and had forbidden his generals to readjust their lines. After the assault began, he then refused to sanction retreat and designated specific cities as "fortresses" to be defended to the last man. That did no more than increase the total casualties. Like a tightening vise, Allied armies closed on the heartland of Germany.

On January 16, Hitler retreated to the bombproof *Führerbunker* under the Reich Chancellery in Berlin, from which he continued to issue orders, most of them divorced from reality. Pledging the imminent appearance of a secret weapon that would yet reverse the tide of battle, he insisted that his generals must not retreat a single inch. When they were forced to do so anyway, he fired them and replaced them with less qualified understudies.

Throughout this farce the generals remained steadfast in their public commitment to his authority; even the rank and file for the most part continued to do what they were told was their duty.[1]

As for Grossadmiral Karl Dönitz, he displayed nearly as much fanaticism as the Führer himself. The historian and Hitler biographer Ian Kershaw lumps Dönitz in with Goebbels and Himmler as "among the most brutal and radical fanatics" of the Nazi regime. As late as March 4, the admiral wrote to Hitler, "Only if we stand and fight have we any chance of turning around our fate." In that spirit, Dönitz sought to revive the war on commerce with a new generation of U-boats, virtually all of them equipped with the new *schnorchel*. Their greatest impact was in the Bay of Biscay. Lorient and St. Nazaire were still in German hands, and when U-boats without a *schnorchel* sought to make their way from there to the open Atlantic, Allied, and especially British, air forces often spotted and attacked when they were only a few hours out of port. The *schnorchel* allowed the U-boats to transit the Bay of Biscay submerged with a better chance of escaping to the open ocean.[2]

Even more revolutionary were the new Type XXI and Type XXIII U-boats. Until late in 1944, "submarines" of every nation were actually "submersibles"—that is, they were essentially surface vessels that could submerge briefly to attack or escape. The new U-boats built in 1944 and 1945 were the first true submarines. They could remain under water for days at a time, and, due to their novel teardrop-shaped hull design, travel at seventeen and a half knots under water, faster than any convoy. Fantasizing that "new successes were within our grasp," Dönitz prevailed on Hitler to make the new U-boats the top national industrial priority. With some misgivings, Dönitz accepted the proposal of the munitions czar, Albert Speer, to build them the way the Americans did their merchant ships—with assembly line procedures. His misgivings were justified, for the boats thus produced had so many problems that production was delayed. As a result, only two of the larger Type XXI U-boats ever embarked on a war patrol. Many more of the smaller Type XXIII U-boats saw service in the first few months of 1945, but they carried only two torpedoes each and had no impact on Germany's accelerating downward trajectory.[3]

As for the German surface navy, the number of surviving combatants in January 1945 could be counted on the fingers of two hands. Virtually all of them were in the Baltic. They included the *Bismarck*'s former consort, the *Prinz Eugen*, both of the original *Panzerschiffe* (*Admiral Scheer* and *Lützow*), and three cruisers, two of which were in the dockyards at Kiel undergoing repair and one, the *Nürnberg*, in Copenhagen, where she would remain until the war was over due to a lack of fuel. Dönitz designated this handful of survivors the "Second Battle Group" and ordered them to support the fight against the Russians, advancing along the southern rim of the Baltic.[4]

The Russians were proving at least as ruthless in their advance westward as the Germans had been three and a half years earlier going eastward. With good reason, German civilians feared falling into Russian hands. On January 27, the Red Army took Memel, Lithuania, and that triggered a desperate effort by civilian refugees in East Prussia and Pomerania to escape. In bitter winter weather, tens of thousands fled by train, by wagon, by handcart, and on foot, often pulling sleds, most of them making toward the Baltic ports of Pillau, Danzig, and Gotenhafen. Dönitz decided that "the salvation of the German eastern population [was] the one essential task" of the Kriegsmarine, and to effect it, he initiated Operation Hannibal, a kind of German Dunkirk.[5]

Virtually every vessel that could still float was pressed into service. They included transports, the few remaining warships, and even the Siebel ferries that had been built back in 1940 for the invasion of England. Crammed with desperate refugees, they headed across the Baltic for western Germany or Denmark, which, along with Norway, remained under German control. Dönitz asked the Allies to guarantee safe passage for these ships, but since many of them carried soldiers as well as civilians, his request was denied. In midwinter these ships put to sea loaded, indeed overloaded, with an eclectic cargo of wounded soldiers, female auxiliary enlisted units (called *Marinehelferinnen*), and thousands of civilians, many of them women and children, as well as a handful of high-ranking officers, especially SS officers, who were desperate to avoid capture by the Russians.

One of the largest ships committed to the evacuation was the former liner *Wilhelm Gustloff*, which left Gotenhafen in the Gulf of Danzig on January 30. According to her manifest, she carried six thousand passengers, though desperate refugees crowding up the ramps and even climbing aboard from small craft swelled the actual numbers to well over eight thousand and perhaps as many as ten. On board, too, were the coffins of Paul von Hindenburg, the former German military hero and president of the Reich until 1934, and his wife, which had been exhumed from their memorial tomb near Tannenberg to prevent them from being vandalized.[6]

In rough seas and amidst intermittent snow flurries, the captain of the *Wilhelm Gustloff*, Friedrich Petersen, decided it was not necessary to zigzag, and when she passed in front of the Russian submarine S-13 near midnight, the sub's commander, Alexander Marinesko, could hardly believe his luck. After carefully stalking her, Marinesko fired four torpedoes. One misfired; the others all struck the liner flush on her side. Though several Kriegsmarine vessels were nearby, including the cruiser *Hipper*, herself burdened with seventeen hundred refugees, fewer than a thousand of those on the *Wilhelm Gustloff* could be rescued. As many as nine thousand died, three times as many as on the *Titanic* and the *Lusitania* combined. It was the greatest maritime disaster in history. Eleven days later Marinesko also sank the liner *General von Steuben*, carrying another six thousand refugees. Despite such disasters, during the first three months of 1945, German ships transported as many as a million people (Dönitz claimed it was two million) across the Baltic to western Germany and Denmark.[7]

Among the ships engaged in this sealift was the pocket battleship *Lützow*, whose fate encapsulates the brief history of the Kriegsmarine. Commissioned in April 1933, two months after Hitler became chancellor, she was christened the *Deutschland* to symbolize the revival of German naval power. After the war began, Hitler ordered that her name be changed, fearing that the loss of a ship named *Deutschland* would be a propaganda coup for his enemies. She served as a commerce raider in the Atlantic, participated in the invasion of Norway, and attacked the North Cape convoys before returning to the Baltic as a training ship. Now, as the Third Reich collapsed, she carried refugees from the path of the advancing Russians. In April she was in Kiel, where she had been commissioned twelve years before almost to the day, when a British Avro Lancaster bomber landed a twelve-thousand-pound "Tallboy" bomb flush on her deck and she sank at her moorings.

With her turrets still above water, she fired her main battery guns in defense of the shipyard until her ammunition was exhausted. Then her crew detonated explosives that blew her apart on May 4. Three days later, Germany surrendered.*

ALL THAT SPRING, as Hitler fumed and plotted in his bunker, his erstwhile henchmen jockeyed for position to see which of them would succeed him as Führer. When Hitler learned that Himmler, mastermind of the Final Solution, and Göring, the sybaritic and sycophantic commander of the Luftwaffe, had each plotted to succeed him, even reaching out to neutrals to orchestrate a capitulation, he was infuriated. He rewrote his Final Testament to designate the loyal Admiral Dönitz, who was free of such conspiracies, as his successor. That same day he married his mistress, Eva Braun, and the following day, bent, pale, and visibly trembling, he entered his private suite in the *Führerbunker*, gave his new bride a cyanide pill, and shot himself in the head.[8]

The next day, Dönitz received a radio message from Martin Bormann, notifying him that he was now Führer. Though Dönitz later insisted that he immediately sought to bring the war to an end, his first instinct was to consolidate his position and appoint a new cabinet. He even went on the radio to insist that "the military struggle continues." Significantly, he did not call off the U-boat war. Only days before he had declared: "We soldiers of the navy know how we have to act. Our military duty, which we unerringly fulfill, whatever happens around us, leaves us standing as a rock of resistance, bold, hard, and loyal." It was such sentiments that won him the dubious distinction of being named Hitler's successor.[9]

As a strategy, or what passed for one, Dönitz sought to hold off the Russians long enough to reach some kind of accommodation with the British and Americans, thus in his view saving Germany from the plague of Bolshevism. He ordered the army in the east to fight on while he sent deputies to open negotiations with Field Marshal Montgomery. Montgomery had no authority to treat with representatives of the German government,

---

* That was not quite the end of the story. After the Soviets occupied Kiel, they raised the *Deutschland/Lützow* and used her for target practice in the Baltic, where she sank for the last time on July 22, 1947.

though he agreed to accept the surrender of units in northern Germany. He insisted, however, that Denmark and Holland must be included in the agreement, and he demanded "the simultaneous surrender of all warships and merchantmen." That last demand caused Dönitz to pause, since German ships were still carrying refugees from the path of the Russians. "The demand that we should surrender our ships," he wrote, "disturbed me greatly."[10]

If Montgomery overstepped his authority by treating with emissaries of the German government, the politically savvy Eisenhower was more careful. The Germans, he insisted, must agree to "an immediate, simultaneous and unconditional surrender on all fronts." Without such an agreement, Eisenhower warned, he would close his lines to the thousands of Germans— both military and civilian—who were fleeing the Red Army. Out of options, and with the Russians already inside Berlin, Dönitz agreed, ordering the Wehrmacht generals to sign an official surrender document at Reims on May 7. The Russian representatives added their signatures the next day, and hostilities ended officially at midnight on May 8–9.[11]

After 2,075 days, the war in Europe was over.

———————

THE WAR WAS REACHING A CRISIS MOMENT in the Pacific as well. While Hitler dreamed feverishly of Armageddon in the *Führerbunker*, more than six thousand miles away Americans stormed ashore on the island of Okinawa, the largest of the Ryukyu Islands that run southward from Kyushu toward Formosa like a kite's tail. The Okinawans were not ethnically Japanese and spoke their own dialect, yet because the Ryukyus had been integrated into the empire in 1879, the island was considered part of the homeland. Consequently, when the Americans landed there on April 1, it was an existential crisis for Japan's leaders. Once again a looming fight was declared to be "the decisive battle in defense of the Homeland."[12]

By now, of course, Japan had few weapons for such a battle. The Japanese army, as many as five million strong, remained a powerful force, though it was highly variegated in terms of quality and equipment. About half of it was in the Home Islands, with most of the rest in China and Manchuria. Okinawa itself had a garrison of about seventy-five thousand, plus another twenty-five thousand indifferently trained militia recruited from the native population of 450,000. They would put up a desperate fight, as Japanese garrisons had done on Peleliu, Iwo Jima, and elsewhere. Yet despite brave language about throwing the invaders into the sea, the Japanese knew that American command of the sea and of the air meant that if they were to defend Okinawa, it would require truly desperate measures.[13]

Back in October, during the American invasion of Leyte, Vice Admiral Taijiro Onishi, commander of the First Air Fleet in the Philippines, had organized what was called a "special attack" (*tokkōtai*) unit composed of pilots who would crash-dive their airplanes into American ships, sacrificing their lives in order to destroy an American warship. As noted in Chapter 25, the handful of planes that crashed into the American jeep carriers off Leyte Gulf did nearly as much damage to the Americans as Kurita's entire fleet. With only twelve planes, Onishi's little squadron had sunk the *St. Lô* and crippled five other small carriers, three of them so badly they had to go back to the United States for repairs.

Suicide attacks made the most of the poorly trained pilots on whom Japan now depended, and because every flight was a one-way trip, it doubled the range of their aircraft. Then, too, by demanding the ultimate sacrifice for country and emperor, it embodied the ideals of *yamato-damashii*. Onishi was not the first to suggest this desperate protocol, but he was the one who actually put it into practice.[14]

In the several weeks after the Battle of Leyte Gulf, *tokkōtai* pilots wounded several *Essex* and *Independence*-class carriers, and on January 6, thirty Japanese planes crashed into no fewer than fifteen American ships in a single day, killing 167 Americans and wounding 500 more. From the Japanese perspective, these successes by "body crash" units constituted the only bright spot after the failures of the Leyte Gulf campaign. Onishi rationalized the sacrifice of so many young men by calculating that conventional attacks on American ships by such novice pilots were all but suicidal anyway and far less likely to be effective or to change the direction of the war. If, on the other hand, the Americans suffered heavy ship losses in their assault on the Japanese homeland, they might yet prove willing to accept a negotiated settlement to the war. Such arguments helped Onishi convince the navy high command, including navy minister Yonai, that suicide tactics should be employed on a larger scale.[15]

This photo depicts the moment on October 25, 1944, when a Japanese kamikaze struck the American escort carrier *St. Lô.* The perceived success of the first group of kamikazes in the Philippines campaign convinced the Japanese to embrace *tokkōtai* as a general policy.

U.S. National Archives photo no. 80-G-270516

The Kamikaze Special Attack Unit was formed officially on March 5, 1945, only days before much of downtown Tokyo was incinerated by the first of the B-29 firebomb attacks. Its name derived from the divine wind (*kami-kaze*) that had twice destroyed the invasion fleets of Kublai Khan in the thirteenth century. This time, the Japanese would provide their own divine intervention with the kamikaze squadrons. The commander of the program was Yamamoto's former chief of staff, Vice Admiral Matome Ugaki, with Onishi acting as his chief of staff. Ugaki and Onishi gathered hundreds of airplanes from all over Japan and from as far away as Manchuria and Korea, concealing them at scores of small airfields on Kyushu. Though they hoped to assemble as many as thirty-five hundred airplanes, repeated air strikes by Mitscher's carriers whittled their assets down to about half that.[16]

Finding pilots was easier. Naval cadets, many of them teenagers at the outset of their pilot training, assembled to hear a hortatory speech from one or another senior officer, then were handed a form that asked them to select from one of three options:

1. I do not want to join the *tokkōtai*
2. I would like to join the *tokkōtai*
3. It is my fervent desire to join the *tokkōtai*

Virtually everyone chose option three. As one of them put it matter-of-factly, "When we became soldiers we offered our lives to the Emperor.... Therefore 'special attack' is just another way of performing our military obligation."[17]

Besides piloted aircraft, Ugaki's command also included rocket-propelled flying bombs called *ohka* (literally, "cherry blossoms"), which the Americans, who could not understand such a practice, called *baka*, or "stupid." Like the German Fritz-X guided missiles that had destroyed the Italian battleship *Roma* in the Mediterranean, *ohka* were carried into battle suspended beneath a conventional bomber, usually a two-engine Betty, and released fifteen or twenty miles from the target. The difference was that instead of being radio-controlled like the German version, the Japanese *ohka* were guided to the target by volunteer pilots. Once detached, the *ohka* flew at better than five hundred miles per hour, making them all but invulnerable to AA fire. The problem was getting the lumbering Bettys to within fifteen or twenty miles of the American ships to launch them. In one early attack by nine Bettys carrying *ohka*, American Hellcat fighters shot down eight of the mother ships before they got close enough to launch, though the one *ohka* that did launch succeeded in sinking a destroyer. Subsequent attacks damaged other American ships, but the losses were not enough to be strategically meaningful.[18]

The kamikazes were far more numerous, and therefore much more dangerous. For a kamikaze attack, the Japanese typically used a Zero, once the premier fighter plane in the Pacific, though now significantly inferior to the newer American fighter aircraft. Each Zero carried a 550-pound bomb; thus burdened, it lost much of its famous maneuverability. Because of that, they had to be escorted to the target by conventional fighters flown by more experienced pilots. Early on, the kamikazes attacked in groups of three or four, with two or three fighters as an escort. Off Iwo Jima, such groups managed to sink the escort carrier *Bismarck Sea* and severely damage the fleet carrier *Saratoga*. Typically, however, the returning pilots reported much greater accomplishments. Based on their reports, Ugaki informed Tokyo that his kamikazes had destroyed "seven enemy carriers, two battleships, and one cruiser."[19]

For the Okinawa campaign, Ugaki planned to pull out all the stops and send not three or four kamikazes at a time but hundreds of them in a swarm attack that would overwhelm the Americans. During a preliminary attack on March 30, one kamikaze successfully crashed into Spruance's flagship, the *Indianapolis*. Spruance himself was unhurt, but the *Indianapolis* had to be sent back to the United States for repair, and Spruance shifted his flag to the battleship *New Mexico*.* It proved to be only the prologue.[20]

THE FULL-SCALE KAMIKAZE ASSAULTS, called *kikusui*, began on April 6. That morning, Ugaki sent off a total of seven hundred planes from airfields across Kyushu. Only about half of them (355) were kamikazes. The rest were either conventional bombers or fighter escorts assigned to fend off the Hellcats so that the kamikazes could get through to the American ships. The kamikazes did not lack for targets. The sea around Okinawa was crowded with ships; the invasion fleet for Okinawa was the largest since the D-Day landings off Normandy. Admiral Morison, who was a witness, recalled that in addition to the warships, "every visible expanse of water was covered with LSTs and landing and control craft."[21]

Though the kamikaze pilots had been instructed to focus on the carriers, only a few did so. Forty to seventy miles out from the main body of the invasion fleet, Richmond Kelly Turner had positioned an arc of sixteen small destroyers and destroyer escorts as radar pickets to provide early warning of approaching enemy aircraft. They were the first American warships the kamikaze pilots encountered. To these novice pilots, few of whom had ever seen an American warship from the air, the radar pickets may have looked no different from battleships, and, eager to fulfill their sacred task, they pushed over to the attack.[22]

---

* It was not the end of the war for the *Indianapolis*. After undergoing repairs at Mare Island Navy Yard in California, she was charged with delivering the first atomic bomb, Little Boy, to Tinian in July. After completing the delivery, she was en route to the Philippines on July 30 when she was hit by two torpedoes from the I-58. She sank in twelve minutes, with some 300 men of her crew going down with her; 900 others suffered exposure, dehydration, and nearly constant shark attacks for most of four days before 317 of them were rescued.

The three picket destroyers closest to Kyushu that April morning were the *Bush*, the *Calhoun*, and the *Emmons*, and they became the focus of as many as fifty kamikazes. Four crashed into the *Bush*, and five more hit the *Emmons*; others plunged into the sea nearby, either victims of accurate AA fire or simply unable to hit their targets. All three American ships sank with heavy loss of life. Elsewhere that day, the kamikazes also sank one LST, two Victory ships, and two ammunition ships, and they damaged ten others, including the battleship *Maryland*. One group of kamikazes did attack the American carriers that Ugaki considered the primary target, but virtually all of them were shot down by Hellcats flying CAP, and only one managed to hit the carrier *Hancock*. Serious as the damage was, it was not enough to halt the invasion.[23]

Ugaki was not discouraged. Once again, the damage reports from returning pilots—those who had flown the mission as escorts—exaggerated the results. "The sea around Okinawa," Ugaki recorded in his diary, "turned into a sea of carnage." If not quite as dramatic as that, the damage was real enough, and over the next several weeks the kamikazes took a heavy toll on the American fleet.[24]

In subsequent attacks, the eager kamikaze pilots continued to focus on the picket destroyers. One of those pickets, the destroyer USS *Laffey*, endured perhaps the most persistent aerial onslaught of the war. On the morning of April 16, the *Laffey*, a new destroyer that had been named for the one lost at Guadalcanal, occupied Picket Station Number 1, thirty miles off the northern tip of Okinawa. At 8:20 a.m. her radar operator reported that there were at least fifty inbound bogies "closing fast from the north." Half of them broke off to find other targets, but the rest headed for the *Laffey*. "Here they come!" a lookout cried, and for the next hour and twenty minutes the kamikazes attacked the destroyer from every point of the compass.[25]

The *Laffey*'s gunners threw up more than a thousand rounds of AA fire per minute, and with significant assistance from friendly fighters, they downed the first nine of the attackers. Then at 8:39 a Val bomber struck the *Laffey* a glancing blow forward, careened across her deck, and exploded off her fantail. Minutes later, a Judy crashed into a 20 mm battery amidships.

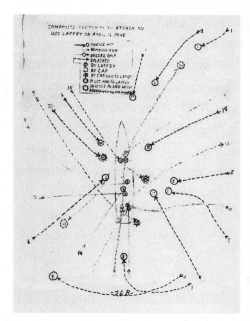

The *Laffey*'s captain, Commander Julian Becton, included this sketch with his after-action report to depict the attack by twenty-two Japanese planes on the morning of April 16, 1944. Incredibly, the *Laffey* survived.

Action Report, USS Laffey, USNA

Then another Val approaching from astern only twenty to thirty feet above the sea smashed into a 5-inch gun mount. The damage control teams worked frantically to contain the fires while the *Laffey* maneuvered radically at 32 knots. A bomb that struck the port side propeller guard jammed the rudder at hard over, so the *Laffey* "circled madly like a wounded fish," in the words of Lieutenant Frank Manson. Two more planes crashed into the crippled and burning destroyer. The assaults were continuous and they seemed to last forever, yet at 9:47 they ended.[26]

Able at last to take a free breath, the *Laffey*'s skipper, Commander Julian Becton, surveyed the damage: "Our whole topside was strewn with plane wreckage from bow to stern—engines, landing gear, wings, the remains of Jap pilots. What a mess." He estimated that the *Laffey* had been struck by eight kamikazes and four bombs; thirty-two crewmen had been killed and another seventy-one wounded. Yet somehow the *Laffey* still floated. She was towed to Okinawa for some quick repairs, and then proceeded under her own power to Saipan and eventually the American West Coast. Though her war was over, the *Laffey* floats still, and is open to visitors at

Sailors on Mitscher's flagship, the USS *Bunker Hill*, go calmly about their duties despite a strike by two kamikazes on May 11, 1945. The *Bunker Hill* lost 389 killed and another 264 wounded in that attack, including a dozen men from Mitscher's staff. She returned to the United States under her own power for repairs and was still there when the war ended.

U.S. National Archives photo no. 80-G-323712

the Patriot's Point Museum in Mount Pleasant, South Carolina, alongside the *Yorktown*.[27]

There were more massed kamikaze attacks that month, and they continued into May. On May 11, two kamikazes hit Mitscher's flagship, the carrier *Bunker Hill*, and the admiral was forced to transfer his flag to the *Enterprise*. When, three days later, it, too, was hit, he transferred again to the *Randolph*. Serious as all these strikes were, they did not compel the Allies to call off the invasion or even interfere with the support of operations ashore.

Soon enough, Ugaki was forced to acknowledge, at least to himself, that the kamikazes were not going to turn the war around. Returning pilots had reported sinking dozens of American carriers, though Ugaki mused in his diary that if that were true, there wouldn't be "so many undamaged carriers still operating." By May it was clear that despite the terrible cost, the kamikaze campaign had failed. Even so, it continued for another full month; Japan had no other resources to hurl at their opponents. It put Ugaki in a stoical frame of mind. On the last day of April he wrote, "In the midst of the decisive battle, I don't regret this passing of the spring. Spring will come again, but what I fear is that a chance to recover the war situation won't come again." That same day in Berlin, Hitler shot himself.[28]

The Japanese conducted ten massed kamikaze attacks from April 6 to June 22, sending a total of 1,465 planes, and of course an equal number of pilots, at the Americans. They sank thirty-six American ships and damaged three hundred more. Okinawa fell anyway, making the invasion of Japan itself not only likely but imminent.[29]

In the midst of the campaign, Ugaki composed a haiku, which he entered in his diary:

> Flowers of the special attack are falling
> When the spring is leaving
> Gone with the spring
> Are young boys like cherry blossoms
> Leaving cherry trees only with leaves.[30]

JAPAN'S SURFACE NAVY was nearly as bereft of ships that April as the Kriegsmarine. Both of the hermaphrodite battleship/carriers that had survived the Battle of Leyte Gulf, *Ise* and *Hyuga*, had been crippled by American air attacks, and in any case they lacked both airplanes and sufficient fuel to go to sea. That left Japan with only one capital ship, the *Yamato*, available for active service. Some in the Navy Ministry argued that the *Yamato* should be held back to defend the homeland when the time came. Others found it intolerable that the navy's signature ship should remain idle while young pilots hurled themselves to destruction in defense of Okinawa. Champions of this latter view received a powerful, indeed irresistible boost from the emperor himself when, during the formal presentation of the plan for defending Okinawa with kamikazes, Hirohito asked: "Where is the Navy?" It may have been simply a question, but to Japanese naval officers it was a sharp slap to the face. It was intolerable that some spoke derisively of the *Yamato* as "a floating hotel for idle, inept admirals." Admiral Kusaka explained to a subordinate that the *Yamato* must sortie because her "reputation is open to criticism." It was the fear of being shamed that led the Japanese to send the *Yamato* to the battle for Okinawa.[31]

With only enough fuel (much of it synthesized from vegetable oil) for a one-way trip, the *Yamato* would steam south from the Inland Sea, expend all of her ammunition against the invaders off Okinawa, then beach herself on the island so that her 3,500-man crew could join the army in the fight against the invaders. Virtually everyone realized that without air cover, it was a near certainty that the *Yamato* would never make it to Okinawa, and even if she did, the idea that sailors could leap from her decks to fight American soldiers and Marines ashore was utter fantasy. It was a gesture: a last, bold, hopeless attack, like the banzai charges on so many of the Pacific Islands. In acknowledgment of that, the orders to Vice Admiral Seiichi Itō stated explicitly that "this is a *tokkōtai* operation."[32]

Officially, at least, the *Yamato* group was to act as a decoy, to attract the Americans away from their own carriers and make those carriers vulnerable to the kamikazes. That explanation fooled few. Itō told his officers, "We are being given an appropriate chance to die." As the crew of the *Yamato* prepared the sortie, her officers gathered to drink the traditional sake toast prior to departure. When they raised their glasses, the navigation officer accidentally dropped his and it shattered on the deck. There was profound silence as the officer dropped his head in shame. It was a terrible omen.[33]

LATER THAT NIGHT, the *Threadfin*, one of two American subs monitoring the exit from the Inland Sea, reported a large surface contact accompanied by several smaller contacts exiting the Bungo Channel. In receipt of the news, Spruance's first instinct was to alert Admiral Morton Deyo to ready his battleships for a surface engagement. Mitscher, however, was not about to miss this opportunity. He ordered a dawn search by long-range carrier planes that yielded results at 8:30 a.m. on April 7, when a pilot reported one large battleship, one light cruiser, and eight destroyers in the East China Sea. Mitscher ordered a full carrier strike by 280 planes from nine carriers. Only then did he radio Spruance, sending a TBS message asking, "Will you take them or shall I?" Spruance replied, "You take them." By then the planes were already en route.[34]

The *Yamato* never had a chance. The American planes circled high above the ten Japanese ships and carefully picked out their targets. Just past noon, they plunged to the attack. Early on, an American torpedo struck the light cruiser *Yahagi* in her engine room, leaving her dead in the water. All but defenseless after that, she was hit by as many as twelve bombs and seven torpedoes before her captain ordered abandon ship as she sank. Most of the escorting destroyers were hit as well, and four of them sank. The focus of American attention, however, was the *Yamato*.[35]

In addition to her main battery guns, the *Yamato* possessed six 6-inch guns, twenty-four 5-inch guns, and no fewer than 162 small 1-inch guns. Even her big 18.1-inch guns could fire a new anti-air shell that converted those guns into enormous shotguns scattering shell fragments all over the sky. Daunting as all that ordnance was, it could not protect her from the American planes. In a coordinated attack, the bombers and torpedo planes struck repeatedly at the *Yamato* in waves that arrived fifteen to twenty minutes apart. One of the few Japanese officers who survived the attack recalled watching "silvery streaks of torpedoes...silently converging on us from all directions." The young officer was awestruck by the "incessant explosions, blinding flashes of light, thunderous noises, and crushing weights of blast pressure."[36]

During the first several attacks, multiple torpedoes struck the *Yamato* on her port side, and she took on a perceptible list. Bombs exploded all along her deck, hurling AA gun tubs into the air and turning her superstructure into a mass of twisted metal. After planes in the third wave put five more torpedoes into her hull, her list increased dangerously. Admiral Itō had to order her boiler rooms and engine rooms flooded, sacrificing the men who occupied them, to prevent her from rolling over, though of course that left her dead in the water with no power. Then a fourth attack arrived...and a fifth...and a sixth. The *Yamato*'s list eventually increased to eighty degrees—she was clearly doomed. To ensure the rest of the crew was not trapped below deck when she rolled over, Itō called all hands topside. He solemnly shook hands with his chief of staff and retired to his cabin. Around 2:30, the ship simply exploded: "huge fingers of flame went flashing and skyrocketing into the dark clouds," with the smoke rising more than a mile

The explosion that marked the demise of the Japanese battleship *Yamato* on April 7, 1945, also marked the end of the Imperial Japanese Navy. The size of the explosion can be discerned from the silhouette of the nearby Japanese destroyer.

Naval History and Heritage Command

into the air. It could be seen from Kyushu, a hundred miles away. When the smoke cleared, the *Yamato* was gone. During the entire two hours of the air attacks, the Americans had lost ten airplanes.[37]

EVEN AS THE IMPERIAL JAPANESE NAVY DIED, Allied naval strength in the Pacific continued to increase. More newly constructed vessels arrived from shipyards in the United States, and other ships arrived from the European theater, including a significant contingent from the British. With the war in Europe coming to an end, Churchill was eager to dispatch a Royal Navy task force to the Pacific, in large part to obtain leverage that might affect the future of Britain's former colonies, especially Hong Kong and Singapore. When Churchill brought up the idea at the Octagon Conference in Quebec in September 1944, the Americans were less than enthusiastic. Admiral King, blunt as usual, insisted the British were not needed, not wanted, and more likely to be a burden than an asset. The presence of a Royal Navy task force in the Pacific, he insisted, would complicate an already complicated chain of command, and only add to the American logistical burden. He noted that British ships tended to be short-legged, which would make effective cooperation between the two navies difficult. Without saying so, it was also evident that King and others resented the idea that after the U.S. Navy had borne the battle against the Japanese for

Few officers had a more varied wartime
career than Admiral Sir Philip Vian. It was
Vian, then a captain, who had chased the
Altmark into Jøssing Fjord back in 1940; he
commanded several of the key convoys to
Malta in the Mediterranean in 1942–43; he
led the carrier force off Salerno in 1943 and
the Eastern Assault Force at Normandy in
1944. In 1945 he commanded the Royal
Navy carrier strike force in the Pacific.

Imperial War Museum

three years, the British now planned to jump in at the last moment and
claim a share of the victory. Despite such misgivings, Roosevelt told
Churchill that the Americans were happy to accept the British offer.[38]

The British Pacific Fleet (BPF), as it was formally styled, was a significant force on paper. It included two battleships, one of which was the *King
George V*, which had hunted down the *Bismarck* back in 1941, and six aircraft carriers, four of which were kept on active service. Though overall command belonged to Admiral Sir Bruce Fraser, he raised his flag ashore in
Sydney and operational command of the task force fell to Admiral Bernard
Rawlings, "a cultured British gentleman of the old school," according to
an American who served on his staff. Admiral Sir Philip Vian commanded the carrier force, which was labeled Task Force 113. Despite its
apparent strength, however, King's skepticism about its utility proved well
founded. Veterans of years of war in the North Sea and Mediterranean, the

British found the vast distances involved in the Pacific theater daunting. Despite the presence of twenty-two British tankers, the practice of underway refueling, which had become routine for the Americans, proved especially challenging. Vian himself acknowledged that the British effort to refuel at sea was "an awkward, unseaman-like business compared with the American method." In addition to such logistic difficulties, Royal Navy ships were not air-conditioned, and temperatures below deck sometimes surpassed a hundred degrees Fahrenheit.[39]

For the Okinawa campaign, Spruance assigned Vian's carriers the job of suppressing Japanese airfields on the islands of Miyako and Ishigaki south of Okinawa. This they did, cratering the airfields so they could not be used by the few planes Japan had left. Still, it was evident even to Vian that the task was largely a sideshow. The British carriers did prove superior to their American counterparts in one respect. On April 1, the day the Americans landed on Okinawa, a kamikaze made a direct hit on the *Indefatigable*, yet because of her armored flight deck, something the American carriers did not have, it had relatively little impact and, true to her name, the *Indefatigable* was operating at full capacity within an hour. A more serious attack on the *Formidable* two weeks later did more damage, but that ship, too, was back to full operational status within six hours. The carriers of Task Force 113 launched strikes against targets on Formosa as well as in the Ryukyus, but the demands of constant service in an alien environment soon began to show. The *Illustrious*, which had conducted the air attack on Taranto back in 1940, became so unseaworthy she was obliged to sail for home in mid-April. By the end of May, all of Rawlings's ships were in need of a refit, and they returned to Sydney. The planes of Vian's strike force had flown 4,691 sorties and destroyed 75 Japanese planes against losses of 26. Yet the British also lost 134 aircraft to operational accident or kamikaze strikes. Churchill had succeeded in putting a Royal Navy task force in the Pacific, but its performance did relatively little to promote his political goals.[40]

THE BATTLE FOR OKINAWA lasted for nearly three months, and in the midst of it there were important political developments. On April 7, the same day the *Yamato* went down in the East China Sea, Prime Minister

Koiso resigned and was replaced by Kantaro Suzuki, an eighty-year-old retired admiral who had opposed war with the United States from the beginning. Suzuki appointed several other retired admirals to his cabinet, a fact that provoked Ugaki to muse, "The Navy, now without ships, is going to fight at the critical time by forming a cabinet.... Ha Ha!"[41]

Five days later, the United States, too, underwent a leadership change when on April 12 Franklin Roosevelt, only sixty-three years of age, succumbed to a cerebral hemorrhage at his Warm Springs, Georgia, cottage. Hitler, who was himself less than three weeks from death by his own hand, experienced a flash of joy when he heard the news, telling those around him that this would turn the war around.

Resistance on Okinawa ended on June 22, and that also ended the massed kamikaze attacks. Despite the desperate hand-to-hand fighting ashore, because of the kamikazes the U.S. Navy lost more men killed during the campaign (4,907) than did either the U.S. Army (4,675) or Marines (2,928). Of course, the Japanese suffered the most. Perhaps 70,000 Japanese soldiers perished in the three months between April 1 and June 22, plus another 11,000 who died in the so-called "mopping-up operations" afterward. More than 100,000 civilians died as well. Among the dead were both of the opposing commanders: General Mitsuru Ushijima and General Simon Bolivar Buckner, who had drawn much criticism for his management of the lengthy and bloody campaign.[42]

By any rational index, by the end of June Japan was defeated. The American B-29s had turned her cities into ash, and American submarines cut off even the most basic imports. Though LeMay remained focused on strategic bombing of Japanese cities, Nimitz persuaded him to devote some planes to laying more than thirteen thousand mines in and around Japan's harbors, and aerial mine-laying further stifled Japanese imports. American submarines roamed at will in the western Pacific, including in the Sea of Japan, where nine American submarines under Commander Earl Hydeman sank thirty-one ships in three weeks in June. In July, the submarine *Barb*, commanded by Gene Fluckey, sent a boat party ashore on Sakhalin Island, planted explosives on a coastal railroad, and blew up a passing train. Japan had become a passive target, absorbing punishment and unable to strike back.[43]

None of that meant that Japan was close to surrender. The militarists remained dominant in the government, and what passed for a "peace party" in Japan, including Prime Minister Suzuki, consisted of individuals who believed that Japan should consider negotiations to reach a settlement in which the nation retained not only its identity and sovereignty but also at least some of its foreign conquests. None advocated surrender. The Japanese government assumed that after Okinawa it would take the Americans several months to initiate another offensive, and that would provide time to seek alternatives, such as asking the Soviets to broker an armistice. Despite a cautious withdrawal toward the coast, Japanese armies continued to fight ferociously in China, as they did in Burma and the Philippines. The Army General Staff massed as many as ten thousand aircraft in Kyushu to resist the expected American invasion. Finally, the cult of defiance and the code of *bushido* were so powerful in the Japanese military that most military leaders were perfectly willing to accept that every living soul in Japan should be sacrificed rather than endure the shame of surrender.[44]

On July 26, the Allied heads of government met at Potsdam in occupied Germany. Without consulting the Russians, the British and Americans released the Potsdam Declaration, aimed at Japan's leaders. After pledging that Japanese soldiers would be allowed to return to their homes and that the Allies did not intend to enslave the Japanese people, it ended with an ultimatum: "We call upon the government of Japan to proclaim now the unconditional surrender of all Japanese armed forces" or face "prompt and utter destruction." Because the Japanese had no knowledge of the Manhattan Project or of the still-secret Soviet agreement to join the war against Japan in August, they assumed this was simply another negotiating posture. Noting the absence of Russian participation in the declaration, they retained hope that the Russians might yet be willing to act as intermediaries.[45]

The American plan for the invasion and conquest of Japan's homeland—Operation Downfall—assumed correctly that the Japanese would "continue the war to the utmost extent of their capabilities." Recalling the determination of civilians on Saipan to kill themselves rather than be taken prisoner and their experience with the kamikazes, the Americans expected to encounter "a fanatically hostile population." As if to confirm that, the Japanese passed an act making all males over fifteen and females between seventeen and forty part of the military for the defense of the home islands. Japanese authorities urged citizens to defend the homeland with spears, rocks, even their bare fists. If their hands were cut off, they were to try to bite their foes. Ultra intercepts indicated a buildup of Japanese units in Kyushu in numbers large enough to suggest that the planned American landing there would be extremely costly. Absent some almost supernatural intervention, it seemed possible, even likely, that the war would have to end with a campaign of virtual extermination.[46]

The supernatural intervention arrived in the form of a mushroom cloud.

The detonation of the first atomic bomb, on August 6, did not prompt an immediate surrender; despite the reports from Hiroshima, Japanese military leaders remained defiant. They, as well as others in the government, continued to insist that Japan must fight to the bitter end. The war minister, General Korechika Anami, insisted that it would be better for the entire population of Japan to be exterminated than to accept surrender. Three days later, another atomic bomb devastated Nagasaki, and the Soviet Union declared war. Those events compelled a reconsideration. American use of the atomic bombs in August 1945 has often been explained and rationalized on the grounds that by forestalling an invasion, they saved several hundred thousand American lives. It might also be argued that they also saved many millions of Japanese lives.

On August 9, only hours after the Soviet invasion of Manchuria and the explosion of the second atomic bomb, the emperor called a meeting of the Supreme Council. He listened quietly as his advisors debated what to do. Even now, General Yoshijirō Umezu, chief of the Imperial General Staff, insisted that while Soviet intervention was "unfavorable," it did not preclude a successful outcome to the war. When at last Prime Minister Suzuki asked the emperor to state his views, Hirohito told them that Japan must "bear the unbearable" and accept the Potsdam conditions so long as the imperial throne was preserved. Then he left the room.

In theory the emperor's pronouncement was decisive, and the Japanese government notified the Allies that it would accept the Potsdam protocols. After that, however, several days passed without any further communication.

The B-29 raids had been suspended due to bad weather and President Harry Truman was unwilling to restart them, fearing it would signal American rejection of the peace. After several days of silence from Tokyo, however, Truman authorized the raids to begin again on August 13. The delays were a result of continued resistance to the notion of surrender within the Japanese army. Japanese commanders in China and Indochina controlled nearly two million soldiers, and for several days it was uncertain that they would obey the order to surrender, even from the emperor. In Tokyo itself, a group of junior officers plotted to seize control of the emperor's recorded radio address announcing surrender in order to prevent it from being broadcast. Meanwhile, firebombs once again rained down on Japan's cities.

Finally at noon on August 15, Hirohito's address was broadcast to the nation. It was a stunning moment for his subjects, who until that moment had never heard the emperor's voice. He told them that "the war situation has developed not necessarily to Japan's advantage," and because of that, Japan would accept "the provisions of the Joint Declaration." The reverence for the emperor was so great that once those words went out over the airwaves, the militarists' plots collapsed. That night Truman ordered American commanders in the field to cease hostile action.[47]

It was over.

EPILOGUE

Tokyo Bay, 1945

A	T 8:55 A.M. ON SUNDAY MORNING, September 2, 1945, the American *Gleaves*-class destroyer *Lansdowne*, a veteran of Pacific battles from Guadalcanal to Okinawa, eased up alongside the USS *Missouri*, anchored in Tokyo Bay. The newest—and the last—of the American battleships, the *Missouri* had been commissioned in June 1944, just as the campaign for Saipan was getting under way. Sleek and modern as she was, she had been designed for a form of naval warfare that was already passing into history. Though she had participated in the campaigns for both Iwo Jima and Okinawa, and had been hit by a kamikaze during the latter campaign, this morning was to be her great historic moment, and in anticipation of it her crew had scrubbed her into inspection-ready condition: her brass gleamed and her nine 16-inch guns pointed skyward at a forty-five-degree angle, as if in salute. She flew the American flag at the gaff, though on this day she also flew the national flags of Great Britain, the Soviet Union, and China.

After the *Lansdowne*'s crew hooked onto the *Missouri*'s companion ladder, Mamoru Shigemitsu, head of Japan's Foreign Ministry, dressed impeccably in formal court dress, including a black top hat, gingerly stepped across the brow to the *Missouri*'s ladder and began to climb. He did so with some difficulty, as he had lost a leg years before in Korea to a terrorist's bomb and worn a wooden prosthesis ever since. Even after he attained the deck of the *Missouri*, he moved forward haltingly, with a perceptible limp, relying on a cane to support himself. It was poignant that Shigemitsu headed the official Japanese delegation given that from the start he had opposed the ambitions of the militarists in the Army General Staff. Now that their madness had been fully exposed, he was tasked with signing the surrender document.

Behind him was the head of the Japanese Army General Staff, Yoshijirō Umezu, who wore his green field uniform with the gold aiguillettes of his staff position draped across his chest. Unlike Shigemitsu, Umezu had been a fierce champion of continuing the war and was devastated by the emperor's decision to surrender. He insisted to the very end that Japan should continue fighting until the British and Americans offered better terms. He submitted only when the emperor personally ordered him to prove his loyalty by accepting this bitter duty.

Umezu's navy counterpart, Soemu Toyoda, was not in the Japanese delegation, nor in fact were any of the admirals who had played key roles in the Pacific War: Ozawa, Kondō, Kurita, or Ugaki. Instead, the navy was represented by two relatively junior rear admirals. One was Sadatoshi Tomioka, who, like Shigemitsu, had opposed the attack on Pearl Harbor as well as the Midway campaign, and who had spent most of the war as a member of the Operations Bureau in the Naval General Staff. The other was Ichiro Yokoyama, who had been Japan's last prewar attaché to the United States and had spent the first year of the war in American custody before being exchanged for his American counterpart.

Once all members of the Japanese delegation arrived on the deck of the *Missouri*, American staff officers marshaled them into three ranks, with Shigemitsu and Umezu in front. The eleven delegates stood there stoically with frozen expressions while official photographers recorded the moment for history. For Umezu in particular, it was extraordinarily painful.

Twenty feet in front of them, on the other side of an ordinary mess table covered with a green cloth, were the representatives of the nine nations that had participated in the war against Japan. Douglas MacArthur, who presided over the ceremony, stood in the forefront, wearing a long-sleeved khaki uniform that was unadorned but for a circle of five silver stars on each collar. Behind him the representatives of America's allies also wore simple open-collar khaki uniforms, except for the British representative, Admiral Bruce Fraser, who stood out in what were known as tropical whites: a short-sleeved white shirt, knee-length white shorts, and white shoes and socks.

Thomas Blamey represented Australia, and Conrad Helfrich, who had presided over the short and disastrous life of the ABDA command, was there to represent the Netherlands. Even the Soviet Union, which had been in the Pacific War for only three weeks, was represented by Lieutenant General Kuzma Derevyanko, who also stood out in his dark Russian Army uniform with gold epaulettes. The moment was especially meaningful for the Chinese representative, General Hsu Yung-chang (Xu Yongchang). China had been at war with Japan since 1937 and had suffered between fifteen and twenty million dead, more than thirty times the number of Americans killed and second only to the Russian toll of twenty-six million.

Arrayed along the bulkhead as witnesses were more officers in khaki, most of them Americans, including William Halsey, Charles Lockwood, John S. McCain, and Richmond Kelly Turner. Above them, crowding the rails and sitting atop the ship's gun turret, were hundreds of ordinary sailors, jostling one another to get a better view of this historic moment. Some dangled their legs over the edge of the turret. Very likely, any of the Japanese delegates who saw them out of the corner of their eye deplored such undisciplined familiarity, which would not have been tolerated in the Imperial Navy.

MacArthur made it clear at once that this was not a parley or a discussion. "The issues involving divergent ideals and ideologies," he announced, "have been determined on the battlefields of the world, and hence are not for our discussion or debate." After declaring his "earnest hope" that "a better world shall emerge out of the blood and carnage of the past," he invited "the representatives of the Emperor of Japan and the Japanese government and the Japanese Imperial General Headquarters to sign the Instrument of Surrender at the places indicated."

Shigemitsu went first, limping up to the table and removing his hat. Looking and failing to find a place to put it, he set it down on the table. Then he sat in the solitary chair facing the men whose countries had vanquished his own. Leaning forward, he carefully signed his name in Japanese kanji characters before returning to his place. One by one, the other Japanese delegates followed suit. Solemn as the occasion was, MacArthur affected a casual pose throughout, alternately clasping his hands behind his back and thrusting them in his pockets in a comfortable slouch.

Chester Nimitz signs the Instrument of Surrender on board USS *Missouri* on
September 2, 1945. Behind him are (left to right) Douglas MacArthur, William F.
Halsey, and Forrest Sherman (looking at MacArthur).

U.S. National Archives photo no. 80-G-701293

After all eleven of the Japanese representatives had affixed their names,
MacArthur pronounced that he would sign next "on behalf of all the nations
at war with Japan." As he affixed his signature, two gaunt witnesses stood by
as observers. American General Jonathan Wainwright and British General
Arthur Percival had each been taken prisoner in the early days of the Pacific
War—Wainwright at Corregidor and Percival at Singapore. They had spent
four years in Japanese captivity yet they had each survived to witness this
moment. Chester Nimitz signed next, and he was followed by the representatives of China, Britain, the Soviet Union, Australia, Canada, France, the
Netherlands, and New Zealand. It took some time, during which no one
spoke except in muted whispers. When it was done, MacArthur stepped
back to the microphone. Speaking slowly in his stentorian baritone, aware
that his audience was not the few hundred who were gathered on the deck
of the *Missouri* but history itself, he solemnly announced, "Let us pray that
peace be now restored to the world, and that God will preserve it always.
These proceedings are closed."[1]

AFTERWORD

THE SECOND WORLD WAR was fought in a score of theaters, from Norway to Ceylon, Burma to Morocco, and Dunkirk to the Solomon Islands. It was punctuated by epic and sanguinary struggles at Stalingrad, Guadalcanal, Tunisia, the Hürtgen Forest, Kursk, Iwo Jima, and elsewhere. The Allies prevailed in this global contest due to three circumstances. The first was the determination of the British, personified by their indomitable prime minister, who fought the Axis powers alone for a full year from June 22, 1940, to June 22, 1941, and prevented a German victory in the first summer of the war. The second was the resilience of the Red Army, which shed its blood profligately during the next two years to keep the Germans from overrunning the Continent. The third was Allied naval superiority, itself a product of American material resources. While "boots on the ground" were essential in this war (as they are in every war), it was supremacy at sea that eventually proved decisive.

As this narrative has shown, operational success constituted one important aspect of the Allied naval victory. Technological breakthroughs—in aircraft, torpedoes, code breaking, radar, and eventually atomic energy—were also central to the story. In the end, however, the single greatest contributor to maritime success was the ability of Allied—and especially American—shipyards and shipyard workers to exploit superior natural resources and build transports and warships of every type faster than the Axis could sink them. The British and Russian sacrifices from 1939 to 1944 kept the Axis at bay long enough for the economic powerhouse of American factories and shipyards to produce the wherewithal necessary for the Allies to overwhelm the Axis.

The First World War was supposed to have been the war to end all wars. Expectations for the Second World War were more realistic, yet that conflict did change the world. Germany and Japan were devastated, of course, but so were China and Russia, as well as much of France and nearly all of Eastern Europe. Even Britain, where no enemy had managed to set foot, was a pale shadow of its former self in 1945. Only the United States, protected by two vast oceans, emerged not only relatively unscathed but stronger, both economically and militarily. The end of the war marked the onset of a new chapter in world history, one that is still being written.

OF THE SIX NATIONAL LEADERS whose oversize personalities or unassailable authority dominated the Second World War, three did not live to see its end, all of them dying within days of one another in April 1945: Roosevelt of a cerebral hemorrhage on the twelfth, Mussolini at the hands of Communist partisans on the twenty-eighth, and Hitler by his own hand on the thirtieth.

Churchill, Stalin, and Hirohito all survived the war, though they had quite different postwar experiences. Churchill was turned out of 10 Downing Street almost immediately by a population that, for all its admiration of his inspirational leadership and indomitable will, had been worn down by nearly six years of "blood, toil, tears, and sweat." Churchill was still a member of Parliament, however, and he returned as prime minister in 1951. Despite increasingly poor health, he held that post for another four years until he resigned in 1955. He remained a beloved national figure, won the Nobel Prize in Literature for his six-volume history of the Second World War, and died quietly at home at the age of ninety-one in 1965.

Stalin could not be turned out of office, of course, and he was determined to pursue territorial compensation for the horrific sacrifices made by the Red Army in the war: approximately ten million killed, more than the total of German, Italian, Japanese, British, and American losses combined. His intransigence concerning Eastern Europe in general, and Poland in particular, provoked a pushback from the West, and the Cold War emerged hard on the heels of the Second World War. That conflict was reaching its apex in 1953 when Stalin died of a stroke on March 4 at the age of seventy-four.

Despite being on the losing side, Hirohito remained on the Chrysanthemum Throne as emperor of Japan. Though the U.S. had rejected Japanese demands that Hirohito remain as the supreme authority in Japan, the American response that he would be subordinate to the Allied Supreme Commander at least implied that he could remain as a figurehead. During the war, virtually all of the important policy decisions had been made by generals. That remained true after the war, though now, instead of the warlords of the Imperial Army, it was the Allied plenipotentiary, Douglas MacArthur, who ruled in the emperor's name. Hirohito remained on the throne for another forty-four years and died in January 1989 at the age of eighty-seven.

To assuage those in the Allied camp who insisted that Hirohito must be called to account, the Americans portrayed General Hideki Tojo as the true architect of Japan's war of aggression. Aware that he was about to be arrested, Tojo asked a doctor to outline the precise location of his heart on his chest with charcoal, and subsequently shot himself where the doctor had indicated. The bullet nevertheless missed his heart and he survived. After recovering, he was arrested and tried for war crimes by the International Military Tribunal for the Far East. At that trial he accepted full responsibility for the conduct of the war, and he was hanged on December 23, 1948.

Erich Raeder was also arrested and tried for war crimes before the International Military Tribunal at Nuremberg. Having been part of the national leadership when the war began, he received a life sentence, though he was released nine years later, in September 1955, in consideration of his poor health. He lived out the rest of his life quietly, writing his memoirs and attending occasional veterans' reunions, and he died at the age of eighty-four on November 6, 1960.

Dönitz, too, was found guilty of war crimes at Nuremberg. The court made much of his conduct of unrestricted submarine warfare, citing it as a violation of the 1936 agreement for the humane use of submarines. The defense presented an affidavit from Admiral Chester Nimitz, who acknowledged that American submarine commanders in the Pacific had operated under nearly identical protocols. As a result, Dönitz received a sentence of only ten years, though he actually served one more year than Raeder. He was released in October 1956 and lived quietly in a small town in northern Germany. Until the day he died, he insisted that he was merely a professional naval officer doing his duty. He died of a heart attack on Christmas Eve, 1980, at the age of eighty-nine.

Many of the Japanese naval leaders did not survive the war. Yamamoto had been shot down over Bougainville in 1943, and Nagumo shot himself as the Americans overran Saipan in 1944. Some who did survive the conflict chose to kill themselves immediately afterward. A few, such as Takijirō Ōnishi, committed ritual seppuku and disemboweled themselves; others made a symbolic final attack against the hated Americans. On August 15, the day that Hirohito's radio message was broadcast, Matome Ugaki, who had supervised the kamikaze attacks, made a final entry in his diary, climbed into the cockpit of a plane, and flew off to make a suicide attack of his own. A dozen other pilots insisted on going with him. Ugaki radioed back that he was preparing to crash-dive on the enemy, but no kamikaze attack is recorded as having taken place that day, and the wreckage of his plane was subsequently found on Iheyajima Island, near Okinawa.

General Umezu, who had signed the Instrument of Surrender on behalf of the Imperial General Staff, was subsequently arrested, tried, and found guilty of waging a war of aggression. Sentenced to life in prison, he died of cancer three years later, four days after his sixty-seventh birthday. Admiral Soemu Toyoda, who had presided over the last days of the Imperial Navy, was also arrested and charged with war crimes. Despite having sanctioned the kamikaze blitz, and his insistence—especially after the atomic bombs— that Japan should fight to the last man, he was found not guilty by the tribunal and released, the only high-ranking individual in the Japanese armed forces to be acquitted. He lived another decade, dying in 1957 of a heart attack at the age of seventy-two.

Jisaburō Ozawa, the admiral who had endured defeat in the Philippine Sea and commanded the sacrificial force in the Battle of Leyte Gulf, was not arrested. He simply went home, kept his own counsel, and died twenty years later, in 1966, at the age of eighty. Similarly, Takeo Kurita, who had steamed away from Leyte Gulf when he seemed to be on the brink of victory, was never arrested. He became a masseur and lived quietly with his daughter's family, tending her garden. He wrote no memoir and agreed to only one interview—in 1954—in which he acknowledged that he had made a mistake by disengaging off Samar and confessed that he had been "extremely fatigued" during the battle. Twice a year he made a pilgrimage to the Yasukuni Shrine, but otherwise refrained from talking about the war at all. He died of natural causes in 1977 at the age of eighty-eight.

France had its own postwar reckoning. Immediately after the war, those who had been part of the resistance or simply resented the Vichy regime exacted a fearful revenge on their collaborationist countrymen. Though records are incomplete, as many as ten thousand individuals were tried by actual or ersatz courts, condemned to die, and executed. More formally, in what was called the *épuration légale* (literally "legal purge"), the French High Court of Justice sentenced another six thousand to death for treason, though all but 767 of them had their sentences commuted. Among the more prominent Frenchmen to be executed was Pierre Laval, the pro-German head of state who had haughtily declared that France would defend itself against the Allied invasion of North Africa. Also condemned to death by the court was Admiral Jean de Laborde, who had refused to allow the fleet at Toulon to join the Allies in 1942. Unlike Laval, de Laborde's sentence was commuted to life imprisonment, and he was released from confinement only a year later, in June 1947. He lived another thirty years and died in July 1977 at the age of ninety-eight.

Raffaele de Courten, the last commander of the Regia Marina, joined Victor Emmanuel and Badoglio at Brindisi in 1944 and remained as minister of marine in the Italian government until December 1946, when he resigned in protest of the Paris peace treaties that stripped Italy of its overseas colonies as well as Istria, which was granted to Yugoslavia. In 1952 he became president of a shipping company, retired in 1959, and died in 1978 one month shy of his ninetieth birthday.

AMONG THE VICTORS, Bertram Ramsay, hero of both Dunkirk and D-Day, did not live to see the end of the war. When the Germans began the

Ardennes counteroffensive that became the Battle of the Bulge in December 1944, Ramsay decided to fly from Paris to Montgomery's headquarters to see how he could help. His plane took off successfully but almost immediately lost power and plunged into the ground, killing everyone on board.

Andrew Cunningham, who presided over the Allied victory in the Mediterranean, survived the war and became First Sea Lord. In that capacity he oversaw the Royal Navy's transition to peace after 1945, nursing the service through the draconian budget cuts of the postwar years. He was made Baron Cunningham of Hyndhope in 1945, and Viscount Cunningham in 1946. He retired to the country the next year, sat occasionally in the House of Lords, and died in June 1963 at the age of eighty. Appropriately, he was buried at sea in the English Channel off Portsmouth.

Philip Vian, who had chased the *Altmark* into Jøssing Fjord in 1940, helped to sink the *Bismarck* in 1941, fought off incessant air and surface attacks while escorting convoys to Malta in 1942–43, commanded British naval forces off Normandy in 1944, and led a Royal Navy carrier force into the Pacific in 1945, became commander in chief of the Home Fleet in 1948 and retired as a five-star Admiral of the Fleet in 1952. He then became a successful banker in London and died at his home in 1968 at the age of seventy-three.

Ernest J. King, the grim-faced, no-nonsense American chief of naval operations, also retired after the war and lived in Washington, where he served as president of the Naval Historical Foundation. He suffered a massive stroke in 1947 and thereafter spent much of his time in the naval hospital in Bethesda outside Washington or at his retirement home in Kittery, Maine. He was in Kittery when he died of a heart attack on June 25, 1956, at the age of seventy-seven.

Chester Nimitz replaced King as chief of naval operations in 1945 and presided over the dramatic reduction of the U.S. Navy from its wartime peak of some sixty-five thousand ships (including armed landing craft) to just over a thousand in 1947. He retired from the navy that year and moved first to Berkeley, California, and then to Yerba Buena Island in San Francisco Bay, midpoint of the Oakland Bay Bridge. He died there in February 1966 at the age of eighty.

Many of those who knew Raymond Spruance remarked that his demeanor was suggestive of a university professor. It was appropriate, then, that after the war Spruance became the twenty-sixth president of the U.S. Naval War College in Newport, Rhode Island, a post he held until his retirement two years later. He served as U.S. ambassador to the Philippines until 1955, then, like his friend and mentor Chester Nimitz, moved to California, living on Pebble Beach near Monterey. He died there in December 1969 at the age of eighty-three and is buried near Nimitz in the Golden Gate National Cemetery.

The man with whom Spruance traded command of the Big Blue Fleet in the Pacific, William F. Halsey, received a fifth star as a fleet admiral in 1945. The decision was controversial in that only four such billets were authorized by law, and with King, Nimitz, and Admiral William D. Leahy (FDR's chief of staff) holding down three of them, only one other individual was eligible. In the end, Truman selected Halsey over Spruance because of his role in boosting national morale by conducting early carrier raids in 1942. Accepting a large advance from McGraw-Hill, Halsey dictated his memoirs to Joseph Bryan, the son of a former fraternity brother at the University of Virginia. The resulting book, with its self-serving comments about the Battle of Leyte Gulf, did little to enhance his public reputation, and by 1953 Halsey concluded that it had been a mistake to write it. He moved to New York, where he served on the board of the International Telephone and Telegraph Company (ITT), and died of a heart attack on August 16, 1959. He is buried in Arlington National Cemetery.

As for the rest—the captains, commanders, and lieutenants; the pilots, gunners, enginemen, and boatswains; the sub crews, code breakers, radio and radar operators; the shipyard workers, merchant mariners, and the thousands of others, of every nationality, veterans of every navy, who had fought the war at sea—they went home to pick up their lives.

ACKNOWLEDGMENTS

As always, I owe a debt of thanks to the many people who aided or supported me during the preparation of this book. It was Tim Bent, my editor at Oxford University Press, who persuaded me that I should tackle this topic. Nearly five years ago, he and I were discussing possible projects on the role of navies in the Second World War when Tim's colleague and friend Dave McBride, who has the office next door, poked his head around the corner and told me that I should do *all* of it. Tim immediately supported the idea and convinced me that I could. Tim and I have worked together on five books now, and his gentle blue pen and warm sense of humor have weaned me from many stylistic eccentricities (but not all!). He has been a wise counselor and an indefatigable cheerleader throughout.

Once again it was a genuine pleasure to work with the highly professional staff at Oxford University Press. The president and publisher of OUP, Niko Pfund, has been a strong supporter throughout. And I am indebted to the production editor, Amy Whitmer, as well as to Tim's assistant, Mariah White. Sue Warga was a virtual lifesaver as a copy editor, saving me from innumerable gaffes and errors. Sarah Russo and Erin Meehan in publicity and marketing have been a pleasure to work with. Somehow they all manage to retain a sense of fun and wit even as they do serious work.

At overseas archives and repositories, I am indebted to Richard Porter, friend and former colleague at the Britannia Royal Naval College in Dartmouth, England, who guided me with Royal Navy sources and provided the image of Admiral Sir Charles Forbes. Thanks also to Megan Vassey and Kat Southwell at the Australian War Memorial in Canberra; to Lisa and Neera, the otherwise anonymous assistants at the Imperial War Museum in London; to the helpful staff at the Bundesarchiv in Berlin; and to Dee Corbell, friend of many years, who went out of her way to translate documents and track down elusive items for me in France.

In the United States, my first bow must go to the helpful and cheerful staff of the Nimitz Library at the U.S. Naval Academy in Annapolis, Maryland, including (but not limited to) Jennifer Bryan of the Special Collections Department and Linda McLeod in Circulation. The Nimitz Library possesses what is almost certainly the most complete collection of publications on naval history in the world. Thanks also to Reagan Grau, archivist at the Nimitz Education and Research Center at the National Museum of the Pacific War in Fredericksburg, Texas; Lindsey Barnes at the National World War II Museum in New Orleans; and Holly Reed and Michael Bloomfield at the U.S. National Archives in College Park, Maryland. Janis Jorgenson was once again extraordinarily helpful in the photo archives of the U.S. Naval Institute in Annapolis, Maryland, and Robert Hanshew was the very model of a generous colleague in helping me in track down items at the Naval History and Heritage Command in the Washington Navy Yard in Washington, D.C., despite doing so in the midst of a house move.

Several individuals helped me better understand the language and cultural nuances of other national navies. These included Yoji Koda (Japan), Edward Chen (China), and Johannes (John) Hensel (Germany). Jeff Ward was once again a consummate perfectionist in rendering the two dozen maps in the book.

I have spent virtually all of my adult life as a naval historian, and one of the most rewarding aspects of it has been the community of scholars who have mentored me, assisted me, argued with me, and altogether made my endeavors richer and more fulfilling. The list is too long to include everyone, and I hope a blanket acknowledgment will be forgiven. For this particular project, several individuals read portions of the manuscript, including Tom Cutler, Richard Frank, James Hornfischer, and Jon Parshall, all of whom I consider friends. Any errors that remain are, of course, entirely my responsibility. Invaluable support came also from family members, especially Jeff, Suz, Will, and Bee in California, and from our friends Edith and Harold Holzer in New York, and John and Jeanne Marszalek in Mississippi, all of whom have been supportive (and patient) sounding boards.

Finally, I once again profess my great admiration of and deep affection for my wife, Marylou, whose contribution to this book comes close to being that of a co-author.

ABBREVIATIONS USED IN NOTES

Action Reports	*U.S. Navy Action and Operational Reports from World War II*. Originals at National Archives and Records Administration; also available on microfilm (Bethesda, MD University Publications of America, 1990)
BOMRT	Battle of Midway Round Table (Midway42.org)
CINCPAC	Commander in Chief, Pacific (at National Archives)
DDE	Dwight David Eisenhower
FDR	Franklin D. Roosevelt
FRUS	*Foreign Relations of the United States* [U.S. State Department], Washington, DC: Government Printing Office, 1961, 1970
GCM	George C. Marshall
JMH	*Journal of Modern History*
NARA	National Archives and Records Administration, College, Park, Maryland
NHF	Naval Historical Foundation
NHHC	Naval History and Heritage Command, Washington Navy Yard, Washington, DC
NMPW	National Museum of the Pacific War, Fredericksburg, Texas
NWC	U.S. Naval War College, Newport, Rhode Island
NWCR	*Naval War College Review*
NWWIIM-EC	The National World War II Museum (Eisenhower Center), New Orleans, Louisiana
PDDE	*The Papers of Dwight David Eisenhower*, ed. Alfred D. Chandler (Baltimore: Johns Hopkins University Press, 1996)
Proceedings	*United States Naval Institute Proceedings*
UMD	Hornbake Library, University of Maryland
USNA	Nimitz Library, United States Naval Academy
USNI	United States Naval Institute Press
WSC	Winston S. Churchill

Prologue

1. *Times* (London), January 21, 1930, 16.
2. Ibid., 14.
3. *Proceedings of the London Naval Conference of 1930 and Supplementary Documents* (Washington, DC: Government Printing Office, 1931), 26–27.
4. Raymond G. O'Connor, *Perilous Equilibrium: The United States and the London Naval Conference of 1930* (New York: Greenwood Press, 1962), ch. 2; Sadao Asada, *From Mahan to Pearl Harbor: The Imperial Japanese Navy and the United States* (Annapolis: Naval Institute Press, 2006), 130; John H. Maurer and Christopher M. Bell, eds., *At the Crossroads Between Peace and War: The London Naval Conference of 1930* (Annapolis: USNI, 2013).
5. *Proceedings of the London Naval Conference*, 83.
6. Ibid., 85.
7. Asada, *From Mahan to Pearl Harbor*, 139, 153, 139–47.
8. *Proceedings of the London Naval Conference*, 115.

Chapter 1: *Unterseebooten*

1. Gunter Prien, *I Sank the Royal Oak* (London: Grays Inn Press, 1954), 15–121.
2. Angus Konstam, *Scapa Flow: The Defences of Britain's Great Fleet Anchorage, 1914–1945* (Oxford: Osprey, 2009).
3. Stephen Roskill, *The War at Sea, 1939–1945* (London: Her Majesty's Stationery Office, 1954), 1:70–74.
4. Prien, *I Sank the Royal Oak*, 182–83.
5. Karl Doenitz, *Memoirs: Ten Years and Twenty Days* (Annapolis: USNI, 1958, 1959), 3.
6. Ibid., 5; Friedrich Ruge, "German Naval Strategy Across Two Wars," *Proceedings*, February 1955, 152–66.
7. Doenitz, *Memoirs*, 5–8; Erich Raeder, *My Life* (Annapolis: USNI, 1960), 138; Clay Blair, *Hitler's U-Boat War: The Hunters, 1939–1942* (New York: Random House, 1996), 31; Eberhard Rössler, *The U-Boat* (London: Cassell, 1981), 88–101; William A. Wiedersheim, "Factors in the Growth of the Reichsmarine, 1919–1939," *Proceedings*, March 1948, 317–24.

8. Wiedersheim, "Factors in the Growth of the Reichsmarine," 319.

9. Edward P. Von der Porten, *The German Navy in World War II* (New York: Thomas Y. Crowell, 1969); Joseph Maiolo, *The Royal Navy and Nazi Germany, 1933–1939: A Study in Appeasement and the Origins of the Second World War* (London: Macmillan, 1998); D. C. Watt, "The Anglo-German Naval Agreement of 1935: An Interim Judgment," *JMH* 2 (1956): 155–75. The 1936 Admiralty report is quoted in Terry Hughes and John Costello, *The Battle of the Atlantic* (New York: Dial Press, 1977), 31.

10. Rössler, *The U-Boat*, 102–21; Wiedersheim, "Factors in the Growth of the Reichsmarine," 320; Doenitz, *Memoirs*, 7; Raeder, *My Life*, 138.

11. Rössler, *The U-Boat*, 122; Karl H. Kurzak, "German U-Boat Construction," *Proceedings*, April 1955, 274–89; Raeder, *My Life*, 280. Dönitz quotes his August 28, 1939, memo in his *Memoirs*, 43–44.

12. Francis M. Carroll, Athenia *Torpedoed: The U-Boat Attack That Ignited the Battle of the Atlantic* (Annapolis: USNI, 2012), 31; Peter Kemp, *Decision at Sea: The Convoy Escorts* (New York: Elsevier-Dutton, 1978), 1–8.

13. Doenitz, *Memoirs*, 47.

14. Prien, *I Sank the* Royal Oak, 123–24.

15. Ibid., 124.

16. Ibid., 187.

17. Alexandre Korganoff, *The Phantom of Scapa Flow* (Skepperton, Surrey: Ian Allen, 1974), 48–76; Prien, *I Sank the* Royal Oak, 189.

18. Prien, *I Sank the* Royal Oak, 190.

19. Ibid., 191.

20. Gerald S. Snyder, *The* Royal Oak *Disaster* (London: William Kimber, 1976), 94–96. Benn is quoted on 109.

21. Snyder, *The* Royal Oak *Disaster*, 113–31; Prien, *I Sank the* Royal Oak, 190.

22. There are several books on the sinking of the *Royal Oak* by the U-47. In addition to Gunter Prien's own dramatized memoir (*I Sank the* Royal Oak), first published in Germany in 1940 as wartime propaganda and published in English in 1954, other books offer alternative theories about the event. Alexander McKee's *Black Saturday* (1959) implies that a conspiracy was partly responsible for what he deems an otherwise inexplicable event; Alexandre Korganoff's *The Phantom of Scapa Flow* (1974) tells the tale from the German perspective as a daring and dangerous adventure by a plucky crew; Gerald S. Snyder's *The* Royal Oak *Disaster* (1976) is more even-handed and includes the perspective of the victims on the *Royal Oak* as well as those on the U-47. The most recent retelling is H. J. Weaver's *Nightmare at Scapa Flow: The Truth About the Sinking of H.M.S.* Royal Oak (Peppard Common, Oxfordshire: Cressrelles, 1980).

23. The description of the effect of depth charges is from the oral history of Slade Benson of USS *Nautilus*, Walter Lord Collection, NHHC, box 18. The crew's reaction is from Korganoff, *The Phantom of Scapa Flow*, 119–23.

24. Blair, *Hitler's U-Boat War: The Hunters*, 90, 108.

25. Doenitz, *Memoirs*, 51–53.

Chapter 2: *Panzerschiffe*

1. Erich Raeder, *My Life* (Annapolis: USNI, 1960), 283–84; David Miller, *Langsdorff and the Battle of the River Plate* (Barnsley, South Yorkshire: Pen and Sword, 2013), 88–89.

2. Eugen Millington-Drake, *The Drama of the* Graf Spee *and the Battle of the Plate: A Documentary Anthology, 1914–1964* (London: Peter Davies, 1964), 97–99. Millington-Drake's anthology is by far the most useful source for assessing both the rampage of the *Graf Spee* and the subsequent battle of the river Plate.

3. The contemporary was Commander A. D. Campbell, quoted in Millington-Drake, *The Drama of the* Graf Spee, 97.

4. Ibid., 99–100, 123–25.

5. Ibid.; Eric Grove, *The Price of Disobedience: The Battle of the River Plate Reconsidered* (Annapolis: USNI, 2000), 26. That night, Langsdorff transferred Captain Harris and the *Clement*'s chief engineer to a neutral Greek freighter.

6. Karl Doenitz, *Memoirs: Ten Years and Twenty Days* (Annapolis: USNI, 1958, 1959), 5; Raeder, *My Life*, 3, 239–44, 251–52, 255–63; Leonard Seagren, "The Last Fuehrer," *Proceedings*, May 1954, 525; Keith W. Bird, *Erich Raeder: Admiral of the Third Reich* (Annapolis: USNI, 2006), 31–90; Clay Blair, *Hitler's U-Boat War: The Hunters, 1939–1942* (New York: Random House, 1996), 41.

7. David Wragg, *"Total Germany": The Royal Navy's War Against the Axis Powers, 1939–45* (Barnsley, South Yorkshire: Pen and Sword, 2016), 6; D. L. Kauffman, "German Naval Strategy in World War II," *Proceedings*, January 1954, 2.

8. Raeder, *My Life*, 201–14; Erich Raeder, *Struggle for the Sea* (London: William Kimber, 1959), 27, 40–41; Friedrich Ruge, "German Naval Strategy Across Two Wars," *Proceedings*, February 1955, 157.

9. Terry Hughes and John Costello, *The Battle of the Atlantic* (New York: Dial Press, 1977), 34–35; Edward P. Von der Porten, *The German Navy in World War II* (New York: Thomas Y. Crowell, 1969), 29.

10. Andrew Roberts, *The Storm of War: A New History of the Second World War* (New York: Harper, 2011), 36–37.

11. Hughes and Costello, *The Battle of the Atlantic*, 35; Raeder, *My Life*, 282, 286.

12. Blair, *Hitler's U-Boat War: The Hunters*, 66–69; Ruge, "German Naval Strategy Across Two Wars," 158; Raeder, *My Life*, 287.

13. Millington-Drake, *The Drama of the* Graf Spee, 101–2. The characterization of Pound is in a letter from Robert Bower to Stephen Roskill in March 1970, and is quoted by Correlli Barnett in *Engage the Enemy More Closely* (New York: W. W. Norton, 1991), 52.

14. Millington-Drake, *The Drama of the* Graf Spee, 102–4; James Levy, "Ready or Not? The Home Fleet at the Outset of World War II," *NWCR* 52 (Autumn 1999): 92.

15. Millington-Drake, *The Drama of the* Graf Spee, 103; Stephen Roskill, *The War at Sea, 1939–1945* (London: Her Majesty's Stationery Office, 1954), 1:114; Dudley Pope, *The Battle of the River Plate* (Annapolis: USNI, 1956), 46–47.

16. Admiralty memo of October 5, 1939, printed in Millington-Drake, *The Drama of the* Graf Spee, 102–3.

17. Millington-Drake, *The Drama of the* Graf Spee, 116–7; Roskill, *The War at Sea*, 1:115–16.
18. Millington-Drake, *The Drama of the* Graf Spee, 114–16. The quotation is from F. W. Raseneck's memoir, *Panzerschiff* Admiral Graf Spee, which Millington-Drake quotes on 116.
19. Millington-Drake, *The Drama of the* Graf Spee, 120–25.
20. Langsdorff memo, dated Nov. 26, 1939, quoted in Millington-Drake, *The Drama of the* Graf Spee, 133.
21. Millington-Drake, *The Drama of the* Graf Spee, 141.
22. Ibid., 142.
23. Cecil Hampshire, "British Strategy in the River Plate Battle," *Proceedings*, December 1958, 86–87. Copies of Harwood's orders are in Millington-Drake, *The Drama of the* Graf Spee, 147 and 165. See also Grove, *The Price of Disobedience*, 57.
24. Hampshire, "British Strategy," 87.
25. Langsdorff's comment was recorded by Commander Raseneck and is quoted in Millington-Drake, *The Drama of the* Graf Spee, 189.
26. Miller, *Langsdorff and the Battle of the River Plate*, 119–20; Millington-Drake, *The Drama of the* Graf Spee, 191, 204–5, 216.
27. Miller, *Langsdorff and the Battle of the River Plate*, 120.
28. Millington-Drake, *The Drama of the* Graf Spee, 227; Miller, *Langsdorff and the Battle of the River Plate*, 127–28.
29. Hampshire, "British Strategy," 90.
30. The diplomatic documents relevant to the *Graf Spee*'s brief stay in Montevideo are in the *Uruguayan Blue Book* (London: Hutchinson, 1940).
31. Langsdorff is quoted in Grove, *The Price of Disobedience*, 121.
32. Ibid., 170.
33. Willi Frischauer and Robert Jackson, *"The Navy's Here!": The* Altmark *Affair* (London: Victor Gollancz, 1955), 212–13. Published in the United States as *The* Altmark *Affair* (New York: Macmillan, 1955).
34. Philip Vian, *Action This Day: A War Memoir* (London: Frederick Muller, 1960), 26. Churchill discusses his role in this episode in *The Gathering Storm* (Boston: Houghton-Mifflin, 1949), 526–27, 561–64.
35. Ibid., 28–29; Frischauer and Jackson, *"The Navy's Here,"* 223–43.
36. David J. Bercuson and Holger Herwig, *The Destruction of the* Bismarck (Woodstock, NY: Overlook Press, 2001), 24.
37. Raeder, *My Life*, 290–91, 306–7.

Chapter 3: Norway

1. Martin Fritz, *German Steel and Swedish Iron Ore, 1939–1945* (Goteborg: Institute of Economics, 1974), 30–39, 41–48; Geirr H. Haarr, *The German Invasion of Norway, April 1940* (Annapolis: USNI, 2009), 27.
2. Erich Raeder, *My Life* (Annapolis: USNI, 1960), 308–9; Hitler's order of March 1 is in *Fuehrer Conferences on Naval Affairs, 1939–1945* (Annapolis: USNI, 1990), 83–84. See also Anthony Martienssen, *Hitler and His Admirals* (New York: E. P. Dutton, 1949), 50. The name translates as Operation Weser Exercise, the Weser

being a river in Germany. It was likely meant to imply an internal exercise rather than a foreign invasion.

3. Several scholars have assessed Churchill's role as naval strategist. See, for example, Max Hastings, *Winston's War: Churchill, 1940–1945* (New York: Alfred A. Knopf, 2010); Stephen S. Roskill, *Churchill and the Admirals* (London: Collins, 1977); and Christopher M. Bell, *Churchill and Sea Power* (New York: Oxford University Press, 2013).

4. Bell, *Churchill and Sea Power*, 173–79; Correlli Barnett, *Engage the Enemy More Closely: The Royal Navy in the Second World War* (New York: W. W. Norton, 1991), 93–94, 100–102; Haarr, *The German Invasion of Norway*, 28.

5. Raeder, *My Life*, 309.

6. Raeder's concerns are evident in his March 9 report to Hitler, which is printed in *Fuehrer Conferences*, 84–87, and in Martienssen, *Hitler and His Admirals*, 51–53. See also T. K. Derry, *The Campaign in Norway* (London: Her Majesty's Stationery Office, 1952), 18–21; and Raeder, *My Life*, 311.

7. Peter Dickens, *Narvik: Battles in the Fjords* (Annapolis: USNI, 1974), 17.

8. David Brown, ed., *Naval Operations of the Campaign in Norway, April–June 1940* (London: Frank Cass, 2000), 5–7; Dickens, *Narvik*, 18; Clay Blair, *Hitler's U-Boat War: The Hunters, 1939–1942* (New York: Random House, 1996), 147.

9. The most comprehensive history of the naval battles for Norway is Geirr Haarr's *The German Invasion of Norway, April 1940* (Annapolis: USNI, 2009). Haarr discusses the sinking of the *Glowworm* on 90–97. The Royal Navy's official account is in Brown, ed., *Naval Operations*, 128–38, as well as Richard Porter and M. J. Pearce, eds., *Fight for the Fjords: The Battle for Norway, 1940* (Plymouth: University of Plymouth Press, 2012), which is part of the Britannia Naval Histories of World War II series. The loss of the *Glowworm* is covered on 36–37.

10. Porter and Pearce, eds., *Fight for the Fjords*, 40; Dickens, *Narvik*, 30.

11. Haarr, *The German Invasion of Norway*, 307–14; Porter and Pearce, eds., *Fight for the Fjords*, 49–51; Dickens, *Narvik*, 34–40; Vincent P. O'Hara, *The German Fleet at War, 1939–1945* (Annapolis: USNI, 2004), 24–26; Brown, ed., *Naval Operations*, 19–21; Stephen Roskill, *The War at Sea, 1939–1945* (London: Her Majesty's Stationery Office, 1954), 165–66.

12. Dickens, *Narvik*, 17.

13. Haarr, *The German Invasion of Norway*, 323–28; Brown, ed., *Naval Operations*, 19; Dickens, *Narvik*, 36–39; O'Hara, *The German Fleet at War*, 28–31.

14. Porter and Pearce, eds., *Fight for the Fjords*, 65–66; Dickens, *Narvik*, 42; Krigsmuseum, *Narvik* (Narvik: Krigsminnemuseum, n.d.), 4; Gardner, ed., *Evacuation of Dunkirk*, 52.

15. Porter and Pearce, eds., *Fight for the Fjords*, 66–68.

16. Ibid., 61–62; Dickens, *Narvik*, 46–47; O'Hara, *The German Fleet at War*, 33.

17. Porter and Pearce, eds., *Fight for the Fjords*, 61–64; Dickens, *Narvik*, 39; Haarr, *The German Invasion of Norway*, 336–46; O'Hara, *The German Fleet at War*, 25–36.

18. Porter and Pearce, eds., *Fight for the Fjords*, 61–64; Blair, *Hitler's U-Boat War: The Hunters*, 149.

19. Haarr, *The German Invasion of Norway*, 346–50; Dickens, *Narvik*, 78, 87–90; O'Hara, *The German Fleet at War*, 32–40.

20. Barnett, *Engage the Enemy More Closely*, 109, 122; Andrew Roberts, *The Storm of War: A New History of the Second World War* (New York: Harper, 2011), 40.

21. Brown, ed., *Naval Operations*, 32–36.

22. Porter and Pearce, eds., *Fight for the Fjords*, 77–86; Dickens, *Narvik*, 119–21, 124, 141; Haarr, *The German Invasion of Norway*, 357–71.

23. Derry, *The Campaign in Norway*, 145–46.

24. Porter and Pearce, eds., *Fight for the Fjords*, 103; Roskill, *The War at Sea*, 1:187.

25. Brown, ed., *Naval Operations*, 101, 111; Derry, *The Campaign in Norway*, 145–47.

26. Hastings, *Winston's War*, 11–19.

27. Derry, *The Campaign in Norway*, 171–72, 200–201.

28. Ibid., 207–11.

29. Earl F. Ziemke, "The German Decision to Invade Norway and Denmark," in *Command Decisions*, ed. Kent Roberts Greenfield (Washington, DC: Office of the Chief of Military History, 1960), 71; Raeder, *My Life*, 314.

30. O'Hara, *The German Fleet at War*, 54–59; Haarr, *The German Invasion of Norway*, 1. On the value of the ore mines of French Lorraine, see Marcus D. Jones, *Nazi Steel: Friedrich Flick and German Expansion in Western Europe, 1940–1944* (Annapolis: USNI, 2012).

31. John Winton, *Carrier Glorious: The Life and Death of an Aircraft Carrier* (London: Leo Cooper, 1986), 166–73.

32. Brown, ed., *Naval Operations*, 127–29; Porter and Pearce, eds., *Fight for the Fjords*, 128–29; Barnett, *Engage the Enemy More Closely*, 136–38; Fritz-Otto Busch, *The Drama of the Scharnhorst* (London: Robert Hale, 1956), 47–50.

Chapter 4: France Falls

1. Winston Churchill, *Their Finest Hour*, vol. 2 of *The Second World War* (Boston: Houghton Mifflin, 1949), 42; Walter Lord, *The Miracle of Dunkirk* (New York: Viking Press, 1982), 2.

2. Stephen S. Roskill, *The War at Sea* (London: Her Majesty's Stationery Office, 1954), 1:213–14.

3. W. S. Chalmers, *Full Cycle: The Biography of Admiral Sir Bertram Home Ramsay* (London: Hodder and Stoughton, 1959), 21.

4. Ibid., 29; David Divine, *The Nine Days of Dunkirk* (New York: W. W. Norton, 1959), 31.

5. Lord, *Miracle of Dunkirk*, 47.

6. Robert Carse, *Dunkirk, 1940* (Englewood Cliffs, NJ: Prentice-Hall, 1970), 40, 65.

7. Roskill, *The War at Sea*, 1:216–17; Carse, *Dunkirk, 1940*, 24–25; Robin Prior, *When Britain Saved the West: The Story of 1940* (New Haven: Yale University Press, 2015), 112, 114.

8. The destroyer officer was Lieutenant Graham Lumsden of HMS *Keith*, who is quoted in *The Mammoth Book of Eyewitness Naval Battles* (New York: Carroll and Graf, 2003), 432.

9. Carse, *Dunkirk, 1940*, 54; Correlli Barnett, *Engage the Enemy More Closely: The Royal Navy in the Second World War* (New York: W. W. Norton, 1991), 159–60.

10. Lord, *Miracle of Dunkirk*, 117; W. J. R. Gardner, ed., *The Evacuation from Dunkirk: Operation Dynamo, 26 May–4 June 1940* (London: Frank Cass, 2000), 27–28; Prior,

When Britain Saved the West, 115. The survivor's comment was recorded by journalist Gordon Buckles and is quoted in Lawrence, *Eyewitness Naval Battles*, 434.

11. Gardner, ed., *The Evacuation from Dunkirk*, 28.

12. M. J. Whitley, *German Coastal Forces of World War Two* (London: Arms and Armour, 1992), 23.

13. Prior, *When Britain Saved the West*, 120–21.

14. Ibid., 123–24, 260; Gardner, ed., *Evacuation from Dunkirk*, 36; Roskill, *The War at Sea*, 1:222–23.

15. Prior, *When Britain Saved the West*, 128–29.

16. Churchill, *Their Finest Hour*, 115; Lord, *Miracle of Dunkirk*, 227.

17. Churchill, *Their Finest Hour*, 141, 115.

18. It is noteworthy that the French had no operational aircraft carriers in 1940. Its sole carrier, the *Béarn*, was consigned to transport duties in the West Indies, and its projected replacement, the *Joffre*, was never completed. A good summary of French naval strength at the outbreak of war is John Jordan, "France: The Marine Nationale," in *On Seas Contested*, ed. Vincent P. O'Hara, W. David Dickson, and Richard Worth (Annapolis: USNI, 2010), 16–20.

19. The pertinent sections of the armistice agreement are quoted by Arthur Marder in *From the Dardanelles to Oran* (London: Oxford University Press, 1974), 196. Marder discusses the nuances of the word *contrôle* on 214–15. See also Churchill, *Their Finest Hour*, 158; Roskill, *The War at Sea*, 1:240–41; Warren Tute, *The Deadly Stroke* (New York: Coward, McCann and Geoghegan, 1973), 34; and George E. Melton, *From Versailles to Mers el-Kebir: The Promise of Anglo-French Naval Cooperation, 1919–1940* (Annapolis: USNI, 2015).

20. Roskill, *The War at Sea*, 1:240–41; Marder, *From the Dardanelles to Oran*, 200.

21. Barnett, *Engage the Enemy More Closely*, 211–12; Marder, *From the Dardanelles to Oran*, 228–29; Michael Simpson, "Force H and British Strategy in the Western Mediterranean, 1939–1942," *Mariner's Mirror* 83 (1977): 63–64.

22. The order is printed in Marder, *From the Dardanelles to Oran*, 233–37.

23. Marder, *From the Dardanelles to Oran*, 212.

24. Barnett, *Engage the Enemy More Closely*, 221–22; Andrew Browne Cunningham, *A Sailor's Odyssey* (New York: E. P. Dutton, 1951), 244–55, quotations from 244 and 250. See also Marder, *From the Dardanelles to Oran*, 260–64; and René-Emile Godfroy, *L'Aventure de la Force X à Alexandrie, 1940–1943* (Paris: Librarie Plon, 1953).

25. Barnett, *Engage the Enemy More Closely*, 232; Peter C. Smith, *Critical Conflict: The Royal Navy's Mediterranean Campaign in 1940* (Barnsley, South Yorkshire: Pen and Sword, 2011), 124–26.

26. The peroration to Churchill's famously defiant speech is in Churchill, *Their Finest Hour*, 118.

27. Marder, *From the Dardanelles to Oran*, 205; Smith, *Critical Conflict*, 129.

28. Marder, *From the Dardanelles to Oran*, 242–44.

29. Roskill, *The War at Sea*, 1:244; Marder, *From the Dardanelles to Oran*, 239–40. Churchill's message is quoted in *Their Finest Hour*, 236.

30. Jack Greene and Alessandro Massignani, *The Naval War in the Mediterranean, 1940–1943* (London: Chatham, 2002), 58–61; Raymond De Belot, *The Struggle*

for the Mediterranean, 1939–1945 (Princeton: Princeton University Press, 1951), 26–29.

31. Somerville is quoted in Simpson, "Force H and British Strategy," 64. See also Smith, *Critical Conflict*, 131.

32. Churchill, *Their Finest Hour*, 233–34.

33. Peter Smith discusses this issue thoughtfully and at length in *Critical Conflict*, 151–227. See also Barnett, *Engage the Enemy More Closely*, 204–5, 257–58; and Simpson, "Force H and British Strategy," 65–67.

34. Churchill, *Their Finest Hour*, 237–39; Greene and Massignani, *The Naval War in the Mediterranean*, 61; Max Hastings, *Winston's War: Churchill, 1940–1945* (New York: Alfred A. Knopf, 2010), 66.

35. Henri Noguères, *Le Suicide de la Flotte Française à Toulon* (Paris: Robert Laffont, 1961).

Chapter 5: The Regia Marina

1. Marc Antonio Bragadin, *The Italian Navy in World War II* (Annapolis: USNI, 1957), 3–14; James J. Sadkovich, *The Italian Navy in World War II* (Westport, CT: Greenwood Press, 1994), 1–44; Peter C. Smith, *Critical Conflict: The Royal Navy's Mediterranean Campaign in 1940* (Barnsley, South Yorkshire: Pen and Sword, 2011), 26–33.

2. Jack Greene and Alessandro Massignani, *The Naval War in the Mediterranean, 1940–1942* (London: Chatham, 2002), 51; Alan J. Levine, *The War Against Rommel's Supply Lines, 1942–1943* (Westport, CT: Praeger, 1999), 4–6.

3. Correlli Barnett, *Engage the Enemy More Closely: The Royal Navy in the Second World War* (New York: W. W. Norton, 1991), 224–25; Smith, *Critical Conflict*, 29–31. The characterization of the conflict as a guerilla war is from Giorgio Giorgerini, *La Battaglia dei Convogli in Mediterraneo* (Milan: Murcia, 1977), quoted in Sadkovich, *The Italian Navy in World War II*, 45.

4. Sadkovich, *The Italian Navy in World War II*, 55–63; Friedrich Ruge, *Der Seekrieg* (Annapolis: USNI, 1957), 134. Ciano's diary entry is from July 13, 1940, in Galeazzo Ciano, *Diary, 1937–1943* (New York: Enigma Books, 2002), 370. The authority quoted here is Robert S. Ehlers Jr. in *The Mediterranean Air War: Airpower and Allied Victory in World War II* (Lawrence: University Press of Kansas, 2015), 17–18, 53.

5. Ehlers, *The Mediterranean Air War*, 17–18; Raymond De Belot, *The Struggle for the Mediterranean, 1939–1945* (Princeton: Princeton University Press, 1951), 42; Andrew B. Cunningham, *A Sailor's Odyssey* (New York: E. P. Dutton, 1951), 258–59, 262.

6. Bragadin, *The Italian Navy in World War II*, 28–29; Sadkovich, *The Italian Navy in World War II*, 58–59; Greene and Massignani, *The Naval War in the Mediterranean*, 74; Smith, *Critical Conflict*, 34–76.

7. Sadkovich, *The Italian Navy in World War II*, 55–58. The quotation is in a letter from Parker to the author Peter Smith in Apr. 1979, and is quoted by Smith in *Critical Conflict*, 67. Cunningham's official report and his "Narrative of Operations," dated Jan. 29, 1941, are in John Grehan and Martin Mace, eds., *The War at Sea in the Mediterranean, 1940–1944* (Barnsley, South Yorkshire: Pen and Sword, 2014), 1–12.

8. Greene and Massignani, *The Naval War in the Mediterranean*, 93–97.

9. Ciano, *Diary, 1937–1943* (entry of Sept. 9, 1940), 381.

10. Greene and Massignani, *The Naval War in the Mediterranean*, 95, 101–14.

11. Thomas P. Lowry and John W. G. Wellham, *The Attack on Taranto: Blueprint for Pearl Harbor* (Mechanicsburg, PA: Stackpole Books, 1995), Appendix B.

12. Cunningham to Secretary of the Admiralty, Jan. 16, 1941, in *The Fleet Air Arm in the Second World War* (Farnham, Surrey: Ashgate, 2012), 1:314–27.

13. Ibid., 1:318; Stephen Roskill, *The War at Sea* (London: Her Majesty's Stationery Office, 1954), 1:301. The Mount Etna comment is from pilot Charles Lamb, who is quoted in Richard R. Lawrence, *The Mammoth Book of Eyewitness Naval Battles* (New York: Carroll and Graf, 2003), 523–24.

14. Lowry and Wellham, *Attack on Taranto*, 73–82; report of Cunningham to Secretary of Admiralty, Jan. 16, 1941, in *Fleet Air Arm*, 1:319; Greene and Massignani, *The Naval War in the Mediterranean*, 106–7; Sadkovich, *The Italian Navy in World War II*, 90–95; Cunningham, *A Sailor's Odyssey*, 286; Ciano, *Diary, 1937–1943* (entry of Nov. 12, 1940), 395.

15. Lowry and Wellham, in *Attack on Taranto* (87–100), overstate the connection between Taranto and the subsequent Japanese attack on Pearl Harbor.

16. Cavagnari's dismissal is covered in Robert Mallett, *The Italian Navy and Fascist Expansionism, 1935–1940* (London: Frank Cass, 1998); Winston S. Churchill, *Their Finest Hour* (Boston: Houghton Mifflin, 1949), 544.

17. Smith, *Critical Conflict*, 259–61, 271–81.

18. Ibid., 280, 282–84.

19. Somerville's report, dated Dec. 18, 1940, is in Grehan and Mace, eds., *The War at Sea in the Mediterranean*, 27–46; Sadkovich, *The Italian Navy in World War II*, 96–97.

20. Smith, *Critical Conflict*, 307, 315–22.

21. De Belot, *The Struggle for the Mediterranean*, 87–88; Ruge, *Der Seekrieg*, 147–51; Cunningham, *A Sailor's Odyssey*, 298.

22. "Conference Between the C-in-C Navy and the Fuehrer," Sept. 14, 1940, in *Fuehrer Conferences on Naval Affairs, 1939–1945* (Annapolis: USNI, 1990), 137–38. See also Egbert Kieser, *Hitler on the Doorstep: Operation "Sea Lion": The German Plan to Invade Britain, 1940* (Annapolis: USNI, 1997), 254–57.

23. Ciano, *Diary* (Oct. 12, 1940), 300.

24. "Evaluation of the Mediterranean Situation," Nov. 14, 1940, in *Fuehrer Conferences*, 154–56.

25. "Report to the Fuehrer," Feb. 13, 1942, and "Report by the C-in-C, Navy to the Fuehrer," Mar. 12, 1942, both in *Fuehrer Conferences*, 261–65, 265–68.

26. Sadkovich, *The Italian Navy in World War II*, 120–24. Marc Antonio Bragadin notes in his book that "the writer can state personally that at least in some cases, and at least during the first year of the war, Mussolini directly influenced the decisions of Supermarina on the side of prudence." Bragadin, *The Italian Navy in World War II*, 83.

27. Roskill, *The War at Sea*, 2:52–53. See also Rowena Reed, "Central Mediterranean Sea Control and the North African Campaigns," *NWCR* 32 (July-Aug. 1984): 85, 88–89.

28. The memo is printed in S. W. C. Pack, *The Battle of Cape Matapan* (New York: Macmillan, 1961), 19. Iachino wrote later that German pressure was "the determining cause" of the sortie. Iachino, *Gaudo e Matapan*, 263–67, reprinted in *Dark Seas: The Battle of Cape Matapan*, Britannia Royal Naval College series, ed. G. H. Bennett, J. E. Harrold, and R. Porter (Plymouth: University of Plymouth Press, 2012), 141 n. 2. On Italy's fuel oil situation, see Greene and Massignani, *The Naval War in the Mediterranean*, 142–44.

29. De Belot, *The Struggle for the Mediterranean*, 100–102; Ronald Seth, *Two Fleets Surprised: The Story of the Battle of Cape Matapan, March, 1941* (London: Geoffrey Bles, 1960), 13–19; Pack, *Battle of Matapan*, 60–63.

30. Pack, *Battle of Cape Matapan*, 64.

31. Greene and Massignani, *The Naval War in the Mediterranean*, 141; J. Valerio Borghese, *Sea Devils: Italian Navy Commandos in World War II* (Annapolis: USNI, 1995), 27, 78–82 (originally published in 1950 as *Decima Flottiglia Mas*).

32. Cunningham, *A Sailor's Odyssey*, 312–13, 321.

33. The role of the Bletchley Park code breakers is in John Winton, *ULTRA at Sea: How Breaking the Nazi Code Affected Allied Naval Strategy During World War II* (New York: William Morrow, 1988), 14–16. Cunningham's report, dated Nov. 11, 1941, is printed in Grehan and Mace, eds., *The War at Sea in the Mediterranean*, 48. See also Greene and Massignani, *The Naval War in the Mediterranean*, 146–48; Seth, *Two Fleets Surprised*, 34–37; Cunningham, *A Sailor's Odyssey*, 325–26.

34. Greene and Massignani, *The Naval War in the Mediterranean*, 148–49; S. W. C. Pack, *Night Action off Cape Matapan* (Shepperton, Surrey: Ian Allan, 1972), 34–35.

35. Iachino makes much of this shortcoming in *Gaudo e Matapan*. See Pack, *Battle of Cape Matapan*, 65.

36. Seth, *Two Fleets Surprised*, 42–43; Cunningham, *A Sailor's Odyssey*, 327. The verbatim sighting reports are in Appendix D of Bennett, Harrold, and Porter, eds., *Dark Seas*, 110–111.

37. "Sighting Reports," Appendix D of Bennett, Harrold, and Porter, eds., *Dark Seas*, 111; Seth, *Two Fleets Surprised*, 62–66; Cunningham, *A Sailor's Odyssey*, 327.

38. Greene and Massignani, *The Naval War in the Mediterranean*, 151–52; "Sighting Reports," Appendix D of Bennett, Harrold, and Porter, eds., *Dark Seas*, 114.

39. Seth, *Two Fleets Surprised*, 68–69.

40. Vincent P. O'Hara, *Struggle for the Middle Sea: The Great Navies at War in the Mediterranean Sea, 1940–1945* (Annapolis: USNI, 2009), 90–91; Angelo Iachino, *Gaudo e Matapan*, in *Dark Seas*, 130; Seth, *Two Fleets Surprised*, 92, 100; Greene and Massignani, *The Naval War in the Mediterranean*, 153.

41. Seth, *Two Fleets Surprised*, 107; Pack, *Battle of Cape Matapan*, 116.

42. Seth, *Two Fleets Surprised*, 108; Pack, *Battle of Cape Matapan*, 117–20.

43. Cunningham, *A Sailor's Odyssey*, 332.

44. O'Hara, *Struggle for the Middle Sea*, 94; Cunningham, *A Sailor's Odyssey*, 332; Seth, *Two Fleets Surprised*, 117, 119–21.

45. From the narrative of Chief Engineer G. S. Parodi, included in Seth, *Two Fleets Surprised*, 145–46.

46. Cunningham's report, Nov. 11, 1941, in Grehan and Mace, *The War at Sea in the Mediterranean*, 51; Greene and Massignani, *The Naval War in the Mediterranean*, 158; Cunningham, *A Sailor's Odyssey*, 334.

47. Sadkovich, *The Italian Navy in World War II*, 130; Ehlers, *The Mediterranean Air War*, 80.

48. Cunningham, *A Sailor's Odyssey*, 373.

49. Ibid., 380–89; Ehlers, *The Mediterranean Air War*, 84.

50. Tedder is quoted by Ehlers in *The Mediterranean Air War*, 129.

Chapter 6: The War on Trade, I

1. Karl Doenitz, *Memoirs: Ten Years and Twenty Days* (Annapolis: USNI, 1959), 111–13, 125; Lars Hellwinkel, *Hitler's Gateway to the Atlantic: German Naval Bases in France, 1940–1945* (Annapolis: USNI, 2014), 12–25; Eberhard Rössler, *The U-Boat: The Evolution and Technical History of German Submarines* (London: Cassell, 1981), 126.

2. Doenitz, *Memoirs*, 104–5.

3. Correlli Barnett, *Engage the Enemy More Closely: The Royal Navy in the Second World War* (New York: W. W. Norton, 1991), 199–200; Doenitz, *Memoirs*, 137–41.

4. Clay Blair, *Hitler's U-Boat War: The Hunters, 1939–1942* (New York: Random House, 1996), 87–93, 149–62. Dönitz is quoted on 159.

5. Doenitz, *Memoirs*, 137–40.

6. Terry Hughes and John Costello, *The Battle of the Atlantic* (New York: Dial Press, 1977), 97.

7. Blair, *Hitler's U-Boat War: The Hunters*, 168–75; Kevin M. Moeller, "A Shaky Axis," *Proceedings*, June 2015, 30–35; Hughes and Costello, *The Battle of the Atlantic*, 102–3.

8. Arnold Hague, *The Allied Convoy System, 1939–1945* (Annapolis: USNI, 2000), 26–28. Hague includes a list of convoy designations as Appendix 1.

9. Antony Preston and Alan Raven, *Flower Class Corvettes* (Norwich: Bivouac Books, 1973); Chris Howard Bailey, *The Battle of the Atlantic: The Corvettes and Their Crews* (Annapolis: USNI, 1994), 6. The passages from Monsarrat are from his book *Three Corvettes* (London: Cassell, 1945), 22, 27; italics added.

10. Peter Kemp, *Decision at Sea: The Convoy Escorts* (New York: Elsevier-Dutton, 1978), 12; Hughes and Costello, *The Battle of the Atlantic*, 36–37.

11. Bernard Edwards, *Convoy Will Scatter: The Full Story of Jervis Bay and Convoy HX84* (Barnsley, Yorkshire: Pen and Sword, 2013), 15–17; Bruce Allen Watson, *Atlantic Convoys and Nazi Raiders: The Deadly Voyage of HMS Jervis Bay* (Westport, CT: Praeger, 2006), 46. Tales of service by men in the "Wavy Navy" can be found in J. Lennox Kerr and David James, eds., *Wavy Navy, by Some Who Served* (London: George G. Harrap, 1950).

12. Marc Milner, *North Atlantic Run: The Royal Canadian Navy and the Battle for the Convoys* (Annapolis: USNI, 1985), 26–27; W. A. B. Douglas, Roger Sarty, and Michael Whitby, *No Higher Purpose* (St. Catharines, ON: Vanwell, 2002), 181.

13. Winston Churchill, *Their Finest Hour*, vol. 2 of *The Second World War* (Boston: Houghton Mifflin, 1949), 406; WSC to FDR, July 31, 1940, Aug. 15, 1940, both in

Roosevelt and Churchill: Their Secret Wartime Correspondence, ed. Francis L. Loewenheim, Harold Langley, and Manfred Jones (New York: E. P. Dutton, 1975), 107–10; George VI to FDR, June 26, 1940, in John W. Wheeler-Bennett, *King George VI: His Life and Reign* (New York: St. Martin's Press, 1958), 511. See also Philip Goodhart, *Fifty Ships That Saved the World: The Foundation of the Anglo-American Alliance* (Garden City, NY: Doubleday, 1965).

14. WSC to FDR, Aug. 15, 1940, in *Roosevelt and Churchill*, 109.
15. Hague, *Allied Convoy System*, 28.
16. Ibid., 29; Stephen Roskill, *The War at Sea, 1939–1945* (London: Her Majesty's Stationery Office, 1954), 1:93.
17. Hague, *Allied Convoy System*, 45; Edwards, *Convoy Will Scatter*, 19.
18. Hague, *Allied Convoy System*, 25; Samuel McLean and Roger Sarty, "Gerald S. Graham's Manuscript Diary of His Voyage in HMS *Harvester*, 1942," *Northern Mariner*, April 2016, 177, 180.
19. Paul Lund and Harry Ludlam, *Night of the U-Boats* (London: W. Foulsham, 1973), 41–57.
20. Ibid., 32–40.
21. McLean and Sarty, "Gerald S. Graham's Manuscript Diary," 180.
22. Bernard Ireland, *Battle of the Atlantic* (Annapolis: Naval Institute Press, 2003), 54–55.
23. Lund and Ludlum, *Night of the U-Boats*, 79–86.
24. Ibid., 94.
25. The convoy survivor was Henry Revely, who wrote *The Convoy That Nearly Died: The Story of ONS 154* (London: William Kimber, 1979), 13. Kretschmer's war diary is quoted in Doenitz, *Memoirs*, 108. A slightly different translation appears in Blair, *Hitler's U-Boat War: The Hunters*, 198.
26. Lund and Ludlam, *Night of the U-Boats*, 93–151, 180; Blair, *Hitler's U-Boat War: The Hunters*, 199–200.
27. Lund and Ludlam, *Night of the U-Boats*, 174–75; Hughes and Costello, *Battle of the Atlantic*, 109–11.
28. Blair, *Hitler's U-Boat War: The Hunters*, 212–13; Hughes and Costello, *The Battle of the Atlantic*, 62.
29. Walter Karig, "Murmansk Run," *Proceedings*, Jan. 1946, 32.
30. Erich Raeder, *My Life* (Annapolis: USNI, 1960), 273, 345–46.
31. Theodor Krancke and H. J. Brennecke, *The Battleship Scheer* (London: William Kimber, 1956), 21–30.
32. Edwards, *Convoy Will Scatter*, 10–11, 15, 19; Watson, *Atlantic Convoys*, 76.
33. Watson, *Atlantic Convoys*, 87.
34. Krancke, *Battleship Scheer*, 40.
35. Edwards, *Convoy Will Scatter*, 43–45; Krancke, *Battleship Scheer*, 40; Watson, *Atlantic Convoys*, 89–95.
36. Edwards, *Convoy Will Scatter*, 76–84; Krancke, *Battleship Scheer*, 44–47.
37. Watson, *Atlantic Convoys*, 95.
38. Ibid., 101.
39. Edwards, *Convoy Will Scatter*, 61–65; Calum MacNeil, *San Demetrio* (Sydney: Angus and Robertson, 1957), 37, 81–82.

40. MacNeil, *San Demetrio*, 86, 88.
41. Ibid., 88.
42. Ibid., 94, 99–100. The story of the *San Demetrio* became a popular motion picture in 1943 under the title *San Demetrio London*, directed by Charles Freund.
43. Krancke, *Battleship* Scheer, 199.
44. Raeder, *My Life*, 249–50; Vincent P. O'Hara, *The German Fleet at War, 1939–1945* (Annapolis: USNI, 2004), 70–74; Fritz-Otto Busch, *The Drama of the* Scharnhorst (London: Robert Hale, 1956), 32–34.
45. August K. Muggenthaler, *German Raiders of World War II* (New York: Prentice-Hall, 1977); Bernard Edwards, *Beware Raiders! German Surface Raiders in the Second World War* (Annapolis: USNI, 2001); Friedrich Ruge, *Der Seekrieg* (Annapolis: USNI), 1957), 174–83; Olivier Pigoreau, *The Odyssey of the* Komet: *Raider of the Third Reich* (Paris: Histoire et Collections, 2016), 13.
46. Bernhard Rogge with Wolfgang Frank, *Under Ten Flags: The Story of the German Commerce Raider* Atlantis (London: Weidenfeld and Nicolson, 1955), 16–21; Joseph P. Slavick, *The Cruise of the German Raider* Atlantis (Annapolis: USNI, 2003), 27–45; Ulrich Mohr and A. V. Sellwood, *Ship 16: The Story of the Secret German Raider* Atlantis (New York: John Day, 1956).
47. Rogge, *Under Ten Flags*, 19, 23–25; Slavick, *The Cruise of the German Raider* Atlantis, 44–48.
48. Eiji Seki, *Mrs. Ferguson's Tea-set, Japan, and the Second World War: The Global Consequences Following Germany's Sinking of the SS* Automedon *in 1940* (Folkestone, Kent: Global Oriental, 2007), 6–17; Rogge, *Under Ten Flags*, 99–103; Slavick, *The Cruise of the German Raider* Atlantis, 109–111; Roskill, *The War at Sea*, 1:381. The member of the German boarding party was Ulrich Mohr, quoted in *Ship 16*, 153.
49. Wesley Olson, *Bitter Victory: The Death of HMAS* Sydney (Annapolis: USNI, 2000), 271–72; Michael Montgomery, *Who Sank the* Sydney? (New York: Hippocrene Books, 1981); G. Herman Gill, *Royal Australian Navy, 1939–1942* (Canberra: Australian War Memorial, 1957), 453–57. The German perspective is in Joachim von Gösseln, "The Sinking of the *Sydney*," *Proceedings*, March 1953, 251–55.
50. Blair, *Hitler's U-Boat War: The Hunters*, 251–53.
51. Ibid., 256–58.

Chapter 7: The Bismarck

1. Erich Raeder, *My Life* (Annapolis: USNI, 1960), 272–75.
2. Iain Ballantyne, *Killing the* Bismarck: *Destroying the Pride of Hitler's Fleet* (Barnsley, South Yorkshire: Pen and Sword, 2010), 21–24; David Bercuson and Holger H. Herwig, *The Destruction of the* Bismarck (Woodstock, NY: Overlook Press, 2001), 21–22.
3. Bercuson and Herwig, *Destruction of the* Bismarck, 29–30; Raeder, *My Life*, 351.
4. Raeder, *My Life*, 351–52.
5. Albert Vulliez and Jacques Mordal, *Battleship* Scharnhorst (Fair Lawn, NJ: Essential Books, 1958), 110–11. Raeder's diary entry from Mar. 6, 1941, is quoted in Bercuson and Herwig, *Destruction of the* Bismarck, 43.
6. Raeder, *My Life*, 351–53; Bercuson and Herwig, *Destruction of the* Bismarck, 50–59.
7. Bercuson and Herwig, *Destruction of the* Bismarck, 50–59.

8. Ibid.

9. Correlli Barnett, *Engage the Enemy More Closely: The Royal Navy in the Second World War* (New York: W. W. Norton, 1991), 50; Bercuson and Herwig, *Destruction of the Bismarck*, 84–89.

10. Bercuson and Herwig, *Destruction of the* Bismarck, 62–63; Barnett, *Engage the Enemy More Closely*, 283.

11. Russell Grenfell, *The Bismarck Episode* (New York: Macmillan, 1949), 22–25, 29–30.

12. Ibid., 33–35.

13. Bercuson and Herwig, *Destruction of the* Bismarck, 101–4.

14. Grenfell, *The Bismarck Episode*, 40–41, 46–47; Bercuson and Herwig, *Destruction of the* Bismarck, 129–30.

15. Bercuson and Herwig, *Destruction of the* Bismarck, 138–9; Grenfell, *The Bismarck Episode*, 47.

16. According to the almanac, sunrise at the latitude of the Denmark Strait on May 20 was 4:00 a.m. Parker's prayer is in Bernard Ash, *Someone Had Blundered: The Story of the Repulse and the Prince of Wales* (Garden City, NY: Doubleday, 1961), 75.

17. On the battle between *Bismarck* and *Hood*, see Bercuson and Herwig, *Destruction of the* Bismarck, 147–149, and Burkard Müllenheim-Rechberg, *Battleship Bismarck: A Survivor's Story* (Annapolis: USNI, 1980), 105–7. Russell Grenfell, in *The Bismarck Episode*, pulls no punches in criticizing Holland's dispositions and concludes that "British tactics appear to have been unskillfully conceived and directed" (62).

18. Müllenheim-Rechberg, *Battleship* Bismarck, 104–6, 109–10.

19. Bercuson and Herwig, *Destruction of the* Bismarck, 162–64; Müllenheim-Rechberg, *Battleship* Bismarck, 113; Grenfell, *The Bismarck Episode*, 32–34, 66; Stephen Roskill, *The War at Sea* (London: Her Majesty's Stationery Office, 1954), 1:401–6.

20. Müllenheim-Rechberg, *Battleship* Bismarck, 114–15. Some postwar sources assert that the heated discussion between Lütjens and Lindemann concerned Lindemann's desire to return to port, but most of the evidence, including that of Müllenheim-Rechberg, cited here, indicates that it was about Lindemann's eagerness to continue the fight.

21. Winston Churchill, *The Grand Alliance*, vol. 3 of *The Second World War* (Boston: Houghton-Mifflin, 1950), 307. Twenty years later, Tovey claimed that Pound had threatened to court-martial both Leach and Wake-Walker, and was dissuaded only when Tovey threatened to resign if he did so. Tovey to Roskill, Dec. 14, 1961, in Roskill Papers, quoted by Barnett, *Engage the Enemy More Closely*, 299. For his part, Churchill wrote after the war, "Admiral Wake-Walker decided not to renew the action.... In this he was indisputably right." Churchill, *The Grand Alliance*, 310.

22. Bercuson and Herwig, *Destruction of the* Bismarck, 147–49, 163, 168; Raeder, *My Life*, 358.

23. Barnett, *Engage the Enemy More Closely*, 247–48.

24. Grenfell, *The Bismarck Episode*, 87–95; Bercuson and Herwig, *Destruction of the* Bismarck, 186–93; Müllenheim-Rechberg, *Battleship* Bismarck, 133; Anthony Martienssen, *Hitler and His Admirals* (New York: E. P. Dutton, 1949), 111.

25. Müllenheim-Rechberg, *Battleship* Bismarck, 134–35, 138.

26. Bercuson and Herwig, *Destruction of the* Bismarck, 225–26, 230–31; Grenfell, *The Bismarck Episode*, 97–98.

27. Müllenheim-Rechberg, *Battleship* Bismarck, 147.

28. Grenfell, *The* Bismarck *Episode*, 101–4; Barnett, *Engage the Enemy More Closely*, 303–5.

29. Bercuson and Herwig, *Destruction of the* Bismarck, 237–39.

30. Ibid., 231, 236–41; Grenfell, *The* Bismarck *Episode*, 118–20, 132–33.

31. Bercuson and Herwig, *Destruction of the* Bismarck, 251–52, 256; Grenfell, *The* Bismarck *Episode*, 133–34.

32. Bercuson and Herwig, *Destruction of the* Bismarck, 257–59; Grenfell, *The* Bismarck *Episode*, 138–47.

33. Grenfell, *The* Bismarck *Episode*, 154.

34. Müllenheim-Rechberg, *Battleship* Bismarck, 168–69; Bercuson and Herwig, *Destruction of the* Bismarck, 259–66. Radio reports made by or to the *Bismarck* are in *Fuehrer Conferences on Naval Affairs, 1939–1945* (Annapolis: USNI, 1990), 209–13.

35. Grenfell, *The* Bismarck *Episode*, 160–61, 164–69.

36. Ibid., 177–79; Müllenheim-Rechberg, *Battleship* Bismarck, 204–5.

37. Grenfell, *The* Bismarck *Episode*, 184–87.

38. Müllenheim-Rechberg, *Battleship* Bismarck, 211–14.

39. Bercuson and Herwig, *Destruction of the* Bismarck, 297; Churchill, *The Grand Alliance*, 319.

40. Friedrich Ruge, *Der Seekrieg: The German Navy's Story* (Annapolis: USNI, 1957), 172; Raeder, *My Life*, 358.

41. Andrew Roberts, *The Storm of War: A New History of the Second World War* (New York: Harper, 2011), 160.

Chapter 8: The Rising Sun

1. Sadao Asada, *From Mahan to Pearl Harbor: The Imperial Japanese Navy and the United States* (Annapolis: USNI, 2006), 153–56, 164–66.

2. Stephen E. Pelz, *Race to Pearl Harbor: The Failure of the Second London Naval Conference and the Onset of World War II* (Cambridge, MA: Harvard University Press, 1974), 27–29; Sadao Asada, "The Japanese Navy and the United States," in *Pearl Harbor as History*, ed. Dorothy Borg and Shumpei Okamoto (New York: Columbia University Press, 1973), 229–31. The 69.75 percent figure comes from Table 2 in Asada, *From Mahan to Pearl Harbor*, 298.

3. Stephen Howarth, *The Fighting Ships of the Rising Sun* (New York: Atheneum, 1983), 170–72.

4. Craig Symonds, *The Battle of Midway* (New York: Oxford University Press, 2011), 27–29. I am grateful to Admiral Yoji Koda (Ret.) of the Japanese Maritime Self-Defense Force for his insight about the complicated politics of the Imperial Japanese Navy in the prewar period.

5. Howarth, *Fighting Ships of the Rising Sun*, 176–77; Asada, *From Mahan to Pearl Harbor*, 170–71.

6. Tsuneo Watanabe, ed., *Who Was Responsible? From Marco Polo Bridge to Pearl Harbor* (Tokyo: Yomiuri Shimbun, 2006), 21–22, 49; Howarth, *Fighting Ships of the Rising Sun*, 191.

7. Richard J. Smethurst, *A Social Basis for Prewar Japanese Militarism* (Berkeley: University of California Press, 1974), xvii; Howarth, *Fighting Ships of the Rising Sun*, 177.

8. Pelz, *Race to Pearl Harbor*, 15–17; Howarth, *Fighting Ships of the Rising Sun*, 190–91.

9. Hiroyuki Agawa, *The Reluctant Admiral: Yamamoto and the Imperial Navy* (Tokyo: Kodansha International, 1979), 70–76; Symonds, *Midway*, 23–27; Katō is quoted by Sadao Asada in "The Japanese Navy and the United States," 240.

10. Alfred Thayer Mahan, *The Influence of Sea Power upon History, 1660–1783* (Boston: Little, Brown, 1890). The first chapter summarizes Mahan's philosophy of battleship dominance. Sadao Asada discusses the impact of Mahan on Japanese strategic thinking in ch. 2 of *From Mahan to Pearl Harbor*, 26–46.

11. Mark R. Peattie, *Sunburst: The Rise of Japanese Naval Air Power, 1909–1941* (Annapolis: USNI, 2001), 83; Agawa, *Reluctant Admiral*, 93; Symonds, *Midway*, 30.

12. Agawa, *Reluctant Admiral*, 13.

13. Peattie, *Sunburst*, 80–81, 86–89; Asada, *From Mahan to Pearl Harbor*, 185; Symonds, *Midway*, 32–33.

14. Thomas Wildenberg, *All the Factors of Victory: Admiral Joseph Mason Reeves and the Origin of Carrier Airpower* (Washington, DC: Brassey's, 2003), 1–10; Craig C. Felker, *Testing American Sea Power: U.S. Navy Strategic Exercises, 1923–1940* (College Station: Texas A&M University Press, 2007), 121.

15. David C. Evans and Mark R. Peattie, *Kaigun: Strategy, Tactics, and Technology in the Imperial Japanese Navy, 1887–1941* (Annapolis: USNI, 1997), 250–63; Pelz, *Race to Pearl Harbor*, 30–32; Asada, "The Japanese Navy," 239.

16. Evans and Peattie, *Kaigun*, 238–39; Mark R. Peattie, "Japanese Naval Construction, 1919–41," in Phillips P. O'Brien, ed., *Technology and Naval Combat in the Twentieth Century and Beyond* (London: Frank Cass, 2001), 97.

17. Ibid., 266–70.

18. Asada, "The Japanese Navy," 239.

19. Howarth, *Fighting Ships of the Rising Sun*, 192–93, 198–203.

20. Agawa, *Reluctant Admiral*, 95–96; W. D. Puleston, *The Armed Forces of the Pacific* (New Haven: Yale University Press, 1941), 45.

21. Watanabe, *Who Was Responsible?*, 71. See also Howarth, *Fighting Ships of the Rising Sun*, 178; Asada, *From Mahan to Pearl Harbor*, 170–72; Smethurst, *A Social Basis of Prewar Japanese Militarism*, xiii–xiv.

22. Frank Dorn, *The Sino-Japanese War, 1937–41* (New York: Macmillan, 1974), 33–37.

23. Peattie, *Sunburst*, 91–92; Jon Parshall and Anthony Tully, *Shattered Sword: The Untold Story of the Battle of Midway* (Washington, DC: Potomac Books, 2005), 78.

24. Asada, *From Mahan to Pearl Harbor*, 238. The text of the Fundamental Principles is available in David J. Lu, *Japan: A Documentary History* (New York: M. E. Sharpe, 1997), 418–20.

25. Kitaro Matsumoto, *Design and Construction of the Yamato and Musashi* (Tokyo: Haga, 1961), 337–54; Akira Yoshimura, *Build the Musashi! The Birth and Death of the World's Greatest Battleship* (Tokyo: Kodansha International, 1991), 37.

26. Janusz Skulski, *The Battleship Yamato: Anatomy of a Ship* (Annapolis: USNI, 1988; Matsumoto, *Design and Construction of the Yamato and Musashi*; Yoshimura, *Build the Musashi!*, 46–47.

27. Agawa, *Reluctant Admiral*, 91.

28. The figure of 200,000 killed is from Dorn, *The Sino-Japanese War*, 92–95. Dorn accompanied the Japanese army during this campaign. Other sources cite a figure as low as 90,000 or as high as 300,000. Iris Chang, in *The Rape of Nanking: The Forgotten Holocaust of World War II* (New York: Penguin, 1997), asserts the higher number, though her claim provoked a backlash from right-wing elements in Japan, some of whom insisted that the so-called rape of Nanking never happened at all. For a discussion of this controversy see Masahiro Yamamoto, *Nanking: Anatomy of an Atrocity* (Westport, CT: Praeger, 2000). The most recent study is Peter Harmsen, *Nanjing, 1937: Battle for a Doomed City* (Havertown, PA: Casemate, 2015). On the reaction of Swanson and FDR to the *Panay* crisis, see Frank Freidel, *Franklin D. Roosevelt: A Rendezvous with Destiny* (Boston: Back Bay Books, 1990), 291.

29. The text of the Tripartite Agreement is in Lu, ed., *Japan: A Documentary History*, 424–25.

30. Fujiwara Akira, "The Role of the Japanese Army," in *Pearl Harbor as History*, ed. Dorothy Borg and Shumpei Okamoto (New York: Columbia University Press, 1973), 190–91, 194.

31. Asada, *Mahan to Pearl Harbor*, 237. One memo being circulated at the time read: "On the assumption that war with the United States is inevitable, we should make adequate preparation for war." See Watanabe, ed., *Who Was Responsible?*, 90.

32. Ibid., 239. See also William L. Langer and S. Everett Gleason, *The Undeclared War, 1940–1941* (New York: Harper and Brothers, 1953), 7.

33. Agawa, *Reluctant Admiral*, 219–22, 225.

Chapter 9: A Two-Ocean Navy

1. Robert F. Cross, *Sailor in the White House: The Seafaring Life of FDR* (Annapolis: USNI, 2003); Joseph E. Persico, *Roosevelt's Secret War: FDR and World War II* (New York: Random House, 2001), 161.

2. Frank Freidel, *Franklin D. Roosevelt: A Rendezvous with Destiny* (Boston: Little, Brown, 1990), 92–98.

3. Stephen E. Pelz, *Race to Pearl Harbor: The Failure of the Second London Naval Conference and the Onset of World War II* (Cambridge, MA: Harvard University Press, 1974), 77–81.

4. The definitive book on the war plans, and particularly Plan Orange, is Edward Miller, *War Plan Orange: The U.S. Strategy to Defeat Japan, 1897–1945* (Annapolis: USNI, 1991).

5. Major Ellis's 1921 article is available at www.biblio.org/hyperwar/USMC/ref/AdvBaseOps.

6. Skipper Steeley, *Pearl Harbor Countdown: Admiral James O. Richardson* (Gretna, LA: Pelican, 2008), 84; Craig C. Felker, *Testing American Sea Power: U.S. Navy Strategic Exercises, 1923–1940* (College Station: Texas A&M University Press, 2007), 57–59.

7. Freidel, *Franklin D. Roosevelt*, 291; *Time* magazine, March 28, 1938; Patrick Abbazia, *Mr. Roosevelt's Navy: The Private War of the U.S. Atlantic Fleet, 1939–1942* (Annapolis: USNI, 1975), 3–4.

8. FDR to WSC, Feb. 1, 1940, and WSC to FDR, Dec. 7, 1940, both in *Roosevelt and Churchill: Their Secret Wartime Correspondence*, ed. Francis L. Loewenheim, Harold Langley, and Manfred Jones (New York: Saturday Review/E. P. Dutton, 1975), 93, 122.

9. Abbazia, *Mr. Roosevelt's Navy*, 62–68; Thomas A. Bailey and Paul B. Ryan, *Hitler vs. Roosevelt: The Undeclared Naval War* (New York: Free Press, 1979), 32–33, 41, 70. Wheeler is quoted on 45.

10. Abbazia, *Mr. Roosevelt's Navy*, 71–74.

11. Ibid., 80. In making such decisions, FDR relied on power he essentially granted to himself. On May 21, 1940, he activated the Office of Emergency Management, which gave him the authority to manage the several branches of the military services. Freidel, *Franklin D. Roosevelt*, 341–42.

12. Pelz, *Race to Pearl Harbor*, 317–18; Mark R. Peattie, "Japanese Naval Construction, 1919–41," in *Technology and Naval Combat in the Twentieth Century and Beyond*, ed. Phillips P. O'Brien (London: Frank Cass, 2001), 101.

13. James R. Leutze, *Bargaining for Supremacy: Anglo-American Naval Collaboration, 1937–1941* (Chapel Hill: University of North Carolina Press, 1977), 117.

14. Stark to Knox, Nov. 12, 1940, quoted in Craig L. Symonds, *Neptune: The Allied Invasion of Europe and the D-Day Landings* (New York: Oxford University Press, 2014), 11.

15. Symonds, *Neptune*, 12–13.

16. United States–British Staff Conversations Report, March 27, 1941, printed as exhibit #49 (copy no. 98 of 125), U.S. Congress, *Pearl Harbor Attack Hearings* (Washington, DC: Government Printing Office, 1946), 15:1487–96. See also Symonds, *Neptune*, 13–17.

17. Robert W. Love Jr., "Ernest Joseph King," in *The Chiefs of Naval Operations*, ed. Robert W. Love Jr. (Annapolis: USNI, 1980), 139; Abbazia, *Mr. Roosevelt's Navy*, 136.

18. Abbazia, *Mr. Roosevelt's Navy*, 136; Ernest J. King and Walter Muir Whitehill, *Fleet Admiral King, a Naval Record* (New York: W. W. Norton, 1952), 313, 319.

19. Gordon Prange, with Donald M. Goldstein and Katherine V. Dillon, *At Dawn We Slept: The Untold Story of Pearl Harbor* (New York: McGraw-Hill, 1981), 39–40, 47; Steeley, *Pearl Harbor Countdown*, 165–82.

20. *Complete Presidential Press Conferences of Franklin D. Roosevelt* (New York: Da Capo Press, 1972), 17:285–86. See also H. W. Brands, *Traitor to His Class: The Privileged Life and Radical Presidency of Franklin D. Roosevelt* (New York: Anchor Books, 2009), 590.

21. Kimmel protested the removal of so many ships from his Pacific Fleet command. Stark explained to him that "the possible effect of this transfer as regards Japan is realized, but must be accepted if we are to take an effective part in the Atlantic." U.S. Congress, *Pearl Harbor Attack Hearings*, 15:2163. See also Harold Ickes, *The Secret Diary of Harold Ickes* (New York: Simon and Schuster, 1954), 3:523 (entry of May 25, 1941); Prange, *At Dawn We Slept*, 130–33.

22. Abbazia, *Mr. Roosevelt's Navy*, 159–65, 176.

23. Bailey and Ryan, *Hitler and Roosevelt*, 138–40.

24. FDR to Ickes, July 1, 1941, in Ickes, *Secret Diary*, 3:567.

25. Robert E. Sherwood, *Roosevelt and Hopkins: An Intimate History* (New York: Harper Collins, 1948), 242–44.

26. T. R. Fehrenbach, *F.D.R.'s Undeclared Naval War* (New York: David McKay, 1967), 254–55; Abbazia, *Mr. Roosevelt's Navy*, 223–24.

27. Abbazia, *Mr. Roosevelt's Navy*, 223–31.

28. *FDR's Fireside Chats* (Norman: University of Oklahoma Press, 1992), 189, 196; Abbazia, *Mr. Roosevelt's Navy*, 229.

29. *Fuehrer Conferences on Naval Affairs, 1939–1945* (Annapolis: USNI, 1990), 231–35.

30. Jon Meacham, *Franklin and Winston: An Intimate Portrait of an Epic Friendship* (New York: Random House, 2004), 105–6; Sherwood, *Roosevelt and Hopkins*, 276–78.

31. Abbazia, *Mr. Roosevelt's Navy*, 255–61.

32. Action Report, USS *Kearny*, October 20, 1941, USNA. Available at www.destroyers .org/bensonlivermore/USS%Kearny/Kearnyreport.html.

33. Abbazia, *Mr. Roosevelt's Navy*, 270–72.

34. Ibid., 276–79.

35. "Report by the C-in-C, Navy," Sept. 17 and Nov. 13, 1941, both in *Fuehrer Conferences on Naval Affairs*, 231–35, 235–39.

36. Abbazia, *Mr. Roosevelt's Navy*, 298–300.

37. Ickes, *Secret Diary*, 3:650 (entry of Nov. 23, 1941).

38. Memorandum of Conversation, July 24, 1941, *Documentary History of the Franklin D. Roosevelt Presidency* (Dayton, OH: University Publications of America/ LexisNexis, 2001), 9:265–73.

39. James C. Thomson Jr., "The Role of the Department of State," in *Pearl Harbor as History: Japanese American Relations, 1931–1941*, ed. Dorothy Borg and Shumpei Okamoto (New York: Columbia University Press, 1973), 101. The story of Acheson's role in derailing FDR's oil policy is in Jonathan Utley, *Going to War with Japan* (Knoxville: University of Tennessee Press, 1985), 95–101, 126–33, 151–56. The quotation is on 154. See also Jonathan W. Jordan, *American Warlords: How Roosevelt's High Command Led America to Victory in World War II* (New York: Random House, 2015), 97.

40. Prange, *At Dawn We Slept*, 3–8; Sadao Asada, *From Mahan to Pearl Harbor: The Imperial Japanese Navy and the United States* (Annapolis: USNI, 2006), 272–76.

41. Prange, *At Dawn We Slept*, 205; U.S. Congress, *Report on the Joint Committee on the Investigation of the Pearl Harbor Attack* (New York: Da Capo Press, 1972), 32–35. In his diary, Stimson insisted that Hull told him, "I have washed my hands of it. It is now in the hands of you and Knox—the Army and the Navy." Hull subsequently denied ever saying such a thing, though it may have reflected his attitude. See Barbara Wohlstetter, *Pearl Harbor: Warning and Decision* (Stanford: Stanford University Press, 1962), 234, 258.

42. Prange, *At Dawn We Slept*, 406; Wohlstetter, *Pearl Harbor*, 228–46, 259.

Chapter 10: Operation AI: The Attack on Pearl Harbor

1. Jisaburō Ozawa, "Outline Development of Tactics and Organization of the Japanese Carrier Air Force," in *Pacific War Papers: Japanese Documents of World War II*, ed.

Donald M. Goldstein and Katherine V. Dillon (Washington, DC: Potomac Books, 2004), 78–79; Mark R. Peattie, *Sunburst: The Rise of Japanese Naval Air Power, 1909–1941* (Annapolis: USNI, 2001), 149, 151.

2. Hiroyuki Agawa, *The Reluctant Admiral: Yamamoto and the Imperial Navy*, trans. John Bester (Tokyo: Kodansha International, 1979), 264; Gordon Prange interview of Genda (Sept. 5, 1966), Prange Papers, box 17, Hornbake Library, University of Maryland, College Park; Matome Ugaki, *Fading Victory: The Diary of Admiral Matome Ugaki, 1941–1945* (Annapolis: USNI, 1991), 13 (diary entry of Oct. 22, 1941).

3. Atsushi Oi, "The Japanese Navy in 1941," in *Pacific War Papers*, 16; Peattie, *Sunburst*, 76.

4. John Campbell, *Naval Weapons of World War II* (London: Conway Maritime, 1985); Craig L. Symonds, *The Battle of Midway* (New York: Oxford University Press, 2011), 38–39.

5. Gordon Prange, with Donald M. Goldstein and Katherine V. Dillon, *At Dawn We Slept: The Untold Story of Pearl Harbor* (New York: McGraw-Hill, 1981), 382.

6. Jonathan Parshall and Anthony Tully, *Shattered Sword: The Untold Story of the Battle of Midway* (Washington, DC: Potomac Books, 2005), 130; John Campbell, *Naval Weapons of World War II*; Peattie, *Sunburst*, 95.

7. Prange, *At Dawn We Slept*, 390; Walter Lord, *Day of Infamy* (New York: Holt, Rinehart, and Winston, 1957), 19.

8. Prange, *At Dawn We Slept*, 393–94.

9. Ibid., 22; Lord, *Day of Infamy*, 17–19, 26.

10. Husband E. Kimmel, *Admiral Kimmel's Story* (Chicago: Henry Regnery, 1955), 25; Prange, *At Dawn We Slept*, 409.

11. Prange, *At Dawn We Slept*, 440.

12. Robert E. Sherwood, *Roosevelt and Hopkins: An Intimate History* (New York: Enigma Books, 2008, orig. 1948), 334.

13. Prange, *At Dawn We Slept*, 490–92.

14. Lord, *Day of Infamy*, 27–28, 38, 43.

15. Prange, *At Dawn We Slept*, 501.

16. Ibid., 397, 504.

17. Paul H. Backus, "Why Them and Not Me?" in Paul Stilwell, *Air Raid: Pearl Harbor!* (Annapolis: USNI, 1981), 163.

18. Prange, *At Dawn We Slept*, 268–70.

19. Ibid., 515.

20. Lord, *Day of Infamy*, 219–20; Prange, *At Dawn We Slept*, 515; Andrieu D'Albas, *Death of a Navy: Japanese Naval Action in World War II* (New York: Devin-Adair, 1957), 35–37.

21. Sherwood, *Roosevelt and Hopkins*, 347; Winston S. Churchill, *The Grand Alliance* (Boston: Houghton Mifflin, 1950), 603–4; Lynne Olson, *Citizens of London* (New York: Random House, 2010), 143–44.

22. Frank Freidel, *Franklin D. Roosevelt: Rendezvous with Destiny* (Boston: Little, Brown, 1990), 406.

23. Brian P. Farrell, *The Defense and Fall of Singapore, 1940–1942* (Stroud, Gloucestershire: Tempus, 2005), 139–42; D'Albas, *Death of a Navy*, 38–43.

24. Farrell, *The Defense and Fall of Singapore*, 141; Geoffrey Bennett, *The Loss of the* Prince of Wales *and* Repulse (Annapolis: USNI, 1973), 131.

25. Farrell, *The Defense and Fall of Singapore*, 142–43.

26. Russell Grenfell, *Main Fleet to Singapore* (New York: Macmillan, 1952), 92–93; Arthur Nicholson, *Hostage to Fortune: Winston Churchill and the Loss of the* Prince of Wales *and* Repulse (Stroud, Gloucestershire: Sutton, 2005), 33–48.

27. Christopher M. Bell, *Churchill and Sea Power* (New York: Oxford University Press, 2013), 239–47.

28. Bennett, *The Loss of the* Prince of Wales *and* Repulse, 31–34.

29. Ibid., 43; David Thomas, *The Battle of the Java Sea* (New York: Stein and Day, 1968), 67–71.

30. Bernard Ash, *Someone Had Blundered: The Story of the "Repulse" and the "Prince of Wales"* (Garden City, NY: Doubleday, 1962), 210, 217.

31. Thomas, *The Battle of the Java Sea*, 88.

32. Farrell, *The Defense and Fall of Singapore*, 143.

33. Grenfell, *Main Fleet to Singapore*, 118.

34. Thomas Wildenberg, *Billy Mitchell's War with the Navy: The Interwar Rivalry over Air Power* (Annapolis: USNI, 2014), 70–94.

35. Thomas, *The Battle of the Java Sea*, 92–95. The lieutenant was Geoffrey Brooke, who is quoted in Richard R. Lawrence, *The Mammoth Book of Eyewitness Naval Battles* (New York: Carroll and Graf, 2003), 462.

36. Ash, *Someone Had Blundered*, 246; Bennett, *The Loss of the* Prince of Wales *and* Repulse, 52.

37. Churchill, *The Grand Alliance*, 620.

Chapter 11: Rampage

1. The British historian is David A. Thomas, *The Battle of the Java Sea* (New York: Stein and Day, 1968), 147. See also Ian W. Toll, *Pacific Crucible: War at Sea in the Pacific, 1941–1942* (New York: W. W. Norton, 2012), 237–40.

2. Stark to Kimmel, Dec. 15, 1941, and Stark to Pye, Dec. 22, 1941, both in Nimitz Papers, box 1:49–50, 72, NHHC; John B. Lundstrom, *Black Shoe Carrier Admiral: Frank Jack Fletcher at Coral Sea, Midway, and Guadalcanal* (Annapolis: USNI, 2006), 23, 31.

3. Thomas, *Battle of the Java Sea*, 117–19; Lodwick H. Alford, *Playing for Time: War on an Asiatic Fleet Destroyer* (Bennington, VT: Merriam Press, 2006), 95; Jeffrey R. Cox, *Rising Sun, Falling Skies: The Disastrous Java Sea Campaign of World War II* (Oxford: Osprey, 2014), 155–61.

4. Craig L. Symonds, *The Battle of Midway* (New York: Oxford University Press, 2011), 65–75; Toll, *Pacific Crucible*, 203–27.

5. Thomas, *Battle of the Java Sea*, 120; Toll, *Pacific Crucible*, 233–34.

6. Cox, *Rising Sun, Falling Skies*, 129, 137.

7. The Anglo-American conversations about a unified command in the Pacific are in Craig L. Symonds, *Neptune: The Allied Invasion of Europe and the D-Day Landings* (New York: Oxford University Press, 2014), 38–41. See also Stephen W. Roskill, *The War at Sea, 1939–1945* (London: Her Majesty's Stationery Office, 1956), 2:6.

8. Alford, *Playing for Time*, 116, 118; Cox, *Rising Sun, Falling Skies*, 178; G. Herman Gill, *Royal Australian Navy, 1939–1942* (Canberra: Australia War Memorial, 1957), 515, 553.

9. Toll, *Pacific Crucible*, 252–54; Thomas, *Battle of the Java Sea*, 105–7; James D. Hornfischer, *Ship of Ghosts* (New York: Bantam Books, 2006), 7–13.

10. Hubert V. Quispel, *The Job and the Tools* (Rotterdam: WYT & Sons, 1960), 37–38; Thomas, *Battle of the Java Sea*, 157; Cox, *Rising Sun, Falling Skies*, 257; Gill, *Royal Australian Navy*, 556–57.

11. Churchill is quoted in Andrew Roberts, *The Storm of War: A New History of the Second World War* (New York: Harper, 2011), 205.

12. Andrieu D'Albas, *Death of a Navy: Japanese Naval Action in World War II* (New York: Devin-Adair, 1957), 65–66; Paul S. Dull, *A Battle History of the Imperial Japanese Navy, 1941–1945* (Annapolis: USNI, 1978), 54; Alford, *Playing for Time*, 69–79; Cox, *Rising Sun, Falling Skies*, 216–22.

13. Roskill, *The War at Sea*, 2:9.

14. Thomas, *Battle of the Java Sea*, 128–30; Cox, *Rising Sun, Falling Skies*, 209–11.

15. F. C. van Oosten, *The Battle of the Java Sea* (Annapolis: USNI, 1976), 27.

16. Thomas, *Battle of the Java Sea*, 140–47; Dull, *Battle History of the Imperial Japanese Navy*, 55–60; Cox, *Rising Sun, Falling Skies*, 232–40.

17. Dwight R. Messimer, *Pawns of War: The Loss of the USS* Langley *and the USS* Pecos (Annapolis: USNI, 1983), 51–79; Cox, *Rising Sun, Falling Skies*, 265–79.

18. Ibid., 281–82; Hara, Tameichi, with Fred Saito and Roger Pineau, *Japanese Destroyer Captain: Pearl Harbor, Guadalcanal, Midway—the Great Naval Battles as Seen Through Japanese Eyes* (Annapolis: USNI, 1967), 64–65.

19. Roskill, *The War at Sea*, 2:13–14; Thomas, *Battle of the Java Sea*, 159; Cox, *Rising Sun, Falling Skies*, 253.

20. Thomas, *Battle of the Java Sea*, 160.

21. Ibid., 153, 170; Cox, *Rising Sun, Falling Skies*, 263–64.

22. Cox, *Rising Sun, Falling Skies*, 283–85.

23. Ibid., 259–60.

24. Hara, *Japanese Destroyer Captain*, 72; Thomas, *Battle of the Java Sea*, 178–80.

25. Thomas, *Battle of the Java Sea*, 187–89; Cox, *Rising Sun, Falling Skies*, 296.

26. Thomas, *Battle of the Java Sea*; 191, 196, 198–99, 201–2; Cox, *Rising Sun, Falling Skies*, 297–300; P. C. Boer, *The Loss of Java* (Singapore: NUS Press, 2011), 194–95, 197.

27. Gill, *Royal Australian Navy*, 614–15.

28. Hara, *Japanese Destroyer Captain*, 74–75; Thomas, *Battle of the Java Sea*, 209–13; Cox, *Rising Sun, Falling Skies*, 312–16; Hornfischer, *Ship of Ghosts*, 92.

29. Hornfischer, *Ship of Ghosts*, 47–48; Gill, *Royal Australian Navy*, 615–16.

30. Hornfischer, *Ship of Ghosts*, 100–102.

31. Roskill, *The War at Sea*, 2:16; Hornfischer, *Ship of Ghosts*, 108.

32. Quoted in Hornfischer, *Ship of Ghosts*, 116.

33. Hornfischer, *Ship of Ghosts*, 122–25; Gill, *Royal Australian Navy*, 621.

34. Hornfischer, *Ship of Ghosts*, 128; W. G. Winslow, *The Fleet the Gods Forgot: The U.S. Asiatic Fleet in World War II* (Annapolis: USNI, 1982), 195. Waller, who had also played an important role in the Battle of Cape Matapan (see Chapter 5), was also

honored after the war for "gallantry and resolution," and HMAS *Waller*, an Australian submarine commissioned in 1999, is named for him.

35. Roskill, *The War at Sea*, 2:18; Toll, *Pacific Crucible*, 260; Thomas, *Battle of the Java Sea*, 148–49.

36. Gordon Prange interview of Watanabe Yasuji (Sept. 25, 1964), Prange Papers, box 17, UMD; H. P. Willmott, *The Barrier and the Javelin: Japanese and Allied Pacific Strategies, February to June 1942* (Annapolis: USNI, 1983), 43–44; Matome Ugaki, *Fading Victory: The Diary of Admiral Matome Ugaki* (entry of Jan. 5, 1942), trans. Masataka Chiyada, ed. Donald M. Goldstein and Katherine V. Dillon (Annapolis: USNI, 1991), 68.

37. Quoted in Willmott, *The Barrier and the Javelin*, 79; Prange interview of Watanabe (Feb. 3–4, 1966), Prange Papers, box 17, UMD.

38. Donald MacIntyre, *Fighting Admiral: The Life of Admiral of the Fleet Sir James Somerville* (London: Evans Brothers, 1961), 186–88.

39. Dull, *A Battle History of the Imperial Japanese Navy*, 108–9; Roskill, *The War at Sea*, 2:26–27.

40. Mark R. Peattie, *Sunburst: The Rise of Japanese Naval Air Power, 1909–1941* (Annapolis: USNI, 2001), 67–70; Dull, *A Battle History of the Imperial Japanese Navy*, 109–10.

41. Symonds, *The Battle of Midway*, 95–6.

42. Somerville is quoted in MacIntyre, *Fighting Admiral*, 179. For a detailed analysis of British naval strategy in this campaign see Angus Britts, *Neglected Skies: The Demise of British Naval Power in the Far East, 1922–42* (Annapolis: USNI, 2017).

Chapter 12: The War on Trade, II

1. Stephen W. Roskill, *The War at Sea, 1939–1945* (London: Her Majesty's Stationery Office, 1956), 2:28.

2. Ed Offley, *The Burning Shore: How Hitler's U-Boats Brought World War II to America* (New York: Basic Books, 2014), 57–58; Michael Gannon, *Operation Drumbeat* (New York: Harper and Row, 1990), 97–99.

3. Clay Blair, *Silent Victory* (Philadelphia: J. B. Lippincott, 1975), 106–7. See also Joel Holwitt, *"Execute Against Japan": The U.S. Decision to Conduct Unrestricted Submarine Warfare* (College Station: Texas A&M University Press, 2013), esp. 141–49.

4. Karl Doenitz, *Memoirs: Ten Years and Twenty Days* (Annapolis: USNI, 1959), 154, 161; Robert S. Ehlers Jr., *The Mediterranean Air War: Airpower and Allied Victory in World War II* (Lawrence: University of Kansas Press, 2015), 97–98.

5. J. Valerio Borghese, *Sea Devils: Italian Navy Commandos in WWII* (Annapolis: USNI, 1995), 131–60.

6. Vian's report, dated Mar. 31, 1942, is printed in John Grehan and Martin Mace, eds., *The War at Sea in the Mediterranean, 1940–1944* (Barnsley, South Yorkshire: Pen and Sword, 2014), 180–94. Vian discusses the battle in his memoir, *Action This Day* (London: Frederick Muller, 1960), 89–91. See also S. W. C. Pack, *The Battle of Sirte* (Annapolis: USNI, 1975), 54–82. Fans of the literature of C. S. Forester may be aware that his novel *The Ship* is based on Vian's defense of convoy MW-10.

7. Winston S. Churchill, *The Hinge of Fate*, vol. 4 of *The Second World War* (Boston: Houghton Mifflin, 1950), 273.

8. Corelli Barrett, *Engage the Enemy More Closely* (New York: W. W. Norton, 1991), 272–76; Doenitz, *Memoirs*, 152–54, 161.

9. "Report of Admiral Commanding Submarines," May 14, 1942, and Apr. 21, 1943, in *Fuehrer Conferences on Naval Affairs, 1939–1945* (Annapolis: USNI, 1990), 280–83, 316. The Navy Training Manual is quoted by Samuel Eliot Morison in *The Battle of the Atlantic, September 1939–May 1943*, vol. 1 of *History of United States Naval Operations in World War II* (Boston: Little, Brown, 1947), 127–28.

10. See Appendix R in Roskill, *The War at Sea*, 1:615–18; Doenitz, *Memoirs*, 178, 197.

11. W. J. R. Gardner, *Decoding History: The Battle of the Atlantic and Ultra* (Annapolis: USNI, 1999), 130–33.

12. Jak P. Mallmann Showell, *German Naval Codebreakers* (Annapolis: USNI, 2003), 39, 88–93; Offley, *The Burning Shore*, 83; David Kahn, *The Codebreakers: The Story of Secret Writing* (New York: Macmillan, 1967), 465–66.

13. David Kahn, *Seizing the Enigma: The Race to Break the German U-Boat Codes, 1939–1943* (Boston: Houghton Mifflin, 1991), 195–96.

14. Ibid., 53, 62–66, 68–71.

15. John Winton, *Ultra at Sea* (New York: William Morrow, 1988), 22–24; Kahn, *Seizing the Enigma*, 1–14, 161–68; David Syrett, *The Defeat of the German U-Boats: The Battle of the Atlantic* (Columbia: University of South Carolina Press, 1994), 20; Terry Hughes and John Costello, *The Battle of the Atlantic* (New York: Dial, 1977), 153–54.

16. F. W. Winterbotham, *The Ultra Secret* (New York: Harper and Row, 1974), 24–26; Offley, *The Burning Shore*, 87–88; Kahn, *Seizing the Enigma*, 184.

17. Syrett, *The Defeat of the German U-Boats*, 19–20.

18. Gannon, *Operation Drumbeat*, 152; Gardner, *Decoding History*, 165; Hughes and Costello, *Battle of the Atlantic*, 165–66.

19. Jürgen Rohwer, "The Operational Uses of 'Ultra' in the Battle of the Atlantic," in *Intelligence and International Relations*, ed. Christopher Andrew and Jeremy Noakes (Exeter: University of Exeter, 1987), 283–84. See also David Syrett's introduction to his edited volume *The Battle of the Atlantic and Signals Intelligence* (Aldershot: Navy Records Society, 1998), xvi.

20. Hughes and Costello, *Battle of the Atlantic*, 180–83.

21. Gardner, *Decoding History*, 137. For the numbers, see Appendix O in Roskill, *The War at Sea*, 2:485.

22. Peter Cremer, *U-Boat Commander: A Periscope View of the Battle of the Atlantic* (Annapolis: USNI, 1982), 53–61; Clay Blair, *Hitler's U-Boat War: The Hunters, 1939–1942* (New York: Random House, 1996), 453–54.

23. Gannon, *Operation Drumbeat*, 206–9.

24. Ernest J. King and Walter Muir Whitehall, *Fleet Admiral King: A Naval Record* (New York: W. W. Norton, 1952), 349–55; Walter R. Borneman, *The Admirals: Nimitz, Halsey, Leahy, and King* (New York: Little, Brown, 2012), 212.

25. Historians divide on the issue of King's reluctance to establish coastal convoys. Michael Gannon (*Operation Drumbeat*, 1990) holds King almost criminally negli-

gent, while Clay Blair (*Hitler's U-Boat War: The Hunters*, 1996) ardently defends him and insists that most of the criticism of King originated with the British, who thought King paid too much attention to the Pacific Theater. The newest analysis of the U-boat war against the American eastern seaboard is Ken Brown, *U-Boat Assault on America: The Eastern Seaboard Campaign, 1942* (Annapolis: USNI, 2017).

26. Blair, *Hitler's U-Boat War: The Hunters*, 439; Gannon, *Operation Drumbeat*, 466–67. The four ships sunk by Hardegen on January 18/19 were *Brazos*, *City of Atlanta*, *Ciltvaira*, and *Malay*.

27. Blair, *Hitler's U-Boat War: The Hunters*, 475; Doenitz, *Memoirs*, 203; Cremer, *U-Boat Commander*, 69; Michael L. Hadley, *U-Boats Against Canada: German Submarines in Canadian Waters* (Kingston, ON: McGill-Queen's University Press, 1985), 52–74.

28. Blair, *Hitler's U-Boat War: The Hunters*, 481.

29. Homer H. Hickam, *Torpedo Junction: U-Boat War off America's East Coast, 1942* (Annapolis: USNI, 1989), 114–29.

30. See the table of ship losses in Blair, *Hitler's U-Boat War: The Hunters*, 695.

31. Hickam, *Torpedo Junction*, 108–13.

32. Blair, *Hitler's U-Boat War: The Hunters*, Appendix 4, 727–30; Cremer, *U-Boat Commander*, 78. Hemingway called upon his experience in the Hooligan Navy for a novel that was published posthumously as *Islands in the Stream* (New York: Charles Scribner's Sons, 1970).

33. Hickam, *Torpedo Junction*, 149–57, 179, 188–95.

34. Ibid., 165–67.

35. On the *milch* cows, see Blair, *Hitler's U-Boat War: The Hunters*, 534n (Cremer's exploits are detailed on 545–46). A detailed tabulation of U-boat sinkings is in Jürgen Rohwer, *Axis Submarine Successes, 1939–1945* (Annapolis: USNI, 1983).

36. Carl Boyd and Akihiko Yoshida, *The Japanese Submarine Force and World War II* (Annapolis: USNI, 1995), 65–67; *New York Times*, Jan. 21, Jan. 24, and Feb. 24, 1942, all stories page 1.

37. Hickam, *Torpedo Junction*, 230.

38. "Report by Chief of Staff," Jan. 22 and Jan. 29, 1942, in *Fuehrer Conferences on Naval Affairs*, 259–60; Cremer, *U-Boat Commander*, 53; Roskill, *The War at Sea*, 2:100–101, 116; Doenitz, *Memoirs*, 206.

39. Jan Drent, "The Trans-Pacific Lend-Lease Shuttle to the Russian Far East, 1941–46," *The Northern Mariner*, January 2017, 33–34, 45–46. Most of the ships in these convoys were Liberty Ships that had been built in American yards and then transferred to Russian service.

40. "Memorandum Concerning the Report of the C-in-C, Navy," Jan. 12, 1942, *Fuehrer Conferences on Naval Affairs*, 256–57.

41. Roskill, *The War at Sea*, 2:150; Erich Raeder, *My Life* (Annapolis: USNI, 1960), 360–61.

42. Roskill, *The War at Sea*, 2:156–57.

43. London *Times*, Feb. 14, 1942; Raeder, *My Life*, 361.

44. Richard M. Leighton and Robert W. Coakley, *Global Logistics and Strategy, 1940–1943* (Washington, DC: Office of the Chief of Military History, 1955), 555; Michael G. Walling, *Forgotten Sacrifice: The Arctic Convoys of World War II* (Oxford: Osprey,

2012), 9–36; Richard Woodman, *The Arctic Convoys, 1941–1945* (London: John Murray, 1994), 24–32; Walter Karig, "Murmansk Run," *Proceedings*, Jan. 1946, 27.

45. Roskill, *The War at Sea*, 118–20.

46. Richard M. Leighton and Robert W. Coakley, *Global Logistics and Strategy, 1940–1943* (Washington, DC: Office of the Chief of Military History, 1955), 557.

47. Winton, *Ultra at Sea*, 53–65; Roskill, *The War at Sea*, 2:120–23, 127; Max Hastings, *Winston's War: Churchill, 1940–1945* (New York: Knopf, 2010), 207.

48. Broome picked up the convoy at sea from an eclectic group of escorts that included one Polish and one Free French destroyer. See Woodman, *The Arctic Convoys*, 195–200, and Jack Broome, *Convoy Is to Scatter* (London: William Kimber, 1972), 103.

49. Walling, *Forgotten Sacrifice*, 153–54; Roskill, *The War at Sea*, 2:137; Winton, *Ultra at Sea*, 60–65.

50. Woodman, *The Arctic Convoys*, 213; Walling, *Forgotten Sacrifice*, 156–57; Broome, *Convoy Is to Scatter*, 160. The German attackers also put a torpedo into the Russian tanker *Azerbaijan*, though it remained afloat.

51. Woodman, *Arctic Convoys*, 211–12; Winton, *Ultra at Sea*, 63–65, 68; Broome, *Convoy Is to Scatter*, 178.

52. Broome, *Convoy Is to Scatter*, 182–83.

53. Winton, *Ultra at Sea*, 68–69; Broome, *Convoy Is to Scatter*, 182; Woodman, *The Arctic Convoys*, 255; Walling, *Forgotten Sacrifice*, 170, 173–79. The quotation is from the memoir of William A. Carter, *Why Me, Lord?* (Millsboro, DE: William A. Carter, 2007), 174. The Allies did send a shipment of supplies on the American cruiser USS *Tuscaloosa* in August, but a warship could carry only a small cargo, and it was more a token of goodwill than a genuine supply mission.

54. On Pantelleria, see James J. Sadkovich, *The Italian Navy in World War II* (Westport, CT: Greenwood Press, 1994), 256–65. The precise numbers for shipping losses remain elusive. The most detailed and authoritative source is Jürgen Rohwer's *Axis Submarine Successes, 1939–1945* (Annapolis: USNI, 1983), which is a chronological list of all ships sunk by U-boats during the war. Rohwer, however, does not keep a running total and lumps losses in the North Sea, in the North Atlantic, and off the eastern coast of the United States into a single category, so differentiating requires a hand count. Clay Blair itemizes the ships lost in Operation Paukenschlag in Appendix 4 of *Hitler's U-Boat War: The Hunters* (727–32). More user friendly are the tables in Morison, *The Battle of the Atlantic* (412) and Roskill, *The War at Sea* (2:485), though their estimates lack the advantage of more recent research. Roskill also attributes most losses to U-boats, while Morison attributes some of those losses to mines and aircraft.

Chapter 13: Stemming the Tide

1. Theodore Taylor, *The Magnificent Mitscher* (Annapolis: USNI, 1954), 112.

2. Duane Schultz, *The Doolittle Raid* (New York: St. Martin's Press, 1988), 5–10.

3. James A. Doolittle oral history (Aug. 3, 1987), and Henry Miller oral history (May 23, 1973), both USNI.

4. E. B. Potter, *Nimitz* (Annapolis: USNI, 1976), 16–30; William F. Halsey and J. Bryan III, *Admiral Halsey's Story* (New York: McGraw-Hill, 1947), 101.

5. Henry Miller oral history (May 23, 1973), 1:37, and James Doolittle oral history (Aug. 3, 1987), 27, both USNI; Mitscher to Nimitz, April 28, 1942, Action Reports: Part I, CINCPAC, reel 2.

6. Lowell Thomas and Edward Jablonsky, *Doolittle: A Biography* (Garden City, NY: Doubleday, 1976), 178–79; James H. Doolittle and Carroll V. Glines, *I Could Never Be So Lucky Again: An Autobiography by General James H. "Jimmy" Doolittle* (New York: Bantam Books, 1991), 4; Halsey and Bryan, *Admiral Halsey's Story*, 101.

7. John B. Lundstrom, *The First Team: Pacific Naval Air Combat from Pearl Harbor to Midway* (Annapolis: USNI, 1984), 148; Thomas and Jablonsky, *Doolittle: A Biography*, 181; Doolittle oral history (Aug. 3, 1987), USNI, 19.

8. Quentin Reynolds, *The Amazing Mr. Doolittle* (New York: Appleton-Century-Crofts, 1953), 209–12; Doolittle and Glines, *I Could Never Be So Lucky Again*, 10–11.

9. Carroll V. Glines, *Doolittle's Tokyo Raiders* (New York: D. Van Nostrand, 1964), 337; Gordon Prange interview of Watanabe (Sept. 25, 1964), Prange Papers, box 17, UMD.

10. Elliot Carlson, *Joe Rochefort's War* (Annapolis: USNI, 2011), esp. 172–84, 211; John Winton, *Ultra in the Pacific: How Breaking Japanese Codes and Ciphers Affected Naval Operations Against Japan* (London: Leo Cooper, 1993), 6; Rochefort oral history (Aug. 14, 1969), USNI, 99, 104.

11. Craig L. Symonds, *The Battle of Midway* (New York: Oxford University Press, 2011), 145; Wilfrid Jasper Holmes, *Double-Edged Secrets: U.S. Naval Intelligence Operations in the Pacific During World War II* (Annapolis: USNI, 1979), 65; Carlson, *Joe Rochefort's War*, 268–70.

12. Frederick C. Sherman, *Combat Command: The American Aircraft Carriers in the Pacific War* (New York: E. P. Dutton, 1950), 92; Frederick D. Parker, *A Priceless Advantage: U.S. Navy Communications Intelligence and the Battle of Coral Sea, Midway, and the Aleutians* (Washington, DC: Center for Cryptologic History, National Security Agency, 1993), 25; "Running Summary, April 18, 1942," and "Estimate of the Situation, April 22, 1942," both in Nimitz Papers, box 1, 501–5, 516, NHHC; Edwin Layton, with Roger Pineau and John Costello, *"And I was There"... Pearl Harbor and Midway—Breaking the Secrets* (New York: William Morrow, 1985), 367–68; John Prados, *Combined Fleet Decoded: The Secret History of American Intelligence and the Japanese Navy in World War II* (New York: Random House, 1995), 300; Rochefort oral history (Sept. 21, 1969), USNI, 174–75.

13. John Lundstrom, *The First South Pacific Campaign: Pacific Fleet Strategy, December 1941–June 1942* (Annapolis: USNI, 1976), 98; H. P. Willmott, *The Barrier and the Javelin: Japanese and Allied Pacific Strategies, February to June 1942* (Annapolis: USNI, 1983), 171–200.

14. Nimitz to King, June 17, 1942, Action Reports: Part I, CINCPAC, reel 2, 3; Samuel Eliot Morison, *Coral Sea, Midway and Submarine Actions, May 1942–August 1942* (Boston: Little, Brown, 1975), 25–26; John Lundstrom, *Black Shoe Carrier Admiral: Frank Jack Fletcher at Coral Sea, Midway, and Guadalcanal* (Annapolis: USNI, 2006) 146, 149; Willmott, *The Barrier and the Javelin*, 217–18.

15. Richard W. Bates, *The Battle of the Coral Sea, May 1 to May 11 Inclusive, 1942: Strategical and Tactical Analysis* (Washington, DC: Bureau of Naval Personnel, 1947),

7–12; Lundstrom, *First South Pacific Campaign*, 103–4, as well as his article "A Failure of Radio Intelligence: An Episode in the Battle of the Coral Sea," *Cryptologia* 7, no. 2 (1983): 108–110, 115; and Willmott, *The Barrier and the Javelin*, 234–35.

16. Lundstrom, *The First Team*, 193; Lundstrom, *Black Shoe Carrier Admiral*, 165; Stuart D. Ludlum, *They Turned the War Around at Coral Sea and Midway* (Bennington, VT: Merriam, 2000), 77.

17. Ludlam, *They Turned the War Around*, 74–79; Lundstrom, *The First Team*, 199, 205.

18. Lundstrom, *The First Team*, 191; Paul S. Dull, *A Battle History of the Imperial Japanese Navy, 1941–1945* (Annapolis: USNI, 1978), 124.

19. Pederson to Buckmaster, May 16, 1942, Action Reports: Part I, CINCPAC, reel 2; Ludlum, *They Turned the War Around*, 86; Morison, *Coral Sea and Midway*, 49–51. The pilot quoted is Noel Gayler in his oral history (Feb. 15, 2002), NHF, 6.

20. Buckmaster to Nimitz, May 25, 1942, Action Reports: Part I: CINCPAC, reel 2, 10; Sherman, *Combat Command*, 109–111, 114; Gustave Sembritzky oral history (OH00601), NMPW.

21. King initially kept the loss of the *Lexington* a secret, reporting to the press only that she had been damaged.

22. Buckmaster to Nimitz, May 25, 1942, Action Reports: Part I: CINCPAC, reel 2, 7, 40.

23. Matome Ugaki, *The Diary of Admiral Matome Ugaki*, ed. Donald Goldstein and Katherine Dillon (Annapolis: USNI, 1991), 125 (diary entry of May 10, 1942).

24. *New York Times*, May 9, 1942, 1.

25. Holmes, *Double-Edged Secrets*, 90; Rochefort oral history (Oct. 5, 1969), 211, and Dyer oral history (Sept. 14, 1983), 241, both USNI.

26. *Traffic Intelligence Summaries, Combat Intelligence Unit, Fourteenth Naval District (16 July 1941–30 June 1942)*, Special Collections, Nimitz Library, USNA, 3:326.

27. "Estimate of the Situation," May 26, 1942, Nimitz Papers, box 1:516, 520, NHHC.

28. Marc Mitscher, who commanded the *Hornet*, was an aviator, but he was under the strategic direction of Raymond Spruance. See Thomas B. Buell, *The Quiet Warrior: A Biography of Admiral Raymond A. Spruance* (Boston: Little, Brown, 1974), and Lundstrom, *Black Shoe Carrier Admiral*.

29. Donald Goldstein and Katherine Dillon, eds., *The Pearl Harbor Papers: Inside the Japanese Plans* (Washington, DC: Brassey's, 1993), 348.

30. Jonathan P. Parshall and Anthony P. Tully, *Shattered Sword: The Untold Story of the Battle of Midway* (Washington, DC: Potomac Books, 2005), 63–66.

31. Symonds, *Battle of Midway*, 102–6, 212–13; Parshall and Tully, *Shattered Sword*, 48–51; Gordon W. Prange with Donald Goldstein and Katherine Dillon, *Miracle at Midway* (New York: McGraw-Hill, 1982), 162–64, 170; Willmott, *The Barrier and the Javelin*, 81–82.

32. Symonds, *Battle of Midway*, 231–32; Prange, *Miracle at Midway*, 206; Parshall and Tully, *Shattered Sword*, 149.

33. Symonds, *Battle of Midway*, 236–38; Parshall and Tully, *Shattered Sword*, 153; Ryūnosuke Kusuka interview with Gordon Prange (1966), Prange Papers, box 17, UMD.

34. "CINC First Air Fleet Detailed Battle Report," Feb. 1, 1943, *ONI Review*, May 1947; Kusaka interview with Prange, Prange Papers, box 17, UMD; Parshall and Tully, *Shattered Sword*, 132, 159, 161–66; Symonds, *Battle of Midway*, 238–44.

35. Symonds, *Battle of Midway*, 244; Parshall and Tully, *Shattered Sword*, 165–66.

36. Symonds, *Battle of Midway*, 274–75.

37. Ibid., 260–61, 267–73.

38. "Memorandum for the Commander in Chief," June 7, 1942, Action Reports: Part I, CINCPAC, reel 2; George Gay, *Sole Survivor: The Battle of Midway and its Effects on His Life* (Naples, FL: Naples Ad/Graphics, 1979), 119–21.

39. Symonds, *Battle of Midway*, 287, 301–2; Parshall and Tully, *Shattered Sword*, 233–35.

40. Symonds, *Battle of Midway*, 52–54.

41. For a fuller discussion of the "flight to nowhere," see Symonds, *Battle of Midway*, 245–65, plus Appendix F, 389–91.

42. John S. Thach oral history (Nov, 6, 1970), 252, USNI; Richard Best interview (Aug. 11, 1995), 17, NMPW; Norman (Dusty) Kleiss oral history (Sept. 3, 2010), BOMRT; Parshall and Tully, *Shattered Sword*, 250. Jon Parshall, who has conducted the most thorough analysis of this attack, concludes that including the small 100-pound bombs, a total of twelve American bombs hit the *Kaga*. See BOMRT, Aug. 25, 2010.

43. Best to Walter Lord, Jan. 27, 1966, Lord Collection, box 18, NHHC; Richard Best interview (Aug. 11, 1995), 42, NMPW.

44. Max Leslie to Smith, Dec. 15, 1964, Prange Papers, box 17, UMD; Parshall and Tully, *Shattered Sword*, 264.

45. Symonds, *Battle of Midway*, 321–26; John S. Thach Oral History (Nov. 6, 1970), USNI Oral History Collection, 1:268.

46. Symonds, *Battle of Midway*, 347–50.

47. Gallaher to Walter Lord, Feb. 26, 1967, Walter Lord Collection, box 18, NHHC; Parshall and Tully, *Shattered Sword*, 326–29.

Chapter 14: Two Beleaguered Islands

1. The Soviet Union also had a naval presence in the Black Sea that consisted of one battleship, one heavy cruiser, and five light cruisers. C. W. Koburger Jr., *Naval Warfare in the Baltic, 1939–1945* (Westport, CT: Praeger, 1994), 27–33; V. I. Achlasov and N. B. Pavlovich, *Soviet Naval Operations in the Great Patriotic War, 1941–1945* (Annapolis: USNI, 1981), 8, 25; I. S. Isakov, *The Red Fleet in the Second World War* (London: Hutchinson, 1947), 26–27; Friedrich Ruge, *The Soviets as Naval Opponents, 1941–1945* (Annapolis: USNI, 1979), 16, 20–21.

2. Alan J. Levine, *The War Against Rommel's Supply Lines, 1942–1943* (Westport, CT: Praeger, 1999), 27–28; Peter C. Smith, *Pedestal: The Convoy That Saved Malta* (London: William Kimber, 1970), 17–20.

3. Richard B. Frank, *Guadalcanal: The Definitive Account of the Landmark Battle* (New York: Penguin, 1990), 25–28.

4. Bruce Gamble, *Fortress Rabaul: The Battle for the Southwest Pacific, January 1942—April 1943* (Minneapolis: Zenith Press, 2010), 210–11; James D. Hornfischer, *Neptune's Inferno: The U.S. Navy at Guadalcanal* (New York: Bantam Books, 2011), 4; Ian Toll, *The Conquering Tide: War in the Pacific Islands, 1942–1944* (New York: W. W. Norton, 2015), xxiv–xxxi; Frank, *Guadalcanal*, 31; Patrick Lindsay, *The Coast Watchers: The Men Behind Enemy Lines Who Saved the Pacific* (North Sydney, Australia: William Heinemann, 2010), 197.

5. Ronald H. Spector, *Eagle Against the Sun: The American War with Japan* (New York: Free Press, 1985), 184–87; Ernest J. King and Walter Muir Whitehill, *Fleet Admiral King: A Naval Record* (New York: W. W. Norton, 1952), 387.

6. Frank, *Guadalcanal*, 32–36.

7. Richard M. Leighton and Robert W. Coakley, *Global Logistics and Strategy, 1940–1943* (Washington, DC: Office of the Chief of Military History, 1955), 202; Samuel Eliot Morison, *The Struggle for Guadalcanal, August 1942–February 1943*, vol. 5 of *A History of United States Naval Operations in World War II* (Boston: Little, Brown, 1949), 15.

8. Hornfischer, *Neptune's Inferno*, 32–35; George C. Dyer, *The Amphibians Came to Conquer: The Story of Admiral Richmond Kelly Turner* (Washington, DC: Naval Historical Center, 1969), 1:258–67. The contemporary was Admiral Harry Hill, who is quoted in James D. Hornfischer, *The Fleet at Flood Tide: America at Total War in the Pacific, 1944–1945* (New York: Bantam Books, 2016), 25.

9. King to Fletcher, March 30, 1942, Nimitz Papers, series 1, box 1, and Nimitz to King, May 29, 1942, King Papers, series 1, box 2, both NHHC. See also John B. Lundstrom, *Black Shoe Carrier Admiral: Frank Jack Fletcher at Coral Sea, Midway, and Guadalcanal* (Annapolis: USNI, 2006), 107.

10. Hornfischer, *Neptune's Inferno*, 32–35.

11. Frank, *Guadalcanal*, 64–65; Lindsay, *The Coast Watchers*, 197. Tsukahara is quoted by Bruce Gamble in *Fortress Rabaul*, 217.

12. The witness was Joe James Custer, who wrote *Through the Perilous Night: The Astoria's Last Battle* (New York: Macmillan, 1944), 120.

13. Lundstrom, *Black Shoe Carrier Admiral*, 366; Ian W. Toll, *The Conquering Tide: War in the Pacific Islands, 1942–1944* (New York: W. W. Norton, 2015), 31–33.

14. Lundstrom, *Black Shoe Carrier Admiral*, 358–60; Gamble, *Fortress Rabaul*, 218.

15. Turner to Ghormley, Aug. 7, 1942 (9:30 p.m.), Action Reports, Part I, CINCPAC, reel 1. This message is also printed in Lundstrom, *Black Shoe Carrier Admiral*, 370.

16. Lundstrom, *Black Shoe Carrier Admiral*, 368, 386.

17. John J. Domagalski, *Lost at Guadalcanal: The Final Battles of the* Astoria *and* Chicago *as Described by Survivors and in Official Reports* (Jefferson, NC: McFarland, 2010), 71; Dyer, *The Amphibians Came to Conquer*, 358–59.

18. The critic is Richard W. Bates, in *The Battle of Savo Island, August 9th, 1942: Strategical and Tactical Analysis* (Newport, RI: Naval War College, 1950), 55–61; Domagalski, *Lost at Guadalcanal*, 80.

19. Toshikazu Ohmae, "The Battle of Savo Island," *Proceedings*, Dec. 1957, 1270.

20. Ibid., 1271.

21. Ibid.; Hornfischer, *Neptune's Inferno*, 58; Morison, *The Struggle for Guadalcanal*, 19. Turner is quoted in Dyer, *The Amphibians Came to Conquer*, 1:372.

22. Ohmae, "The Battle of Savo Island," 1273; Domagalski, *Lost at Guadalcanal*, 84.

23. Morison, *The Struggle for Guadalcanal*, 37; Hornfischer, *Neptune's Inferno*, 59–60.

24. Ohmae, "The Battle of Savo Island," 1275; U.S. Office of Naval Intelligence, *The Battles of Savo Island and the Eastern Solomons* (Washington, DC: Naval Historical Center, 1994, orig. 1943), 10; Domagalski, *Lost at Guadalcanal*, 92.

25. Ohmae, "The Battle of Savo Island," 1273; Morison, *The Struggle for Guadalcanal*, 44–46; John Costello, *The Pacific War* (New York: HarperCollins, 1981), 325–27.

26. Ohmae, "The Battle of Savo Island," 1275; Hornfischer, *Neptune's Inferno*, 63, 75–87; Frank, *Guadalcanal*, 105, 111–13; Domagalski, *Lost at Guadalcanal*, 144; Custer, *Through the Perilous Night*, 161–62; Office of Naval Intelligence, *Battles of Savo Island and Eastern Solomons*, 21, 24, 40–43.

27. Mikawa's statement is included as postscript to Ohmae, "Battle of Savo Island," 1276. See also Morison, *The Struggle for Guadalcanal*, 53.

28. Fletcher to Ghormley, Aug. 9, 1942 (3:15 a.m.), and COMSOPAC (Ghormley) to CINCPAC (Nimitz), Aug. 9, 1942 (8:30 a.m.), both in Action Reports, NARA, reel 1. See also Lundstrom, *Black Shoe Carrier Admiral*, 384–87.

29. *New York Times*, Aug. 18, 1942, 1.

30. Morison, *Struggle for Guadalcanal*, 61–64; Lundstrom, *Black Shoe Carrier Admiral*, 399–405; King to Stark, Sept. 14, 1943, in Hornfischer, *The Fleet at Flood Tide*, 28. In defending Fletcher, Lundstrom finds fault with Turner not only for the confusion during the battle but also for the unprofessional finger-pointing afterward.

31. Lewis Richie, *The Epic of Malta* (London: Odhams, 1943), 5; Ernle Bradford, *Siege: Malta, 1940–1943* (New York: William Morrow, 1986), 240–41. The quoted survivor was Jack Belden, who authored *Still Time to Die* (New York: Harper and Brothers, 1943), 186.

32. Erich Raeder, *My Life* (Annapolis: USNI, 1960), 364; Gerhard Weinberg, *A World at Arms: A Global History of World War II* (Cambridge: Cambridge University Press, 1994), 229.

33. Levine, *The War Against Rommel's Supply Lines*, 20–24; Michael Pearson, *The Ohio and Malta: The Legendary Tanker That Refused to Die* (Barnsley, South Yorkshire: Leo Cooper, 2004), 12–13. The visiting American admiral was H. Kent Hewitt, quoted here from his *Memoirs* (Newport, RI: Naval War College Press, 2004), 192.

34. Robert S. Ehlers Jr., *The Mediterranean Air War: Airpower and Allied Victory in World War II* (Lawrence: University of Kansas Press, 2015), 173–74; Smith, *Pedestal*, 32–37.

35. Charles A. Jellison, *Besieged: The World War II Ordeal of Malta, 1940–1942* (Hanover, NH: University Press of New England, 1984), 167, 218–25; Richard Woodman, *Malta Convoys, 1940–1943* (London: John Murray, 2000), 369–72, 377; Bradford, *Siege*, 247–48; James J. Sadkovich, *The Italian Navy in World War II* (Westport, CT: Greenwood Press, 1994), 256–64. See the report of Henry Harwood to the Admiralty, June 2, 1942, in John Grehan and Martin Mace, eds., *The War at Sea in the Mediterranean, 1940–1944* (Barnsley, South Yorkshire: Pen and Sword, 2014), 175–80. Significantly, Harwood warned the Admiralty, "Before another Malta convoy is run, air superiority in the island must be assured." Jackson is quoted in Smith, *Pedestal*, 40, and Parks in Jeremy Harwood, *World War II at Sea* (Minneapolis: Zenith, 2015), 124.

36. Peter Shankland and Anthony Hunter, *Malta Convoy* (New York: Ives Washburn, 1961), 70–72; Sam Moses, *At All Costs* (New York: Random House, 2006), 100, 107; Pearson, *The Ohio and Malta*, 33.

37. Smith, *Pedestal*, 43; Dennis A. Castillo, *The Santa Marija Convoy* (Lanham, MD: Lexington Books, 2012), 198.

38. Woodman, *Malta Convoys*, 392–94; Moses, *At All Costs*, 132–36; Smith, *Pedestal*, 82–90. The witness is quoted on 83–84. Rosenbaum was recalled to Berlin and awarded the Knight's Cross.

39. Castillo, *The Santa Marija Convoy*, 199; Sadkovich, *The Italian Navy*, 289; Moses, *At All Costs*, 142. The witness who described the AA fire was Anthony Krimmins, a radio broadcaster on board the escort flagship *Nigeria*, who is quoted in Smith, *Pedestal*, 95–96.

40. The witness who thought *Indomitable* resembled a sardine can was telegraphist Charles McCoombe, quoted in Smith, *Pedestal*, 134; Moses, *At All Costs*, 144.

41. Syfret's Report to the Admiralty, Aug. 25, 1942, in Grehan and Mace, eds., *Air War in the Mediterranean*, 153–61; Smith, Pedestal, 91–92, 121–22; Moses, *At All Costs*, 131.

42. Shankland and Hunter, *Malta Convoy*, 150–53; Smith, *Pedestal*, 144–51; Pearson, *The* Ohio *and Malta*, 72–73.

43. Pearson, *The* Ohio *and Malta*, 70; Smith, *Pedestal*, 155–60.

44. Bradford, *Siege, Malta*, 263–66; Shankland, *Malta Convoy*, 167–72.

45. Shankland and Hunter, *Malta Convoy*, 173–82; Woodman, *Malta Convoys*, 419–20; Smith, *Pedestal*, 193–96. The German admiral was Eberhard Weichold, who is quoted in Smith, *Pedestal*, 199.

46. Shankland and Hunter, *Malta Convoy*, 197–203.

47. Woodman, *Malta Convoys*, 382; Shankland and Hunter, *Malta Convoy*, 209–14; Smith, *Pedestal*, 227–30.

48. Shankland and Hunter, *Malta Convoy*, 241; Syfret's Report to the Admiralty, Aug. 25, 1942, in Grehan and Mace, eds., *Air War in the Mediterranean*, 158.

49. Syfret's Report to the Admiralty, Aug. 25, 1942, in John Grehan and Martin Mace, eds., *War at Sea in the Mediterranean, 1940–1944* (South Yorkshire, England: Pen and Sword Maritime, 2014), 153–61.

50. Levine, *The War Against Rommel's Supply Lines*, 27–28; I. S. O. Playfair, *The Mediterranean and Middle East*, vol. 4 of *History of the Second World War* (London: Her Majesty's Stationery Office, 1966), 1–4.

Chapter 15: A Two-Ocean War

1. Craig L. Symonds, *Neptune: The Allied Invasion of Europe and the D-Day Landings* (New York: Oxford University Press, 2014), 146–48; Frederic Lane, *Ships for Victory: A History of Shipbuilding Under the U.S. Maritime Commission in World War II* (Baltimore: Johns Hopkins University Press, 1951), 3–6.

2. J. R. M. Butler, *Grand Strategy II*, vol. 3 of *History of the Second World War* (London: Her Majesty's Stationery Office, 1964), esp. Appendix III, 675–81; Forrest Pogue, *George C. Marshall, Ordeal and Hope, 1939–1942* (New York: Viking Press, 1966); Symonds, *Neptune*, 51–54.

3. Churchill outlined his strategic views in a memorandum written aboard *Duke of York*, Dec. 16–20, 1941, that can be found in *FRUS*, Special Conferences Series, 1:30. See also Symonds, *Neptune*, 29–42.

4. Bernard Fergusson, *The Watery Maze: The Story of Combined Operations* (New York: Holt, Rinehart and Winston, 1961), 175–81; Robin Neillands, *The Dieppe Raid: The Story of the Disastrous 1942 Expedition* (Bloomington: Indiana University Press, 2005).

5. Maurice Matloff and Edwin M. Snell, *Strategic Planning for Coalition Warfare* (Washington, DC: Department of the Army, 1953), 278; Samuel Eliot Morison,

Operations in North African Waters (New York: Little, Brown, 1947), 15; Symonds, *Neptune*, 67–70. FDR's memo, dated July 16, 1942, is in Robert E. Sherwood, *Roosevelt and Hopkins: An Intimate History* (New York: Harper Collins, 1948), 471.

6. Andrieu d'Albas, *Death of a Navy: Japanese Naval Action in World War II* (New York: Devin-Adair, 1957), 172; Richard B. Frank, *Guadalcanal: The Definitive Account of the Landmark Battle* (New York: Penguin, 1990), 139–40; Gerhard Weinberg, *A World in Arms: A Global History of World War II* (Cambridge: Cambridge University Press, 1994), 347.

7. Richard Camp, "Flying in the Eye of the Guadalcanal Storm," *Naval History*, August 2017, 14–19. The Marine staff officer was Otto K. Williams in his oral history (OH00821), NMPW, 28.

8. The staff officer is quoted in John F. Wukovits, *Tin Can Titans* (Boston: Da Capo, 2017), 76. The American carrier raid on Lae and Salamaua on March 10 had sunk three large transports and damaged another. Craig L. Symonds, *The Battle of Midway* (New York: Oxford University Press, 2011), 86–87; Samuel E. Morison, *The Struggle for Guadalcanal, August 1942–February 1943* (Boston: Little Brown, 1949), 81.

9. Frank, *Guadalcanal*, 151–56.

10. Morison, *Struggle for Guadalcanal*, 82; D'Albas, *Death of a Navy*, 172–73. While Fletcher was ever sensitive to the fueling needs of his command (some said too much so), this particular refueling protocol was Ghormley's idea. On August 22 he wrote Fletcher: "Important [that] fueling be conducted soonest possible and if practicable one carrier task force at a time retiring for that purpose." COMSOPAC to CTF 61, Aug. 22, 1942, Chester Nimitz Papers [Graybook], NHHC, 1:808. See the Order of Battle in Frank, *Guadalcanal*, 167–74.

11. Morison, *Struggle for Guadalcanal*, 87–88; John B. Lundstrom, *Black Shoe Carrier Admiral: Frank Jack Fletcher at Coral Sea, Midway, and Guadalcanal* (Annapolis: USNI, 2006), 435–41.

12. Tameichi Hara, *Japanese Destroyer Captain* (Annapolis: USNI, 1967), 100.

13. James D. Hornfischer, *Neptune's Inferno: The U.S. Navy at Guadalcanal* (New York: Bantam Books, 2012), 114–15; Morison, *Struggle for Guadalcanal*, 97–99; Lundstrom, *Black Shoe Carrier Admiral*, 438–42, 445–46, 461; Frank, *Guadalcanal*, 176–84. The quotation is from Arthur Brown oral history, NMPW, 5.

14. COMSOPAC to CTF 17, Aug. 24, 1942 (1102), Nimitz Papers, box 1 (809), NHHC. Slonim is quoted in Lundstrom, *Black Shoe Carrier Admiral*, 451.

15. Hornfischer, *Neptune's Inferno*, 115–16; Raizo Tanaka, "The Struggle for Guadalcanal," in *The Japanese Navy in World War II*, ed. David C. Evans (Annapolis: USNI, 1969, 1986), 168–69; Morison, *Struggle for Guadalcanal*, 104–5; D'Albas, *Death of a Navy*, 176–77.

16. Lundstrom, *Black Shoe Carrier Admiral*, 460–64.

17. John Costello, *The Pacific War* (New York: HarperCollins, 1981), 344.

18. In 1949, Samuel Eliot Morison attributed the attack on *Wasp* to the I-19, but credited the I-15 with the hits on both *North Carolina* and *O'Brien*. Most historians followed Morison's lead on this. More than thirty years later, in an article in the *Naval Institute Proceedings*, Captain Ben Blee offered evidence that all three ships were hit by a single spread from the I-19, which is the view now embraced by virtually all naval scholars.

See Morison, *Struggle for Guadalcanal*, 130–38, and Ben Blee, "Whodunnit?" *Proceedings*, June 1982, 42–47. I thank Richard B. Frank for his help in unraveling this piece of naval historiography. For the convoy load, see Costello, *The Pacific War*, 347.

19. Clark, *Calculated Risk* (New York: Harper and Brothers, 1950), 45–46.

20. Symonds, *Neptune*, 72–73.

21. I. S. O. Playfair, *The Mediterranean and Middle East*, vol. 4: *The Germans Come to the Help of Their Ally* (London: Her Majesty's Stationery Office, 1966), 4:113; Vincent P. O'Hara, *Torch: North Africa and the Allied Path to Victory* (Annapolis: USNI, 2015), 77; Symonds, *Neptune*, 83–84.

22. Symonds, *Neptune*, 76–78; O'Hara, *Torch*, 20–29. The quotation is from Playfair, *The Mediterranean and Middle East*, 4:127.

23. The American task organization tables are in Samuel Eliot Morison, *Operations in North African Waters, October 1942–June 1943* (Annapolis: USNI, 2010, orig. 1947), 36–40. The British order of battle is in Playfair, *The Mediterranean and the Middle East*, 4:139.

24. George E. Mowry, *Landing Craft and the War Production Board, April 1942 to May 1944*, Historical Reports on War Administration, Special Study No. 11 (Washington, DC: War Production Board, 1944), 1–4; O'Hara, *Torch*, 27–29; Jerry E. Strahan, *Andrew Jackson Higgins and the Boats That Won World War II* (Baton Rouge: LSU Press, 1994), 57–58, 64; Morison, *Operations in North African Waters*, 29.

25. Morison, *Operations in North African Waters*, 137.

26. Morison, *Struggle for Guadalcanal*, 147–48; Costello, *The Pacific War*, 349–50.

27. Louis Brown, *A Radar History of World War II* (Bristol: Institute of Physics, 1999), 370; Charles Cook, *The Battle of Cape Esperance: Encounter at Guadalcanal* (Annapolis: USNI, 1968), 16–18; Frank, *Guadalcanal*, 294.

28. Hornfischer, *Neptune's Inferno*, 169–70; Morison, *Struggle for Guadalcanal*, 151–52, 156; Cook, *Battle of Cape Esperance*, 39–42; Frank, *Guadalcanal*, 300–301.

29. Hornfischer, *Neptune's Inferno*, 171–73; Morison, *Struggle for Guadalcanal*, 157–58; Frank, *Guadalcanal*, 301.

30. Cook, *Battle of Cape Esperance*, 70; Morison, *Struggle for Guadalcanal*, 159–60.

31. Hornfischer, *Neptune's Inferno*, 175; Morison, *Struggle for Guadalcanal*, 160. Costello (*The Pacific War*, 351) renders Gotō's imprecation as "Stupid bastards."

32. Cook, *Battle of Cape Esperance*, 77–78.

33. Morison, *Struggle for Guadalcanal*, 163–66; Frank, *Guadalcanal*, 303–4.

34. Morison, *Struggle for Guadalcanal*, 171; Costello, *The Pacific War*, 352.

35. Thomas Alexander Hughes, *Admiral Bill Halsey: A Naval Life* (Cambridge, MA: Harvard University Press, 2016), 94, 175–76; Ian W. Toll, *The Conquering Tide: War in the Pacific Islands, 1942–1944* (New York: W. W. Norton, 2015), 145–46.

36. Hughes, *Admiral Bill Halsey*, 94; Hornfischer, *Neptune's Inferno*, 216–17; Morison, *Struggle for Guadalcanal*, 182–83, 201.

37. Morison, *Struggle for Guadalcanal*, 199. The Japanese order of battle is on 206–7; a simplified version is in Hornfischer, *Neptune's Inferno*, 226.

38. Frank, *Guadalcanal*, 352–54; Hornfischer, *Neptune's Inferno*, 226; Morison, *Struggle for Guadalcanal*, 204.

39. Hornfischer, *Neptune's Inferno*, 226–27; Morison, *Struggle for Guadalcanal*, 209–10.

40. Hornfischer, *Neptune's Inferno*, 223–29; Morison, *Struggle for Guadalcanal*, 212, 219–21; Toll, *The Conquering Tide*, 150–53.

41. Morison, *Struggle for Guadalcanal*, 213. The American pilots claimed six bomb hits, though the Japanese reported only three. Hornfischer, *Neptune's Inferno*, 228–30.

42. Hornfischer, *Neptune's Inferno*, 230–32; Morison, *Struggle for Guadalcanal*, 215–19; Toll, *The Conquering Tide*, 151–52.

43. Costello, *The Pacific War*, 364–66.

44. Ibid., 364; Hughes, *Admiral Bill Halsey*, 195–96; Hornfischer, *Neptune's Inferno*, 235–36; Toll, *The Conquering Tide*, 154.

Chapter 16: The Tipping Point

1. I. S. O. Playfair, *The Mediterranean and Middle East*, vol. 4: *The Germans Come to the Help of Their Ally* (London: Her Majesty's Stationery Office, 1966), 4:15–17, 27–30.

2. Alan J. Levine, *The War Against Rommel's Supply Lines* (Westport, CT: Praeger, 1999), 33–34; Winston Churchill, *The Hinge of Fate* (Boston: Houghton Mifflin, 1950), 588–89; James J. Sadkovich, *The Italian Navy in World War II* (Westport, CT: Greenwood Press, 1994), 278–83, 302–6; Playfair, *The Mediterranean and Middle East*, 4:25, 101n.

3. Richard M. Leighton and Robert W. Coakley, *Global Logistics and Strategy, 1940–1943* (Washington, DC: Office of the Chief of Military History, 1955), 204; Stephen Roskill, *The War at Sea, 1939–1945* (London: Her Majesty's Stationery Office, 1956), 213; Vincent P. O'Hara, *Torch: North Africa and the Allied Path to Victory* (Annapolis: USNI, 2015), 73–75; the order of battle is in Appendix III, 305–13.

4. O'Hara, *Torch*, 78–79.

5. Several sources attribute the attack on the *Thomas Stone* to Korvettenkapitän Franz-Georg Reschke in the U-205. British sources, however, clearly indicate that it was an air attack. See Playfair, *The Mediterranean and Middle East*, 4:131; and O'Hara, *Torch*, 330, note 11.

6. Oakes Combat Report, Dec. 17, 1942, is available at www.ww2survivorstories.com; O'Hara, *Torch*, 79–80.

7. The situation was complicated by a group of pro-Allied Frenchmen who at Murphy's instigation had seized several points in Algiers but could not hold them long enough to be relieved by the invaders. See William L. Langer, *Our Vichy Gamble* (Hamden, CT: Archon Books, 1947), esp. 345–49. See also George F. Howe, *Northwest Africa: Seizing the Initiative in the West*, vol. 11 of *The United States Army in World War II* (Washington, DC: Office of the Chief of Military History, 1957), 249–50; Churchill, *The Hinge of Fate*, 611–15, 623; and Paul Auphan and Jacques Mordal, *The French Navy in World War II* (Annapolis: USNI, 1959), 219.

8. Playfair, *The Mediterranean and Middle East*, 4:130; Orr Kelly, *Meeting the Fox: The Allied Invasion of Africa from Operation Torch to Kasserine Pass to Victory in Tunisia* (New York: John Wiley and Sons, 2002), 55.

9. Auphan and Mordal, *The French Navy in World War II*, 226–27; O'Hara, *Torch*, 123–26, 132–35.

10. Kelly, *Meeting the Fox*, 69–70; Leslie W. Bailey, *Through Hell and High Water: The Wartime Memories of a Junior Combat Infantry Officer* (New York: Vantage Press, 1994), 45–50.

11. Craig L. Symonds, *Neptune: The Allied Invasion of Europe and the D-Day Landings* (New York: Oxford University Press, 2014), 89; Auphan and Mordal, *The French Navy in World War II*, 222; O'Hara, *Torch*, 91; Kelly, *Meeting the Fox*, 75.

12. Playfair, *The Mediterranean and Middle East*, 4:145, 160–61; O'Hara, *Torch*, 99–105.

13. Symonds, *Neptune*, 74–75.

14. Ibid., 81–83; Playfair and Molony, *The Mediterranean and Middle East*, 130; Samuel Eliot Morison, *Operations in North African Waters* (Boston: Little, Brown, 1965, orig. 1947), 43–45.

15. Hewitt to C-in-C Atlantic, Nov. 28, 1942, Battle Action Reports (Mss. 416), USNA, box 3 (hereafter Hewitt Report); H. Kent Hewitt, *The Memoirs of H. Kent Hewitt*, ed. Evelyn M. Cherpak (Newport, RI: Naval War College Press, 2004), 149–50; Morison, *Operations in North African Waters*, 84.

16. Hewitt Report; Symonds, *Neptune*, 90–91; Morison, *Operations in North African Waters*, 63, 65, 79.

17. Symonds, *Neptune*, 92.

18. Auphan and Mordal, *The French Navy in World War II*, 232–34; O'Hara, *Torch*, 195–205; Morison, *Operations in North Africa*, 100.

19. Vincent P. O'Hara credits this battle as "the largest surface, air, and subsurface naval action fought in the Atlantic Ocean during World War II," and offers a detailed account in *Torch*, 195–218. See also Morison, *Operations in North African Waters*, 101–7. The French admiral is Gabriel Auphan, in *The French Navy in World War II*, 233, 236.

20. The *Massachusetts* used up 60 percent of its 16-inch ammunition, and the cruisers *Wichita* and *Tuscaloosa* had each fired more than twelve hundred 8-inch shells; the *Brooklyn* expended 2,691 of its 6-inch shells. See O'Hara, *Torch*, 213–18.

21. Patton to Beatrice Patton, Nov. 8, 1942, and diary entry, Nov. 8, both in *The Patton Papers, 1940–1945*, ed. Martin Blumenson (Boston: Houghton Mifflin, 1974), 2:103, 105.

22. DesRon 19 to C-in-C, Atlantic, Nov. 20, 1944, Action Reports (Mss 416), box 3, USNA.

23. Symonds, *Neptune*, 92–93; Morison, *Operations in North African Waters*, 144–48.

24. Levine, *Rommel's Supply Line*, 80; Playfair and Molony, *The Mediterranean and Middle East*, 28; Sadkovich, *The Italian Navy*, 283, 286, 303–6.

25. Raeder's report, Nov. 17, 1942, is in *Fuehrer Conferences on Naval Affairs, 1939–1945* (Annapolis: USNI, 1990), 300.

26. Levine, *Rommel's Supply Line*, 58–60, 84–86.

27. Ibid., 83–84.

28. Ibid., 76, 81, 83–86, 89.

29. For a breakdown of the post-invasion Allied convoys, see Table 13 in Leighton and Coakley, *Global Logistics and Strategy*, 485.

30. DDE to Smith, Nov. 10, DDE to GCM, Nov. 17, and DDE to Thomas T. Handy, Dec. 7, 1942, all in *PDDE*, 2:686, 729–32, 812.

31. Several French warships in Tunisia were seized by the Germans. Weygand's comment is in his foreword to Auphan and Mordal, *The French Navy in World War II*, v.

32. RADM John L. Hall discusses Michelet's circumstances in his oral history, Columbia University, 119–20. For Godfroy, see Playfair, *The Mediterranean and the Middle East*, 4:164.

33. Tameichi Hara, *Japanese Destroyer Captain* (Annapolis: Naval Institute Press, 1967), 149–50.

34. James D. Hornfischer, *Neptune's Inferno: The U.S. Navy at Guadalcanal* (New York: Bantam Books, 2011), 250–52.

35. Ibid., 246.

36. The characterization of Abe as excessively cautious comes from Hara (*Japanese Destroyer Captain*, 126), whose judgment may have been affected by what happened in the battle.

37. Samuel Eliot Morison, *The Struggle for Guadalcanal: August 1942–February 1943* (Boston: Little, Brown, 1949), 237–43; Hornfischer, *Neptune's Inferno*, 263–74; Frank, *Guadalcanal*, 436–40; Timothy S. Wolters, *Information at Sea* (Baltimore: Johns Hopkins University Press, 2013), 202–3.

38. Richard B. Frank, *Guadalcanal: The Definitive Account of the Landmark Battle* (New York: Penguin, 1990), 436–38; Hara, *Japanese Destroyer Captain*, 130–31.

39. Morison, *Struggle for Guadalcanal*, 244. The exec on the *O'Bannon* is quoted by John F. Wukovits, *Tin Can Titans* (Boston: Da Capo Press, 2017), 52. Parker is quoted by James Hornfischer, *Neptune's Inferno*, 302, but see also 275, 292. And see F. Julian Becton, with Joseph Morschauser, *The Ship That Would Not Die* (Englewood Cliffs, NJ: Prentice Hall, 1980), 9. The sequence of orders on *Helena* is from C. G. Morris and Hugh B. Cave, *The Fightin'est Ship: The Story of the Cruiser* Helena (New York: Dodd, Mead, 1944), 91.

40. Robert M. Howe Oral History, NMPW, 4; Becton, *The Ship That Would Not Die*, 9–10.

41. Howe Oral History, NWPW, 5; J. G. Coward, "Destroyer Dust," *Proceedings*, Nov. 1948, 1375; Hornfischer, *Neptune's Inferno*, 282–89, 299, 301–2 (Du Bose is quoted on 302).

42. Frank, *Guadalcanal*, 454–55; Thomas G. Miller Jr., *The Cactus Air Force* (New York: Harper and Row, 1969), 184–89.

43. Matome Ugaki, *Fading Victory: The Diary of Matome Ugaki* (Pittsburgh: University of Pittsburgh Press, 1991), 278 (diary entry of Nov. 17).

44. Morris, *The Fightin'est Ship*, 95; Dan Kurzman, *Left to Die: The Tragedy of the USS Juneau* (New York: Pocket Books, 1994), 1–4, 10–26.

45. Raizo Tanaka, "The Struggle for Guadalcanal," in *The Japanese Navy in World War II*, ed. David C. Evans (Annapolis: USNI, 1969, 1986), 192–95.

46. Hornfischer, *Neptune's Inferno*, 335–36, 347–50.

47. Ibid., 357–62; Wolters, *Information at Sea*, 203.

48. Louis Brown, *A Radar History of World War II* (Bristol: Institute of Physics, 1999), 370.

49. Frank, *Guadalcanal*, 582–94.

Chapter 17: The War on Trade, III

1. Shipping losses are compiled in Appendix 20 of Clay Blair, *Hitler's U-Boat War: The Hunted* (New York: Random House, 1996), 820. The quotation is from WSC to FDR, Oct. 31, 1942, in *Roosevelt and Churchill: Their Secret Wartime Correspondence*, ed. Francis L. Loewenheim, Harold D. Langley, and Manfred Jones (New York: E. P. Dutton, 1975), 262.

2. *Proceedings of the London Naval Conference of 1930 and Supplementary Documents* (Washington, DC: Government Printing Office, 1931), 83.

3. James P. Duffy, *The Sinking of the* Laconia *and the U-Boat War: Disaster in the Mid-Atlantic* (Santa Barbara, CA: Praeger, 2009), 53, 71–84.

4. Léonce Peillard, *The* Laconia *Affair* (New York: G. P. Putnam's Sons, 1963), 166–70; Blair, *Hitler's U-Boat War: The Hunted*, 58–64.

5. Duffy, *The Sinking of the* Laconia, 96; Peillard, *The* Laconia *Affair*, 190; Blair, *Hitler's U-Boat War: The Hunted*, 65.

6. Karl Doenitz, *Memoirs: Ten Years and Twenty Days* (Annapolis: USNI, 1958, 1990), 29–94; Blair, *Hitler's U-Boat War: The Hunted*, 767.

7. Stephen S. Roskill, *The War at Sea, 1939–1945* (London: Her Majesty's Stationery Office, 1956), 2: 290–98; A. E. Sokol, "German Attacks on the Murmansk Run," *Proceedings*, Dec. 1952, 1333; Erich Raeder, *My Life* (Annapolis: USNI, 1960), 370.

8. Keith Bird, *Erich Raeder: Admiral of the Third Reich* (Annapolis: USNI, 2006), 196–97; Winston S. Churchill, *The Hinge of Fate*, vol. 4 of *The History of the Second World War* (Boston: Houghton Mifflin, 1950), 275–76.

9. John Winton, *The Death of the* Scharnhorst (New York: Hippocrene Books, 1983), 5–6; Raeder, *My Life*, 369–70.

10. "Conference Between the C-in-C Navy and the Fuehrer," Jan. 11, 1943, in *Fuehrer Conferences on Naval Affairs* (Annapolis: USNI, 1990), 307; Bird, *Erich Raeder*, 202–3.

11. Raeder, *My Life*, 374; Doenitz, *Memoirs*, 299–300, 311; "Minutes of Conference Between the C-in-C Navy and the Fuehrer," Feb. 13, 1943, in *Fuehrer Conferences*, 310.

12. Jürgen Rohwer, *The Critical Convoy Battles of March 1943* (Annapolis: USNI, 1977), 47; Doenitz, *Memoirs*, 315–16; Blair, *Hitler's U-Boat War: The Hunted*, 24–25, 40.

13. Blair, *Hitler's U-Boat War: The Hunted*, 25; Peter Padfield, *The War Beneath the Sea: Submarine Conflict During World War II* (New York: John Wiley and Sons, 1995), 280–81, 286.

14. Doenitz, *Memoirs*, 316; Blair, *Hitler's U-Boat War: The Hunted*, 234–35.

15. John M. Waters Jr., *Bloody Winter* (Annapolis: USNI, 1967, 1984), 178–94.

16. Rohwer, *Critical Convoy Battles*, 50–51; Blair, *Hitler's U-Boat War: The Hunted*, 260–65.

17. Several books cover the battle for HX-229/SC-122 in detail. See in particular Rohwer, *Critical Convoy Battles*, 55–62, 109–85 (plus Appendix 9); Martin Middlebrook, *Convoy* (New York: William Morrow, 1977), 126–278 (plus Appendix 4); and Michael Gannon, *Black May: The Epic Story of the Allies' Defeat of the German U-Boats in May 1943* (New York: HarperCollins, 1998). The junior officer witness is Ensign Frank Pilling, who is quoted in Middlebrook, *Convoy*, 188.

18. Doenitz, *Memoirs*, 329.

19. Blair, *Hitler's U-Boat War: The Hunted*, 271, 768–69. Michael Gannon concludes that the Royal Navy officers in Trade Plot were less concerned because the metrics showed that the U-boats were failing. See Gannon, *Black May*, xvii–xxviii.

20. William T. Y'Blood, *Hunter Killer: U.S. Escort Carriers in the Battle of the Atlantic* (Annapolis: USNI, 1983), 35–39; Herbert A. Werner, *Iron Coffins: A Personal Account of the German U-Boat Battles of World War II* (New York: Holt, Rinehart and Winston, 1969), 120.

21. Dönitz's War Diary, March 5, 1943, is printed as Appendix 4 in Rohwer, *Critical Convoy Battles*, 212–14; Doenitz, *Memoirs*, 324–25; Blair, *Hitler's U-Boat War: The Hunted*, 191.

22. The crewman on the *Sapelo* was E. E. Lipke, who described the attack in "A North Atlantic Convoy," *Proceedings*, March 1947, 292.

23. Michael Gannon offers a detailed account of the battle for ONS-5 in *Black May*, 115–240; Gretton is quoted on 233. See also Roskill, *The War at Sea*, 2:373–74; and Peter Gretton, *Crisis Convoy: The Story of HX231* (Annapolis: USNI, 1974), 149–53.

24. Roskill, *The War at Sea*, 2: 375–76.

25. Ibid., 2:377; Doenitz, *Memoirs*, 341.

26. Gretton, *Crisis Convoy*, 159–76.

27. Minutes of a Conference Between Donitz and Hitler on April 11, 1943, in *Fuehrer Conferences on Naval Affairs* (Annapolis: USNI, 1990), 2:20. See also Padfield, *War Beneath the Sea*, 220.

28. Frederic C. Lane, *Ships for Victory: A History of Shipbuilding Under the U.S. Maritime Commission in World War II* (Baltimore: Johns Hopkins University Press, 1951, 2001), 138–44; GCM to FDR, Feb. 18, 1942, Franklin D. Roosevelt Library, Hyde Park, NY, Secretary's File, box 3. The British historian is Max Hastings in *Retribution: The Battle for Japan, 1944–45* (New York: Alfred A. Knopf, 2008), 96.

29. Lane, *Ships for Victory*, 72–74.

30. Ibid., 257.

31. Ibid., 214.

32. Ibid., 145, 207.

33. Craig L. Symonds, *Neptune: The Allied Invasion of Europe and the D-Day Landings* (New York: Oxford University Press, 2014), 159–60; Lane, *Ships for Victory*, 144, 149, 167; Padfield, *War Beneath the Sea*, 276. The quotations are from Knox to Stimson, Feb. 8, 1943, *Papers of George Catlett Marshall*, ed. Larry I. Bland (Baltimore: Johns Hopkins University Press, 1996), 3:535n; King to Stark, Aug. 29, 1942, Commander U.S. Naval Forces Europe [Stark] Subject File, RG 313, box 24, NARA; and WSC to FDR, Oct. 31, 1942, in *Roosevelt and Churchill* (New York: E. P. Dutton, 1975), 262–63. This was the same letter in which Churchill mentioned his "torment" at the loss of so many ships.

34. Clay Blair, *Silent Victory: The U.S. Submarine War Against Japan* (Philadelphia: J. B. Lippincott, 1975), 109–12.

35. The quotation is from the oral history of William Coffey (OH 00833), NMPW, 7. See also Buford Rowland and William B. Boyd, *U.S. Navy Bureau of Ordnance in*

World War II (Washington, DC: Bureau of Ordnance, 1953), 90; Robert Gannon, *Hellions of the Deep: The Development of American Torpedoes in World War II* (University Park, PA: Penn State University Press, 1996), 75–76; Blair, *Silent Victory*, 169–70; and Mark P. Parillo, *The Japanese Merchant Marine in World War II* (Annapolis: USNI, 1993), 204.

36. The story of the *Narwhal* is in Blair, *Silent Victory*, 319; the quotation is from Edward L. Beach, *Submarine!* (New York: Pocket Books, 1946), 21.

37. Samuel Eliot Morison, *Coral Sea, Midway, and Submarine Actions, May 1942–August 1942* (Boston: Little, Brown, 1949), 189.

38. David B. Bell oral history (OH 00646), 20, NMPW.

39. Ibid., 3; Edward M. Hary oral history (OH00830), 2; and Wiley Davis oral history (OH 00843), 1, all NMPW.

40. Blair, *Silent Victory*, 109; Corwin Mendenhall, *Submarine Diary* (Annapolis: Naval Institute Press, 1991), 8 (entry of Dec. 9, 1942); and Coffey oral history, 10, NMPW.

41. Davis oral history, 11; Tim Dearman oral history (OH 00533), 10, both NMPW.

42. The officer who reported feeling sorry for victims was Commander David B. Bell of the *Cuttlefish* in his oral history, 16.

43. The story of Morton's machine-gunning of the survivors of the *Buyo Maru* is in Richard H. O'Kane, *Wahoo: The Patrols of America's Most Famous World War II Submarine* (Novato, CA: Presidio Press, 1987), 150–54. See also Blair, *Silent Victory*, 384–85; and Don Keith, *Undersea Warrior: The World War II Story of "Mush" Morton and the USS* Wahoo (New York: New American Library, 2011), 168–73. The italics are added to the language of the Presidential Unit Citation.

44. Bell oral history, 16. For the statistics about U.S. submarine patrols in 1942–43, see Appendix F in Blair, *Silent Victory*, 900–983. A more detailed breakdown of Japanese shipping losses to American submarines is in *Japanese Naval and Merchant Shipping Losses During World War II by All Causes* (Washington, DC: Government Printing Office, 1947), 29–37 for 1942. The quotation of Blair is from *Silent Victory*, 360.

45. Blair, *Silent Victory*, 275–78; Charles A. Lockwood and Hans Christian Adamson, *Hellcats of the Sea* (New York: Greenberg, 1955), 3–23. The furious skipper was Edward L. Beach, in *Submarine!*, 21.

46. Charles A. Lockwood, *Sink 'Em All: Submarine Warfare in the Pacific* (New York: E. P. Dutton, 1951), 93–95; Blair, *Silent Victory*, 435–39.

47. Samuel Eliot Morison, *Breaking the Bismarcks Barrier, 22 July 1942–1 May 1944* (Boston: Little, Brown, 1950), 66; Blair, *Silent Victory*, Appendix F; Gannon, *Hellions of the Deep*, 89.

48. Blair in *Hitler's U-Boat War: The Hunted*, 338–39, 353–54. The Dönitz quotations are from his *Memoirs*, 342–43, and from Padfield in *War Beneath the Sea*, 371.

Chapter 18: Airplanes and Convoys

1. Wesley Frank Craven and James Lea Cate, *Army Air Forces in World War II*, vol. 4: *The Pacific: Guadalcanal to Saipan* (Chicago: University of Chicago Press, 1950), 136–37; Bruce Gamble, *Fortress Rabaul: The Battle for the Southwest Pacific, January 1942–April 1943* (Minneapolis: Zenith Press, 2010), 303.

2. John Prados, *Storm over Leyte: The Philippine Invasion and the Destruction of the Japanese Navy* (New York: New American Library, 2016), 39–40; Lex McAulay, *Battle of the Bismarck Sea* (New York: St. Martin's Press, 1991), 47–48.

3. Craven and Cate, *Army Air Forces in World War II*, 4:140–41. The Japanese sailor was Masuda Reiji, whose account is included in Haruko Taya Cook and Theodore F. Cook, eds., *Japan at War: An Oral History* (New York: New Press, 1992), 301.

4. Cook and Cook, *Japan at War*, 301–2; McAulay, *Battle of the Bismarck Sea*, 77, 120–22; Thomas E. Griffith, *MacArthur's Airman: General George C. Kenney and the War in the Southwest Pacific* (Lawrence: University of Kansas Press, 1998), 106–8. Masada's account is in Cook and Cook, eds., *Japan at War*, 302.

5. McAulay, *Battle of the Bismarck Sea*, 102–3, 138; Gamble, *Fortress Rabaul*, 310–11; Griffith, *MacArthur's Airman*, 106–7; Samuel Eliot Morison, *Breaking the Bismarcks Barrier*, vol. 6 of *History of United States Naval Operations in World War II* (Boston: Little, Brown, 1950), 62.

6. McAulay, *Battle of the Bismarck Sea*, 136, 155; Gamble, *Fortress Rabaul*, 312–15. Based on the pilots' reports, MacArthur issued a press release claiming that his forces had sunk six destroyers or light cruisers and twenty-two merchant ships. When subsequent evidence showed that these estimates were greatly inflated, MacArthur implied that anyone who challenged his report would be subject to military discipline. Kenney's own postwar memoir, *General Kenney Reports* (New York: Duell, Sloan and Pearce, 1949), 205–6, repeats the inflated numbers.

7. Gamble, *Fortress Rabaul*, 320–21; Matome Ugaki, *Fading Victory: The Diary of Admiral Matome Ugaki, 1941–1945* (Pittsburgh: University of Pittsburgh Press, 1991), 216, 320 (diary entries of Dec. 29, 1942, and Apr. 3, 1943).

8. Ugaki, *Fading Victory* (diary entry of Apr. 16, 1943), 348–49; Gamble, *Fortress Rabaul*, 316–18.

9. Gamble, *Fortress Rabaul*, 323–27; Ian W. Toll, *The Conquering Tide: War in the Pacific Islands, 1942–1944* (New York: W. W. Norton, 2015), 202–3.

10. Stephen S. Roskill, *The War at Sea, 1939–1945* (London: Her Majesty's Stationery Office, 1956), 2:423.

11. Carroll V. Glines, *Attack on Yamamoto* (New York: Orion Books, 1990), 1–2.

12. Edwin T. Layton, with Roger Pineau and John Costello, *"And I Was There": Pearl Harbor and Midway—Breaking the Secrets* (New York: William Morrow, 1985), 475.

13. Glines, *Attack on Yamamoto*, 27–39.

14. The quotation is from P-38 pilot Roger Ames, "The Death of Yamamoto," paper presented at a symposium in Fredericksburg, Texas, April 16, 1988, NMPW.

15. In his report on the incident, Lanphier claimed credit for shooting down the first Betty, the one with Yamamoto on board, and he repeated the claim in a December 1966 article in *Reader's Digest* ("I Shot Down Yamamoto"). Subsequently, however, the testimony of other American pilots and, significantly, of one of the Japanese Zero pilots (Kenji Yanagiya), all of whom witnessed it, indicated that it was Barber, attacking from behind, who had shot down the first Betty, not Lanphier. Besby Holmes's account, entitled "Who Really Shot Down Yamamoto?," appeared in

Popular Aviation, March/April 1967. Both articles are included in Clines, *Attack on Yamamoto*, 63–65, and 70–73 (but see also 152–53). At a symposium held in Fredericksburg, Texas, on April 16, 1988, virtually all of the surviving pilots agreed that it was Barber, not Lanphier, who deserved credit for the first bomber and half credit (along with Holmes) for the second.

16. Glines, *Attack on Yamamoto*, 110–11.

17. Alan J. Levine, *The War Against Rommel's Supply Lines, 1942–1943* (Westport, CT: Praeger, 1999), 147–48; I. S. O. Playfair and C. J. C. Molony, *The Mediterranean and Middle East*, vol. 4: *The Destruction of the Axis Forces in Africa* (London: Her Majesty's Stationery Office, 1966), 240, 246; Richard Hammond, "Fighting Under a Different Flag: Multinational Naval Cooperation and Submarine Warfare in the Mediterranean, 1940–1944," *JMH*, April 2016, 452.

18. Playfair and Molony, *The Mediterranean and Middle East*, 407–8 (Cunningham is quoted on 410); Levine, *The War Against Rommel's Supply Lines*, 150–54, 160. See also Robert S. Ehlers Jr., *The Mediterranean Air War: Airpower and Allied Victory in World War II* (Lawrence: University of Kansas Press, 2015), 278, 282.

19. Italian destroyer losses are in Marc'Antonio Bragadin, *The Italian Navy in World War II* (Annapolis: USNI, 1957), 249. The exchange between Dönitz and Riccardi is in "Conference at Supermarina, 12 May 1943," in *Fuehrer Conferences on Naval Affairs* (Annapolis: USNI, 1990), 323.

20. Playfair and Molony, *The Mediterranean and Middle East*, 411–16; Ehlers, *The Mediterranean Air War*, 287.

21. Ibid., 424, 460; Andrew B. Cunningham, *A Sailor's Odyssey* (New York: E. P. Dutton, 1951), 529–30. According to Robert S. Ehlers Jr. (*The Mediterranean Air War*, 2), the Allies captured a total of 101,784 Germans, 89,442 Italians, and 47,017 others whose nationality was unspecified, all of them unwounded. The records do not record the number of wounded who were also taken prisoner. U.S. records show a total of 270,000 taken prisoner, which may be slightly inflated. "Conference at Supermarina, 12 May 1943," 322.

22. Rick Atkinson, *An Army at Dawn: The War in North Africa, 1942–1944* (New York: Henry Holt, 2002), 536–39.

23. Minutes of a meeting of the Combined Chiefs of Staff, Jan. 18, 1943, in *FRUS*, Special Conferences Series, 1:598, 628–34, 678, 689. See also Carlo D'Este, *Bitter Victory: The Battle for Sicily, 1943* (New York: E. P. Dutton, 1988), 31–52.

24. The passage is from the diary of Eisenhower's naval aide Harry Butcher (entry of July 11, 1943), Harry C. Butcher, *My Three Years with Eisenhower* (New York: Simon and Schuster, 1946), 357.

25. Denis Smyth, *Deathly Deception: The Real Story of Operation Mincemeat* (New York: Oxford University Press, 2013); Bragadin, *The Italian Navy in World War II*, 253; "Report to the Fuehrer, 14 May 1943," in *Fuehrer Conferences*, 327.

26. Samuel Eliot Morison, *Sicily-Salerno-Anzio, January 1943–June 1944* (Boston: Little, Brown, 1954), 229.

27. Minutes of several meetings of the Combined Chiefs of Staff, May 13, 14, and 21, 1943, *FRUS*, Special Conferences Series, 3:41–44, 53–54, 348.

Chapter 19: Husky

1. Bernard Fergusson, *The Watery Maze: The Story of Combined Operations* (New York: Holt, Rinehart, and Winston, 1961), 221; Carlo D'Este, *Bitter Victory: The Battle for Sicily* (New York: E. P. Dutton, 1988), 76–77.

2. D'Este, *Bitter Victory*, 115–16; C. J. C. Molony, *The Mediterranean and Middle East*, vol. 5: *The Campaign in Sicily* (London: Her Majesty's Stationery Office, 1973), 5:25; Cunningham to Pound, Apr. 28, 1942, quoted in John Winton, *Cunningham* (London: John Murray, 1998), 311; Diary of George Patton (entry of Apr. 29, 1942), in *The Patton Papers, 1940–1945*, ed. Martin Blumenson (Boston: Houghton Mifflin, 1974), 2:236.

3. Stephen S. Roskill, *The War at Sea, 1939–1945* (London: Her Majesty's Stationery Office, 1961), 3 (part 1): 107.

4. Molony, *The Mediterranean and Middle East*, 5:29–34. See the order of battle in Appendix B (584–91) in D'Este, *Bitter Victory*.

5. Andrew B. Cunningham, *A Sailor's Odyssey* (New York: E. P. Dutton, 1951), 493, 524.

6. Ibid., 547–48, 553; Philip Vian, *Action This Day: A War Memoir* (London: Frederick Muller, 1960), 106; Molony, *The Mediterranean and Middle East*, 5:53; I. S. O. Playfair, *The Mediterranean and Middle East*, vol. 4: *The Germans Come to the Help of Their Ally* (London: Her Majesty's Stationery Office, 1966), 4: Appendix 5, 482.

7. Truscott's after-action report is quoted in Samuel Eliot Morison, *Operations in North African Waters* (Boston: Little, Brown, 1947), 123.

8. Craig L. Symonds, *Neptune: The Allied Invasion of Europe and the D-Day Landings* (New York: Oxford University Press, 2014), 152–55; Winston S. Churchill, *Closing the Ring* (Boston: Houghton Mifflin, 1951), 28.

9. Lucian Truscott, *Command Missions: A Personal Story* (New York: E. P. Dutton, 1954), 202.

10. Symonds, *Neptune*, 150; Charles C. Roberts Jr., *The Boat That Won the War: An Illustrated History of the Higgins LCVP* (Annapolis: USNI, 2017).

11. Samuel Eliot Morison, *Sicily-Salerno-Anzio, January 1943–June 1944* (Boston: Little, Brown, 1954), 106; Symonds, *Neptune*, 210, 210n.

12. D'Este, *Bitter Victory*, 157; Cunningham, *A Sailor's Odyssey*, 534–35; H. Kent Hewitt, "Naval Aspects of the Sicilian Campaign," *Proceedings*, July 1953, 707.

13. Rear Admiral Alan Goodrich Kirk oral history, Columbia University, 198.

14. Truscott, *Command Missions*, 203–4.

15. Ibid.

16. Roskill, *The War at Sea*, 3 (part 1): 116–17; Kirk and Patton are quoted in Morison, *Sicily-Salerno-Anzio*, 16–17, 22, 61; Hall's quotation is from his oral history, Columbia University, 173; and Hewitt's is from his article "Naval Aspects of the Sicilian Campaign," 714.

17. Rick Atkinson, *The Day of Battle: The War in Sicily and Italy, 1944–1945* (New York: Henry Holt, 2007), 75–78.

18. Action Report, Western Naval Task Force, Operation Husky, NHHC, 36; Atkinson, *The Day of Battle*, 65–66; Cunningham, *A Sailor's Odyssey*, 544; Truscott, *Command Missions*, 209.

19. U.S. Office of Naval Intelligence, *Sicilian Campaign* [*Combat Narrative*] (Washington, DC: U.S. Navy, 1945), 117–18; Morison, *Sicily-Salerno-Anzio*, 65–66.

20. Albert N. Garland and Howard M. Smith, *The Mediterranean Theater of Operations: Sicily and the Surrender of Italy* (Washington, DC: Office of the Chief of Military History, 1965), 125; U.S. Office of Naval Intelligence, *The Sicilian Campaign*, 28; Hugh Pond, *Sicily* (London: William Kimber, 1962), 72.

21. Morison, *Sicily-Salerno-Anzio*, 80.

22. Truscott, *Command Missions*, 196, 212; Jack Belden, *Still Time to Die* (New York: Harper and Bros., 1943), 251–52; D'Este, *Bitter Victory*, 255–57.

23. Garland and Smith, *The Mediterranean Theater of Operations: Sicily and the Surrender of Italy*, 128; Morison, *Sicily-Salerno-Anzio*, 81.

24. U.S. Office of Naval Intelligence, *The Sicilian Campaign*, 7, 24, 33; D'Este, *Bitter Victory*, 254–59, 264n; Molony, *The Mediterranean and Middle East*, 5:63.

25. Molony, *The Mediterranean and Middle East*, 5:59–62; Atkinson, *Day of Battle*, 87; Mark Zuehlke, *Operation Husky: The Canadian Invasion of Sicily, July 10–August 7, 1943* (Vancouver: Douglas and McIntyre, 2008), 107.

26. Morison, *Sicily-Salerno-Anzio*, 30–31, 84–85.

27. Ibid., 100–101, 107–8; U.S. Office of Naval Intelligence, *The Sicilian Campaign*, 39–42; Zuehlke, *Operation Husky*, 112.

28. Belden, *Still Time to Die*, 267; John Mason Brown, *To All Hands: An Amphibious Adventure* (New York: Whittlesey House, 1943), 148; Morison, *Sicily-Salerno-Anzio*, 106, 108.

29. D'Este, *Bitter Victory*, 285–89; Atkinson, *Day of Battle*, 100.

30. Robert L. Clifford and William J. Maddocks, "Naval Gunfire Support of the Landings in Sicily," monograph No. 5 (Oct. 1984), 45th Infantry Division Museum, Oklahoma City, 25–26, 30; U.S. Office of Naval Intelligence, *The Sicilian Campaign*, 69; Atkinson, *Day of Battle*, 103; Morison, *Sicily-Salerno-Anzio*, 113, 117.

31. U.S. Office of Naval Intelligence, *The Sicilian Campaign*, 4–10; Hewitt, "Naval Aspects of the Sicilian Campaign," 710.

32. D'Este, *Bitter Victory*, 296; Morison, *Sicily-Salerno-Anzio*, 111–13; George S. Patton, *War as I Knew It* (Boston: Houghton Mifflin, 1947), 59.

33. Morison, *Sicily-Salerno-Anzio*, 118; Hewitt, "Naval Aspects of the Sicilian Campaign," 718.

34. D'Este, *Bitter Victory*, 412–27; Morison, *Sicily-Salerno-Anzio*, 179–85; Butcher (diary entry of Aug. 2, 1943) in Harry C. Butcher, *My Three Years with Eisenhower* (New York: Simon and Schuster, 1946), 376. The American visitor was H. Kent Hewitt; *The Memoirs of Admiral H. Kent Hewitt*, ed. Evelyn Cherpak (Newport, RI: Naval War College Press, 2004), 192.

35. D'Este, *Bitter Victory*, 476–81; Cunningham, *A Sailor's Odyssey*, 554.

36. Morison, *Sicily-Salerno-Anzio*, 209–18.

Chapter 20: Twilight of Two Navies

1. Albert N. Garland and Howard McGaw Smith, *The Mediterranean Theater of Operations: Sicily and the Surrender of Italy* (Washington, DC: Office of the Chief of Military History, 1965), 440–41, 443.

2. WSC to FDR, July 29 and 31, 1943, in Winston S. Churchill, *Closing the Ring* (Boston: Houghton-Mifflin, 1951), 61, 64.

3. DDE to CCS, July 18, 1943, *FRUS*, The Conferences at Washington and Quebec (1943), 1056; Samuel Eliot Morison, *Sicily-Salerno-Anzio, January 1943–June 1944* (Boston: Little, Brown, 1954), 238.

4. CCS to DDE, Aug. 18, 1943, and Conference Minutes, Aug. 21, 1943, both in *FRUS*, The Conferences at Washington and Quebec, 1061, 1072, 1073, 1075; italics added. Garland and Smith, *Sicily and the Surrender of Italy*, 445, 459; D. K. R. Crosswell, *Beetle: The Life of General Walter Bedell Smith* (Lexington: University of Kentucky Press, 2010), 472–73.

5. Garland and Smith, *Sicily and the Surrender of Italy*, 459.

6. Minutes of Meetings held on July 17 and Aug. 1–3, 1943, *Fuehrer Conferences on Naval Affairs* (Annapolis: USNI, 1990), 343–44, 352–53.

7. Minutes of Discussions, Aug. 9 and 11, 1943, in *Fuehrer Conferences*, 359–60; Antonio Bragadin, *The Italian Navy in World War II* (Annapolis: USNI, 1957), 310.

8. DDE to Smith, Sept. 8, 1943, *PDDE*, 3:1401–2; Garland and Smith, *Sicily and the Surrender of Italy*, 466–67, 474–76.

9. Garland and Smith, *Sicily and the Surrender of Italy*, 483; Bragadin, *The Italian Navy in World War II*, 310. The Instrument of Surrender, Aug 26, 1943, is printed in *FRUS*, The Conferences at Washington and Quebec, 1162–64.

10. Bragadin, *The Italian Navy in World War II*, 311; Garland and Smith, *The Mediterranean Theater of Operations*, 480; Jack Greene and Alessandro Massignani, *The Naval War in the Mediterranean, 1940–1943* (Annapolis: USNI, 2002), 299.

11. Greene and Massignani, *The Naval Air War in the Mediterranean*, 299; Garland and Smith, *Sicily and the Surrender of Italy*, 508.

12. Eisenhower's radio announcement is in *PDDE*, 3:1402n.

13. Garland and Smith, *Sicily and the Surrender of Italy*, ch. 9; Ralph S. Mavrogordata, "Hitler's Decision on the Defense of Italy," in *Command Decisions*, ed. Kent Roberts Greenfield (Washington, DC: Office of the Chief of Military History, 1960), 315.

14. Badoglio to DDE, Sept. 8, 1943, *PDDE*, 3:1403.

15. DDE to Badoglio, Sept. 8, 1943, *PDDE*, 3:1403; Garland and Smith, *Sicily and the Surrender of Italy*, 510–12, 524, 543; Greene and Massignani, *The Naval War in the Mediterranean, 1940–1943*, 300–301.

16. Bragadin, *The Italian Navy in World War II*, 312, 313. Bragadin, then a navy commander, was in the room at the time and a witness to the events described.

17. Morison, *Sicily-Salerno-Anzio*, 243; Bragadin, *The Italian Navy in World War II*, 316.

18. The eyewitness is quoted by Greene and Massignani in *The Naval Air War in the Mediterranean*, 305; Bragadin, *The Italian Navy in World War II*, 318; Morison, *Sicily-Salerno-Anzio*, 243; Stephen S. Roskill, *The War at Sea, 1939–1945* (London: Her Majesty's Stationery Office, 1960), 3 (part 1): 167.

19. Morison, *Sicily-Salerno-Anzio*, 236.

20. Garland and Smith, *Sicily and the Surrender of Italy*, 533: Greene and Massignani, *The Naval Air War in the Mediterranean*, 304–5, 307.

21. Benito Mussolini, *Memoirs, 1942–1943*, ed. Raymond Klibansky (New York: Howard Fertig, 1975), 78–79.

22. "Report by the Combined Staff Planners at Quebec," Aug. 26, 1943, in *FRUS*, The Conferences at Washington and Quebec, 1134.
23. Morison, *Sicily-Salerno-Anzio*, 253; H. Kent Hewitt, "The Allied Navies at Salerno," *Proceedings*, Sept. 1953, 965; John L. Hall Jr. oral history, Columbia University, 147.
24. Mavrogordata, "Hitler's Decision on the Defense of Italy," 317–19.
25. Carlo D'Este, *Fatal Decision: Anzio and the Battle for Rome* (New York: HarperCollins, 1991), 36–38, 41; Morison, *Sicily-Salerno-Anzio*, 250, 265. There was a brief (fifteen-minute) bombardment of the British beaches, but none at all on the American beaches.
26. Morison, *Sicily-Salerno-Anzio*, 266–68. The anonymous GI is quoted by Rick Atkinson in *The Day of Battle: The War in Sicily and Italy, 1943–1944* (New York: Henry Holt, 2013), 205.
27. Andrew B. Cunningham, *A Sailor's Odyssey* (New York: E. P. Dutton, 1951), 571; Roskill, *The War at Sea*, 3 (part 1): 172, 177; Morison, *Sicily-Salerno-Anzio*, 276–78.
28. Corelli Barnett, *Engage the Enemy More Closely* (New York: W. W. Norton, 1991), 659–60; Cunningham, *A Sailor's Odyssey*, 571; Roskill, *The War at Sea*, 3 (part 1): 155; Atkinson, *Day of Battle*, 213.
29. DDE to GCM, Sept. 13, 1943, *PDDE* 3:1411; C. J. C. Molony, *The Mediterranean and Middle East* (London: Her Majesty's Stationery Office, 1973), 5:28; Atkinson, *The Day of Battle*, 205.
30. Hewitt, "The Allied Navies at Salerno," 969.
31. Morison, *Sicily-Salerno-Anzio*, 290; Roskill, *The War at Sea*, 3 (part 1): 178–79; Cunningham, *A Sailor's Odyssey*, 568–69, 571.
32. Morrison, *Sicily-Salerno-Anzio*, 296; Greene and Massignani, *The Naval War in the Mediterranean*, 302.
33. Cunningham, *A Sailor's Odyssey*, 571.
34. Hitler's comment is in "Notes Taken at Conferences on Feb. 26, 1943," *Fuehrer Conferences on Naval Affairs*, 311.
35. David Woodward, *The Tirpitz and the Battle for the North Atlantic* (New York: W. W. Norton, 1953), 147–48; Michael Ogden, *The Battle of North Cape* (London: William Kimber, 1962), 43; John Winton, *The Death of the Scharnhorst* (New York: Hippocrene Books, 1983), 40–41.
36. Roskill, *The War at Sea*, 3 (part 1): 65–66; Woodward, *The Tirpitz and the Battle for the North Atlantic*, 152–53; Barnett, *Engage the Enemy More Closely*, 734–36.
37. Woodward, *The Tirpitz and the Battle for the North Atlantic*, 154–56; G. H. Bennett, J. E. Harrold, and R. Porter, *Hunting Tirpitz: Royal Naval Operations Against Bismarck's Sister Ship*, Britannia Naval Histories of World War II (Plymouth: University of Plymouth Press, 2012), 196–97; Roskill, *The War at Sea*, 3 (part 1): 67.
38. Albert Vulliez and Jacques Mordal, *Battleship Scharnhorst* (Fair Lawn, NJ: Essential Books, 1958), 198–202; Woodward, *The Tirpitz and the Battle for the North Atlantic*, 156–57. Both Lt. Cameron and Lt. Place survived the war as POWs and were awarded the Victoria Cross.
39. Woodward, *The Tirpitz and the Battle for the North Atlantic*, 150–59; Roskill, *The War at Sea*, 3 (part 1): 68; "Conference Minutes of the C-in-C Navy," Sept. 25, 1943, *Fuehrer Conferences*, 369; Barnett, *Engage the Enemy More Closely*, 737.

40. Churchill, *Closing the Ring*, 163–64; Christopher M. Bell, *Churchill and Sea Power* (New York: Oxford University Press, 2013), 262–63; Max Hastings, *Winston's War: Churchill, 1940–1945* (New York: Alfred A. Knopf, 2010), 211, 218; Winton, *Death of the* Scharnhorst, 45–46.

41. Winton, *Death of the* Scharnhorst, 46–47; Churchill, *Closing the Ring*, 270–74.

42. B. B. Schofield, *The Russian Convoys* (Philadelphia: Dufour Editions, 1964), 164.

43. In the archival version, this memo is incorrectly dated January 8, 1944, but accurately dated Dec. 19–20 in the published version. *Fuehrer Conferences on Naval Affairs*, 373–74.

44. Karl Doenitz, *Memoirs: Ten Years and Twenty Days* (Annapolis: USNI, 1958), 375; Ogden, *The Battle of North Cape*, 101; Vulliez and Mordal, *Battleship* Scharnhorst, 212; Winton, *Death of the* Scharnhorst, 79.

45. Ogden, *The Battle of North Cape*, 97–103; A. J. Watts, *The Loss of the* Scharnhorst (London: Ian Allan, 1970), 26–27; Vulliez and Mordal, *Battleship* Scharnhorst, 216.

46. Ogden, *The Battle of North Cape*, 103; Schofield, *The Russian Convoys*, 172. After the war, Dönitz wrote, "Although I myself thought it would be a mistake to employ the *Scharnhorst* alone, my staff and I saw no reason to interfere with the Commander-in-Chief's [Bey's] operational instruction." Karl Doenitz, *Memoirs: Ten Years and Twenty Days* (Annapolis: USNI, 1958), 378.

47. Schofield, *The Russian Convoys*, 172; Winton, *The Death of the* Scharnhorst, 67; Roskill, *The War at Sea*, 3 (part 1): 80.

48. Winton, *The Death of the* Scharnhorst, 85–86.

49. Watts, *The Loss of the* Scharnhorst, 26–27, 38; Vulliez and Mordal, *Battleship* Scharnhorst, 220; Doenitz, *Memoirs*, 380; Derek Howse, *Radar at Sea: The Royal Navy in World War 2* (Annapolis: USNI, 1993), 188; Ogden, *The Battle of North Cape*, 122–25; Winton, *Death of the* Scharnhorst, 82–83.

50. Schofield, *The Russian Convoys*, 178–79; Roskill, *The War at Sea*, 3 (part 1): 85.

51. Vulliez and Mordal, *Battleship* Scharnhorst, 225.

52. Ibid., 228–34; Roskill, *The War at Sea*, 3 (part 1): 87; Ogden, *The Battle of North Cape*, 186; Winton, *Death of the* Scharnhorst, 77. The gun layer was George Gilroy, who is quoted in Richard R. Lawrence, *The Mammoth Book of Eyewitness Naval Battles* (New York: Carroll and Graf, 2003), 481.

53. Watts, *The Loss of the* Scharnhorst, 48–50; Schofield, *The Russian Convoys*, 179. Merry is quoted in Winton, *Death of the* Scharnhorst, 1.

Chapter 21: Breaking the Shield

1. James C. Shaw, "Introduction," in Samuel Eliot Morison, *Aleutians, Gilberts, and Marshalls* (Boston: Little, Brown 1954); Ian Toll, *The Conquering Tide: War in the Pacific Islands, 1942–1944* (New York: W. W. Norton, 2015), 300–305; Alex Vraciu oral history (OH03808), NMPW, 22.

2. Morison, *Aleutians, Gilberts, and Marshalls*, 22–66.

3. Bob Barnett oral history (OH00702), NMPW; Robert Sherrod, *Tarawa: The Story of a Battle* (Fredericksburg, TX: Admiral Nimitz Foundation, 1973, orig. 1944), 57; John L. Chew, "Some Shall Escape," *Proceedings*, Aug. 1945, 887; John F. Wukovits, *Tin Can Titans* (Boston: Da Capo, 2017), 123.

4. The most complete full-length biography of MacArthur is D. Clayton James, *The Years of MacArthur* (New York: Houghton Mifflin, 1970); an excellent single-volume work is William Manchester, *American Caesar: Douglas MacArthur, 1880–1964* (Boston: Little, Brown, 1978). For a brief, incisive portrait, see Richard B. Frank, *MacArthur: Lessons in Leadership* (New York: Palgrave Macmillan, 2007).

5. Max Hastings, *Retribution: The Battle for Japan, 1944–45* (New York: Alfred A. Knopf, 2008), 23.

6. Thomas Alexander Hughes, *Admiral Bill Halsey: A Naval Life* (Cambridge, MA: Harvard University Press, 2016), 259.

7. William F. Halsey and J. Bryan, *Admiral Halsey's Story* (New York: McGraw-Hill, 1947), 154–55, 189–90; Jonathan W. Jordan, *American Warlords: How Roosevelt's High Command Led America to Victory in World War II* (New York: Random House, 2016), 320–21; Toll, *The Conquering Tide*, 220–22.

8. Samuel Eliot Morison, *Breaking the Bismarcks Barrier* (Boston: Little, Brown, 1950), 284–86; Hyakutake is quoted by John Miller Jr. in *Cartwheel: The Reduction of Rabaul* (Washington, DC: Office of the Chief of Military History, 1959), 239.

9. U.S. Office of Naval Intelligence, *The Bougainville Campaign and the Battle of Empress Augusta Bay*, Combat Narratives (Washington, DC: U.S. Navy, 1945), 47–48; Morison, *Breaking the Bismarcks Barrier*, 338–39.

10. C. G. Morris and Hugh B. Cave, *The Fightin'est Ship: The Story of the Cruiser* Helena (New York: Dodd Mead, 1944), 117; Ralph Bailey oral history (OH00770), NWPW.

11. Miller, *Cartwheel*, 91, 98.

12. Timothy S. Wolters, *Information at Sea: Shipboard Command and Control in the U.S. Navy from Mobile Bay to Okinawa* (Baltimore: Johns Hopkins University Press, 2013), 204–5; Louis Brown, *A Radar History of World War II: Technical and Military Imperatives* (Bristol, England: Institute of Physics, 1999), 368–71; Morison, *Breaking the Bismarcks Barrier*, 160–75; Harry A. Gailey, *Bougainville, 1943–1945: The Forgotten Campaign* (Lexington: University Press of Kentucky, 1991), 29.

13. Morris, *The Fightin'est Ship*, 151–156.

14. Ibid., 156. The correspondent was Duncan Norton-Taylor, who is quoted in Wukovits, *Tin Can Titans*, 145. John J. Domagalski, *Sunk in Kula Gulf* (Washington, DC: Potomac Books, 2012), 74, 85–90; Morison, *Breaking the Bismarcks Barrier*, 255–57; Chew, "Some Shall Escape," 888.

15. Morison, *Breaking the Bismarcks Barrier*, 180–91. The quotation is on 194.

16. John Miller Jr. covers the ground campaign for Munda in *Cartwheel*, 91–164. See also Toll, *The Conquering Tide*, 231–34. The Halsey quotation is from Halsey and Bryan, *Admiral Halsey's Story*, 170.

17. Douglas MacArthur, *Reminiscences* (New York: McGraw-Hill, 1964), 169; Morison, *Breaking the Bismarcks Barrier*, 226–27, 238.

18. Morison, *Breaking the Bismarcks Barrier*, 261–68; Frank, *MacArthur*, 82.

19. Miller, *Cartwheel*, 217–21; Morison, *Breaking the Bismarcks Barrier*, 269–75.

20. Gailey, *Bougainville*, 4; Morison, *Breaking the Bismarcks Barrier*, 300; Miller, *Cartwheel*, 246.

21. Morison, *Breaking the Bismarcks Barrier*, 290–91. A list of Allied air strikes is included as Appendix A in *The Bougainville Campaign and the Battle of Empress Augusta Bay*, 77–78.

22. Morison, *Breaking the Bismarcks Barrier*, 290, 3-2-3. The quotation from the navigator is on 299.

23. Miller, *Cartwheel*, 236; *The Bougainville Landing and the Battle of Empress Augusta Bay*, 38–43; Gailey, *Bougainville*, 68–69.

24. Tameichi Hara, *Japanese Destroyer Captain: Pearl Harbor, Guadalcanal, Midway—the Great Naval Battles as Seen through Japanese Eyes* (Annapolis: USNI, 1967), 218.

25. Morison, *Breaking the Bismarcks Barrier*, 305–6; Miller, *Cartwheel*, 248–49; E. B. Potter, *Admiral Arleigh Burke: A Biography* (New York: Random House, 1990), 94.

26. Hara, *Japanese Destroyer Captain*, 223.

27. Potter, *Admiral Arleigh Burke*, 97–98; *The Bougainville Landing and the Battle of Empress Augusta Bay*, 60–63; Morison, *Breaking the Bismarcks Barrier*, 315–18.

28. Hara, *Japanese Destroyer Captain*, 224–25; Morison, *Breaking the Bismarcks Barrier*, 320–22.

29. Potter, *Admiral Arleigh Burke*, 99; Halsey and Bryan, *Admiral Halsey's Story*, 183.

30. Morison, *Breaking the Bismarcks Barrier*, 323–30 (the quotation is on 329); Miller, *Cartwheel*, 232.

31. Miller, *Cartwheel*, 225, 225n; Potter, *Admiral Arleigh Burke*, 102–6.

32. Morison, *Breaking the Bismarcks Barrier*, 401, 406–7; Masatake Okumiya, *Zero* (New York: Dutton, 1956), 222–24.

33. Jordan, *American Warlords*, 281–82. Far from resenting Somerville's candor, King seemed to respect it. He made a point afterward to tell him that if he ever wanted to talk things over, he should feel free to drop in anytime.

34. Philip A. Crowl and Edmund G. Love, *Seizure of the Gilberts and Marshalls* (Washington, DC: Office of the Chief of Military History, 1955), 13–14; MacArthur, *Reminiscences*, 173; Jordan, *American Warlords*, 318–19.

35. MacArthur was correct to suspect that King sought to elevate the navy's role in the war. In his memoir King acknowledged that he "made a determined effort to see that [the new campaign] would be undertaken by the Marine Corps and the Navy." Ernest J. King and Walter Muir Whitehill, *Fleet Admiral King, a Naval Record* (New York: W. W. Norton, 1952), 481.

36. Samuel Eliot Morison, *Aleutians, Gilberts, and Marshalls* (Boston: Little, Brown, 1951), 85; Ashley Halsey Jr., "The CVL's Success Story," *Proceedings*, April 1946, 527. Knox's announcement was reported in the *New York Times*, Nov. 27, 1943.

37. Crowl and Love, *Seizure of the Gilberts and Marshalls*, 24; Morison, *Aleutians, Gilberts, and Marshalls*, 91.

38. The full title of Buell's biography is *The Quiet Warrior: A Biography of Admiral Raymond A. Spruance* (Boston: Little, Brown, 1974). The interviewer was Gordon Prange (Sept. 5, 1964), in Prange Papers, UMD, box 17.

39. Joseph H. Alexander, *Across the Reef: The Marine Assault of Tarawa*, Marines in World War II Commemorative Series (Washington, DC: Marine Corps Historical Center, 1993), 3.

40. As Morison put it, "Either they must exterminate the enemy within a few days or be thrown out." Morison, *Aleutians, Gilberts, and Marshalls*, 109.

41. Holland M. Smith, *Coral and Brass* (New York: Charles Scribner's Sons, 1949), 120; Henry I. Shaw, Bernard C. Nalty, and Edwin T. Turnbladh, *Central Pacific Drive* (Washington, DC: Headquarters U.S. Marine Corps, 1966), 30–31; Maynard M. Nohrden, "The Amphibian Tractor, Jack of All Missions," *Proceedings*, Jan. 1946, 17; James R. Stockman, *The Battle for Tarawa* (Washington, DC: Historical Section U.S. Marine Corps, 1947), 4; Crowl and Love, *Seizure of the Gilberts and Marshalls*, 31–33.

42. Alexander, *Across the Reef*, 9.

43. Sherrod, *Tarawa*, 52, 62; John Wukovits, *One Square Mile of Hell: The Battle for Tarawa* (New York: Penguin, 2006), 103–4.

44. Sherrod, *Tarawa*, 41.

45. Alexander, *Across the Reef*, 13; Fred H. Allison, "We Were Going to Win . . . or Die There," *Naval History*, Oct. 2016, 35.

46. Alexander, *Across the Reef*, 39; Wukovits, *One Square Mile of Hell*, 108. In addition to the seventeen Japanese (one officer and sixteen enlisted men), 129 Korean laborers also survived.

47. Smith, *Coral and Brass*, 126–28; James D. Hornfischer, *Last Stand of the Tin Can Sailors* (New York: Bantam Books, 2004), 67.

48. *New York Times*, Nov. 27, 1943. *With the Marines at Tarawa* is available on YouTube.

Chapter 22: Large Slow Target

1. James L. McGuinness, "The Three Deuces," *Proceedings*, Sept. 1946, 1157; Roy Carter oral history, USNA, 6–8. See also Clendel Williams, *Echoes of Freedom: Builders of LSTs, 1942–1945* (Kearney, NE: Morris, 2011), 3; Craig L. Symonds, *Neptune: The Allied Invasion of Europe and the D-Day Landings* (New York: Oxford University Press, 2014), 152–53.

2. George E. Mowry, *Landing Craft and the War Production Board, April 1942 to May 1944* (Washington, DC: War Production Board, 1944), 11–13, 21–22, 34; Symonds, *Neptune*, 157–58.

3. Mowry, *Landing Craft and the War Production Board*, 14–15, 17; Frederic C. Lane, *Ships for Victory: A History of Shipbuilding Under the U.S. Maritime Commission in World War II* (Baltimore: Johns Hopkins University Press, 1951), 183–84, 311; Symonds, *Neptune*, 158–59.

4. H. Kent Hewitt, "The Allied Navies at Salerno," *Proceedings*, Sept. 1953, 961; Symonds, *Neptune*, 154–55, 63.

5. Jonathan W. Jordan, *American Warlords: How Roosevelt's High Command Led America to Victory in World War II* (New York: Random House, 2016), 312–13.

6. Conference Minutes, Sept. 24, 1943, *Fuehrer Conferences on Naval Affairs, 1939–1945* (Annapolis: USNI, 1990), 369.

7. Martin Blumenson, *Anzio: The Gamble That Failed* (Philadelphia: J. B. Lippincott, 1963), 34.

8. Minutes kept at Tehran, Nov. 28, 1943, *FRUS*, Special Conferences Series, 2:487, 490, 500; WSC to British Chiefs of Staff, Dec. 19, 1943, in Winston S. Churchill, *Closing the Ring*, vol. 5 of *The Second World War* (Boston: Houghton Mifflin, 1951), 429.

9. I have borrowed some language here from Martin Blumenson, who wrote, "An unfettered Churchill would beguile himself and others by a dazzling vision." Blumenson, *Anzio*, 8–9. Churchill claimed later that he would have preferred a three-division assault, but feared that overreaching would get him no forces at all. Churchill, *Closing the Ring*, 435. See also Samuel Eliot Morison, *Sicily-Salerno-Anzio, January 1943–June 1944* (Boston: Little, Brown, 1954), 324–25.

10. Henry L. Stimson, *On Active Service in Peace and War*, with McGeorge Bundy (New York: Harper and Brothers, 1947), diary entry of Nov. 4, 1943; Carlo D'Este, *Fatal Decision: Anzio and the Battle for Rome* (New York: HarperCollins, 1991), 93; Symonds, *Neptune*, 164–65; Churchill, *Closing the Ring*, 432.

11. C. J. C. Molony, *The Mediterranean and Middle East*, vol. 5: *The Campaign in Sicily* (London: Her Majesty's Stationery Office, 1973), 5:644; D'Este, *Fatal Decision*, 98–99; WSC to Chiefs of Staff, Dec. 26, 1943, in *Closing the Ring*, 434.

12. A naval order of battle is included as Appendix III in Morison, *Sicily-Salerno-Anzio*, 395–97.

13. Lucas is quoted in Blumenson, *Anzio*, 61–62.

14. D'Este, *Fatal Decision*, 4, 122–24.

15. Blumenson, *Anzio*, 83–86.

16. D'Este, *Fatal Decision*, 328–29; Theodore C. Wyman, "Red Shingle," *Proceedings*, Aug. 1947, 923–24.

17. WSC to Dill, Feb. 8, 1944, in Churchill, *Closing the Ring*, 487; Blumenson, *Anzio*, 20.

18. DDE to CCS, Jan. 23, 1944, in *PDDE*, 3:1673–75.

19. JCS to DDE, Jan. 25, 1944, in *PDDE*, 3:1691–92n; DDE to JCS, Mar. 9, 1944, in *PDDE*, 3:1763. See also Symonds, *Neptune*, 180–83.

20. Field Marshal Lord Alanbrooke [Alan Brooke], *War Diaries, 1939–1945*, entry of Mar. 29, 1944 (London: Weidenfeld and Nicholson, 2001), 535. The proposal to swap LSTs from the Med is in DDE to the British COS, February 18, 1944, *PDDE*, 3:1732, and GCM to DDE, Mar. 25, 1944, in *Papers of George Catlett Marshall*, ed. Larry I. Bland (Baltimore: Johns Hopkins University Press, 1996), 4:374–75. See also Symonds, *Neptune*, 183.

21. Churchill, *Closing the Ring*, 435.

22. DDE to JCS, Mar. 9, 1944, in *PDDE*, 3:1763–64; DDE to GCM, Mar. 20 and 21, 1944 (italics added), and DDE, Memo for Diary, Mar. 22, 1944, all in *PDDE*, 3:1775, 1777, 1783. See also Symonds, *Neptune*, 178–84.

23. DDE Memo for Diary (Feb. 7, 1944), in *PDDE*, 3:1711–12.

24. Philip A. Crowl and Edmund G. Love, *Seizure of the Gilberts and Marshalls*, The War in the Pacific (Washington, DC: Department of the Army, 1955), 166. I previously used the metaphor of a necklace in Craig L. Symonds, *The Battle of Midway* (New York: Oxford University Press, 2011), 71.

25. Crowl and Love, *The Seizure of the Gilberts and Marshalls*, 206–9; E. B. Potter, *Nimitz* (Annapolis: USNI, 1976), 265.

26. Henry I. Shaw, Bernard C. Nalty, and Edwin T. Turnbladh, *Central Pacific Drive* (Washington, DC: Headquarters U.S. Marine Corps, 1966), 3:109–11; Samuel Eliot Morison, *Aleutians, Gilberts, and Marshalls, June 1942—April 1944* (Boston:

Little, Brown, 1951), 210; Robert D. Heinl Jr., "The Most-Shot-At Island in the Pacific," *Proceedings*, Apr. 1947, 397–99.

27. Mowry, *Landing Craft and the War Production Board*, 30; Morison, *Aleutians, Gilberts, and Marshalls*, 208–9; Shaw et al., *Central Pacific Drive*, 108–9; Symonds, *Neptune*, 164.

28. Shaw et al., *Central Pacific Drive*, 135; Crowl and Love, *The Seizure of the Gilberts and Marshalls*, 313.

29. Shaw et al., *Central Pacific Drive*, 157; Crowl and Love, *The Seizure of the Gilberts and Marshalls*, 290, 312–13.

30. Shaw et al., *Central Pacific Drive*, 156; Morison, *Aleutians, Gilberts, and Marshalls*, 243–44, 246.

31. James D. Hornfischer, *The Fleet at Flood Tide: America at Total War in the Pacific, 1944–1945* (New York: Bantam Books, 2016), 23; Morison, *Aleutians, Gilberts and Marshalls*, 215–22; H. E. Smith, "I Saw the Morning Break," *Proceedings*, Mar. 1946, 403.

32. Bertram Vogel, "Truk—South Sea Mystery Base," *Proceedings*, Oct. 1948, 1269–75.

33. *New York Times*, June 5 and 6, 1944.

Chapter 23: D-Day

1. W. S. Chalmers, *Full Cycle: The Biography of Admiral Sir Bertram Home Ramsay* (London: Hodder and Stoughton, 1959), 134–36.

2. "Training Schedule of U.S. Naval Advanced Amphibious Training," General File 2002.570, NWWIIM-EC; Ralph A. Crenshaw oral history, NWWIIM-EC, 5.

3. Nigel Lewis, *Exercise Tiger: The Dramatic True Story of a Hidden Tragedy of World War II* (New York: Prentice Hall, 1990), 4.

4. Ibid., 73–74; Craig L. Symonds, *Neptune: The Allied Invasion of Europe and the D-Day Landings* (New York: Oxford University Press, 2014), 210–12.

5. Lewis, *Exercise Tiger*, 66; Symonds, *Neptune*, 212–13.

6. Lewis, *Exercise Tiger*, 79.

7. Eugene V. Eckstam, "Exercise Tiger," in *Assault on Normandy: First Person Accounts from the Sea Services*, ed. Paul Stilwell (Annapolis: USNI, 1994), 43.

8. Lewis, *Exercise Tiger*, 219–34. The exact number killed is somewhat in dispute. The numbers given here are from the official navy report. Subsequent studies suggest that the actual number may be as high as 739, which is the number inscribed on the monument on Slapton Sands. See Symonds, *Neptune*, 210–18.

9. Eisenhower's concern is in DDE to GCM, Apr. 29, 1944, *PDDE*, 3:1838–39. See also Com 12th Fleet (Stark) to COMINCH (King), May 2, 1944, both in ComUSNavEur, Message File, RG 313, box 13, NA.

10. Symonds, *Neptune*, 221.

11. Ibid., 225–26.

12. Ibid., 226–27.

13. "Suggested Operating Procedures for LCT," Flotilla Nine, in George Keleher File, NWWIIM-EC.

14. Anthony Beevor, *D-Day: The Battle for Normandy* (New York: Penguin, 2009), 11.

15. Carlo D'Este, *Eisenhower: A Soldier's Life* (New York: Henry Holt, 2002), 782 n. 38.

16. Max Hastings, *Overlord: D-Day and the Battle of Normandy* (New York: Simon and Schuster, 1984), 348. The quotation is from the oral history of Curtis Hansen, NWWIIM-EC, 6.

17. Symonds, *Neptune*, 252–53.
18. Ibid., 252.
19. Rick Atkinson, *The Guns at Last Light* (New York: Henry Holt, 2013), 57.
20. Executive Officer's Report, USS *Nevada*, June 23, 1944, Action Reports, USNA; Joseph H. Esclavon oral history (14) and Edwin Gale oral history (11), both NWWIIM-EC. See also L. Peter Wren and Charles T. Sele, *Battle Born: The Unsinkable USS Nevada* (n.p.: Xlibris, 2008), 43–47.
21. Symonds, *Neptune*, 272–76.
22. Bryant's plea was overhead by the reporter Cecil Carnes, who published it in the *Saturday Evening Post*. It is also included in Samuel E. Morison, *The Invasion of France and Germany* (Boston: Little, Brown, 1957), 143.
23. Action Reports, USS *McCook*, June 27, 1944, USS *Doyle*, June 8, 1944, and USS *Carmick*, June 23, 1944, USNA. See also Symonds, *Neptune*, 290–98.
24. Action Report, USS *Carmick*, June 23, 1944, USNA.
25. Atkinson, *Guns at First Light*, 73; Adrian Lewis, *Omaha Beach: Flawed Victory* (Chapel Hill: University of North Carolina Press, 2001), 25; Action Report, USS *Carmick*, June 23, 1944, USNA.
26. Symonds, *Neptune*, 306.
27. Roy Carter oral history, USNA, 13; Robert T. Robertson oral history, NWWIIM-EC, 9. See also Symonds, *Neptune*, 316–17.
28. On Omaha Beach, the LSTs brought in 8,502 tons of supplies per day during the three days before Mulberry A opened. During the three days that Mulberry A functioned, the LSTs brought in only 200 tons more per day (8,700 tons). In the week after the Mulberry was destroyed, the LSTs brought in 13,211 tons per day. See Symonds, *Neptune*, 328.
29. Karl Doenitz, *Memoirs: Ten Years and Twenty Days* (Annapolis: USNI, 1958), 396.
30. Doenitz, *Memoirs*, 422–23.
31. Stephen Roskill, *The War at Sea* (London: Her Majesty's Stationery Office, 1961), 3 (part 2): 123–35.
32. DDE to GCM, Sept. 14, 1944, *PDDE*, 2143–44. See also Terry Copp, *Cinderella Army: The Canadians in Northwest Europe, 1944–1945* (Toronto: University of Toronto Press, 2006), 42–43, 47.
33. Karl Dönitz and Gerhard Wegner, "The Invasion and the German Army," in *Fighting the Invasion: The German Army at D-Day*, ed. David C. Isby (London: Greenhill, 2000), 87.
34. Denis Whitaker and Shelagh Whitaker, *Tug of War: The Allied Victory that Opened Antwerp* (Toronto: Stoddert Publishing, 2000), 272–77, 285–94, 326–29, 349–53. See also, Roskill, *The War at Sea*, 3 (part 2), 147–52.
35. Whitaker and Whitaker, *Tug of War*, 355–83.

Chapter 24: Seeking the Decisive Battle

1. Samuel Eliot Morison, *New Guinea and the Marianas* (Boston: Little, Brown, 1964), 6–12.
2. William T. Y'Blood, *Red Sun Setting: The Battle of the Philippine Sea* (Annapolis: USNI, 1981), 16.

3. John Prados, *Storm over Leyte: The Philippine Invasion and the Destruction of the Japanese Navy* (New York: New American Library, 2016), 126. Toyoda is quoted in Charles A. Lockwood with Hans Christian Adamson, *Battles for the Philippine Sea* (New York: Thomas Y. Crowell, 1967), 47.

4. Harold J. Goldberg, *D-Day in the Pacific: The Battle of Saipan* (Bloomington: Indiana University Press, 2007), 50; James D. Hornfischer, *The Fleet at Flood Tide: America at Total War in the Pacific, 1944–1945* (New York: Bantam, 2016), 85. See the table (Appendix II) of naval forces involved in Morison, *New Guinea and the Marianas*, 407–11.

5. Morison, *New Guinea and the Marianas*, 171; Hornfischer, *The Fleet at Flood Tide*, 60–61. The witness was Private 1/c Carl Matthews, who is quoted in Goldberg, *D-Day in the Pacific*, 48.

6. Goldberg, *D-Day in the Pacific*, 51.

7. On Japanese pilot training, see Atsushi Oi, "The Japanese Navy in 1941," in *The Pacific War Papers: Japanese Documents of World War II*, ed. Donald M. Goldstein and Katherine V. Dillon (Washington, DC: Potomac Books, 2004), 23; and Mark R. Peattie, *Sunburst: The Rise of Japanese Naval Air Power, 1909–1941* (Annapolis: USNI, 2001), 133–34.

8. Morison, *New Guinea and the Marianas*, 214; Y'Blood, *Red Sun Setting*, 17; Craig L. Symonds, *The Battle of Midway* (New York: Oxford University Press, 2011), 40–42.

9. Goldberg, *D-Day in the Pacific*, 95; Morison, *New Guinea and the Marianas*, 232–37. On June 15, Ugaki noted in his diary: "Land-based planes must sink at least one-third of the enemy carriers before the decisive battle takes place." Matome Ugaki, *Fading Victory* (Annapolis: USNI, 1991), 402.

10. Morison, *New Guinea and the Marianas*, 221, 224–25, 241, 243; Lockwood and Adamson, *Battles of the Philippine Sea*, 82–82. Though Lockwood doesn't say so (his book being published in 1967), the American subs were directed toward these sightings by decrypts forwarded from Pearl Harbor. See Prados, *Storm over Leyte*, 25.

11. Goldberg, *D-Day in the Pacific*, 92; Charles F. Barber oral history, NWC, 19–20; Hornfischer, *The Fleet at Flood Tide*, 168, 170.

12. Morison, *New Guinea and the Marianas*, 250; Hornfischer, *The Fleet at Flood Tide*, 100; J. J. Clark with Clark Reynolds, *Carrier Admiral* (New York: Davis McKay, 1967), 166.

13. Hornfischer, *The Fleet at Flood Tide*, 172–73.

14. Y'Blood, *Red Sun Setting*, 93, 96; Hornfischer, *The Fleet at Flood Tide*, 175; Morison, *New Guinea and the Marianas*, 252.

15. J. Periam Danton, "The Battle of the Philippine Sea," *Proceedings*, Sept. 1945, 1025; Y'Blood, *Red Sun Setting*, 106; Alex Vraciu oral history (Oct. 9, 1994), NMPW, 74.

16. Danton, "The Battle of the Philippine Sea," 1024–5.

17. Hornfischer, *The Fleet at Flood Tide*, 182. The gunnery officer was Lt. William Van Dusen, who is quoted in Bruce M. Petty, *Saipan: Oral Histories of the Pacific War* (Jefferson, NC: McFarland, 2002), 162; Morison, *New Guinea and the Marianas*, 269–71.

18. Y'Blood, *Red Sun Setting*, 1118–19; Vraciu oral history, NMPW, 77; Morison, *New Guinea and the Marianas*, 267.

19. The Japanese called the battle "Battle for the Marianas." Danton, "The Battle of the Philippine Sea," 1025–26; Vraciu oral history, NMPW, 68–69.

20. Lockwood and Adamson, *Battle of the Philippine Sea*, 92–95; Y'Blood, *Red Sun Setting*, 127–29. *Cavalla* is now a museum submarine at Galveston, Texas.

21. Hornfischer, *The Fleet at Flood Tide*, 212–14; Y'Blood, *Red Sun Setting*, 148–49; Theodore Taylor, *The Magnificent Mitscher* (New York: W. W. Norton, 1954), 232.

22. Hornfischer, *The Fleet at Flood Tide*, 222–25; Y'Blood, *Red Sun Setting*, 177–80.

23. Hornfischer, *The Fleet at Flood Tide*, 225–26; Norman Delisle oral history (OH00468), NMPW, 7.

24. Hornfischer, *The Fleet at Flood Tide*, 229–31; Taylor, *The Magnificent Mitscher*, 236–37.

25. Ugaki, *Fading Victory*, 416 (diary entry of June 21, 1944).

26. Theodore Taylor discusses the various reactions to Spruance's decision in *The Magnificent Mitscher*, 238–40. Nimitz is quoted by Thomas J. Cutler in *The Battle of Leyte Gulf, 23–26 October 1944* (New York: HarperCollins, 1994), 20.

27. Goldberg, *D-Day in the Pacific*, 202.

28. Prados, *Storm over Leyte*, 31–33; Max Hastings, *Retribution: The Battle for Japan, 1944–45* (New York: Alfred A. Knopf, 2008), 39. As late as February, 1945, Emperor Hirohito declared that it would be premature to seek peace "unless we make one more military gain." Quoted in Richard Frank, *Downfall: The End of the Imperial Japanese Empire* (New York: Random House, 1999), 90.

29. Prados, *Storm over Leyte*, 13; Hastings, *Retribution*, 24.

30. Samuel Eliot Morison, *Leyte: June 1944–January 1945* (Boston: Little, Brown, 1958), 11; Prados, *Storm over Leyte*, 7–18.

31. Morison, *Leyte*, 11; William F. Halsey with J. Bryan, *Admiral Halsey's Story* (New York: McGraw-Hill, 1947), 197–98.

32. Gerald E. Wheeler, *Kinkaid of the Seventh Fleet* (Washington, DC: Naval Historical Center, 1995), 343–45.

33. Dean Moel oral history (OH001257), NMPW, 4.

34. Thomas Alexander Hughes, *Admiral Bill Halsey: A Naval Life* (Cambridge, MA: Harvard University Press, 2016), 345.

35. Morison, *Leyte*, 58–60.

36. Prados, *Storm over Leyte*, 52–53.

37. Milan Vego, *The Battle for Leyte, 1944* (Annapolis: USNI, 2006), 64–65.

38. Morison, *Leyte*, 160–69; Prados, *Storm over Leyte*, 52–53, 258; Vego, *The Battle for Leyte*, 55–59.

39. Prados, *Storm over Leyte*, 170.

40. Tomiji Koyanagi, "With Kurita in the Battle of Leyte Gulf," *Proceedings*, Feb. 1953, 119–21 (italics added); Prados, *Storm over Leyte*, 66, 100.

41. Koyanagi, "With Kurita," 120; Prados, *Storm over Leyte*, 66, 100.

Chapter 25: Leyte Gulf

1. Samuel Eliot Morison, *Leyte: June 1944–January 1945* (Boston: Little, Brown, 1958), 75; Waldo Heinrichs and Marc Gallicchio, *Implacable Foes: War in the Pacific* (New York: Oxford University Press, 2017), 34–35.

2. Morison, *Leyte*, 30–47. A vivid portrayal of the fighting for Peleliu is E. B. Sledge, *With the Old Breed at Peleliu and Okinawa* (Novato: Presidio Press, 1981).

3. There are many excellent histories of the Battle of Leyte Gulf. Among them (listed here in alphabetical order) are Thomas J. Cutler, *The Battle of Leyte Gulf* (New York: Harper/Collins, 1994); Morison, *Leyte*; John Prados, *Storm over Leyte: The Philippines Invasion and the Destruction of the Japanese Navy* (New York: New American Library, 2016); Evan Thomas, *Sea of Thunder* (New York: Simon and Schuster, 2006); Milan Vego, *The Battle for Leyte: Allied and Japanese Plans, Preparations, and Execution* (Annapolis: USNI, 2006); and H. P. Willmott, *The Battle of Leyte Gulf: The Last Fleet Action* (Bloomington: Indiana University Press, 2005). Books that focus on particular aspects of the battle include James Hornfischer, *Last Stand of the Tin Can Sailors* (New York: Bantam Books, 2004), which dramatically covers the Battle off Samar, and Anthony Tully, *Battle of Surigao Strait* (Bloomington: Indiana University Press, 2009).

4. Morison, *Leyte*, 142, 156; see the Task Organization Table on 415–32.

5. Ibid., 133–35.

6. Ibid., 137; Prados, *Storm over Leyte*, 164, 167. The text of MacArthur's speech was broadcast over the Voice of Freedom and printed in *Fortune* magazine, June 1945, 157–58.

7. Morison, *Leyte*, 168–69; Prados, *Storm over Leyte*, 261; Cutler, *The Battle of Leyte Gulf*, 84–85.

8. Tully, *The Battle of Surigao Strait*, 44–45; Prados, *Storm over Leyte*, 125–27.

9. The unidentified Japanese officer is quoted in Max Hastings, *Retribution: The Battle for Japan, 1944–45* (New York: Alfred A. Knopf, 2008), 134. Kurita's remarks are in Masanori Ito and Roger Pineau, *The End of the Imperial Japanese Navy* (New York: W. W. Norton, 1956), 120 (italics added). See also Prados, *Storm over Leyte*, 177–78.

10. Patrol Report, USS *Darter* (Nov. 5, 1944), USNA; John G. Mansfield, *Cruisers for Breakfast: War Patrols of the U.S.S.* Darter *and U.S.S.* Dace (Tacoma, WA: Media Center, 1997), 149–50.

11. William F. Halsey with J. Bryan, *Admiral Halsey's Story* (New York: McGraw-Hill, 1947), 210; Patrol Report, USS *Darter* (Nov. 5, 1944), 22, USNA; Mansfield, *Cruisers for Breakfast*, 153–54. The sighting report was sent first to submarine commander RADM Ralph Christie at Fremantle, who forwarded it to Halsey and Kinkaid.

12. Patrol Report, USS *Dace* (Nov. 6, 1944), 37, and USS *Darter* (Nov. 6, 1944), 30, both USNA. In all, 684 men were rescued from the *Atago*, while 360 were lost. Mansfield, *Cruisers for Breakfast*, 163.

13. Patrol Report, USS *Dace* (Nov. 6, 1944), 38, USNA.

14. Cutler, *Battle of Leyte Gulf*, 135–36.

15. Halsey and Bryan, *Admiral Halsey's Story*, 214; Tully, *Battle of Surigao Strait*, 68–69, 72–74; Prados, *Storm over Leyte*, 231.

16. Cutler, *Battle of Leyte Gulf*, 70–71, 116–17.

17. Ibid., 122–28; Morison, *Leyte*, 177–82.

18. Prados, *Storm over Leyte*, 47, 203–8, 218; Cutler, *Battle of Leyte Gulf*, 146–49; Tomiji Koyanagi, "With Kurita in the Battle of Leyte Gulf," *Proceedings*, February 1953, 123.

19. Koyanagi, "With Kurita," 123.

20. Carl Solberg, *Decision and Dissent: With Halsey at Leyte Gulf* (Annapolis: USNI, 1995), 112; Vego, *The Battle for Leyte*, 248–49; Halsey and Bryan, *Admiral Halsey's Story*, 216–17; Prados, *Storm over Leyte*, 222; Thomas Alexander Hughes, *Admiral Bill Halsey* (Cambridge, MA: Harvard University Press, 2016), 360–62.

21. Halsey and Bryan, *Admiral Halsey's Story*, 217; Prados, *Storm over Leyte*, 223.

22. Hornfischer, *Last Stand of the Tin Can Sailors*, 138–39; Prados, *Storm over Leyte*, 223–25.

23. Cutler, *Battle of Leyte Gulf*, 160–61, 170–71; Tully, *Battle of Surigao Strait*, 82–85.

24. Halsey and Bryan, *Admiral Halsey's Story*, 214.

25. Morison, *Leyte*, 195; Cutler, *Battle of Leyte Gulf*, 206–13; Hornfischer, *Last Stand of the Tin Can Sailors*, 129; Solberg, *Decision and Dissent*, 125; Hughes, *Admiral Bill Halsey*, 362–64; Theodore Taylor, *The Magnificent Mitscher* (New York: W. W. Norton, 1954), 161–62.

26. Prados, *Storm over Leyte*, 215, 234; Morison, *Leyte*, 187, 189.

27. Nishimura's son had been killed in the Philippines earlier in the war, and it is possible that this added to his lugubrious attitude toward his mission. Tully, *Battle of Surigao Strait*, 101–7; Heinrichs and Gallicchio, *Implacable Foes*, 183; Willmott, *Battle of Leyte Gulf*, 140–41. Masanori Ito, who spoke with many of Nishimura's contemporaries, concluded that "Nishimura had determined to push toward Leyte Gulf at all cost"; *The End of the Imperial Japanese Navy*, 135.

28. Tully, *Battle of Surigao Strait*, 94; Prados, *Storm over Leyte*, 236; Willmott, *Battle of Leyte Gulf*, 142–43.

29. Jesse Oldendorf, "Comments on the Battle of Surigao Strait," *Proceedings*, April 1959, 106; Tully, *Battle of Surigao Strait*, 87; Morison, *Leyte*, 201.

30. The 24th and 56th Destroyer Squadrons also attacked Nishimura's column. Morison, *Leyte*, 222; Prados, *Storm over Leyte*, 236–39; Cutler, *Battle of Leyte Gulf*, 190–93; Willmott, *Battle of Leyte Gulf*, 147.

31. Willmott, *Battle of Leyte Gulf*, 148–51; Oldendorf, "Comments," 106; Morison, *Leyte*, 221, 228; Tully, *Battle of Surigao Strait*, 176–78, 217–18; Heinrichs and Gallicchio, *Implacable Foes*, 182–83.

32. Morison, *Leyte*, 238; Prados, *Storm over Leyte*, 242–50.

33. Taylor, *Magnificent Mitscher*, 262–63; Prados, 254; Cutler, *Battle of Leyte Gulf*, 237; Hornfischer, *Last Stand of the Tin Can Sailors*, 212.

34. Cutler, *Battle of Leyte Gulf*, 221; Ito and Pineau, *The End of the Imperial Japanese Navy*, 135–36; Hornfischer, *Last Stand of the Tin Can Sailors*, 158.

35. On Sprague, see John F. Wukovits, *Devotion to Duty: A Biography of Admiral Clifton A. F. Sprague* (Annapolis: USNI, 1995). Wukovits discusses the origin of Sprague's nickname on 14, the estrangement between Sprague's wife and her brother on 40–41, and the Battle off Samar on 159–80. Hornfischer, *Last Stand of the Tin Can Sailors*, 135–37; Prados, *Storm over Leyte*, 299.

36. Prados, *Storm over Leyte*, 272.

37. Robert C. Hagen with Sidney Shalett, "We Asked for the Jap Fleet—and We Got It," *Saturday Evening Post*, May 26, 1945, 10.

38. Ibid., 74; Cutler, *Battle of Leyte Gulf*, 227–32, 239, 248; Hornfischer, *Last Stand of the Tin Can Sailors*, 203–10, 276–77, 293–302; J. Henry Doscher Jr., *Little Wolf at Leyte* (Austin, TX: Sunbelt Media, 1996), 42.

39. Morison, *Leyte*, 280; Hornfischer, *Last Stand of the Tin Can Sailors*, 241; Willmott, *Battle of Leyte Gulf*, 161. I cannot let pass the opportunity to note here that Lieutenant Paul Garrison, who conducted ten dry runs on the Japanese battleships, was the author's uncle.

40. Cutler, *Battle of Leyte Gulf*, 236; Hornfischer, *Last Stand of the Tin Can Sailors*, 239–40.

41. Prados, *Storm over Leyte*, 272–74; Hornfischer, *Last Stand of the Tin Can Sailors*, 213.

42. Halsey and Bryan, *Admiral Halsey's Story*, 219; Solberg, *Decision and Dissent*, 152–53.

43. Interestingly, the way Halsey remembered this message, and the way he quoted it in his 1947 memoir, is: "THE WHOLE WORLD WANTS TO KNOW WHERE IS TASK FORCE 34." Halsey blamed the error on "the little squirt" in Pearl Harbor who chose the phrase "the world wonders" as terminal padding. The major error, however, was by the radioman on Halsey's own flagship, Lt. (j.g.) Robert Balfour, who failed to delete the padding, and by Lt. Burt Goldstein, who sent it up to the bridge that way. Halsey and Bryan, *Admiral Halsey's Story*, 220–21; Solberg, *Decision and Dissent*, 154.

44. Halsey and Bryan, *Admiral Halsey's Story*, 220–21; Solberg, *Decision and Dissent*, 154; Hughes, *Admiral Bill Halsey*, 370–71.

45. Solberg, *Decision and Dissent*, 154–55.

46. Willmott, *Battle of Leyte Gulf*, 171–72; Hornfischer, *Last Stand of the Tin Can Sailors*, 318; James A. Field, *The Japanese at Leyte Gulf: The Sho Operation* (Princeton: Princeton University Press, 1947), 123.

47. Field, *The Japanese at Leyte Gulf*, 125–26; Ito and Pineau, *The End of the Imperial Japanese Navy*, 166; Koyanagi, "With Kurita," 126; Tameichi Hara, *Japanese Destroyer Captain* (Annapolis: USNI, 1967), 256. There is considerable dispute about the "sighting report" that Kurita claimed to have received. H. P. Willmott in particular wonders if there ever was such a report and suggests that Kurita may have invented it later as "a deliberate attempt to cover [his] tracks." Willmott, *Battle of Leyte Gulf*, 188–91.

48. Morison, *Leyte*, 288; Cutler, *Battle of Leyte Gulf*, 259; Hornfischer, *Last Stand of the Tin Can Sailors*, 322–23.

49. Morison, *Leyte*, 296–99; Prados, *Storm over Leyte*, 296, 327; and Cutler, *Battle of Leyte Gulf*, 262–63, all emphasize Kurita's exhaustion. The interviewer cited here was Masanori Ito, who quotes Kurita in his book *The End of the Imperial Japanese Navy*, 160. Milan Vego (*Battle for Leyte*, 270) concludes that Kurita went north "in search of the enemy carriers." H. P. Willmott (*Battle of Leyte Gulf*, 185) is skeptical, writing, "The various arguments paraded through time as the possible basis for Kurita's decision simply do not make sense...not least the decision to go north to seek out the enemy." Several decades later, Kurita suggested that his true objective was to avoid further loss of life, though that comment was likely a reflection of the postwar mood of reconciliation.

50. Cutler, *Battle of Leyte Gulf*, 268–73.
51. Koyanagi, "With Kurita," 128.

Chapter 26: The Noose Tightens

1. Richard H. O'Kane, *Clear the Bridge: The War Patrols of the U.S.S.* Tang (Chicago: Rand McNally, 1977), 314–20, 445–54.
2. Ibid., 321–40, 455–65. O'Kane was later awarded the Medal of Honor. See also Clay Blair, *Silent Victory: The U.S. Submarine War Against Japan* (Philadelphia: J. B. Lippincott, 1975), 766–70.
3. Blair, *Silent Victory*, 814–15; David Jones and Peter Nunan, *U.S. Subs Down Under* (Annapolis: USNI, 2005), 233–34.
4. Blair, *Silent Victory*, 787.
5. William R. McCants, *War Patrols of the USS* Flasher (Chapel Hill, NC: Professional Press, 1994), 322; Wiley Davis oral history (OH00843), NMPW, 7.
6. Joseph Enright, Shinano! *The Sinking of Japan's Supership* (New York: St. Martin's Press, 1987), 114; McCants, *War Patrols of the USS* Flasher, 245; Davis oral history, NMPW, 10.
7. F. G. Hoffman, "The American Wolf Packs: A Case Study in Wartime Adaptation," *Joint Force Quarterly* 80 (Jan. 2016).
8. Mark P. Parillo, *The Japanese Merchant Marine in World War II* (Annapolis: USNI, 1993), 204 (see especially the tables on 237–47, including Table A.5, on 239); Richard B. Frank, *Downfall: The End of the Imperial Japanese Empire* (New York: Random House, 1999), 78; Samuel Eliot Morison, *New Guinea and the Marianas* (Boston: Little, Brown, 1954), 16; Frederic C. Lane, *Ships for Victory: A History of Shipbuilding Under the U.S. Maritime Commission in World War II* (Baltimore: Johns Hopkins University Press, 1951), including the tables on 5 and 7.
9. Wiley Davis oral history (OH00843), NMPW, 10; Preston Allen oral history (OH00825), NMPW, 6.
10. Parillo, *The Japanese Merchant Marine*, 128–31; Max Hastings, *Retribution: The Battle for Japan, 1944–45* (New York: Alfred A. Knopf, 2008), 37; Richard H. O'Kane, Wahoo: *The Patrols of America's Most Famous Submarine* (Novato, CA: Presidio, 1987), 316–30.
11. Frank, *Downfall*, 81; Hastings, *Retribution*, 17; Parillo, *The Japanese Merchant Marine*, 131; McCants, *War Patrols of the USS* Flasher, 304–12, 332–33; Blair, *Silent Victory*, 794–96, 799.
12. Parillo, *The Japanese Merchant Marine*, 174–77, 209. Also see the war patrol tables in Blair, *Silent Victory*, 898–982, especially those for 1944, which are on 942–67.
13. Blair, *Silent Victory*, 773–74.
14. Curtis E. LeMay and Bill Yenne, *Superfortress: The Story of the B-29 and American Air Power* (New York: McGraw-Hill, 1988), 59–73.
15. Ibid., 74–91.
16. Ibid., 103–4.
17. Enright, *Shinano*, 34–39; LeMay and Yenne, *Superfortress*, 103; Daniel T. Schwabe, *Burning Japan: Air Force Bombing Strategy Change in the Pacific* (Sterling, VA: Potomac Books, 2015), 100–102.

18. Enright, *Shinano*, 71–72.
19. Lynn L. Moore, "*Shinano*: The Jinx Carrier," *Proceedings*, Feb. 1953, 142–49.
20. Enright, *Shinano*, 10–15.
21. Ibid., 90–100.
22. Ibid., 190–95; Blair, *Silent Victory*, 778–79.
23. William F. Halsey and J. Bryan, *Admiral Halsey's Story* (New York: McGraw-Hill, 1947), 229–31.
24. Ibid, 236.
25. C. Raymond Calhoun, *Typhoon: The Other Enemy* (Annapolis: USNI, 1981), 36; Halsey, *Admiral Halsey's Story*, 237.
26. Arthur Brown oral history, NMPW, 12; Halsey, *Admiral Halsey's Story*, 237–38; Calhoun, *Typhoon*, 52, 54, 59. Lower barometric recordings have been made since. The current record is 25.96 inches, made in 2006 south of Guam very near the location of "Halsey's Typhoon."
27. Calhoun, *Typhoon*, 201; Hughes, *Admiral Bill Halsey*, 382–83.
28. Don McNelly oral history (OH01256), 12, NMPW.
29. Ibid., 167. Nimitz's letter of Feb. 13, 1945, and King's endorsement of Nov. 23, 1945, are both in Calhoun, *Typhoon*, 209, 216–23. Gerald Bogan oral history, USNI, 125–26.
30. Thomas B. Buell, *The Quiet Warrior: A Biography of Admiral Raymond A. Spruance* (Boston: Little, Brown, 1974), 323.
31. Samuel Eliot Morison, *Victory in the Pacific* (Boston: Little, Brown, 1960), 157; Hastings, *Retribution*, 290; LeMay and Yenne, *Superfortress*, 111.
32. Samuel Harris, *B-29s over Japan: A Group Commander's Diary* (Jefferson, NC: McFarland, 2011), 201 (diary entry of Feb. 7, 1945).
33. Ernest J. King and Walter Muir Whitehill, *Fleet Admiral King: A Naval Record* (New York: W. W. Norton, 1952), 596.
34. Spruance to CMC, Jan. 5, 1952, quoted in William S. Bartley, *Iwo Jima: Amphibious Epic* (Washington, DC: Historical Branch, U.S. Marine Corps, 1954), 21.
35. Blair, *Silent Victory*, 825–27; William Coffey oral history (OH00833), NMPW, 14.
36. Spruance to Hoover, Nov. 30, 1944, quoted in Thomas B. Buell, *The Quiet Warrior* (Boston: Little, Brown, 1974), 318–19. Airplane losses are listed in Morison, *Victory in the Pacific*, 25.
37. Morison, *Victory in the Pacific*, 12–13.
38. Bartley, *Iwo Jima*, Appendix III (218–21); Robert S. Burrell, *The Ghosts of Iwo Jima* (College Station: Texas A&M University Press, 2006), 83–84; Morison, *Victory in the Pacific*, 15–16, 38–39. The quotation is from 73.
39. Morison, *Victory in the Pacific*, 53–55.
40. LeMay and Yenne, *Superfortress*, 121–22; Frank, *Downfall*, 45–46; Samuel Harris, *B-29s over Japan*, 218 (diary entry of Mar. 7, 1945).
41. LeMay and Yenne, *Superfortress*, 123; Frank, *Downfall*, 6–7; Schwabe, *Burning Japan*, 120–21; Harris, *B-29s over Japan*, 218 (diary entry of Mar. 9). Particularly vivid descriptions of the March 9–10 bombing attack on Tokyo are in Frank, *Downfall*, 3–19; and Hastings, *Retribution*, 296–305.
42. Buell, *The Quiet Warrior*, 324.

43. A useful corrective to the view that the seizure of Iwo Jima was essential to Allied victory is Burrell, *Ghosts of Iwo Jima*, esp. 106–11.

44. "United States Strategic Bombing Survey," July 1, 1946 (Summary Report), 17; Parillo, *The Japanese Merchant Marine*, 225.

45. *New York Times*, March 11, 1945, 1, 13.

Chapter 27: Denouement

1. Ian Kershaw, *The End: The Defiance and Destruction of Hitler's Germany, 1944–45* (New York: Penguin, 2011), 167–86.

2. Ibid., 264, 396, 400; Karl Doenitz, *Memoirs: Ten Years and Twenty Days* (Annapolis, USNI, 1958, 1990), 355–58, 421–22. See also Brian McCue, *U-Boats in the Bay of Biscay* (Washington, DC: National Defense University, 1990).

3. Barry Turner, *Karl Doenitz and the Last Days of the Third Reich* (London: Icon Books, 2015), 37–43; Doenitz, *Memoirs*, 355–58 (quotation on 427).

4. Doenitz, *Memoirs*, 372–73, 399.

5. Kershaw, *The End*, 391–92; Turner, *Karl Doenitz and the Last Days*, 142–46; Cathryn J. Prince, *Death in the Baltic: The World War II Sinking of the* Wilhelm Gustloff (New York: Palgrave Macmillan, 2013), 47–51, 66–67; Doenitz, *Memoirs*, 431.

6. Prince, *Death in the Baltic*, 47–86; A. V. Sellwood, *The Damned Don't Drown: The Sinking of the* Wilhelm Gustloff (Annapolis: USNI, 1973), 16–17.

7. Prince, *Death in the Baltic*, 129–49, 169; Sellwood, *The Damned Don't Drown*, 116–24; Doenitz, *Memoirs*, 434.

8. Turner, *Karl Doenitz and the Last Days*, 2–11; Kershaw, *The End*, 346; Walter Kempowski, ed., *Swansong, 1945* (New York: W. W. Norton, 2014), 210–11.

9. Doenitz, *Memoirs*, 445; Kershaw, *The End*, 306.

10. Doenitz, *Memoirs*, 437, 457–88.

11. Kershaw, *The End*, 363–73; Doenitz, *Memoirs*, 462–63.

12. Samuel Eliot Morison, *Victory in the Pacific, 1945* (Boston: Little, Brown, 1965), 93.

13. Charles S. Nichols and Henry I. Shaw Jr., *Okinawa: Victory in the Pacific* (Washington, DC: Historical Branch, U.S. Marine Corps, 1955), 1–11.

14. Robert Stern, *Fire from the Sky: Surviving the Kamikaze Threat* (Annapolis: USNI, 2010), 32–37; Max Hastings, *Retribution: The Battle for Japan, 1944–45* (New York: Alfred A. Knopf, 2008), 164–73.

15. Stern, *Fire from the Sky*, 33, 53, 69–80, 85, 119.

16. Raymond Lamont-Brown, *Kamikaze: Japan's Suicide Samurai* (London: Arms and Armour, 1997), 7–24; Maxwell Taylor Kennedy, *Danger's Hour: The Story of the USS Bunker Hill and the Kamikaze Pilot Who Crippled Her* (New York: Simon and Schuster, 2008), 125–26, 175.

17. Rikihei Inoguchi and Tadashi Nakajima, *The Divine Wind: Japan's Kamikaze Force in World War II* (Annapolis: USNI, 1958), 83.

18. Ibid., 154.

19. Tameichi Hara with Fred Saito and Roger Pineau, *Japanese Destroyer Captain* (Annapolis: USNI, 1967), 259.

20. Morison, *Victory in the Pacific*, 138.

21. Philip Vian, *Action This Day: A War Memoir* (London: Frederick Muller, 1960), 178; Morison, *Victory in the Pacific*, 148.

22. F. Julian Becton with Joseph Morschauser III, *The Ship That Would Not Die* (Englewood Cliffs, NJ: Prentice-Hall, 1980), 227.

23. Morison, *Victory in the Pacific*, 237.

24. Matome Ugaki, *Fading Victory: The Diary of Admiral Matome Ugaki, 1941–1945*, ed. Donald M. Goldstein and Katherine V. Dillon (Annapolis: USNI, 1995), 573 (entry of Apr. 6, 1945); Morison, *Victory in the Pacific*, 189–97.

25. Becton, *The Ship That Would Not Die*, 233–37; John Wukovits, *Hell from the Heavens: The Epic Story of the USS* Laffey *and World War II's Greatest Kamikaze Attack* (Philadelphia: Da Capo Press, 2015), 151.

26. Becton, *The Ship That Would Not Die*, 241. Manson is quoted by Wukovits in *Hell from the Heavens*, 177.

27. Action Report and deck log of the USS *Laffey*, Apr. 27, 1945, both USNA. Postwar estimates suggest that *Laffey* was actually hit by six kamikazes and five bombs. See Becton's own account, *The Ship That Would Not Die*, 236–62; and Wukovits, *Hell from the Heavens*, 151–209.

28. Ugaki, *Fading Victory* (diary entries of Apr. 6, 13, and 30, 1945), 573, 583, 602.

29. For a compilation of the kamikaze attacks off Okinawa, see the table in Morison, *Victory in the Pacific*, 233.

30. Ugaki, *Fading Victory* (diary entry of May 11, 1945), 610.

31. Hara, *Japanese Destroyer Captain*, 259; Russell Spurr, *A Glorious Way to Die: The Kamikaze Mission of the Battleship* Yamato, *April 1945* (New York: Newmarket Press, 1981), 109.

32. Spurr, *A Glorious Way to Die*, 105.

33. Ibid., 96; Hara, *Japanese Destroyer Captain*, 264; Mitsuru Yoshida, "The End of Yamato," *Proceedings*, Feb. 1952, 118.

34. Spurr, *A Glorious Way to Die*, 205–8, 217–21.

35. Ibid., 231–36; Hara, *Japanese Destroyer Captain*, 278.

36. Yoshida, "The End of *Yamato*," 122, 124, 128.

37. Hara, *Japanese Destroyer Captain*, 284.

38. Stephen S. Roskill, *The War at Sea, 1939–1945* (London: Her Majesty's Stationery Office, 1961), 3 (part 2): 188; Ernest J. King and Walter Muir Whitehill, *Fleet Admiral King, a Naval Record* (New York: W. W. Norton, 1952), 569.

39. Hastings, *Retribution*, 400–402; Vian, *Action This Day*, 175.

40. Hastings, *Retribution*, 402; Vian, *Action This Day*, 177–78, 185, 190; Roskill, *The War at Sea*, 3 (part 2): 343–46.

41. Ugaki, *Fading Victory* (diary entry of Apr. 8, 1945), 577.

42. The numbers are from Hastings, *Retribution*, 402. See also Waldo Heinrichs and Marc Gallicchio, *Implacable Foes: War in the Pacific, 1944–1945* (New York: Oxford University Press, 2017), 465–66.

43. Richard B. Frank, *Downfall: The End of the Imperial Japanese Empire* (New York: Random House, 1999), 79.

44. Hastings, *Retribution*, 426–27, 439–40, 453; Heinrichs and Gallicchio, *Implacable Foes*, 525, 528.

45. Hastings, *Retribution*, 470–78; Heinrich and Gallicchio, *Implacable Foes*, 524–25.
46. Frank, *Downfall*, 118; Heinrichs and Gallicchio, *Implacable Foes*, 525.
47. Hastings, *Retribution*, 505–15; Frank, *Downfall*, 321–22; Anthony Beevor, *The Second World War* (New York: Little, Brown,), 775.

Epilogue: Tokyo Bay, 1945

1. *New York Times*, September 2, 1945, 1, 3; James D. Hornfischer, *The Fleet at Flood Tide* (New York: Random House, 2016), 468–69. Color footage of the surrender ceremony is available at www.youtube.com/watch?v=v5MMVd5XOK8.

BIBLIOGRAPHY

Archival Sources

National Archives and Records Administration (NARA), College Park, Maryland
    Action Reports: *U.S. Navy Action and Operational Reports from World War II*
        Part I, CINCLANT (16 reels)
        Part II, Third Fleet and Fifth Fleet (16 reels)
        Part III, Fifth Fleet and Fifth Fleet Carrier Task Forces (12 reels)
    Record Group 38: CNO Files, CINCPAC Files
    Record Group 313: Naval Operational Forces
    Records of the German Navy, 1850–1945

National Museum of the Pacific War, Fredericksburg, Texas
    Oral histories
    Conference transcripts

National World War II Museum (Eisenhower Center), New Orleans, Louisiana
    Oral histories

Naval History and Heritage Command, Washington Navy Yard, Washington, DC
    Ernest J. King Papers
    Chester Nimitz Diary
    Chester Nimitz Papers
    Walter Lord Collection

University of Maryland (Hornbake Library), College Park, Maryland
    Gordon Prange Papers

U.S. Naval Academy, Annapolis, Maryland
    Action reports
    Oral histories

U.S. Naval Institute, Annapolis, Maryland
    Oral histories

U.S. Naval War College, Newport, Rhode Island
   Bates, Richard W. *The Battle of Savo Island, August 9th, 1942. Strategical and Tactical Analysis.* 1950.
   H. Kent Hewitt Papers

Newspapers
   Japan Times
   New York Times
   The Times (London)
   Chicago Tribune

Printed Primary and Secondary Works
The following printed sources are grouped into topics. Though some books could reasonably be included in more than one list, they are listed here only once. It may therefore be necessary to check more than one topic category in order to find a particular book.
   A. General Works
   B. National Navies
      Royal Australian Navy
      The Royal Canadian Navy
      The French Navy (Marine Nationale)
      The German Navy (Kriegsmarine)
      The Imperial Japanese Navy
      The Italian Navy (Regia Marina)
      The Royal Netherlands Navy
      The Royal Navy
      The Soviet Navy (The Red Fleet)
      The United States Navy
   C. Operational Theaters and Special Topics:
      The Mediterranean
      The Norway Campaign
      The Pacific
      Naval Codes and Code Breaking
      The War on Trade
   D. Articles

A. General Works
Atkinson, Rick. *An Army at Dawn: The War in North Africa, 1942–1943.* New York: Henry Holt, 2002.
———. *The Day of Battle: The War in Sicily and Italy, 1943–1944.* New York: Henry Holt, 2007.
———. *The Guns at Last Light: The War in Western Europe, 1944–1945.* New York: Henry Holt, 2013.
Baldwin, Hanson. *Battles Lost and Won: Great Campaigns of World War II.* New York: Harper and Row, 1966.
Ballantine, Duncan S. *U.S. Naval Logistics in the Second World War.* Princeton: Princeton University Press, 1949.

Beevor, Antony. *The Second World War*. New York: Little, Brown, 2012.

Belden, Jack. *Still Time to Die*. New York: Harper and Brothers, 1943.

Brown, Louis. *A Radar History of World War II: Technical and Military Imperatives*. Bristol, England: Institute of Physics, 1999.

Campbell, John. *Naval Weapons of World War II*. London: Conway Maritime, 1985.

Cressman, Robert. *The Official Chronology of the U.S. Navy in World War II*. Annapolis: Naval Institute Press, 2000.

Fergusson, Bernard. *The Watery Maze: The Story of Combined Operations*. New York: Holt, Rinehart, and Winston, 1961.

Goodhart, Philip. *Fifty Ships That Saved the World: The Foundation of the Anglo-American Friendship*. Garden City, NY: Doubleday, 1965.

Greenfield, Kent Roberts, ed. *Command Decisions*. Washington, DC: Office of the Chief of Military History, 1960.

Guerlac, Henry E., ed. *Radar in World War II*. Vol. 8 (Sections A–C and D–E) of *The History of Modern Physics, 1800–1950*. Los Angeles: Tomash, 1987.

Harwood, Jeremy. *World War II at Sea*. Minneapolis: Zenith, 2015.

Howse, Derek. *Radar at Sea: The Royal Navy in World War II*. Annapolis: Naval Institute Press, 1993.

Jordan, Gerald, ed. *Naval Warfare in the Twentieth Century, 1900–1945*. London: Croom Helm, 1977.

Kempowski, Walter. *Swansong: A Collective Diary of the Last Days of the Third Reich, 1945*. New York: W. W. Norton, 2015.

Kershaw, Ian. *The End: The Defiance and Destruction of Hitler's Germany, 1944–1945*. New York: Penguin, 2011.

Koburger, C. W., Jr. *Naval Warfare in the Baltic, 1939–1945*. Westport, CT: Praeger, 1994.

Leighton, Richard M., and Robert W. Coakley. *Global Logistics and Strategy, 1940–1943*. Washington, DC: Office of the Chief of Military History, 1955.

Leutze, James R. *Bargaining for Supremacy: Anglo-American Naval Collaboration, 1937–1941*. Chapel Hill: University of North Carolina Press, 1977.

MacGregor, David. "Innovation in Naval Warfare in Britain and the United States Between the First and Second World Wars." Ph.D. dissertation, University of Rochester, 1989.

Maurer, John H., and Christopher M. Bell, eds. *At the Crossroads Between Peace and War: The London Naval Conference of 1930*. Annapolis: Naval Institute Press, 2013.

O'Brien, Phillips Payson, ed. *Technology and Naval Combat in the Twentieth Century and Beyond*. London: Frank Cass, 2001.

O'Connor, Raymond G. *Perilous Equilibrium: The United States and the London Naval Conference of 1930*. New York: Greenwood Press, 1962.

Pelz, Stephen E. *Race to Pearl Harbor: The Failure of the Second London Naval Conference and the Onset of World War II*. Cambridge, MA: Harvard University Press, 1974.

Proceedings of the London Naval Conference of 1930 and Supplementary Documents. Washington, DC: Government Printing Office, 1931.

Roberts, Andrew. *The Storm of War: A New History of the Second World War*. New York: Harper, 2011.

Rohwer, Jurgen. *Chronology of the War at Sea, 1939–1945*. Annapolis: Naval Institute Press, 1972, 2005.

Symonds, Craig L. *Neptune: The Allied Invasion of Europe and the D-Day Landings*. New York: Oxford University Press, 2014. Published in paperback as *Operation Neptune: The D-Day Landings and the Allied Invasion of Europe*. New York: Oxford University Press, 2014.

Weinberg, Gerhard L. *A World at Arms: A Global History of World War II*. Cambridge: Cambridge University Press, 1994.

B. National Navies

The Royal Australian Navy

Beaumont, Joan. *Australia's War, 1939–1945*. St. Leonards, Australia: Allen and Unwin, 1996.

Gill, G. Herman. *Royal Australian Navy, 1939–1942*. Canberra: Australian War Memorial, 1968.

Gillison, Douglas. *Royal Australian Air Force, 1939–1945*. Canberra: Australian War Memorial, 1962.

H.MA.S. Sydney. 2 vols. Sydney: Halstead Press, 1953.

Johnston, George H. *Action at Sea: The Saga of the* Sydney. Boston: Houghton Mifflin, 1942.

McKie, Ronald. *Proud Echo: The Last Great Battle of HMAS* Perth. Sydney: Angus and Robertson, 1953.

Montgomery, Michael. *Who Sank the* Sydney? New York: Hippocrene Books, 1981.

Olson, Wesley. *Bitter Victory: The Death of HMAS* Sydney. Annapolis: Naval Institute Press, 2000.

Stevens, David, ed. *The Royal Australian Navy*. New York: Oxford University Press, 2001.

The Royal Canadian Navy

Copp, Terry. *Cinderella Army: The Canadians in Northwest Europe, 1944–1945*. Toronto: University of Toronto Press, 2006.

Douglas, W. A. B., Roger Sarty, and Michael Whitby, et al. *No Higher Purpose* (vol. 2, part 1), *and Blue Water Navy* (vol. 2, part 2): *The Official Operational History of the Royal Canadian Navy in the Second World War, 1943–1945*. St. Catherines, Ontario: Vanwell, 2002 and 2007.

Graves, Donald E. *In Peril on the Sea: The Royal Canadian Navy and the Battle of the Atlantic*. Toronto: Robin Brass Studio, 2003.

Halford, Robert G. *The Unknown Navy: Canada's World War II Merchant Navy*. St. Catherines, Ontario: Vanwell, 1995.

Johnson, Mac. *Corvettes Canada: Convoy Veterans of WWII Tell Their True Stories*. Toronto: McGraw-Hill Ryerson, 1994.

Macpherson, Ken. *Corvettes of the Royal Canadian Navy, 1939–1945*. St. Catherines, ON: Vanwell, 1993.

Milner, Marc. *North Atlantic Run: The Royal Canadian Navy and the Battle for the Convoys*. Annapolis: Naval Institute Press, 1985.

Whitaker, Denis, and Whitaker, Shelagh. *Tug of War: The Allied Victory that Opened Antwerp*. Toronto: Stoddert Publishing, 2000.

Zuehlke, Mark. *Operation Husky: The Canadian Invasion of Sicily, July 10–August 7, 1943*. Vancouver: Douglas and McIntyre, 2008.

The French Navy (Marine Nationale)

Auphan, Paul, and Jacques Mordal. *The French Navy in World War II*. Translated by A. C. J. Sabalot. Annapolis: Naval Institute Press, 1959.

Delage, Edmond. *Six ans de guerre navale, 1939–1945*. Paris: Editions Berger-Levrault, 1950.

Godfroy, René-Emile. *L'aventure de la Force X à Alexandrie, 1940–1943*. Paris: Librairie Plon, 1953.

Heckstall-Smith, Anthony. *The Fleet That Faced Both Ways*. London: Anthony Blend, 1963.

Jenkins, E. H. *A History of the French Navy, from Its Beginnings to the Present Day*. Annapolis: Naval Institute Press, 1973.

Melton, George E. *From Versailles to Mers el-Kébir: The Promise of Anglo-French Naval Cooperation, 1919–40*. Annapolis: Naval Institute Press, 2015.

Noguères, Henri. *Le suicide de la flotte française à Toulon*. Paris: Robert Laffont, 1961.

Tute, Warren. *The Deadly Stroke*. New York: Coward, McCann and Geoghegan, 1973.

The German Navy (Kriegsmarine)

Ballantyne, Iain. *Killing the Bismarck: Destroying the Pride of Hitler's Fleet*. Barnsley, South Yorkshire: Pen and Sword, 2010.

Bercuson, David J., and Holger H. Herwig. *The Destruction of the Bismarck*. New York: Overlook Press, 2001.

Bird, Keith W. *Erich Raeder: Admiral of the Third Reich*. Annapolis: Naval Institute Press, 2006.

Boldt, Gerhard. *Hitler: The Last Days*. New York: Coward, McCann, and Geoghegan, 1947.

Brennecke, Jochen. *The Hunters and the Hunted: German U-Boats, 1939–1945*. New York: W. W. Norton, 1958. Reprinted, Annapolis: Naval Institute Press, 2003.

Busch, Fritz-Otto. *The Drama of the Scharnhorst: A Factual Account from the German Viewpoint*. London: Robert Hale, 1956.

Doenitz, Karl. *Memoirs: Ten Years and Twenty Days*. Annapolis: Naval Institute Press, 1959.

Edwards, Bernard. *Beware Raiders! German Surface Raiders in the Second World War*. Annapolis: Naval Institute Press, 2001.

Fritz, Martin. *German Steel and Swedish Iron Ore, 1939–1945*. Goteborg: Institute of Economic History, 1974.

Fuehrer Conferences on Naval Affairs, 1939–1945. Foreword by Jak P. Mallman Showell. Annapolis: Naval Institute Press, 1990.

Garrett, Richard. Scharnhorst *and* Gneisenau: *The Elusive Sisters*. London: David and Charles, 1978.

Guani, Alberto. *The Uruguayan Blue Book: Documents Relating to the Sinking of the* Admiral Graf Spee *and the Internment of the Merchant Vessel* Tacoma. London: Hutchinson, 1940.

Jones, Marcus D. *Nazi Steel: Friedrich Flick and German Expansion in Western Europe, 1940–1944*. Annapolis: Naval Institute Press, 2012.

Kieser, Egbert. *Operation "Sea Lion": The German Plan to Invade Britain, 1940*. Translated by Helmut Bögler. Annapolis: Naval Institute Press, 1997.

Korganoff, Alexandre. *The Phantom of Scapa Flow*. Skepperton, Surrey: Ian Allen, 1974.

Krancke, Theodor, and H. J. Brennecke. *The Battleship* Scheer. Translated by Edward Fitzgerald. London: William Kimber, 1956. Republished as *Pocket Battleship: The Story of the* Admiral Scheer. New York: W. W. Norton, 1958.

Martienssen, Anthony. *Hitler and His Admirals*. New York: E. P. Dutton, 1949.

McKinstry, Leo. *Operation Sea Lion: The Failed Nazi Invasion That Turned the Tide of War*. New York: Overlook Press, 2014.

Miller, David. *Langsdorff and the Battle of the River Plate*. Barnsley, South Yorkshire: Pen and Sword, 2013.

Muggenthaler, August Karl. *German Raiders of World War II*. Englewood Cliffs, NJ: Prentice-Hall, 1977.

Müllenheim-Rechberg, Burkard. *Battleship* Bismarck, *a Survivor's Story*. Translated by Jack Sweetman. Annapolis: Naval Institute Press, 1980.

Noli, Jean. *The Admiral's Wolf Pack*. Garden City, NY: Doubleday, 1974.

O'Hara, Vincent P. *The German Fleet at War, 1939–1945*. Annapolis: Naval Institute Press, 2004.

Peillard, Léonce. *Sink the* Tirpitz*!* Translated by Oliver Coburn. New York: G. P. Putnam's Sons, 1968. Originally published as *Coulez le* Tirpitz. Paris: Robert Laffont, 1965.

Potter, John Deane. *Fiasco: The Break-out of the German Battleships*. New York: Stein and Day, 1970.

Prien, Gunther. *I Sank the* Royal Oak. Translated by the Comte de la Vatine. London: Grays Inn Press, 1954. Originally published in German in 1940.

Prince, Cathryn J. *Death in the Baltic: The World War II Sinking of the* Wilhelm Gustloff. New York: St. Martin's Press, 2013.

Raeder, Erich. *My Life*. Annapolis: U.S. Naval Institute, 1960.

———. *Struggle for the Sea*. London: William Kimber, 1959.

Rogge, Bernhard, with Frank Wolfgang. *Under Ten Flags: The Story of the German Commerce Raider* Atlantis. London: Weidenfeld and Nicolson, 1955.

Rössler, Eberhard. *The U-Boat: The Evolution and Technical History of German Submarines*. London: Cassell, 1981.

Ruge, Friedrich. *Der Seekrieg: The German Navy's Story, 1939–1945*. Annapolis: U.S. Naval Institute, 1957.

Sellwood, A. V. *The Damned Don't Drown: The Sinking of the* Wilhelm Gustloff. Annapolis: Naval Institute Press, 1996. Originally published 1973.

Slavick, Joseph P. *The Cruise of the German Raider* Atlantis. Annapolis: Naval Institute Press, 2003.

Steinhoff, Johannes. *Messerschmitts over Sicily*. Baltimore, MD: Nautical and Aviation Publishing, 1969.

Stern, Robert C. *Type VII U-Boats*. Annapolis: Naval Institute Press, 1991.

Sweetman, John. Tirpitz: *Hunting the Beast*. Annapolis: Naval Institute Press, 2000.

Turner, Barry. *Karl Doenitz and the Last Days of the Third Reich*. London: Icon Press, 2015.

Von der Porten, Edward P. *The German Navy in World War II*. New York: Thomas Y. Crowell, 1969.

Vulliez, Albert, and Jacques Mordal. *Battleship* Bismarck. Fair Lawn, New Jersey: Essential Books, 1958.

———. *Battleship* Scharnhorst. Fair Lawn, NJ: Essential Books, 1958.

Watts, A. J. *The Loss of the* Scharnhorst. London: Ian Allan, 1970.

Whitley, M. J. *German Capital Ships of World War Two*. London: Arms and Armour, 1989.

———. *German Coastal Forces of World War II*. London: Arms and Armour, 1992.

Williamson, Gordon. *Wolf Pack: The Story of the U-Boat in World War II*. Oxford: Osprey, 2005.

Winton, John. *The Death of the* Scharnhorst. New York: Hippocrene Books, 1983.

Woodward, David. *The* Tirpitz *and the Battle for the North Atlantic*. New York: W. W. Norton, 1953.

The Imperial Japanese Navy

Agawa, Hiroyuki. *The Reluctant Admiral: Yamamoto and the Imperial Navy*. Tokyo: Kodansha International, 1979.

Asada, Sadao. *From Mahan to Pearl Harbor: The Imperial Japanese Navy and the United States*. Annapolis: Naval Institute Press, 2006.

Boyd, Carl, and Akihiko Yoshida. *The Japanese Submarine Force and World War II*. Annapolis: Naval Institute, 1995, 2002.

Chang, Iris. *The Rape of Nanking: The Forgotten Holocaust of World War II*. New York: Basic Books, 1997.

Cook, Haruko Taya, and Theodore F. Cook, eds. *Japan at War: An Oral History*. New York: New Press, 1992.

D'Albas, Andrieu. *Death of a Navy: Japanese Naval Action in World War II*. New York: Devin-Adair, 1957.

Dorn, Frank. *The Sino-Japanese War, 1937–41*. New York: Macmillan, 1974.

Dull, Paul. *A Battle History of the Imperial Japanese Navy, 1941–1945*. Annapolis: Naval Institute Press, 1978.

Enright, Joseph F., with James W. Ryan. Shinano! *The Sinking of Japan's Secret Supership*. New York: St. Martin's Press, 1987.

Evans, David C., ed. and trans. *The Japanese Navy in World War II: In the Words of Former Japanese Naval Officers*. Annapolis: Naval Institute Press, 1969.

Evans, David C., and Mark R. Peattie. *Kaigun: Strategy, Tactics, and Technology in the Imperial Japanese Navy, 1887–1941*. Annapolis: Naval Institute Press, 1997.

Goldstein, Donald M., and Katherine V. Dillon, eds. *Pacific War Papers: Japanese Documents of World War II*. Washington, DC: Potomac Books, 2004.

Hara, Tameichi, with Fred Saito and Roger Pineau. *Japanese Destroyer Captain: Pearl Harbor, Guadalcanal, Midway—the Great Naval Battles as Seen Through Japanese Eyes*. Annapolis: Naval Institute Press, 1967.

Hashimoto, Mochitsura. *Sunk: The Story of the Japanese Submarine Fleet, 1941–1945*. New York: Henry Holt, 1954.

Howarth, Stephen. *The Fighting Ships of the Rising Sun: The Drama of the Imperial Japanese Navy, 1895–1945*. New York: Atheneum, 1983.

Inoguchi, Rikihei, and Tadashi Nakajima, with Roger Pineau. *The Divine Wind: Japan's Kamikaze Force in World War II*. Annapolis: Naval Institute Press, 1958.

Ito, Masanori, with Roger Pineau. *The End of the Imperial Japanese Navy*. New York: W. W. Norton, 1956.

Lamont-Brown, Raymond. *Kamikaze: Japan's Suicide Samurai*. London: Arms and Armour, 1997.

Lu, David J., ed. *Japan: A Documentary History*. New York: M. E. Sharpe, 1997.

Matsumo, Kitaro. *Design and Construction of the* Yamato *and* Musashi. Tokyo: Haga, 1961.

Okakura, Yoshisaburo. *The Japanese Spirit*. London: Constable, 1909.

Okumiya, Masatake. *Zero*. New York: Dutton, 1956.

Parillo, Mark R. *The Japanese Merchant Marine in World War II*. Annapolis: Naval Institute Press, 1993.

Peattie, Mark R. *Sunburst: The Rise of Japanese Naval Air Power, 1909–1941*. Annapolis: Naval Institute Press, 2001.

Skulski, Janusz. *The Battleship Yamato: Anatomy of a Ship*. Annapolis: Naval Institute Press, 1988.

Smethurst, Richard J. *A Social Basis for Prewar Japanese Militarism: The Army and the Rural Community*. Berkeley: University of California Press, 1974.

Spurr, Russell. *A Glorious Way to Die: The Kamikaze Mission of the Battleship* Yamato, *April 1945*. New York: Newmarket Press, 1981.

Ugaki, Matome. *Fading Victory: The Diary of Matome Ugaki, 1941–1945*. Edited by Donald M. Goldstein and Katherine V. Dillon. Translated by Masataka Chihaya. Annapolis: Naval Institute Press, 1991.

Watanabe, Tsuneo, ed. *Who Was Responsible? From Marco Polo Bridge to Pearl Harbor*. A Project of the Yomiuri Shimbun War Responsibility Reexamination Committee. Tokyo: Yomiuri Shimbun, 2006.

Wohlstetter, Roberta. *Pearl Harbor: Warning and Decision*. Stanford: Stanford University Press, 1962.

Yamamoto, Masahiro. *Nanking: Anatomy of an Atrocity*. Westport, CT: Praeger, 2000.

Yoshimura, Akira. *Build the* Musashi: *The Birth and Death of the World's Greatest Battleship*. Tokyo: Kodansha International, 1991.

The Italian Navy (Regia Marina)

Borghese, J. Valerio. *Sea Devils: Italian Navy Commandos in World War II*. Annapolis: Naval Institute Press, 1995. Originally published as *Decima Flottiglia Mas*. Milan: Garzanti, 1967.

Bragadin, Marc'Antonio. *The Italian Navy in World War II*. Translated by Gale Hoffman. Annapolis: Naval Institute Press, 1957.

Ciano, Galeazzo. *Diary, 1937–1943*. New York: Enigma Books, 2002.

Mallett, Robert. *The Italian Navy and Fascist Expansionism, 1935–1940*. London: Frank Cass, 1998.

Mussolini, Benito. *Benito Mussolini Memoirs, 1942–1943, with Documents Relating to the Period*. Edited by Raymond Klibansky. New York: Howard Fertig, 1975.

Sadkovich, James J. *The Italian Navy in World War II*. Westport, CT: Greenwood Press, 1994.

The Royal Netherlands Navy

Boer, P. C. *The Loss of Java*. Singapore: NUS Press, 2011.

Kroese, A. *The Dutch Navy at War*. London: G. Allen and Unwin, 1945.

Quispel, Hubert V. *The Job and the Tools*. Rotterdam: Netherlands United Shipbuilding Bureau, 1960.

Thomas, David A. *The Battle of the Java Sea.* New York: Stein and Day, 1968.

Van Oosten, F. C. *The Battle of the Java Sea.* Annapolis: Naval Institute Press, 1976.

The Royal Navy

Ash, Bernard. *Someone Had Blundered: The Story of the* Repulse *and the* Prince of Wales. Garden City, NY: Doubleday, 1961.

Atkin, Ronald. *Pillar of Fire: Dunkirk, 1940.* Edinburgh: Birlinn, 1990.

Ballantyne, Iain. *Killing the* Bismarck: *Destroying the Pride of Hitler's Fleet.* Barnsley, South Yorkshire: Pen and Sword, 2010.

Barker, A. J. *Dunkirk: The Great Escape.* New York: David McKay, 1977.

Barnett, Correlli. *Engage the Enemy More Closely: The Royal Navy in the Second World War.* New York: W. W. Norton, 1991.

Battle of the River Plate. London: His Majesty's Stationery Office, 1940.

Bell, Christopher M. *Churchill and Sea Power.* New York: Oxford University Press, 2013.

Bennett, C. H., J. E. Harrold, and R. Porter, eds. *Dark Seas: The Battle of Cape Matapan.* Britannia Naval Histories of World War II. Plymouth: University of Plymouth Press, 2012.

———. *Hunting* Tirpitz: *Royal Navy Operations Against* Bismarck's *Sister Ship.* Britannia Naval Histories of World War II. Plymouth: University of Plymouth Press, 2012.

Bennett, Geoffrey. *The Loss of the* Prince of Wales *and* Repulse. Annapolis: Naval Institute Press, 1973.

Britts, Angus. *Neglected Skies: The Demise of British Naval Power in the Far East, 1922–42.* Annapolis: Naval Institute Press, 2017.

Broome, John E. *Convoy Is to Scatter.* London: William Kimber, 1972.

Carse, Robert. *Dunkirk, 1940.* Englewood Cliffs, NJ: Prentice-Hall, 1970.

Chalmers, W. S. *Full Cycle: The Biography of Admiral Sir Bertram Home Ramsay.* London: Hodder and Stoughton, 1959.

Churchill, Winston S. *The Second World War.* 6 vols. Boston: Houghton Mifflin, 1948–1953. Identified in notes by individual volume title.

Cunningham, Andrew Browne. *A Sailor's Odyssey.* New York: E. P. Dutton, 1951.

———. *The Cunningham Papers: The Mediterranean Fleet, 1939–1942.* Edited by Michael Simpson. Navy Records Society, vol. 140. Aldershot, Hants: Navy Records Society, 1999.

Divine, David. *The Nine Days of Dunkirk.* New York: W. W. Norton, 1959.

Frischauer, Willi, and Robert Jackson. *"The Navy's Here!" The* Altmark *Affair.* London: Victor Gollancz, 1955. Published in the United States as *The* Altmark *Affair.* New York: Macmillan, 1955.

Gardner, W. J. R., ed. *The Evacuation from Dunkirk: "Operation Dynamo," 26 May–4 June 1940.* London: Frank Cass, 2000.

Grenfell, Russell. *The* Bismarck *Episode.* New York: Macmillan, 1949.

———. *Main Fleet to Singapore.* New York: Macmillan, 1952.

Grove, Eric. *The Price of Disobedience: The Battle of the River Plate Reconsidered.* Annapolis: Naval Institute Press, 2000.

Hastings, Max, *Winston's War: Churchill, 1940–1945.* New York: Alfred A, Knopf, 2010.

Hellswinkell, Lars. *Hitler's Gateway to the Atlantic: German Naval Bases in France, 1940–1945.* Annapolis: Naval Institute Press, 2014.

Jackson, Robert. *Dunkirk: The British Evacuation 1940*. New York: St. Martin's Press, 1976.

Jones, Ben, ed. *The Fleet Air Arm in the Second World War: Norway, the Mediterranean, and the Bismarck*. Aldershot, England: Ashgate, 2012.

Kennedy, Ludovic. *Pursuit: The Chase and Sinking of the Bismarck*. New York: Viking Press, 1974.

Kerr, J. Lennox, and David James, eds. *Wavy Navy, by Some Who Served*. London: George G. Harrap, 1950.

Konstam, Angus. *Scapa Flow: The Defenses of Britain's Great Fleet Anchorage, 1914–1945*. Oxford, England: Osprey, 2009.

Lord, Walter. *The Miracle of Dunkirk*. New York: Viking Press, 1982.

MacIntyre, Donald. *Fighting Admiral: The Life of Admiral of the Fleet Sir James Somerville*. London: Evans Brothers, 1961.

Marder, Arthur J. *From the Dardanelles to Oran: Studies of the Royal Navy in War and Peace, 1915–1940*. New York: Oxford University Press, 1974.

McKee, Alexander. *Black Saturday: The Tragedy of the Royal Oak*. London: Souvenir Press, 1959.

Millington-Drake, Eugen. *The Drama of the Graf Spee and the Battle of the Plate: A Documentary Anthology, 1914–1964*. London: Peter Davies, 1964.

Nicholson, Arthur. *Hostages to Fortune: Winston Churchill and the Loss of the Prince of Wales and Repulse*. Stroud, Gloucestershire: Sutton, 2005.

Preston, Antony, and Alan Raven. *Flower Class Corvettes*. London: Arms and Armour, 1982. Published in paperback as *Ensign 3: Flower Class Corvettes*, Norwich, UK: Bivouac Books, 1973.

Prior, Robin. *When Britain Saved the West: The Story of 1940*. New Haven: Yale University Press, 2015.

Roskill, Stephen W. *Churchill and the Admirals*. London: Collins, 1977.

———. *Naval Policy Between the Wars: II: The Period of Reluctant Rearmament, 1930–1939*. Annapolis: Naval Institute Press, 1976.

———. *The War at Sea, 1939–1945*. 3 vols. London: Her Majesty's Stationery Office, 1954–1961.

Smyth, Denis. *Deathly Deception: The Real Story of Operation Mincemeat*. New York: Oxford University Press, 2010.

Snyder, Gerald S. *The Royal Oak Disaster*. London: William Kimber, 1976.

Somerville, John. *The Somerville Papers*. Edited by Michael Simpson. Navy Records Society, vol. 134. Aldershot, Hants: Navy Records Society, 1996.

Vian, Philip. *Action This Day: A War Memoir*. London: Frederick Muller, 1960.

Weaver, H. J. *Nightmare at Scapa Flow: The Truth About the Sinking of HMS Royal Oak*. Kestrels House, Oxfordshire: Cressrelles, 1980.

Wheeler-Bennett, John W. *King George VI: His Life and Reign*. New York: St. Martin's Press, 1958.

Winton, John. *Carrier Glorious: The Life and Death of an Aircraft Carrier*. London: Leo Cooper, 1986.

———. *Cunningham: The Greatest Admiral Since Nelson*. London: John Murray, 1998.

———. *The War at Sea: The British Navy in World War II*. New York: William Morrow, 1967.

Woodman, Richard. *The Battle of the River Plate: A Grand Delusion*. Annapolis: Naval Institute Press, 2008.

Wragg, David. *"Total Germany": The Royal Navy's War Against the Axis Powers, 1939–45*. Barnsley, South Yorkshire: Pen and Sword, 2016.

The Soviet Navy (The Red Fleet)

Achkasov, V. I., and N. B. Pavlovich. *Soviet Naval Operations in the Great Patriotic War, 1941–1945*. Annapolis: Naval Institute Press, 1981. Originally published as Sovetskoe voenno-morskoe iskusstvo v Velikoĭ Otechestvennoĭ voĭne. Moscow: Voenizdat, 1973.

Bray, Jeffrey K. *Mine Warfare in the Russo-Soviet Navy*. Laguna Hills, CA: Aegean Park Press, 1995.

Breyer, Siegfried. *Soviet Warship Development*, vol. 1, *1917–1937*. London: Conway Maritime Press, 1992.

Isakov, I. S. *The Red Fleet in the Second World War*. London: Hutchinson, 1947.

Meister, Jürg. *Soviet Warships of the Second World War*. London: Macdonald and Jane's, 1977.

Ruge, Friedrich. *The Soviets as Naval Opponents, 1941–1945*. Annapolis: Naval Institute Press, 1979.

The United States Navy

Abbazia, Patrick. *Mr. Roosevelt's Navy: The Private War of the U.S. Atlantic Fleet, 1939–1942*. Annapolis: Naval Institute Press, 1975.

Alexander, Joseph H. *Across the Reef: The Marine Assault of Tarawa*. Marines in World War II Commemorative Series. Washington, DC: Marine Corps Historical Center, 1993.

——. *Utmost Savagery: The Three Days of Tarawa*. Annapolis: Naval Institute Press, 1995.

Alford, Lodwick H. *Playing for Time: War on an Asiatic Fleet Destroyer*. Bennington, VT: Merriam Press, 2008.

Bailey, Leslie W. *Through Hell and High Water: The Wartime Memories of a Junior Combat Infantry Officer*. New York: Vantage Press, 1994.

Becton, F. Julian, with Joseph Morschauser. *The Ship That Would Not Die*. Englewood Cliffs, NJ: Prentice-Hall, 1980.

Blair, Clay. *Silent Victory: The U.S. Submarine War Against Japan*. Philadelphia: J. B. Lippincott, 1975.

Borneman, Walter R. *The Admirals: Nimitz, Halsey, Leahy and King, The Five-Star Admirals Who Won the War at Sea*. New York: Little, Brown, 2012.

Buell, Thomas B. *Master of Sea Power: A Biography of Fleet Admiral Ernest J. King*. Boston: Little, Brown, 1980.

——. *The Quiet Warrior: A Biography of Admiral Raymond A. Spruance*. Boston: Little, Brown, 1974.

Butcher, Harry C. *My Three Years with Eisenhower: The Personal Diary of Captain Harry C. Butcher, USNR, Naval Aide to General Eisenhower, 1942 to 1945*. New York: Simon and Schuster, 1946.

Calhoun, C. Raymond. *Typhoon: The Other Enemy*. Annapolis: Naval Institute Press, 1981.

Clark, J. J., with Clark G. Reynolds. *Carrier Admiral*. New York: David McKay, 1967.

Clark, Mark Wayne. *Calculated Risk*. New York: Harper and Brothers, 1950.

Cross, Robert F. *Sailor in the White House: The Seafaring Life of FDR*. Annapolis: Naval Institute Press, 2003.

Crosswell, D. K. R. *Beetle: The Life of General Walter Bedell Smith*. Lexington: University of Kentucky Press, 2010.

Davis, Burke. *Get Yamamoto*. New York: Random House, 1969.

———. *Sunk in Kula Gulf: The Final Voyage of the USS* Helena *and the Incredible Story of Her Survivors in World War II*. Washington, DC: Potomac Books, 2012.

Doolittle, James H., with Carroll V. Glines. *I Could Never Be So Lucky Again: An Autobiography by General James H. "Jimmy" Doolittle*. New York: Bantam Books, 1991.

Doscher, J. Henry, Jr. *Little Wolf: The Story of the Heroic USS* Samuel B. Roberts, *DE413 in the Battle of Leyte Gulf During World War II*. Austin, TX: Eakin Press, 1996.

Drury, Bob, and Tom Clavine. *Halsey's Typhoon: The True Story of a Fighting Admiral, and Epic Storm, and an Untold Rescue*. New York: Atlantic Monthly Press, 2007.

Dyer, George Carroll. *The Amphibians Came to Conquer: The Story of Admiral Richmond Kelly Turner*. 2 vols. Washington, DC: Naval Historical Center, 1972.

Eisenhower, Dwight David. *The Papers of Dwight David Eisenhower*. 8 vols. Edited by Alfred D. Chandler Jr. Baltimore: Johns Hopkins University Press, 1970.

Fehrenback, T. R. *F.D.R.'s Undeclared War, 1939–1941*. New York: David McKay, 1967.

Felker, Craig C. *Testing American Sea Power: U.S. Navy Strategic Exercises, 1923–1940*. College Station: Texas A&M University Press, 2007.

Frank, Richard B. *Guadalcanal: The Definitive Account of the Landmark Battle*. New York: Random House, 1990.

Freidel, Frank. *Franklin D. Roosevelt: A Rendezvous with Destiny*. Boston: Little, Brown, 1990.

Gannon, Robert. *Hellions of the Deep: The Development of American Torpedoes in World War II*. University Park, PA: Penn State University Press, 1996.

Glines, Carroll V. *Attack on Yamamoto*. New York: Orion Books, 1990

———. *Doolittle's Tokyo Raiders*. New York: D. Van Nostrand, 1964.

Griffith, Thomas E., Jr. *MacArthur's Airman: General George C. Kenney and the War in the Southwest Pacific*. Lawrence: University Press of Kansas, 1998.

Halsey, William F., and J. Bryan III. *Admiral Halsey's Story*. New York: McGraw-Hill, 1947.

Hewitt, H. Kent. *The Memoirs of Admiral H. Kent Hewitt*. Edited by Evelyn M. Cherpak. Newport, RI: Naval War College Press, 2004.

Holwitt, Joel Ira. *"Execute Against Japan": The U.S. Decision to Conduct Unrestricted Submarine Warfare*. College Station: Texas A&M University Press, 2009.

Hornfischer, James D. *Last Stand of the Tin Can Sailors*. New York: Bantam Books, 2004.

———. *Neptune's Inferno: The U.S. Navy at Guadalcanal*. New York: Bantam Books, 2011.

———. *Ship of Ghosts: The Story of the USS* Houston, *FDR's Legendary Lost Cruiser, and the Epic Saga of Her Survivors*. New York: Bantam Books, 2006.

Hoyt, Edwin P. *The Men of the* Gambier Bay. Middlebury, VT: Paul S. Eriksson, 1979.

Hughes, Thomas Alexander. *Admiral Bill Halsey: A Naval Life*. Cambridge, MA: Harvard University Press, 2016.

Ickes, Harold L. *The Secret Diary of Harold L. Ickes*. New York: Simon and Schuster, 1954.

Jones, David, and Peter Nunan. *U.S. Subs Down Under: Brisbane, 1942–1945*. Annapolis: Naval Institute Press, 2005.

Jordan, Jonathan W. *American Warlords: How Roosevelt's High Command Led America to Victory in World War II*. New York: Random House, 2016.

Kennedy, Maxwell Taylor. *Danger's Hour: The Story of the USS* Bunker Hill *and the Kamikaze Pilot Who Crippled Her*. New York: Simon and Schuster, 2008.

Kenney, George C. *General Kenney Reports: A Personal History of the Pacific War*. New York: Duell, Sloan and Pearce, 1949.

Kimmel, Husband E. *Admiral Kimmel's Story*. Chicago: Henry Regnery, 1955.

King, Ernest J., and Walter Muir Whitehill. *Fleet Admiral King: A Naval Record*. New York: W. W. Norton, 1952.

Kleiss, N. Jack. *Never Call Me a Hero: A Legendary American Dive-Bomber Pilot Remembers the Battle of Midway*. New York: William Morrow, 2017.

Langer, William L. *Our Vichy Gamble*. Hamden, CT: Archon Books, 1947, 1965.

Langer, William L., and S. Everett Gleason. *The Undeclared War, 1940–1941*. New York: Harper and Brothers, 1953.

Lockwood, Charles A., and Hans Christian Adamson. *Battles of the Philippine Sea*. New York: Thomas Y. Crowell, 1967.

———. *Hellcats of the Sea*. New York: Greenberg, 1955.

Love, Robert William, Jr., ed. *The Chiefs of Naval Operations*. Annapolis: Naval Institute Press, 1980.

———. *History of the U.S. Navy*. Vol. 2. Mechanicsburg, PA Stackpole Books, 1992.

Loxton, Bruce, with Chris Coulthard-Clard. *The Shame of Savo: Anatomy of a Naval Disaster*. Annapolis: Naval Institute Press, 1994.

Ludlum, Stuart D. *They Turned the War Around at Coral Sea and Midway: Going to War with* Yorktown's *Air Group Five*. Bennington, VT: Merriam, 2000.

Lundstrom, John B. *Black Shoe Carrier Admiral: Frank Jack Fletcher at Coral Sea, Midway, and Guadalcanal*. Annapolis: Naval Institute Press, 2006.

MacArthur, Douglas. *Reminiscences*. New York: McGraw Hill, 1964. Reprinted, Annapolis: Naval Institute Press, 2001.

Manchester, William. *American Caesar: Douglas MacArthur, 1880–1964*. Boston: Little, Brown, 1978.

Mansfield, John G., Jr. *Cruisers for Breakfast: War Patrols of the U.S.S.* Darter *and U.S.S.* Dace. Tacoma, WA: Media Center, 1997.

McCants, William R. *War Patrols of the USS* Flasher. Chapel Hill, NC: Professional Press, 1994.

Miller, Edward S. *War Plan Orange: The U.S. Strategy to Defeat Japan, 1897–1945*. Annapolis: Naval Institute Press, 1991.

Monroe-Jones, Edward, and Michael Green, eds. *The Silent Service in World War II: The Story of the U.S. Navy Submarine Force in the Words of the Men Who Lived It*. Philadelphia: Casemate, 2012.

Morison, Samuel Eliot. *History of United States Naval Operations in World War II*. 15 vols. Boston: Little, Brown, 1947–62. Reprinted, Annapolis: Naval Institute Press, 2010. [Identified in notes by individual volume title.]

Morris, C. G., and Hugh B. Cave, *The Fightin'est Ship: The Story of Cruiser* Helena. New York: Dodd Mead, 1944.

Mowry, George E. *Landing Craft and the War Production Board, April 1942 to May 1944.* Washington, DC: War Production Board, 1944.

O'Connell, Robert L. *Sacred Vessels: The Cult of the Battleship and the Rise of the U.S. Navy.* Boulder, CO: Westview Press, 1991.

O'Kane, Richard H. *Clear the Bridge: The War Patrols of the U.S.S.* Tang. Chicago: Rand McNally, 1977.

Patton, George S. *The Patton Papers, 1940–1945.* Edited by Martin Blumenson. Boston: Houghton Mifflin, 1974.

———. *War as I Knew It.* Boston: Houghton Mifflin, 1947.

Persico, Joseph E. *Roosevelt's Secret War: FDR and World War II.* New York: Random House, 2001.

Petty, Bruce M. *Saipan: Oral Histories of the Pacific War.* Jefferson, NC: McFarland, 2002.

Potter, E. B. *Admiral Arleigh Burke.* New York: Random House, 1990.

———. *Bull Halsey.* Annapolis: Naval Institute Press, 1985.

———. *Nimitz.* Annapolis: Naval Institute Press, 1976.

Regan, Stephen D. *In Bitter Tempest: The Biography of Admiral Frank Jack Fletcher.* Ames: Iowa State University Press, 1994.

Reynolds, David. *From Munich to Pearl Harbor: Roosevelt's America and the Origins of the Second World War.* Chicago: Ivan R. Dee, 2001.

Roberts, Charles C., Jr. *The Boat That Won the War: An Illustrated History of the Higgins LCVP.* Annapolis: U.S. Naval Institute, 2017.

Roosevelt, Franklin D. *Complete Presidential Press Conferences of Franklin D. Roosevelt.* New York: DaCapo Press, 1972.

———. *Documentary History of the Franklin D. Roosevelt Presidency.* George McJimsey, general editor. Dayton, OH: University Publications of America, 2001.

Roscoe, Theodore. *United States Destroyer Operations in World War II.* Annapolis: U.S. Naval Institute, 1953.

Rowland, Buford, and William B. Boyd. *U.S. Navy Bureau of Ordnance in World War II.* Washington, DC: Bureau of Ordnance, 1953.

Sasgen, Peter. *Hellcats: The Epic Story of World War II's Most Daring Submarine Raid.* London: NAL Caliber, 2010.

Schultz, Duane. *The Doolittle Raid.* New York: St. Martin's Press, 1988.

Sherman, Frederick C. *Combat Command: The American Aircraft Carriers in the Pacific War.* New York: E. P. Dutton, 1950.

Sherwood, Robert E. *Roosevelt and Hopkins: An Intimate History.* New York: Enigma Books, 2008. Originally published 1948.

Smith, Holland M., with Percy Finch. *Coral and Brass.* New York: Charles Scribner's Sons, 1949.

Solberg, Carl. *Decision and Dissent: With Halsey at Leyte Gulf.* Annapolis: Naval Institute Press, 1995.

Spector, Ronald H. *Eagle Against the Sun: The American War with Japan.* New York: Macmillan, 1985.

Stanton, Doug. *In Harm's Way: The Sinking of the USS* Indianapolis *and the Extraordinary Story of Its Survivors*. New York: Henry Holt, 2001.

Steely, Skipper. *Pearl Harbor Countdown: Admiral James O. Richardson*. Gretna, LA: Pelican, 2008.

Stillwell, Paul, ed. *Air Raid: Pearl Harbor! Recollections of a Day of Infamy*. Annapolis: Naval Institute Press, 1981.

———. *Assault on Normandy: First Person Accounts from the Sea Services*. Annapolis: Naval Institute Press, 1994.

Stockman, James R. *The Battle for Tarawa*. Washington, DC: Historical Section, U.S. Marine Corps, 1947.

Taylor, Theodore. *The Magnificent Mitscher*. Annapolis: Naval Institute Press, 1954.

Tuohy, William. *The Bravest Man: The Story of Richard O'Kane and U.S. Submarines in the Pacific War*. Phoenix Mill, Gloucestershire, UK: Sutton, 2001.

Twomey, Steve. *Countdown to Pearl Harbor: The Twelve Days to the Attack*. New York: Simon and Schuster, 2016.

U.S. Navy Department. *Annual Reports of the Secretary of the Navy*. Washington, DC: Government Printing Office, 1935–45.

U.S. Navy, Office of Naval Intelligence. *Battle of Cape Esperance* and *Battle of Santa Cruz Islands*. Washington, DC: Office of Naval Intelligence, 1943.

———. *Battle of Savo Island* and *The Battle of the Eastern Solomons*. Washington, DC: Office of Naval Intelligence, 1943.

———. *Battle of Tassafaronga* and *Japanese Evacuation of Guadalcanal*. Washington, DC: Office of Naval Intelligence, 1944.

———. *Bougainville Campaign and the Battle of Empress Augusta Bay*. Washington, DC: Office of Naval Intelligence, 1945.

Wheeler, Gerald E. *Kinkaid of the Seventh Fleet: A Biography of Admiral Thomas C. Kinkaid, U.S. Navy*. Washington, DC: Naval Historical Center, 1995.

Wildenberg, Thomas. *All the Factors of Victory: Admiral Joseph Mason Reeves and the Origins of Carrier Airpower*. Washington, DC: Brassey's, 2003.

———. *Billy Mitchell's War with the Navy: The Interwar Rivalry over Air Power*. Annapolis: Naval Institute Press, 2014.

Winslow, W. G. *The Fleet the Gods Forgot: The U.S. Asiatic Fleet in World War II*. Annapolis: Naval Institute Press, 1982.

Wohlstetter, Roberta. *Pearl Harbor: Warning and Decision*. Stanford: Stanford University Press, 1962.

Wolters, Timothy S. *Information at Sea: Shipboard Command and Control in the U.S. Navy, from Mobile Bay to Okinawa*. Baltimore: John Hopkins University Press, 2013.

Wren, L. Peter, and Charles T. Sehe. *Battle Born: The Unsinkable USS* Nevada, *BB-36*. Xlibris, 2008.

Wukovits, John. *Devotion to Duty: A Biography of Admiral Clifton A. F. Sprague*. Annapolis: Naval Institute Press, 1995.

———. *Hell from the Heavens: The Epic Story of the USS* Laffey *and World War II's Greatest Kamikaze Attack*. Boston: Da Capo Press, 2015.

———. *One Square Mile of Hell: The Battle for Tarawa*. New York: Penguin, 2006.

———. *Tin Can Titans*. Boston: Da Capo Press, 2017.

C. Operational Theaters and Special Topics

The Mediterranean

Ansel, Walter. *Hitler and the Middle Sea*. Durham: Duke University Press, 1972.

Beevor, Antony. *Crete: The Battle and the Resistance*. Boulder, Colo.: Westview Press, 1994.

Blumenson, Martin. *Anzio: The Gamble That Failed*. Philadelphia: J. B. Lippincott, 1963.

Bradford, Ernle. *Siege: Malta, 1940–1943*. New York: William Morrow, 1986.

Brown, John Mason. *To All Hands: An Amphibious Adventure*. New York: Whittlesey House, 1943.

Castillo, Dennis A. *The Santa Marija Convoy: Faith and Endurance in Wartime Malta*. Lanham, MD: Lexington Books, 2012.

Clayton, Tim, and Phil Craig. *The End of the Beginning: From the Siege of Malta to the Allied Victory at El Alamein*. New York: Free Press, 2002.

Clifford, Robert L., and William J. Maddocks. *Naval Gunfire Support in the Landings at Sicily*. Oklahoma City, OK.: 45th Infantry Division Museum, 1984.

De Belot, Raymond. *The Struggle for the Mediterranean, 1939–1945*. Princeton: Princeton University Press, 1951.

D'Este, Carlo. *Bitter Victory: The Battle for Sicily, 1943*. New York: E. P. Dutton, 1988.

———. *Fatal Decision: Anzio and the Battle for Rome*. New York: HarperCollins, 1991.

Ehlers, Robert S., Jr. *The Mediterranean Air War: Airpower and Allied Victory in World War II*. Lawrence: University of Kansas Press, 2015.

Garland, Albert N, and Howard McGaw Smith. *The Mediterranean Theater of Operations: Sicily and the Surrender of Italy*. Washington, DC: Office of the Chief of Military History, 1965.

Greene, Jack, and Alessandro Massignani. *The Naval War in the Mediterranean, 1940–1943*. London: Chatham, 2002.

Grehan, John, and Martin Mace, eds. *The War at Sea in the Mediterranean, 1940–1944*. Despatches from the Front. Barnsley, South Yorkshire: Pen and Sword Maritime, 2014.

———. *The War in Italy, 1943–1944*. Despatches from the Front. Barnsley, South Yorkshire: Pen and Sword, 2014.

Hickey, Des, and Gus Smith. *Operation Avalanche: The Salerno Landings, 1943*. New York: McGraw-Hill, 1984.

Holland, James. *Fortress Malta: An Island Under Siege, 1940–43*. New York: Miramax Books, 2003.

Howe, George F. *Northwest Africa: Seizing the Initiative in the West*. Washington, DC: Office of the Chief of Military History, 1957.

Jellison, Charles A. *Besieged: The World War II Ordeal of Malta, 1940–1942*. Hanover, NH: University Press of New England, 1984.

Katz, Robert. *The Battle for Rome: The Germans, the Allies, the Partisans, and the Pope, September 1943–June 1944*. New York: Simon and Schuster, 2003.

Kelly, Orr. *Meeting the Fox: The Allied Invasion of Africa from Operation Torch to Kasserine Pass to Victory in Tunisia*. New York: John Wiley and Sons, 2002.

Levine, Alan J. *The War Against Rommel's Supply Lines, 1942–1943*. Westport, CT: Praeger, 1999.

Linklater, Eric. *The Campaign in Italy*. London: Her Majesty's Stationery Office, 1951, 1977.

Molony, C. J. C. *The Mediterranean and Middle East*, vol. 5, *The Campaign in Sicily 1943, and the Campaign in Italy, 3rd September 1943 to 31st March 1944*. History of the Second World War. London: Her Majesty's Stationery Office, 1973.

Moses, Sam. *At All Costs*. New York: Random House, 2006.

O'Hara, Vincent P. *In Passage Perilous: Malta and the Convoy Battles of June 1942*. Bloomington: Indiana University Press, 2013.

———. *Struggle for the Middle Sea: The Great Navies at War in the Mediterranean Theater, 1940–1945*. Annapolis: Naval Institute Press, 2015.

———. *Torch: North Africa and the Allied Path to Victory*. Annapolis: Naval Institute Press, 2015.

Pack, S. W. C. *The Battle of Cape Matapan*. New York: Macmillan, 1961.

———. *The Battle of Sirte*. Annapolis: Naval Institute Press, 1975.

———. *Night Action off Cape Matapan*. Skeppterton, Surrey: Ian Allan, 1972.

Pearson, Michael. *The Ohio and Malta: The Legendary Tanker That Refused to Die*. Barnsley, South Yorkshire: Leo Cooper, 2004.

Playfair, I. S. O. *The Mediterranean and Middle East*, vol. 4, *The Destruction of the Axis Forces in Africa*. History of the Second World War. London: Her Majesty's Stationery Office, 1966.

Pond, Hugh. *Sicily*. London: William Kimber, 1962.

Pope, Dudley. *Flag 4: The Battle of Coastal Forces in the Mediterranean, 1939–1945*. Annapolis: Naval Institute Press, 1954.

Porch, Douglas. *The Path to Victory: The Mediterranean Theater in World War II*. New York: Farrar, Straus and Giroux, 2004.

Seth, Ronald. *Two Fleets Surprised: The Story of the Battle of Cape Matapan*. London: Geoffrey Bles, 1960.

Shankland, Peter, and Anthony Hunter. *Malta Convoy*. New York: Ives Washburn, 1961.

Smith, Peter C. *Critical Conflict: The Royal Navy's Mediterranean Campaign in 1940*. Barnsley, South Yorkshire: Pen and Sword, 2011. Originally published as *Action Imminent*. London: William Kimber, 1980.

———. *Pedestal: The Convoy That Saved Malta*. London: William Kimber, 1970.

Truscott, Lucian K., Jr. *Command Missions: A Personal Story*. New York: E. P. Dutton, 1954.

U.S. Department of the Army. *Anzio Beachhead, 22 January–25 May 1944*. Washington, D.C.: Center of Military History, 1990.

U.S. Navy Office of Naval Intelligence. *The Sicilian Campaign, 10 July–17 August 1943*. Washington, DC: United States Navy Publication Branch, 1945.

The Norway Campaign

Brown, David, ed. *Naval Operations of the Campaign in Norway, April–June, 1940*. London: Frank Cass, 2000.

Derry, T. K. *The Campaign in Norway*. London: Her Majesty's Stationery Office, 1952.

Dickens, Peter. *Narvik: Battles in the Fjords*. Annapolis: Naval Institute Press, 1974, 1997.

Haarr, Geirr H. *The German Invasion of Norway, April 1940*. Annapolis: Naval Institute Press, 2009.

Porter, Richard, and M. J. Pearce, editors. *The Fight for the Fjords: The Battle for Norway, 1940*. Britannia Naval Histories of World War II. Plymouth: University Press of Plymouth, 2012.

Scarfe, Ronald. *In the Norwegian Trap: The Battle for and in Norwegian Waters*. London: Francis Aldor, 1940.

The Pacific

Attiwill, Kenneth. *Fortress: The Story of the Siege and Fall of Singapore*. Garden City, NY: Doubleday, 1960.

Barber, Noel. *A Sinister Twilight: The Fall of Singapore, 1942*. Boston: Houghton Mifflin, 1968.

Burrell, Robert S. *The Ghosts of Iwo Jima*. College Station: Texas A&M University Press, 2006.

Clemans, Martin. *Alone on Guadalcanal: A Coastwatcher's Story*. Annapolis: Naval Institute Press, 1998.

Cook, Charles. *The Battle of Cape Esperance: Encounter at Guadalcanal*. Annapolis: Naval Institute Press, 1968, 1992.

Coombe, Jack D. *Derailing the Tokyo Express: The Naval Battles for the Solomon Islands That Sealed Japan's Fate*. Harrisburg, PA: Stackpole Books, 1991.

Cox, Jeffrey R. *Rising Sun, Falling Skies: The Disastrous Java Sea Campaign of World War II*. Oxford: Osprey, 2014.

Craven, Wesley Frank, and James Lea Cate. *The Army Air Forces in World War II*, vol. 4, *The Pacific: Guadalcanal to Saipan, August 1942 to July 1944*. Chicago: University of Chicago Press, 1950.

Crenshaw, Russell Sydnor, Jr. *South Pacific Destroyer: The Battle for the Solomons from Savo Island to Vella Gulf*. Annapolis: Naval Institute Press, 1998.

Crowl, Philip A., and Edmund G. Love. *Seizure of the Gilberts and Marshalls*, vol. 5, part 6 of *The War in the Pacific*. Washington, DC: Office of the Chief of Military History, 1955.

Custer, Joe James. *Through the Perilous Night: The Astoria's Last Battle*. New York: Macmillan, 1944.

Cutler, Thomas J. *The Battle of Leyte Gulf, 23–26 October 1944*. New York: HarperCollins, 1994.

Domagalski, John J. *Lost at Guadalcanal: The Final Battles of the Astoria and Chicago as Described by Survivors and in Official Reports*. Jefferson, NC: McFarland, 2010.

———. *Sunk in Kula Gulf: The Final Voyage of the USS Helena and the Incredible Story of Her Survivors in World War II*. Washington, DC: Potomac Books, 2012.

Farrell, Brian P. *The Defense and Fall of Singapore, 1940–1942*. Stroud, Gloucestershire: Tempus, 2005.

Field, James A. *The Japanese at Leyte Gulf: The Sho Operation*. Princeton: Princeton University Press, 1947.

Frank, Richard B. *Downfall: The End of the Imperial Japanese Empire*. New York: Random House, 1999.

Gailey, Harry A. *Bougainville, 1943–1945: The Forgotten Campaign*. Lexington: University Press of Kentucky, 1991.

Gamble, Bruce. *Fortress Rabaul: The Battle for the Southwest Pacific, January 1942–April 1943*. Minneapolis: Zenith Press, 2010.

Goldberg, Harold J. *D-Day in the Pacific: The Battle of Saipan*. Bloomington: Indiana University Press, 20007.

Hastings, Max. *Retribution: The Battle for Japan, 1944–45*. New York: Alfred A. Knopf, 2008.

Heinl, Robert D., Jr., and John A. Crown. *The Marshalls: Increasing the Tempo*. Washington, DC: U.S. Marine Corps Historical Branch, 1954.

Heinrichs, Waldo, and Marc Gallicchio. *Implacable Foes: War in the Pacific, 1944–1945*. New York: Oxford University Press, 2017.

Hornfischer, James D. *Neptune's Inferno: The U.S. Navy at Guadalcanal*. New York: Bantam Books, 2011.

———. *The Last Stand of the Tin Can Sailors: The Extraordinary World War II Story of the U.S. Navy's Finest Hour*. New York: Bantam Books, 2004.

Lockwood, Charles A. *Sink 'Em All: Submarine Warfare in the Pacific*. New York: E. P. Dutton, 1951.

Lord, Walter. *Day of Infamy*. New York: Holt, Rinehart and Winston, 1957.

———. *Incredible Victory*. New York: Harper-Collins, 1967.

Lundstrom, John. *The First South Pacific Campaign: Pacific Fleet Strategy, December 1941– June 1942*. Annapolis: Naval Institute Press, 1976.

———. *The First Team: Pacific Naval Air Combat from Pearl Harbor to Midway*. Annapolis: Naval Institute Press, 1984.

McAulay, Lex. *Battle of the Bismarck Sea*. New York: St. Martin's Press, 1991.

Messimer, Dwight R. *Pawns of War: The Loss of the USS* Langley *and the USS* Pecos. Annapolis: Naval Institute Press, 1983.

Miller, John, Jr. *Cartwheel: The Reduction of Rabaul*, vol. 5, part 5, of *The War in the Pacific*. Washington, DC: Office of the Chief of Military History 1959.

Miller, Thomas G., Jr. *The Cactus Air Force*. New York: Harper and Row, 1969.

Parshall, Jonathan, and Anthony Tully. *Shattered Sword: The Untold Story of the Battle of Midway*. Washington, DC: Potomac Books, 2005.

Prados, John. *Storm over Leyte: The Philippine Invasion and the Destruction of the Japanese Navy*. New York: New American Library, 2016.

Prange, Gordon W., with Donald M. Goldstein and Katherine V. Dillon. *At Dawn We Slept: The Untold Story of Pearl Harbor*. New York: McGraw-Hill, 1981.

———. *Miracle at Midway*. New York: McGraw-Hill, 1982.

Prefer, Nathan. *MacArthur's New Guinea Campaign*. Conshohocken, PA.: Combined Books, 1995.

Puleston, W. D. *The Armed Forces of the Pacific: A Comparison of the Military and Naval Power of the United States and Japan*. New Haven: Yale University Press, 1941.

Schwabe, Daniel T. *Burning Japan: Air Force Bombing Strategy Change in the Pacific*. Lincoln, NE: University of Nebraska Press [Potomac Books], 2015.

Shaw, Henry L, Bernard C. Nalty, and Edwin T. Turnbladh, *Central Pacific Drive*, vol. 3 of *History of U.S. Marine Corps Operations in World War II*. Washington, DC: Historical Branch, U.S. Marine Corps, 1966.

Sherrod, Robert. *On to Westward: The Battles of Saipan and Iwo Jima*. New York: Duell, Sloan, and Pearce, 1945. Reprinted, Baltimore: Nautical and Aviation Press, 1990.

———. *Tarawa: The Story of a Battle.* New York: Duell, Sloan, and Pearce, 1944. Reprinted, Fredericksburg, TX: Admiral Nimitz Foundation, 1973.

Sledge, E. B. *With the Old Breed at Peleliu and Okinawa.* Novato, CA: Presidio Press, 1981.

Smith, Larry. *Iwo Jima: World War II Veterans Remember the Greatest Battle of the Pacific.* New York: W. W. Norton, 2008.

Stern, Robert C. *Fire from the Sky: Surviving the Kamikaze Threat.* Annapolis: Naval Institute Press, 2010.

Symonds, Craig L. *The Battle of Midway.* New York: Oxford University Press, 2011.

Thomas, Evan. *Sea of Thunder: Four Commanders and the Last Great Naval Campaign, 1941–1945.* New York: Simon and Schuster, 2006.

Thomas, Lowell, and Edward Jablonski. *Doolittle: A Biography.* Garden City, NY: Doubleday, 1976.

Toll, Ian W. *The Conquering Tide: War in the Pacific Islands, 1942–1944.* New York: W. W. Norton, 2015.

———. *Pacific Crucible: War at Sea in the Pacific, 1941–1942.* New York: W. W. Norton, 2012.

Tully, Anthony P. *Battle of Surigao Strait.* Bloomington: Indiana University Press, 2009.

U.S. Congress. *Pearl Harbor Attack: Hearings Before the Joint Committee on the Investigation of the Pearl Harbor Attack.* Washington, DC: Government Printing Office, 1946.

U.S. Navy Department. *The Assault on Kwajalein and Majuro* [Combat Narratives]. Washington, DC: Office of Naval Intelligence, 1945.

———. *Iwo Jima: Amphibious Epic.* Washington, DC: U.S. Marine Corps Historical Branch, 1954.

———. *The Battles of Savo Island, 9 August 1942 and the Eastern Solomons, 23–25 August 1942.* Washington, DC: Naval Historical Center, 1994.

———. *The Java Sea Campaign* [Combat Narratives]. Washington, DC: Office of Naval Intelligence, 1943.

Utley, Jonathan, *Going to War with Japan.* Knoxville: University of Tennessee Press, 1985.

Vego, Milan. *The Battle for Leyte, 1944: Allied and Japanese Plans, Preparations, and Execution.* Annapolis: Naval Institute Press, 2006.

Warren, Alan. *Singapore: Britain's Greatest Defeat.* London: Hambleton and London, 2002.

Willmott, H. P. *The Barrier and the Javelin: Japanese and Allied Pacific Strategies, February to June 1942.* Annapolis: U.S. Naval Institute, 1983.

———. *The Battle of Leyte Gulf: The Last Fleet Action.* Bloomington: Indianan University Press, 2005.

———. *Empires in the Balance: Japanese and Allied Pacific Strategies to April 1942.* Annapolis: Naval Institute Press, 1982.

Yahara, Hiromichi. *The Battle for Okinawa.* Translated by Roger Pineau and Masatoshi Uehara. New York: John Wiley and sons, 1995.

Y'Blood, William T. *Red Sun Setting: The Battle of the Philippine Sea.* Annapolis: Naval Institute Press, 1981.

Naval Codes and Code Breaking

Bennett, Ralph. *ULTRA and Mediterranean Strategy*. New York: William Morrow, 1989.

Carlson, Elliot. *Joe Rochefort's War: The Odyssey of the Codebreaker Who Outwitted Yamamoto at Midway*. Annapolis: Naval Institute Press, 2011.

Gardner, W. J. R. *Decoding History: The Battle of the Atlantic and Ultra*. Annapolis: Naval Institute Press, 1999.

Holmes, Wilfrid Jasper. *Double-Edged Secrets: U.S. Naval Intelligence Operations in the Pacific During World War II*. Annapolis: Naval Institute Press, 1979.

Kahn, David. *The Codebreakers: The Story of Secret Writing*. New York: Macmillan, 1967.

———. *Seizing the Enigma: The Race to Break the German U-Boat Codes, 1939–1943*. Boston: Houghton Mifflin, 1991.

Layton, Edwin T., with Roger Pineau and John Costello. *"And I Was There": Pearl Harbor and Midway—Breaking the Secrets*. New York: William Morrow, 1985.

Navy Records Society. *The Battle of the Atlantic and Signals Intelligence: U-Boat Situations and Trends, 1941–1945*. Ed. by David Syrett. Aldershot, England: Ashgate, 1998.

Parker, Frederick D. *A Priceless Advantage: U.S. Navy Communications Intelligence and the Battles of Coral Sea, Midway, and the Aleutians*. Washington, DC: Center for Cryptologic History, National Security Agency, 1993.

Prados, John. *Combined Fleet Decoded: The Secret History of American Intelligence and the Japanese Navy in World War II*. New York: Random House, 1995.

Showell, Jak P. Mallmann. *German Naval Code Breakers*. Annapolis: Naval Institute Press, 2003.

Winton, John. *Ultra at Sea: How Breaking the Nazi Code Affected Allied Naval Strategy During World War II*. New York: William Morrow, 1988.

The War on Trade

Bailey, Chris Howard. *The Battle of the Atlantic: The Corvettes and Their Crews: An Oral History*. Annapolis: Naval Institute Press, 1994.

Blair, Clay. *Hitler's U-Boat War: The Hunters, 1939–1942*. New York: Random House, 1996.

———. *Hitler's U-Boat War: The Hunted, 1942–1945*. New York: Random House, 1998.

———. *Silent Victory: The U.S. Submarine War Against Japan*. Philadelphia: J. B. Lippincott, 1975.

Bray, Jeffrey K. *Ultra in the Atlantic: Allied Communication Intelligence and the Battle of the Atlantic*. Laguna Hills, CA: Aegean Park Press, 1994.

Brown, Ken. *U-Boat Assault on America: The Eastern Seaboard Campaign, 1942*. Annapolis: Naval Institute Press, 2017.

Carroll, Francis M. *Athenia Torpedoed: The U-Boat Attack That Ignited the Battle of the Atlantic*. Annapolis: Naval Institute Press, 2012.

Carter, William A. *Why Me, Lord? The Experiences of a U.S. Navy Armed Guard Officer in World War II's Convoy PQ 17 on the Murmansk Run*. Millsboro, DE: William A. Carter, 2007.

Cremer, Peter. *U-Boat Commander: A Periscope View of the Battle of the Atlantic*. Annapolis: Naval Institute Press, 1982.

Dimbleby, Jonathan. *The Battle of the Atlantic: How the Allies Won the War.* New York: Oxford University Press, 2016.

Duffy, James P. *The Sinking of the* Laconia *and the U-Boat War: Disaster in the Mid-Atlantic.* Santa Barbara, CA: Praeger, 2009.

Duskin, Gerald L., and Ralph Segman. *If the Gods Are Good: The Epic Sacrifice of the HMS* Jervis Bay. Annapolis: Naval Institute Press, 2004.

———. *Convoy Will Scatter: The Full Story of* Jervis Bay *and Convoy HX84.* Barnsley, South Yorkshire: Pen and Sword, 2013.

Gannon, Michael. *Operation Drumbeat: The Dramatic True Story of Germany's First U-Boat Attacks Along the American Coast in World War II.* New York: Harper and Row, 1990.

Gannon, Robert. *Hellions of the Deep: The Development of American Torpedoes in World War II.* University Park: Pennsylvania State University Press, 1996.

Gretton, Peter. *Convoy Escort Commander.* London: Cassell, 1964.

———. *Crisis Convoy: The Story of HX231.* Annapolis: Naval Institute Press, 1974.

Hadley, Michael L. *U-Boats Against Canada: German Submarines in Canadian Waters.* Kingston, ON: McGill-Queen's University Press, 1985.

Hague, Arnold. *The Allied Convoy System, 1939–1945.* Annapolis: Naval Institute Press, 2000.

Hickam, Homer, Jr. *Torpedo Junction: U-Boat War off America's East Coast, 1942.* Annapolis: Naval Institute Press, 1989.

Hughes, Terry, and John Costello. *The Battle of the Atlantic.* New York: Dial Press, 1977.

Ireland, Bernard. *Battle of the Atlantic.* Barnsley, South Yorkshire: Pen and Sword, 2003.

Keith, Don. *Undersea Warrior: The World War II Story of "Mush" Morton and the USS* Wahoo. New York: New American Library, 2011.

Kelshall, Gaylord T. M. *The U-Boat War in the Caribbean.* Annapolis: Naval Institute Press, 1988, 1994.

Kemp, Peter. *Decision at Sea: The Convoy Escorts.* New York: Elsevier-Dutton, 1978.

Lund, Paul, and Harry Ludlam. *Night of the U-Boats.* London: W. Foulsham, 1973.

MacIntyre, Donald. *The Battle of the Atlantic.* New York: Macmillan, 1961.

MacNeil, Calum. *San Demetrio.* Sydney: Angus and Robertson, 1957.

McCue, Brian. *U-Boats in the Bay of Biscay: An Essay in Operational Analysis.* Washington, DC: National Defense University, 1990.

Middlebrook, Martin. *Convoy.* New York: William Morrow, 1977.

Mohr, Ulrich, and A. V. Sellwood. *Ship 16: The Story of the Secret German Raider* Atlantis. New York: John Day, 1956.

Offley, Ed. *The Burning Shore: How Hitler's U-Boats Brought World War II to America.* New York: Basic Books, 2014.

Ogden, Michael. *The Battle of North Cape.* London: William Kimber, 1962.

O'Kane, Richard H. Wahoo: *The Patrols of America's Most Famous World War II Submarine.* Novato, CA: Presidio Press, 1987.

Padfield, Peter. *War Beneath the Sea: Submarine Conflict During World War II.* New York: John Wiley and Sons, 1995.

Peillard, Léonce. *The* Laconia *Affair.* Translated from the French by Oliver Coburn. New York: G. P. Putnam's Sons, 1963.

Pope, Dudley. *The Battle of the River Plate.* London: William Kimber, 1956.

Revely, Henry. *The Convoy That Nearly Died: The Story of ONS 154*. London: William Kimber, 1979.

Rohwer, Jurgen. *The Critical Convoy Battles of March 1943: The Battle for HX229/SC122*. Annapolis: Naval Institute Press, 1977.

Royal Navy Central Office of Information. *The Battle of the Atlantic: The Official Account of the Fight Against the U-Boats, 1939–1945*. London: His Majesty's Stationery Office, 1946.

Schofield, B. B. *The Russian Convoys*. Philadelphia: Dufour Editions, 1964.

Seki, Eiji. *Mrs. Ferguson's Tea-set, Japan, and the Second World War: The Global Consequences Following Germany's Sinking of the SS Automedon in 1940*. Folkestone, Kent: Global Oriental, 2007.

Syrett, David. *The Defeat of the German U-Boats: The Battle of the Atlantic*. Columbia: University of South Carolina Press, 1994.

U.S. Department of the Navy. *Japanese Naval and Merchant Shipping Losses During World War II by All Causes*. Washington, DC: U.S. Government Printing Office, 1947.

Walling, Michael G. *Forgotten Sacrifice: The Arctic Convoys of World War II*. Oxford, England: Osprey, 2012.

Waters, John M. *Bloody Winter*. Annapolis: Naval Institute Press, 1967, 1984.

Watson, Bruce Allen. *Atlantic Convoys and Nazi Raiders: The Deadly Voyage of the HMS Jervis Bay*. Westport, CT: Praeger, 2006.

Woodman, Richard. *The Arctic Convoys, 1941–1945*. London: John Murray, 1994.

———. *Malta Convoys, 1940–1943*. London: John Murray, 2000.

Y'Blood, William T. *Hunter-Killer: U.S. Escort Carriers in the Battle of the Atlantic*. Annapolis: Naval Institute Press, 1983.

D. Articles

Allison, Fred H. "We Were Going to Win . . . or Die There." *Naval History*, October 2016, 32–39.

Assmann, Kurt. "The Invasion of Normandy." Translated by Roland E. Krause. *U.S. Naval Institute Proceedings*, April 1952, 400–413.

Blee, Ben. "Whodunnit?" *U.S. Naval Institute Proceedings*, June 1982, 42–47.

Camp, Richard. "Flying in the Eye of the Guadalcanal Storm." *Naval History*, August 2017, 14–19.

Chew, John L., as told to Charles Lee Lewis. "Some Shall Escape." *U.S. Naval Institute Proceedings*, August 1945, 887–903.

"CINC First Air Fleet Detailed Battle Report." *ONI Review*, May 1947.

Coward, J. G. "Destroyer Dust." *U.S. Naval Institute Proceedings*, November 1948, 1373–83.

Danton, J. Periam. "The Battle of the Philippine Sea." *U.S. Naval Institute Proceedings*, September 1948, 1023–1027.

Davis, H. F. D. "Building Major Combatant Ships in World War II." *U.S. Naval Institute Proceedings*, May 1947, 565–79.

Drent, Jan. "The Trans-Pacific Lend-Lease Shuttle to the Russian Far East, 1941–46." *The Northern Mariner/Le Marin du Nord*, January 2017, 31–58.

Field, James A. "Leyte Gulf: The First Uncensored Japanese Account." *U.S. Naval Institute Proceedings*, March 1951, 255–65.

Fukaya, Hajime. "The Shokakus: Pearl Harbor to Leyte Gulf." Translated by Martin E. Holbrook. *U.S. Naval Institute Proceedings*, June 1953, 638–41.

Hagen, Robert C., with Sidney Shalett. "We Asked for the Jap Fleet—And We Got It." *Saturday Evening Post*, May 26, 1945, 9–10, 72, 74, 76.

Halsey, Ashley, Jr. "The CVL's Success Story." *U.S. Naval Institute Proceedings*, April 1946, 523–31.

Hammond, Richard. "Fighting Under a Different Flag: Multinational Naval Cooperation and Submarine Warfare in the Mediterranean, 1940–1944." *Journal of Military History*, April 2016, 447–76.

Hampshire, A. Cecil. "British Strategy in the River Plate Battle." *U.S. Naval Institute Proceedings*, December 1958, 85–91.

Heinl, Robert D., Jr. "The Most Shot-At Island in the Pacific." *U.S. Naval Institute Proceedings*, April 1947, 397–99.

Hewitt, H. Kent. "The Allied Navies at Salerno: Operation Avalanche, September, 1943." *U.S. Naval Institute Proceedings*, September 1953, 959–976.

———. "Naval Aspects of the Sicilian Campaign." *U.S. Naval Institute Proceedings*, July 1953, 705–23.

Hoffman, F. G. "The American Wolf Packs: A Case Study in Wartime Adaptation." *Joint Force Quarterly*, January 2016.

Holmes, Besby. "Who Really Shot Down Yamamoto?" *Popular Aviation Magazine*, March/April 1967.

Karig, Walter. "Murmansk Run." *U.S. Naval Institute Proceedings*, January 1946, 25–33.

Kauffman, D. L. "German Naval Strategy in World War II." *U.S. Naval Institute Proceedings*, January 1954, 1–12.

Koyanagi, Tomiji. "With Kurita in the Battle of Leyte Gulf." Translated by Toshikazu Ohmae. Edited by Roger Pineau. *U.S. Naval Institute Proceedings*, February 1953, 119–33.

Kurzak, Karl Heinz. "German U-Boat Construction." *U.S. Naval Institute Proceedings*, April 1955, 374–89.

Lanphier, Thomas G. "I Shot Down Yamamoto." *Reader's Digest*, December 1966, 82–87.

Levy, James. "Ready or Not? The Home Fleet at the Outset of World War II." *Naval War College Review*, Autumn 1999, 90–108.

Lipke, E. E. "A North Atlantic Convoy." *U.S. Naval Institute Proceedings*, March 1947, 289–91.

McGuinness, James L. "The Three Deuces." *U.S. Naval Institute Proceedings*, September 1946, 1157–61.

McLean, Samuel, and Roger Sarty, "Gerald S. Graham's Manuscript Diary of His Voyage in HMS *Harvester*, 1942." *The Northern Mariner/Le Marin du Nord*, April 2016, 173–96.

Moore, Lynn L. "*Shinano*: The Jinx Carrier." *U.S. Naval Institute Proceedings*, February 1953, 142–49.

Nohrden, Maynard M. "The Amphibian Tractor, Jack of All Missions." *U.S. Naval Institute Proceedings*, January 1946, 13–17.

Ohmae, Toshikazu. "The Battle of Savo Island." Edited by Roger Pineau. *U.S. Naval Institute Proceedings*, December 1957, 1263–1278.

Oldendorf, Jesse. "Comments on the Battle of Surigao Strait." *U.S. Naval Institute Proceedings*, April, 1959, 104–7.

Reed, Rowena. "Central Mediterranean Sea Control and the North African Campaigns." *Naval War College Review*, July–August 1984, 82–96.

Ruge, Friedrich. "German Naval Strategy Across Two Wars." *U.S. Naval Institute Proceedings*, February 1955, 152–66.

Seagren, Leonard. "The Last Fuehrer." *U.S. Naval Institute Proceedings*, May 1954, 523–37.

Simpson, Michael. "Force H and British Strategy in the Western Mediterranean, 1939–1942." *Mariner's Mirror*, February 1977, 62–75.

Smith, H. E. "I Saw the Morning Break." *U.S. Naval Institute Proceedings*, March 1946, 403–15.

Smith, Julian C. "Tarawa." *U.S. Naval Institute Proceedings*, November 1953, 1163–75.

Sokol, A. E. "German Attacks on the Murmansk Run." *U.S. Naval Institute Proceedings*, December 1952, 1327–41.

Stirling, Yates. "Naval Preparedness in the Pacific Area." *U.S. Naval Institute Proceedings*, May 1934, 601–8.

Sweetman, Jack. "Leyte Gulf." *U.S. Naval Institute Proceedings*, October 1994, 56–58.

Vogel, Bertram. "Truk—South Sea Mystery Base." *U.S. Naval Institute Proceedings*, October 1948, 1269–75.

Von Gosseln, Joachim. "The Sinking of the *Sydney*." *U.S. Naval Institute Proceedings*, March 1953, 251–55.

Weems, George B. "Solomons Battle Log." *U.S. Naval Institute Proceedings*, August 1962, 80–91.

Wiedersheim, William A. III. "Factors in the Growth of the Reichsmarine (1919–1939)." *U.S. Naval Institute Proceedings*, March 1948, 317–24.

Wyman, Theodore C. "Red Shingle." *U.S. Naval Institute Proceedings*, August 1947, 923–29.

Yoshida, Mitsuru. "The End of *Yamato*." Translated by Masaru Chikuami. Edited by Roger Pineau. *U.S. Naval Institute Proceedings*, February 1952, 117–29.

INDEX

Aaron Ward (USN destroyer), 367
ABDA (American, British, Dutch, and
  Australian forces), 220–23
  demise of, 234–35
  weakness of, 223
Abe, Hiroaki (IJN admiral), 328, 330,
  367–69
Abe, Toshio (IJN naval officer), 599–600
Abercrombie (RN monitor), 456
Acasta (RN destroyer), 59–60
Acheson, Dean (US diplomat), 193
Achilles (RN cruiser), 31–37
Achse, Operation (1943), 446, 455
Admiral Scheer (German pocket
  battleship), 26, 615
  and North Cape convoys, 261, 263
  raid in 1940, 120–26
  illus., 120
Ady, Howard (USN pilot), 286
Africa Shell (Dutch tanker), 29–30
Agnew, William G. (RN officer), 240, 353
Ainsworth, Walden (USN admiral),
  478–79
Air Solomons (AirSols), 411, 482, 485
Ajax (RN cruiser), 19, 31–37
Akagi (IJN carrier), 159, 160, 162, 197,
  224, 291
Akitsushima (IJN seaplane tender), 302
Akiyama, Teruo (IJN admiral), 478–79
Alabama (Confederate raider), 24

Albacore (British carrier plane), 98
Albacore (USN submarine), 548–49
Alexander, Harold (British general), 422,
  502, 504
Algiers, Allied invasion of, 351–54
Allen, Roland C. (RN officer), 117
Altmark (German supply ship), 27,
  37–38, 40
Ambrosio, Vittorio (Italian general), 447
amphibious ships. *See* landing craft and
  landing ships
amphtracks. *See* landing craft and landing
  ships
Anamann, Edwardo, 37
Anders, Wladyslaw (Polish general), 515
Andrea Doria (Italian battleship), 451
Andrews, Adolphus (USN admiral),
  255–58
Anglo-American strategic disputes, 323
Anglo-German Naval Agreement (1935),
  1–2, 7, 22
Antwerp, Allied capture of, 536–37
Anvil, Operation, 508–9, 535–36
Anzio, Italy, Allied landings at (1944),
  501–7, 514–15
  illus., 505
Aoba (IJN cruiser), 340
Arcadia Conference, 252, 322
Archerfish (USN submarine), 597,
  599–600, 600n

Ardent (RN destroyer), 59–60

Area Zebra (D-Day assembly point), 526–27

Arizona (USN battleship), 205
  illus., 206

Ark Royal (RN carrier), 26, 34–35, 54, 71, 76, 83, 88–89
  and the pursuit of the *Bismarck*, 146–48
  sunk, 242
  illus., 146

Armed Merchant Cruisers (AMC), 110–11
  illus., 110

Arnold, Henry H. "Hap" (USAAF general), 271, 604

Asdic, 7–8, 15–16, 115–18, 121, 129, 379

Assyrian (British steamer), 115

Astoria (USN cruiser), 309

Atago (IJN cruiser), 369, 567–68

Athenia (British liner), 10

Atlantic Charter, 188

Atlantis [formerly *Goldenfels*] (German raider), 127–28

atomic bombs, 634

Attacker (RN carrier), 456–57

Attilio Regolo (Italian cruiser), 451

Attu Island, 285, 470–71

Auchinleck, Claude (British general), 58

Audacity (RN carrier), 250

Augusta (USN cruiser), 188, 356

Auphan, Gabriel (French admiral), 362–63

Aurora (RN cruiser), 353

Austin, Bernard L. (USN admiral), 484

Australia. See Royal Australian Navy

Australia (Australian cruiser), 304

Automedon (British steamer), 128

auxiliary carriers (Allied)
  in Battle of the Atlantic, 250, 382
  at Salerno, 456–57
  at Leyte Gulf, 556–57, 580–83

auxiliary cruisers (German), 126–28

Avalanche, Operation. *See* Salerno, invasion of

Avenger (USN torpedo plane), 382, 469

Axum (Italian submarine), 317

Azalea (RN corvette), 109, 521–22

B-29 bomber (US), 595–97, 603–5, 609–11

Backhouse, Roger (RN admiral), 62

Badoglio, Pietro (Italian PM), 443, 444–49, 454, 455

Badung Strait, Battle of (1942), 226

Balalae, atrocity at, 410n

Balao-class submarines (US), 590–91
  illus., 591

Balikpapan (Borneo), 217–18

Baltic Sea, 8–9, 23, 42–43, 294–95, 615–17, 615n

Baltimore (USN cruiser), 553

Barb (USN submarine), 632

Barbarosa, Operation (invasion of USSR), 91–92, 151

Barber, Charles (USN officer), 543

Barber, Rex T. (US pilot), 412–14

Barbey, Daniel E. (USN admiral), 481

Barham (RN battleship), 93, 242

Barnett, Corelli (historian), 55, 73

bases-for-destroyers agreement (1940), 111–12

Batfish (US submarine), 593

Battle of the Atlantic, 103–29, 241, 245–58, 373–76, 378–91
  See also commerce raiding, German; convoys and convoy defense; and codes and code breaking, British

Battle of the Bulge (1944–45), 613

Battle off Samar (1944), 578–83, 585–87
  See also Leyte Gulf, Battle of

battlecruisers, xvi, 22

Battler (RN carrier), 456–57

Bayntun (USN destroyer escort), 382

Béarn (French carrier), 76n

Beatty, David (RN admiral), xvi

Beatty (USN destroyer), 439

Beatus (British steamer), 117

Beaverford (British steamer), 123–24

Becton, Julian (USN officer), 264

Beer, Robert (USN officer), 532
Begonia (RN corvette), 109
Belfast (RN cruiser), 466
Bell, David B. (USN sub captain), 394
Bell, Frederick S. (RN officer), 33–34
Belleau Wood (USN carrier), 600
Bellinger, Patrick (USN admiral), 202–3
Benn, William G. (RN officer), 14
Bennehoff, Olton R. (transport
    captain), 351
Bergamini, Carlo (Italian admiral), 449–51
    illus., 450
Best, Richard (USN pilot), 291
Betio, invasion of. *See* Tarawa
Beuke, Heinz-Ehler (U-boat captain), 358
Bey, Erich (German naval officer),
    464–68
Birmingham (USN cruiser), 571
Biscayne (USN command ship), 456
Bismarck (German battleship), 22–23, 129
    characteristics, 130–31
    sortie of, 133, 138–40
    illus., 133, 149
    map, 136
Bismarck Sea (USN carrier), 609, 621
Bismarck Sea, Battle of (1943), 404–7
    illus., 406
Blair, Clay (historian), 384, 397
Blamey, Thomas (Australian general),
    481, 639
Blanchard, J. W. (US sub captain),
    548–49
Bleichrodt, Heinrich (U-boat captain),
    116–19, 257
Bletchley Park, 95, 247–50
    and North Cape convoys, 262–64
    See also codes and code breaking
Blücher (German cruiser), 45, 49, 59
Bluebell (RN corvette), 109, 116, 118, 129
Blumenson, Martin (historian), 506
Bode, Howard (USN officer), 304–8, 310
Bogan, Gerald (USN admiral), 568–72,
    574, 603
Bogue (USN/RN carrier), 382

Boise (USN cruiser)
    in Solomon Islands, 339–42
    in Mediterranean, 439–40
Bolzano (Italian cruiser), 453
Bonte, Frederick (German naval officer),
    49–54
Bormann, Martin (Hitler's Secretary, 617
Bougainville, invasion of (1943), 481–85
Bourrasque (French destroyer), 67–68
    illus., 66
Bovey, Henry C. (RN officer), 142
Boyle, William (RN admiral). *See* Cork
    and Orrery, Lord
Bramble (RN destroyer), 376
Breeman (USN destroyer escort), illus., 383
Bret Harte (US liberty ship), illus., 388
Bretagne (French battleship), 71, 75
Briarwood (British steamer), 122
British Expeditionary Force (BEF). *See*
    Dunkirk
Broke (RN destroyer), 353
Brooklyn (USN cruiser), 356
Broome, Jack (RN officer), 263–65
Bryant, Carleton (USN admiral), 531
Buckmaster, Elliott (USN officer), 292–93
Buckner, Simon Bolivar (USA general),
    632
Buell, Thomas B. (historian), 490
Buie, Paul (USN officer), 548
Bulldog (RN destroyer), 248
Bunker Hill (USN carrier), 548, 625
    illus., 625
Burke, Arleigh (USN officer), 484–85,
    486–87, 487n, 574
Burnett, Robert (RN admiral), 465–68
Burrough, Harold (RN admiral), 317, 351
Bush (USN destroyer), 623
Buttercup (RN corvette), 109
Buyo (Japanese transport), 396

Cabot (USN carrier), 569
Cactus Air Force (Guadalcanal), 326–27,
    331–32, 343, 364, 403
    becomes AirSols, 411

Caine Mutiny (novel), 602n
Caio Duilio (Italian battleship), 87, 451
Cairo (RN cruiser), 317
Calabria, Battle of (1940), 82–83
Calhoun (USN destroyer), 623
Calhoun, Raymond (USN officer), 601–2
California (USN battleship), 205–6
Callaghan, Daniel (USN admiral), 364–68
   illus., 36
Cameron, Donald (RN officer), 461
Cambeltown (RN destroyer), 324
Campioni, Inigo (Italian admiral), 82–83,
   85, 89
   and Battle of Cape Spartivento, 88–89
Canada. *See* Royal Canadian Navy
Canberra (Australian cruiser), 304, 308
Cape Engaño, Battle of (1944), 584–85
   See also Leyte Gulf
Cape Esperance, Battle of (1942), 337–42
Cape Matapan, Battle of (1941),
   93–101, 126
Cape Spartivento, Battle of (1940), 88–89
Cape St. George, Battle of (1943), 486–87
Caprella (British tanker), 119
Carlisle (RN cruiser), 242
Carmick (USN destroyer), 532
Carney, Robert B. (USN officer),
   572, 584
Carpender, Arthur S. (USN admiral), 556
Cartwheel, Operation (1943), 471–72,
   475–87
Casablanca
   American invasion of, 355–58, 363
   Allied conference at, 417–18
   illus., 418
Cassino (Italy), 500, 503–4, 515
Castellano, Giuseppe (Italian general),
   444–46, 448, 454
casualties
   in World War II, xi
   at Mers el-Kébir, 76
   in Battle of Cape Matapan, 101
   during evacuation of Crete, 102
   on HMS *Hood*, 139

   on USS *Reuben James*, 192
   at Pearl Harbor, 206–7
   on *Prince of Wales*, 215
   on USS *Houston*, 234
   in PQ-17, 265
   in Solomon Islands, 347
   in North Africa, 417n
   on Tarawa, 495, 496
   at Anzio, 506
   on Peleliu, 563
   on Iwo Jima, 606, 606n
   on Okinawa, 632
   during Exercise Tiger (Slapton
     Sands), 522
Cattaneo, Carlo (Italian admiral), 99–101
Cavagnari, Domenico (Italian Admiral), 88
Cavalla (US submarine), 543, 549
Central Pacific Drive, 487–96, 509–13
   See also Tarawa, Marshall Islands,
     and Saipan
Chamberlain, Neville (British PM), 2, 9,
   57–58
Channel dash (1942), 258–60
Cheek, Mike (USN intel. officer), 574
Chiang Kai-shek (Chinese general),
   169, 499
Chicago (USN cruiser), 304, 307–8
Chikuma (Japanese cruiser), 585
China, 639
   Japan's invasion of (1937), 165–66,
     169–70
   US support for, 554
Chitose (IJN carrier), 559
Chiyoda (Japanese carrier), 559
Chokai (IJN cruiser), 585
Christie, Ralph Waldo (USN admiral),
   590, 595
Christopher Newport (US steamer), 264
Churchill (RN destroyer, formerly USS
   Herndon), 112
Churchill, Winston S. (British PM), 37, 642
   and Anzio, 501–8
   and Battle of the Atlantic, 124, 373
   and the *Bismarck*, 140, 150–51

and France, 61–62, 68–77
and grand strategy, 324–25, 444, 503–4
and the Mediterranean, 88, 243, 320, 444
and Norway, 42, 47, 50, 52, 54–57, 58
and the Pacific, 629
named Prime Minister, 58
relations with admirals, 41–42, 56–57, 73, 89, 137, 140, 243, 334, 462–63
and Singapore, 210, 215, 223
and the Soviet Union, 452, 463
and the United States, 11–12, 188, 208, 314
illus., 40, 418
Ciano, Galeazzo (Italian foreign minister), 81–82, 84, 87
Cilicia (RN Armed Merchant Cruiser), 110
Citadel, Operation (1943), 402
Claggett, Bladen (USN sub captain), 567–68
Clan Ferguson (British ammunition ship), 317
Clark, Mark Wayne (US general)
and the Italian campaign, 455, 457, 501, 505–6, 514–15
and Operation Torch, 334
Clemens, Martin (British coast watcher), 297
Clement (British steamer), 19–20, 22
Coast Guard, U.S., 255–56, 258
Coastal Command (RAF), 105
codes and code breaking, 95
American, 194, 194n, 274–75, 364, 404, 409, 595
(at Midway, 282–83, 286; and Yamamoto, 410–11)
British, 145n, 245–50, 383–84, 466
German, 128, 143, 381, 383–84, 466
Japanese, 274–75
Cobalto (Italian submarine), 316
Cobra, Operation, 535
Collins, J. Lawton (USA general), 520–21, 524

Columbus (German liner), 178
Combat Information Center (CIC), 478
Combined Chiefs of Staff (CCS), 323, 454, 487
Comfort (RN destroyer), 67
commerce raiding, American, 241, 394–98, 542, 589–95
commerce raiding, British, 240–41
commerce raiding, German
by auxiliary cruisers, 126–28
in the Pacific, 128
by surface raiders, 19–20, 24–31, 120–26
by U-boats, 114–20, 129
See also U-boats
commerce raiding, Japanese, 240, 257–58
Conolly, Richard L. (USN admiral)
and Italy, 456
in the Pacific, 504, 512
and Sicily, 431–32, 434
Conte di Cavour (Italian battleship), 86
illus., 87
contre-torpilleurs (French large destroyers), 70
Convallaria (Swedish steamer), 117
convoys and convoy defense, 107–13, 114–20, 261–62
Atlantic convoys:
HG-72, 114
HG 73, 250
HG-76, 250
HX-79, 118–19, 120
HX-79A, 119
HX-84, 121–24
HX-112, 129
HX-133, 249
HX-150, 189
HX-156, 191
HX-229, 380–82, 383
MW-10, 242
OB-318, 248
ON-166, 380
ON-24, 189
ONS-5, 384–85, 399

convoys and convoy defense (*continued*)
    ONS-154, 380
    SL-125, 349
    SC-7, 114–18, 120
    SC-42, 249
    SC-48, 189
    SC-122, 381, 383
    SC-130, 385–86, 399
  Japanese convoys, 593–94
  Mediterranean convoys, 348–49, 361
  North Cape convoys:
    JW-51B, 376–77
    PQ-17, 263–65
    QP-13, 265
    JW-54A, 464
    JW55B, 464
  on the U.S. coast, 252–53, 257–58
  See also Pedestal
Cook, Charles (USN seaman), 341
Cooper, N.C. (RN pilot), 147
Coral Sea, Battle of (1942), 274–81
  map, 277
Cork and Orrery, Lord [William Boyle],
  56–58
Corsi, Luigi (Italian officer), 100
corvettes (RN escort ships), 109–10
  illus., 108
Cornwall (RN cruiser), 236–38
Cossack (RN destroyer), 37–38, 55
Costello, John (historian), 332
Courage, Rafe E. (RN officer), 54
Courageous (RN carrier), 16
Courbet (French battleship), 71
Coward, Jesse (USN naval officer), 576–77
Cowie (USN destroyer), 439
Cowpens (USN carrier), 602
Cremer, Peter (U-boat captain), 251,
  254, 257
Crete, 102
Crutchley, Victor (RN admiral), 303–4, 310
Cumberland (RN cruiser), 31–34
Cunningham, Andrew Browne (RN
  admiral), 71, 401, 454

in Battle of Cape Matapan, 94–101
in Battle of Cape Spartivento, 88–89
death of, 646
First Sea Lord, 463
and the French Navy, 72–73
and Italy, 458
in the Mediterranean, 82–83, 87, 90
and Operation Torch, 334
and Sicily, 422–25, 430
illus., 72
Cunningham, John (RN admiral), 463,
  502, 504
Curtin, John (Australian PM), 556
Cushing (USN destroyer), 367
Cuttlefish (USN submarine), 394
Cyclops (British steamer), 252–53

D-Day (Allied invasion of Europe). *See*
  Overlord
D'Este, Carlo (historian), 433n
D'Oyly-Hughes, Guy (RN officer), 60
Da Zara, Alberto (Italian admiral), 318,
  451–52
  illus., 453
Dace (USN submarine), 567–68, 589
Dagabur (Italian submarine), 316
Dakar, Senegal, 77
Dalrymple-Hamilton, Frederick (RN
  officer), 144
Danis, Anthony L. (USN officer), 189
Darby, William O. (US Army Ranger), 457
Darlan, Jean-François (French admiral),
  70–71, 352, 354, 363
Darter (USN submarine), 567–68, 589
Darwin, Australia, 224
Daspit, Dan (USN sub captain), 398
Dau, Heinrich (German naval officer),
  37–38
Dauntless (USN dive bomber),
  289–90, 292
Davison, Ralph (USN admiral), 569–72
De Courten, Raffaele (Italian admiral),
  444, 447, 453–54, 645

de Gaulle, Charles (French general),
363, 417
de Laborde, Jean (French admiral),
362–63, 645
de Lafond, Gervais (French admiral), 356
De Ruyter (Dutch cruiser), 223, 229–31
Dempsey, Miles (British general) 436, 524
Denmark, 42–43, 70
Denver (USN cruiser), 484
Derevyanko, Kuzma (USSR
general), 639
destroyer escorts, 382–83
illus., 383
Deucalion (British steamer), 317
Deutschland [later *Lützow*] (German
pocket battleship), 6–7, 18–19, 30
in Baltic, 460–61, 615–17, 615n
map of cruise (1939), 28
and North Cape convoys, 261–62
in Norway campaign, 45, 49
renamed *Lützow*, 45
Devastator (USN torpedo bomber),
288–89
Dewey (USN destroyer), 601–2
Deyo, Morton (USN admiral), 627
Dickinson, Norman (RN officer), 115–18
Dieppe, raid on, 267, 324
dive-bombers
American, 289–90, 292
British, 49, 85
German, 101, 198, 295
Japanese, 198–99, 292
Dönitz, Karl (German admiral), 5–10,
17, 21
and the Battle of the Atlantic, 103–20,
241–58, 374–76, 380–82,
384–86, 398–99
as commander of Kriegsmarine, 378–86
as Führer, 617–18, 643–44
and Hitler, 241, 258, 399, 460,
464, 500
and the Italians, 415–16, 445–46
and the Mediterranean, 244, 415–16

and Normandy, 535
and North Cape convoys, 465–66
and Operation Paukenschlag
(Drumbeat), 241, 250–58
tonnage strategy of, 104, 244–45
illus., 6
Dönitz, Peter (U-boat officer), 385
Doolittle, James H. (USAAF general),
270–74, 282
Doorman, Karel (Dutch admiral),
221–23, 225
and Battle of the Java Sea, 228–31
illus., 226
Doric Star (British steamer), 30–31
Dorsetshire (RN cruiser), 150, 236–38
illus., 150
Douglas-Pennant, Cyril (RN admiral), 524
Downfall, Operation (US invasion of
Japan), 633
Dresden, Allied air raid on, 609–10
Drumroll [or Drumbeat]. *See*
Paukenschlag
Duke of York (RN battleship), 263–64,
335, 465–68
DUKW ("ducks"), 429–30
illus., 429
Duncan, Donald (USN officer), 269–70
Dunkirk, evacuation of (1940), 62–69
Dunkerque (French battlecruiser),
71–75, 77
illus., 75
Duprez, E.J.H.L. (French naval officer),
530
Dutch East Indies, 170–71, 209–10,
220–35
Dynamo, Operation. *See* Dunkirk

E-boats. *See schnellbooten*
Eagle (RN carrier), 82–83, 85, 315
Eastern Solomons, Battle of (1942),
329–31
Eck, Heinz-Wilhelm (U-boat captain),
397n

Eckstam, Gene (USN officer), 522

Eden, Anthony (British foreign secretary), 210

Edwards, J. M. (British merchant captain), 29

Eggert, Joseph R. (USN officer), 546

Eisenhower, Dwight D. (US general), 183
  and Anzio, 501–2
  and the campaign in Europe, 536, 618
  and Italian surrender, 444, 448, 454–55
  and LSTs for Normandy, 507–9, 522–23
  and North Africa (Torch), 334, 337, 362
  and Overlord, 519–20, 525–26
  and Salerno, 454–55, 457
  and Sicily (Husky), 420, 422, 424, 433, 440

Eidsvold (Norwegian warship), 50

El Alamein, Battle of (1942), 348–49

Electra (RN destroyer), 230

Elliott (USN transport), 301

Ellis, Earl "Pete" (USMC officer), 176

Ellis, Robert (RN officer), 144

Emden (German cruiser), 6, 8

Emmons (USN destroyer), 623

Empire Thrush (British steamer), 254

Empress Augusta Bay, Battle of (1943), 482, 484–85

Encounter (RN destroyer), 230–31

Endrass, Engelbert (U-boat commander), 5, 11, 117, 250

Enigma machine (German), 246–50, 383–84
  illus., 246

Eniwetok Island, US invasion of (1944), 513

English, Robert H. (USN admiral), 398

Enright, Joseph (USN sub captain), 597, 599–600, 600n

Enterprise (USN carrier), 202, 218, 272
  at Midway, 283–93
  in Solomon Islands, 330, 342, 344–45, 346

escort carriers. *See* auxiliary carriers

Eskimo (RN destroyer), 56

Esmonde, Eugene (RN pilot), 142

Essex (USN carrier), 469

Etajima (Japanese naval academy), 154, 160, 167

Euryalus (RN cruiser), 441

Evans, Ernest (USN officer), 580–81

Exercise Tiger (1944), 520–23

Exeter (RN cruiser)
  in Battle of the Java Sea, 229–31
  in Battle of the Plate, 32–37
  in South Pacific, 222–23, 225

Fanshaw Bay (USN carrier), 580–83

Fédala, American landings at, 355–58
  map, 357

Fegan, Edward S. F. (RN officer), 121–22

Fenno, Frank (USN sub captain), 397

Ferrini, Renato (Italian naval officer), 317

Fife, James (USN admiral), 590, 595

Fifth Fleet (USN), 490, 509, 603
  redesignated as Third Fleet, 555–56

Finland, 42, 294–95

Finschhafen, 481

Fiume (Italian cruiser), 100

Fisher, Douglas (RN officer), 100

Flasher (USN submarine), 594

Fleet Faction (Japan), 155–58, 164–67

Fletcher, Frank Jack (USN admiral), 217
  and Battle of Eastern Solomons, 328–32
  and the Battle of Midway, 287
  and the Coral Sea, 275–81
  and Guadalcanal, 299–300, 302–3, 309–10
  illus., 299

Flower class corvettes. *See* corvettes

Fluckey, Eugene (USN sub captain), 632

Flying Fish (US submarine), 543

Forager, Operation. *See* Saipan

Forbes, Charles (RN admiral), 4–5, 124, 133–34

in Norway campaign, 54
illus., 55
Formidable (RN carrier), 95, 97–98, 236, 630–31
Fougueux (French destroyer), 356
Fowey (RN sloop), 116–17
Franklin (USN carrier), 600
Fraser, Bruce (RN admiral), 462–63, 630, 638
sinks *Scharnhorst*, 465–68
French Navy, 69–70
attacked by British, 69–77
at D-Day, 530
and North Africa, 353–58
scuttled, 77, 362–63
Fritz-X guided missile. *See* FX-1400
Frost, Laurence H. (USN officer), 187
Fubuki (IJN destroyer), 233, 341
Fuchida, Mitsuo (IJN officer), 205
fuel. *See* oil
Furious (RN carrier), 54–55, 57
Fusō (IJN battleship), 163, 565–66, 569, 577
FX-1400 guided missile ("Fritz-X"), 450, 457, 459

Gambier Bay (USN carrier), 582, 587
Gamble, Bruce (historian), 408
Garrison, Paul B. (USN officer), 582
Gato-class USN submarines, 398
Geddes, George C. (RN officer), 522
gekokujō, concept of, 157–58
Genda, Minoru (IJN officer), 196
General von Steuben (German liner), 616
Gensoul, Marcel-Bruno (French admiral), 74–76
Gentian (RN corvette), 108
George V, xiii–xvi
George VI, 111
German Navy. *See* Kriegsmarine
Ghormley, Robert (USN admiral), 182, 298–99, 300, 302, 309, 330, 342

Gibraltar, 351
Gilbert Islands, US invasion of (1943), 489–96
Giordani (Italian tanker), 359
Giraud, Henry (French general), 417
Giulio Cesare (Italian battleship), 83, 452–53
Glasfurd, Charles E. (RN officer), 60
Glassford, William (USN admiral), 221
Glorious (RN carrier), 54, 57
sinks, 59–60, 69
Glowworm (RN destroyer), 46–47
Gneisenau (German battlecruiser), 4, 22
and the Channel dash, 258–60
as commerce raider, 126, 129, 131–32
decommissioned, 460
in Norway campaign, 43–45, 48–49, 59–60
Goddard, Victor (British army officer), 62
Godfoy, René-Emile (French admiral), 72–73, 363, 417
Goebbels, Josef (German propaganda minister), 10, 16, 376–77
Goldenfels. *See Atlantis*
Gomorrah, Operation (1943), 402
Gordon, Oliver (RN officer), 230
Göring, Hermann (German Luftwaffe commander)
antipathy to the navy, 376–77
and the Battle of the Atlantic, 105
and the Blitz, 90, 105
and Dunkirk, 64–65
and Norway, 42, 54
and succession, 617
Gorizia (Italian cruiser), 453
Gort, Lord [John Vereker] (British general), 62, 66–68
Gotō, Aritomo (Japanese admiral), 339–42
Government Code & Cypher School (British), 247
See also Bletchley Park

Graf Spee (German pocket battleship),
  18–20, 24–34
  map of cruise, 28
  scuttled, 35–36
Grafton (RN destroyer), 67
Graziani, Rodolfo (Italian general),
  83–84, 90
Greece
  British support of, 92–93, 101–2
  German intervention in, 101–2
  Italian invasion of, 91–92
Greer (USN destroyer), 187–88
Gretton, Peter (RN officer), 316,
  385, 386
Grew, Joseph (US diplomat), 165
Grider, George (USN sub captain), 594
Guadalcanal, battles for, 295–311
  Japanese attacks on, 328–33, 342–46
  Japanese evacuation of, 372
  supply of, 326–28, 363–64
  See also Savo Island and Naval Battle of
    Guadalcanal
gunfire support. *See* naval gunfire
    support
Gurkha (RN cruiser), 54
Gustav Line (in Italy), 500–1, 503, 515
  map, 501
Gwin (USN destroyer), 479

Haakon VII (King of Norway), 58
Hagen, Robert (USN officer), 580–81
Haguro (IJN cruiser), 229–31, 483, 549,
  585
Hale, J. W. (RN pilot), 86
Halifax, Lord (British foreign minister), 56
Hall, John Lesslie Jr. (USN admiral), 432,
  436, 455, 524
Halsey, William F. (USN admiral),
  639, 647
  and the Doolittle raid, 272–74
  and Leyte Gulf, 562–63. 568–69,
    572–74, 578, 583–85, 586–88
  and MacArthur, 474–75, 557–58

misses fight at Midway, 283
  in the Solomon Islands, 342–46, 478,
    485–86
  and the typhoon, 600–3
  illus., 343
Hamaguchi, Osachi (Japanese PM), 156
Hambleton (USN destroyer), 358
Hamburg, bombing of (1943), 402
Hancock (USN carrier), 623
Hannibal, Operation (German
    evacuation, 1945), 615–17
Hara, Chūichi (IJN admiral)
  in the Coral Sea, 278–81
  in Solomon Islands, 328–31
Hara, Tameichi (IJN naval officer), 585
Hardegen, Richard (U-boat captain),
  252–54
Hardy (RN destroyer), 53
Harris, F.P.C. (British merchant captain),
  19–20, 25
Hart, Thomas C. (USN admiral), 211, 217,
  221–23
  illus., 222
Hartenstein, Werner (U-boat captain),
  374–75
Haruna (IJN battleship), 342
Harwood, Henry (RN officer)
  described, 31
  in Battle of the Plate, 32–37, 139
  in Mediterranean, 89, 334
Hastings, Max (historian), 474
Hatsukazi (IJN destroyer), 484
Havock (RN destroyer), 54
hedgehog (ASW system), 379–80
  illus., 379
Heerman (USN destroyer), 581
Heinl, Robert (historian), 510
Helena (USN cruiser)
  in Battle of Cape Esperance, 339–42
  lost, 479, 479n
  in Naval Battle of Guadalcanal, 366–68
Helfrich, Conrad (Dutch admiral),
  220–22, 225, 226, 639

criticizes Waller, 232
relations with Doorman, 227–28
illus., 222
Henderson Field (Guadalcanal), 326–29,
    332–33, 339, 342, 343–44, 364,
    369, 403
illus., 327
Hepburn, Arthur J. (USN admiral), 310
Hermes (RN carrier), 76, 238
Hewitt, H. Kent (USN admiral)
    and Anvil, 535
    and Anzio, 499
    and Operation Torch, 354
    and Salerno, 454–59
    and Sicily, 424–25, 440
Heye, Helmuth (German naval officer),
    23, 46–47
HF/DF (huff duff), 245
Hiei (IJN battleship), 365–68
Higgins boats, 336, 351–52, 355,
    434–35, 483, 513
    at Normandy, 526–27, 530
    illus., 427
    See also landing craft
Hilfskreuzers. See commerce raiding,
    German
Hill, Harry (USN admiral), 493
Himmler, Heinrich (SS leader), 617
Hipper (German cruiser)
    in Baltic, 616
    as commerce raider, 126
    decommissioned, 460
    and North Cape convoys, 263, 376
    in Norway campaign, 45–47
Hirohito (Japanese emperor), 156, 626,
    634–35, 643
Hiryū (IJN carrier), 198, 217,
    224, 292
Hitler, Adolf, 1, 8–10, 260–61
    and Britain, 18–19, 23, 90
    and the defense of Italy, 455, 500
    and large surface ships, 376–78, 460
    and Norway, 38, 39, 58–59

relations with Raeder, 22, 38–40, 59,
    120, 141–42, 151, 186, 188,
    259–60, 376–78
relations with Dönitz, 258, 378, 399,
    464, 500
relations with Mussolini, 91–92, 445–46
and the Soviet Union, 91, 151, 186,
    295, 613
suicide of, 617, 642
Hitokappu Bay (Japan), 195–96
Hiyo (IJN carrier), 550
Hobart (Australian cruiser), 304
Hoel (USN destroyer), 581
Holland. *See* Royal Netherlands Navy
Holland, Cedric (RN officer), 74–75
Holland, Lancelot (RN admiral), 137–39
Holmes, Besby (US pilot), 412
Honolulu (USN cruiser), 479
Hood (RN battlecruiser), xvi, 71, 124, 131
    and fight with *Bismarck*, 137–39
Hoover, Gilbert (USN officer), 369
Hoover, John (USN admiral), 606–7
Hopkins, Harry (US advisor), 187, 203
Hornet (USN carrier), 202
    and Doolittle raid, 269–70
    at Midway, 283–90
    in Solomon Islands, 333, 342, 344–46
    illus., 273, 345
Hōshō (IJN carrier), 160, 161
Hosogaya, Bushirō (IJN admiral), 471
Hotspur (RN destroyer), 53
Houston (USN cruiser), 222–23, 225, 554
    in Battle of the Java Sea, 229–31
    in Battle of Sunda Strait, 233–34
Howarth, Stephen (historian), 157
Hsu Yung-Chang [Xu Yongchang]
    (Chinese general), 639
Huebner, Charles (USA general), 524
Huffmeier, Friedrich (German naval
    officer), 461
Hull (USN destroyer), 602
Hull, Cordell (US Sec'y of State), 194
Hunter (RN carrier), 456–57

Hunter (RN destroyer), 53
Husky, Operation. *See* Sicily
Hyakutake, Harukichi (Japanese
    general), 475
Hydeman, Earl T. (US sub captain),
    592, 632
Hydrangea (RN corvette), 129
Hyperion (RN destroyer), 178
Hypo. *See* codes and code breaking,
    American
Hyuga (Japanese warship), 585, 626

Iachino, Angelo (Italian admiral), 89. 449
    and the Battle of Cape Matapan,
        93–101
Icarus (US Coast Guard cutter), 256
Ichiki, Kiyonao (Japanese army officer),
    328
Ickes, Harold (US presidential advisor),
    192
Illustrious (RN carrier), 84, 93
    in the Pacific, 630–31
    and raid on Taranto, 85–86
Imperial Japanese Navy (IJN)
    attrition of, 469, 593–94, 626
    in Indian Ocean, 235–38 (map, 237)
    military aircraft of, 198–99
    offensive southward, 208–9, 216–35
        (map, 219)
    politics of, 154–61
    and strategic planning, 514, 539–40
Indefatigable (RN carrier), 630–31
Independence (USN carrier), 486
Indianapolis (USN cruiser), 607,
    622, 622n
Indochina, 193
Indomitable (RN carrier), 210–11, 236,
    314n, 315–16
Inoue, Shigeyoshi (IJN admiral), 161, 281
Intrepid (USN carrier), 568, 600
Inukai, Tsuyoshi (Japanese PM), 157
Iowa (USN battleship), 502n
iron ore, importance of, 39–41
Ironclad (US steamer), 265

Ise (IJN battleship), 163, 585, 626
island hopping strategy in the Pacific,
    480–81
Italia (Italian battleship), 451
Italian Air Force. *See* Regia Aeronautica
Italian Navy. *See* Regia Marina
Ithuriel (RN destroyer), 316
Itō, Seiichi (IJN admiral), 627–28
Ivanhoe (RN destroyer), 67
Iwo Jima, Battle of (1945), 605–9
    illus., 608

Jackson, Edward (Malta governor), 313
Jamaica (RN cruiser), 376
Jan Wellem (German supply ship), 53
Japan
    army politics, 156–57
    economic resources, 153, 172, 192–94,
        542, 558–59
    national policies, xix, 166, 179, 235
    and peace talks, 553
    strategic planning of, 403–4, 475,
        514, 539
    U.S. bombing of, 595–97, 603–5,
        609–12 (map, 596)
    and war in China, 165–67, 169–70
    See also Imperial Japanese Navy
Java (Dutch cruiser), 229–31
Java Sea, Battle of, 228–31
Jean Bart (French battleship), 71,
    355–56, 363
    illus., 356
jeep carriers. *See* auxiliary carriers
Jeffers (USN destroyer), 440
Jervis (RN destroyer), 101
Jervis Bay (RN Armed Merchant
    Cruiser), 114, 121–22, 124
Jintsu (IJN cruiser), 331
John D. Ford (USN destroyer), 218
John Harvey (US liberty ship), 459n
Johnston (USN destroyer), 580–82
Joint Chiefs of Staff (US), 507–8, 514
Joseph Hewes (USN transport), 358
Juin, Alphonse (French general), 352, 515

Juneau (USN cruiser), 368–69
Jun'yō (IJN carrier), 364, 595
Jupiter (RN destroyer), 230–31
Jutland, Battle of (1916), xvi

Kaga (IJN carrier), 162, 197, 224, 275,
    290–92
    illus., 162
Kahoolawe Island, 510
Kami, Shigenori (IJN officer), 561
kamikaze tactics, 345n, 587, 600, 609,
    620–626, 632
Karlsruhe (German cruiser), 7, 49
Kasserine Pass, Battle of (1943), 362
Kate (Nakajima Type 99 bomber),
    198–99, 292
    illus., 199
Katō, Kanji (IJN admiral), xi, 155–56,
    159–60
Kawaguchi, Kiyotake (Japanese general),
    372
Kearney (US destroyer), 189–91
    illus., 190
Kellogg-Briand Peace Pact, xv
Kennedy, John F. (USN officer),
    480n
Kenney, George (US general), 404–7,
    482
Keppel (RN destroyer), 264
Kernevel (U-boat HQ), 103, 103n,
    116–19, 249
Kershaw, Ian (historian), 614
Kesselring, Albert (German general), 312,
    359–60
    in Italy, 455, 459, 500, 503, 505–6,
    514–15
Kidō Butai (Japan's carrier Strike Force),
    196
    in Indian Ocean, 236–38
    (map, 237)
    and Pearl Harbor, 200–8
    and South Asia, 224, 227
Kimmel, Husband (USN admiral), 184,
    202–3, 217

Kimura, Masatomi (IJN admiral), 404
Kinashi, Takaichi (IJN sub captain), 332
King, Ernest J. (USN admiral)
    and Allied strategy, 420, 488–89, 523,
    554–55, 605, 629
    characterized, 183–84
    as COMINCH and CNO, 252–53
    as commander, Atlantic fleet, 183–86
    and convoy controversy, 252–53, 391
    death of, 646
    and Fletcher, 331–32
    and Guadalcanal, 297–300, 310
    and Halsey, 603
    and MacArthur, 474
    illus., 183
King George V (RN battleship), 137,
    145–49, 630
    illus., 134
Kinkaid, Thomas (USN admiral), 342,
    346, 590
    and Leyte Gulf, 580, 582–83
    and the Seventh Fleet, 555–57
Kirishima (IJN battleship), 365, 368,
    369–72
Kirk, Alan G. (USN admiral)
    and D-Day, 528
    and Sicily, 431–32
Kirkpatrick, Charles C. (USN sub
    captain), 397
Kiska Island, 285, 470–71
Kitkun Bay (USN carrier), 582
Klakring, Burt (US sub captain), 592
Knorr, Dietrich (German U-boat
    captain), 53
Knox, William Franklin "Frank" (US Sec'y
    of Navy), 183–84, 257, 391, 489
Kobayashi, Michio (Japanese pilot), 292
Kōdōha (Faction in Japanese army),
    156–57, 161, 165, 174
Koga, Mineichi (IJN admiral), 413, 475,
    483, 514, 539
    illus., 413
Koiso, Kuniaki (Japanese general), 553,
    632

Köln (German cruiser), 4, 7

Kolombangara, Battle of (1943), 479–80

Komandorski Islands, Battle of (1943), 471

Komet (German raider), 128

Kondō, Nobutake (IJN admiral), 285–86, 328, 346, 364, 365, 371, 638

Kongō (IJN battleship), 163, 342, 585

Königsberg (German cruiser), 49

Kormoran (German raider) 128

Kosco, George (USN aerologist), 601

Kortenaer (Dutch destroyer), 230

Kosler, Herman (USN sub captain), 549

Koyanagi, Tomiji (IJN officer), 560–61, 572, 586, 588

Krancke, Theodor (German admiral), 521
  as commerce raider, 120–26
  and Hitler, 377
  illus., 123

Krebs (German trawler), 247

Kretschmer, Otto (U-boat captain), 117–18, 129

Kriegsmarine, 1–2, 5–10, 20–24, 38, 43–54
  Channel dash, 258–60
  surface navy, 130–33, 140,
  See also commerce raiding, German

Kriegstransporters (KT boats), 360–61

Kula Gulf, Battle of (1943), 478–79

Kure Naval Arsenal (Japan), 167

Kuribayashi, Tadamichi (Japanese general), 608–9

Kurita, Takeo (IJN admiral), 224–25, 485, 638, 644–45
  and Leyte Gulf, 559, 560–61, 566, 567, 571–75, 576, 578–83, 585–87, 585–88
  illus., 566

Kusaka, Jin'ichi (IJN admiral), 475, 477–78, 565, 626–27

Kusaka, Ryūnosuke (IJN admiral), 565

Kwajalein Island, U.S. invasion of, 509–13

Kyokusei Maru (Japanese transport), 404

L'Alcyon (French destroyer), 357

Laconia (British liner), 374–75

Lae, 481

Laffey [DD-459] (USN destroyer), 367–68

Laffey [DD-724] (USN destroyer), 623–25
  illus., 624

Laforey (RN destroyer), 456

Land, Emory Scott (USN admiral), 386–87

landing craft and landing ships
  description of, 425–30
  effectiveness of, 459, 477, 498
  landing protocols of, 434–35, 437, 457, 477, 506, 511–12
  shortage of, 454–55, 498–99, 500–9, 522–23
  Specific types:
  landing craft assault (LCA), 336, 427
  landing craft, infantry (LCI), 429 (illus., 428)
  landing craft, mechanized (LCM or Mike boat), 426
  landing craft, personnel (LCP), 336
  landing craft, tank (LCT), 427 (illus., 428)
  landing craft, tracked (LVT or amphtracks), 492–93, 494, 511–13 (illus., 511)
  landing craft, vehicle and personnel (LCVP), 427 (*See also* Higgins boats)
  landing ship, medium (LSM), 564
  landing ship, tank (LST)
    and Anzio, 500–1, 503, 505–6
    crews of, 512
    described, 426–27, 497–98
    and Kwajalein, 512–13
    and Normandy, 507–9, 522–23, 533–34
    and Sicily, 437, 477
    Winstons (British tank carriers), 336–37

See also individual LSTs
  (illus., 427, 499, 523, 525, 534)
Lane, Frederic C. (historian), 389
Langley (USN carrier/seaplane tender),
  226–27
Langsdorff, Hans (German naval officer),
  19–20, 24–37
Lansdowne (USN destroyer), 637
Languedoc (British steamer), 116
Lanphier, Thomas G. (US pilot), 412–14
La Paz (British tanker), 257
Larcom, Charles (RN officer), 147
Lasswell, Alva "Red" (USMC code
  breaker), 410
Laub (USN destroyer), 439
Laval, Pierre, (French PM), 352, 645
Layton, Edwin (USN officer), 203,
  275, 410
Leach, John (RN officer)
  and the *Bismarck*, 138–49
  in South China Sea, 211–15
Leander (New Zealand cruiser), 479
Lee, Willis (USN admiral), 342, 544
  and Leyte Gulf, 573–74, 583
  and Naval Battle of Guadalcanal,
    370–72
  illus., 370
Leeson, Robert A. (USN officer), 576
Leipzig (German cruiser), 460
Leith (RN sloop), 117
LeMay, Curtis (USAAF general),
  609–12
Lemp, Fritz-Julius (U-boat commander),
  10, 248, 248n
Lend-Lease Act (1941), 185
Leslie, Max (USN pilot), 292
Lexington [CV-2] (USN carrier), xix, 162,
  269, 275
  in Battle of Coral Sea, 276, 278, 280–81
Lexington [CV-16] (USN carrier), 470,
  548, 550, 572, 600
Leygues, Georges (French Minister of
  Marine), xx

Leyte Gulf, Battle of (1944), 559–61,
  564–87
  map, 570
Li Wo (RN gunboat), 224–25
Libeccio (Italian destroyer), 86
liberty ships, 387–89
  illus., 388
Lincoln (RN destroyer, formerly USS
  Yarnall), 112
  illus., 112
Lindemann, Ernst (German naval officer),
  131–48, 151
Liscome Bay (USN carrier), 495–96
Littorio (Italian battleship), 86, 243
Lockwood, Charles (USN admiral),
  397–98, 590, 595, 639
London Naval Arms Limitation
  Conference (1930), xiii–xxii, 156
Long Lance torpedoes. *See* torpedoes,
  Japanese
Lorraine (French battleship), 72
Louisville (USN cruiser), 575, 577
Lowry, Frank J. (USN admiral), 504
Loyal (RN destroyer), 456
LST-77 (illus.), 427
LST-197, 506
LST-289 (illus.), 523
LST-313, 437, 439
LST-353, 541
LST-499 (illus.), 525
LST-507, 521
LST-531, 522
LST-543, 533
Lucas, John P. (USA general),
  504–6, 514
Ludlow (USN destroyer), 357
Lütjens, Günther (German
  admiral), 126
  in Norway campaign, 47–49
  and the *Bismarck* sortie, 131–49, 151
Lützow (German pocket battleship). *See*
  Deutschland
Lyster, Lumley (RN admiral), 85

MacArthur, Douglas (US general),
216–17, 297–98
characterized, 472–74
and Japanese surrender, 638–40, 643
and the Philippine invasion, 564, 600–1
in Southwest Pacific, 480–81, 487
strategic views of, 488–89, 496,
554–57
illus., 473, 555
Mackesy, Piers (British general), 56–57
MacKinnon, Lachlan (RN convoy
commodore), 115–18
MacNeil, Calum (British sailor), 124
Maddox (USN destroyer), 437
Mahan, Alfred Thayer (USN admiral/
writer), 160, 173, 586
Malaya, Japanese invasion of, 209–10
Malta, 92–93, 265
described, 311–12
siege of, 242, 294–95, 312–13
supply convoys to, 79–80, 82, 242–43,
313–20
See also Pedestal
Marat [formerly *Petropavlovsk*] (USSR
battleship), 295
Marinesko, Alexander (USSR sub
captain), 616
Market Garden, Operation, 536
Marshall, George C. (US general), 183, 387
strategic views of, 323, 325, 420, 460
Marshall Islands
described, 509–10
US invasion of (1944), 510–13
US raid on (1942), 218
Maryland (USN battleship), 205, 493,
576, 623
Mason, Dudley W. (tanker captain), 314,
317–20
Massachusetts (USN battleship), 335,
355–56
Matsobara, Takisaburo (IJN officer), 549
Matsumoto, Hiroshi (Japanese army offi-
cer), 344

Matsunaga, Sadaichi (IJN admiral), 212–13
Maund, Loben E. H. (RN officer), 146–47
May 15 Incident in Japan (1932), 157–58
Maya (IJN cruiser), 568
McCain, John S. (USN admiral), 307,
573, 583, 587, 639
McCampbell, David (USN pilot), 548
McCawley (USN command ship), 303
McClintock, David H. (USN sub
captain), 567–68, 568n
McClusky, Clarence Wade (USN pilot),
290–91
illus., 291
McGrigor, Rhoderick (RN admiral), 436
McIntyre, Ross (FDR's doctor), 502n
McMahon, Barney (USN sub captain),
606
McMorris, Charles H. (USN admiral),
470
Mediterranean, 69, 79–90, 92–102
convoys in, 242–44, 359–61
map, 80–81
U-boats in, 242
See also Malta, North Africa,
Pedestal, and Sicily
Merrill, Aaron (USN admiral), 482–85
Merrill, Wayne (USN sub captain), 593
Merry, Vernon (RN officer), 468
Mers-el-Kébir, British attack on, 71,
73–77
Meyer, Hans (German naval officer),
461–62
Michelier, Félix (French admiral), 363
Middleton, Troy (US general), 431, 436
midget submarines
British, 461–62
Japanese, 204
Midway, Battle of (1942), 282–93
map, 284
Mikawa, Gunichi (IJN admiral)
at Naval Battle of Guadalcanal, 364
at Savo Island, 305–10
illus., 306

Milan (French destroyer), 356

Miller, Henry (USN pilot), 271–72

mines, 23–24, 316

Minoru, Yokota (IJN sub captain), 369

Missouri (USN battleship), 637–40

Mitchell, John W. (US pilot), 411–112

Mitchell, William "Billy" (USA general), 213

Mitscher, Marc "Pete" (USN admiral)
  and AirSols, 411
  and Battle of the Philippine Sea, 544–46, 548–52
  and the Doolittle raid, 269–70
  and Leyte Gulf, 562, 574
  and Midway, 290
  and Okinawa, 627
  and TF 58, 513–14, 540
  illus., 547

Mogami (IJN cruiser), 565, 577

Mohan (British steamer), 121

Molotov, Vyacheslav (Soviet diplomat), 324

Monaghan (USN destroyer), 602

Monrovia (USN command ship), 440

Monsarrat, Nicholas (RN officer/novelist), 109

Montcalm (French cruiser), 530

Monte Cassino. *See* Cassino

Monterey (USN carrier), 602

Montgomery, Bernard Law (British general)
  and the campaign in Europe, 536
  and German surrender, 617–18
  in North Africa, 348–49, 414
  and Sicily, 422–23, 425, 441

Moon, Don (USN admiral), 520–23, 524, 526

Moore, Henry (RN officer), 264

Moore, Woodrow Wilson (US pilot), 407

Moosbrugger, Frederick (USN officer), 480

Morgan, Frederick (British general), 507

Morgenthau, Henry (US advisor), 193

Morison, Samuel Eliot (historian), xi, 342, 356, 366–67, 452, 479, 485, 622

Morocco, U.S. landings in (1942), 354–58

Morton, Dudley "Mush" (USN sub captain), 395–97, 397n, 407, 594
  illus., 396

Mukden Incident (1932), 157

Mulberries (artificial harbors), 534–35

Müllenheim-Rechberg, Burkard (German naval officer), 139

Müchen (German weather ship), 247

Munda (Japanese base), 478, 480

Murphy, Robert (US diplomat), 352

Murray, George D. (USN officer), 342

Musashi (IJN battleship), 169, 542
  and Battle of Leyte Gulf, 558–59, 571–72
  illus., 571

Mussolini, Benito (Italian dictator), 78–79, 642
  confidence in air forces, 81
  invades Greece, 90–92
  removed from power, 442, 443
  rescued by Germans, 453–54
  urges invasion of Egypt, 83–84

Mutsu (IJN battleship), 163

Mutsuki (Japanese transport), 331

Myōkō (IJN cruiser), 483, 485, 571

Nachi (IJN cruiser), 229–31, 577

Nagano, Osami (IJN admiral), 172, 235, 305
  illus., 171

Nagara (IJN cruiser), 371

Nagumo, Chūichi (IJN admiral), 196–97
  in Battle of Midway, 285–89
  in Indian Ocean, 224, 236–38
  and Pearl Harbor, 200–2, 207
  in Solomon Islands, 330–31, 347
  suicide of, 552
  illus., 197

Nanking (Nanjing), "rape of" (1937), 169, 177

Narvik, Norway, 40, 42, 49–58
  illus., 51

Narwhal (USN submarine), 392–93
Nashville (USN cruiser), 273, 564
Naval Battles of Guadalcanal, 363–372
naval gunfire support
　in Europe, 536
　at Normandy, 526–27, 530, 531–32
　　　(map, 528–29)
　in the Pacific, 510, 607–9
　at Salerno, 456–59
　in Sicily, 439–40
　at Tarawa, 493–94, 495
Neff, Ziggy (USN pilot), 548
Nelson (RN battleship), 124, 335, 454
Nelson, Horatio Lord (RN admiral), 70,
　　157–58
Neosho (USN oiler), 279
Neptune, Operation (naval aspect of
　　Overlord), 519–20
　Channel crossing, 523–24, 526–30
　rehearsals, 520–23
　supply effort, 533–35
Netherlands. *See* Royal Netherlands Navy
Nevada (USN battleship), 205–7, 530
New Guinea, operations on, 404
New Jersey (USN battleship), 562, 572,
　　574, 584
New Mexico (USN battleship), 622
New York (USN battleship), 335
New Zealand Navy, 31, 31n
Nigeria (RN cruiser), 317
Niizuki (IJN destroyer), 479
Nimitz, Chester (USN admiral), 218,
　　271–72, 478, 643–44, 646
　and Battle of the Coral Sea, 275–81
　and Battle of Midway, 283
　and Central Pacific Drive, 510, 514,
　　　552, 554–57, 563
　and Halsey, 272, 603
　and Leyte Gulf, 583–84, 587–88
　and MacArthur, 474
　and surrender, 640
　and Yamamoto, 410–11, 411n
　illus., 271, 555, 640

Nishimura, Shōji (IJN admiral), 227, 565,
　　566–67, 569, 575–76
Nishiro, Shigeru (IJN officer), 578
Nisshim Maru (Japanese tanker), 594
Nomura, Kichisaburo (Japanese admiral/
　　diplomat), 158, 193–94
Norden bombsight (US), 604–5
Norfolk (RN cruiser), 135
Norge (Norwegian warship), 50
Norness (Panamanian tanker), 253
North, Dudley (RN admiral), 74, 77
North Africa, Allied invasion of (1942), 347
　Allied victory in, 417
　invasion convoys, 349–52, 354
　planning, 325–26, 334–37
　map, 350
North Carolina (USN battleship),
　　329–30, 332
Northampton (USN cruiser), 345–46
Norway
　German invasion of (1940), 39–58
　Hitler's obsession with (1942), 258–59
　map, 44
Nubian (RN destroyer), 101, 456
Nürnberg (German cruiser), 615

Oakes, Walter M. (US army officer),
　　351–52
Ōbayashi, Sueo (IJN officer), 344
O'Bannon (USN destroyer), 367
O'Brien (USN destroyer), 332
Ohio (US/RN tanker), 313–14, 317–20
　illus., 320
ohka (piloted bombs), 621
oil (petroleum)
　Italian shortage of, 79–80, 92, 359
　Japanese shortage of, 153, 172,
　　　192–94, 542, 558–59, 594
　transport along US coast, 253–58
　US assets, 192–94, 192n, 192–9, 562
O'Kane, Richard (USN sub captain), 396,
　　589–90
　illus., 396

Okinawa, US invasion of (1945), 618–19, 626–32,

Oklahoma (USN battleship), 205–6

Oldendorf, Jesse (USN admiral), 556, 574, 575–77

Oliver, Geoffrey (RN commodore), 456, 524

Omaha Beach (Normandy), 530–33

Ōmori, Sentarō (IJN admiral), 483–85

Onishi, Taijiro (IJN admiral), 619–20, 644

Operation AI. *See* Pearl Harbor

Oran, Allied invasion of, 352–53

Oribe (RN destroyer), 385

Orion (German raider), 128

Orion (RN cruiser), 98

Osmeña, Sergio (Philippines president), 564

Ostfriesland (German battleship), 213

Ota, Kioski (Japanese soldier), 493

Outerbridge, William W. (USN officer), 204

Overlord, Operation (1944), 499, 507–9, 519–20

rehearsals for, 520–23

Ozawa, Jisaburō (IJN admiral), 224, 240, 347, 408, 638, 644

and the Battle of the Philippine Sea, 541, 543–46, 549

and Leyte Gulf, 559, 565, 572

Pacific Ocean Area (POA), 297–98

Palembang (Sumatra), 225–26

Panay (USN gunboat), 169, 177

Pantelleria, Battle of (1943), 265

Panzerschiffe. See pocket battleships

Parillo, Mark (historian), 611

Paris (French battleship), 71

Park, Keith (RAF Air Marshal), 313

Parker, Edward N. (USN officer), 367

Parker, Hyde (RN admiral), 70

Parker, W. G. (RN chaplain), 138

Parks, Lew (US sub captain), 592

Patterson (USN destroyer), 307

Patton, George S. (American general)

in Europe, 535

in North Africa, 358

in Sicily, 432, 440–41

Paukenschlag, Operation (1942), 250–58

Pearl Harbor, Japanese attack on (1941), 195–208

map, 201

illus., 206

Peary (USN destroyer), 224

Pedestal, Operation (1942), 313–20, 333

map, 315

See also Malta

Peleliu, US invasion of (1944), 563

Pelican (RN destroyer), 385

Penelope (RN cruiser), 5

Penn (RN destroyer), 319

Pennsylvania (USN battleship), 205

Percival, Arthur Ernest (British general), 209, 223, 640

Perth (Australian cruiser), 229–34

Pétain, Philippe (French general), 352

Petersen, Friedrich (German liner captain), 616

petroleum. *See* oil

Petropavlovsk. See Marat

Pettigrew, Hugh (Canadian merchant captain), 123

Philadelphia (USN cruiser), 456

illus., 458

Philippines

Japanese invasion of, 216–17

and US strategy, 554–55

Philippine Sea, Battle of (1944), 538, 543–52, 598

map, 545

illus., 547

Phillips, Tom (RN admiral), 211–15

Piet Hein (Dutch destroyer), 226

Place, Basil (RN officer), 462

Plan Orange (US), 175–76, 216

pocket battleships (German), 7, 18–20, 22, 26–27

Pola (Italian cruiser), 99–100
Pollard, Charles (British sailor), 125
Port Moresby, New Guinea, 275–81
Portland (USN cruiser), 367–68
Potsdam Declaration (1945), 633
Pound, Dudley (RN admiral), 25–26, 62, 68, 71, 140
   death of, 463, 463n
   and PQ-17, 264–65
   relations with Churchill, 41–42, 210
   illus., 25
Pownall, Henry (British general), 221
Prados, John (historian), 539
Preuss, Joachim (U-boat captain), 190
Pridham-Whippell, Henry Daniel (RN admiral), 96–99
Prien, Gunther (U-boat captain)
   attacks convoys, 114
   killed, 129
   sinks the *Royal Oak*, 3–5, 10–16, 18
Prince of Wales (RN battleship), 188, 403
   and the *Bismarck*, 137–49
   in the South China Sea, 210–15
   illus., 214
Princeton (USN carrier), 482, 485–86, 569–70, 587
Prinz Eugen (German cruiser), 133, 139–44, 259, 615
Provence (French battleship), 71, 75
PT boats. *See* torpedo boats, American
Puller, Lewis B. "Chesty" (USMC officer), 344
Punta Stilo, Battle of. *See* Calabria, Battle of
Pye, William S. (USN admiral), 217–18

Q-ships, 256
Quebec Conference, 454, 487
Queen Elizabeth (RN battleship), 242

Rabaul (Japanese base), 220, 276, 298, 301, 305, 328, 404, 408, 472
   US air attacks on, 482–83, 485–87
   illus., 486

radar, 27, 46, 83, 138, 143, 145, 316, 379
   at Midway, 292
   at Pearl Harbor, 204–5
   in Solomon Islands, 338–42, 366, 478, 483–84
Raeder, Erich (German admiral), 16, 18, 35
   and a balanced navy, 22–23, 468
   death of, 643
   described, 21
   and the Mediterranean, 91–92, 295–96, 359–60
   and Norway, 39–41, 59
   relations with Hitler, 22, 38, 39–40, 59, 141–42, 186, 188, 191, 241, 259–60
   and surface raiders, 20–21, 23–24, 120–26, 129, 130–33, 259, 263–64
   illus., 21
Ramillies (RN battleship), 88–89, 236
Ramsay, Bertram (RN admiral)
   and the campaign in Europe, 536
   death of, 645–46
   described, 62
   and Dunkirk, 63–69
   and Operation Torch, 334
   and Overlord/Neptune, 519–21, 523, 526
   and Sicily, 425
   illus., 63
Randolph (USN carrier), 625
Ranger (USN carrier), 333, 335, 355–56
Raseneck, F. W. (German naval officer), 33
Rauenfels (German ammunition ship), 54
Rawalpindi (RN auxiliary cruiser), 45
Rawlings, Bernard (RN admiral), 630
Red Banner Fleet (Soviet Union), 294–95
Redfin (US submarine), 543
Redman, John (USN officer), 275
Redman, Joseph (USN officer), 275
Reeves, Mason (USN admiral), 162, 176
Regia Aeronautica, 81–82, 450

Regia Marina, 78–80
  commando raids by, 242
  fuel shortages of, 79–80, 92, 318, 415
  relations with Regia Aeronautica,
      81–82, 93–94, 98, 318
  surrender of, 444–53
  See also Calabria and Matapan,
      Battles of
Reid, Jewell "Jack" (USN officer), 286
Rejewski, Marian (Polish
      mathematician), 247
Renown (RN battleship), 26, 34–35
  in Norway campaign, 45, 47–49
Repulse (RN battlecruiser), 124, 145,
      210–11, 213–15
  illus., 214
Resolution (RN battleship), 71, 236
Reuben James (USN destroyer), 191–92
Revenge (RN battleship), 236
Reynaud, Paul (French president), 61
Rhododendron (RN corvette), 109
Riccardi, Arturo (Italian admiral), 88, 92,
      318, 444
  and Dönitz, 415–16
Richardson, James O. (USN admiral), 184
Richelieu (French battleship), 71, 76
Richmond (USN cruiser), 470
Riefkohl, Frederick (USN officer), 304,
      308–9
Ring, Stanhope (USN pilot), 288, 290
Rioult, Andre Georges (French admiral),
      353
River Plate, Battle of (1939), 33–37
Robert, Georges (French admiral), 76n
Robert Rowan (US liberty ship), 437
  illus., 438
Roberts (RN monitor), 436–37
Roberts, Andrew (historian), 151
Roberts, David W. (USN officer), 234
Robin Moor (US steamer), 186
Rochefort, Joseph (USN officer/
      codebreaker, 274–75
  and Midway, 282–83

Rodney (RN battleship), 54, 124, 144–49
Rohwer, Jürgen (historian), 249
Rogge, Bernhard (German raider
      captain), 127–28
Roma (Italian battleship), 449, 450–51
  illus., 451
Römer, Wolfgang (U-boat captain), 378
Rommel, Erwin (German general), 90,
      295, 312–13, 362, 446
  logistics problems of, 359–60, 414–16
Rooks, Albert (USN officer), 230–33
Roope, Gerard B. (RN officer), 46–47,
      47n
Roosevelt, Franklin D. (US president),
      502n, 609
  and aid to Britain, 111–12, 185–86, 187
  and American neutrality, 177–79,
      181–82, 185–88, 190–92
  and Churchill, 177, 188, 208, 314
  death of, 632, 642
  described, 173–74
  and the French, 363
  naval buildup, 173–75, 177, 179, 182–83
  and Pearl Harbor, 208
  and pre-war Japan, 192–94, 200, 203
  and unconditional surrender, 417–18
  and U.S. shipbuilding, 386–87, 498
  and wartime strategy, 270, 324, 352,
      553–55
  illus., 181, 418, 555
Roosevelt, Theodore (US president), 173
Roper (USN destroyer), 256
Rosenbaum, Helmut (U-boat captain), 315
Roskill, Stephen (historian), xi, 221, 409
Rowland, James (RN officer), 129
Royal Navy (Britain), xiv–xv, 25–27,
      41–42, 52–57, 59–60
  and the *Bismarck*, 133–52
  and Dunkirk, 67–68
  and France, 69–77
  and the Indian Ocean, 236–38
      (map, 237)
  and the Mediterranean, 78–102

Royal Navy (Britain) (*continued*)
   and the North Cape convoys, 260–66,
     462–68
   in the Pacific, 629–31
   See also Battle of the Atlantic
Royal Australian Navy, 100–1, 128, 221,
   231–34
Royal Canadian Navy, 111, 189
Royal Navy Voluntary Reserves
   (British), 111
Royal Netherlands Navy, 220–34
Royal Oak (RN battleship), 4–5, 12–15
   illus., 13
Royal Sovereign (RN battleship), 236, 452
Ryder, Charles (American general), 354
Ryūjō (IJN carrier), 160, 224, 225, 328–31
Ryukyu Islands (Japan), 618

Saipan, U.S. invasion of (1944), 541,
   552–54
Saitō, Yoshitsugu (Japanese general), 552
Salerno, Allied invasion of (1943), 454–60
Salt Lake City (USN cruiser), 471
Samuel B. Roberts (USN destroyer),
   581, 590
San Demetrio (British tanker), 124–25
San Francisco (USN cruiser), 339–40,
   367–68, 369
San Juan (USN cruiser), 304
Sanders, Harry (USN officer), 531
Sansonetti, Luigi (Italian admiral), 97, 447
Santa Cruz Islands, Battle of (1942),
   344–46
Santee (USN carrier), 587
Sapelo (USN tanker), 384–85
Saratoga (USN carrier), xix, 162, 176,
   202, 217, 331–32, 482, 485–86,
   609, 621
Savage (RN destroyer), 467
Savannah (USN cruiser), 440, 456–57
Savo Island, Battle of (1942), 305–11
   map, 305
Scapa Flow (British naval base), 4–5, 10–15
Scarborough (RN sloop), 115-

Scarlett-Streatfield, Norman (RN pilot), 87
Schacht, Harro (U-boat captain), 257
Scharnhorst (German battlecruiser), 22
   and the Channel dash, 258–60
   as commerce raider, 126, 129, 131–32
   destruction of, 464–68
   and North Cape convoys, 460–62
   in Norway campaign, 43–45, 47–47,
     59–60
   illus., 48, 465
Scheer, Reinhard (German admiral), xx
Schepke, Joachim (U-boat captain),
   117–18, 129
schnellboot. See torpedo boats, German
schnorchel (on U-boats), 535, 614
schuitjes (Dutch canal boats), 65
Scientist (British steamer), 127
Scimitar (RN destroyer), 521
Scoresby (British steamer), 116
Scott, Norman (USN admiral), 304, 337
   and Battle of Cape Esperance,
     338–42
   and Naval Battle of Guadalcanal,
     365, 368
   illus., 337
Sea Bees (US construction battalion),
   332, 481
Sea Lion, Operation (invasion of
   England), 90–91, 124
Seafire (RN fighter plane), 457, 457n
Seahorse (US submarine), 543
Seal (RN submarine), 105
Seatrain New Jersey (USN tank landing
   ship), 337
Semmes, Raphael (Confederate naval
   officer), 24–25
Sembrisky, Gustave (USN sailor), 280
Sendai (IJN cruiser), 484
Seventh Fleet (USN), 555–56, 564
Sheffield (RN cruiser), 83, 147,
   376, 466
Sherbrooke, Robert (RN officer), 55
Sherman, Forrest P. (USN officer),
   333, 333n

Sherman, Frederick (USN officer), 280, 333n

Sherrod, Robert (US correspondent), 493

Shibazaki, Keiji (IJN admiral), 491, 494, 495

Shigemitsu, Mamoru (Japanese diplomat), 637–39

Shigure (IJN destroyer), 484

Shima, Kiyohide (IJN admiral), 575

Shimada, Shigetarō (IJN admiral), 553

Shinano (IJN carrier), 558, 597–600

shipping, shortage of, 296, 311, 323
    construction of, 386–91, 511
    at Guadalcanal, 325–26, 327
    in the Mediterranean, 359
    for Torch, 334–37

Shōhō (IJN carrier), 278–79
    illus., 279

Shōkaku (IJN carrier), 198
    in the Coral Sea, 276–81
    Midway battle, kept out of, 285
    in Solomon Islands, 346–47
    sunk, 549

Short, Walter C. (US general), 202

Shubrick (USN destroyer), 440

Siam, Japanese invasion of, 209

Sibuyan Sea, Battle of (1944), 569–72
    See also Leyte Gulf

Sicily, Allied invasion of (1943)
    Allied decision, 418–20
    Allied plans, 422–23, 424 (map, 423)
    the invasion, 430–38
    landings, 435–38

Siebel ferries (German transports), 361

Sims (USN destroyer), 279

Singapore, 209, 223

Sirte, Second Battle of (1942), 242–43

Slapton Sands, 520–23

sloop-of-war (RN escort vessel), 110

Slonim, Gil (USN officer), 330

Smith, Holland M. (USMC general), 490, 492, 492n, 495, 607
    illus., 490

Smith, Julian (USMC general), 492n, 492–93

Smith, Ralph C. (USA general), 492n, 495

Smith, Walter Bedell (USA general), 444–46

Solomon Islands, Allied campaign in (1943), 296–97, 471–72, 475–87
    map, 476

Somerville, James (RN admiral), 71–72, 488
    and Battle of Cape Spartivento, 88–89
    in the Indian Ocean, 236–38
    and Mers-el-Kébir, 73–76
    and pursuit of the *Bismarck*, 143–48
    relations with Churchill, 89

sonar, 7, 187, 379

Sōryū (IJN carrier), 198, 217, 224, 292

South Dakota (USN battleship), 346, 369–70, 548

Southampton (RN cruiser), 93

Southwest Pacific Area (SoWesPac), 297–98

Spaatz, Carl "Tooey" (USAAF general), 432–33

Sparke, P.J.D. (RN pilot), 86

Speer, Albert (German minister of armaments), 614

Spence (USN destroyer), 484, 602

Spey (RN corvette), 351–52

Spitsbergen, German attack on (1943), 460

Sprague, Clifton "Ziggy" (USN admiral), 579–80, 582–83, 586, illus., 579

Sprague, Thomas L. (USN admiral), 579

Spruance, Raymond A. (USN admiral)
    and Battle of the Philippine Sea, 540, 543–46, 549, 552
    death of, 647
    and the Fifth Fleet, 490–91, 513
    and Iwo Jima, 605, 607, 622, 627
    and Midway, 283–88

Stagg, James M. (RAF officer/
    meteorologist), 525–26
Stalin, Josef (Soviet premier), 261, 361, 419,
    452, 463, 472, 517–18, 642–43
Stalingrad, Battle of (1942–43), 295
Stalker (RN carrier), 456–57
Stark, Harold "Betty" (USN admiral)
    sends war warning, 194, 202
    superseded, 252
    and U.S. strategy, 179, 180–81, 180n,
        191, 203
    illus., 181
Station Hypo. *See* codes and code
    breaking, American
Sterlett (USN submarine), 606
Sterope (Italian tanker), 415
Stimson, Henry
    as Sec'y of State, xix-xx, 174, 373–74
    as Sec'y of War, 488, 503
St. Lô (USN carrier), 580, 587, 619
    illus., 620
St. Louis (USN cruiser), 479
Strasbourg (French battlecruiser), 71,
    76, 77
Streonshalh (British steamer), 32
Stringbags. *See* Swordfish
Strong, Stockton B. (USN officer), 344
Stubbs, William (British merchant
    captain), 30
submarines, xix-xx
    Italian submarines, 106–7, 425
    rules for use (1936), 8
    USN submarines, 391–98, 391n,
        589–95, 595, 599–600
    See also U-boats
Suffolk (RN cruiser), 135, 143, 145
Sunda Strait, Battle of (1942), 231–34
Superfortress bomber. *See* B-29
Surigao Strait, Battle of (1944), 575–78
    See also Leyte Gulf, Battle of
Suwanee (USN carrier), 587
Suzuki, Kantaro (Japanese PM), 632,
    633–34
Swanson, Claude (US Sec'y of Navy), 177

Swarts, J. S. (USN officer), 522
Swett, James E. (USMC pilot), 409
Swordfish (British aircraft), 84–85
    attack on *Bismarck*, 142, 146–48
    attack on Taranto, 85–86
    illus., 84, 146
Sydney (Australian cruiser), 128
Syfret, Neville (RN admiral), 314,
    316–17, 349

Tacoma (German steamer), 36
Tairoa (British steamer), 3
Takagi, Takeo (Japanese admiral), 227
    in Battle of the Coral Sea, 276–81
    in Battle of the Java Sea, 228–31
    illus., 228
Taiho (IJN carrier), 541, 548n,
        548–49, 558
Takao (IJN cruiser), 369, 568, 568n
Talbot, George (RN admiral), 524
Talbot, Paul H. (USN officer), 218
Tambula (British hospital ship), 437
Tanaka, Raizo (IJN admiral), 328,
        369, 371
Tang (USN submarine), 589–90, 592
    illus., 591
Tanjong Priok naval base (Java), 232
Taranto, Italy
    Allied occupation of, 452
    British attack on, 85–88
Tarawa, invasion of (1943), 491–95
    illus., 492, 494
Tartar (RN destroyer), 456
Tassafaronga, Battle of (1943), 371
Taussig, Joseph (USN officer), 207
Taylor, Maxwell (USA general), 448
TBS (talk between ships), 339–40, 339n,
        484, 526
Tedder, Arthur (British air marshal), 102
    and Italy, 456
    and Sicily, 432–33
Tehran Conference (1943), 501–2, 508
Tennant, William (RN officer),
        64–65, 215

Tennessee (USN battleship), 205
Texas (USN battleship), 335, 531
Thailand. *See* Siam
Thatcher (USN destroyer), 484
Third Fleet (USN), 555–56, 603
  See also Fifth Fleet
Thomas, J. F. (USN officer), 207
Thomas Stone (USN transport), 351
Threadfin (USN submarine), 627
Tillman (USN destroyer), 439
Tinosa (USN submarine), 398
Tirpitz (German battleship), 22–23,
    129, 294, 324
  and the Channel dash, 258–60
  characteristics of, 130–31
  damaged, 460–62
  and North Cape convoys, 261–63
  illus., 262
Tojo, Hideki (Japanese general), 172,
    192, 553
tokkōtai. See kamikaze
Tokyo Express, 328, 337, 342–43,
    364, 477
Tomioka, Sadatoshi (IJN admiral),
    638
Tomonaga, Joichi (Japanese pilot),
    286–87, 292
Topp, Erich (U-boat captain), 191
Torch, Operation. *See* North Africa
  map, 350
torpedoes
  American, 392–93, 398
  British, 86–87, 105–6, 380
  German, 17, 53–54, 105–6, 378
  Japanese, 163, 199–200, 226, 230
torpedo boats
  American (PT boats), 480n, 576
  German (*schnellbooten*), 67, 457,
    521–22, 535
  Italian (*motoscafo turismos*), 94–95,
    317–18, 535
torpedo planes
  American, 288–89, 469 (*See also*
    Devastator and Avenger)

British, 85–88, 142–43
  (*See also* Swordfish)
  Japanese, 199–200 (*See also* Kate)
Tovey, John (RN admiral)
  described, 114
  and the North Cape convoys, 263
  and pursuit of the *Bismarck*, 134–37,
    142, 144–49
  reassigned, 462–63
  illus., 134
Towers, John (USN admiral), 513
town class destroyers, 112
  illus., 112
Toyoda, Soemu (IJN admiral), 539–40,
    638, 644
  and Leyte Gulf, 560–61, 566, 572,
    575, 578
Trade Plot (RN convoy HQ),
    113–14, 121
traffic analysis (British), 245
  See also code breaking
Tramontane (French destroyer),
    353
treaty cruisers, xviii
Treaty Faction (Japan), 155–58
Trevanian (British steamer), 2
Trident Conference, 419–20, 444
Triton (USN submarine), 397
Tromp (Dutch cruiser), 226
Trondheim, invasion of (1940), 46–47,
    54, 56
Troubridge, Thomas (RN admiral),
    351, 436
Trout (USN submarine), 397
Truman, Harry S. (US president),
    635
Truscott, Lucien (USA general), 425–26,
    431, 434, 514–15
Tsukahara, Nishizo (IJN admiral),
    301
Tulagi, 276
Turing, Alan (British code
    breaker), 248
Turner, Bradwell (RN officer), 38

Turner, Richmond Kelly (USN admiral),
639
at Guadalcanal, 299–300, 302–3,
309–10
at Okinawa, 622
at Tarawa, 492
illus., 303
Tuscaloosa (USN cruiser), 255
Twining (USN destroyer), 547–48
Twining, Nathan (USA general), 482
Two-Ocean Navy Act (1938), 179, 323

U-boats (German), 2, 6–7
attack protocols, 10–13
in Battle of the Atlantic, 103–7, 113,
116–20, 378, 380–82, 384–86
coastal "ducks," 8
in the Mediterranean, 242–44, 315, 425
in Norway campaign, 53–54
and the *schnorchel*, 535
shortage of, 106–7, 244, 251, 251n, 378
Type VII, 8–9 (illus., 9)
Type IX, 251–53
Type XIV (milch cows), 257
Type XXI and XXIII, 614
off the US coast, 250–58
U.S. Navy
fleet exercises of, 176, 176n
fleet organization, 182–83
in the Pacific, 480–81, 488–89, 496, 510,
514, 552, 554–57, 563, 554–57
personnel, 489
undeclared war in Atlantic, 187–88,
190–92
war plans of, 175–76, 181–82, 487–88
See also specific operations
Ugaki, Matome (IJN admiral), 197, 204,
285, 408, 412, 638, 644
and the kamikazes, 620–26, 632
in the Philippine Sea, 542–43, 552
Uganda (RN cruiser), 457
Ulithi (USN base), 562, 573, 601,
603, 607

Ultra (code classification), 248–50
Umezu, Yoshijirō (Japanese general),
634, 638, 644
Unicorn (RN repair ship), 457
Ushijima, Mitsuru (Japanese general),
632
Utah (USN target ship), 205–6
Utley, Jonathan, 193

Val (Japanese Type 99 dive-bomber),
198–99, 292, 302
Valiant (RN battleship), 71, 94,
242, 458–59
Vandegrift, Arthur (USMC general),
299–300, 302, 333
illus., 303
Vanoc (RN destroyer), 129
Vella Gulf, Battle of (1943), 480
Vella Lavella, Battle of (1943), 481
Vereker, John (British general). *See*
Gort, Lord
Verity (RN destroyer), 129
Versailles Treaty, xv, xx, xxii, 5
Hitler renounces, 1
Vestal (USN repair ship), 205
Vian, Philip (RN admiral), 646
and the *Bismarck*, 144–49
in the Mediterranean, 242–43, 425,
430, 434–35, 456–57
in Norwegian campaign, 37–38
in the Pacific, 630–31 (illus., 630)
Vichy France, 70
Victor Emanuel III (King of Italy), 442,
449, 454
Victorious (RN carrier), 142–48, 264, 630
Vidette (RN destroyer), 385
Vincennes (USN cruiser), 309
Vinson, Carl (US congressman), 174
Vinson-Trammel Act (1934), 174–75
Virginia (US steamer), 257
Vittorio Veneto (Italian battleship), 93
in Battle of Cape Matapan, 96–101
illus., 94

von Arnim, Hans-Jürgen (German general), 416
von Hindenberg, Paul (German president), 616
von Liebenstein, Gustav (German naval officer), 442
von Vietinghoff, Heinrich (German general), 455, 457–58
Vraciu, Alex (USN pilot), 546–47, 548

Wahoo (USN submarine), 395–97, 594
    illus., 396
Waimarana (British steamer), 317
Wainwright (USN destroyer), 262–64
Wainwright, Jonathan (USA general), 640
Waite, George (British merchant captain), 124–25
Wakatsuki, Reijirō (Japanese PM), xxi–xxii
Wake Island, 217
Wake-Walker, Frederic (RN officer)
    and Dunkirk, 64
    and the hunt for Bismarck, 135, 140, 143–44, 149
Wakeful (RN destroyer), 67
Walcheren Island, Allied capture of, 536–37
Waldron, John C. (USN pilot), 288–90
Walker, John (RN officer), 250
Walkerling, Heinz (U-boat captain), 381
Waller, Hector (Australian naval officer), 231
    in Battle of Java Sea, 231
    in Battle of Sunda Strait, 231–34
    in the Mediterranean, 100–1
    illus., 232
War Production Board (US), 498, 511
War Shipping Administration (US), 386–87
Warburton-Lee, Bernard (RN officer), 50–54
Ward (USN destroyer), 204
Warspite (RN battleship), 83, 93, 304
    in Battle of Cape Matapan, 96–101

in European campaign, 536
in Indian Ocean, 236
in Mediterranean, 441, 458–59
at Narvik, 54–55
Washington (USN battleship), 263, 342, 370–71, 574–75
Washington Naval Arms Limitation Conference (1921–22), xv, xviii, 161–62, 510
Wasp (USN carrier), 243, 269, 326, 332–33
    illus., 333
Watchtower, Operation. See Guadalcanal
Wavell, Archibald (British general), 220–21
Wavy Navy. See Royal Navy Voluntary Reserves
Weinberg, Gerhard (historian), 312
Werner, Herbert (U-boat captain), 382
West Virginia (USN battleship), 205–6, 576–77
Weygand, Maxime (French general), 363
Weyler, George L. (USN admiral), 556n
Whitworth, William (RN admiral), 45–49, 54–56
Wichita (USN cruiser), 355
Wilhelm Gustloff (German liner), 616
Wilhelm Heidkamp (German destroyer), 53
Wilhelmshaven (German naval base), xx
Wilkins, Charles "Weary" (USN sub captain), 392–93
Wilkinson, Theodore S. (USN admiral), 481, 483
Wilkinson, Thomas (RN officer), 224–25
William D. Porter (USN destroyer), 502n
Williamson, Kenneth (RN pilot), 86, 87
Willis, Algernon (RN admiral), 454–55
Willoch, Odd Isaksen (Norwegian naval officer), 50
Wilson, Henry Maitland (British general), 502, 508
Wilson, Woodrow (US president), 173
Winant, John G. "Gil" (US ambassador), 208

Windsor, G. R. (British merchant captain), 127
Winn, Rodger (RN officer), 249
Winooski (USN tanker), 358
wolf pack tactics
  in the Atlantic, 104–5, 114, 116–20, 245, 250
  in the Pacific, 393–94, 592
Wolverine (RN destroyer), 129, 316
Women's Royal Navy Service (WRNS), 245
Wouk, Herman (novelist), 602n
Wyman, Theodore (USN officer), 506

X-craft (British midget subs), 461–62

Yahagi (IJN cruiser), 628
Yamagumo (IJN destroyer), 577
Yamamoto, Isoroku (Japanese admiral), 158–61, 164, 172
  killed, 410–14
  and Midway, 285–86
  and Pearl Harbor attack, 172–4, 195–96
  and Solomon Islands campaign, 328, 346–47, 369, 407–10
  illus., 159
Yamato (IJN battleship), 167–69, 285, 328, 542
  and Battle of Leyte Gulf, 558–59, 585, 587
  destruction of, 626–29
  illus., 168
Yamashiro (IJN battleship), 565–66, 577
yamato-damashii, concept of, 158, 159, 619
Yarnall (US destroyer), 112
Yasukuni Shrine (Japan), 157
Yates, George D. (RN officer), 50
Yatsushiro, Sukeyoshi (IJN admiral), 218
Yokosuka Shipyard (Japan), 597
Yokoyama, Ichiro (IJN admiral), 638
Yonai, Mitsumasa (IJN admiral), 553, 560–61, 619
York (RN cruiser), 94–95
Yorktown (USN carrier CV-5), 202, 218, 253, 269
  at Midway, 283–93
Yorktown (USN carrier CV-10), 470, 470n

Zam Zam (Egyptian steamer), 127–28
Zara (Italian cruiser), 100
Zero (Japanese fighter plane), 166, 198
Zhukov, Georgy (USSR general), 208, 295, 322
Zuihō (IJN carrier), 344, 346–47, 559
Zuikaku (IJN carrier), 198, 558
  in the Coral Sea, 276–81
  Midway battle, kept out of, 285
  in Philippine Sea, 550
  sunk, 584–85